THE OXFORD HAN

PHILOSOPHY OF CRIMINAL LAW

THE OXFORD HANDBOOK OF

PHILOSOPHY OF CRIMINAL LAW

Edited by

JOHN DEIGH AND DAVID DOLINKO

OXFORD
UNIVERSITY PRESS

Oxford University Press is a department of the University of Oxford. It furthers
the University's objective of excellence in research, scholarship, and education
by publishing worldwide. Oxford is a registered trade mark of Oxford University
Press in the UK and certain other countries.

Published in the United States of America by Oxford University Press
198 Madison Avenue, New York, NY 10016, United States of America.

© Oxford University Press 2011

First issued as an Oxford University Press paperback, 2019

All rights reserved. No part of this publication may be reproduced, stored in
a retrieval system, or transmitted, in any form or by any means, without the
prior permission in writing of Oxford University Press, or as expressly permitted
by law, by license, or under terms agreed with the appropriate reproduction
rights organization. Inquiries concerning reproduction outside the scope of the
above should be sent to the Rights Department, Oxford University Press, at the
address above.

You must not circulate this work in any other form
and you must impose this same condition on any acquirer.

Library of Congress Cataloging-in-Publication Data
The Oxford handbook of philosophy of the criminal law / edited by John Deigh and David Dolinko.
p. cm.
Includes index.
ISBN 978-0-19-531485-4 (hardcover : alk. paper); 978-0-19-007424-1 (paperback : alk. paper)
1. Criminal law—Philosophy.   I. Deigh, John.   II. Dolinko, David.
III. Title: Handbook of philosophy of the criminal law.
K5018.O96 2011
345'.001—dc22   2010023180

INTRODUCTION

Over the last sixty years scholarly work in legal philosophy has grown tremendously, generating a wealth of new ideas and spreading widely into new areas of research. Not only have there been major developments in the field's core area, jurisprudence, but different branches of law have also become burgeoning centers of significant philosophical study. The criminal law, being the branch with the longest tradition of writings on philosophical problems, has also been foremost, among the different branches, in producing a rich contemporary literature on both its traditional problems and new ones that have emerged as the work in this area has grown. Research on these problems has attracted the interest of philosophers, legal theorists, criminologists, and other students of the criminal law. Its originality and influence has created demand for an authoritative handbook that covers the different topics under which the problems fall. We have put together the volume before you to meet this demand.

The volume contains seventeen original essays by leading thinkers in the philosophy of the criminal law. These essays represent the state of current research on the major topics in the field that arise from issues in the substantive criminal law. We have not included essays dealing with topics generated by the law of criminal procedure. While a philosophical literature on the latter topics, particularly the criminal law's standard of proof, has begun to emerge, the range of such topics is still too narrow to warrant including a separate section of essays on them in a handbook. Thus, to preserve the coherence of the volume, we decided to restrict its essays to philosophical topics in substantive criminal law. In this way, since all of these topics are interrelated, we expected that each of the essays would be enriched and deepened by its connections to many of the others. We have not been disappointed.

The oldest of these topics is punishment. Indeed, until midway through the last century, work on philosophical topics in the criminal law was largely confined to the study of questions about the justification of punishment. That study boasts a long history that traces back to Plato's *Protagoras* and *Laws*. In the modern period, one can find some discussion of these questions in Hobbes's *Leviathan* and Locke's *Second Treatise of Government*, but sustained discussion of them did not begin until the second half of the eighteenth century with the work of Beccaria and Bentham. This discussion has continued and evolved into contemporary debates over the place of retribution, deterrence, and reform in a just penal system. The literature these debates comprise is now vast.

Unlike the study of punishment, the study of other topics in the criminal law was largely ignored by modern philosophers and left instead to writers who applied the traditional methods of legal scholarship: exposition of common law, interpretation of statutes, harmonization of apparently conflicting elements in some branch of law, and the like. Things began to change, however, with the appearance, in the years following World War II, of H. L. A. Hart's essays on responsibility. Increasingly, philosophers took up Hart's questions about attributions of responsibility to criminal offenders and initiated studies of other related aspects of the criminal law. At the same time, scholars in the legal academy who specialized in criminal law began to incorporate these philosophical writings into their own works, to deal with the same questions philosophers were examining, and to adopt some of the philosophers' methods. George Fletcher's landmark book *Rethinking Criminal Law*, published in 1978, is a prime example of this latter development.

A third wave of philosophical writing concerning the criminal law began with the appearance in 1957 of the Wolfenden Report , which contained the recommendations of the Committee on Homosexual Offences and Prostitution for reforming British law governing sexual conduct. In making these recommendations, the Committee revived John Stuart Mill's argument in *On Liberty* and applied it to the criminal law's restrictions on individual liberty in the area of sexual relations. This application of Mill's argument sparked severe criticism from Lord Devlin, and Devlin's criticism in turn elicited a strong response from Hart in defense of the Report's appeal to Mill. The controversy between Devlin and Hart has led to extensive and searching discussion by moral philosophers, scholars of the criminal law, and legal and political theorists, among others, of the criminal law's scope and limits and the relevance of customary morality to the definition of criminal offenses. These issues received comprehensive and masterful treatment in Joel Feinberg's four-volume work *The Moral Limits of the Criminal Law*, published successively in 1984, 1985, 1986, and 1988. Unsurprisingly, though, they continue to stir debate.

Today the literature in the philosophy of the criminal law has expanded greatly. It now covers many questions beyond the three aforementioned mainstays of the field: (1) what justifies the infliction of harm, as punishment, on criminals; (2) on what basis are criminals properly held responsible for their unlawful actions; and (3) what are the proper limits to the criminal law. In addition, it deals, inter alia, with questions about prosecuting omissions (e.g., what can justify such prosecutions if an unlawful act is a necessary element of any crime?), puzzles about criminal attempts (e.g., what qualifies an attempt as criminal and why should punishment for an attempt be less than for the corresponding completed offense?), questions about accomplice liability (e.g., what constitutes complicity in another's crime and how severe should its punishment be in comparison with the punishment imposed on the principal offender?), and questions about the place, if any, of clemency and mercy in a just penal system (e.g., how can mercy be consistent with justice in the infliction of punishment?). All these questions and more are discussed in the essays collected in this volume.

The first three deal with questions concerning the justifiability of "the state's outlawing certain acts as criminal offenses. Gerald Dworkin, in his essay, "The Limits of the Criminal Law", takes up the general question of what must be true of an act to justify the state's outlawing it as a criminal offense. Wayne Sumner's essay "Criminalizing Expression: Hate Speech and Obscenity", examines the same question as it applies specifically to certain acts of speech and against the background of the right to free speech that is granted by the Canadian Charter of Rights and Freedoms. The third of the initial essays, by Mitchell Berman, tackles the puzzling nature of blackmail. Why is it criminal, given that neither the act the blackmailer threatens to do (giving certain photos or documents that reveal information about the victim to others) nor the offer the blackmailer makes to the victim (to sell those photos or documents to him or her) is by itself a crime? In investigating this puzzle, Berman both explains its source and offers a solution.

The next three essays deal with issues concerning the general requirement in the criminal law of conduct as a necessary element of an offense. Douglas Husak, in his essay, "The Alleged Act Requirement in Criminal law", disputes the very existence of such a requirement. Andrew Ashworth, in in his essay "Attempts", considers the problems inherent in specifying what acts count as criminal attempts and what the rationale is for making such acts offenses when they are in themselves harmless. And Christopher Kutz's essay, "Complicity", examines the conditions of accomplice liability, how the criminal law conceives of assistance or encouragement someone gives another in the commission of a crime as itself a crime, what intentions the person giving assistance or encouragement must have to be liable as an accomplice, and under what conditions an accomplice's guilt is as great or even greater than that of the offender he assists or encourages.

Because the acts of someone who assists or encourages another in the commission of a crime do not directly cause whatever harms the crime results in, accomplice liability raises questions about the necessity of a causal connection between the assistance or encouragement and such harm and the criteria of causation the criminal law uses to establish this connection. Kutz deals with these questions in arguing for the greater importance to determining liability of the accomplice's intentions. General questions about the criteria of causation in the criminal law and how they compare to similar questions in tort law are then thoroughly discussed in the volume's seventh essay, Michael Moore's "Causation in the Criminal Law".

The next six essays cover different topics related to criminal responsibility. John Deigh's essay, "Responsibility" surveys the different theories of criminal responsibility against the background of the question whether universal determinism, if true, would vitiate such responsibility. Larry Alexander, in his essay "Culpability", expounds and argues for a theory of criminal responsibility that restricts the factors determining a person's culpability for wrongdoing, as much as possible, to ones that cannot be the result of mere chance. To believe that culpability may be due to factors that result from mere chance is to endorse the idea of moral luck, and for Alexander such luck is anathema to regarding people as responsible for their actions. Kimberly Ferzan focuses in her essay, "Justification and Excuse," on the distinction between defenses in which the defendant in a criminal trial offers reasons purporting to justify his act and defenses in which the defendant, while conceding that his act was wrong, offers reasons for excusing him from responsibility for it. The distinction has generated an important literature in criminal law theory and has been the site of several disputes among leading theorists over how to draw the distinction, which defenses qualify as justifications and which qualify as excuses, and what the rationale is for drawing this distinction. Ferzan gives a rich account of this literature and the nature of these disputes. Joshua Dressler's essay, "Duress," examines many of the questions Ferzan considers as they apply to the defense of duress. His overall conclusion is that the defense is best understood as an excuse rather than a justification. And Walter Sinnott-Armstrong and Ken Levy, in their essay, 'Insanity Defenses', review the controversies that surround the plea of insanity as an exculpatory defense. The last of these six essays is Marcia Baron's "Gender Issues in the Criminal Law" critically discusses two defenses, provocation and self-defense, whose traditional requirements raise questions about gender bias in the criminal law and how best to remedy it. In addition, Baron discusses similar questions that the crime of rape, in light of its traditional definition, raises.

The volume's final four essays concern the topic of punishment. David Dolinko, in his essay "Punishment", comprehensively surveys the philosophical literature on this topic, clarifying the different problems about punishment discussed in this literature and explaining the different positions legal philosophers have taken in proposing solutions to them. Capital punishment is the topic of the next essay Carol Steiker's "The Death Penalty and Deontology". After a brief review of retributivist arguments in support of permitting, if not requiring, capital punishment for certain offenses, Steiker examines and evaluates various retributivist arguments for its abolition. Finding these inconclusive at best, Steiker examines additional abolitionist arguments that, like retributivist arguments, appeal to considerations besides the death penalty's record as a deterrent to lethally violent crimes. These, too, she argues, require further development. Anthony Duff, in his essay "Mercy", discusses the tension between doing justice and showing mercy in sentencing criminal offenders. And Steve Garvey, in his "Alternatives to Punishment", the volume's final essay first considers proposals for supplementing or replacing the practice of punishing criminal offenders with that of preventive detention of such offenders or others recognized as dangerous to others. Then, in the final section of his essay, Garvey takes up the controversial program of restorative justice, whose advocates have promoted it as a better alternative to punishment.

We have deliberately refrained from setting for our contributors the precise parameters of their essays. Rather, it seemed to us best to allow each to adopt the format he or she felt most comfortable with, and we have accordingly given each wide latitude in deciding the kind of essay to include in the volume. As a result, there is a good deal of variation in the formats of these essays. Some discuss the particular answers their authors give to the issues they raise, while others present overviews of the range of approaches one finds in the literature. Some address broad topics; others focus on narrower issues. All of them, we believe, will stimulate interest in, and reflection on, the intriguing conceptual and normative problems that abound in the field of criminal law.

John Deigh
David Dolinko

Austin, Texas and Los Angeles, California
May 2010

TABLE OF CONTENTS

Notes on Contributors

Larry Alexander is the Warren Distinguished Professor at the University of San Diego School of Law. He is the author or coauthor of five books, the editor of four anthologies, and the author or coauthor of 180 articles, essays and chapters. His most recent book (with Kimberly Ferzan) is *Crime and Culpability: A Theory of Criminal Law* (Cambridge University Press, 2009). He is coeditor of the journal *Legal Theory* and is on the editorial boards of *Ethics, Law & Philosophy*, *Criminal Law & Philosophy*, and the *Ohio State Journal of Criminal Law*.

Andrew Ashworth is Vinerian Professor of English Law at the University of Oxford and a Fellow of All Souls College, having previously (1988–97) been Edmund-Davies Professor of Criminal Law and Criminal Justice at King's College, London. His principal books are *Principles of Criminal Law*, 6th ed. (2009), *Sentencing and Criminal Justice*, 5th ed. (2010), *The Criminal Process*, 4th ed., with M. Redmayne (2010), and *Human Rights and Criminal Justice*, 3rd ed., with B. Emmerson and A. Macdonald (forthcoming). He was a member (1999–2010) and chairman (2007–10) of the Sentencing Advisory Panel for England and Wales.

Marcia Baron is Rudy Professor of Philosophy at Indiana University. Her publications include *Kantian Ethics Almost without Apology* (Cornell, 1995), *Three Methods of Ethics: A Debate*, coauthored with Philip Pettit and Michael Slote (Blackwell, 1997), and articles on (among other topics) justifications and excuses, friendship and impartiality, patriotism, feminist criticisms of Kant's ethics, remorse and agent-regret, self-deception, and manipulativeness.

Mitchell N. Berman holds the Richard Dale Endowed Chair in Law and is Professor of Philosophy (by courtesy) at the University of Texas at Austin. He has written on diverse subjects in the philosophy of criminal law, constitutional theory, and jurisprudence.

John Deigh is Professor of Law and Philosophy at the University of Texas at Austin. He writes on topics in moral, political, and legal philosophy. He is the author of *The Sources of Moral Agency* (1996), *Emotions, Values, and the Law* (2008), and *An Introduction to Ethics* (2010).

David Dolinko is Professor of Law at the University of California, Los Angeles. His research interests focus on the philosophical underpinnings of criminal law.

He has published articles on retributivism, capital punishment, and the privilege against self-incrimination.

Joshua Dressler holds the Frank R. Strong Chair in Law at Ohio State University, Michael E. Moritz College of Law. He is the Editor-in-Chief of the second edition of the *Encyclopedia of Crime and Justice* and the author of two treatises and two casebooks in the fields of criminal law and procedure and numerous articles on criminal responsibility.

R. A. Duff was educated at Oxford and taught for forty years in the Philosophy Department at the University of Stirling. He now also holds a half-time position at the University of Minnesota Law School. He has published books and articles on criminal punishment, on the structure of criminal law, on criminal attempts, and on the criminal trial.

Gerald Dworkin is Distinguished Professor of Philosophy at the University of California, Davis. He is the author of many books and articles in the areas of moral, political, and legal philosophy.

Kimberly Kessler Ferzan is the Associate Dean for Academic Affairs and Professor of Law at Rutgers University School of Law Camden. She is also the cofounder and codirector of the Institute for Law and Philosophy and is Associate Graduate Faculty in the Philosophy Department at Rutgers New Brunswick. She is coauthor, with Larry Alexander, of *Crime and Culpability* (Cambridge University Press, 2009) and coeditor of *Criminal Law Conversations* (Oxford University Press, 2009).

Stephen P. Garvey is Professor of Law and Associate Dean for Academic Affairs at Cornell Law School. His current scholarly interest focuses on the substantive criminal law. He has also written on prison labor, shaming penalties, and jury decision-making in capital cases.

Douglas Husak (Ph.D., J.D., Ohio State University, 1976) is Professor of Philosophy at Rutgers University. He has published three books in criminal law theory: *Philosophy of Criminal Law* (1987); *Overcriminalization* (2008); and *The Philosophy of Criminal Law: Selected Essays* (2010).

Christopher Kutz is Professor of Law in the Jurisprudence and Social Policy Program and Director of the Kadish Center for Law, Morality and Public Affairs at Berkeley Law School, University of California, Berkeley. He is the author of *Complicity: Ethics and Law for a Collective Age* (Cambridge, 2000) and many articles in criminal law, jurisprudence, and political theory.

Ken Levy is Assistant Professor of Law at LSU Law Center in Baton Rouge, Louisiana. He has published articles in criminal theory and analytic philosophy.

Michael Moore holds the Charles R. Walgreen, Jr., Chair at the University of Illinois at Urbana-Champaign, where he is Professor of Law and Philosophy. He has published many books and articles in philosophy of criminal law, including *Causation and Responsibility* (2009), *Placing Blame* (1997), *Act and Crime* (1993), and *Law and Psychiatry* (1984).

Walter Sinnott-Armstrong is Chauncey Stillman Professor of Practical Ethics in the Philosophy Department and the Kenan Institute for Ethics at Duke University. He has published widely in normative moral theory, metaethics, applied ethics, philosophy of law, epistemology, informal logic, and philosophy of religion.

Carol Steiker is the Howard J. and Katherine W. Aibel Professor of Law at Harvard Law School. She attended Harvard-Radcliffe Colleges and Harvard Law School, where she served as president of the *Harvard Law Review,* the second woman to hold that position in its then ninety-nine-year history. She is the author of numerous scholarly works in the fields of criminal law, criminal procedure, and capital punishment. She served as coauthor, with Sanford Kadish and Stephen Schulhofer, of the casebook *Criminal Law and Its Processes*, 8th ed. (2007), as editor of *Criminal Procedure Stories* (Foundation, 2006), and on the Board of Editors of the *Encyclopedia of Crime and Justice*, 2nd ed. (Macmillan, 2002).

L. W. Sumner is University Professor Emeritus in the Department of Philosophy at the University of Toronto. He is the author of four books: *Abortion and Moral Theory* (1981); *The Moral Foundation of Rights* (1987); *Welfare, Ethics, and Happiness* (1996); and *The Hateful and the Obscene: Studies in the Limits of Free Expression* (2004). He is a Fellow of the Royal Society of Canada and recipient of the 2009 Molson Prize in Social Sciences and Humanities from the Canada Council for the Arts. He currently has a book forthcoming on assisted death.

THE OXFORD HANDBOOK OF

PHILOSOPHY OF CRIMINAL LAW

CHAPTER 1

....

THE LIMITS OF THE
CRIMINAL LAW

....

GERALD DWORKIN

It is obvious that the criminal law, like other normative systems for the regulation of behavior, has various kinds of limits. For example, it cannot affect the behavior of those who are not capable of understanding or conforming to its edicts. These include infants, the demented, the comatose. Even for those who are capable of understanding and conforming, the sanctions of the law may prove not to change potential conduct. It is very unlikely, for example, that those contemplating suicide would be affected by the knowledge that committing (or even attempting) suicide is punishable by a fine or imprisonment.

Even when the criminal law is capable of influencing conduct in one direction or another, it may carry with it other consequences that are sufficiently harmful that we would choose not to have such a law. The law may be efficacious but, on balance, bad.

Again, there are laws that while efficacious, and on balance beneficial, might involve means that violate rights that people have, and are rejected for that reason. So crimes that can only be detected by entrapment, that is, consensual corruption, might be rejected because it is thought that we ought not to be in the business of testing people's virtue.

Laws might be limited by constitutional provisions. Thus while we might want to prevent certain kinds of hate speech, and sanctions would deter such conduct, it might be a violation of the First Amendment.

Laws may pass through all the above filters but be too expensive (in terms of cost and time) to enforce.

Some limits are conceptual (laws forcing people to volunteer), some run up against limitations of human nature (laws forbidding self-defense), some run afoul of requirements of rationality (a law against committing suicide), some are norma-tive (laws requiring people to retreat when faced with home invaders). The limits I am going to consider are a special kind of normative limit. They are concerned with drawing a principled line between those actions that may be legitimately restricted by a democratic state and those that citizens must be left free to commit without fear of criminal sanctions.

It is important to note at the outset that there are two issues that should be kept distinct. The issue of legitimacy is the issue of what kinds of actions are within the legitimate scope of coercive action. This is the issue of *jurisdiction*. This is not the same as the question of what actions the state ought to require or forbid. This con-cerns which acts within the state's jurisdiction it ought to legislate about. This is the issue of the proper *exercise* of legitimate state power. Both of these are normative in character, but the former is the more fundamental. If the state is not entitled to coerce in some realm, the issue of whether it should is moot.

1

My first question is what it means to draw a *principled* line between those actions that are legitimately coercible and those that are not. The first thing to note is that any claim about the status of particular types of acts, for example, rape or drug sell-ing, has to be true in virtue of some general property that these acts share. If the selling of drugs should be legally permissible, it will be in terms of some property such as "a voluntary transaction between consenting adults, which does not affect in a significant manner the rights or interests of others." And if this is the right char-acterization of the act (for the purpose of drawing the limits of the law) then we have a general principle that explains and justifies (if correct) the kinds of grounds that underlie a limit thesis.

The second thing to note is that as a principle, it governs the kinds of *reasons* a state must have in order to justify coercive restrictions. But does any normative position count, in this context, as a principled reason or line? When Devlin says: "The line that divides the criminal law from the moral is not determinable by the application of any clear-cut principle…the boundary is fixed by balancing in the case of each particular crime the pros and cons of legal enforcement in accordance with the sorts of considerations I have been outlining,"[1] he is arguing precisely that it is a matter not of principle but of balancing particular factors to arrive at a judg-ment about whether some conduct should be criminalized or not.

So the contrast we are looking for is not one with no line at all, but one with a line that is justified by some general rule or norm that precludes (in general) look-ing at the particular factors in the situation. Mill's harm principle is a clear case of a principled line. "If anyone does an act hurtful to others, there is a prima facie case for punishing him by law." It is important to see that this is compatible, for Mill, with actually not punishing him because, say, "it is a kind of case in which he is on the whole likely to act better when left to his own discretion than when controlled in any way in which society have it in their power to control him; or because the attempt to exercise control would produce other evils, greater than those which it would prevent."[2] In these cases, it is still true that the act is of a type that is within the legitimate sphere of state coercion. Mill's principle is supposed to settle the issue of the state's jurisdiction, not the question of when the state should exercise its power within the jurisdiction.

Note also that both Mill and Devlin appeal to consequences. But Devlin thinks that we must balance the consequences for each proposed type of immoral conduct, whereas Mill thinks that we can set up general categories (e.g., harm to others) and draw a line permitting limiting such acts in advance. It is true that the argument for such a line is itself a consequentialist one "grounded on the permanent interests of man as a progressive being," but unless one is going to rule out as unprincipled any view that is founded on the balance of benefits over harms, this view draws a principled line.

There are other issues that could be addressed, for example, whether there are some constraints that ought to be placed on the kind of principle we are searching for. Liberal theorists have sometimes argued that the principles should be, in some sense, neutral. So, for example, the Rawlsian might argue for principles that "all citizens may reasonably be expected to endorse." A Scanlonian argues for principles that are "not reasonably rejectable." The idea is to avoid, if possible, appealing to any controversial conception of the good.

For our purposes, we shall only consider the controversy between those who might be called "particularists" and those who are "generalists," that is, between those who think we cannot in advance have general rules for what is legitimately coercible and those who think we can.

2

Let us begin by considering in very abstract terms what the possibilities for an argument for or against generalism might look like.

A Best Explanation of the Data

There might be a body of judgments widely shared in a community about what kinds of acts it is legitimate to restrict and what kinds it is not. We might agree that laws against certain kinds of force (murder and robbery), certain kinds of deception (fraudulent inducement), certain kinds of bodily infringement (rape and assault), certain kinds of speech (hate speech or blackmail), certain kinds of infringement of property rights (trespass and theft) are legitimately within the coercive power of the state. We might agree about this even if we thought that some of these acts ought not to be legislated against. So we might think that the state may properly legislate against intentional deception but that certain instances of this would be better left alone, for example, lies by a husband to his wife about his age.

There might also be widespread agreement that certain kinds of conduct are not legitimately coercible: who we have dinner with, what color clothes we wear, most of the things we say and write, what kind of church we attend, sexual acts between consensual adults in private, what risks we may take with our life and limb, and so forth.

There may, of course, be cases that are in dispute within the community. May one person kill another at the latter's request? May we force people to wear motorcycle helmets? What kinds of people may we refuse to rent our apartments to? Must we rescue people who are drowning in front of us?

The generalist believes that he can formulate general categories—the harmful, the evil, the offensive—that will capture and explain why we are entitled to interfere with the acts in the first category and not with those in the second. As to the disputed cases, he may have enough confidence in the categories that he lets them decide those cases.

The particularist denies that we can have a small number of clear and precise categories that can capture and explain all the data. Note that this is quite a different view from that of the generalist, who believes that the particular categories ought to be added to or subtracted from in order to account for our judgments. He is disagreeing with the generalist about his theory not whether such a theory is possible.

B Criticism of Theoretical Arguments

There are arguments for specific generalist positions that do not start from a data base and try to explain it. Instead they proceed from some values or ideal of a just society and attempt to show that certain legitimacy principles follow (or at least cohere with) the values or ideals. As an example of this, consider the structure of Feinberg's *Moral Limits of the Criminal Law*.

He begins from a foundation of liberalism in autonomy. "The spirit of liberalism" lies in its "concern for humanity...limited only by its respect for autonomy."[3] He also assumes that only certain parts of morality may be enforced by the criminal law. For Feinberg it is a question of "*which* judgments on behavior may rightly receive the stamp of moral certification from the criminal law, *not* whether in applying that stamp the criminal law is enforcing some moral judgments or other."[4]

As Postema claims, Feinberg's view "takes as morally fundamental the claims persons are entitled to make in their own names and for their own sakes. Whenever demands of morality in this domain are ignored or defied, there are assignable persons who are entitled to complain, 'to voice grievances in protest, and press for some sort of remedy or censure.' The morality of Feinberg's liberalism is 'grievance morality.'"[5]

One way of arguing against the idea of principled restrictions is to consider arguments such as Feinberg's and show that they are not sound. Obviously, this would have to be done for all the plausible arguments (Mill, Dworkin, Ripstein, etc.), and at that, one would have only shown that the arguments produced so far in the history of the topic are not good ones.

C Impossibility Arguments

These are arguments that attempt to show directly that no system of principles could be developed. Something like this has been put forward by particularists like Dancy with respect to any moral principles. If there are no moral principles, then there are no moral principles that determine the legitimacy of state coercion. Philosophical anarchists believe there are no such principles, not because they think there could not be but because they think in fact the state has no right to coerce. Particularists, like Devlin, think the state does have a right to coerce but that there is no set of principles that explain and justify the kinds of actions that may be coerced. To my knowledge, nobody has developed an argument to show that there could not be principled restrictions.

3

I turn now to what I will call the demarcation problem. Every theory about the limits of the criminal law assumes that conduct that is to be forbidden must be wrong, immoral, a violation of rights, or something along these lines. Crimes are those wrongs that are punished by the law. This may be because the wrong is wrong independently of the law—malum in se—or because it is made wrong by being criminalized: malum prohibitum. In this sense, the idea that the law enforces morality is necessarily true.

The disputes concern different views of the nature of morality, disputes about whether immorality per se is sufficient to bring acts within the jurisdiction of state coercion, and disagreements about whether all of morality or only subsets may be enforced.

This agreement raises two problems. Why is immorality of some kind a necessary condition for bringing acts within the jurisdiction of the state? Why is immorality—perhaps accompanied by other features of the act—sufficient for settling jurisdiction?

After all, with respect to the former, one might have thought the fact that an action was unaesthetic, for example, the constructing of a building out of character with its surroundings, might have been enough to warrant sanctions. Or the fact that an action was profoundly self-destructive—where this is not thought of as a wrong to the self—might have warranted its being forbidden.

With respect to the latter, one might have thought that it requires some argument to the effect that the state has standing to punish people for their wrongs.

When we do not punish various forms of deception, for example, a husband lying about his age to his wife, is it the case that by being a lie the act is within the jurisdiction of the state but there are various reasons of a pragmatic character for not interfering? Or does this kind of immorality not lie within the jurisdiction of the state?

The first distinction that must be made is between positive and critical morality. The positive morality of a society is the set of moral rules, principles, codes that are actually accepted or believed to be true by (most of?) the citizens of the society. In that sense, it is part of the positive morality of our society that heroin use, assisted suicide, and rape are immoral. The critical morality is the set of rules, and so on, that one believes are the correct, best justified, true views concerning moral matters for the society. While I think the question of when positive morality (even if incorrect) may be enforced is an interesting one—for example, may Israel prevent buses from running on the Sabbath—my discussion will be confined to the enforcement of critical morality.

In an earlier essay, I argued that the fact that certain acts were wrong implied that they were not to be done. I then continued: "this provides a reason—perhaps conclusive, perhaps not—for discouraging the performance of such actions."[6]

But, as Postema has argued, it does not follow from this claim that the state may enforce morality. First, one needs an argument, and second, such an argument will involve substantive moral premises to show that the state has standing to legislate and punish those who commit acts of a certain type. In the following, I will explore various views about standing and the arguments connected with them.

The general issue of standing is the question of why if an act is immoral, or harmful to others, or offensive, or harmful to self, or degrading to the person who does it, this gives the state any right or license to criminalize the act and to punish those who perform it. One aspect of this issue is the demarcation problem, that is, may the mere fact that an act is wrong or immoral put the conduct within the jurisdiction of the state, or is it only some subset of immorality that plays this role? In particular, Feinberg has argued that only what he calls a violation of "grievance" morality brings an act within the scope of state power—although that does not settle the issue of whether the state ought to actually enforce it. The latter issue brings in many practical and normative considerations that must be evaluated to see whether a compelling case can be made for enforcement.

Different theorists pick out different predicates (harm, immoral, degrading) and give different answers to the issue of standing. As far as I can see, the types of argument are limited to the following.

A Arguments from the Nature of the State

Hobbes argues that to remedy various evils, we contract out of the state of nature and accept what the sovereign regards as necessary to the prevention of various evils. The state has jurisdiction because we create it to have such jurisdiction.

Kant argues that having an institution such as the state is necessary for a regime of rights, which in turn is necessary for a certain kind of moral relationship to hold between free and equal persons.

A rule-utilitarian will argue that best consequences follow from having a state that will enforce certain rules of morality. The rules are those such that general observance would produce the best consequences. Of course, not all such rules should be legally enforced, but the issue of those that should is also determined by which rule(s) concerning the types of acts to be enforced would produce best consequences.

B Arguments from the Nature of the Category

By "the category" I mean the concept used to pick out those acts that may be coerced. So, for example, Feinberg argues that a violation of grievance morality, and only grievance morality, involves the individual having a claim against others to prevent a violation of the rights of the individual that have been infringed. It is a personal claim, and a claim to the protection of others.

Devlin argues that any violation of the accepted morality of a society threatens the existence of the society and the moral integrity of the community, and since a society always has the right to preserve its existence, and the appropriate instrument for that protection is the state, this gives the state standing.[7]

Postema argues that the relevant concept is the public morality of a community: "members of the community have a stake in the moral integrity of the moral life of the community and…that legal enactment and enforcement of the community's public morality is an appropriate method of protecting that stake."[8]

In all these cases, the theorist has two tasks; first, to show that there is an argument from the nature or value of the concept to the standing of the state to enforce, and second, to show that the concept is a necessary condition for such standing, that is, alternative notions do not have similar arguments to standing.

Thus, Feinberg has to show, first, that grievance morality entitles the state to enforce the grievance, and second, that it is entitled to enforce only acts that fall within grievance morality. The former follows if we accept his analysis of what it is to have a right. The harder task is to limit the scope of state jurisdiction just to those individual wrongs. Why, for example, may the state not enforce ideals (e.g., dignity and dwarf-tossing) or harms such as corruption of someone's character? The hardest cases for him are those such as Irving Kristol's consensual gladiatorial contests. Feinberg treats these as cases of harmless immorality by appealing to the Volenti principle (to him who consents, no wrong has been done). Although the interests of the gladiator who is killed have been damaged, no wrong has been done to him. He cannot complain. He is not entitled to call on the state to protect him. Even were this true, it does not follow that the rest of us may not call on the state to prevent these contests.

4

Here is an outline of the argumentative strategy Feinberg uses.

1. There is a strong inclination, which Feinberg shares, to think it legitimate to criminalize gladiatorial contests.
2. The only liberty-limiting principles are harm to others and the offense principle.
3. Try and show that criminalizing gladiatorial contests falls under the harm principle. The spectators are being morally corrupted with respect to dispositions about the suffering of other people. Therefore, the interests of others become vulnerable.
4. This argument may fail, because people may be able to compartmentalize their attitudes so that they distinguish between killing volunteers for profit and other kinds of non-consented-to killings.
5. Invoke the idea that doubts about the voluntariness of the gladiators are sufficient to justify criminalizing gladiatorial contests (call this "bold liberalism").
6. Concede that an evil such as this is a relevant reason for coercion, that is, the act is within the legitimate sphere of state coercion, but that it, in fact, will never be weighty enough to outweigh the case for liberty (call this "moderate liberalism").

Now, in fact, there is an alternative strategy for holding onto bold liberalism. One could give up the Volenti principle. In the gladiator case, this would involve bringing it under the harm principle, by denying that the mere fact that one has consented to some harm, namely, the risk of death, makes it, either because the harm is treated as self-inflicted or because the action is treated as if it were one of harmless wrongdoing, a case of action that the state cannot legitimately coerce. If, as some have contended, there are certain rights that cannot be alienated, then one retains the right not to be harmed (even if one has consented to the harm), and consequently, the action is one that the state can legitimately coerce despite the consent. So the issue becomes one of relative costs to the theory. Does Feinberg lose more than he gains by abandoning the Volenti principle?

The first thing to note is that it would surely be a mistake to abandon the Volenti principle in general. It is clear that consent is a moral power to alter the normative status of various acts. What would otherwise be theft is a gift if I consent to your possession of a good of mine. What would otherwise be rape is merely sex if mutual consent is present. What would otherwise be battery is consent if I say that you may perform surgery on me. Feinberg is surely right to argue that often the issue of whether I have been wronged depends on whether, and how freely, I have consented to what you do to me.

It is an essential part of his arguments against paternalism as well. Otherwise the manufacturer and distributor of cigarettes to willing purchasers is on a par with the person who puts poison in your food.

So the essential question is not whether the Volenti principle is ever valid but whether it has limits. Are there kinds of acts that are still wrongs even if they have been (freely) consented to? Are there limits to what a person may (permissibly) consent to?

We should recall that even Mill, that stalwart opponent of paternalism, made an exception to voluntary slavery. It is an argument to the effect that the decision to become a slave represents not simply a decision to abandon autonomy (retaining the possibility of regaining it) but to enter a situation in which one cannot rethink the decision and decide to regain one's autonomy. Given Mill's theory of value, according to which the development of autonomous individuals is required for util-ity, a utilitarian theory cannot accept such a permanent abandonment of future autonomy. Whatever the nature of the argument, it is clearly an instance where Mill abandons the Volenti principle. Consent in *this* type of case cannot perform its normal task of immunizing what is done against legal sanction.

It is true that we have in this case not a use of the criminal law to threaten but rather a denial of the civil law to enforce a contract. But I see no reason to suppose that Mill could not support the former as an additional tool to prevent voluntary slavery.

Arthur Ripstein, in a recent article on the harm principle, argues for a limita-tion on the Volenti principle in terms of sovereignty. Here is his argument:

> The sovereignty principle provides a different account, one that takes off from the respects in which the familiar exceptions to the consent principle are distinctive. Because it regards independence as relational, the sovereignty principle must also regard consent as a relationship between persons, rather than as a sort of blanket abandonment of rights. If you court danger by walking alone through a dangerous neighborhood after dark, you don't thereby give anyone who attacks you the right to do so; if you consent to my napping in your bed, you don't thereby consent to anyone else doing so, even if I invite them to. The sovereignty principle dictates that consent be understood as a transfer of rights between two persons, and any such transfer is something the two of them do together. The idea of independent people doing something together precludes two people from jointly terminating the independence of one of them. The sovereignty principle has no resources to prohibit suicide, since it doesn't involve domination. But it doesn't need to prohibit suicide in order to deny that consent is a defense to murder. The problem is with one person giving another the power of life and death over them, not with the fact that the victim chooses to die.[9]

The problem with this argument is that it seems too strong. For it applies just as well to cases of physician-assisted suicide and euthanasia, which I believe the law can legitimately permit in certain circumstances.

I want to consider one more case that bears on the Volenti principle. This is the case of dwarf-tossing. This is a "bar sport" in which dwarfs are fitted out with pad-ding and helmets, and have handles attached to their backs. The contest is to see who can throw them the furthest. My view is that this is a plausible case for making illegal.

So the issue remains whether one can find limits to the Volenti principle that enable us to reconcile the following views:

1. It is legitimate to forbid slavery contracts and gladiatorial contests, and perhaps cases like dwarf-tossing.
2. It is legitimate, in some circumstances, to legally permit assisted suicide and euthanasia.
3. The Volenti principle is valid for many cases of harm to which people consent.

Why is the Volenti principle valid at all? Why does it seem plausible in many cases? The obvious explanation is that consent is a moral power to change the moral status of acts. But it is not clear exactly what the explanation of that power is. There are alternative models.

On one model, by consenting I give up something and transfer it to you. I had the right to use this hat. I had the sole power to determine how it would be used. By giving you the hat, by consenting to your possession of it, I give up my right to determine use and transfer it to you. It is a corollary of this transfer that I no longer have a right to complain when you destroy the hat or wear it in a way of which I do not approve.

On another model, that of Kant, consent involves two people "uniting their wills." It is not a matter of my giving up something. As Ripstein puts it, it is "not that the consenting person has surrendered something, but rather that by uniting his or her will with that of another person, he or she has made that other person's action an exercise of his or her own purposiveness." So when I consent to your doing something to me, it is as if we are acting jointly. I have the same responsibility for what you do as if I were doing it to myself.[10]

On a third model—Larry Alexander's—consenting just *is* giving up one's right to complain about the crossing of a moral boundary.[11]

These models can have various moral implications. For example, on the last model it does not follow from the fact that *you* have waived the right to complain that others may not have the right to complain on your behalf. The fact that you are willing to undergo debasing and humiliating conduct (dwarf-tossing) does not settle the issue of whether we cannot criticize you and the others for such an agreement. Whether we can, in addition, make it legally difficult for the consented-to action to take place will depend on whether some principle such as moral paternalism or legal moralism can be justified. The former is the view that it is permissible for the state to interfere with consensual acts in order to make the parties morally better off or to make the parties better morally. The latter is the view that it is permissible for the state to interfere simply on the grounds that the conduct in question is immoral.

Suppose we accept the Alexander view that the source of the change of moral status is the waiving of one's right to complain about what is done to one. This has a weaker and a stronger version. The weaker is just that you no longer have the status to complain, but it may still be that your rights have been violated. The stronger is that you no longer have the status to complain because your rights cannot be violated if you waive them. The Volenti principle seems better explained by the latter reading. It is clearly the one Feinberg uses in his arguments. The law is limited to the protection of people's rights. Only if there is someone who has been wronged may we intervene; mere wrongdoing is not enough. What the law may enforce is grievance morality. Satisfaction of the Volenti principle removes the case from grievance morality.

If we accept Feinberg's premises, then to make them compatible with interference with gladiators and dwarfs we must interpret the Volenti principle in such a way that it is not satisfied in these cases. This means that there are some acts, fully consented to, that leave rights intact (although it may be the case that the person has forfeited his right to complain about the violation). This, of course, is just the doctrine of inalienable rights.

Now, "inalienability" comes in weaker and stronger versions as well. The weaker version is that one cannot abandon one's rights permanently, that is, a general abandonment of one's rights. The stronger version is that cannot abandon them even on a single occasion. Note that the gladiator case differs from the dwarf case just in the fact that the former involves permanent abandonment (at least it risks that) whereas the latter might only involve abandoning one's rights to dignity on a single occasion.

Another ambiguity is between rights that can neither be forfeited nor waived and rights that can be forfeited but not waived. Thus one might have a right to life that could be forfeited by one's attempting to take the life of another, but not waived, by, say, consenting to be killed by another.

Finally, we must distinguish between waiving the exercise of a right one continues to possess and waiving the right itself.[12] If I ask your assistance in committing suicide, I do not waive my right to life; I relinquish the exercise of that right.

What kind of theory could explain the judgments in the four cases—gladiatorial contest, voluntary slavery, dwarf-tossing, justified euthanasia?

First, no inalienable rights theory will do. If the right to life is inalienable, then both the gladiator and the euthanasia cases must be classified as violations of the individual's right to life. If the judgment about euthanasia is correct, then rational persons must, in certain circumstances, be entitled to lift the moral barrier against being killed by others.

Second, it does not look plausible that a single theory explains both the slavery and dwarf-tossing cases. The intuition behind not allowing people to enter into slavery contracts is that it is wrong for people to renounce their autonomy on a permanent and irrevocable basis. The intuition behind the dwarf-tossing case is that it is wrong for people to allow themselves to be degraded in certain ways. Of course, if one is prepared to allow as a single theory something like a Rossian view that we must weigh the reasons for and against in each case and judge which reasons are weightier, then there could be a theory. But it would not be informative.

In my view, we are left with a problem to be solved. Of course, if one does not share my judgments about the cases, then there will be no problem to be solved.[13]

5

The last issue I want to discuss is that of so-called neutrality. This is supposed to be a kind of metaprinciple that restricts the kinds of first-order principles that can be considered for regulating criminalization. It is obviously a substantive claim, and it is closely associated with liberal views, so it is sometimes called "liberal neutrality."

The basic idea is to restrict the kinds of reasons that the state may appeal to when criminalizing conduct. The state, as a state of all its citizens, is supposed to be appropriately neutral about the citizens' views about what constitutes a good, ideal, worthwhile way of living one's life. In its criminal law—not necessarily its tort or contract law—the state ought not to favor one group of citizens' moral, religious, aesthetic preferences over those of others. This is compatible with using the law to enforce a system of rights that safeguards the ability of each citizen to define and pursue her own conception of the good life.

This claim has been justified in many different ways. Some, like Locke in his argument for religious toleration, argue that it is impossible to promote certain goods by coercive means. Some, like Rawls, argue that for political purposes only views acceptable to all behind a veil of ignorance are legitimate. Some, like Mill, argue that the state is not competent to determine what is good in some area, for example, what is in the best interests of any person. Some argue for a modus vivendi, in order to preserve civil peace. Some argue that the imposition of certain ideals is incompatible with the ideal of autonomous individuals choosing for themselves their own mode of living.

I want to concentrate on this last idea—that there is a higher order restriction on the content of criminal laws that stems from a certain ideal of the state as recognizing its citizens as autonomous. The issue then becomes framed in terms of how a state can force people to act counter to their own conception of what is right or wrong, good or bad, worthwhile or not. The solution, following Kant and Rousseau (and in our time, Rawls) is to show that legitimate laws are ones that are, in some sense, acceptable to each citizen. These laws are, in some sense, willed or recognized as valid by the citizens' own powers of reason. And laws that cannot pass this test are illegitimate.

To advance our understanding of this idea, we have to understand what it means for citizens to be autonomous, and we have to understand what types of laws are inconsistent with the ideal of autonomy. In particular, let us consider three paradigms. First, a law making rape illegal is paradigmatic of a law that clearly is consistent with autonomy. Second, a law that prevents people from advocating socialism is paradigmatic of a law that is clearly inconsistent with autonomy. Third, a law that makes gladiatorial contests for public exhibition illegal is a law whose status is unclear.

"Autonomy" is a term with many meanings and is used in connection with different theoretical tasks. For our purposes, it must be distinguished from notions of liberty or freedom. For any law—whether legitimate or not—limits people's liberty.

It must also be distinguished from notions of rational or prudent action. For people may have a right to do what is nonrational or imprudent. The concept we want has to do with preserving the ability of persons to make their own judgments about what kind of life to lead, and to be able to use those judgments to inform their actions and decisions. This is the conception advanced by, among others, Joseph Raz. He defines autonomous persons as "those who can shape their life and determine its course…creators of their own moral world."[14] There are certain conditions that are necessary for a person to be autonomous—adequate options, sufficient mental abilities, and freedom from coercion and manipulation. Finally, Raz interprets autonomy so that its value is dependent on being directed at good options. A person may be autonomous even if he pursues what is bad, but his autonomy only has value if he chooses the good. This does not mean, according to Raz, that when a person uses his autonomy to pursue bad ends we are always entitled to interfere with him. Coercion, being an interference with autonomy, may only be imposed to promote greater autonomy, and not every pursuit of bad ends will produce more loss of autonomy than coercion does.

It is obvious that this theory assumes that autonomy is a value that sometimes justifies coercion. But then it is hardly neutral between those who value autonomy highly and those who either do not value it at all or value it much less. Some liberal theorists have gone further in specifying the relevant sense of autonomy as one that respects "neutrality." The idea here is that in justifying laws, the legislature is not allowed to make assumptions about what kinds of life it is good or best for people to lead. Examples of laws that, it is arguable, are only justifiable by making such assumptions are laws that require people to worship in a particular church on the grounds that only those who are saved lead a good life, or laws that prevent people from taking certain drugs on the ground that such drugs cause people to be disconnected from reality and only such a connection allows people to lead a good life, or laws that make prostitution illegal solely on the grounds that sex for money is not a worthwhile activity.

This idea of neutrality is antiperfectionistic. In Peter deMarneffe's words, "It holds that the fact that an activity is not excellent or admirable or part of the best possible human life, or that it is shameful, base, or degrading, or that it inhibits the full development and exercise of the higher human capacities is not alone sufficient to justify the government in prohibiting this activity."[15]

The problem here is that while one may agree with any of the particular claims made above, it is not clear that there is some concept of neutrality that is independently specifiable, independently justifiable, and clear enough to make the distinctions we want. When Mill justifies his antipaternalism on the "permanent interests of man as a progressive being" and holds that these interests include our developing our individuality, our own way of life, isn't he violating the neutrality principle by making a claim about what kind of life it is good or best for persons to live? Don't (some) egalitarians believe that some distribution is legitimate, just on the grounds that a more equal distribution is a more just one?

DeMarneffe has argued recently that even if we cannot find a conception of neutrality that is such that it specifies a morally relevant property that is possessed only by legitimate laws and never by illegitimate ones, we can at least specify a list of reasons that are nonneutral, and therefore that cannot be appealed to in justifying a law.[16] But this appeal to "I don't know what neutrality is but I know nonneutrality when I see it" is, at least, theoretically unsatisfying. As the philosopher said, "I know it works in practice, but does it work in theory?"

NOTES

1. P. Devlin, *The Enforcement of Morals* (London: Oxford University Press, 1965), pp. 21–22.

2. J. S. Mill, *On Liberty* (Liberal Arts Press, 1958), pp. 14–15.

3. J. Feinberg, *The Moral Limits of the Criminal Law: Harmless Wrongdoing* (New York: Oxford University Press, 1988), p. 28.

4. Ibid., p. 13.

5. G. Postema, "Politics Is About the Grievance: Feinberg on the Legal Enforcement of Morals," *Legal Theory* 11, 2005, p. 294.

6. G. Dworkin, "Devlin Was Right: Law and the Enforcement of Morality," *William and Mary Law Review* 40, 1999, p. 943.

7. P. Devlin, *The Enforcement of Morals*.

8. "Public Faces, Private Places," reprinted in G. Dworkin, *Morality, Harm and the Law* (Boulder, Co.: Westview Press, 1994), p. 88.

9. A. Ripstein, "Beyond the Harm Principle," *Philosophy and Public Affairs* 34, 2006, 236n.

10. Personal communication.

11. L. Alexander, "The Moral Magic of Consent," *Legal Theory* 2, 1996, p. 165.

12. All of these distinctions are made by Feinberg in a (neglected) article, "Voluntary Euthanasia and the Inalienable Right to Life," *Philosophy and Public Affairs* 7, 1977, pp. 93–123.

13. For some fascinating case materials and interesting discussion of the Volenti Principle, see Vera Bergelson, "Consent to Harm," *Pace Law Review,* forthcoming.

14. J. Raz, *The Morality of Freedom* (Oxford: Clarendon Press, 1986), p. 154.

15. P. deMarneffe, "The Possibility and Desirability of Neutrality," unpublished manuscript.

16. Ibid.

CHAPTER 2

CRIMINALIZING EXPRESSION: HATE SPEECH AND OBSCENITY

L. W. SUMNER

> Since many acts may be "harmful," and since society has many other
> means for controlling or responding to conduct, criminal law should be
> used only when the harm caused or threatened is serious, and when the
> other, less coercive or less intrusive means do not work or are
> inappropriate.
>
> Government of Canada, *The Criminal Law in Canadian Society* (1982).

THE costs of the criminal law are high. Not just the social or economic costs of the criminal justice system, though they are indeed high, especially in countries with a special zeal for incarcerating their citizens, but also the costs to offenders who are subjected to its uniquely severe sanctions. It is the costs of criminal law that make its use as a means of regulating conduct so difficult to justify. That justificatory threshold is commonly thought to be particularly difficult to surmount when the conduct in question is speech or expression. When, if ever, is the harm caused or threatened by expression serious enough to warrant control by means of criminal sanctions? And when, if ever, are less coercive or intrusive means unworkable or inappropriate? These are the questions I plan to explore in this chapter, with hate speech and obscenity as my two test cases. Throughout the discussion I will use Canadian free speech law and jurisprudence as my reference point, since (as we shall see) the Canadian courts have been particularly obliging in raising and responding to the principal philosophical issues concerning the criminal regulation of expression.

1 THE MORAL LIMITS OF THE CRIMINAL LAW

If we are seeking a principled approach to the legal regulation of expression, then a natural place to start is with John Stuart Mill's classic essay "On Liberty." Mill addresses this issue directly in the second chapter of his essay, where he argues that the pursuit of truth (or knowledge) is best enhanced by affording unlimited freedom for the circulation of ideas, regardless of how unpopular or offensive they might be. Mill's trenchant defense of free inquiry and free discussion has been much cited, and also much criticized, since it was first published a century and a half ago. So the most obvious way for me to proceed would be to see how well his arguments stand up when applied to my two test cases. However, there are problems with this approach. The least of them is that Mill himself never discussed either (what we now regard as) hate speech or obscenity, so we would be left to speculate whether he would want to include these forms of expression within the bounds of his "liberty of discussion." More important, Mill limits his topic to the free circulation of opinions—above all, opinions about "morals, religion, politics, social relations, and the business of life."[1] Many instances of hate speech readily qualify as the expression of such opinions, though it is doubtful that all do.[2] But the category of opinion seems scarcely to apply to pornography, virtually all of which nowadays is visual. Furthermore, Mill's self-imposed restriction to opinions is no accident since his entire case for freedom of expression is truth based; it therefore can be applied only to forms of expression that have a truth value. And therein lies its most serious limitation.

In his classic treatment of free speech issues, Frederick Schauer identified three principal values commonly thought to be protected by rights of free expression: truth, democracy, and individual autonomy or self-fulfillment.[3] The selfsame values are now routinely rehearsed by courts in their adjudication of free speech issues.[4] Anyone who has read Mill's political philosophy will agree that he cannot be accused of overlooking the value of either democracy or self-fulfillment, or of failing to appreciate the contribution of free expression to both of them. But these values play little role in his truth-based arguments in chapter 2 of "On Liberty." Furthermore, Mill's preoccupation with truth (or knowledge) leaves no room for appreciating the grounds most commonly offered for regulating hate speech or obscenity, which look not to the stamping out of falsehood or error but to the prevention of harm (to minorities, women, children, etc.). There is little in Mill's treatment of "liberty of discussion" that speaks to these issues. To bring the resources of "On Liberty" to bear on them, we need to look beyond Mill's specific arguments in chapter 2 to the main theme of the work as a whole.

That theme, Mill tells us at the outset, is "the nature and limits of the power which can be legitimately exercised by society over the individual."[5] What Mill is seeking is a general principle that will define the limits of social interference with the activities of individual citizens or, what comes to the same thing, the limits of individual liberty of action. The kinds of social interference he has in mind include not only the formal mechanisms available to the state through its legal system—paradigmatically the use of criminal sanctions—but also the more informal ways dissident minorities can be suppressed or silenced by dominant social groups: what Mill calls "the tyranny of the majority." Among the activities susceptible to these forms of interference, it is clear that Mill attached a special importance to the expression or discussion of opinions, since he allocated the longest chapter of his essay exclusively to this case. However, it is but one example of the freedoms Mill defended, which is why its treatment is embedded within the larger theme of liberty of action in general.

Mill's statement of his principle of liberty is well known: "the only purpose for which power can be rightfully exercised over any member of a civilized community, against his will, is to prevent harm to others. His own good, either physical or moral, is not a sufficient warrant."[6] Because this principle defines the limits of individual liberty in terms of harm to others, it has come to be known as the *harm principle*. The harm principle states that in the social realm, where harm to others is involved, individuals may rightfully be subject to coercion or control, while in their purely personal conduct, where no such harm is involved, their liberty must be protected. As such, the harm principle excludes two other possible justifications for the coercive regulation of individual conduct: the *paternalism principle* (prevention of harm to self) and the *moralism principle* (prohibition of harmless conduct on the ground that it is, or is commonly thought to be, immoral).

According to Mill, the personal sphere protected by the harm principle comprises (1) the "inward domain of consciousness," including conscience, thought, feeling, opinion, and the like; (2) living out our own plan of life (as long we do not thereby harm others); and (3) voluntary association with others (again for purposes that do not harm third parties).[7] These "parts of life" are to be protected against social interference by means of rights to such things as freedom of conscience, privacy (as we would now put it), and freedom of association. For our purposes, what is noteworthy about this list is what it does not include: the activity of "expressing and publishing opinions." Mill clearly does not mean to exclude this activity from the protected region of liberty. But he does flag its special status by recognizing that "it belongs to that part of the conduct of an individual which concerns other people."[8] In other words, while Mill argues for an extensive freedom to express and discuss opinions, he does not base his argument for that freedom on the claim that these activities belong to the personal domain by virtue of posing no risk of harm to others. But this means that Mill's treatment of freedom of expression (or discussion) is anomalous within the overall argumentative scheme of "On Liberty": it is the only activity falling within the social (rather than the personal) sphere to which Mill allocates a lengthy dedicated discussion and the only one for which he urges (nearly) absolute protection against social interference. His reason for giving expression this privileged status is that liberty of discussion "being almost of as much importance as the liberty of thought itself, and resting in great part on the same reasons, is practically inseparable from it."[9]

Mill's point is obvious: the freedom to hold any opinion you wish is worth little without the companion freedom to advocate, discuss, and circulate it. However, his recognition that the latter activities are, by virtue of their capacity for harming others, social rather than personal has far-reaching implications for his defense of freedom of discussion. Whatever falls within the personal realm receives principled protection: social interference, whether by official or unofficial means, is here absolutely prohibited. The case is quite different for social acts: "As soon as any part of a person's conduct affects prejudicially the interests of others, society has jurisdiction over it, and the question whether the general welfare will or will not be promoted by interfering with it, becomes open to discussion. But there is no room for entertaining any such question when a person's conduct affects the interests of no persons besides himself."[10] Mill is not here suggesting that interference is warranted whenever an activity falls within the social realm; on the contrary, "it must by no means be supposed, because damage, or probability of damage, to the interests of others, can alone justify the interference of society, that therefore it always does justify such interference. In many cases, an individual, in pursuing a legitimate object, necessarily and therefore legitimately causes pain or loss to others."[11] Under the harm principle, harm to others is a necessary condition for social interference with an activity but not a sufficient one.

Since the expression of opinions falls within the social and not the personal realm, the question whether it should be interfered with in any way should be "open to discussion" and settled by reference to the general welfare. If we assume that this is the way Mill sees the question, then it becomes possible to understand what he is trying to do in chapter 2 of "On Liberty." The burden of his argument is that while the expression of opinion is indeed a social act, a policy of interference with it will nonetheless be inimical to the general welfare. For Mill, therefore, the question whether a policy of interfering with expression, or with a particular category of expression, is justified can be answered only by undertaking a consequentialist cost-benefit calculation. For those who tend to regard Mill as a free speech absolutist, this may be a surprising result, but it will be so only if they conflate two different aspects of his doctrine. The liberty of discussion Mill advocates is indeed (nearly) absolute; however, it is also the conclusion of a (truth-based) cost-benefit balancing. Besides this consequentialist foundation, the other principal lesson to be drawn from Mill's principled framework is the centrality of the harm question. On Mill's view, coercive interference with any form of conduct (therefore any form of expression) can be justified only if *both* of the following principles are satisfied:

> *Harm principle*: The conduct in question causes or threatens harm to others.
> *Consequentialist principle*: Interference with the conduct will yield a better balance of benefits over costs than noninterference.

Both principles impose justificatory burdens on any agency, such as the state, that would restrict expression. The first burden is that of showing that the expression in question poses a significant risk of harm to parties other than those who are voluntary consumers of it.[12] Because liberty is a benefit for those who possess it, every restraint is (as Mill puts it), qua restraint, an evil. Especially where forms of expressions are concerned, we begin with an initial presumption of freedom, against which it is the burden of the state to make a convincing case by providing reliable evidence of the link between the expression in question and the harm it causes. It follows immediately that if there are forms of expression that pose no (or no significant) risk of harm to others, then the freedom to engage in them must be inviolable. Much work still remains to be done, of course, to determine what constitutes harm, when one individual's actions pose a risk of harm to others, and when that risk should be deemed significant. But once that work is done, a finding that some form of expression is harmless (in the relevant sense) is a guarantee of the right to circulate it.

The more difficult cases are those in which the risk of harm is a factor and in which it must therefore be decided whether that risk justifies (some form of) social interference. The second, consequentialist, condition does not provide a simple algorithm for deciding whether, and when, the state is entitled to enforce restrictions on forms of expression in those cases in which the harm principle is satisfied. However, the consequentialist condition does suggest the kinds of factors that will be relevant. First, the restriction must have some reasonable expectation of success. While it may be thought desirable to inhibit or suppress some form of expression by legal means, it is a further question whether doing so is possible. To the extent that the restrictions can be readily circumvented, by an underground market or by technological innovations such as the Internet, the case for them is weakened. Second, there must be no less costly policy available for securing the same results. Even when it promises to be effective in preventing some significant social harm, suppression abridges personal liberty and deprives consumers of whatever benefits they may derive from the prohibited forms of expression. Suppression should therefore be the last, not the first, resort of government for preventing the harm in question. Where other "less coercive or intrusive means" promise comparable results, they should be preferred. Where a narrower infringement of freedom of expression will be equally effective, it, too, should be preferred. Third, the expected benefits of the restriction must, on balance, justify its costs. Censorship can compromise other important social values, such as vigorous engagement in public debate. It can have a "chilling effect" on legitimate forms of expression (literary, artistic, etc.). However well intended the restriction might be, in practice it will be administered by police, prosecutors, judges, and bureaucrats who may use it to justify targeting unpopular, marginal forms of literature with no significant capacity for social harm. Given the inevitable gap between the de jure and de facto policy, the additional protection of vulnerable groups provided by legal restraints on expression must be great enough to justify the collateral costs.

These conditions raise a high justificatory threshold for restrictions on freedom of expression. Whether a policy of imposing content restrictions on hate speech or obscenity can surmount this threshold remains to be determined. The argumentative framework Mill deploys in "On Liberty" does not answer this question for us, but it does help us to get the question right. Furthermore, something very like it has been adopted by the Canadian courts in their adjudication of free speech issues. Section 2(b) of the Canadian Charter of Rights and Freedoms gives constitutional protection to the right to free expression, while section 1 stipulates that all of the specific rights enumerated in the Charter are subject to "such reasonable limits pre-scribed by law as can be demonstrably justified in a free and democratic society." The Charter is therefore a convenient vehicle for raising the question whether the regulation of hate speech or obscenity, by means of criminal sanctions, is a "reason-able limit" on the right of free expression.

In the two following sections, we will examine the answers the Canadian Supreme Court has given to these questions in the leading Canadian hate speech and obscenity cases. It is worth outlining in advance the methodology—set out in its 1986 *Oakes* decision—the Court employed in both instances.[13] In order for a limit on a Charter right to be "reasonable," it must pass two tests, one concerning its end, and the other concerning the means it employs to achieve that end:

1. *Legislative objective:* The purpose of the legislation must be sufficiently "pressing and substantial" to justify limiting the right.
2. *Proportionality:* The means employed by the legislation must be propor-tional to the objective to be achieved. The proportionality test subdivides into three parts:
   a. *Rational connection:* There must be reasonable grounds for expecting the legislation to be effective in achieving its objective.
   b. *Minimal impairment:* The legislation must limit the right no more than is necessary in order to achieve its objective.
   c. *Proportional effects:* The costs of the limitation must not exceed the benefits to be gained from achieving the objective.

Only in very rare instances has the Court found a piece of legislation so wanting in legitimate rationale as to fail the first test.[14] The main issue at stake in its section 1 adjudication, therefore, has been the application of the proportionality test, which requires that the expected benefits of the legislation be balanced against its expected costs. The rational connection requirement is intended to ensure that the benefits promised by the legislation will actually be delivered; legislation will fail at this step if it can be shown to be ineffective or, worse, actually counterproductive. Minimal impairment then moves us to the cost side, where the question now is whether the legislation impairs the right in question to a greater extent than is necessary in order to yield its expected benefits; the usual ground of failure at this step is overbreadth. Finally, the proportional effects requirement brings the cost and benefit sides together, in order to determine whether the benefits of the legislation are worth securing in the face of its predictable costs.

The similarities between the *Oakes* tests and Mill's conditions for a justified limit on individual liberty are obvious. The first test—legislative objective—is the analogue of Mill's harm principle, since it raises a justificatory threshold that a right-infringing piece of legislation must surmount in advance of any cost-benefit balancing.[15] Mill's consequentialist principle then has its counter-part in the second *Oakes* test of proportionality, with its balancing of the expected costs and benefits of the legislation in question.[16] In this way both Mill and the Court identify the same central issues for determining whether—and, if so, when—the criminal regulation of hate speech or obscenity can be justified: the risk of harm posed by these forms of expression and the cost-benefit balance of measures designed to prevent this harm. To these issues, therefore, we now turn.

2 HATE SPEECH

In common with most European countries (but unlike the United States), Canada regulates hate speech by means of criminal law. Section 319(2) of the Criminal Code, first enacted in 1970, prohibits the willful promotion of hatred against groups identified by such characteristics as race and religion.[17] In *Keegstra* (1990), a constitutional challenge was raised against this section, primarily on the ground that it was an unjustifiable infringement of section 2(b) of the Charter. In its judgment, the Court upheld the constitutionality of the hate promotion law by a narrow four-to-three majority. Both sides on the Court agreed that hateful expression was covered by section 2(b), thus that the law did indeed infringe the Charter right. The issue therefore was whether this infringement was "demonstrably justified" under the terms of section 1. In applying the *Oakes* tests, both sides also agreed that the objective of the law—which they took to be the protection of vulnerable minorities against the harms likely to result from the spread of contempt or enmity—was "pressing and substantial." The main points of contention, therefore, were the first two parts of the proportionality test.

Writing for the dissenting minority, Justice Beverley McLachlin argued that the hate speech law could not reasonably be expected to achieve its own objective since the criminal prosecution of hatemongers would provide them with a public platform for the advocacy of their opinions and might also make them objects of public sympathy; for these reasons the enforcement of the law might actually be self-defeating. McLachlin also contended that the law was overbroad, largely because of the potentially wide scope of the key notion of hatred, and that it therefore could have a substantial chilling effect on legitimate forms of expression. She therefore concluded that it failed both the rational connection and minimal impairment requirements in the proportionality test.

Chief Justice Brian Dickson, writing for the majority, defended the law on both counts. He argued that the prosecution of hatemongers can have the beneficial effect of endorsing the values of tolerance and equality and of expressing social condemnation of hate speech. In response to the contention of overbreadth, he urged a narrow interpretation of the key concept of hatred confining it to the most intense and extreme feelings of antipathy toward the target groups. He also pointed to the array of defenses the law makes available to the accused. In these respects, Dickson argued, the legislation was crafted so as to minimize its impact on expressive freedom.

In *Keegstra*, therefore, the Court kept its focus squarely on the two central issues: the harms of hate speech and the expected consequences of the law designed to prevent these harms. Since both issues are broadly empirical, it seems reasonable to expect opinions on them to be based on the best available evidence. As far as the first issue is concerned, I have reviewed the available evidence elsewhere and will only briefly summarize the results here.[18] In contrast with the putative links between pornography and harms to women, which I will examine in the next section, social scientists have given relatively little attention to the harms of hate speech. In sorting through what is available, it is convenient to distinguish two different (though not mutually exclusive) causal pathways by means of which hate messages targeting a particular minority might harm the members of that minority. The harm is *direct* if it results from exposure to the messages by members of the target group themselves. This may occur when individuals are subjected to verbal abuse in the form of racist epithets or insults, but also when hate messages intrude on the lives of their targets in the form of anonymous telephone calls or notes, graffiti spray-painted in public spaces, crosses burned in front yards, pamphlets delivered through the mail, the desecration of sacred places, or other means. Hate messages directed at members of their target group are not meant to engage the audience in a rational debate or persuade them of some important truths. Rather, they are meant to hurt—by insulting, humiliating, or intimidating—and there is reliable evidence that they often succeed.

The harms of hate speech, however, do not end with its direct impact on its victims. *Indirect* harms work through the mediation of attitudes and conduct on the part of an audience other than the target groups themselves. The two broader social conditions to which hate messages are most frequently said to contribute are the social inequality of target minorities and violence against members of these minorities. These outcomes are not, of course, really distinct, since the experience of living in fear of racist or homophobic violence is itself one form of social inequality. However, for analytic purposes I will deal with them separately, first with inequality and then, finally, with violence.

Most hate messages preach the inferiority of the groups they choose to single out and advocate one or another form of discrimination against the members of those groups. Actual discriminatory practices against minorities would therefore count as success for the producers and distributors of these messages. But because members of hate groups typically have little power to impose such practices beyond the confines of their own narrow circles, success will necessarily require enlisting a much wider public in the cause. That, in turn, will require an impact on the attitudes of nonmembers of the target minorities—members, that is, of the dominant social groups. It is plausible to suppose that hate speech makes some contribution toward the unequal social status of minorities such as blacks, Asians, Jews, aboriginals, and gays and lesbians. But no serious scientific attempt has been made to factor out and measure the extent of this contribution, nor is it easy to see how this could be done. It seems that in the territory of equality, few advances are possible beyond what common sense and experience can teach us.

Things are rather different when we turn to the issue of violence. Hate violence takes the form of assault on a person or damage to property motivated by hostility toward the group with which the person or property is associated. Most legal jurisdictions now classify certain cases of murder, assault, public mischief, and the like as hate crimes on the basis of evidence of such motivation. Whereas the literature on the effects of hate speech may be limited, there is ample evidence of the damage hate crimes can do, both to their immediate victims and to other members of the target communities. None of this, of course, is surprising: we know that being the victim of racist or homophobic violence is a harm, just as we know the same for sexual violence. The question is whether there is a causal relationship between hate speech and hate crimes.

Many hate messages either imply or openly advocate the legitimacy of violence against minorities. By so doing, it is arguable—indeed highly plausible—that they contribute to a climate that fosters hate crimes and that members of vulnerable minorities experience as threatening or intimidating. The extent of this contribution is, of course, difficult to measure with any degree of certainty, but we can at least point to one tangible link in the causal chain from speech to crime. While some hate messages are disseminated by isolated individuals, most of them are generated by organized hate groups. For these groups the primary purpose of the materials they circulate, largely now through websites, is not to contribute to a broad public debate concerning Jews or blacks or gays. Rather, the materials are used to reinforce the shared ideology that binds the group together and to recruit new group members. For a hate group, hate speech is its creed or ideology, and its call to action. That action frequently involves acts of violence against members of target groups or their property. It is impossible to determine with any accuracy what proportion of the overall incidence of hate crimes can be attributed to individuals affiliated with hate groups. However, there have been a number of prominent instances of hate violence in recent years where the perpetrator has had a personal history of involvement with a hate group.[19] When the group has advocated violence against members of a particular minority and one of its adherents comes to practice just such violence, it is difficult to resist the cause-and-effect conclusion. If that conclusion is at least sometimes justified, then hate messages can do more than merely legitimize or endorse violence against target minorities—they can also encourage or even instigate it.

If there is good reason to think that hate speech has the potential to cause (both direct and indirect) harm to vulnerable minorities, then Mill's harm principle is satisfied, and the issue turns on the cost-benefit balance of criminal measures designed to prevent such harm. The offense defined by the Canadian hate speech law is the willful promotion of hatred. The effect of requiring that the promotion of hatred be "willful" is to make the offense one of specific intent: the speaker must "intend or foresee as substantially certain a direct and active stimulation of hatred against an identifiable group."[20] The *Keegstra* Court was very clear that the offense consists in the intent of the speech rather than its (probable or certain) effect: no evidence need be adduced of any hatred actually promoted by the speech in question.

What, then, is it to promote hatred? In *Keegstra*, Dickson glossed the verb as follows: "Given the purpose of the provision to criminalize the spreading of hatred in society, I find that the word 'promotes' indicates active support or instigation. Indeed the French version of the offense uses the verb 'fomenter,' which in English means to foment or stir up. In 'promotes' we thus have a word that indicates more than simple encouragement or advancement."[21] In this, Dickson effectively identified the promotion of hatred with its incitement. "Incite" derives from the Latin root *citare*, which means to set in rapid motion, rouse, or stimulate ("excite" has the same root). The *Oxford English Dictionary* offers the following as approximate synonyms for "incite": spur on, stir up (see "foment," above), animate, stimulate, provoke, instigate. What these various notions seem to have in common is the idea of (1) galvanizing someone into action by (2) appealing to the passions rather than to reason. Inciting to action thus contrasts with counselling, or advising, or persuading: it works through getting the subject worked up or agitated rather than by offering a convincing argument.

The *Keegstra* Court therefore effectively defined hate speech (for the purpose of the hate promotion law) as speech intended to incite feelings of extreme enmity against members of one of the protected groups. Despite Dickson's resolute defense of the law, it is easy to see why the minority on the Court found it problematic. First there is the fact that in order to commit the offense, one need not actually incite any hatred. In defense of this provision, Dickson wrote that "it is clearly difficult to prove a causative link between a specific statement and hatred of an identifiable group. In fact, to require direct proof of hatred in listeners would severely debilitate the effectiveness of s. 319(2) in achieving Parliament's aim."[22] The law does require that the speech in question be public—or, rather, "other than in private conversation"—but it is not clear that it requires that there be any audience at all. Putting hateful messages on my telephone answering machine or my personal website would doubtless be an offense even if no one ever dialled my number or accessed my site. Furthermore, in those cases where the speech does have listeners, the reaction of the audience is immaterial. I commit the offense if I am able to galvanize my audience to hate the people I happen to hate on the basis of their skin color or the god they choose to worship or the partners they choose to sleep with, but I also commit it if I succeed only in putting my audience to sleep or reducing them to helpless laughter.

Leaving this issue aside, it is also worth noting that the crime of inciting hatred is somewhat anomalous. The notion of incitement has its uses in the law beyond this particular context. *Black's Law Dictionary* defines "incite" as "to provoke or stir up (someone to commit a criminal act, or the criminal act itself)" and includes incitement, along with attempt, conspiracy, and solicitation, in the roster of inchoate offenses. Now, it is in the nature of an inchoate offense that its unlawful status is, as it were, parasitic on a principal or substantive offense. Attempted murder, therefore, is an offense in its own right because murder is, and conspiracy to defraud is an offense because fraud is. Likewise, in the criminal law in general incitement is a criminal act only where the act incited is itself criminal. However, incitement of hatred is a conspicuous exception to this rule. Hatred is not itself a criminal offense, not even when it is directed at a group defined by such markers as race, religion, or sexual orientation. So it is somewhat odd, to say the least, that it should be unlawful to incite someone to a state or condition that is not itself unlawful. It is difficult to think of other examples in the criminal law, though assisting (counselling, aiding, or abetting) a suicide does come to mind. Here the principal act is not criminal, though assisting it is. But at least in this case it is an act, on the part of a second party, on which the collateral offense is defined. The further oddity of the crime of inciting hatred is that the thing incited is a feeling, or emotion, or attitude rather than a concrete act. The problem here is not that hatred is incapable of being incited: one can incite feelings in another just as much as, or in addition to, acts. Indeed, as indicated earlier, it seems part of the very meaning of incitement that the other is moved to act by the arousal of passion. No, the difficulty lies in figuring out why inciting a feeling, where there is no requirement of any subsequent criminal act, itself deserves the status of a criminal act.

The offense defined by the hate promotion law is therefore doubly removed from the harms of discrimination and violence that it aims to prevent. Because the offense consists entirely in the intent to incite hatred, there is no requirement that any hatred has actually been incited, and even if the incitement has been successful there is no requirement that it has resulted in, or even increased the likelihood of, any criminal, or otherwise antisocial, act. We should not conclude from this, however, either that hate speech should be subject to no regulation or that the notion of incitement has no role to play in such regulation. In Canada, virtually all discussion of hate speech regulation has focused on section 319(2) of the Criminal Code—the hate promotion law that was at stake in the *Keegstra* case. Much less attention has been devoted to section 319(1), which prohibits the incitement of hatred against an identifiable group "where such incitement is likely to lead to a breach of the peace."[23] In framing its hate speech restrictions, the legislature elected to define two distinct offenses, one of inciting hatred and the other of promoting hatred. While both speak of stirring up or provoking a feeling or passion, only the former requires the crucial further link to an unlawful act. Unlike the hate promotion law, the hate incitement law therefore retains an important element of the notion of incitement as an inchoate offense. In this way the incitement offense requires what the promotion offense does not: some contribution to the (actual or potential) commission of an unlawful act (such as a hate crime against members of a protected minority). In this respect, it seems designed to deal with the final category of indirect harm identified above: instances in which speakers use inflammatory rhetoric to inspire listeners to commit acts of racist or homophobic violence.

It is worth noting here that Mill himself acknowledged that restrictions on incitement to violence could satisfy his conditions for justifiable limits to free speech. Having concluded his absolutist defense of "the fullest liberty of professing and discussing, as a matter of ethical conviction, any doctrine, however immoral it may be considered,"[24] he then turned to the question "whether the same reasons do not require that men should be free to act upon their opinions." Unsurprisingly, in answering this question he invoked the harm principle and applied it to the special case of the expression of opinions: "even opinions lose their immunity, when the circumstances in which they are expressed are such as to constitute their expression a positive instigation to some mischievous act. An opinion that corn-dealers are starvers of the poor, or that private property is robbery, ought to be unmolested when simply circulated through the press, but may justly incur punishment when delivered orally to an excited mob assembled before the house of a corn-dealer, or when handed about among the same mob in the form of a placard."[25] Here we have the familiar ingredients of unlawful incitement: the use of fiery speech to ignite strong passions, which will in turn drive listeners to commit unlawful acts. Mill touches on the same themes in his treatment of the doctrine of tyrannicide, where he defends the right to circulate it as a general thesis but then continues: "I hold that the instigation to it, in a specific case, may be a proper subject of punishment, but only if an overt act has followed, and at least a probable connexion can be established between the act and the instigation."[26]

By "instigation," Mill evidently means something very similar to what we normally understand as incitement. Similar, but not quite identical. As Mill makes clear, he would treat instigation as an offense "only if an overt act has followed." But this requirement is at odds with the common conception of inchoate offenses, whose commission does not require that the principal offense actually be carried out. This is necessarily true in the case of attempts, which by their very nature preclude the successful commission of the act, but it can be contingently true of all other inchoate offenses: the conspiracy to defraud may be overheard in wiretapped conversations, the solicitation to murder may be made to an undercover police officer, and the exhortation to beat up on Jews or Asians may be greeted with shrugs and yawns. Mill may still be right in requiring "a probable connexion...between the act and the instigation," but this requirement would be satisfied if it could be shown that the incitement at least created a significant risk that the offense would be committed. This condition is what the Canadian Parliament seems to have had in mind in stipulating that the incitement must be "likely to lead to a breach of the peace," whether or not any such breach actually occurs.

I noted earlier that messages disseminated by hate groups can have the function both of recruiting new members and of motivating adherents to commit hate crimes against members of target groups. The latter function makes for a much more direct causal relationship between the message and the violence, one that is not mediated by shifts in the overall climate of public opinion about minorities. However, this function also opens up the possibility of treating the communication of hate messages, under certain circumstances, as incitement to this violence. Where hate crimes have been committed by members, or former members, of known hate groups and have clearly been inspired by hate messages disseminated by those groups, there seems no reason not to regard those groups as having incited the violence and as being liable to prosecution on that basis. The Canadian offense of inciting hatred seems to target just such cases.

3 OBSCENITY

Where hate speech is concerned, the approach followed consistently by the Canadian courts has been remarkably faithful to Mill's principles, focusing as it has on harm (to others) and on the cost-benefit balance of criminal law designed to prevent such harm. Obscenity law, however, has been a different matter. For the greater part of a century, the test of obscenity in Canadian law was that laid down by Lord Cockburn in *Hicklin,* an 1868 case in England: "whether the tendency of the matter charged as obscenity is to deprave and corrupt those whose minds are open to such immoral influences."[27] Under this test, the rationale of the obscenity law was a peculiar combination of moralism (combatting immoral influences) and paternalism (protecting willing consumers against depravity and corruption). By the 1950s, however, the *Hicklin* test had come to be widely regarded as inadequate, and in 1959 the Canadian Parliament adopted a statutory definition of obscenity in terms of "the undue exploitation of sex."[28] But this was scarcely more satisfactory, for the courts then had the unhappy task of determining when the "exploitation of sex" in a book or magazine or movie was "undue." In an effort to make this task more manageable, in 1962 the Canadian Supreme Court fell back on the test of "contemporary community standards."[29] As refined by subsequent court decisions, this test became a matter of the limits of community tolerance: "it is a standard of *tolerance,* not taste, that is relevant. What matters is not what Canadians think is right for themselves to see. What matters is what Canadians would not abide other Canadians seeing because it would be beyond the contemporary Canadian standard of tolerance to allow them to see it."[30]

The community standards test for obscenity has never been decisively displaced in either Canada or the United States. However, new approaches to pornography and obscenity in the 1970s and 1980s, pioneered by feminists, gradually began to make it seem beside the point, just as the earlier moralism/paternalism of the *Hicklin* test had come to seem misdirected. What concerned feminists about pornography was not that it might breed moral corruption, or that it might offend the sensibilities of the community, but that it might encourage and legitimize sexual violence against women. In Robin Morgan's memorable dictum, "pornography is the theory, rape is the practice." This concern was stimulated in the first instance by anecdotal evidence of women sexually assaulted by men who had allegedly been turned on or inspired by viewing pornography, but it soon spawned a veritable social science industry of research into the causal links between pornography and sexual violence and inequality. Whatever the results of that research (which remain contested to this day), the emphasis was now squarely on harm to others: harm done to women (or children) proximately by men but more remotely by the producers and distributors of pornography. In Canada, these themes began to creep into case decisions in the 1980s, focusing particularly on the depiction of "degrading or dehumanizing treatment" of women.

By the time the Canadian Supreme Court revisited the obscenity issue in its 1992 *Butler* decision,[31] basically two distinct tests for obscenity were in play in the Canadian courts: the older community standards test and the more recent harm test. One of the tasks confronting the *Butler* court was to sort out the relationships between these tests. Justice John Sopinka, writing for the majority, attempted to resolve the potential conflict between the tests by taking community standards to be the measure of harm. Acknowledging that the harmfulness (or otherwise) of pornography is very much a matter of opinion, Sopinka appealed to community standards to resolve the issue: "Because this is not a matter that is susceptible of proof in the traditional way and because we do not wish to leave it to the individual tastes of judges, we must have a norm that will serve as an arbiter in determining what amounts to an undue exploitation of sex. That arbiter is the community as a whole."[32] In *Butler*, therefore, the Supreme Court definitively established community standards as the measure of harm for erotic materials, thus as the sole test of obscenity in Canadian criminal law. The community's intolerance of (some particular form of) pornography was to be taken as an indicator, or perhaps a criterion, of the harmfulness of the material. If the material exceeds the community's limits of tolerance then it is harmful, and if it does not then it is not.

The problems inherent in this use of the community standards test are evident. In order for the test to yield any results at all, we need to assume that there is a national community in Canada, that this community has a uniform standard of tolerance for erotic materials, and that this standard can somehow be discerned by judges in the absence of evidence—all of these assumptions being subject to legitimate doubt. But even if we can discover the community's level of tolerance for some erotic materials, what assurance do we have—or could we have—that this will track the harmfulness of these materials? Why could the community not tolerate materials which pose a genuine risk of harm (e.g., by eroticizing sexual violence against women)? Or why could it not refuse to tolerate materials with no risk of harm (e.g., because they depict gay or lesbian sex)? Nowhere else in the criminal law, where harm to others is the basis for an offense, is the public's intolerance of a particular form of conduct used as evidence of, or a criterion for, the harmfulness of that conduct. Sopinka's forced marriage of the community standards test and the harm principle was doomed from the outset.

If harm is the issue, as it ought to be, then the community standards test is at best a distraction, an irrelevancy, a red herring. But the case against the test runs deeper than its failure to track the real issue. When Mill wrote "On Liberty," the danger against which he thought individual liberty principally needed protection was what he called the "tyranny of the majority," which included "the tyranny of the prevailing opinion and feeling…[and] the tendency of society to impose…its own ideas and practices as rules of conduct on those who dissent from them…and compel all characters to fashion themselves upon the model of its own."[33] The harm principle was Mill's proposed line of defense against this tyranny: unless it is possible to demonstrate a significant risk of social harm, there is no case for a restraint of liberty. In protecting individuals against the tyranny of the majority, the harm principle forbids restraint on the basis of a community standard of tolerance.

The rationale behind the harm principle is obvious: since harm is (by definition) an evil, no one has an unqualified right to inflict it on others. The fact that some activity is socially harmful is therefore easily recognizable as a reason (in principle) for its legal regulation. There is no similar rationale for the community standards test: the fact that the majority is not prepared to tolerate some activity is, taken by itself, no reason at all for restricting it. Indeed, it appears to confuse the existence of intolerance with the justification for it; whereas harm can count as a reason for refusing to tolerate an activity, the mere fact that it is not tolerated cannot. The task of the courts is to determine what forms of expression must be tolerated by the public, however offensive or unpopular they might be. This task cannot be carried out simply by ascertaining what forms of expression the public is in fact prepared to tolerate. The idea that important individual rights can be circumscribed by the tolerance level of the majority is misconceived since one of the principal functions of rights (and of their constitutional entrenchment) is to safeguard minorities against the intolerance of the majority.

It was only a matter of time before the Canadian Supreme Court would come to acknowledge that the *Butler* test for obscenity was an awkward, unstable, transitional compromise between the old and the new way of thinking about the regulation of expression. The acknowledgment came in its 2005 *Labaye* decision.[34] The appellant in the case was the owner of a private "swingers club" in Montreal who had been charged with keeping a common bawdy house "for the practice of acts of indecency." Up to that point, community standards had been used by the courts as the test of indecency, as well as obscenity. But in *Labaye,* the Supreme Court resolved to apply a harm test directly rather than through the medium of the community's level of tolerance. Its conclusion that the activities in the club were not indecent was based primarily on the fact that they posed no discernible risk of harm to the public, as they were well hidden from view. But what was most noticeable in the Court's decision was its decisive rejection of community intolerance as a ground for criminal regulation of conduct. While the Court has not revisited the obscenity issue since *Butler,* were it to do so, it could scarcely fail to take the same line. The community standards test is now effectively obsolete in Canadian obscenity law, having been supplanted by Mill's harm principle.

If the Court were to reconsider the obscenity issue, it is not clear what it would now make of the harm question. As I indicated earlier, it seems reasonable to expect limits on liberty to be based on reliable evidence of harm. Yet in *Butler,* the Court was very undemanding concerning social science evidence of a causal relationship between pornography and harms to women. After conceding that the evidence was "subject to controversy," Sopinka sidestepped the evidential issue by saying that "while a direct link between obscenity and harm to society may be difficult, if not impossible, to establish, it is reasonable to presume that exposure to images bears a causal relationship to changes in attitudes and beliefs."[35] In the end, it was enough for Sopinka that the legislature had a "reasonable basis" for choosing to intervene by means of criminal law.

Suppose that this is not enough for us and we seek a more solid evidential foundation for an obscenity law. What, then, does the evidence show? Unlike the case of hate speech, here we have an abundance of social science results on which to rely—far too many to summarize readily in a limited space.[36] Again, it helps somewhat to categorize different types of potential harm. The pornography industry employs primarily women (but also some men) to produce a product primarily for men (but also for some women). The possible victims of harm can then be either women in the industry (*participant* harms) or women at large (*third-party* harms).[37] And the harm done to women by pornography, as in the case of the indirect harms of hate speech, might take the form either of exploitation or discrimination (inequality) or sexual assault (violence). Though most women, especially in developed countries, are not coerced into making pornography, the industry is largely unregulated (because semilegal), and the possibility of exploitation (or even sexual assault) is therefore real. However, the appropriate response to this risk would appear to be to regulate the industry, not to drive it underground by criminalizing its product. As for third-party harms, there is no reliable evidence that the availability of pornography contributes to women's inequality in a society; in fact, the North American and western European countries with the greatest degree of gender equality tend also to have the most liberal markets in pornography. There is also no reliable evidence that nonviolent pornography encourages or contributes to sexual violence against women. However, there is some reason to think that pornography that eroticizes sexual violence might make male viewers more likely to approve or endorse such violence.

An obscenity law is therefore on the strongest evidential ground when it specifically targets violent pornography (which was the outcome of the *Butler* case in Canada). Ironically, however, this very fact casts doubt on the necessity of such a law. Pornography that eroticizes sexual violence against women is objectionable because of the misogynist attitude it expresses toward women. Misogynist attitudes, however, can also be expressed in visual or verbal materials with no erotic content whatever (for instance, in novels or films portraying female characters as brainless). What this suggests is that the focus on the erotic, which is the hallmark of an obscenity law, may be fundamentally misdirected. Pornography is problematic when it constitutes hate speech concerning women. But in that case, the appropriate vehicle for its legal regulation may be a hate speech law that (unlike the Canadian law) includes women as a protected social group. However, if we contemplate subsuming obscenity law in hate speech law in this way, then we might also contemplate taking the further step, discussed in the previous section, of narrowing the offense to the incitement of a hate crime against women. In that case, the producers or distributors of misogynist pornography would be vulnerable to prosecution for incitement if it could be shown that their publications inspired acts of sexual violence against women or materially increased the risk of such acts. In this way, both the hate promotion law and the obscenity law could be subsumed in legislation prohibiting the incitement of hate violence.

4 CONCLUSION

My initial questions were whether the harm caused or threatened by hate speech or obscenity is serious enough to warrant criminal regulation of these forms of expression and whether other, less coercive, means of responding to them might be equally effective with less cost to expressive freedom. Since these are broadly empirical matters, and since the empirical evidence on them is scarcely conclusive, any answers to these questions are bound to be contestable. However, the conditions for the justifiable restriction of speech derived from Mill and operationalized by the Canadian Supreme Court do point to some tentative conclusions. The case for criminal regulation is weakest where the harms in question (such as the social inequality of visible minorities and women) are widespread and diffuse and the causal link with speech remote and speculative. Where the Canadian hate promotion and obscenity laws are concerned, it is difficult to justify coercion (especially the extreme form of coercion exemplified by the criminal law) rather than reliance on such less intrusive measures as education, antiracism and antisexism campaigns, counterspeech, and so on. The case is stronger, however, for legislation, such as the hate incitement law, that is more narrowly aimed at speech that constitutes an instigation to an unlawful act, especially to a hate crime. Even here it could be argued that no law specifically regulating speech is necessary, if in general it is unlawful to incite the commission of a criminal offense. However this might be, singling out hate speech or obscenity in this way need not fail Mill's conditions and may be appropriate for the support it provides for vulnerable social groups.

NOTES

1. John Stuart Mill, "On Liberty," in John M. Robson, ed., *Essays on Politics and Society*, Collected Works of John Stuart Mill, vol. 18 (Toronto: University of Toronto Press, 1977), pp. 244–5. All subsequent references to "On Liberty" are to this edition.

2. Does calling someone a "kike" or a "nigger" express an opinion? Does publishing a cartoon depicting a derogatory ethnic or racial stereotype? Does burning a cross or text-messaging a death threat?

3. Frederick Schauer, *Free Speech: A Philosophical Enquiry* (Cambridge: Cambridge University Press, 1982), chs. 2–5.

4. For the Canadian courts see *R. v. Keegstra*, (1990) 3 S.C.R. 697 at 762–4, 863–4. This case will be subsequently referred to as *Keegstra*.

5. "On Liberty," p. 217.

6. "On Liberty," p. 223.

7. "On Liberty," pp. 225–6.

8. "On Liberty," pp. 225–6.

9. "On Liberty," p. 226; cf. 227, where Mill refers to "the Liberty of Thought: from which it is impossible to separate the cognate liberty of speaking and of writing."

10. "On Liberty," p. 276.

11. "On Liberty," p. 292.

12. Voluntary consumers of a product do not count as "others" for the purpose of the harm principle. Restricting access to the product in order to prevent harm to its consumers would be an instance of paternalism, which is condemned by the harm principle.

13. *R. v. Oakes*, (1986) 1 S.C.R. 103.

14. However, in 1985 the Court struck down a Sunday closing law on the ground that its stated objective—"to compel the observance of the Christian sabbath"—was not sufficiently important to justify limiting the right to freedom of conscience and religion. (*R. v. Big M Drug Mart*, (1985) 1 S.C.R. 295) And in 1992 the Court was unable to find a pressing and substantial objective for the "spreading false news" statute, but elected to give it the benefit of the doubt and struck it down instead on proportionality (overbreadth). *R. v. Zundel*, (1992) 2 S.C.R. 731.

15. It must be acknowledged that the *Oakes* requirement of a "pressing and substantial objective" is less demanding than Mill's principle, since it does not limit legitimate legislative objectives to the prevention of harm to others. The Canadian Supreme Court has explicitly rejected any such limitation, by determining that the harm principle is not a "principle of fundamental justice" within the meaning of section 7 of the *Charter*. In so determining, the Court recognized the legitimacy of other legislative objectives, including the prevention of harm to self (paternalism) and the prohibition of harmless acts such as cannibalism and bestiality on the basis of their "offensiveness to deeply held social values" (moralism). *R. v. Malmo-Levine*, (2003) 3 S.C.R 571. However, in its adjudication of free speech issues the Court has recognized no permissible objective for regulation other than the prevention of harm to vulnerable third parties (principally women, in the case of obscenity, and visible minorities, in the case of hate speech). In the domain of free expression, therefore, the approach of the Court has been squarely based on the harm principle.

16. It must also be acknowledged that, while the Court has committed itself to cost-benefit balancing in its section 1 analysis, it has never endorsed outright consequentialism. In particular, it has never committed itself to approving legislation whose expected benefits barely exceed its expected costs, as opposed to requiring a higher threshold for the justified infringement of a constitutionally protected right. I owe this point to Tom Hurka, and discuss it more fully in L. W. Sumner, *The Hateful and the Obscene: Studies in the Limits of Free Expression* (Toronto: University of Toronto Press, 2004), sec. 3.2. However, it does not play a crucial role in the Court's free speech decisions.

17. *Criminal Code*, R.S., 1985, c. C-46: Section 319(2): "Every one who, by communicating statements, other than in private conversation, wilfully promotes hatred against any identifiable group is guilty of (a) an indictable offense and is liable to imprisonment for a term not exceeding two years; or (b) an offense punishable on summary conviction....(7) In this section, 'identifiable group' means any section of the public distinguished by colour, race, religion, ethnic origin or sexual orientation."

18. See Sumner, *The Hateful and the Obscene*, sec. 5.5.

19. In 1999 Benjamin Smith, an adherent of the World Church of the Creator, killed two people and wounded twelve during a shooting rampage in Indiana and Illinois in which he was targeting blacks, Jews, and Asians. Later that same year, Buford Furrow, who had been affiliated with Aryan Nation-Church of Jesus Christ, shot five people in a

Jewish community center in Los Angeles and then killed a Filipino postal worker an hour later.

20. *Keegstra*, 777.

21. *Keegstra*, 776–7.

22. *Keegstra*, 776.

23. Section 319(1): "Every one who, by communicating statements in any public place, incites hatred against any identifiable group where such incitement is likely to lead to a breach of the peace is guilty of (a) an indictable offense and is liable to imprisonment for a term not exceeding two years; or (b) an offense punishable on summary conviction."

24. "On Liberty," p. 228n.

25. "On Liberty," p. 260. In contemporary terms, Mill rejects content restrictions on speech but is willing to accept (some) "time, manner, or circumstance" restrictions.

26. "On Liberty," p. 228n.

27. *R. v. Hicklin*, (1868) L.R. 3 Q.B. 360 at 371.

28. This definition remains in place to the present day. The full text of s. 163(8) of the Criminal Code reads as follows: "For the purposes of this Act, any publication a dominant characteristic of which is the undue exploitation of sex, or of sex and any one or more of the following subjects, namely, crime, horror, cruelty and violence, shall be deemed to be obscene."

29. The leading Canadian case was *Brodie v. The Queen*, (1962) S.C.R. 681; see Justice Judson's opinion at 705. Judson adapted the community standards test from an opinion by Justice Fullagar in a 1948 Australian case: *R. v. Close*, (1948) V.L.R. 445. Curiously, he made no mention of the very similar test formulated by Justice Brennan in the more recent American case of *Roth*: "whether to the average person, applying contemporary community standards, the dominant theme of the material taken as a whole appeals to prurient interest." *Roth v. United States*, (1956) 354 U.S. 476 at 489. The U.S. Supreme Court further fine-tuned its community standards test in *Miller v. California*, (1973) 413 U.S. 15. There the test of obscenity is "(a) whether 'the average person, applying contemporary community standards" would find that the work, taken as a whole, appeals to the prurient interest; (b) whether the work depicts or describes, in a patently offensive way, sexual conduct specifically defined by the applicable state law; and (c) whether the work, taken as a whole, lacks serious literary, artistic, political, or scientific value." There are material differences between the Canadian and American community standards tests for obscenity (for instance, for the purpose of the Canadian test the "community" must be national, while for the American test it is meant to be local), but these need not concern us since they do not go to the heart of the problems with the reliance on community standards.

30. *Towne Cinema Theatres Ltd. v. The Queen*, (1985) 1 S.C.R. 494 at 508 (emphasis in original).

31. *R. v. Butler*, (1992) 1 S.C.R. 452 (hereinafter referred to as *Butler*).

32. *Butler*, 484.

33. "On Liberty," p. 220.

34. *R. v. Labaye*, (2005) 3 S.C.R. 728.

35. *Butler*, 502.

36. I have surveyed this literature in *The Hateful and the Obscene*, secs. 5.1–5.3.

37. I omit possible harms to children, since we are dealing here with obscenity, not child pornography (which in Canada, as in most jurisdictions, is regulated by a different law). I also omit any possible harms to men (should there be any).

REFERENCES

Government of Canada, *The Criminal Law in Canadian Society* (Ottawa, 1982).

John Stuart Mill, "On Liberty," in John M. Robson, ed., *Essays on Politics and Society*, vol. 18 of *Collected Works of John Stuart Mill* (Toronto: University of Toronto Press, 1977).

Frederick Schauer, *Free Speech: A Philosophical Enquiry* (Cambridge: Cambridge University Press, 1982).

L. W. Sumner, *The Hateful and the Obscene: Studies in the Limits of Free Expression* (Toronto: University of Toronto Press, 2004).

CHAPTER 3

·····

BLACKMAIL

·····

MITCHELL N. BERMAN

GENERALLY, the permissibility of a conditional threat tracks the permissibility of the conduct threatened. That is, if it is permissible to X, it is ordinarily permissible to conditionally threaten to X. Call this bargaining. And if it is impermissible to Y, it is ordinarily impermissible to conditionally threaten to Y. Call this extortion. But these relationships hold true only ordinarily, not invariably. In rare contexts, it might be permissible to conditionally threaten what it would be impermissible to do. Nuclear deterrence is the most salient example. And sometimes it is impermissible to conditionally threaten what it would be permissible to do. Call this fourth cell in our implicit two-by-two matrix *blackmail:* its central case, of course, consists of a threat to disclose embarrassing information that one has a right to reveal unless paid to remain silent.

What, if anything, justifies the criminalization of blackmail, and what should be the contours of the offense, have long been among the most delighting and devilish puzzles of criminal law theory. Indeed, one long-standing participant in the debate ventured some years ago that explaining why blackmail is properly criminalized remains "one of the most elusive intellectual puzzles in all of law."[1] This chapter presents an opinionated summary of the state of the literature. It has two principal aims, and a subsidiary one. Most ambitiously, I hope both to resolve the blackmail puzzle and to draw forth from that proposed solution some lessons of broader import. If I fail in pursuit of those first twinned objectives, I hope nonetheless to analyze the nature of the blackmail puzzle, and the successes and failures of other proposed solutions to it, in ways that will prove productive for future theorists of blackmail.

The chapter proceeds in five sections. Section I clears ground by introducing distinctions, vocabulary, and simple hypotheticals that will aid the analyses that follow. It also provides a rudimentary account of the methodology I recommend for evaluating competing blackmail theories. Section II summarizes and criticizes many of the most notable contributions to the blackmail literature—those that seek to explain and justify blackmail's criminalization, as well as a few contrarian theories that maintain that blackmail's criminalization cannot be justified.

The next two sections introduce, develop, and defend a version of the solution to the puzzle that I first put forth a decade ago—a coercion-centered account that I termed the "evidentiary theory of blackmail."[2] Section III reviews previous coercion-centered accounts of blackmail and presents the evidentiary theory as an improvement that better explains and justifies what the literature generally treats as the paradigmatic case of blackmail: a conditional threat to reveal the target's marital infidelities unless paid to remain silent. Section IV then applies the evidentiary account beyond this central case to types of blackmail whose criminalization might plausibly be thought either less secure or less well supported by the evidentiary theory, including threats to reveal criminal wrongdoing (crime-exposure blackmail), threats to sell one's information to ordinary media outlets (market-price blackmail), and threats to do things other than to reveal secrets (noninformational blackmail). Finally, Section V briefly explores some reasons to believe that the puzzle warrants the substantial intellectual attention it has received, partly by sketching out some implications the evidentiary theory bears beyond the case of blackmail.

I Preliminaries

Before we start, a few words about objective, vocabulary, and methodology.

First, I have defined blackmail as an impermissible conditional threat to do that which is permissible. I have also suggested that the existence of this subclass of conditional threats is puzzling precisely because it frustrates our expectation that a conditional threat gains its normative character from the normative character of the conduct threatened—an expectation that reflects attachment to what we may call *the threat principle*. This needs to be more precise. What we call a conditional threat is (with rare exceptions I will put aside) a biconditional proposal consisting of a conditional threat and a conditional offer, and the proposal itself could take its normative character from the conduct threatened, the conduct offered, or even the condition imposed. So the threat principle provides that the proposal qua conditional threat is presumptively permissible *vel non* in virtue of the permissibility *vel non* of the conduct threatened. Qua conditional offer, the presumptive permissibility of the proposal derives from that of the conduct offered. And qua solicitation, the proposal takes its normative character from that of the action demanded or requested.

In any event, permissibility is not a free-floating concept; it makes necessary (if implicit) reference to a normative system. Thus do we frequently agree that some morally impermissible conduct ought to remain legally permissible, or perhaps criticize the state for making legally impermissible that which we deem morally permissible. Blackmail is not a uniquely legal concept; it is perfectly familiar to describe some conduct as blackmail when speaking in an extralegal or wholly moral register. Accordingly, I propose to distinguish two different forms of blackmail: *legal blackmail* is the unlawful conditional threat to do that which is legal; *moral blackmail* is the morally wrongful conditional threat to do that which is morally permissible. Moreover, each form of blackmail presents an independent puzzle.

We can illustrate the distinct puzzles of legal and moral blackmail with the following simple paired cases, both of which represent paradigms of the offense.[3]

Gay-disclosure:

A is an adult gay man. The product of a religious and socially conservative upbringing, A struggles with feelings of shame about his sexual orientation, and has come out to only a few close friends. B, an acquaintance who sees A leave a gay bar in another town, outs A to his friends and coworkers.

Gay-threat:

Instead of disclosing A's sexual orientation, B threatens to do so unless A pays B $10,000—a considerable sum to A.

Adultery-disclosure:

H is cheating on his wife, W. B, an acquaintance who learns of H's infidelity and suspects W's ignorance of it, tells W that H is unfaithful.

Adultery-threat:

Instead of disclosing H's adultery to W, B threatens to do so unless H pays B $10,000—a considerable sum to H.

Plausibly, the following propositions best match existing law and widespread moral intuitions: (1) *gay-disclosure* and *adultery-disclosure* are both lawful; (2) *gay-threat* and *adultery-threat* are both criminal; (3) *gay-threat* and *adultery-threat* are both morally wrongful; (4) *gay-disclosure* is morally wrongful; and (5) *adultery-disclosure* is morally permissible.

Assuming arguendo that these descriptions are accurate,[4] then *adultery-threat* is legal blackmail and moral blackmail. *Gay-threat*, in contrast, is legal blackmail but moral extortion. (Keep in mind that "legal [moral] blackmail" does not signify blackmail that is legally [morally] permissible; it refers to a form of conditional threat that is wrongful from a legal [moral] point of view despite the fact that the conduct threatened is permissible from that same point of view.) *Gay-threat* presents only the puzzle of legal blackmail—why the law criminalizes only the wrongful threat and not the wrongful disclosure. *Adultery-threat* presents the puzzles both of legal blackmail and moral blackmail—how a threat to perform a morally permissible act becomes morally wrongful.

Legal theorists who have entered the debate over blackmail have concentrated on the puzzle of legal blackmail—that is, the questions of whether and when we should outlaw conditional threats to do what is, and should remain, legally permissible. While this focus is understandable, we should not be satisfied with answers to those questions that do not also shed light on the puzzle of moral blackmail—that is, the questions of when, and if so how, the conditional threat to perform a morally permissible action can become itself morally impermissible—either all things considered, or pro tanto.[5] Given the intimate yet complex relationship between law and morals, even those interested only in the legal puzzle and not the moral puzzle should hesitate to affirm any proposed solution to the former that leaves the latter untouched, for it may turn out that the key to the moral puzzle unlocks the legal puzzle as well.

By "blackmail theory," I will mean any sort of argument that seeks to solve one or both of these blackmail puzzles, by explaining either what justifies criminalizing threats to perform lawful acts (or why criminalization of such threats cannot be justified) or how threats to perform morally permissible acts can become wrongful (or why they can't). (Notice that the two puzzles call for different types of solution. An analysis that vindicates legal blackmail is normative or prudential; one that vindicates moral blackmail is, depending on one's metaethics, metaphysical or perhaps conceptual.) In evaluating competing blackmail theories, my approach is broadly coherentist. Conceivably, a given theory will be defective for relying on faulty reasoning, say, or by generating absurd consequences. However, the (claimed) shortcomings of most theories are of a different sort. I expect that most readers of this chapter start with strong intuitions that at least some conduct conventionally classified as blackmail is immoral and properly criminalized. Blackmail grabs our interest precisely because these judgments conflict with other initial judgments of ours—regarding, for example, the relationship between acts and threats, the content of various of our moral rights, and the principles that constrain the criminal sanction—and yet the confidence with which we hold them makes us reluctant to give them up.

Very roughly, then, the task for a blackmail theorist is to work back and forth among our judgments about the rightness or wrongness of particular acts and threats and about the more general principles that govern criminal law and moral evaluation to reach a set of claims that maximally commands our assent.[6] It is this coherentist approach to the subject that both permits us to deem it a mark against a particular theory that it cannot explain the moral impermissibility or the criminalizability of types of conduct that presently fall within the generally accepted contours of blackmail and reminds us to consider it *only* as a mark against—what I will often call a "difficulty"—but surely not as a decisive objection, or refutation. (When I charge a theory with being "underinclusive," I am measuring its implications against the baseline of what I will take to be widespread judgments regarding which types of conditional threats are properly criminalized or are morally wrongful, as the case may be.) The most satisfactory theory of blackmail might well require us to revise particular pretheoretical judgments regarding which conditional threats and which unconditional acts are permissible, but the satisfactoriness of a theory will vary depending upon just which pretheoretical judgments it requires us to abandon.[7]

II A CRITICAL OVERVIEW OF BLACKMAIL THEORIES

Though the criminalization of blackmail is not, strictly speaking, a paradox,[8] it is undeniably puzzling—puzzling enough to have seduced an array of distinguished commentators, including law professors and judges, moral philosophers, and economists. This section summarizes and critiques a broad sampling of the answers these participants have supplied. Subsection A examines theories that justify criminalization of blackmail by reference to the supposedly adverse systemic consequences that could be expected in a regime that tolerated blackmail. Subsection B investigates several others according to which blackmail is criminalizable because it is a nonconsequentialist wrong with which the criminal law is properly concerned.[9] Subsection C discusses some theorists' efforts to establish that current law and prevailing intuitions are wrong, and that blackmail's criminalization cannot be justified. Given the vast number of contributions to the debate and, in many cases, their subtlety, this overview is necessarily abbreviated notwithstanding its considerable length. Its ambition is not to canvass all theories or even to conclusively refute the many it does discuss, but to introduce the most influential or interesting existing accounts and to convey a strong flavor of what I view as the principal difficulties each confronts.[10] (This is a long section. A reader who is less interested in a review of the literature yet wishes to understand my own account and its implications can safely skim this discussion or jump straight to Section III. Conversely, a reader uninterested in my account may content herself with this section and Subsection III.A.)

A Accounts That Justify Criminalization by Reference to Its Systemic Consequences

The most familiar consequentialist analysis of blackmail argues that it is properly criminalized because it is economically inefficient. Other consequentialist approaches view blackmail as justifiably criminalized because, and insofar as, it encourages force or fraud (on Richard Epstein's account) or invasions of privacy (on Jeffrie Murphy's).

1. *Blackmail is economically inefficient.*

Following the most common line, I have located the blackmail puzzle in its constituting an exception to the general rule (*the threat principle*) that the permissibility of a conditional threat tracks the permissibility of the act threatened. However, blackmail is unusual in another respect, too. Ex post, the successful blackmail transaction looks like a garden-variety voluntary exchange: the blackmail "victim" buys the blackmailer's promise not to disclose certain information to which the blackmailer is privy. And, ex ante, the blackmailer's threat to disclose the information unless the deal is consummated looks just like any seller's threat to withhold a good or service unless the potential buyer meets the seller's price. But voluntary transactions are generally favored in the law. So a second blackmail puzzle concerns why it, in contrast to most other voluntary transactions, is illegal.

Because economists particularly value voluntary transactions, this second puzzle has attracted some of the most distinguished theorists of law and economics. Almost all have weighed in favor of continued criminalization of blackmail—at least in its paradigmatic case.[11] Of course, one route to this conclusion denies the premise that blackmail transactions are voluntary in the morally relevant sense. In fact, the evidentiary theory discussed in Section III takes this tack by conceiving of blackmail as a form of coercion: a moral wrong that potentially vitiates the consent of the offeree. This is not, however, the approach favored by economically minded theorists. Although adherents of the law and economics approach by and large approve criminalization of blackmail, few if any agree that the deal between blackmailer and victim is "involuntary."[12] Instead, they argue that blackmail, unlike most other voluntary transactions, is economically inefficient. This subsection (II.A.1) presents the economic thesis and then raises three objections: that it does not, on its terms, justify criminalizing adventitious blackmail; that when supplemented to take adequate account of incentive effects, blackmail might be socially desirable; and that, even if not desirable (on the economists' relatively thin criteria of value), criminalization is not obviously the best means to reduce its incidence.

The economic defense of blackmail's criminalization was first advanced thirty years ago in a paper—unpublished but widely distributed and discussed—by Douglas Ginsburg and Paul Schectman,[13] and endorsed some years later by Ronald Coase.[14] Its central claim is that the usual blackmail transaction produces deadweight economic losses by redistributing real resources from the blackmailee to the blackmailer without making the victim better off. On the surface, this is obviously false: in exchange for money, the threatener does give something of value to the victim: the promise not to reveal the information, and perhaps other things as well—letters, photographs, negatives. But this transfer is not supposed to count because it incorrectly accepts as a given that the threatener possesses the information. Instead, Ginsburg and Schectman urge us to view the transaction at its outset; B is contemplating the venture and has yet to unearth the damaging information. B calculates that, for $200 invested in research, he can uncover information for the suppression of which A will pay him $300.... No rational economic planner would tolerate the existence of an industry dedicated to digging up dirt, at real resource cost, and then reburying it.[15]

And if it shouldn't be tolerated, these theorists conclude, it should be prohibited.

The first difficulty with the argument is that it seems not to justify criminalizing blackmail based on information that the blackmailer happened on adventitiously—that is, without expending resources with the intent to discover information that might be leveraged into a blackmail threat.[16] This is a mark against the account insofar as adventitious blackmail strikes us, even on reflection, as wrongful and properly criminalized. But it is not a fatal flaw. As emphasized at the outset, until we settle on a persuasive account of blackmail's wrongfulness, we should not naturalize the contours of the offense under present law, nor should we treat our case-specific intuitions as fixed. It is revealing, however, that the theorists do not bite this bullet.

Instead of agreeing that their theory could not explain the criminalization of adventitious blackmail, Ginsburg and Schectman argued that the transaction costs still justify prohibiting blackmail even when the information the blackmailer threatens to disclose is adventitiously obtained. "Although we focused attention on the resources that a potential B would expend in order to 'dig up dirt' about A," they explained, our essential point was that by viewing the blackmail transaction ex ante, the waste involved would be made apparent.

Thus, it is of no moment that a particular B may have come by compromising information accidentally. Should A refuse to pay him, B has no reason to begin incurring expenses, such as are necessary to secure publication of the information, except insofar as he is looking to future opportunities for blackmail. The resources he expends in order to publish the information (and presumably to get credit as the source of it) are justified only from his ex ante perspective on the *next* blackmailing opportunity—regardless of whether B sets out to find it or waits for it again to come knocking at his door. Thus, assuming that the first blackmail opportunity arrives by accident, when B asks for payment to suppress what he knows, he has become an entrepreneur of blackmail; for B then to carry out his threat to reveal the information is an investment decision, not a part of the earlier accident.[17]

This response does not withstand scrutiny. First and least significantly, insofar as it rests on the premise that the blackmailer's costs of carrying out his threat are substantial, it is likelier that, as Steven Shavell has observed, "[t]he direct cost to a blackmailer of actually carrying out his threat is ordinarily trivial; it takes almost no effort to mail a photograph or a document to someone."[18] Second, it is equally dubious that "B has no reason" to incur expenses except to bolster his reputation. To the contrary, if A rejects B's proposal, B might carry out his threat out of spite. And as Ginsburg and Schectman themselves acknowledged, there is "no reason in economic theory to dishonor [B's] preference for making A suffer."[19] Third, even if B incurs nontrivial costs to carry out his threat and even if he does so solely in order to strengthen his reputation as a credible threatener, Ginsburg and Schectman are wrong to conclude that "[t]he resources [B] expends…are justified only from his ex ante perspective on the next *blackmailing* opportunity."[20] Rather, any expenses incurred might well be justified by the blackmailer's anticipation of the next *bargaining* opportunity, whatever it may be. Ginsburg and Schectman claim that "B's only potential gain…in establishing his credibility as someone willing to incur a cost if not obliged…*is an asset only insofar as B* is an entrepreneur of blackmail, i.e., someone who expects to engage in similar future transactions."[21] But this is unpersuasive. A reputation as someone willing to forego a benefit or incur costs if not obliged is extraordinarily valuable in the "legitimate" business world, for it allows one to secure a disproportionately large share of the potential benefits of exchange. And such a reputation can be exploited in any transactional domain regardless of the specific contexts in which it was forged or reinforced. In sum, Ginsburg and Schectman have not effectively rebutted Lindgren's objection that the basic economics argument cannot justify prohibition of participant or opportunistic blackmail.[22]

A second respect in which the argument from efficiency is either infirm or incomplete is that a narrow focus on the resource gains and losses of the blackmailer and blackmailee alone cannot establish that the practice of blackmail (whether adventitious or nonadventitious) is inefficient, for the fact (if true) that a given transaction reduces the aggregate wealth of the actual parties to the exchange does not prove that the transaction reduces the overall wealth of society. If the threat and practice of blackmail encouraged socially useful activity or discouraged socially harmful behavior, then a regime that permitted blackmail might be wealth maximizing relative to a regime in which blackmail is prohibited. Although theorists of law and economics have been aware of this problem for decades—William Landes and Richard Posner explored one aspect of the question in their very first collaboration, over thirty-five years ago[23]—they are far from persuasively demonstrating that blackmail is all things considered inefficient.

Consider, for example, Shavell's own contribution. While agreeing that the criminality of adventitious blackmail "cannot be explained by the need to discourage wasteful efforts to obtain information," Shavell has argued that "there is still an obvious incentive-based reason for making blackmail illegal: to avoid being blackmailed by [persons who happen on information accidentally], potential *victims* will exercise excessive precautions or reduce their level of innocent, yet embarrassing, activities."[24] It is unclear that the prospect of being blackmailed over innocent activities would be sufficiently great in a regime of legalized blackmail to have any significant effect on the incidence or manner of their performance. But even assuming that it would, Shavell's account succeeds at most in justifying continued prohibition of adventitious blackmail *of innocent conduct the incidence of which society has no interest in reducing*. It provides no argument for prohibiting conditional threats to reveal information about socially undesirable behavior where such information was obtained costlessly.

Posner himself has undertaken the most thorough analysis to date of whether blackmail confers a countervailing social benefit.[25] Adopting a purportedly exhaustive seven-part typology of acts or conditions that a blackmailer might threaten to reveal,[26] he concluded that in none of the cases could we be confident that there would be a countervailing social benefit. On this basis, he agreed that blackmail is on average wealth reducing and therefore should be prohibited by the criminal law.

Posner's typology is not as exhaustive as he suggests. He provides no account of threats to do anything other than disclose information or of demands for something other than pecuniary gain. Far more troubling, though, is the tentative, even dubious, nature of some of Posner's central conclusions. For example, he concedes that the social welfare arguments against his "category two" and "category five" blackmail—threats to reveal that a victim has engaged either in a criminal act for which he was not caught and punished, or in disreputable or immoral acts that do not violate any commonly enforced law—are inconclusive.[27] But he disfavors legalizing such forms of blackmail by privileging "a presumption against the expenditure of scarce political capital on an effort to change laws that are not demonstrably inefficient" over a contrasting "presumption against government intervention in private affairs that is not demonstrably efficient."[28] That would be a fair conclusion were the question whether we should campaign for blackmail's decriminalization (in whole or part). But it is nonresponsive to one who seeks theoretical understanding.

Finally, even if nonadventitious blackmail were shown to reduce social wealth, and even if the theory's apparent failure to cover adventitious blackmail could be rectified or deemed appropriate on reflection, proponents of the argument from economic efficiency have not yet persuasively explained why the fact that the practice of blackmail is, on balance, wealth reducing, justifies its criminalization. On the consequentialist assumptions that underpin the economic approach, recourse to the heavy artillery of the criminal law could not be justified if the incidence of blackmail could be comparably well reduced by means that incur less social cost, in terms, inter alia, of tax dollars expended and the human suffering of persons caught and punished. Put another way, criminalization of blackmail cannot be justified as a means to promote utility or wealth-maximization unless its marginal benefits—relative, say, to making blackmail agreements unenforceable as a matter of contract law (as is presently the case) or making blackmail a tort—outweigh the marginal social costs.

One commentator, Joseph Isenbergh, has concluded that they do not. Isenbergh begins by observing that "A gains no real control over disclosure from an unenforceable bargain with B. And if B cannot assure A of any increased control over disclosure, B cannot extract much from A, and therefore has little reason to invest much effort in bargaining."[29] Therefore, there is likely to be little blackmail in a regime that seeks to deter blackmail simply by making blackmail agreements unenforceable as a matter of contract law.

Of course, there could be less blackmail still in a regime that made blackmail agreements unenforceable *and* barred blackmail through the criminal law. Noting the rarity of blackmail in the case law, Posner has speculated that the few reported cases accurately reflect a low incidence of the crime. Anticipating that their would-be victims would refuse to pay blackmail, he surmises, a vast number of would-be blackmailers choose not to risk the criminal penalty.[30] This is possible. However, an alternative hypothesis strikes me as more likely—namely, that blackmail is much more frequent than the incidence of reported cases would indicate, and that the low rate of prosecution reflects the substantial willingness of victims to pay. After all, an economically rational blackmailer should be able to conceive and propose a blackmail price low enough to substantially reduce the probability that his victim will report the blackmailer to the police rather than accept the deal. Thus, although the social cost of the blackmail prohibition is apparently low (commensurate with the infrequency of prosecution and conviction), the deterrent value of the criminal ban is likely to be as small or smaller. Because the goal from an economic standpoint is not to achieve *maximum* but *optimal* deterrence, taking account of all costs and benefits (as measured by utilitarian or wealth-maximizing metrics), it is hard to conclude that blackmail's criminalization is a good buy.

But the economic case *against* criminalization is even stronger, for the blackmail ban might be positively counterproductive. As Isenbergh has explained, if blackmail is made a crime, A gains considerable control over disclosure from entering into a bargain with B, because B, by incurring the criminal exposure of a blackmailer, can now sell A a much higher likelihood of silence.... The criminal prohibition of blackmail, therefore, makes the blackmail bargains entered into across the threshold of prohibition highly enforceable.[31]

And if the would-be blackmailer anticipates that a consummated bargain will be reasonably enforceable, he is more likely to commit the resources necessary to undertake the activity. In short, making blackmail a criminal offense might deter some blackmail that would not be deterred in a regime that merely made the blackmail deal unenforceable as a matter of contract law. But, if so, its deterrent effect is likely to be small. The ban might be moderately economically efficient or moderately inefficient. On the other hand, criminalizing blackmail might actually increase its incidence. In that event, resort to the criminal law is necessarily inefficient, maybe substantially so.

In my view, the most comprehensive formal game-theoretic analysis of the question reaches equivocal results. Fernando Gómez and Juan-José Ganuza conclude in a recent article that making blackmail contracts unenforceable but voidable—so that a blackmailer who promises, for payment, not to disclose the blackmailee's secret does not incur an obligation to pay damages for breach, but can be compelled in restitution to return the blackmailee's payments—will not likely reduce the incidence of blackmail relative to a regime in which blackmail was lawful and blackmail contracts fully enforceable.[32] This argument would lend some support to the economic case for blackmail's criminalization. But it confronts at least two significant problems.

First, Gómez and Ganuza's conclusion that criminalization would reduce blackmail relative to the particular alternative contract solution they consider (that contracts will be unenforceable but voidable) depends on at least two dubious assumptions. The first one is that if the blackmailer discloses after being paid for silence, the blackmailee incurs no disclosure-related costs in suing for restitution.

But disclosure might not be a simple binary matter. For example, if the blackmailer discloses a husband's infidelity to his wife, the husband might nonetheless incur additional reputational costs were he to broadcast his indiscretions more widely by going to court. Their second dubious assumption is that the blackmailee's financial costs of pursuing recovery are nil. To the contrary, given the American rule (not followed in Spain, whence Gómez and Ganuza write) that litigants generally bear their own costs, and given anticipated difficulties in establishing that payments have been made, let alone in what amount, the blackmailee's expected financial payoff from filing suit will be substantially less than his actual payments, and possibly even negative. For both these reasons, Gómez and Ganuza are not warranted in concluding that, if the blackmailer discloses after payment, the blackmailee's clear dominant strategy is to file suit. Consequently, the presence or absence of the prospect of large damage awards might nontrivially affect the effective enforceability of blackmail deals, and thus the incidence of blackmail.

The second flaw in the Gómez and Ganuza analysis cuts at least as deeply. Their model, to repeat, compares the likely incidence of blackmail under two regimes—one in which blackmail is criminalized, the other in which it is lawful but blackmail contracts are unenforceable and voidable. There is, however, a second way that contract law might try to reduce the incidence of blackmail: it could withhold all legal recognition of such agreements, meaning that a blackmailee who acceded to a blackmail demand could neither sue for damages in the event of disclosure nor recoup his payments in restitution. Because this would be the more effective way for contract law to try to combat blackmail, it would seem to provide the more illuminating comparison for those trying to determine whether, on economic principles, resort to the criminal law is justified. For reasons that are unclear, it is not the comparison on which Gómez and Ganuza focus. Still, they do consider this alternative contract regime as a qualification to their model. And when they do, their conclusions are revealing.

First, they rightly recognize that, in a static game, the blackmailer might have little or no incentive to keep his promise, thus giving the blackmailee insufficient confidence to accept the blackmail deal—which was Isenbergh's claim.[33] Whether the same conclusion would obtain in a dynamic setting, most notably if the blackmailer is a repeat player who might benefit from reputation effects in his dealings with other potential blackmailees, is less clear. Gómez and Ganuza claim, reasonably, that it doesn't. But even if so, it is far from obvious that, on economic grounds alone, criminalization is warranted even in the case of repeat and professional blackmailers, for the state has other ways to discourage them. For instance, in addition to making blackmail contracts void, the state could possibly ban blackmail advertising[34] or withhold the benefits of incorporation from firms engaged in blackmailing. Finally, the authors suggest that blackmail might also survive its nonrecognition by contract law when the blackmailer and blackmailee have a long-term relationship in which the former reiterates relatively small demands at intervals, and if the blackmailee has a low discount factor. But they do acknowledge that this is complex and requires further analysis.[35] In light of all this, it seems to me that

Gómez and Ganuza considerably overstate the extent to which their formal analysis undermines Isenbergh's argument that any inefficiency entailed by blackmail can be adequately discouraged simply by making contracts of silence entered into between a blackmailer and his victim either voidable or entirely unregulated, and by excepting contracts with an adventitious blackmailer.[36]

2. Blackmail as the "hand-maiden to corruption and deceit."

Rejecting the problematic premise that the economic inefficiency of a practice provides a sufficient basis for criminalizing it, Richard Epstein argued some twenty-five years ago that blackmail is criminal because it has a necessary tendency to induce *other* acts of theft and deception, whose criminalization is wholly *unpuzzling*.[37]

Epstein "begin[s] with a brief account of the moral theory of criminal responsibility"[38]—to wit, that there is no criminal liability without mens rea and actus reus. Blackmail easily satisfies the mens rea requirement. Blackmail's criminalization is problematic, then, because of the actus reus requirement, which Epstein views as limited, in a manner not fully spelled out, to the threat or use of force or fraud.[39] Accordingly, the criminalization of blackmail is puzzling because (ordinarily) it entails neither force nor fraud.[40] Of course, one could "argue that the threat to disclose is illegal precisely because the disclosure itself, if made, *ought* to be illegal."[41] But this argument won't do, Epstein concludes, for it "jettisons the basic theory of criminal responsibility by holding that deliberate acts, not involving the use of force or fraud, may themselves be regarded as criminal."[42]

Epstein maintains that the solution to the blackmail puzzle appears when we consider "what…the world [would] look like if blackmail were legalized." Under such a regime, there would then be an open and public market for a new set of social institutions to exploit the gains from this new form of legal activity. Blackmail, Inc. could with impunity place advertisements in the newspaper offering to acquire for top dollar any information with the capacity to degrade or humiliate persons in the eyes of their families or business associates.

And, Epstein proposes, the existence of Blackmail, Inc. would produce at least two undesireable consequences. First, the greater prevalence of blackmail would lead to more blackmail victims and, consequently, greater incidences of theft and fraud by victims desperate to obtain the funds necessary to pay the blackmailer. Second, because Blackmail, Inc. would "recognize[] that its ability to extract future payments from V [the victim] depends upon T [the third party to whom the disclosure would be made] being kept in the dark," it would inevitably "instruct [V] in the proper way to arrange his affairs in order the keep the disclosures from being made."[43] In short, Epstein concludes, "[b]lackmail is made a crime not only because of what it is, but because of what it necessarily leads to…. [I]t is the hand-maiden to corruption and deceit."[44]

This particular rendition of Epstein's conclusion is misleading. The real thrust of *Blackmail, Inc.* is that blackmail is properly made a crime *not* because of "what it is," but *only* because of "what it necessarily leads to." Epstein's assertion that force and fraud exhaust the concerns of the criminal law entails that criminalization of blackmail would be impermissible *but for* the frauds and thefts it engenders (given that blackmail does not itself constitute fraud or force). Now, lots of conduct that Epstein would never think justifiably criminalized leads to fraud and theft and other core moral wrongs. Some number of persons have stolen and robbed innocent victims for money to buy jewelry and electronics, for example, but it would be fanciful to think it consistent with Epstein's "moral theory of criminal responsibility" to criminalize the production or sale of such goods. Once Epstein qualifies his moral theory to permit the state to criminalize not only acts of force and fraud themselves but also conduct that has some causal relationship to such acts, he must both insist that the linkage be of a fairly circumscribed sort and persuasively establish that blackmail satisfies whatever narrow causal standard he has in mind, lest his concession open the door to criminalization of just about everything.

Epstein does not, in his brief chapter, specify just how closely or substantially or intimately given nonforceful, nonfraudulent conduct must cause or facilitate other forceful or fraudulent conduct to justify its criminalization. But he does repeatedly intimate—his theory relies, after all, on claims regarding what blackmail "*necessarily* leads to"[45]—that blackmail's relationship to such activity is close and substantial indeed. Recall that Epstein focuses on two ways that blackmail produces the wrongs with which the criminal law is properly concerned: it induces blackmail victims to steal and defraud to gain the funds to pay the blackmailer's demands; and it coaches victims in how best to perpetuate the frauds they are already perpetrating against others. Let us consider these two mechanisms in reverse.

Plainly, the second argument depends on the assumption that the blackmail victim, V, is in fact engaged in fraud against some third party, T. Epstein expressly so claims: "not to put too fine a point on it, V is engaged in a type of long term, systematic fraud against T that if disclosed would allow T some type of relief against V—be it a divorce or a money judgment."[46] But that puts *much* too fine a point on it. Take, for example, our two paradigm cases: *adultery-threat* and *gay-threat*. The adulterer is engaged in fraud against his wife, but our hypothetical gay man is defrauding nobody. Not all deception is fraudulent. Indeed, not all secrets that a blackmailer might threaten to disclose are even deceptions. One example that recurs in the literature concerns a blackmail threat to reveal, to the man's friends and coworkers, that some unfortunate soul is an inveterate bedwetter. Clearly the bedwetter is engaged in no fraud. And unless he has affirmatively denied bedwetting (perhaps he walks to work wearing a sandwich board that declares "I do not wet my bed"?), he has not even deceived anyone. He has simply not disclosed an embarrassing secret that he'd prefer people not know. I expect that most people would view as especially worthy of criminalization conditional threats to divulge embarrassing secrets whose continued suppression would not wrong anybody else. But Epstein's second argument provides no support for their criminalization.[47]

Epstein's first argument is hardly more successful, though for different reasons. To start, it cannot help justify criminalization of blackmail threats that involve demands for anything other than cash or its equivalent. So Epstein's theory would not support making it a crime to demand sexual compliance for the nondisclosure of embarrassing information the victim has no moral obligation to divulge (e.g., that she was born out of wedlock). But even when we turn to blackmail demands for money, Epstein's theory is infirm.

Epstein claims that the second of the two ways that blackmail breeds fraud and deception is bound to occur: "This is not a case, like driving, where we are uncertain whether a teenager will speed if granted a license. Continued fraud against T is a pre-condition for blackmail against V."[48] We have criticized that second argument not by denying that Blackmail, Inc. will very likely come to participate in the deception, but by denying that the deception in which it participates will necessarily constitute fraud (or even that it's necessarily properly described as deception). However Epstein's claims regarding the likelihood that Blackmail, Inc. will encourage its victims to engage in criminal activity to pay its bill are markedly—and appropriately—more modest. "What," he asks, "is to prevent Blackmail, Inc. from hinting, ever so slightly, that it thinks strenuous efforts to obtain the necessary cash should be undertaken? Do we believe that V would never resort to fraud or theft given this kind of pressure…?"[49] No, of course not. But the standard to which Epstein appeals is much too lenient. Surely nothing prevents Jewelry, Inc. from hinting, ever so slightly, that a besotted young man should make strenuous efforts to purchase the ring his fiancée has admired. Nor do we believe that he would never resort to criminality given that kind of pressure.

My point is not to equate the two cases. Rather, it's to emphasize that Epstein cannot rest content with establishing merely that the practice of blackmail will pre-dictably cause some increase in force or fraud by blackmailees. That is not good enough to justify subjecting to criminal sanction persons who do not themselves engage in force or fraud if Epstein's core principle of criminal responsibility—crim-inal sanctions must be limited, in the first instance, to actual instances of force or fraud—is to retain real bite.

3. *Blackmail encourages invasions of privacy.*

A third theory, proposed by Jeffrie Murphy,[50] exhibits similarities to both of the approaches already discussed. Like Epstein, Murphy focuses on the antisocial con-duct that blackmail's legalization can be expected to encourage. Like proponents of the economic analysis, Murphy seems principally motivated to explain and justify the distinction between blackmail and "other hard economic transactions."[51] Like both earlier approaches, however, Murphy's theory does not comport with strong intuitions regarding proper outcomes.

Murphy's argument proceeds in three steps. He begins by pronouncing twin assumptions about the moral underpinnings of the criminal law:

> The first is that immorality should be a necessary condition for criminalization but not a sufficient condition. The second is that utilitarian considerations, though unsatisfactory in explicating the concept of immorality, are a reasonable basis on which to answer the question "Which of all immoral actions should be criminalized?"[52]

He then asserts that blackmail and hard economic transactions "are both intrinsically immoral (and immoral for the same reason—e.g., taking an unfair advantage
of the victim's vulnerability)." Lastly, he explains that utilitarian considerations provide good reasons for (1) criminalizing the blackmail of persons who are not public
figures—namely, that if blackmail were legalized, would-be blackmailers would
have incentives to invade the privacy of average persons where presently no such
incentives exist,[53] and (2) not criminalizing hard economic transactions—namely,
that there is no apparent way to draw sensible and enforceable lines between
immoral and morally acceptable transactions.[54]

Like the economic argument, Murphy's theory is rendered underinclusive by its
inability to justify criminalization of adventitious blackmail because any invasions
of privacy that such forms of blackmail occasion are unaffected by blackmail laws.[55]
An even greater difficulty is that Murphy cannot rest on a bare assertion that blackmail is immoral because it takes unfair advantage of a victim's vulnerability.[56]
Consider the example Murphy offers of a paradigmatic "hard economic
transaction":

> I know that your son, whom you love more than anything else in the world, is
> dying of leukemia. I also know two other things: (1) that he is a great baseball fan
> who would love to have a baseball autographed by Babe Ruth to cheer him during
> his final days and (2) that $6,000 is all the money you have in the world. Now
> I happen to own the last such baseball available in the world, and I will make you
> a proposition—namely, to sell you this baseball for $6,000.[57]

Well, yes, that does sound hard. And let's agree arguendo that it's immoral. But
Murphy does not claim that the baseball's owner has a moral obligation to *give* it to
the dying boy: presumably he is morally free to sell it to the boy's parents for a "fair"
price. If so, and if the analogy holds, then the blackmailer should also be free to sell
what he has to offer—his silence—whether that price is set by the "market" or by
another means. That is, "fair-price blackmail" would seem to be morally unproblematic, and not permissibly criminalized (in principle). Neither conclusion is
demonstrably erroneous. But, on balance, Murphy's analysis generates conclusions
that do not cohere well with either present law or what I take to be widespread
moral intuitions.

B The Inherent Wrongfulness of Blackmail

The consequentialist theories of blackmail are not entirely without merit. The practice of blackmail might well produce the costs on which these theories focus: greater
invasions of individual privacy, more fraud and deception, waste of social resources.
But the defects of these accounts also loom large: they generally fail to justify criminalization of large swaths of conduct (adventitious blackmail, for example) that
strike other participants to the debate as properly criminalized; they frequently
incorporate dubious empirical assumptions; and they often fail to ground their
diagnoses of blackmail's harms in persuasive theories of the proper scope of the

criminal law. Moreover, most readers are likely to feel that the accounts discussed in Subsection I.A. just have the wrong tone, for they fail to make sense of the widespread conviction that blackmail is morally wrongful. For all these reasons, it is no surprise that many theorists try to establish that blackmail is properly criminalized precisely because it is morally wrongful.

Broadly speaking, there are two routes to the conclusion that blackmail is morally wrongful: the first derives its wrongfulness from the wrongfulness of the conduct threatened (or offered); the second locates wrongfulness in the proposal itself such that blackmail can be morally wrongful even if it would not be wrongful for the blackmailer to do as he threatens (or as he offers). If the conduct that a blackmailer threatens can be assumed to be wrongful (think *gay-disclosure*), then the wrongfulness of the conditional threat follows from the threat principle, and the theorist's challenge is only to resolve the puzzle of legal blackmail: to explain why the unconditional performance of the conduct threatened and the making of the conditional threat, albeit both morally wrongful (even if not equally so), properly call forth different legal responses. If the conduct threatened might not be wrongful (think *adultery-disclosure*), then the challenge is greater: to explain both what renders the threat wrongful and why its wrongfulness is the type of wrongfulness that the state ought to (or may) criminalize, given that not all wrongdoing is properly subject to legal sanction.

1. *The puzzle of legal blackmail.*

We have supposed that *gay-disclosure* and *gay-threat* are both morally wrongful and, furthermore, that the wrongfulness of the latter derives from (but is not necessarily reducible to) that of the former. What reasons could we have for criminalizing the threat if we decline to criminalize the unconditional disclosure? The existing literature suggests several.

First, the disclosure and the threat to disclose differently implicate free speech values. Although contemporary First Amendment doctrine nominally protects the freedom not to speak as fully as the freedom to speak,[58] we might reasonably believe that the values undergirding the First Amendment are generally better served by more rather than less speech or, in any event, that they are implicated little, if at all, by the offered sale of one's silence. If so, this would be a reason to permit morally wrongful disclosures but not to permit those morally wrongful conditional threats to disclose.[59]

Second, while the unconditional disclosure is a one-shot affair, the conditional threat to disclose ordinarily lends itself to repetition. The repetitive nature of the blackmail proposal is likely to instill in the blackmailee continued fear and anxiety that the one-time disclosure cannot likewise create.[60] Indeed, George Fletcher has argued that the blackmailer's continued power over the blackmailee permits him a dominance the deterrence and punishment of which are central purposes of the criminal law.[61]

Third, the disclosure and the threat directly harm different types of interest. The disclosure inflicts emotional and reputational injuries; the conditional threat implicates interests in property. Conceivably, the latter sorts of interest are more important or more properly the concern of the state. Something like this idea seems to undergird Leo Katz's contribution to the blackmail literature.[62] In the context of *adultery-threat*, Katz poses the blackmail puzzle thus: "If revealing the infidelities is only a minor immorality, then how can the taking of money which the victim prefers to that minor immorality be anything more than a minor immorality itself?"[63] And his answer follows from the following general principle (which he derives from a characteristically clever hypothetical involving a battery and a theft):[64] "when the defendant has the victim choose between either of two immoralities which he must endure, the gravity of the defendant's wrongdoing is to be judged by what he actually did (or sought to achieve), not by what he threatened to do."[65] Blackmail is a serious offense because it is a form of robbery or (at the least) theft, a graver wrong than the disclosure of an embarrassing secret.[66]

Fourth, the disclosure might implicate, to a far greater degree than the threat, a range of concerns related to the practical administration of the criminal laws. For example, it could be that wrongful disclosures (but not wrongful threats) are so common that "effective enforcement [of a law proscribing the disclosures] might be possible only by making demands on the criminal justice system that would significantly compromise its ability to deal with more serious offenses."[67] Or we may believe ourselves unable to craft a law prohibiting the wrongful disclosures that does not incur an excessive risk of overdeterring permissible disclosures or producing erroneous convictions.

None of these answers is perfect alone. The free speech rationale would seem to predict a greater variation in blackmail laws across jurisdictions than we find and, moreover, would not address the puzzle of noninformational legal blackmail. The argument based on the threat's repetitive nature is underinclusive insofar as it cannot justify the criminalization of blackmail proposals that do not reasonably create apprehension of repeated demands.[68] The arguments that posit that threat to property interests is greater than threat to reputational and emotional interests are, to my mind, more asserted than defended. The arguments that emphasize different practical administrative concerns point to conceivable differences that would matter but require further development to establish that these conceivable differences are likely actually to obtain.

But if not perfect, they are pretty good, especially in combination. The biggest problem with these answers is that *they don't address the puzzle of moral blackmail*. Thus does Lindgren object that Katz's solution "merely assumes away the paradox, which is in part that often what the blackmailer threatens to do is a moral right."[69] This oversight is problematic for at least two reasons. First and most obviously, it risks substantial underinclusiveness. If these accounts cannot be supplemented, we will be unable to explain and justify criminalization in cases like *adultery-threat*. Second, until we have resolved the puzzle of moral blackmail, we cannot have full confidence in proposed solutions even to the legal puzzle, for when the solution to the puzzle of moral blackmail does emerge it might provide us with resources, presently unseen, for a more satisfactory solution to the puzzle of legal blackmail as well.

2. The puzzle of moral blackmail.

Unfortunately, few solutions have been specifically proposed to the puzzle of moral blackmail. That is not so surprising. After all, the distinctness of the two puzzles is almost universally overlooked. Moreover, the puzzle of legal blackmail alone—that is, the puzzle that arises if we assume the moral wrongfulness of the conduct threatened, and therefore of the threat—is by far the easier nut to crack. Even if controversial, it is not truly puzzling to explain or justify the criminalization of attempts to secure property of another by means of morally wrongful threats. So the puzzle of legal blackmail principally reduces to the question of why not to criminalize the wrongful act (usually an informational disclosure). But if that's the question, at least some of the reasons just canvassed—for example, the consideration sounding in free speech values, and concerns about practical administration of the law by the police and judiciary—should spring readily to mind. To be sure, we might also reasonably ask whether, given the decision to keep the acts threatened lawful, some potential victims of disclosure might not be better off in a regime that permitted conditional offers of silence, and thus whether it might not be utility enhancing or otherwise prudent to legalize the conditional threats notwithstanding their conceded wrongfulness. But this is a very practical question, hardly a puzzle let alone a paradox. The puzzle of moral blackmail guards its secret much more securely.

One possible solution to the problem of moral blackmail was advanced by James Lindgren in his influential 1984 article. Lindgren began by noting (infelicitously) that "the heart of the [blackmail] problem is that two separate acts, each of which is a moral and legal right, can combine to make a moral and legal wrong."[70] He then claimed to unravel this puzzle by observing that the blackmail threat differs from ordinary and legitimate threats in commercial transactions in that only the former entails using leverage properly belonging to another person (e.g., the adulterer's spouse) for one's own gain. What makes the blackmailer's conduct distinct and wrongful, Lindgren argues, is that he interposes himself parasitically in an actual or potential dispute in which he lacks a sufficiently direct interest. What right has he to make money by settling other people's claims?

At the heart of blackmail, then, is the triangular nature of the transaction, and particularly this disjunction between the blackmailer's personal benefit and the interests of the third parties whose leverage he uses. In effect, the blackmailer attempts to gain an advantage in return for suppressing someone else's actual or potential interest. The blackmailer is negotiating for his own gain with someone else's leverage or bargaining chips.[71]

Lindgren's approach has been subjected to extensive criticism that need not be repeated here in full. It is fair to conclude that his theory enjoys claims to rough—though surely not perfect[72]—descriptive accuracy. But it is also true—as Lindgren has conceded[73]—that the normative grounding of his bargaining-chip explanation is obscure. That is, Lindgren provides no reason why use of someone else's leverage for individual gain should be made unlawful, let alone criminal. Furthermore, if the use of such leverage *is* wrongful, it's not clear why the *squandering* of another's chips—by deciding neither to threaten nor to make a given disclosure—is not likewise wrongful and thus properly criminalizable.

Another alternative is Fletcher's dominance theory. I earlier agreed that it can contribute to a solution to the puzzle of legal blackmail by helping to explain why a wrongful conditional threat can inflict greater harm than would unconditional performance of the wrongful conduct threatened. But perhaps Fletcher also means it to explain why the conditional threat is wrongful even if the conduct threatened would not be. If so, it faces a steeper hill to climb.

Plainly, that a relationship includes elements of dominance and subordination cannot suffice to justify intervention from the criminal law. Innumerable relationships—parent and child, employer and employee, teacher and student, and so on—exhibit aspects of dominance and subordination, yet raise no suspicion in the eyes of the law. Indeed some such relationships—for example, prison guard and inmate—are products of the criminal law. So the existence of such a dynamic cannot be a sufficient condition for criminalization. As one of Fletcher's early critics objected, "It must be the case, therefore, that the blackmailer's actions are somehow intrinsically wrong and unjustified."[74] Fletcher appeared to agree with this observation but thought the wrongfulness of blackmail obvious and overdetermined:

> Many words and expressions at hand express what is wrong with blackmail. In fact, too many things are wrong with it. Blackmail represents coercion of the victim, exploitation of the victim's weakness, and trading unfairly in assets or chips that belong to others. It represents an undesirable and abusive form of private law enforcement. It leads to the waste of resources so far as blackmailers are induced to collect information that they are willing to suppress for a fee.[75]

In short, Fletcher seems to suggest, *of course* blackmail is wrong and unjustified.

But Fletcher's litany of blackmail's evils cannot fully do the work he expects of it precisely because each assertion is so hotly contested. What makes blackmail "coercive" or "exploitative" in a morally meaningful sense? Why is trading on another's chips "unfair"? What moral significance should we attribute to the fact, if true, that, on balance, blackmail wastes resources? These are challenging questions. And they weigh with particular force when, as in *adultery-threat,* the conduct threatened is presumptively morally permissible. Mere reference to theories that elicit, but do not convincingly resolve, these questions cannot satisfactorily answer what Fletcher seems to acknowledge is the crucial question for his own theory—namely, what about the blackmailer's actions creates a *wrongful* type of dominance?

C Blackmail Is Not Justifiably Criminalized

The analysis to this point suggests the following provisional conclusions. First, we cannot adequately explain and justify blackmail's criminalization by attending only to its supposed social consequences. We reasonably expect that blackmail's (nonconsequentialist) moral wrongfulness should somehow feature into a satisfactory explanation of, and justification for, its criminalization. Second, if we assume that the conduct a blackmailer threatens is wrongful, then it is not terribly hard to provide reasons for treating the threat differently. Third, those reasons do not seem fully to account for the contours of the crime and (worse) do not yet explain the threat's moral wrongfulness if (as the puzzle supposes) the act threatened is not morally wrongful. That is, if we are close to a solution of the puzzle of legal blackmail, we remain very far from a solution to the puzzle of moral blackmail.

In light of these difficulties, several theorists have concluded that blackmail is not properly criminalized. The most familiar arguments are libertarian in nature. A second argument, recently advanced by Russell Christopher, urges that decriminalizing blackmail is the only way to avoid a logical contradiction. In short, the first argument contends that decriminalization is demanded by a due respect for individual liberty; the second thinks it's demanded by a regard for logical consistency.

1. *Liberty.*

In his 1962 classic *Man, Economy, and State,* the Austrian economist Murray Rothbard observed in passing that libertarianism would not permit the criminalization of blackmail: "Blackmail would not be illegal in the free society. For blackmail is the receipt of money in exchange for the service of not publicizing certain information about the other person. No violence or threat of violence to person or property is involved."[76] Libertarian writers since Rothbard have reiterated the claim.[77] One in particular, Walter Block, has pressed the argument with particular industriousness, producing nearly a score of papers over the past two decades.[78] These articles generally argue for decriminalization on two tracks. In predominant part, they aim to show that particular procriminalization theories fail for the usual sorts of reasons—because they rest on unsupported or implausible premises, employ fallacious reasoning, or the like. In addition, they argue that decriminalization is compelled on general principle because (1) justice permits the state to criminalize only the use or threat of violence against person or property right, and (2) blackmail does not involve the use or threat of violence against person or property right.[79] Recently, Block has complained that, while he has assiduously criticized the arguments advanced by members of the procriminalization camp, his opponents have not returned the favor.[80] I fear that that asymmetry in attention is likely to persist.

Libertarians' criticisms of particular theories purporting to justify blackmail's criminalization warrant careful attention and response in proportion to their cogency and force. (Of course, whether successful criticisms should drive the proponents of criminalization to accept that blackmail should in fact be decriminalized, rather than to try harder to unearth the justification for criminalization that they believe is waiting to be discovered, is a dicier matter—one that, I suggested in Section I, depends in large part on the strength of their pretheoretical conviction that this is conduct the state should, or may, prohibit on pain of criminal punishment.) But the libertarians' affirmative argument for decriminalization does not demand equivalent attention, for the strength of the libertarian argument is also, in a sense, its weakness. The libertarian conclusion rests on a fairly straightforward and easily articulated and understood major premise that the overwhelming majority of contemporary theorists of the criminal law simply reject.[81] Block seems to believe that his adversaries are obligated either to accept the libertarian premise regarding the very limited legitimate scope of the criminal sanction or to construct full-blown refutations of it in their writings on blackmail. But that is unreasonable to demand in papers directed to the blackmail puzzle. It seems perfectly acceptable for theorists to view their challenge as justifying blackmail consistent with mainstream theories of punishment; they should not be obligated in addition to argue for those theories against all competitors.[82]

If blackmail theorists need not be expected to mount a frontal assault on libertarian criminal theory, it is not the case that they lack recourse to competing theories.[83] For example, the dominant contemporary Anglo-American theory of criminal punishment—the dominant answer to the question of what justifies the state in imposing criminal punishment—is almost certainly a retributively constrained pluralistic consequentialism. That is, it views the state as justified in imposing and threatening the criminal sanction to achieve a wide range of social goods (including realization of deserved punishment), while requiring that the state take substantial (but not absolute) pains not to punish individuals in excess of their ill-desert. A theory of this sort comfortably legitimizes punishment in cases like *gay-threat*: it is plausible to conclude (1) that aggregate welfare is promoted if the state can successfully reduce attempts to take property by threatening to wrong the property owner; (2) that cases like *gay-threat* represent precisely such an attempt; and (3) that by threatening to act wrongfully toward the blackmailee, the threatener in *gay-threat* is morally blameworthy, and thus has ill-desert.

Block asserts that "[b]lackmail no more 'takes' property from another than the baker 'takes' money from his customer in return for bread. In both the bakery and blackmail cases, there is not a 'taking' but rather a voluntary trade which was mutually agreed upon at the time of sale."[84] Yet on mainstream premises, the asserted equivalence between the two cases is simply false. Block seems to agree (despite the puzzle of moral blackmail) that the blackmailer is not morally justified in doing as he threatens.[85] There is no reason to expect, however, that he thinks the same is true of the baker: presumably Block, like most people, believes that the baker is morally justified in doing as he threatens, namely to keep his bread. So the blackmailer extracts property by a threat to wrong the offeree, whereas the baker does not. On ordinary consequentialist and retributivist theories of the criminal law, this difference would provide prima facie justification for criminalizing the act of the blackmailer (in cases where the conduct threatened would be wrongful) and for describing the blackmailer's acquisition of the blackmailee's property as a "taking" in a morally freighted sense. To put this conclusion in rights terms, we could posit that an individual has a right that others not try to take his property by means of threats to wrong him.

I do not for a moment think that the case for mainstream theories of punishment is so strong that Block is compelled on pain of irrationality to accept them.

But most blackmail theorists who try to develop accounts that might successfully justify blackmail's criminalization are not *trying* to persuade committed libertarians; we understand that we are employing a theory of the justifiability of the criminal sanction broader than they accept. The ambition of mainstream blackmail theorists is reasonably limited: it is to explain why it is consistent with mainstream theories of the justifiability of criminal punishment (which themselves must be argued for, albeit not necessarily by blackmail theorists themselves) to criminalize and punish conditional threats to do what is, and should remain, lawful. Libertarian theorists who advance arguments designed to show that we cannot achieve *that* ambition are as entitled as nonlibertarian theorists to a response—no more, no less. But if they expect responses to arguments that are themselves based on libertarian premises,[86] they are apt to continue to be disappointed.

2. *Logic.*

One might be skeptical that logic alone supplies the appropriate tools to resolve the normative question of whether blackmail should be criminalized. Yet that is just what Russell Christopher argues when introducing the imaginative conceit of "meta-blackmail"—that is, the conditional threat to conditionally threaten what it is permissible to do—and issues a challenge that we determine how the law should treat it.[87] Logically, he says, there are only three possibilities. What he terms the "formalist" solution would punish meta-blackmail more severely than the blackmail proposal on which the meta-blackmail proposal is predicated; a "functionalist" solution would punish the two proposals the same; and a "substantivist" solution would punish meta-blackmail less severely than its corresponding blackmail proposal.

The problem for procriminalization theorists is that these three options are not merely logical possibilities. To the contrary, Christopher argues, each is supported by plausible—even "compelling"—intuitions. The intuition that a threat to perform an unlawful act is ordinarily worse or more serious than the threat to perform a legal act supports the formalist solution; the intuition that the two conditional threats are equivalent in purpose and effect supports the functionalist solution; and the intuition that the meta-blackmail proposal threatens more distant, remote, or attenuated harm than does the ordinary blackmail proposal supports the substantivist solution. Because these three solutions are mutually incompatible, the proponent of criminalization must choose one and provide arguments sufficient to defeat the intuitions that support the other two. Skeptical that this can be accomplished, Christopher urges that the only way out is to decriminalize blackmail. If a conditional threat to perform a legal action were itself legal then the formalist, functionalist, and substantivist perspectives would align in directing that meta-blackmail should be legal, too. The only escape from the trilemma, then, is to legalize blackmail.

It's a clever argument, but not a sound one. Christopher is right that, for any given pair consisting of a particular blackmail proposal and a particular corresponding meta-blackmail proposal, there exist only three possibilities: the latter should be treated more severely, the same, or less severely, than the former. It does not follow, however, that there exist only three possible ways for the law to treat the *class* of blackmail proposals relative to the *class* of their corresponding meta-blackmail proposals. Christopher implicitly assumes that the law must punish all meta-blackmail proposals the same way relative to the blackmail proposals that they threaten—more severely, less severely, or equally severely. But that assumption is mistaken. It could be that different meta-blackmail/blackmail pairs warrant different treatment depending on which of the three intuitions each pair in fact vindicates.

To see this, consider two different meta-blackmail/blackmail pairs. Let Bm_1 be A's conditional threat to immediately reveal H's adultery to W unless paid $X. The corresponding meta-blackmail proposal—$M\text{-}Bm_1$—is A's conditional threat to immediately issue Bm_1 unless paid $X. Let Bm_2 be A's conditional threat to reveal H's adultery to W in ten years unless paid $X. $M\text{-}Bm_2$ is A's conditional threat to issue Bm_2 in ten years unless paid $X.[88]

Consider the latter pair first, and assume with Christopher that the harm threatened is disclosure. $M\text{-}Bm_2$ threatens that harm in twenty years, while Bm_2 threatens it in ten years. So the meta-blackmail proposal threatens more remote and attenuated harm, thereby satisfying the substantivist premise. But for precisely that reason, the pair do not satisfy the functionalist premise: the two threats are not equivalent in function and effect. Matters are reversed with respect to Bm_1 and $M\text{-}Bm_1$. Any difference in the remoteness of the threatened harm in this case is truly de minimis, suggesting that the two proposals are equivalent in function and effect, and likely in all other respects that are relevant to the criminal law. So Bm_1 and $M\text{-}Bm_1$ do satisfy the functionalist premise. Of course, for precisely that reason, they do not satisfy the substantivist one.

The point of these simple illustrations can be generalized: whenever meta-blackmail threatens a more remote or less probable harm than does the simple blackmail proposal to which it corresponds (however rare or common that may be), the substantivist premise obtains and the functionalist premise does not. One proposal cannot *both* threaten more remote or less probable harm than another *and* be fully equivalent to the other on dimensions of purpose, function, and effect. Put in Christopher's terms, either "the lower certainty and probability of the harm of meta-blackmail constitutes a qualitatively significant, non de minimis, difference between meta-blackmail and [its corresponding blackmail proposal],"[89] in which case the proposals are not functionally equivalent, or the differences in probability and remoteness are de minimis, in which case the proposals are functionally equivalent. Both cannot be true, so there is no incompatibility between the functionalist and substantivist perspectives. They do not yield conflicting conclusions regarding the proper treatment of any given corresponding pair of blackmail and meta-blackmail proposals.

The formalist perspective does not change things. The reason why we think that a threat to perform an illegal act is more "serious" than a threat to perform a legal act is that we assume (defeasibly) that the illegal act is more "serious" than the legal one: it is precisely the greater seriousness of the one than the other that presumptively explains and justifies the decision to make one illegal and the other legal. But if a given meta-blackmail threat is functionally equivalent to the blackmail threat that it threatens, then it's simply *not* more serious. And if it is not functionally equivalent because it threatens more remote harm, then it would seem to be less serious. In neither case would it be sensible to adjudge the meta-blackmail threat more serious than the blackmail threat and to punish it more severely. I am open to the possibility (though I wouldn't bet on it) that Christopher can adduce criminal-law-relevant considerations in virtue of which a particular meta-blackmail threat would be more serious all things considered than its corresponding blackmail threat. Were he to do so, then we'd have to conclude that, for that pair, the substantivist and functionalist conclusions are not warranted. But whether he can do so or not, the bottom line remains that the formalist, functionalist, and substantivist perspectives do not yield "jointly incompatible"[90] conclusions regarding the proper legal treatment of any given pair of corresponding meta-blackmail and blackmail proposals. There is no trilemma, and thus no logical tidiness to be gained by decriminalizing blackmail.

III COERCION AND THE EVIDENTIARY THEORY

Although his meta-blackmail conceit is designed to demonstrate, by logic alone and without endorsing any contestable normative, conceptual, or empirical premises, that blackmail ought not to be criminalized, Christopher also surveys and critiques prior efforts to justify its criminalization. In the course of that effort, he opines that a coercion-based approach might work,[91] a view shared by others who think the puzzle not yet solved.[92] The evidentiary theory is just such an approach. Its merits— and possibly its demerits as well—will emerge more clearly after we review a brief and partial history of efforts to explain blackmail as the wrong of coercion.

A Toward a Theory of Blackmail as Coercion

1. *Robert Nozick.*

In *Anarchy, State, and Utopia*, Nozick argues that blackmail differs from ordinary voluntary transactions because blackmail is a species of what Nozick terms "unproductive exchanges."[93] An exchange between A and B is unproductive for Nozick when two conditions are satisfied: (1) A is no better off as a result of the transaction than if he had nothing to do with B, and (2) if B's part of the transaction consists solely of abstaining from performing some action, x, B proposes to perform x solely to sell A his abstention.[94]

Now, it is not obvious that the first condition is satisfied in all cases of blackmail.[95] But waiving that objection and assuming that the blackmail deal is unproductive, the question remains why it should be illegal, let alone criminal. That consequentialists would disfavor such transactions is to be expected. But, as we've seen, not even the law and economics theorists have persuasively justified blackmail's criminalization. How such a justification might be forthcoming compatible with Nozick's brand of libertarianism is hard to fathom. Accordingly, Michael Gorr states the consensus view when concluding that "the reasons which Nozick offers for prohibiting 'unproductive' exchanges could not plausibly be made to cohere with the principles that are generally taken to underlie a libertarian society."[96]

Indeed, the claim that the unproductivity of an exchange is a sufficient basis for it to be criminalized is so implausible, and Nozick's argument for that proposition so cryptic,[97] that it's worth questioning whether his readers have correctly grasped his intent. In fact, I think it likely that Nozick did not mean to contend that the fact that an exchange is "unproductive" provides sufficient reason for the state to make it criminal.

Before introducing the notion of unproductive exchanges, Nozick explores how much compensation is due individuals when the state prohibits conduct in which they might wish to engage. (Whether the conduct at issue threatens the types of harms with which the state may properly concern itself is a separate question.) When the state prohibits an *intentional* boundary-crossing, no compensation is due. The setting of a proper compensation level becomes difficult only when the conduct is itself morally permissible (on libertarian principles) but risks causing a cognizable harm to another. Ideally, the state should replicate the market price for the cessation of the risky conduct—that is, the price on which the persons threatened by the risky conduct and the person who wishes to undertake that conduct would agree in a voluntary transaction.

However, the likely existence of a transactional surplus (that is, the minimum price acceptable to the seller is less than the maximum price acceptable to the buyer) makes it impossible to ascertain the hypothetical market price. Nozick proposes the productive exchange test as a step toward resolving this difficulty. Put briefly, Nozick argues that where the hypothetical voluntary transaction would be an unproductive exchange, the buyer of cessation from the risky conduct should be entitled to the entire transactional surplus. In this circumstance, the state should compensate the individual whose morally permissible conduct it forbids only at a level that would keep him on the same indifference curve. But, to repeat, whether the hypothetical transaction would be productive has no bearing on the antecedent question of whether the conduct is proscribable. In short, then, not only is the productive exchange test an implausible basis for criminalizing blackmail, but perhaps Nozick should no longer be read to contend otherwise.

Even if this is correct, Nozick seems to have something to say about blackmail's criminalization. The definition of an unproductive exchange that Nozick offers in *Anarchy, State, and Utopia* closely tracks the test of coercion he offered some years earlier. In that earlier article,[98] Nozick argued that a proposal is coercive if it's properly deemed a "threat" rather than an "offer." A proposal is a threat if it would put the recipient worse off than his expected baseline, where "[t]he term 'expected' is meant to shift between or straddle *predicted* and *morally required.*"[99] Insofar as we're seeking a justification for the criminalization of blackmail, this approach seems more promising.[100] Roughly, coercion is the wrong of interfering with a person's freedom by putting improper pressure on his range of alternatives. So if a blackmail proposal is coercive, there is at least prima facie reason to believe that it should be made illegal.

But if a coercion-based approach seems promising, Nozick's own analysis does not make fully good on its promise. Most commentators believe that *adultery-disclosure* is morally permissible. If they are correct, then the conditional proposal does not threaten to put the adulterer worse off than his morally required baseline. It may also fail to put him worse off than his expected baseline. But even if it does put him worse off than his expected baseline, the moral significance of this expectation is obscure. Therefore, Nozick seems to leave us with the conclusion that *adultery-threat* is not wrongful and should not be criminalized. That could be the right answer. But the coercion-based approach would be more attractive if it could yield the intuitive conclusion that adultery blackmail is properly criminalized.

2. *Joel Feinberg.*

Unfortunately, the first coercion-based theory of blackmail—Joel Feinberg's[101]—reinforces concerns that such an approach might prove unable to resolve the puzzle of blackmail. Indeed, Feinberg initially suggests that not only will an appeal to coercion not resolve the puzzle of moral blackmail (exemplified by *adultery-threat*), it might not even resolve the seemingly more tractable puzzle of legal blackmail (exemplified by *gay-threat*). Unlike "other types of robbery by coercion," Feinberg observes, the act a blackmailer threatens is lawful.[102] "To preserve the coherence of a criminal code," he further maintains, "if we make disclosure independently illegal then we can ban blackmail because it uses the threat to do something illegal to extract a gain, and if we legalize the disclosure as such, then we must legalize blackmail."[103] That is an unpromising start, to be sure. But—and here's the heart of Feinberg's solution to the legal puzzle—conduct ought not to be considered lawful just because it is not prohibited by the criminal law; "the law of torts too can be said to impose duties."[104] Many of the acts a blackmailer threatens, while (by definition) not criminally prohibited, would be tortious or should be. *Gay-disclosure*, for example, should constitute an actionable invasion of privacy. Therefore, *gay-threat* is a threat to do something that is *not* legally permissible and can be unproblematically punished by the criminal law.

Adultery-threat, however, presents a different story. In accord with what I have assumed (in Section I) to be the dominant view, Feinberg argues that a person who comes to learn of another's adultery will often have neither a moral duty to reveal that fact nor a moral duty to remain silent. Consequently, society could not justifiably impose a legal obligation, criminal or civil, on persons either to disclose or not to disclose the commission of adultery. It follows, Feinberg provisionally concludes, that the corresponding blackmail proposal must be decriminalized. And yet, he acknowledges,

There is an argument that deserves our respect for the judgment that all adultery-blackmail is immoral since it must necessarily violate someone or other's rights. Either the cheated spouse has a right to know, the argument begins, or he does not. If he does have such a right then a third-party observer has a duty to transmit the unhappy news to him, and it would be wrong to conceal it in exchange for money. If he does not have such a right, the argument continues, then it would be wrong to violate the adulterer's privacy by revealing her secrets spitefully if the blackmail threat fails. If the blackmailer has a duty to the husband (in this example) to inform him, then he does not have a duty to the wife to keep silent, and vice-versa, so once he undertakes the path of blackmail, he is bound to default a duty to one or the other.

This argument, Feinberg concludes, has false premises. The third party observer may *neither* have a duty to inform the spouse *nor* a duty not to. It may be "morally risky" to intervene at all, but whether he does so is up to him.... So the blackmailer is within his rights morally, and ought to be within his rights legally, if he informs, and equally within his rights if he does not inform.[105]

In short, *adultery-threat* is neither immoral nor criminalizable.

3. *Michael Gorr.*

Deeming this conclusion "astonishing,"[106] Michael Gorr has tried to salvage Feinberg's basic approach to blackmail by showing why it actually supports the morally intuitive conclusion that *adultery-threat* is both morally wrongful and properly criminalized. Gorr agrees that society should not impose a legal duty either to disclose or not to disclose adultery, but bases his conclusion on epistemic uncertainty: we may not know whether the consequences of such a disclosure would be morally beneficial or would cause unnecessary misery;[107] and we may lack necessary information "about the prior distribution of moral rights and duties among the related parties."[108] But for these considerations, Gorr argues, there would be a morally conclusive reason for imposing on third-party observers a legal requirement either to report the occurrence of adultery or (depending upon the circumstances) to refrain from reporting its occurrence. It follows that, in the absence of such concerns, there would also be a morally conclusive reason for prohibiting the corresponding blackmail proposals since these would constitute attempts to acquire some of the adulterer's assets either by offering to conceal what ought morally to be disclosed or by threatening to disclose what ought morally to be concealed. But, *ex hypothesi*, although such difficulties do serve to inhibit us from imposing duties with respect to the mere disclosure or nondisclosure of the adulterer's activities, they do not prevent us from imposing duties not to engage in the blackmailing of such persons.[109]

In short, because one of the two acts that a blackmailer contemplates is morally wrongful (even though we don't know which one), the making of the biconditional proposal must also be morally wrongful—*either* a wrongful offer of silence *or* a wrongful threat to disclosure. Because the blackmailer employs this wrongful tool in an attempt to extract the blackmailee's property, his conduct is rightly criminal-ized as a form of theft. It is wrongful to "seek[] to acquire the resources of another either by threatening to disclose what ought to be concealed or by offering to con-ceal what ought to be disclosed."[110]

Although Gorr's argument contains some missteps,[111] I believe that he is on to something important. He is right, in my view, to focus not on why the conditional threat is impermissible, given the permissibility of the act threatened, but on why the threatened act *is* permissible.[112] As we will see, his focus on epistemic limitations is also salutary. But his account encounters at least two significant challenges—challenges that the evidentiary theory aims to meet.

First, as Scott Altman has objected, Gorr's account does not support the com-mon intuition that *adultery-threat* wrongs the blackmailee, for as far as his analysis goes, the wrong is as likely done the blackmailee's spouse.[113] Second, Gorr fails ade-quately to explain why embarking on a path that might lead to wrongdoing is itself wrongful. The linchpin of the explanation appears to involve the intent to gain resources belonging to another. But I do not believe that that factor can do the work Gorr demands of it.

Take an example Gorr discusses (from Feinberg) of a merchant who engages in lawful but "underhanded" practices. Gorr concludes that the law should not require people who learn of this fact to disclose it. But, he says, there are good reasons to prohibit conditional threats to disclose it. Because the proposal "involves an attempt by the blackmailer to acquire significant *resources* belonging to his victim," it is properly criminalized as "a form of *theft*."[114] Maybe so. But the conclusion is not adequately supported; some critical step of the argument is missing. Just as the law shouldn't mandate disclosure, nor should it mandate silence: anyone who learns of the merchant's practices by means not themselves improper should have a lawful right to disclose or not. That being so, the proposal that Gorr characterizes as an attempt to acquire the victim's resources can also be recharacterized—say, by the offeror—as an offer to sell something of value to the offeree, namely the offeror's silence. An attempt to acquire resources from willing parties is not theft unless the means of acquiring the resources are in some fashion wrongful. But there's nothing in Gorr's analysis here that explains what makes this particular effort wrongful.

The fundamental problem, I believe, is that Gorr ignores the blackmailer's own beliefs and reasons for acting. This is brought out in Gorr's discussion of *adultery-threat*. Gorr assumes that B either has a moral duty to disclose or a moral duty to remain silent, but that "we" know not which. Suppose that B, however, does know. If he knows that he has a duty to disclose, then he is threatening to do what he knows he may not do. If he knows that he has a duty to remain silent, then he is offering to do what he knows what he may not do. So far, so good.

Now suppose, however, that B, like Gorr and his readers, lacks a belief regarding where his duty lies. On an objectivist or belief-independent view of moral duties, it follows that if B chooses wrongly, he violates his duty. (That, we will see, is not my view, but I am willing to accept its plausibility.) How should B decide what to do? Of course, he should think harder—by investigating the morally relevant facts and by reflecting further on the shape, weight, and grounding of moral principles. But suppose he does this and still doesn't know what morality demands in this case. He must decide somehow. Perhaps a true moral principle biases decisions in favor of inaction: when in doubt, do nothing. However, that is not self-evident, and Gorr says nothing to suggest that he endorses it. (And even if it is and he does, we can massage the hypothetical to provide that B is in equipoise regarding whether the default presumption against inaction is overcome.) Absent that, what—flip a coin? Suppose that B does flip a coin, having decided that he will disclose if it lands heads and remain silent if tails. If the result of his flip leads him to the action that, ex hypothesi, violates his moral duty, then *that* action (silence or disclosure) is wrongful. On the other hand, if the flip directs him to what he ought to do (from the God's-eye perspective) then his action in conformity with (what we might describe as) the coin's directive is not wrongful. Either way, I see no compelling reason to conclude that B violated a moral duty by the action of flipping the coin itself, and Gorr offers none.

If the coin flip is not an independent ground of wrongdoing in this (admittedly exceptional) circumstance, it's not because there is something special about coins. So suppose that B chooses a different decision-making protocol: he delegates the decision to a third party. That third party might be some uninvolved person, T. But if that would be permissible, then why not delegate the decision to H? To be sure, H is certain to opine that B ought not to disclose. So maybe B structures his delegation differently. "I genuinely do not know what I should do," he explains to H. "So if you pay me $1,000 I will remain silent; if you don't, I won't."[115] If H doesn't pay, and B discloses, and B's duty was to remain silent, then the disclosure violates a moral duty. Similarly, if H does pay, and B doesn't disclose, and B's duty was to reveal, then the nondisclosure violates a moral duty. But, again, B's final move—disclosure or silence—might be entirely permissible, and it's not at all clear why the proposal isn't morally equivalent to the coin flip. If it is, then the proposal does not *itself* violate a moral duty. And if that's right, and if we may criminalize only violations of moral duties (as Gorr claims), then we are, on Gorr's own principles, prevented from imposing legal duties not to engage in the blackmailing of such persons.

One obvious response to this puzzling case is to resist the supposition that B doesn't know, or have beliefs regarding, what he should do—to disclose or remain silent. Surely, you might say, it is a very rare case when we are truly in equipoise regarding what the balance of undefeated moral reasons requires—at least in cases when we are aware of pro tanto moral reasons for and against a course of conduct. I agree and will therefore bracket such cases in the development of my account. That is, my analysis will explicitly assume that the actor has a view about which he ought to do and will acknowledge that the inference I wish to draw fails when the case is otherwise. But the unusualness of that situation becomes relevant only if the moral beliefs of the actor are themselves relevant. Because Gorr's analysis of the blackmail puzzle does not appear to make the actor's beliefs regarding what he morally ought to do relevant, he has no apparent basis for acknowledging that a different conclusion lies in this admittedly unusual situation.[116] He therefore seems committed to the conclusion that this odd blackmailer does act morally wrongfully but without offering any reasons for that conclusion beyond the unsatisfactory observation that the blackmailer is seeking to acquire resources of another.

4. Scott Altman.

Altman's own "patchwork theory" of blackmail contains elements of coercion and of exploitation and much else besides. The conception of coercion at its heart is a slight revision of Nozick's. Whereas Nozick proposed that a proposal is coercive if it threatens to put the offeree worse off than either his moral baseline or his statistical one, Altman recommends that the moral baseline be supplemented with a counterfactual one. Thus, he who makes a conditional proposal engages in the moral wrong of coercion if he would have done as he offered—that is, would have given the benefit or withheld the harm—had he been unable to make the proposal, and if the benefit or harm-relief "was important to the recipient."[117]

I think this modification is unlikely to succeed. Suppose that, having tidied her garage in a burst of spring cleaning, A is preparing a load for the dump. Up walks B, a well-known collector of old lawnmowers. A, no fool, offers to sell B the lawnmower for $100. By hypothesis, had she been unable to make the proposal—say, a local law prohibited the unlicensed sale of lawnmowers—A would have cheerfully given it to B for free. That is, Altman's counterfactual baseline test is satisfied. Yet surely A is morally entitled to try to secure for herself some of the benefits B would reap from the lawnmower. It seems quite implausible to suppose that A wrongs B by proposing a sale. Admittedly, Altman can endorse that intuitive conclusion. He need only stipulate that the benefit offered—the lawnmower—is not "important" to B. Likely it isn't. But perhaps it is. Perhaps, for example, B needs this particular model to complete a collection that has been a lifetime in the making. If this makes the benefit important, I fear that Altman is committed to the strongly counterintuitive conclusion that A coerces B. Alternatively, if the benefit remains unimportant, then we need an account of importance that prevents these judgments from being ad hoc and that also captures all the usual cases of blackmail.

B Of Beliefs, Motives, and Conditional Offers: The Evidentiary Theory

The fundamental problem with Altman's theory is the same as with Nozick's "expected baseline" test for coercion. The nonmoral baselines cannot do the moral work required of them. Consequently, the prevailing understanding conceives of coercion as the wrong of trying to induce a victim to act in accordance with the wrongdoer's wishes by conditionally threatening to wrong him if he does not.[118] It is a wrongful interference with the victim's freedom because it puts wrongful pressure on his liberty to do otherwise. This understanding of coercion holds true in any normative system, or across normative domains. That is to say: (1) it is presumptively morally wrong to conditionally threaten what it is presumptively morally wrong to do; (2) it is presumptively criminally wrong to conditionally threaten what it is presumptively criminally wrong to do; (3) it is presumptively unconstitutional to conditionally threaten what it would be presumptively unconstitutional to do; and so on. Indeed, it is precisely this understanding of coercion that is responsible for one-half of the threat principle introduced in Section I—namely, the half that maintains that a threat is impermissible if the act threatened is.

What I have previously called the "evidentiary theory" aims to make good on these prior attempts to develop an account by which conditional threats to engage in morally permissible conduct can be morally coercive, hence properly criminalized. It relies on two components, in addition to the understanding of coercion just put forth and the distinction, already emphasized, between threats that are legally coercive and those that are morally coercive (which distinction underwrites the difference between the puzzles of legal blackmail and moral blackmail). First, the theory claims that the moral wrongfulness of an action can depend not only on objective or external judgments about the act and its likely consequences but also on such subjective or internal features as the actor's beliefs and motives. Second, it argues that a conditional proposal to engage in particular conduct can, under appropriate circumstances, have significant evidential bearing on what the threatener's motives or beliefs would likely be were he to engage in the act threatened (or the act offered). Call these two theses, vague though they are, the *subjectivist thesis* and the *evidentiary thesis,* respectively.

Combining these two independent theses, the theory maintains that we are warranted in adjudging that a conditional threat to engage in presumptively or apparently morally permissible conduct is itself morally wrongful when the fact of the conditional offer of silence permits an inference that the act-token threatened would be wrongful because the proposal-maker would, in undertaking it, act on the wrong sorts of beliefs or motives (or lack the right sorts). Uniquely among blackmail theories of which I am aware, my account is, first and foremost, a solution to the puzzle of *moral* blackmail. If it succeeds in explaining why cases like *adultery-threat* are morally wrongful—and morally wrongful *as threats*—then we can proceed to the puzzle of legal blackmail by considering when threats to engage in moral wrongdoing are properly criminalized even when the wrongdoing threatened reasonably remains lawful.

1. *The moral puzzle—first take.*

Keep in mind that *adultery-disclosure* is a biconditional proposal: a conditional threat to disclose adultery if not paid, and a conditional offer to (promise to) remain silent if paid. I believe that Gorr is right that such a proposal is very likely to be wrongful because it is either a conditional threat to wrongfully disclose or a conditional offer to wrongfully remain silent. My objection was not to this conclusion itself but to Gorr's failure to provide a satisfactory argument for it. I reach the same conclusion via a somewhat different route, by exploiting a subjectivist understanding of what morality commands.

In the past, I have advanced a version of the subjectivist thesis that focused on the actor's motives, or explanatory reasons for actions. To a first approximation, the claim was that an actor behaves in morally blameworthy fashion if he knows or believes that his conduct will cause harm to another unless (1) he also believes that the moral reasons in favor of the conduct outweigh or otherwise defeat the moral reasons against, and (2) those justifying reasons are among (or prominent among) the explanatory reasons for which he acts.

For reasons set out in the end note,[119] I presently favor a version of that thesis that turns on the actor's beliefs, not his motives (though I should note my belief that a sharp distinction between versions is probably overly stylized). The belief-centered version maintains—again, this is only to a first approximation—that it is wrongful to act in the face of apparent moral reasons to do otherwise if one does not genuinely believe, based on reasonable and appropriately thorough moral evaluation, that one's conduct is, at the least, permitted by the balance of undefeated moral reasons.[120] Morality, on this view, does not (or does not always) command us to act (or not to act) in specified ways. It does not (always) say "do Φ" or "don't do Φ." Rather, it can be understood to issue a two-part command of the following rough form: first, that we deliberate seriously and soberly about how the potentially relevant moral considerations bear on our choice predicament, and second, that we act in accordance with what judgments we reach on due deliberation. Accordingly, an actor *wrongs* another if he knowingly causes him harm without reasonably believing that producing that harm is consistent with the balance of undefeated moral reasons under the circumstances.[121] I will employ this belief-centered version of the subjectivist thesis in illustrating the operation of the evidentiary theory, though I emphasize that what is integral to the evidentiary theory (in my view) is the more general subjectivist thesis and not any specific version of it. After all, the subjectivist thesis captures a family of related views (the doctrine of double effect, for example, is a member),[122] and I think it entirely likely that the particular version I've advanced will require further refinement.

With this proposed (loose and partial) account of moral wrongfulness in hand, it's easy enough to see why *adultery-threat* is overwhelmingly likely to be wrongful—one way or the other. Because the blackmailer cannot be reasonably unaware that a decision either to disclose or to remain silent is morally freighted, he is under an obligation to deliberate with seriousness regarding what the balance of undefeated moral reasons directs. If he satisfies that obligation he will come to believe either that he ought to disclose or that he ought to remain silent. If he believes that he ought not to disclose H's infidelity to W, then the proposal constitutes a wrongful conditional threat because it is wrongful to threaten what it's wrongful to do—and regardless of whether he has any genuine intent to carry out the threat. (The stick-up artist commits the wrong of coercion by threatening to shoot even if he plans not to, indeed even if his gun is unloaded or fake.) If he concludes that he ought to disclose, then his proposal constitutes a wrongful conditional offer because he proposes to bind himself to act (by his lights) wrongfully.[123] In this rather simple manner, the wrongfulness of the conditional proposal emerges clearly from the claim that one acts wrongfully by doing what he recognizes there is moral reason not to do unless actually and reasonably believing the conduct is permissible all things considered, conjoined to the commonsensical further propositions that it is wrongful either to conditionally threaten or to conditionally offer what it would be wrongful to do.

If this is correct (and I will consider some objections shortly), then we are poised to address the next question: what, if anything, warrants the standard intuition that *adultery-threat* is especially likely to be wrongful one way and not the other—a wrongful threat, not a wrongful offer? Here is where the evidentiary thesis comes in.

We have already concluded that B is very likely to be engaged in some wrong when extending his conditional proposal—either the wrong of making a coercive threat or the wrong of making a wrongful offer. So if he is not making a morally coercive threat it is not because he is acting wholly permissibly but because he is engaged in a different wrong—the wrong of offering to engage in wrongdoing for a price. And he would be engaged in that wrong only if has come to believe that he ought, all things considered, to tell W of H's infidelity. How would he have reached such a judgment?

Only, I think, by carefully identifying and weighing the sorts of possibly incommensurable factors that Gorr and Feinberg discuss—things like the probable consequences of disclosure for W, for H, and for interested third parties (like their children) and the prior distribution of moral rights and duties as between H and W. Because this is not a simple assessment to make—what one ought to do in cases of this sort can rarely be read straight off the facts that are comfortably at hand—one will reach a responsible judgment only if motivated to look hard and think hard. And except for those rare souls who treat engaging in such careful moral evaluation as a consumption good, the motivation will be supplied (almost without exception) by a commitment or strong disposition to act in accordance with the judgment reached. Yet the very fact of B's conditional proposal, qua conditional offer, substantially undermines the claim that he possesses any such disposition.[124] Simply put: if B is willing to do what he believes he ought not to do it is hard to fathom what reason he would have had for doing the hard work necessary to reach the judgment that he ought to disclose.

To be sure, you might suppose that the same could be said against the supposition that he believes he ought not to disclose: what reason would B have had to undertake the assessment necessary to reach *that* judgment? But for a variety of reasons the cases are not fully symmetrical. I'll offer three, though I doubt they are exhaustive. First, the weight of the moral reasons not to disclose are generally more salient, especially if (as will more often be the case) greater privity obtains between B and H than between B and W. Moreover, even if there is no genuine moral force behind the act/omission distinction—and there may be—it seems true as a matter of empirical psychology that people overwhelmingly employ the distinction as a default principle of moral decision-making. Finally, we needn't entirely speculate as to what B believes disclosure would do to H. The very fact of the threat indicates that B believed that disclosure would be harmful to H. And the magnitude of the demand indicates B's belief that the harm to H would be substantial, for B could not otherwise have thought it reasonably likely that H would accede to it.

In short, B wrongs H if he conditionally threatens to reveal secrets about H that he believes he ought not disclose (or, to be more precise, that he does not affirmatively believe he ought to or may disclose); and the fact of B's offer of silence is evidence that he does not affirmatively believe that he at least may disclose the secret, because arriving at that belief would require a sincere and careful moral analysis and evaluation that one is ordinarily motivated to undertake only if committed or strongly disposed to act in accordance with what such analysis and evaluation deliver, as one who makes the conditional proposal has shown himself not to be.

The puzzle of moral blackmail, recall, asks how it can be morally wrongful to threaten what it would not be morally wrongful to do. The evidentiary theory does not, exactly, provide an answer. Instead, it solves the puzzle by identifying and curing an equivocation in the formulation of the question. In putative cases of moral blackmail, the act-type threatened is morally permissible, not in the sense that all tokens of the type are permissible but in the different sense that many are, or that the act-type can be performed permissibly, or something of this sort. But some individual act-tokens of the act-type are morally wrongful: they are wrongful if they belong to a wrongful act-subtype described by reference to certain subjectivist features like the actor's beliefs or motives. Of course, by virtue of the threat principle (which itself, we have noted, partly derives from the concept of coercion), the conditional threat to engage in a morally wrongful token of the morally permissible act-type is itself morally wrongful. But by the evidentiary thesis, the very fact of the conditional threat is evidence in support of the proposition that the act-token threatened—that is, an act proposed to be undertaken by *this* person on *this* occasion—would be wrongful.

2. *The moral puzzle—objections.*

That's the skeletal account of my solution to the puzzle of moral blackmail. Let us briefly consider two objections.

One might first resist my contention that B will believe either that he ought to disclose or that he ought to remain silent. Perhaps, the thinking goes, B has no view as to whether the balance of morally relevant considerations favors disclosure or silence. Now, the absence of such a view could arise in either of two principal ways: either B has given the matter serious and sustained thought but his deliberation has left him in perfect equipoise regarding what he morally ought to do, or B has simply not reflected on the question with the requisite care. I have already said, when assessing Gorr's account, that I consider the first possibility sufficiently unlikely as to be safely put aside. The second possibility cannot be dismissed in the same way. But a blackmailer who finds himself in this position has already defaulted on his moral obligations. While it would be lunacy to suppose that we are under an obligation to deliberate about *all* our actions, we do have such an obligation whenever we become aware of a prima facie or pro tanto moral reason not to do whatever we happen to be contemplating. And surely B must be aware of such reasons when he contemplates revealing deeply embarrassing information about another. Therefore, the fact, if true, that B hasn't reached a judgment regarding what he ought to do is insufficient to defeat the conclusion that he has issued a morally coercive threat by threatening to wrong H by knowingly causing him harm without reasonably believing that producing that harm is consistent with the balance of undefeated moral reasons under the circumstances.

A second possible objection is, in a sense, a diametric opposite to the first. Whereas the first maintained that B might have no view regarding what he ought to do, the second holds that B might genuinely believe that he has adequate moral reason to do *either* of the things he proposes—to keep silent if H pays up, or to tell W if he doesn't.

I have been assuming that the principal morally appropriate reasons to disclose H's infidelity to W are to promote supposed interests of W and perhaps also to satisfy one's supposed obligations regarding truth-telling. The principal reasons to keep mum are to promote interests of H, and possibly of W as well. But that might not be how B looks at it. B might emphasize a wholly different reason to disclose— to wit, that H deserves to suffer for his transgressions. If B believes that giving H his just deserts constitutes the weightiest reason to disclose (perhaps he believes, too, that W would be more harmed than helped by disclosure), then he might also believe that that interest would be served comparably well either by disclosing H's adultery to W or by keeping silent but compelling H to, let's say, "pay through the nose." On this reasoning, B's biconditional proposal is not, on subjectivist principles, either a wrongful threat or a wrongful offer. To the contrary, it is a way to *ensure* that B will do as the balance of reasons dictates: cause H to suffer as he deserves.

I am prepared to grant that something like this could occur and that, if all relevant details fill out in the right way, B's issuance of the biconditional proposal we have called *adultery-threat* could be morally permissible. I'd merely caution that the likelihood is small and that B's heartfelt protest "but H deserved it!" is far from good enough to make out the case. Two obstacles loom especially large. First, even if (as many people deny) H's suffering or his being punished (in a strict or loose sense) would be a good, not a bad, any suffering or punishment beyond what he deserves is unquestionably a bad. And we have no reason for confidence, and much reason to doubt, that B will structure the proposal with concern not to inflict evil on H in excess of his ill-desert, for B has a pecuniary interest in maximizing H's payment. Second, as antiretributivists have long argued, whether a wrongdoer deserves to suffer (or to be punished) and whether some other agent may purposely bring about that desert object are separate questions: an affirmative answer to the first does not entail an affirmative answer to the second.[125] So B not only must believe that H deserves to suffer whatever humiliation or disgrace the revelation of his infidelity will likely cause him but also must have an adequate account of why he, B, is an appropriate agent of H's distress.

To sum up: it is wrongful to threaten to engage in a wrongful act-token of a presumptively permissible act-type, and it is permissible to threaten to engage in a permissible act-token of a presumptively permissible act-type. But in contexts in which the evidentiary inference is sufficiently strong—*adultery-threat* is one—the very fact of the conditional threat helps support an inference that the act-token being threatened would be wrongful, not permissible. Morally speaking, then, blackmail is a conditional threat by B to harm A (or another party with whom A has a special relationship) under circumstances that (1) are sufficiently morally complex or fraught with factual uncertainty to preclude a confident external assessment regarding what B morally ought to do, and (2) would permit the reasonable inference that in carrying out his threat B would be acting wrongfully in virtue of his not actually believing that there existed adequate moral justification for his action.

3. *The legal puzzle.*

I have just explained why, on the evidentiary theory, *adultery-threat* is likely to be morally wrongful (not *necessarily* wrongful) even if *adultery-disclosure* is likely to be permissible. The question remains whether one or the other ought to be criminalized. A recommendation to criminalize the former but not the latter requires a solution to the puzzle of legal blackmail.

To reiterate a point made earlier, there is nothing puzzling on this account about criminalizing *adultery-threat.* If the conditional threat is an effort to take property by morally wrongful means, then it's just one among the many species of theft, and the case for criminalization seems, at first blush, no more problematic than for, for example, theft by fraud or deception. True, plausible political theories might conclude that this is an unjustifiably expansive use of the criminal sanction. But resolution of this dispute requires normative argument, not puzzle-solving. If there's any puzzle here it concerns only the differential treatment between *adultery-threat* and *adultery-disclosure.*

In fact, though, *adultery-threat* and *adultery-disclosure* differ in several respects that plausibly matter to the criminal law, most of which have already been mentioned. First, as just explained, act-tokens of the act-type represented by *adultery-threat* are much likelier than act-tokens of the act-type represented by *adultery-disclosure* to be morally wrongful. Second, morally wrongful tokens of the two act-types implicate different interests. The wrongful disclosure threatens reputational, emotional, and psychological harms. The wrongful threat implicates property interests (or, when what is demanded is sexual compliance, threatens interests in sexual autonomy). At least some theories of the state or of criminal punishment would think these differences meaningful. Third, disclosure is more likely than the threat to advance plausible social interests in the dissemination of information. Fourth and relatedly, overdeterrence worries are likely to weigh more heavily against criminalizing the disclosure, for any lawful conduct chilled by its proximity to the criminalized conduct is likely to be more valuable. Fifth, because the threat lends itself to repetition, it likely causes greater fear and anxiety and is more likely to create the relationships of dominance and submission that Fletcher helpfully emphasized. Sixth, even when the threat is not repeated, and even when repetition is not feared, the demand is often (probably usually) steep enough to constitute the moral wrong of exploitation, broadly understood as taking unfair or excessive advantage of the victim's vulnerability. For all these reasons, and perhaps for others as well, it would be eminently defensible to criminalize *adultery-threat* while leaving *adultery-disclosure* unregulated. Indeed, a wag might suggest that the greater puzzle is why serious thinkers would continue to think otherwise.

But to say that differential treatment of the pair is defensible is not to conclude that it is optimal. Perhaps the law should criminalize "wrongful disclosure" and then criminalize the conditional threat to wrongfully disclose. Such a solution would dissolve even a hint of the legal puzzle. It would, however, both confront the significant drafting challenge of defining "wrongful disclosure" in a satisfactory way and create significant prosecutorial challenges of establishing wrongfulness (however defined) in each case. Happily, the subjectivist and evidentiary theses together suggest that disclosure-after-threat is a rough proxy for wrongful disclosure. Though undeniably over- and underinclusive, it is more easily administered and better advances the core values underlying the principle of legality. It might also better meet First Amendment concerns.[126] So perhaps the state should criminalize disclosure-after-threat as a proxy for wrongful disclosure, and then also criminalize the threat to engage in disclosure-after-threat. Doing so would neatly moot the puzzle of legal blackmail because the act threatened would no longer be lawful.

Now, you might object that this is an empty formalism, a trick of some sort. But that verdict would be too harsh. This solution is not wholly equivalent to merely criminalizing the conditional threat. Rather, it is functionally equivalent to increasing the punishment for a blackmailer who carries out his threat after making it. And that, law and economics scholars have reasoned, helps augment the deterrent effect of the blackmail ban.[127] By prodding us to rethink our ways to characterize "the act threatened," the evidentiary theory allows us to solve the puzzle of legal blackmail elegantly while also possibly achieving a marginal gain in crime reduction.

IV Beyond the Central Case

Section III has presented the basics of the evidentiary theory by focusing on the modal case of a threat to reveal a target's adultery unless paid to remain silent. But blackmail is a broad class with a diverse membership. The act a (putative) blackmailer threatens need not be to disclose information, and his demand need not be for money (or equivalent). Furthermore, even the subclass of conditional threats to disclose information unless paid hush money is comprised of further subclasses that introduce additional complexities. Should it matter, for example, if the information B threatens to reveal is not merely embarrassing but relates to A's commission of a crime? Or what if B "demands" of A no more than B could get from other market actors for the same information? Some of the evidentiary theory's nuances will emerge, and its conformity with case-specific intuitions will be bolstered (or undermined), by applying the account to a range of such cases. In the discussion that follows I concentrate on whether particular proposals are moral blackmail, as defined above (see Subsection III.B.2), and only secondarily on whether proposals of that subtype ought to be criminalized. The latter question implicates practical problems of legal drafting and institutional enforcement that cannot be resolved by essentially philosophical inquiry and analysis.

A "Hard" Bargains

Explicitly or implicitly, every potential commercial transaction conforms to the same biconditional form as does blackmail. The proposition implicitly conveyed by your local retailer, for example, is this: If you pay me the listed purchase price for any good in my store, I will give it to you; if you do not, I won't. Aside from a formal similarity of structure, that proposition does not look much like blackmail. Matters are thought to get a little murkier, however, in the case of the so-called hard bargain, like that presented by Murphy's hypothetical owner of the baseball autographed by Babe Ruth.[128]

These are easy cases under the evidentiary theory, for the act threatened—to withhold the good or service on offer—is not plausibly wrongful, and the content of the conditional proposal does not support an inference that the seller believes otherwise. To be sure, the price demanded is so steep as possibly to instantiate the wrong of exploitation. And it is this that makes the hard bargain look like blackmail, for many or most blackmail proposals are plausibly adjudged exploitative as well as coercive.[129] But exploitation is usually a less serious moral wrong than coercion and almost certainly a less secure basis for criminalization. The evidentiary theory explains why blackmail is the moral wrong of coercion, and justifies its criminalization on this ground. It does not indict hard bargains.

B Crime-Exposure Blackmail

A special case within informational blackmail arises when the secret that B threatens to reveal would not merely embarrass A, but would subject him to criminal penalty. This variation, which we may inelegantly term "crime-exposure blackmail," has provoked particular attention from law and economics scholars, who query whether permitting blackmail of this type would benefit society as a form of private law enforcement. Their answers vary.[130]

Whatever the uncertainty a utilitarian (or wealth-maximization) analysis might engender, that crime-exposure blackmail should be a crime is, I venture, obvious to most people. Indeed, under the reductivist approach advanced by Feinberg and Gorr, the matter is simple: Because it is wrongful to withhold information about a crime, it is equally wrongful to offer to withhold it for payment.[131] Both the offer and the unconditional performance of the act offered may be criminalized. In fact, however, the criminal law treats the conditional offer substantially more severely. Under the common law, the mere failure to report information about a crime (including the identity of the perpetrator) was misprision of felony, a misdemeanor. Modern statutes have tended to ignore it entirely.[132] In contrast, the conditional threat to do so is blackmail.[133] The evidentiary theory explains this difference exceedingly well, especially when we invoke both versions of the subjectivist thesis—motive-centered as well as belief-centered.

The critical step is to explore why a failure to expose a criminal is legally tolerated and, I believe, at least often not subjected to substantial moral criticism. Plainly, silence can significantly injure the public. It hampers society's efforts to punish and deter the commission of crime, and it permits criminals to reoffend. Our relatively lenient attitudes (in law and morals) toward the nondisclosure stems from our awareness that silence does not always bespeak a disregard for the common good and the welfare of actual and potential victims. It is often explained, at least in large part, by felt duties of friendship and loyalty toward the perpetrator, fear of criminal retaliation, and fear or distrust of the police. To some extent (and on some moral theories), these considerations can reduce or eliminate the wrongfulness of remaining silent. And even to the extent they don't affect wrongfulness, they surely reflect sympathetic motivations that mitigate the actor's blameworthiness.[134]

Consider now the conditional proposal. Had B threatened to expose A unless paid off, we strongly infer that she did not believe that she had an overriding duty of silence and that her motives for violating her civic duty had nothing to do with either loyalty to, or fear of, the culprit. The fact of her blackmail proposal provides circumstantial evidence as to her mental state: we now believe that she was *in fact* activated by more culpable motives than, absent this evidence, we had hypothesized *might have* motivated her. The conditional proposal is not coercive, because its wrongfulness stems from the wrongfulness of the act offered (silence) not from that of the act threatened (disclosure). But because we can infer that this act-token of silence is likely to be (considerably) more wrongful and more blameworthy than we often assume to be true for tokens of this act-type, crime-exposure blackmail should be both a crime and a more serious offense than mere misprision of felony.

Should the preceding analysis change if the individual who threatens to expose A's crime had been A's victim? Suppose B threatens to file a criminal complaint against A unless A provides B reasonable compensation for the harms B actually suffered? The Model Penal Code would grant an affirmative defense to prosecution for threatening to "accuse anyone of a criminal offense…that the property obtained by threat of accusation…was honestly claimed as restitution or indemnification for harm done in the circumstances to which such accusation…relates."[135] This defense was added "in order to assure that one who had a civil complaint for damages against another could not be convicted of extortion for threatening during negotiations to file a criminal charge"— conduct "many regard as legitimate negotiating tactics."[136] Then again, many don't: The 1969 Model Code of Professional Responsibility, for example, provides that "[a] lawyer shall not present, participate in presenting, or threaten to present criminal charges solely to obtain an advantage in a civil matter."[137]

The short answer is that the fact that B is a victim of A and has a valid tort claim against him does not change the analysis. The threat to file a criminal complaint suggests, on the reasoning above, that B's silence would be wrongful, as a violation of civic duty. But this answer is a trifle too short. The longer answer is that, though B's identity as A's victim doesn't *change* the analysis, it does *add* to it in ways that might matter.

This longer answer depends on a distinction mentioned in passing at the outset but not yet developed—that between all things considered and pro tanto wrongfulness.[138] If B's unconditional silence would be wrongful, then the offer of silence is wrongful pro tanto. So the question is whether use of this wrongful tool can be justified by the good its use aims to achieve. Characterizing the good to be achieved as personal advantage to B suggests a negative answer: gain to B is a good, but it lacks the particularly moral value necessary to justify what our analysis suggests is pro tanto wrongdoing. Additionally or alternatively, however, we might characterize the good that B seeks as the realizing of corrective justice, or something similar. This might have the moral character sufficient to justify the commission of the pro tanto moral wrong of offering the moral wrong of silence. *If* it does, then carrying out the offer, on satisfaction of the condition, would also be permissible because backed by the moral weight of promise-keeping. But *whether* it does will likely depend on such factors as the weight of the public's interest in criminal prosecution of this offender for this type of offense, the relative strength of our commitment to retributive and corrective justice, and the relative probabilities that each form of justice will be realized if B contacts the public authorities.

In sum, the moral permissibility of crime-exposure blackmail by the crime victim presents a hard question. The evidentiary theory can help clarify the structure of the analysis. Given reasonable disagreement about the particular moral judgments that enter into the analysis, however, any bottom-line conclusions will inevitably be contestable.[139]

C Market-Price Blackmail

Imagine B has an embarrassing photograph of celebrity A, for which a supermarket tabloid will pay $1,000. Assume no background factors would render B's agreement to sell the photo an uncontroversial moral wrong (e.g., B obtained the photo without committing an immoral act, and has no prior obligation of confidentiality to A). B now approaches A with this proposition: if you pay me $1,000 I'll give you this photograph and its negative; if you do not, I'll sell them on the open market. Theorists have divided over whether this proposal—"market-price blackmail"— should be lawful.[140]

Focus first on whether the proposal is morally permissible. This is an easy call if you think that sale to the tabloid, although lawful, is morally impermissible. In that case, the conditional threat to sell to the tabloid constitutes the moral wrong of coercion. But suppose you believe unconditional sale to the tabloid permissible. Distinguish two routes to this conclusion: (1) although there are good moral reasons not to disclose (disclosure harms A in a morally relevant sense), there are moral reason to disclose of equal or greater strength, or (2) even absent moral reason to disclose, there is no significant moral cost to doing so because, for example, by seeking and achieving celebrity, public figures have assumed the risk of, and possibly even consented to, widespread invasions of their privacy.

Route (1) strikes me as fairly implausible in the mine run of cases, although it can certainly be true in some situations, as when the celebrity is either a public official or a nonofficial who has interjected himself into public or cultural debates and the photographs reveal that his actions are inconsistent with his public position. In cases such as these, the prior conditional offer of silence has at least some evidentiary value. It is probably mildly probative in support of the hypothesis that B does not believe that there is adequate moral reason to disclose (therefore that he acts wrongfully in disclosure) and significantly probative in support of the hypothesis that he would not be motivated by such reasons (therefore that he is morally blameworthy in making the disclosure). If you take route (2)—the unconditional disclosure would be permissible because there is no significant moral reason against it—then the prior conditional offer of silence has no probative value with respect to any morally material question. The act-token threatened is morally permissible, and so is the conditional proposal.

This analysis prevents us from reaching any simple conclusions regarding the moral permissibility of the conditional proposal: it all depends on your view of the permissibility of the unconditional disclosure and, if you believe it permissible, your reasons for that judgment. But even if you conclude, on the basis of the evidentiary analysis, that the conditional proposal would likely be wrongful, whether it should be criminalized is a separate question. And the argument against is clear and weighty, so long as we assume that the unconditional sale to the tabloid remains lawful. Market-price blackmail simply gives a right of first refusal to persons who are harmed and (by hypothesis) wronged by unconditional disclosure. It almost certainly makes them better off and thereby mitigates the moral harms associated with a regime of lawful sale and publication.

Legalization of market-price blackmail does not, however, entail legalization of "supra-market-price blackmail"—the offer to sell exclusive disclosure to A (that is, nondisclosure to others) for a sum substantially in excess of what B could receive for selling the same information on the market. At some price, a supra-market-price blackmail offer can become exploitative. But even short of that level, the state can regulate the price B may charge A for nonpublication—capping it at the market price—for much the same reason the state regulates prices elsewhere. Price regulation, after all, is a common way of limiting the price a monopolist can charge to that which (presumably) would obtain were the market for the monopolist's goods or services competitive. And the blackmailer (market-price, supra-market-price, or otherwise) must be a monopolist (or, at least, an oligopolist) of the information he threatens to reveal, else his offer of secrecy would have little value. However, B's possession of information about A does not make him equally a monopolist with respect to the rest of the world as it does with respect to A himself. To be sure, if B is the only person with photographs of A in a compromising position, he is, by definition, a monopolist supplier. But his monopoly is economically meaningful only to the extent that there are no adequate substitutes for those photos. As far as buyers of information about public figures are concerned, reasonably close substitutes for B's photos of celebrity A do exist—namely, embarrassing or scandalous information (photographs, interviews, etc.) about celebrities C, D, and E. These are not substitutes as far as A is concerned, though. Consequently, consistent with well-established justifications for economic regulation of monopolies, the state could reasonably decide to protect A from monopolistic exploitation by prohibiting B from charging A more than the hypothetical competitive price for the information in question, a price adequately approximated by the existing market price. This is a rationale for prohibiting supra-market-price blackmail that does not depend on a conclusion that it is morally coercive.

D Public-Interest Blackmail

The garden-variety blackmailer demands from his victim a cash payment to which he has no legitimate claim. But the blackmailer need not demand money. Nor need he even seek private advantage (narrowly defined). A recurring question, accordingly, is whether blackmail should be criminalized when the blackmailer's ostensible objective is a public, rather than private, good. We have already touched on this issue when considering the claim that the advantage demanded in a case of victim-initiated crime-exposure blackmail be conceived as the good that corrective justice be done. We now address the question in greater depth by examining three variations on a theme. In each case, assume that the putative blackmailer genuinely and correctly believes that the blackmailee's compliance with the condition would powerfully advance the public interest.

Revise *gay-threat* as follows: A is extremely wealthy, but miserly. B demands, for his silence, that A donate $1 million for Alzheimer's research. We have already assumed arguendo that B acts wrongfully in the original *gay-threat*. I suspect that most people would conclude that B acts wrongfully in this variation (*gay-threat/Alzheimer's*) too, although the question is perhaps debatable—much as people might disagree about the permissibility of the actions of Robin Hood. The important point is that nothing about this case invites doubt that B would be acting wrongfully were he actually to do as he threatens. Accordingly, the making of the conditional threat is morally wrongful, at least pro tanto, and the only question is whether the moral good that B aims to achieve by means of the threat is so great as to supply adequate moral justification, that is, to render this pro tanto wrong not wrongful all things considered. Surely, coercive threats can sometimes be justified. (Consider: A is a brilliant but misanthropic scientist who has already devised a cure for Alzheimer's, which he refuses to divulge for any payment, and B's demand is merely that A divulge it.)

In the second variation (*gay-threat/legislator*), A is a closeted gay congressman who supports antigay legislation, L; B threatens to out A unless A changes his position on L. (L can be whatever you choose subject to the lone constraint that it morally ought not to be enacted). Like *gay-threat/Alzheimer's,* the threat is plausibly made to promote the greater good. Both conceivably qualify as blackmail for the public interest. But in *gay-threat/legislator,* there are plausibly morally sound reasons to make the disclosure—namely, to expose A as a probable hypocrite and political opportunist—to be weighed against the usual moral reasons not to out somebody. Outing legislator A thus looks more like disclosing H's infidelity: a morally fraught decision that calls for careful and serious—and inescapably contestable—moral judgment. Finally, the content of the conditional offer lends support for the inference that, if B were to out A, B would actually have the beliefs and motives necessary to render the disclosure morally permissible and not blameworthy. The offer, if accepted, tends to undermine the moral reasons in favor of disclosure: if A supports L, then he is no longer (or less) hypocritical, and the moral reason to out him disappears (or diminishes in force).[141] So even if we accept that B acts permissibly and for good reasons in both *gay-threat/Alzheimer's,* and *gay-threat/legislator,* there is this difference, born of the facts that the conditional proposal has evidentiary value in the *Alzheimer's* but not the *legislator* case: in *Alzheimer's,* B might be engaging in morally justified coercion, whereas in *legislator,* he might be threatening to engage in a morally justified disclosure, in which case he does not even commit the pro tanto moral wrong of coercion.

In the third and last variation (*adultery-threat/Alzheimer's*), B threatens to reveal H's adultery unless H contributes $1 million to Alzheimer's research. Like ordinary *adultery-threat* and unlike *gay-threat,* the act B threatens is not clearly morally wrongful. Like both *gay-threat/Alzheimer's,* and *gay-threat/legislator,* and unlike *adultery-threat* and *gay-threat, adultery-threat/Alzheimer's* is advanced to serve the public interest. Finally, like *gay-threat/Alzheimer's,* and unlike *gay-threat/legislator,* the conditional proposal itself lacks probative value regarding whether the particular disclosure threatened would be wrongful or permissible. Perhaps B (reasonably) believes disclosure to be wrongful, but also (reasonably) believes that using the wrongful threat for a greater good is justified all things considered, or perhaps he (reasonably) believes disclosure to be permissible, but decides to leverage the threat of a permissible action for an even greater good. I am simply unsure how strong an inference is warranted in a case like this.

The upshot of this quick survey is that there are at least two distinct ways in which a putative blackmail proposal might be morally justified as in the public interest—either carrying out the threat would be permissible, or, although it wouldn't be, making the threat is—and that the first of these two ways may or may not gain advantage from the evidentiary inference. We can hardly expect widespread agreement regarding the moral permissibility of individual cases. Agreement on the optimal criminal statute is likely to be even more elusive.

E Noninformational Blackmail

Most people agree that the concept of blackmail is capacious enough to include some threats to do things other than disclose information. However, not only do they disagree over whether specific threat-tokens qualify, they also lack shared articulated criteria that would, in principle, resolve the disputes. The evidentiary theory explains very well what noninformational blackmail consists of, though the answer is not such as to promise much help in securing agreement about individual cases.

Here's a common example. A and B are neighboring landholders. B informs A that she intends to erect some structure on her land (e.g., a tall fence, an outdoor sculpture, a wind turbine) that has these two properties: it would adversely affect A's enjoyment of his property (e.g., by blocking access to light, or just by being ugly), and it is within B's property rights (i.e., it would not constitute an actionable nuisance). B then offers not to build the structure if A pays her $X. A objects that this is blackmail, a charge that B denies. Both A and B understand themselves to be arguing about morals; A does not mean, and B does not take him to mean, that the proposal is a crime.

On the subjectivist thesis, whether B's construction of the structure would be permissible or wrongful depends on the reasons B would be acting on in building it. The anticipated harm (or, if you prefer, cost or disutility) to A supplies moral reason not to build. This is true notwithstanding that B would be within her rights to build: it is often wrong to exercise one's rights. So the moral permissibility of building depends on there being actual reasons in its favor. Suppose that the structure would be a good in some fashion for B. (To a first approximation, the structure is a good for B if, for example, it serves her interests or advances her welfare, including by satisfying her preferences, though not morally discreditable preferences like that others be made worse off.) The good to B and the bad to A both count in the moral calculus. In circumstances such as these, B is entitled to value the good to her more highly than the bad to A, for that is part of what it means for B to have a right to build on her land. To a very large extent, then, B's valuing of the structure is precisely what confers on it its moral value. If B really doesn't want it—if she values the structure only for its use as threat not for its use in actuality—then no moral reason weighs in favor of its construction and the existence of moral reason against it, in the form of the cost the structure imposes on A, renders its construction morally wrongful. (Notice that, in cases such as these, the motive-centered and belief-centered versions of the subjectivist thesis cannot be easily prised apart: B can believe that there is moral value in the structure, and thus that its construction is morally permissible all things considered, only if she would want it to be constructed.) Call the structure a "spite structure" if its construction would not be supported by permissible reasons.

Per our understanding of coercion (as reflected in the threat principle), the conditional proposal by B is wrongful if what she threatens to build would be a spite structure—a concept that is defined by reference to subjectivist features. But whether it would be is something we ordinarily just don't know.[142] Indeed, I venture that that question is precisely what is in dispute when A and B are arguing over whether the proposal is blackmail.

Whether the bare fact of the conditional offer to forbear construction if paid has substantial evidential bearing on that all-important question is uncertain. For example, if B proposes to erect a wind turbine and the price she "demands" for forbearance reflects the net discounted value of the energy savings it would earn her, there is precious little grounds to infer that, were A to reject the deal and B to build, B would lack the reasons (and therefore the beliefs) necessary to render construction permissible. In other cases, the evidentiary inference is stronger. If B offers not to install an outdoor sculpture if paid, A might well suspect that B doesn't really want the sculpture. Whether the inference is warranted, however, is hard to assess in the abstract. Perhaps B really would enjoy the sculpture, but thinks she'd be equally satisfied with a week-long pilgrimage to Bilbao, a trip that would cost $X more than the sculpture.[143]

F Bribery

A final puzzle is what Sidney DeLong calls the second paradox of blackmail:[144] why is a conditional offer that would be illegal if proposed by the blackmailer legal if initiated by the victim? DeLong locates the moral difference between blackmail and "bribery" (i.e., a proposal initiated by a potential blackail victim) in the social meaning of the narratives paradigmatic of the respective transactions. "[T]he purpose of the law of blackmail," DeLong proposes in a vein similar to Fletcher's, "is to protect the community against the conspiratorial agreement of blackmailer and victim, which isolates and subjects him to a submissive relationship with the blackmailer."[145] In contrast, "[t]hrough bribery, the victim transforms the menace into an ally whose cooperation preserves the victim's place in the larger community."[146]

No doubt this explanation touches on one common distinction between the consequences of blackmail and bribery. But it does not cut as forcefully as DeLong suggests, for the briber risks highlighting his vulnerability to disclosure, thereby increasing the risk that the recipient of his bribe will return for more—next time, as a blackmailer. If, as Fletcher has emphasized, "[d]ominance and subordination are states of anticipation,"[147] it is unclear how much security and peace of mind a potential blackmail victim purchases with his bribe. In any event, the evidentiary analysis reaches the same bottom-line conclusion as DeLong does, namely that the law may sensibly treat the same deal differently depending on which party proposes it.

Of course, when the act the briber solicits is itself wrongful, there is nothing perplexing about making the bribe illegal and punishing both the giver and the receiver—hence the common law crimes of "bribery" (offering a government official payment for favorable treatment) and "extortion under color of public office" (solicitation or acceptance of payment by the official).[148] As noted in Section I, a biconditional proposal can be wrongful in virtue of the wrongfulness of what is demanded or solicited. At the other extreme, it seems reasonably clear that an offer of payment for desisting from an act is morally permissible and ought to be legal when performance of the act in question would be wrongful. Suppose that A, in *gay-threat* and *gay-disclosure*, learns that B has learned that he, A, is gay. If it would be wrongful (as we have supposed) for B to reveal this fact, surely it is permissible for A to ask B to keep mum. If, in addition to requesting, pleading, and cajoling, A offers to pay B to keep quiet, A does risk insulting B. But, at first blush, it does not seem that the offer of payment constitutes any greater wrong than that.

Now, we could imagine that the offer has this sort of evidentiary significance: it implies that A knows some unusual facts (say, that A has proposed marriage to a woman who thinks A is straight) that would make B's outing of A under the circumstances not wrongful, and not merely permissible, but possibly even morally required or preferable. Conceivably. But that strikes me as a rather weak inference. It's just as likely, I should think, that A makes the offer because he has some reason to fear that B would, without the monetary incentive, do the wrong thing. Finally, if the act that the briber offers to buy desistance from is morally uncertain—as when H offers B $1,000 for B's promise not to tell W about H's extramarital affair—then it seems plausible to believe that H compounds the underlying wrong of infidelity, by seeking to make B something like an accessory after the fact. Most likely this is a fairly marginal exacerbation of his initial wrong. Even if not, it is not the sort of wrong that essentially liberal political theories are apt to consider properly criminalized.

A separate question is whether *acceptance* of the bribe should be criminalized. If the nominal bribe really is just a payoff by a blackmailee to a blackmailer savvy enough to convey his threat by innuendo, the law need not respect the formal structure of the transaction; so long as a fact finder concludes that the nominal bribe taker intended to communicate a blackmail threat, he can be deemed a blackmailer and punished accordingly. If the idea of the bribe really did originate with the maker, then the offeree is being offered payment to refrain from what he might well have done in any event. My instinct is that acceptance is hardly virtuous, but nor is it wrongful. Again, it's hard to see what might justify its criminalization, except as a prophylactic rule to ensure that a genuine blackmailer does not escape conviction by insinuating his demands with some subtlety.

V IMPLICATIONS

Blackmail is a serious crime. Moreover, it exerts a grasp on the popular imagination almost surely out of proportion to the actual incidence of its occurrence. Still, one might think the amount of scholarly attention devoted to solving its puzzles disproportionate. (Notice, for example, that blackmail is the lone criminal offense discussed in this handbook, otherwise devoted to concerns of the general part of criminal law.) As Donald Dripps has quipped, there may be more articles on blackmail than prosecutions of it.[149]

Theorists' obsession with the blackmail puzzle is partly explained, I suggest, by a widespread intuition that a solution will require the development of sufficiently new tools or principles, or the deployment of principles and considerations in sufficiently novel ways, as to shed welcome light on other conundrums in law and morality. Thus have Katz and Lindgren opined that "one cannot think about coercion, contracts, consent, robbery, rape, unconstitutional conditions, nuclear deterrence, assumption of risk, the greater-includes-the-lesser arguments, plea bargains, settlements, sexual harassment, insider trading, bribery, domination, secrecy, privacy, law enforcement, utilitarianism and deontology without being tripped up repeatedly by the paradox of blackmail."[150] While their hopes might be a tad extravagant, I, too, believe that blackmail sits at a theoretical crossroads of sorts, making it reasonable to expect that a solution to its puzzles will bear implications beyond its borders. Although it is well beyond the scope of this chapter to detail all the lessons the evidentiary theory might teach outside the blackmail context, this final section offers a very few telegraphic suggestions designed to nourish optimism that broader lessons can be drawn from the evidentiary theory. Indeed, to illustrate the breadth of its possible implications, I start, provocatively, at a very distant remove.

A Subjectivism and Abortion

Some people, coming from two diametrically opposed perspectives, believe that abortion raises a relatively easy moral question. The first perspective maintains that fetuses have the same moral status or worth as do postnatal human beings, and therefore that any interests the pregnant woman might have in terminating the pregnancy, short of her interest in preserving her own life, cannot possibly outweigh the fetus's interest in not being killed. Abortion, on this view, is necessarily and unequivocally wrong (except when necessary to save the life of the mother). The second perspective holds that fetuses (at least during the early stages of pregnancy) lack significant moral status and therefore that the moral reasons not to terminate a pregnancy are trivial or nonexistent. On this view, abortion is unequivocally morally permissible.

A majority of people (at least in the contemporary United States) reject both views. They believe that weighty moral interests lie on both sides of the decision to terminate a pregnancy. The fetus is a living entity that can experience pain and has the potential to become a full human being, but is not yet entitled to moral status remotely approaching that of a neonate. Pregnancy and childbirth, on the other hand, can be painful and dangerous for the mother and can massively disrupt her life plans. On this view, abortion is morally uncertain in roughly the same way as disclosing someone's marital infidelity (though with vastly greater moral stakes on both sides): it is a morally difficult decision that resists a simple verdict regarding what morally ought to be done. The subjectivist thesis dovetails with this common view about the morality of abortion in a given case: a pregnant woman's decision to terminate her pregnancy is morally permissible if and only if she reasonably believes that her particular reasons for terminating the pregnancy outweigh the reasons against.[151] It is precisely her serious reflection and evaluation that confers permissibility on her action.

This account also explains the permissibility of prohibitions on abortion.[152] As just suggested, a woman's decision to terminate a pregnancy can come about in either of two ways, or reflect either of two moral calculi. She can conclude either (1) that, although the interests of hers that would be advanced by abortion are slight, the fetus's interest in continued existence is slighter still, or (2) that, although the fetus's interests are significant, her own interests in avoiding the pain, discomfort, and life disruptions that come with pregnancy, childbirth, and (if the child is not put up for adoption) parentage have overriding moral weight. Similarly, people who support broad prohibitions on abortion can reach that judgment in at least two very different ways. They can conclude either (1) that, although a woman's interests in avoiding pregnancy and childbirth are frequently substantial, as are the equality interests of women as a class, the killing of a fetus is such a profound moral wrong as to render termination (almost) always unjustified, or (2) that, although fetal interests are not terribly strong, whatever impact an unwanted pregnancy has on the life of the mother and on the equality interests of women are even less substantial. On this admittedly simplified picture, we can say that a law prohibiting abortion could be understood by its drafters and proponents as either high-cost/higher-benefit or low-cost/medium-benefit.

If all this is right, then the constitutionality of abortion prohibitions might depend on whether any of the component judgments—regarding the strength or moral quality either of the fetuses' interests or of the pregnant women's—can be regarded as correct or mistaken as a matter of constitutional law. My own view (to be asserted but not defended here) is that judges in the American constitutional regime are competent to reach or endorse judgments on some of these issues but not on others. In particular, the judiciary may—in fact, must—reach a judgment regarding the scope and magnitude of the liberty and equality interests of pregnant women; the proper judgment for them to reach is that such interests are substantial and can be infringed only for powerful reasons. In contrast, the judiciary is not competent to conclude either that fetuses have minimal interests or that fetuses have substantial interests. This is a claim about judicial decision-making, not more broadly about, say, Rawlsian public reason. I do not deny that individuals may reach judgments about the interests or moral character of fetuses and act on such judgments in their capacities as voters or legislators.

It follows that a law prohibiting abortion is unconstitutional (we might say it's constitutionally unreasonable) if it derives from a belief on the part of its supporters that women's interests are flimsy or insubstantial, but constitutional (constitutionally reasonable, hence permissible) if it is based on the belief that fetuses' interests are morally weighty. To put the point differently, the state has a compelling interest in protecting against the destruction of beings that it reasonably believes have a moral status equivalent to, or close to, that of a neonate. So in this unusual case, the judicial question of whether the state's interest *is* compelling is parasitic on what the state *actually believes* about the nature of the thing it is endeavoring to protect (given that, under existing conditions of American pluralism, no actual belief on this subject can be dismissed as constitutionally unreasonable). It is also true that the state has reasons to misrepresent, even to itself, what its animating beliefs and judgments are. So the courts ought not to simply accept without question the state's representations as to its actual beliefs, for doing so would be to substantially underprotect the liberty interests of women at stake. Instead, courts must rely on evidence—including aspects of the provision's enactment history and features of the state's corpus juris—from which they can draw epistemically responsible inferences regarding the actual beliefs and motives that animate the challenged legislation.

The subjectivist view about what it means to act permissibly within a given normative discourse, and a proper focus on evidentiary inference, thus might shed light on matters as far removed from blackmail as the moral permissibility of individual decisions to terminate a pregnancy and the constitutionality of laws that would preclude women from making that choice.

B Evidential Facts and the Criminal Law

The evidentiary thesis recalls Hohfeld's distinction between "operative" and "evidential" facts. According to Hohfeld, "[o]perative, constitutive, causal, or 'dispositive' facts are those which, under the general legal rules that are applicable, suffice to change legal relations."[153] In contrast, "[a]n evidential fact is one which, on being ascertained, affords some logical basis—not conclusive—for inferring some other fact…either a constitutive [i.e., operative] fact or an intermediate evidential fact."[154] Plainly, the blackmailer's conditional threat is an operative fact under the positive law of blackmail. Indeed, to ask why blackmail is a crime while the act threatened is not, is really only to inquire into *why* the threat is an operative legal fact. Ordinarily, a fact is operative under the criminal law because it has prelegal constitutive or causal significance. That the deceased was a human being is an operative fact under the law of homicide, for example, because something of independent importance turns on the fact that it was a *person* (rather than, say, a chicken or a tomato plant) that was killed. The evidentiary theory of blackmail is distinguished by the recognition that the blackmail threat is not this type of operative fact.[155] Fundamentally, the conditional threat is not "operative" at all, but evidential—it "affords some logical basis— not conclusive—for inferring some other fact," namely, that if the threatener were to carry out his threat, he would lack the beliefs about the moral balance necessary to render his action morally permissible. One upshot of the evidentiary theory, then, is a general caution to guard against confusing evidential facts for operative facts.

1. *Why results matter.*

The debate over moral outcome luck is one context in which keeping this distinction in mind could be useful. Those who believe that the fortuitous realization or nonrealization of harm is irrelevant to an actor's moral blameworthiness are often thought to be committed to the proposition that the criminal law should punish complete attempts and complete target offenses the same. Of course, there are various ways to avoid this conclusion.[156] But one of the most powerful, I think, is to recognize that the occurrence or nonoccurrence of harm is often good evidence regarding the actor's culpability with respect to the prospect of harm—a consideration that those opposed to moral outcome luck recognize as the chief determinant of blameworthiness and desert.

The evidentiary value of results is particularly strong, I believe, when an actor acts recklessly with respect to the prospect of harm. Criminal law teachers often press students on the relevance of resulting harm with hypotheticals that posit that two persons act in an identically reckless manner, except that one has the ill fortune to cause a harm. In the real world, though, we don't have direct access to the riskiness of an actor's behavior. All else equal, a reckless driver courts, or is aware of, greater risk the farther he drives, the worse the road conditions, the faster his speed, the more often he darts across lanes, the larger the number of pedestrians in the vicinity, even the greater his own ability. Surely the actual realization of harm will be some evidence regarding these features, much as the outcome of a sporting contest is a strong indicator of the quality of a competitor's performance.[157] Naturally, it will be very far from perfect evidence. In the ordinary case, however, it is not obvious that the criminal justice system will have access to lots of better evidence of the magnitude of a reckless actor's culpability with respect to harm.

2. *Limited duties to act.*

A second and less familiar context in which a presumed operative fact might have overlooked evidential significance concerns the act/omission distinction. To take a standard hypothetical: A, a child, is drowning in a pool, while B (A's father), C (the lifeguard), and D (an Olympic swimmer) all relax poolside. Assuming that all three bystanders could save A but don't, only B and C are guilty of homicide if A dies; in most jurisdictions, D goes scot free because he, alone of the three, lacks a legal duty to act. The question is why this should be.

The most common answers emphasize line-drawing difficulties and also claim that persons have no moral duty to save a stranger. Both arguments strike me as overstated. It is true that a sensible statute should limit the situations in which one has an affirmative duty to those in which the threatened harm to another is grave and the cost or risk to the agent is minimal. Though this means that the resulting law would be more standard than rule, I rather suspect that the inescapable vagueness can be kept within acceptable bounds. And while B's and C's duties to A are almost surely greater than are D's, the claim that strangers have no affirmative moral obligations to others is hard to defend.

Another partial possible explanation emerges if we imagine what the prosecution of D would look like under a well-drafted law. Surely the state will be required to prove that D had some level of culpability with respect to A's peril—probably knowledge, but recklessness at a minimum. In seeking to discharge that burden, the prosecution would be likely to rely heavily on evidence that suggests an ordinary person would have been aware, and on proof that others were in fact aware. That might be good evidence. The problem is that if D was in fact not aware of the peril—perhaps he was deeply engrossed in a book, or was snoozing—he will find it exceedingly difficult to rebut a reasonable inference of awareness, thereby producing erroneous convictions notwithstanding the state's burden of proof. (Consider: if we accept that thirty-eight residents of neighboring buildings were aware of Kitty Genovese's peril, how will the thirty-ninth persuade us that *he* wasn't?)

·   If this captures a genuine concern, then we might view the status relationships that serve as predicates for an affirmative legal duty to act as partially evidentiary, not wholly operative. The fact that B was A's parent, or that C was contractually obligated to look out for A, affords (in Hohfeld's terms) "some logical basis—not conclusive—for inferring some other fact," namely, that B or C was in fact aware of the danger to A and therefore of the need to act. That is, the status relationship reinforces the formal requirement that the state prove awareness; it is a belt-and-suspenders approach to establishing knowledge or recklessness. Accordingly, scholars and law reformers who would like to expand the scope of affirmative duties in criminal law might be well advised to identify other circumstances that would plausibly serve this same evidential function.

C The Evidentiary Theory and Unconstitutional Conditions

One concrete example of the evidentiary theory's potential relevance, this time from outside the criminal law, is provided by the so-called unconstitutional conditions problem—that is, the question of when it should be unconstitutional for a government to condition a benefit it is not compelled to provide on the recipient's relinquishment or waiver of a constitutional right. Here are some diverse examples. A sentence of Y years for crime X would be constitutionally permissible; the state offers sentence Y-n if a defendant waives his constitutional rights to contest his guilt at trial. The Fourth Amendment is held generally to grant persons a right not to be subjected to search absent particularized suspicion; the state offers aid to families with dependent children on the condition that recipients waive their right against suspicionless searches of their homes. The Twenty-First Amendment (let us suppose) authorizes the states to set minimum legal drinking ages at their discretion; Congress offers additional federal highway funds to states that raise their minimum drinking age to twenty-one. Consistent with the Fifth and Fourteenth amendments, states may not effect a physical occupation of private property without just compensation; zoning boards offer landowners variances from land use restrictions if they grant a public easement over their property. The First Amendment protects citizens' right to speak on matters of public concern; the federal government offers public broadcast funds to stations that refrain from editorializing.

Despite the frequency with which the problem arises, courts have yet to provide consistent standards for evaluating when the precept that a state may not do indirectly what it is prohibited from doing directly should take priority over the competing principle that the greater power entirely to withhold the benefit entails the lesser power to grant it on condition. And scholarly commentary on the subject, despite a vast output,[158] has not clarified matters. While scholars broadly agree that the conditional tender of governmental benefits should sometimes be held legitimate and sometimes unconstitutional, there is no consensus regarding whether and why any particular proposition of this form should pass muster.

The evidentiary theory of blackmail has obvious and powerful application to this puzzle.[159] Our conception of coercion dictates that a conditional proposal by the government constitutes a constitutional wrong if what it threatens would be unconstitutional to do. Putative "offers" not to inflict criminal punishment on people if they don't advocate communism, or not to levy a special tax on the condition that an individual not worship Baal, are therefore unconstitutionally coercive (at least pro tanto). Such proposals are not thought to raise the unconstitutional conditions problem only because, as a doctrinal matter, the problem is limited to cases in which the state threatens to withhold a "benefit," and not being imprisoned and not being subject to extraordinary taxes are not generally conceived of as benefits. But what is a benefit turns out to be the conclusion to an argument, not a primitive. Functionally, then, limiting the scope of the problem to cases involving threats to deny benefits is really just a way to cabin inquiry to situations in which the unconstitutionality of the act that government threatens is not patent.

So let us focus on situations where the government threatens to perform an act that appears, on first or second glance, to be constitutionally permissible—situations that represent the constitutional analogue to moral blackmail. Here is where the subjectivist thesis applies, in a motive-centered version. It counsels that the state may not treat a rightholder less well than it otherwise would for the purpose either of punishing the rightholder for exercising her right, or of discouraging exercise of the right in the future by this rightholder or by others.[160] Call it a "penalty" when a disadvantage (relative to this counterfactual baseline) is imposed for one of these proscribed purposes. The state's purpose for carrying out the act threatened (*not* its purposes for *making* the threat)[161] is a constitutive element of that act's being a penalty. If the denial of a benefit would, in this case, be a penalty, then it would be unconstitutional. And, per our understanding of coercion, so, too, would be the conditional proposal.

But would the state in fact have the proscribed purposes were it to do as it threatens? Here is where the evidentiary thesis kicks in. It predicts that the fact and content of the conditional proposal will sometimes support an inference (not, recall, a deduction) that the state would in fact act on the bad purposes in carrying out its threat. In particular, we might think that a rebuttable presumption of bad purpose arises when the putative legitimate purposes for withholding the benefit unconditionally are not the same as the apparent purposes for issuing the conditional offer.

That's a compact and abstract summary of the evidentiary theory's extension to the unconstitutional conditions problem. Here are just three concrete illustrations of its application. In each case, I mean only to provide a first-pass analysis, not to deny that counterarguments to my provisional conclusions are possible and therefore that more detailed and nuanced investigation might be required.

The offer of welfare payments conditioned on the recipient's agreement to warrantless, suspicionless searches seems not to threaten a penalty, hence not to instantiate the constitutional wrong of coercion. The reasoning is this: the state has made the constitutionally acceptable decision to limit welfare payments to one-adult households. The condition permits welfare officials to spot-check to ensure that a recipient household does not contain a second adult. If an applicant rejects the condition, the state may conclude that it lacks adequate assurance that a constitutionally legitimate eligibility condition is satisfied.

In contrast, the federal government's offer of additional highway funds conditioned on a state's enactment of a higher drinking age does threaten a penalty, hence is presumptively unconstitutional. Congress has a perfectly legitimate reason for seeking to induce states to raise their drinking ages. But if a state refuses to do so, then all the federal government's legitimate reasons for building or improving roads in that state still apply, and with equal force. Thus, Congress's reason to withhold some portion of otherwise available funds must be to punish or discourage a state's decision to stand on its constitutional authority over its own drinking age. That would be a penalty (in my stipulated sense). It may not be imposed and may not be threatened.

Third and last, consider the commercial speech doctrine—a region of constitutional law not usually understood to raise the unconstitutional conditions problem. May the state prohibit advertisement of business activities that it could ban, but has not? In *Posadas de Puerto Rico Associates v. Tourism Co.*, a divided Supreme Court upheld extensive state regulation of casino advertising, reasoning that "the greater power to completely ban casino gambling necessarily includes the lesser power to ban advertising of casino gambling."[162] The naïve suggestion of then-Justice Rehnquist that the greater always includes the lesser has attracted justifiable academic scorn. But scholars are too quick to denounce the holding. We can reformulate the advertising ban as a conditional offer of permission to operate a casino on condition that it not be advertised in ways likely to attract the local populace. We might also suppose that, in deciding to permit casino gambling, the Puerto Rico legislature was walking a tightrope: it wanted to attract tourist dollars but only if it could keep gambling by its own citizens within reasonable bounds. The legislature thought it could accomplish these goals if casinos restricted their advertising in specified ways. But if they refused to do so, then the legislature was entitled to conclude that the benefits of legalized gambling would not exceed the costs. Insofar as this really was the legislature's reasoning, then withholding a casino license from an entity that does not agree to abide by the advertising restrictions does not impose a penalty, and the regulations— reconceived as a conditional offer—are not coercive.[163]

CONCLUSION

Blackmail's criminalization does not puzzle the casual observer. Not only does blackmail bear a family resemblance to other varieties of theft whose criminalization rarely raises eyebrows; blackmail just smells likes a nasty practice. Theorists from a wide range of disciplines, however, have long identified a puzzle—that it should ever be illegal to threaten what it is legal to do—and have labored vigorously to propose solutions.

This chapter has suggested that blackmail should be disambiguated into at least two concepts. As a legal concept, blackmail is the unlawful conditional threat to do that which would be lawful if done unconditionally. Analogously, as a moral concept, blackmail is the morally wrongful conditional threat to do that which would be morally permissible if done unconditionally. Some paradigmatic instances of the crime of blackmail involve threats that are not moral blackmail. These are conditional threats to do that which would be morally wrongful, although lawful. Plausible examples include the conditional threat to out a closeted lesbian or gay man, or to reveal that somebody wets his bed or has a peculiar, though not wrongful, sexual fetish. In cases such as these, the wrongfulness of the conditional threat flows unproblematically from the wrongfulness of the act threatened. Moreover, because the wrongful threat is employed to extract money or other valuable resources from the offeree, it's easy enough (if not absolutely uncontroversial) to see why a liberal society may punish it as a form of theft. If there's a legal puzzle lurking, it's only why not to criminalize the disclosure as well. But a range of considerations, including difficulties of statutory line-drafting and free speech values, can answer that question with relative ease.

The puzzle over blackmail's criminalization is much more profound if the act threatened is neither morally impermissible nor morally obligatory, but rather, we might say, morally uncertain. The paradigmatic example is the conditional threat to disclose someone's marital infidelity to his or her spouse unless paid for silence. I have suggested that explaining the propriety of criminalizing this sort of threat requires first that we understand whether, and how or why, the conditional threat is morally wrongful though commission of the act threatened might not be. In other words, resolution of this region of the puzzle of legal blackmail piggybacks on a solution to the puzzle of moral blackmail.

The evidentiary theory of blackmail proposes that the act threatened in cases of moral blackmail would be wrongful if the actor does not himself actually believe that commission of the act (which almost invariably will incur significant moral costs) is morally permissible under the circumstances or (possibly) if he is not actually moved by the reasons that obtain and could supply moral justification. The theory claims in addition that the very fact of the conditional proposal is often good evidence that the actor would have the wrong beliefs or motives in doing as he threatens. The two fundamental bases of the evidentiary theory, then, are, first, that an actor's beliefs about the moral permissibility of his conduct can affect its permissibility (*the subjectivist thesis*), and second, that conditional threats can constitute powerful (albeit not conclusive) circumstantial evidence regarding what beliefs the actor would in fact have were he to do as he threatens (*the evidentiary thesis*). In contexts in which the evidentiary value of the conditional proposal is sufficiently strong, the state may treat the conditional threat as wrongful with confidence sufficient to justify its criminalization. While I hope that the evidentiary account is not demonstrably false, I am certain that it is not demonstrably correct. This chapter has tried to show, however, that it coheres well with intuitions about subclasses of blackmail and that it provides fertile ground for exploring other puzzles in law and morals.

ACKNOWLEDGEMENT

For helpful reactions to this project and my general thesis, I am grateful to participants at the September 2008 Roundtable on the Oxford Handbook of Philosophy of Criminal Law organized and sponsored by the University of Illinois Program in Law and Philosophy, and to participants at the January 2010 Roundtable on Exploitation, Price-Gouging, and Blackmail held at the University of San Diego Institute for Law and Philosophy. I am also indebted to the several scholars whose published criticisms of my account of blackmail have contributed to its possible improvement; to Peter Westen for his valuable challenges and generous encouragement; to Larry Alexander, Jonathan Dancy, and Ada Fee for critical reactions to earlier drafts; and to David Dolinko for excellent and careful editing.

NOTES

1. James Lindgren, *Blackmail: An Afterword,* 141 U. Pa. L. Rev. 1975, 1975 (1993).

2. *See* Mitchell N. Berman, *The Evidentiary Theory of Blackmail: Taking Motives Seriously,* 65 U. Chi. L. Rev. 795 (1998).

3. Contemporary writers routinely treat the threat to disclose one's adultery as the modal case of blackmail. From the late eighteenth century through the better part of the twentieth, the modal case involved a threat to accuse the blackmailee of homosexuality or of particular homosexual conduct. *See* Peter Alldridge, *"Attempted Murder of the Soul": Blackmail, Privacy and Secrets,* 13 Oxford J. L. Stud. 368, 374–77 (1993).

4. It is not essential that you do agree with these claims. These four cases are put forth to illustrate the difference between (what I am calling) legal blackmail and moral blackmail. If you do not share the assessments offered—if, say, you believe that *adultery-disclosure* is morally wrongful or that *gay-disclosure* is morally permissible—then I invite you to substitute cases for which the characterizations in text would be apt.

5. An action is pro tanto wrongful if there is genuine moral reason against it, although its wrongmaking features can be overridden by other considerations that render the action permissible, or even obligatory, all things considered. To characterize an action as prima facie wrongful, in contrast, is to say that it appears to be wrongful, though it might turn out, when all the facts are in, not to be wrongful, not even pro tanto.

6. This description corresponds to the method of narrow reflective equilibrium. Wide reflective equilibrium would seek coherence with, as well, the yet more abstract theoretical considerations that shape or determine the principles. Ultimately, wide reflective equilibrium is what we should strive for, but it is a lot to demand of a blackmail theory.

7. I believe that most blackmail theorists share these methodological commitments. *See, e.g.*, George P. Fletcher, *Blackmail: The Paradigmatic Crime*, 141 U. Pa. L. Rev. 1617, 1617 (1993) (expressly invoking the Rawlsian method of reflective equilibrium). Nonetheless, the approach is worth making explicit precisely because some participants seem otherwise not to appreciate the nature or grounding of some common critical moves. *See, e.g., infra* Section II.C.1.

8. James Lindgren's important 1984 article influentially characterized blackmail as a paradox. *See* James Lindgren, *Unraveling the Paradox of Blackmail*, 84 Colum. L. Rev. 670 (1984). The characterization is disputed in Wendy J. Gordon, *Truth and Consequences: The Force of Blackmail's Central Case*, 141 U. Pa. L. Rev. 1741, 1742–43 (1993).

9. Sections I.A and I.B follow the dominant way of classifying blackmail theories, *see generally Symposium: Blackmail*, 141 U. Pa. L. Rev. 1565–1989 (1993), although to better situate my own evidentiary theory, I break out the prior coercion-based theories into Section III.

10. More comprehensive treatment of many of these theories appears in Berman, *supra* note 2, at 799–833, and Lindgren, *supra* note 8, at 680–701. Exhaustive and nearly up-to-date citation to other critiques of various blackmail theories appears in Ken Levy, *The Solution to the Real Blackmail Paradox: The Common Link between Blackmail and Other Criminal Threats*, 39 Conn. L. Rev. 1051, 1063 n. 21 (2007).

11. For one exception, see Joseph Isenbergh, *Blackmail from A to C*, 141 U. Pa. L. Rev. 1905 (1993) (discussed *infra* notes 29–36 and accompanying text).

12. *See, e.g.*, Richard A. Posner, *Blackmail, Privacy, and Freedom of Contract*, 141 U. Pa. L. Rev. 1817, 1819 (1993) ("One alternative to economic analysis in…the blackmail cases is to play with the meaning of 'voluntary,' for example by confining 'voluntary' acts to those in which severe constraints are absent; but this just adds a layer of uncertainty."); Jennifer Gerarda Brown, *Blackmail as Private Justice*, 141 U. Pa. L. Rev. 1935, 1950 n. 32 (1993).

13. Ginsburg and Schectman subsequently published their paper, with a short postscript, as Douglas H. Ginsburg & Paul Schectman, *Blackmail: An Economic Analysis of the Law*, 141 U. Pa. L. Rev. 1849 (1993). An intellectual precursor was George Daly & J. Fred Giertz, *Externalities, Extortion, and Efficiency*, 65 Am. Econ. Rev. 997 (1975).

14. Ronald H. Coase, *The 1987 McCorkle Lecture: Blackmail*, 74 Va. L. Rev. 655 (1988).

15. Ginsburg & Schectman, *supra* note 13, at 1860.

16. This argument was first advanced by Lindgren, relying on a typology of blackmail advanced in Mike Hepworth, *Blackmail: Publicity and Secrecy in Everyday Life* 73–77 (1975). *See* Lindgren, *supra* note 8, at 694–97.

17. Ginsburg & Schectman, *supra* note 13, at 1875–76.

18. Steven Shavell, *An Economic Analysis of Threats and Their Illegality: Blackmail, Extortion, and Robbery*, 141 U. Pa. L. Rev. 1877, 1889 (1993). Shavell proceeds to note that "[t]he cost to a blackmailer of carrying out his threat probably inheres mainly in any resulting increase in the risk of his being caught and punished. But the blackmailer can usually reveal his information anonymously, using the mail or the telephone." *Id.* Interestingly, Shavell's point is actually even stronger than he seems to realize. The blackmailer's costs of avoiding detection and punishment are not relevant when deciding whether blackmail *should* be punishable.

19. Ginsburg & Schectman, *supra* note 13, at 1864. They proceed to argue, however, that the rational economic planner can ignore B's welfare interest in acting spitefully on the grounds that "some potential gains are not realizable because they are not as great as the cost entailed in their identification." *Id.* But if B's pleasure in harming A counts in the welfare calculus, then a realistic appraisal of the costs incurred by the adventitious blackmailer becomes critical.

20. *Id.* (emphasis added).

21. *Id.* at 1875 (internal quotation omitted; ellipses and emphasis in original).

22. Acknowledging that the economic responses to Lindgren's challenge had been inadequate, Professor Richard McAdams proposed a "second-best" economic defense of the criminal ban against adventitious blackmail. *See* Richard H. McAdams, *Group Norms, Gossip, and Blackmail*, 144 U. Pa. L. Rev. 2237, 226–92 (1996). In McAdams's view, absent social norms, adventitious blackmail produces a suboptimal distribution of adventitiously discovered information while a blackmail ban yields a superoptimal distribution of such information. However, he argues, norms favoring privacy correct the latter inefficiency better than norms favoring disclosure correct the former. Therefore, criminalization of adventitious blackmail is more efficient than legalization.

This analysis strikes me as dubious, for it overlooks the social norms against blackmailing. That is, it seems unlikely that decriminalization of adventitious blackmail would eviscerate the social norms against the practice. But even granting its premise arguendo, the consequences of the argument are more far-reaching than McAdams acknowledges—and more expansive than I believe can be adequately defended. Ostensibly McAdams claims only to "supplement[] the economic theory of blackmail." *Id.* at 2287; *see also id.* at 2267 n. 82. But, in fact, his analysis rests on a very different footing. The economic case against blackmail rests on the premise that it is appropriate to criminalize conduct that results in deadweight economic losses. McAdams recognizes that much adventitious blackmail cannot be justified on that principle. *Id.* at 2287. He also eschews reliance on any administrative difficulties of excepting adventitious blackmail from a general blackmail prohibition. *Id.* at 2270 n. 93. Therefore, the unstated premise of his argument is that the fact that a legal prohibition would likely produce a more "efficient" social distribution of information constitutes a sufficient condition for criminalization. It follows that his theory would tolerate an elaborate regime of criminal laws mandating disclosure of certain categories of information and prohibiting concealment of others.

23. *See* William M. Landes & Richard A. Posner, *The Private Enforcement of Law*, 4 J. Legal Stud. 1, 42–43 (1975) (considering whether a blackmail threat to reveal that the blackmail victim committed a crime might increase social utility—and therefore warrant legalization—by reducing other crimes).

24. Shavell, *supra* note 18, at 1903.

25. *See* Posner, *supra* note 12.

26. Posner's categories are as follows: (1) criminal acts for which the blackmailer's victim has been punished; (2) undetected criminal acts; (3) acts that are wrongful, perhaps tortious, but not criminal; (4) wrongful acts of which the blackmailer (or his principal) was the victim; (5) disreputable or otherwise censurable acts that do not, however, violate any enforced law; (6) involuntary acts or conditions that are a source of potential humiliation; and (7) any of the first six categories, except that the victim did not commit the act for which he is being blackmailed. *Id.* at 1820.

27. *Id.* at 1827, 1835.

28. *Id.* at 1827; *see also id.* at 1835 ("once again, the argument for allowing blackmail is too speculative to make a strong case for decriminalizing this particular form of extortion").

29. Isenbergh, *supra* note 11, at 1928. *See also* Posner, *supra* note 12, at 1841 (noting that the third of his proposed mechanisms by which criminalization deters blackmail "could be achieved without criminal law simply by making blackmail contracts unenforceable as a matter of contract law").

30. *Id.* at 1841.

31. Isenbergh, *supra* note 11, at 1928.

32. Fernando Gómez & Juan-José Ganuza, *Civil and Criminal Sanctions Against Blackmail: An Economic Analysis*, 21 Int'l Rev. Law & Econ. 475 (2002).

33. *Id.* at 492 ("[T]he static analysis of the blackmail puzzle in the absence of legal regulation could lead us to jump to the conclusion that no legal rule is the best legal rule.").

34. Admittedly, whether a ban on such advertising would pass judicial scrutiny under current First Amendment doctrine is uncertain. I have argued, though, that current commercial speech doctrine is flawed and that advertising regulations that can be understood as conditional offers of the form "you may engage in such-and-such commercial activity that we might otherwise prohibit on the condition that you not advertise it" should often be upheld. *See* Mitchell N. Berman, *Commercial Speech and the Unconstitutional Conditions Doctrine: A Second Look at "The Greater Includes the Lesser,"* 55 Vand. L. Rev. 693 (2002).

35. Gómez & Ganuza, *supra* note 32, at 497 n. 42.

36. In light of the difficulty in ascertaining whether given information was costlessly obtained, Isenbergh would, as a proxy, make all contracts to remain silent enforceable as a matter of contract law if the parties knew each other before the blackmail bargain. He would also make an exception to that exception in cases where the subject of the contract for silence is the commission of torts and crimes. Isenbergh, *supra* note 11, at 1925–32.

37. Richard A. Epstein, *Blackmail, Inc.*, 50 U. Chi. L. Rev. 553 (1983).

38. *Id.* at 555.

39. *Id.* at 556–57. Although Epstein appears to locate his preferred moral limits on the criminal law in the actus reus requirement, his is not the orthodox understanding of that requirement. On the various meanings of actus reus, see Paul H. Robinson, *Should the Criminal Law Abandon the Actus Reus–Mens Rea Distinction?*, *in* Action and Value in Criminal Law 187, 190–202 (Stephen Shute et al. eds., 1993). Still, we can understand Epstein as advancing a normative claim that the criminal law should only criminalize the use or threat of force or fraud, and some narrow "principled extension[s]." Epstein, *supra* note 37, at 555.

40. Epstein notes that blackmail can incorporate elements of force or fraud, as for example, when the blackmailer threatens to disclose information gleaned from stolen documents. Epstein, *supra* note 37, at 558. But in such a case, criminalization of blackmail presents no puzzle for "[i]t is easy to regard blackmail as a criminal offense whenever the disclosure is itself regarded as wrongful." *Id.* With Epstein, let us put those cases aside.

41. *Id.* at 560.

42. *Id.*

43. *Id.* at 564.

44. *Id.* at 566. For another account that, like Epstein's, grounds blackmail's wrongfulness in the harms that it proximately causes see Henry E. Smith, *The Harm in Blackmail*, 92 Nw. U. L. Rev. 861 (1998) (emphasizing that blackmail often provokes the blackmailee to suicide, fraud, theft, and even murder).

45. *See supra* text accompanying note 44. *See also* Epstein, *supra* note 37, at 565 (decrying blackmail's "necessary tendency to induce deception and other wrongs").

46. *Id.* at 564. *See also id.* (claiming that Blackmail, Inc. will "participate in the very fraud that V is *necessarily* engaged in against T") (emphasis added).

47. Unless, that is, the practical difficulties in excepting such cases from a general blackmail ban would be insurmountable or too costly, a contention Epstein does not make.

48. *Id.* at 564.

49. *Id.*

50. Jeffrie G. Murphy, *Blackmail: A Preliminary Inquiry,* 63 Monist 156 (1980).

51. *Id.* at 156.

52. *Id.* at (footnotes omitted).

53. Murphy proceeds to qualify this rule for "public figures": because there already exist substantial economic incentives to invade their privacy, blackmail of such figures at rates that do not exceed the market price for the information in question would be permitted. And he qualifies this qualification for "public officials": because concealment of embarrassing information about public officials often disserves citizens' legitimate interests, blackmailing them, even at market-price, should be disallowed. *Id.* at 164–65.

54. *Id.* at 163–66.

55. *See* Lindgren, *supra* note 8, at 689.

56. In fairness, Murphy does not say that "taking an unfair advantage of the victim's vulnerability" constitutes the whole of the immorality of blackmail and hard economic transactions; he says only that it is an *example* of their immorality. But if there are other ways in which blackmail is "intrinsically immoral," Murphy does not hint at what they may be.

57. Murphy, *supra* note 50, at 156–57.

58. *See, e.g., Harper & Row Pub., Inc. v. Nation Enterprises,* 471 U.S. 539, 559 (1985).

59. *See, e.g.,* Hugh Evans, *Why Blackmail Should Be Banned,* 65 Phil. 89, 92–94 (1990).

60. This is a theme that runs through Hepworth, *supra* note 16.

61. George Fletcher predicates his proposed solution to the blackmail paradox on a novel and explicit theory of crime and punishment. *See generally* Fletcher, *supra* note 7. The core concern of the criminal law, he ventures, is to deter and negate conditions of dominance and subordination. *Id.* at 1635. If so, there is no reason to criminalize the mere disclosure of embarrassing information. It's over and done with. The blackmail threat to disclose the same information is another story. Precisely because of "the prospect of repeated demands," *id.* at 1626, blackmail tends to create a continuing relationship of dominance and submission. In consequence, blackmail "is not an anomalous crime but rather a paradigm for understanding both criminal wrongdoing and punishment." *Id.* at 1617.

62. Leo Katz, *Blackmail and Other Forms of Arm-Twisting,* 141 U. Pa. L. Rev. 1567 (1993).

63. *Id.* at 1598 (emphasis omitted).

64. Smithy the burglar breaks into Bartleby's house to commit larceny. Inside, he demands that Bartleby divulge the combination to his safe and threatens to beat Bartleby senseless if he does not comply. Bartleby declares that he could not bear to part with the items in his safe (which have only sentimental value) and regrets he'll have to submit to the beating. Smithy batters Bartleby savagely and leaves. When Louie the burglar breaks into Bartleby's house the next night, the identical scenario transpires—with one exception. Just as Louie is about to strike Bartleby he espies a scrap of paper containing the safe's combination. Despite Bartleby's plea that he would rather be pummelled than lose his goods, Louie opens the safe and leaves with the contents. *Id.* at 1582–83. According to Katz, the law would and should punish Smithy the batterer more severely than Louie the thief.

Whereas victims are concerned solely with harm, the law is concerned with the defendant's culpability, of which harm is but a minor ingredient. *Id.* at 1590.

65. *Id.* at 1598 (emphases omitted).

66. *Id.* at 1599. The same intuition is suggested by remarks in Michael Gorr, *Liberalism and the Paradox of Blackmail,* 21 Phil. & Pub. Affairs 43, 53–54 (1992).

67. *Id.* at 53.

68. Consider a judicial nominee who has committed some minor indiscretion in his past—say, he smoked marijuana, and inhaled—for which he is not ashamed but which he (rightly) fears might doom his nomination if revealed. Assume that Blackmailer approaches Nominee on the eve of the confirmation vote and threatens to disclose his prior drug use to the Senate committee unless the Nominee pays $10,000. Because he could hardly care less were the information to be revealed after he is confirmed, Nominee believes to a moral certainty that he may accede to the demand without thereby initiating a submissive relationship. Under Fletcher's theory, Blackmailer's conduct should not be criminalized—a conclusion contrary to prevailing law as well as, I'd suspect, to common moral intuition.

69. Lindgren, *supra* note 1, at 1977. As it turns out, Lindgren's latter claim demands qualification: the evidentiary theory aims to show that the moral status of the act threatened is far more complex and contingent than Lindgren recognizes. But Lindgren's first claim is surely right: whether the act threatened is a moral right or a moral wrong (or something else), neither proposition can be simply assumed without argument.

70. Lindgren, *supra* note 8, at 670. This formulation of the puzzle is properly criticized in Benjamin E. Rosenberg, *Debate: Another Reason for Criminalizing Blackmail,* 16 J. Pol. Phil. 356, 356 n. 3 (2008).

71. Lindgren, *supra* note 8, at 702.

72. Consider, for example, a threat by Nazis to march in Skokie unless the town's residents buy them off with a large cash payment. I assume that this is blackmail. If so, the Nazis are merely leveraging their own constitutional rights, which they are threatening to exercise as an instrument of cruelty toward the town's many Holocaust survivors. (It could be argued that the Nazis in this hypothetical are really leveraging the informational interests of the public—within or outside of Skokie—that might wish to view the march. But this is a forced and artificial construction. The public could not, after all, compel the Nazis to march if they chose not to, nor could the Nazis be viewed as having even a weak moral obligation to march.)

73. *See* Lindgren, *supra* note 1, at 1988.

74. Fletcher, *supra* note 7, at 1637 (paraphrasing an objection leveled by Stephen Latham).

75. *Id.* (citations omitted).

76. Murray N. Rothbard, *Man, Economy, and State* 443 n. 49 (1962).

77. *See, e.g.,* Eric Mack, *In Defense of Blackmail,* 41 Phil. Stud. 274 (1982); Ronald Joseph Scalise, Jr., *Comment, Blackmail, Legality, and Liberalism,* 74 Tul. L. Rev. 1483 (2000).

78. For a listing of Block's many articles on blackmail, some coauthored, see his website: www.walterblock.com/publications.php.

79. *See, e.g.,* Walter Block, *The Case for De-criminalizing Blackmail: A Reply to Lindgren and Campbell,* 24 W. St. U. L. Rev. 225, 237 (1997) (hereafter "Block, *De-criminalizing Blackmail*") (maintaining that "justice is the essence of law and that justice, in turn, consists mainly of protecting persons and property against violent

incursions"); *id.* at 246 (concluding that "the proper basis of criminality [is] a violation of person or property right through initiatory force"). *But see* Walter Block, *Berman on Blackmail: Taking Motives Fervently,* 3 Fla. St. U. Bus. Rev. 57, 71 (2003) (hereafter "Block, *Berman on Blackmail*") (criminal prohibitions can extend beyond force in the ordinary sense, and that force and violence mean only "violating the rights of person or property"). If this is so, then "through initiatory force" appears redundant.

80. Block, *Berman on Blackmail, supra* note 79, at 59–63.

81. Block's libertarian theory of punishment begins with the premise that "the essence of punishment theory" is an "attempt[] to render the victim whole again." Block, *De-Criminalizing Blackmail, supra* note 79, at 235. On the mainstream view, this is not the essence of punishment theory, though of course many writers outside the libertarian tradition accept this as the essence of *tort* theory. Starting from this point of departure, libertarian punishment theory maintains "that whatever the miscreant does to this victim is done to him, only twice over." Block, *Berman on Blackmail, supra* note 79, at 76. For example, a rapist would be sodomized with a broomstick, twice. *Id.* at 77. This is said to render the victim whole because she is permitted to negotiate with the perpetrator for monetary payment in lieu of punishment.

82. Block takes me to task, *see id.* at 62 n. 12, for refraining from critiquing Rothbard's argument beyond observing that it "stands or falls upon familiar libertarian premises." Berman, *supra* note 2, at 800 n. 10. But my point was to concede that the decriminalization conclusion follows if one accepts libertarian political theory and to suggest that challenging that theory—a theory about which most of my readers could be expected already to have a view—was beyond the proper ambit of a paper on blackmail. Some things must be bracketed to get on with the business at hand, even if the claims that are bracketed are not incontestable or even uncontested.

I rather suspect that Block thinks otherwise because he believes that a theory of blackmail must start from something in the vicinity of first principles. But that is precisely what coherentism denies. Block's apparent failure to appreciate the coherentist methodology would also explain his peculiar claim that Joel Feinberg "arouses Berman's ire since he actually has the audacity to maintain that at least one kind of blackmail, exposing adultery should be legalized. Instead of directly confronting Feinberg on this apostasy, [Berman] dismisses him on the ground that his 'conclusion is startling.'" Block, *Berman on Blackmail, supra* note 79, at 72 (footnotes omitted). On coherentist principles, to point out respects in which a particular account generates conclusions likely not to accord with strong pre-theoretical case-specific judgments of one's expected interlocutors *is* to "directly confront[]" the account; it's just not to *refute* it.

83. For my own ruminations on punishment theory, see Mitchell N. Berman, *Punishment and Justification,* 118 Ethics 258 (2008); Mitchell N. Berman, *Two Kinds of Retributivism, in* The Philosophical Foundations of Criminal Law pp. 433–57 (R. A. Duff & Stuart Green eds., 2011).

84. Block, *De-Criminalizing Blackmail, supra* note 79, at 235.

85. This is not quite as clear as it could be. Compare, e.g., *id.* at 235 & n. 40 (emphasizing that he is not taking a position on the morality of the acts involved in a blackmail proposal) with *id.* at 226 n. 6 (asserting that gossiping about a person's adulterous affairs would not be morally justified).

86. *See, e.g., id.* at 226 (acknowledging that his reply to procriminalization theorists is based on the libertarian principle that the law should concern itself only with protecting against "violation of person and legitimate property rights").

87. Russell L. Christopher, *Meta-Blackmail*, 94 Geo. L.J. 739 (2006). I published a reply to that article, to which Christopher penned a sur-reply. *See* Mitchell N. Berman, *Meta-Blackmail and the Evidentiary Theory: Still Taking Motives Seriously,* 94 Geo. L.J. 787 (2006); Russell L. Christopher, *The Trilemma of Meta-Blackmail: Is Conditionally Threatening Blackmail Worse, the Same, or Better than Blackmail Itself?,* 94 Geo. L.J. 813 (2006) (hereafter "Christopher, *Trilemma*").

88. For a discussion of some difficulties in determining precisely what conditional proposals Christopher would count as a metablackmail threat see Berman, *supra* note 87, at 805 n. 54.

89. Christopher, *Trilemma, supra* note 87, at 827.

90. Christopher, *Meta-Blackmail, supra* note 87, at 747.

91. *Id.* at 769.

92. *See, e.g.,* Stuart P. Green, *Lying, Cheating, and Stealing: A Moral Theory of White-Collar Crime* 212–34 (2006).

93. Robert Nozick, *Anarchy, State, and Utopia* 84–87 (1974).

94. Michael Gorr summarizes Nozick's definition in similar terms, although he does not present the second criterion as a conditional. Under Gorr's definition, it is a sine qua non of an unproductive exchange (in Nozick's sense) that one of the parties sells forebearance from an act. *See* Michael Gorr, *Nozick's Argument against Blackmail*, 58 Personalist 187, 188 (1977). Nozick does not address this point explicitly. As note 100, *infra*, indicates, I think Gorr's is not the better view.

95. Imagine that Adulterer dumps his Mistress who then decides to reveal their affair to his Wife. However, an advertisement for Blackmail, Inc. causes her to reconsider. Although she'd like to hurt her ex-lover, a possible windfall is attractive too. She sells her love letters to the professionals, who in turn sell them to Adulterer. Adulterer's acceptance of the blackmail offer is arguably conclusive evidence that he's better off because of the blackmailer. Aware of such problems, Nozick responds: "To state the point exactly in order to exclude such complications is not worth the effort it would require." Nozick, *supra* note 93, at 85 n. Perhaps Nozick means to agree that the blackmail agreement in such circumstances is not "unproductive." The further implication that such instances should be lawful would make this a profound concession, deeply inconsistent with prevailing law. More probably, Nozick means that he could recraft his test for unproductive exchanges so as to make the deal between Adulterer and Blackmail, Inc. unproductive by definition. But the difficulty in justifying blackmail's criminalization would be exacerbated.

96. Gorr, *supra* note 94, at 187; *see also, e.g.,* Murphy, *supra* note 50, at 158 (observing that Nozick argues that "blackmail should be prohibited because it is an *un*productive economic exchange" and criticizing Nozick for failing to provide any argument for the proposition "that unproductive economic exchanges are *immoral*"). Gordon, *supra* note 8, at 1758 (remarking that Nozick, "usually thought of a deontologic theorist, has grounded his blackmail argument on the idea of 'unproductive exchanges,'" and complaining that the theory's "deontological rationale is opaque").

97. Gordon, *supra* note 8, at 1772 n. 137 (expressing uncertainty whether Nozick presents a deontological or consequentialist argument for the criminalization of blackmail); Kathleen M. Sullivan, *Unconstitutional Conditions*, 102 Harv. L. Rev. 1413, 1447 n. 140, 1449 n. 145 (1989) (noting both that Nozick has "used utilitarian grounds to defend the ban on blackmail" and that his theory "reflects conceptions of negative liberty").

98. Robert Nozick, *Coercion, in* Philosophy, Science, and Method: Essays in Honor of Ernest Nagel 440–72 (Sidney Morgenbesser et al. eds., 1969).

99. *Id.* at 447. Nozick proposes that the normal and morally required course of events usually coincide and, further, that when they do not, the latter ordinarily takes precedence over the former. *Id.* at 449–51.

100. In most cases, the tests for coercion and unproductive exchange come out the same. That is, a consummated exchange is "unproductive" if and only if the proposal that launched the exchange was a "threat." Such is the case, for example, with the illustration Nozick offers to elucidate the second criterion of his definition of unproductive exchange: "If your next-door neighbor plans to erect a certain structure on his land, which he has a right to do, you might be better off if he didn't exist at all. . . . Yet purchasing his abstention from proceeding with his plans will be a productive exchange. Suppose, however, that the neighbor has no desire to erect the structure on the land; he formulates his plan and informs you of it solely in order to sell you his abstention from it. Such an exchange would not be a productive one; it merely gives you relief from something that would not threaten if not for the possibility of an exchange to get relief from it." Nozick, *supra* note 93, at 84–85. As the last sentence suggests, the proposal leading up to the hypothesized unproductive exchange is a threat (i.e., coercive), not an offer.

But the equivalence between coercion and unproductive exchanges does not always hold. Imagine that your coworker announces that his daughter is selling Girl Scout cookies and that he will be taking orders. You subscribe for four boxes of thin mints at $4 per box. Truth is, you don't want the cookies, but you estimated that to decline the offer might cause you some reputational harm, and you valued the cookies and the preservation of your reputation more highly than $16 plus a possible slight diminution of your office status. This is plainly an unproductive exchange—you would have preferred that your coworker had never mentioned his daughter and the cookies. But the proposal to sell you Girl Scout cookies is not a threat (because it doesn't propose to put you worse off than your expected or morally deserved baselines).

101. *See* Joel Feinberg, *The Moral Limits of the Criminal Law: Harmless Wrongdoing* 238–76 (1988).

102. *Id.* at 241.

103. *Id.* at 246.

104. *Id.* at 250.

105. *Id.* at 248–49. Feinberg continues: "*Either* the blackmailer should have a duty to inform (or a duty not to, as the case may be) in which case it would be consistent to prohibit him from threatening to violate that duty unless paid off, *or* he should have no legal duty one way or the other, in which case it would be incoherent to punish him for threatening to do what is within his legal rights." Here Feinberg takes a strong stance on legal blackmail, not only on moral blackmail. As we have seen in Section II.B.1, the judgment that it would be "incoherent" to criminalize what it should not be criminal to do is not supportable, for there can be all sorts of pragmatic reasons not to criminalize conduct that is in principle criminalizable. For present purposes, the important point is Feinberg's position on moral blackmail—in particular, that *adultery-threat* cannot be morally wrongful on the assumption that *adultery-disclosure* isn't.

106. Gorr, *supra* note 66, at 50.

107. *Id.* at 55.

108. *Id.* at 56 (quoting Feinberg, *supra* note 101, at 248).

109. *Id.* at 56–57.

110. *Id.* at 65.

111. For one thing, Gorr is surely incorrect to assert that, if we knew what the blackmailer's moral obligation was, we'd have a "morally conclusive reason" for imposing a

legal obligation either to disclose or to remain silent. We properly refrain from criminalizing lots of conduct that we are confident violates moral obligations, including routine lying and promise-breaking. He is also mistaken about the positive law of invasion of privacy. Although he contends that disclosures of embarrassing but not wrongful behavior will usually be actionable, e.g., *id.* at 47, 62, recovery will generally be disallowed if the embarrassing information is at all a matter of public concern, which includes many matters concerning the private lives of public figures, or if the disclosure is made to a small number of persons, under circumstances in which the information is not likely to become public knowledge. *See* Restatement Second of Torts § 652D. In addition to these errors, Gorr gives seemingly undue attention to the moral and legal character of the act of the blackmailee that the blackmailer might threaten to reveal. From a sensible intermediate conclusion that the blackmail proposal is likely to involve acts that are legally permissible but morally wrongful, he moves too quickly to the conclusion that the challenging cases for a blackmail ban involve threats to disclose actions that are legally permissible, morally wrongful, and "involve[] some significant harm to another person." Gorr, *supra* note 66, at 52. The considerations advanced to support this last condition do not strike me as sound. Consider behavior that plausibly satisfies the first two conditions but not the third—say, a wealthy person's serial purchase of important art for the sole purpose of secretly destroying it. Presumably Gorr believes that there is no significant puzzle over the permissibility of criminalizing a conditional threat to reveal such behavior because such threats are plainly not criminalizable. But this is far from self-evident.

112. In Gorr's estimation, "most theorists have…tended to suppose that there is nothing especially problematic about the fact that we permit blackmailers to *do* what they threaten, and that all that really needs explaining is how, in light of this, it could ever make sense to prohibit the threats themselves. My contention, however, is that this is precisely the wrong way to view the matter and that the key to resolving the paradox of blackmail (and to meeting some of the other important objections to its continued criminalization) is to determine just *why* blackmailers are given the liberty to do the acts that they threaten." *Id.* at 44. Gorr is concerned with why we give people a legal right to do the things that are leveraged into blackmail threats. I think it's more perspicuous to examine why (we believe that) they have a moral right to do those things.

113. Scott Altman, *A Patchwork Theory of Blackmail*, 141 U. Pa. L. Rev. 1639, 1652 (1993).

114. Gorr, *supra* note 66, at 53–54.

115. This might seem fanciful, but I can make it modestly more attractive. Suppose B honestly doesn't know what his duty is. So he determines that the right thing to do, given that uncertainty, is to give the information to the party who would value it most highly. Unfortunately, he can't hold an auction between H and W because to do would be already to give the information to W. So B estimates the value that W would place on it: $X. He then offers the information to H for $X + n. If H accepts the deal, then B has some grounds for concluding that H values it more highly than does W, so he gives it to H not W. If H rejects, then B has grounds for concluding that W values it more highly than does H, so he gives it to W. Again, on an objectivist view of duties, B acts wrongfully if the final action—disclosure or silence—is the objectively wrong thing to do. But it is mysterious why this superficially sensible way of deciding on a course of action in the face of uncertainty is itself wrongful.

116. The basic point is that the unusualness of a particular variable (here, that the blackmailer is in equipoise regarding what he morally ought to do) is relevant only if the parameter that the variable instantiates is itself relevant (here, the blackmailer's beliefs regarding what he morally ought to do). A farfetched example might make this point clearer. Imagine that the blackmailer and blackmailee share the same birthday though they

were born exactly twenty years apart, or that their full names are anagrams of each other. The rarity of such circumstances would provide a basis for concluding that the moral outcomes in such cases differ from the norm only on an account that has resources for recognizing the moral relevance of birth dates or name spellings.

117. Altman, *supra* note 113, at 1642.

118. *See, e.g.,* Alan Wertheimer, *Coercion* (1987); Berman, *The Normative Functions of Coercion Claims,* 8 Legal Theory 45 (2002).

119. There will be a large overlap between the belief-centered and motive-centered accounts. The latter encompasses the former: whenever an actor's beliefs make his conduct wrongful, he will almost invariably have bad motives too. But the converse is not true. My reason for preferring the belief-centered account is not that I think the motive-centered account does not satisfactorily resolve the blackmail puzzle, but only that it may not equally well solve that puzzle by showing blackmail to be a form of coercion. An actor who knowingly causes harm without being animated by morally justifying motives—whether he is animated by inherently bad motives like malice or spite, or inherently neutral motives like bolstering a personal reputation as a credible threatener—acts in a morally blameworthy fashion. I believe that it is permissible (if often imprudent) for the state to criminalize conduct that is both harm-causing and morally blameworthy. (This position is easily supported by retributivist and expressivist considerations, and also by many ordinary consequentialist considerations that would require a little spelling out.) *See* Berman, *supra* note 2, at 833–40. But I also think it plausible that A does not *wrong* B by causing him harm without justifying motives if in fact A ought to engage in the harm-causing conduct and A knows or believes this to be so (even if that knowledge or belief has no motivational force for him). And I think the wrong of coercion most plausibly requires a conditional threat to wrong someone (usually the threatenee, but possibly third parties). So even though I continue to believe that the motive-centered version of the subjectivist thesis can solve the blackmail puzzle, I believe that the belief-centered version better shows blackmail to be a form of coercion.

120. The qualification that the belief must be reasonable ensures that this account of wrongdoing is not subjectivist all the way down; it does not license idiosyncratic moral judgments. In effect, the subjectivist thesis recognizes that there are actions whose moral quality is indeterminate due to reasonable uncertainty regarding empirical and predictive matters and also due to the need for (inescapably individual) evaluative judgment. In such circumstances, the moral command is to do what you believe is right (or permissible) after due deliberation, entailing as a corollary that you act wrongfully only if you fail to heed that directive. This account is not, I think, viciously circular, for morality does not command, on this view, that the actor do as she believes morality commands. Rather, it commands her to reach judgments about what the balance of undefeated moral reasons requires, permits, or forbids (as the case may be), where such reasoning is not, on my view, an attempt to discover preexisting moral reality but, instead, is constructivist in a broad sense. (I am grateful to Jonathan Dancy for pressing the objection from circularity.)

121. Several commentators have criticized my reliance on an under-specified account of harm. *See, e.g.,* Christopher, *Meta-blackmail, supra* note 87, at 765–66; Green, *supra* note 92, at 220; Scalise, *supra* note 77, at 1493 ; Block, *Berman on Blackmail, supra* note 81, at 87. I concede that I lack a developed account of this notoriously elusive concept. So a few quick remarks. *See also* Berman, *supra* note 2, at 797–98. First, I believe that harm is a moralized, not purely descriptive, concept. If, roughly, a harm is a setback to interests of a type that we have moral reasons of a particular character or of a particular stringency not to cause, then it seems no more problematic than other moral concepts that we must be

allowed to employ without awaiting a fully adequate understanding of their content or contours. Second, I believe that the acts threatened in usual blackmail proposals (like the disclosure of embarrassing secrets) inflicts what counts as harm under conventional moral standards. In any event, the structure of the subjectivist thesis recommends that if we doubt whether some setback or disutility constitutes a harm, we should conclude that it does, for if conduct inflicts only marginal harm it is extremely likely to be morally justified all things considered. That is, an error at the first step in the direction of finding too much to be harmful is likely to be corrected at the second.

122. Precisely what the doctrine of double effect (DDE) provides is controversial. In its motive-centered variant, it provides that an act that has good and bad effects is permissible if the good effects outweigh the bad effects; the actor merely permits, but does not will, the bad effects; and the good effects of the action are at least as causally immediate as are the bad effects. The causal-structure variant requires, inter alia, that the bad effect not be a means to the realization of the good effect. *See generally* "Doctrine of Double Effect," Stanford Encyclopedia of Philosophy, http://plato.stanford.edu/entries/double-effect/. For an effort to resolve the blackmail paradox by appealing to a negative implication of DDE—namely, that beneficial side-effects do not redeem an action when the actor's direct intent is to do harm—see Gordon, *supra* note 8. Whereas, as we will see, the evidentiary theory inquires into the beliefs or motives the actor would have in carrying out the action he threatens, Gordon focuses on the blackmailer's motives for making his threat. This causes her to conclude—incorrectly, in my view—that blackmail is wrongful because the actor's "intent is directed to the money." *Id.* at 1765.

123. To put things differently, I am taking issue with Feinberg's claim that, when disclosure and silence are both "morally risky," what a third party chooses to do "is up to him." *See supra* text accompanying note 105. Rather, when in a "morally risky" situation, one has a duty to deliberate with seriousness and then not to act against what he determines to be the balance of moral reason. The choice of action, therefore, is not "up to him" in a phenomenologically robust sense.

124. Let me emphasize: the fact of the offer *undermines* such a proposition but doesn't *disprove* it. Perhaps B, a close friend of W, develops a pressing need for funds (say, B's child needs an emergency operation) in sudden coincidence with his discovery of H's adultery. Lacking any other source of income, B decides, after painful soul-searching, to blackmail H to obtain the desperately needed funds. When H rejects B's offer, B proceeds to spill the beans to W, believing as he had all along that W had a strong moral claim to the information, and even feeling somewhat relieved to be "freed" to perform what he viewed as his moral duty. In this scenario—and by hypothesis only—B does not act wrongfully and even has good motives when making his harm-causing disclosure, notwithstanding his unsuccessful blackmail proposal.

125. For a powerful presentation of this argument see David Dolinko, *Some Thoughts about Retributivism,* 101 Ethics 537 (1991).

126. Note, though, that we should not blithely assume that a law criminalizing wrongful disclosures of embarrassing secrets is unconstitutional. Until the Supreme Court's decision in *Garrison v. Louisiana,* 379 U.S. 64 (1964) (holding that the First Amendment prohibits the prosecution of alleged libels absent proof of knowing or reckless falsehood, when such publications relate to public affairs), a majority of states, by constitution or statute, provided that a valid defense to a criminal libel prosecution required the defendant to establish not only the truth of the libelous publication but that it was "published with good motives and for justifiable ends." *Garrison,* 379 U.S. at 70–72 & n. 7. Although criminal libel was generally justified as a means to protect against breaches of the peace, *see id.* at

67–68, some jurisdictions had expressly conceived of the offense as a means to guard against injury to the libeled party. *See, e.g., Gardner v. State of Arizona*, 139 P. 474, 476–77 (Ariz. 1914). Many state courts invalidated these provisions after *Garrison*. But the *Garrison* Court explicitly left the question open, *see Garrison*, 379 U.S. at 72 n. 8, and ten years later, it again refused to decide "whether truthful publications may ever be subjected to civil or criminal liability consistently with the First and Fourteenth Amendments." *Cox Broadcasting Corp. v. Cohn*, 420 U.S. 469, 491 (1975).

127. Recall Isenbergh's argument that the criminal ban might increase the incidence of blackmail (relative to a regime in which blackmail bargains are entirely void) because, by incurring potential criminal liability, the blackmailer can sell the blackmailee a higher likelihood of silence, increasing likelihood of acceptance. But the blackmailee is less likely to accept in proportion to the likelihood he anticipates that he can report the blackmailer to the police without thereby provoking disclosure. And that outcome becomes more probable if the blackmailer risks liability for disclosure beyond the liability he has already incurred for making the threat. *See* Gómez & Ganuza, *supra* note 32, at 481; Posner, *supra* note 12, at 1839.

128. *See supra* text accompanying note 57.

129. This is a theme of Altman, *supra* note 113.

130. *Compare, e.g.,* Brown, *supra* note 12 (arguing that legalizing blackmail of criminals would probably increase deterrence of other crimes), *with* Posner, *supra* note 12, at 1823–27 (concluding that the effects are ambiguous); Landes & Posner, *supra* note 23 (same); *and* Shavell, *supra* note 18, at 1899–1900 (contending that it is more efficient to maintain a ban on crime-exposure blackmail, supplemented by public authority to offer rewards for the identification of criminals).

131. *See, e.g.,* Feinberg, *supra* note 101, at 243–45. As I noted in Section I, qua offer, a biconditional proposal takes its normative character from that of the act offered, not threatened.

132. *See* P. Glazebrook, *How Long, Then, Is the Arm of the Law to Be?*, 25 Mod. L. Rev. 301, 307 n. 51 (1962) ("No court in the United States has been prepared to adopt the English doctrine in its simplicity, and hold that a mere failure to disclose knowledge of a felony is itself an offence."). However, through the offense of "compounding," the Model Penal Code would make it a misdemeanor to accept money in consideration for failing to report to law enforcement authorities information about the suspected commission of a crime. MPC § 242.5.

133. *See, e.g.,* MPC § 223.4(2).

134. This seems to be the very sentiment underlying Chief Justice Marshall's pronouncement in *Marbury v. Brooks*, 20 U.S. (7 Wheat.) 556: "It may be the duty of a citizen to accuse every offender, and to proclaim every offense which comes to his knowledge; but the law which would punish him in every case for not performing this duty is too harsh for man." And it might have been too harsh in the very case at hand, which involved "the attempt of a father-in-law to conceal the forgeries of a son-in-law, by paying off the notes he had forged." 20 U.S. (7 Wheat.) at 575. *Cf. Haupt v. U.S.*, 330 U.S. 631, 641–42 (1947) (holding, in treason prosecution, that "[i]t was for the jury to weigh the evidence that the acts proceeded from parental solicitude against the evidence of adherence to the German cause" and that the jury could disbelieve defendant's contention that he "merely had the mis-fortune to sire a traitor and all he did was to act as an indulgent father toward a diabolical son").

135. MPC §223.4.

136. *Id.* Comment (f).

137. DR 7–105A. The 1983 Model Rules of Professional Conduct lack any such specific proscription.

138. *See supra* note 5. The argument that follows in text is overly stylized, but an adequate first pass at the problem.

139. Of course, the story is entirely different if what B threatens if not paid reasonable compensation is to file a tort suit, rather than to file a criminal complaint. The action threatened is entirely permissible on the assumption that B has a good faith belief that he has a legally enforceable claim for damages against A. And the offer is permissible too: it's A's claim, he can forego it if he wishes. The conditional proposal not to sue if A pays appropriate damages does not impugn the permissible beliefs or motives we might otherwise expect B to have. The proposal is morally kosher, and it's hard to see a sensible legal objection to it. Relatedly, however, scholars have objected that class action litigation constitutes blackmail. For a careful evaluation, and rejection, of the argument see Charles Silver, *"We're Scared to Death": Class Certification and Blackmail*, 78 N.Y.U. L. Rev. 1357 (2003).

140. *Compare, e.g.,* Murphy, *supra* note 50, at 164–65 (proposing to decriminalize cases of blackmail in which the putative blackmailer seeks from his "victim" only the going market price), Ginsburg & Schectman, *supra* note 13, at 1860 (same), *and* Feinberg, *supra* note 101, at 262–64 (deeming "[d]emands for fair compensation for considerate offers not to publish" instances of "plausibly justified blackmail"), *with* Lindgren, *supra* note 1, at 1987 (opining that market-price blackmail "seems like classic blackmail" and concluding that, "[g]iven the lack of agreement over the rationale for blackmail," its continued criminalization is sound).

141. Fifteen years ago, the *Advocate*, a gay-oriented national magazine, threatened to out Arizona congressman James Kolbe because of his support for the Defense of Marriage Act, which provides that states need not recognize same-sex marriages performed in another state. Kolbe preempted the *Advocate* by announcing his homosexuality in advance of the magazine. *See* John E. Young, *Rep. Kolbe Announces He Is Gay*, Wash. Post, Aug. 3, 1996, at A8. The *Advocate* explained its actions precisely as a way to challenge what they saw as Kolbe's hypocrisy. *See id.* Of course, this is not to say the magazine was correct. A gay politician can oppose a piece of (ostensibly) gay-friendly legislation without being hypocritical just as an African-American politician can with integrity oppose legislation considered to be advantageous to the African-American community as a whole or a Jewish politician can oppose, say, policies favorable to Israel. Indeed, Barney Frank, the openly gay congressman from Massachusetts, declared that he approves of outing "in cases of gross hypocrisy," but opined that Kolbe's was not such a case. *See Kolbe Won't Be Gay Rights "Poster Boy,"* Worcester Tel. & Gaz., Aug. 4, 1996.

142. Consider one of Nozick's illustrations of an unproductive exchange: B proposes to erect a structure on his land "solely in order to sell [A, B's neighbor] his abstention from it." *See supra* note 100. In my view, B does not merely propose an unproductive exchange but engages in the moral wrong of coercion, for the act-token he threatens would be morally wrongful because there is moral reason against it—the disutility that, by hypothesis, B knows A will suffer—and no moral reason in its favor. But we know that B's carrying out of the threat would be wrongful in this case only because Nozick pronounces, ex cathedra, that B would not have good reason were he to do as he threatens. (That, I take it is what Nozick means by specifying that B hatches the plan *solely* to sell abstention from it.) In the ordinary case of putative noninformational blackmail, as in Nozick's, the act-type threatened is not presumptively wrongful. Accordingly, the question becomes whether the conditional proposal itself supplies sufficiently strong evidence about the

beliefs and motives the proposal maker would have were he to do as he threatens to permit an inference that commission of this act-token would be wrongful (or that it wouldn't be).

143. Sometimes the evidentiary value of the conditional proposal arises not from the formal elements of the proposition (the particular conduct threatened, the particular advantage or concession "demanded"), but from the precise terms in which it is presented. That is true, I think, in these hypotheticals crafted by Leo Katz: "Pay me $10,000, or I will give your high-spirited, risk-addicted nineteen-year-old daughter a motorcycle for Christmas"; "Pay me $10,000, or I will hasten our ailing father's death by leaving the Catholic Church." *See* Katz, *supra* note 62, at 1567–68.

144. Sidney W. DeLong, *Blackmailers, Bribe Takers, and the Second Paradox,* 141 U. Pa. L. Rev. 1663 (1993). *See also, e.g.,* Kathryn H. Christopher, *Toward a Resolution of Blackmail's Second Paradox,* 37 Ariz. St. L.J. 1127 (2005).

145. DeLong, *supra* note 144, at 1691.

146. *Id.,* at 1692.

147. Fletcher, *supra* note 7, at 1638.

148. *See generally* James Lindgren, *The Theory, History, and Practice of the Bribery-Extortion Distinction,* 141 U. Pa. L. Rev. 1695 (1993); *see also* MPC § 240.1.

149. Donald A. Dripps, *The Priority of Politics and Procedure over Perfectionism in Penal Law, or Blackmail in Perspective,* 3 Crim. L. & Phil. 247, 249 (2009).

150. Leo Katz & James Lindgren, *Instead of a Preface,* 141 U. Pa. L. Rev. 1565, 1565 (1993).

151. Those who believe that abortion presents an easy moral question (one way or the other) can agree with this statement, though, for them, the requirement that the actor's own beliefs be reasonable will operate wholesale to rule out, or in, a great many individual cases that others would assess retail. Persons who view fetuses as persons in a morally relevant sense will conclude that a belief in abortion's permissibility will be unreasonable (almost) always; persons who view fetuses as without moral status or significance will conclude that such a belief is (almost) invariably reasonable.

152. The following discussion is drawn from Mitchell N. Berman, *Originalism and Its Discontents (Plus a Thought or Two about Abortion),* 24 Const. Comment. 383, 398–99 (2007).

153. Wesley N. Hohfeld, *Some Fundamental Legal Conceptions as Applied in Judicial Reasoning,* 23 Yale L. J. 16, 25 (1923).

154. *Id.* at 27.

155. At least not first and foremost. But the threat can have a dual aspect: it is evidence of the beliefs and motives the threatener would have were he to do as he threatens, and can also exacerbate or amplify the moral wrong because of the fear and anxiety it creates due to its capacity for repetition.

156. For example, the theorist could agree that stiffer punishment for offenses that realize harm serves expressive functions. If she is a side-constrained consequentialist about punishment, she can then tolerate differential punishment so long as the attempter is punished less than what is deserved.

157. As one philosopher of sport observed, usually "it won't do to separate winning and losing from how well one played the game, because the outcome of the game is an especially significant indicator of how well one actually played." Robert L. Simon, *Fair Play: The Ethics of Sport* 36–37 (2d ed. 2004).

158. Noteworthy contributions to the literature include Sullivan, *supra* note 97; Richard A. Epstein, *The Supreme Court, 1987 Term—Foreword: Unconstitutional Conditions, State Power, and the Limits of Consent,* 102 Harv. L. Rev. 4 (1988); Seth Kreimer, *Allocational Sanctions: The Problem of Negative Rights in a Positive State,* 132 U. Pa. L. Rev.

1293 (1984); William Van Alstyne, *The Demise of the Rights-Privilege Distinction in Constitutional Law*, 81 Harv. L. Rev. 1439 (1968); and Robert L. Hale, *Unconstitutional Conditions and Constitutional Rights*, 35 Colum. L. Rev. 321 (1935).

159. The account in text is much simplified. For the fuller argument, see Mitchell N. Berman, *Coercion without Baselines: Unconstitutional Conditions in Three Dimensions*, 90 Geo. L.J. 1 (2001).

160. For the argument that the proposition in text is entailed (or nearly so) by the very concept of a constitutional right, see *id.* at 32–36.

161. This is an essential distinction that critics of the evidentiary analysis of the unconstitutional conditions problem frequently overlook. *See, e.g.,* Samuel R. Bagenstos, *Spending Clause Litigation in the Roberts Court,* 58 Duke L.J. 345, 378–80 (2008) (erroneously stating that "Berman treats a federal funding condition as imposing a penalty whenever *the law* has the purpose of influencing the states' behavior," and inexplicably attributing to me the view that "the Constitution should prohibit states from contracting away some of their freedom of action (for a temporary period) in exchange for what they deem to be adequate consideration") (emphasis added; internal quotation and citation omitted).

162. 478 U.S. 328, 345–46 (1986).

163. A fuller examination of *Posadas* appears in Berman, *supra* note 34.

CHAPTER 4

....

THE ALLEGED ACT
REQUIREMENT IN
CRIMINAL LAW

....

DOUGLAS HUSAK

Does (Anglo-American) criminal law contain an act requirement? Virtually all textbooks and treatises answer affirmatively.[1] A negative rejoinder is given by an increasing number of criminal theorists.[2] How should we decide who is correct? The methodology used to resolve this issue is bound to be contentious and to influence the verdict we reach. For example, if repetition in textbooks and treatises qualifies as evidence for the truth of the statement repeated, there can be little doubt that criminal law *does* contain an act requirement. The assessment of *arguments,* on the other hand, would produce a different outcome entirely. In any event, one preliminary matter that should *not* be contentious is that the question itself must be clarified before we have any prospects of deciding who is correct. Thus I begin with some remarks about what it would *mean* for the criminal law to contain an act requirement. Then I move on to how this question, suitably clarified, might be approached. Given my views about *what* the question means and *how* one should approach it, I will contend that the criminal law does *not* contain an act requirement but something easily confused with it. I will conclude by speculating about why so many distinguished penal theorists mistakenly believe that criminal law contains an act requirement.

Before beginning, I want to emphasize that the determination of whether criminal liability requires an act is not of vital importance. Legal philosophers give far more attention to this issue than is warranted by its substantive significance, as the requirement (if it exists at all) plays a surprisingly small role in a theory of penal responsibility. First, in almost all cases in which liability might be thought to be objectionable because of a supposed conflict with the act requirement, some *other* less controversial doctrine could be invoked to preclude liability. For example, few real or imaginary offenses that dispense with an act would preserve the mens rea requirement. Second, statutes that seem to violate the act requirement can be redrafted to remove the incompatibility. Consider *Robinson v. California*[3]—the most famous U.S. Supreme Court case to affirm the act requirement in criminal law. In 1962, the Court invalidated a statute making it a crime "to be addicted to the use of narcotics." Needless to say, the result in *Robinson* did not retard the subsequent war on drugs; statutes were simply redrafted to prohibit the use of narcotics, with little or no change in substantive outcome.

Perhaps the main practical function of the act requirement is to bar punishment in those relatively unusual cases of strict criminal liability. Imagine, for example, that a driver lurches his wheel to the right and injures a pedestrian. The lurch was caused when he began waving his arms frantically to ward off a swarm of bees that had unexpectedly flown through the window.[4] Suppose the statute for which this driver is prosecuted does not require any culpability—not even negligence—for the injuries that are caused. Nonetheless, liability would be unjustified because of the absence of a voluntary act.[5]

I WHAT DOES IT MEAN FOR CRIMINAL LAW TO CONTAIN AN ACT REQUIREMENT?

Even those penal theorists who express no reservations about the existence of an act requirement in criminal law should acknowledge their confusion about several basic issues. First, commentators are uncertain about what acts are. Second, they are unclear about how the act requirement should be formulated. Since each of these issues is wholly unresolved, I regard the apparent consensus about the act requirement in textbooks and treatises as nothing short of remarkable. One wonders why anyone can express such confidence that the criminal law contains an act requirement when he is so confused about these two basic issues.

One might naturally suppose that attempts to formulate the act *requirement* are best postponed until we understand what acts *are*. Only then can we hope to decide whether criminal liability requires an act. After all, the act requirement requires an *act*, however this requirement is explicated. But how should we begin to grasp the nature of human action? My discussion of the concept of action will be brief, since I do not believe that philosophical inquiry into this topic is likely to be fruitful. Any analysis of action is no less controversial than the act requirement itself. I will conclude that it is unlikely that criminal law contains an act requirement, *whatever* plausible view one takes about the nature of action.

One of many reasons to be skeptical that the philosophy of action will yield clear answers is as follows. I am inclined to believe that many of the things people do are neither clearly action nor inaction but are and will remain on the borderline. Consider coughs, sneezes, burps, yawns, habitual gestures, and a host of equally familiar behaviors. Why insist that each of these events ultimately must be classified as an action or a nonaction? What further evidence do we need in order to place these events on one side of the line or the other? The concept of action, like virtually all concepts, is vague and admits of indeterminacy. Although philosophers differ about how to construe vague predicates, I assume a predicate is vague when there simply is no right answer about whether or not that predicate applies. Of course, one always can resort to stipulation. But the most informative description of the behaviors I have listed is that they resemble clear cases of action in some ways but differ from them in others. An action has been performed more or less, to some degree or another. We are bound to be disappointed if we expect a philosophical analysis of action to inform us whether the imposition of criminal liability in any of these borderline cases would be compatible with the act requirement.

Still, a brief discussion of the philosophy of action is appropriate. Philosophers generally assume that the fundamental issue is to explain the difference between moving my arm and my arm moving. John Austin famously defended the claim that human actions consist in bodily movements caused by a mental state of volition (or by what is more commonly called the will).[6] When I raise my arm, the motion of my limb is caused by a volition, but the will is not involved when my arm is raised by, say, a pulley that has been attached to it. For many years, this conception found little favor among philosophers of action who regarded the existence of the will as highly problematic.[7] More recently, however, the claim that actions are bodily movements caused by volitions has received an extended and sophisticated defense by Michael Moore.[8] His account of the *causal theory of action* contains three components: (1) each human action is partially identical to some bodily movement (and fully identical only to the sequence: volition-causing-bodily-movement); (2) the distinctive mental state causing bodily movements that are actions is volition (a kind of intention not reducible to beliefs, desires, or belief/desire sets); and (3) the relationship between volitions and the bodily movements that are their objects is a causal one, in the standard sense of "cause" (that is, no sui generis "agent-causation" is allowed).[9] According to Moore, volitions are not mysterious; they are functional states that mediate between intentional mental states like beliefs and desires and the bodily movements they cause.

Some philosophers have challenged Moore's account of action.[10] For present purposes, however, the greatest difficulty with this account is not its philosophical adequacy. Instead, we need to inquire how this conception of action could hope to preserve the truth of the act requirement in criminal law. Notice that volitions seem just as causally efficacious in many cases in which people do *not* move their bodies. Consider, for example, the impressive feats of the guards at Buckingham Palace.[11] Although tourists regularly taunt and tease them, these highly disciplined soldiers refuse to budge. Remarkable strength of will is needed to resist the impulse to move. Only an extraordinarily generous interpretation of bodily movements would enable us to say that these guards move their bodies.[12] If we had reason to blame them or to impose liability for their conduct—as would be warranted if the queen were under attack–the supposition that the guards do not move and thus do not *act* (according to the foregoing conception) seems utterly beside the point.

If we employ a conception of action that requires bodily motion, cases involving the absence of motion will seem deviant and problematic. Perhaps we should say that the stoic guards in the above example *do* act, and that some acts do not involve bodily movements.[13] As far as I can see, both philosophical analysis and ordinary language are ambivalent about this matter, and I know of no considerations that are decisive on one side or the other. Rather than struggle with controversial issues in the philosophy of action, I propose to inquire whether *any* plausible conception of action can hope to preserve the truth of the act requirement in criminal law. To answer this question, we need to decide how to understand the act *requirement*. I begin with the assumption that any sensible interpretation of the act requirement should construe it as both descriptive and normative. It purports to accurately describe the great bulk of existing criminal law while recognizing the possibility of a handful of exceptions. In other words, an act is somehow present in all or virtually all cases in which criminal liability is imposed. Possible exceptions to this descriptive generalization, however, are suspect. On closer examination, such cases either are not exceptions at all or involve an illegitimate use of the criminal sanction. The basis for this suspicion is that the act requirement is normative as well as descriptive: it simultaneously expresses a principle to which impositions of criminal liability *ought* to conform in order to be justifiable. At the very least, genuine departures from this requirement, if they are permissible at all, need a special defense. Beyond this single point of agreement, the issue becomes cloudy.

The source of the problem, as we will see, is that liability often is imposed for what almost certainly is *not* an act. If so, perhaps it is mistaken to posit the existence of an act *requirement* at all. R. A. Duff proposes to replace an *act requirement* with an *action presumption*,[14] but I doubt that this suggestion is very helpful. A presumption, as I construe it, differs from a rule in that it is capable of being overridden by a more weighty consideration. On at least some occasions in which liability is imposed for the failure to act, however, it seems misguided to suppose that the act requirement exerts any normative force that needs to be outweighed. The case in favor of imposing liability for the failure to file a tax return, for example, does not depend on producing arguments capable of overriding any residual weight the act presumption exerts. The judgment that no act is involved provides no reason to resist liability.

What *are* the possible exceptions to the act requirement? In other words, what would amount to a *violation* of the act requirement? To answer this question, we need to examine the normative function or role that the act requirement plays in a theory of penal liability. This alleged requirement has been invoked to reject or to cast suspicion on (real or imaginary) attempts to impose liability in various kinds of case. Four such categories of case are prominent. The act requirement has been invoked to question or reject liability for (1) *omissions*; (2) *nonvoluntary actions*; (3) *status of states*; and (4) *thoughts*. When liability has been proposed for any of these four categories, courts and commentators are bound to object that liability would violate the act requirement. Punishment is said to be objectionable *because* it would violate the act requirement.

In order to decide whether liability in any of these kinds of case *would* violate the act requirement, we need to be clear about how that requirement should be understood.[15] In what follows, I will consider two possible formulations of the act requirement. Unfortunately, neither formulation will turn out to be unproblematic. Obviously, additional interpretations might be offered.[16] Since I am skeptical that a good normative argument supports the act requirement and will conclude that it probably should be rejected in favor of a competitive principle, I will not struggle to provide alternative formulations. I encourage commentators who are more persuaded that criminal law contains an act requirement to devise a version that is preferable to those I consider below.

The first formulation of the act requirement is the most simple: criminal liability is and ought to be imposed *for* an act. In other words, nothing but an act is or ought to be the proper *object* of criminal liability. This formulation, although certainly straightforward, is almost certainly false—both descriptively and normatively. Often, the object of criminal liability is *not* an act. Crimes of possession provide the most obvious (but not the only) counterexamples. State penal codes include over one hundred possession offenses, ranging from minor violations to the most serious category of felony punishable by life imprisonment. These include possession of a toy gun, graffiti instruments, public benefit cards, credit card embossing machines, gambling records, usurious loan records, obscene materials, eavesdropping devices, noxious materials, and a host of others.[17] Several of these offenses, of course, are enormously controversial on normative grounds.[18] Still, many crimes of possession—such as that proscribing the private possession of nuclear weapons—seem clearly justifiable. In any event, no one should say that the state of possessing something—like the coins in my pocket—*is* an act. If criminal liability ever is imposed *for* the state of possession—as seems clear—it follows that criminal liability is not always imposed for an act. If the act requirement should be construed to hold that only acts are and ought to be the objects of liability, it is unquestionably false both descriptively and normatively.

The act requirement must be given a different formulation if it is to be preserved. The difficulty, of course, is to formulate the act requirement so that it is plausible both descriptively and normatively. This much is common to any suitable candidate: *some* act is required for criminal liability. But whatever the act required by the act requirement is, it need not be that *for* which liability is imposed. What, then, *is* the relation between the act and the object of liability that will satisfy the act requirement? The act and the object of liability must stand in *some* appropriate relation, but what is the nature of this elusive relation? I will call possible answers to this question attempts to specify the *appropriate relation* between the act and the object of liability that must obtain in order to satisfy the act requirement. Unless this appropriate relation can be specified with some degree of precision, I daresay that commentators will not know what they are talking about when they affirm (or deny) that criminal law includes an act requirement.

What might this appropriate relation be? A clue may be derived from the way possession offenses are treated within the Model Penal Code. Possession offenses are not regarded as counterexamples to the act requirement; they are only counter-examples to the supposition that the act requirement should be construed to hold that acts must be the objects of liability. The Code provides that "possession is an act...if the possessor knowingly procured or received the thing possessed or was aware of his control thereof for a sufficient period to have been able to terminate his possession."[19] Taken literally, this provision is nonsense. The state of affairs in which Smith possesses his socks is not an act, and this state is not magically transformed into an act simply because he is "aware of his control thereof for a sufficient period." I have not been performing continuing acts of possessing each of the shirts in my closet since the moment I knowingly acquired them several years ago. No state of mind or passage of time can perform the alchemy needed to convert nonacts into acts. Thus I conclude that the foregoing provision from the Model Penal Code should not be construed literally. It should not really be interpreted to specify the conditions under which the state of possession *is* or *becomes* an act. Instead, this provision should be interpreted to specify the conditions under which the state of possession becomes compatible with the *act requirement*. If I am correct, the treat-ment of possession offenses in the Model Penal Code suggests a second and more plausible candidate for how the act requirement should be formulated.

In order to reconcile the act requirement with the imposition of liability for nonacts such as possession, the Model Penal Code contains what I take to be a sec-ond formulation of the act requirement: "A person is not guilty of an offense unless his liability is based on conduct that includes a voluntary act or the omission to perform an act of which he is physically capable."[20] This second formulation of the act requirement differs from the first, deleting the "for" relation between the required act and the object of liability that is central to the earlier account. In its place, the Code substitutes the "based on" and "includes" relations. Thus this formulation answers our difficult question by specifying the appropriate relation between the act and the object of liability as the *based on* and the *includes* relations. But exactly what is meant by *basing* liability on conduct that *includes* a voluntary act? These terms are notoriously cryptic, and questions abound. Are these two relations identi-cal or different? That is, can liability be based on a voluntary act that is not included in it? Or does every case in which liability is based on a voluntary act include that act? This version of the act requirement will remain mysterious unless these rela-tions can be clarified.

Notice that the Code does not say that liability must be based on a voluntary act, that is, based on conduct that *is* a voluntary act. Liability need only be based on conduct that *includes* a voluntary act. How should we understand this "includes" relation? In some contexts, this relation is straightforward. Many acts are complex composites of smaller acts and omissions that contain them. Consider a given fight between two boxers: for example, the memorable "rumble in the jungle" heavy-weight championship between Mohammad Ali and George Foreman in Zaire on October 30, 1974. Clearly, the act referred to as "the rumble in the jungle" includes innumerable actions and omissions within its scope. The fighters weaved, bobbed, punched, ducked, rested, and the like. The sense in which the act of fighting includes these acts and omissions is both temporal and spatial. Ali and Foreman ducked *while* they were fighting; their weaving occurred *where* they were fighting. Perhaps the "includes" relation in the Model Penal Code's formulation of the act requirement should be understood similarly—in the same temporal and spatial sense in which the act referred to as "the rumble in the jungle" includes both the act of punching and the omission of resting.

If we accept that criminal liability need only be imposed for conduct that includes a voluntary act, and explicate the sense of *includes* as both spatial and temporal, we will be able to recognize what is unsound about the following argument. Suppose a driver spots a pedestrian she would like to injure crossing the road in front of her. She fails to apply her brakes, and her car runs over the victim. When prosecuted, she alleges that her failure to apply the brakes is an omission, and she had no duty to the pedestrian not to injure him by omission. Obviously, this argument is silly. But what exactly is silly about it? The answer is not that the failure to apply the brakes must be categorized as an action. Even if construed as an omission, the failure to apply the brakes occurred within the larger complex act of driving. Like a prizefight, the act of driving includes many acts and omissions within its temporal and spatial scope. A driver who injures a pedestrian in the course of the complex act of driving cannot defend herself on the ground that the injury was caused by an omission.

As the Commentaries make relatively clear, the main point of this second formulation of the act requirement—which does not require that liability be imposed *for* an act but requires only that liability be imposed for conduct that *includes* a voluntary act—is to allow punishment in what might be called "culpability-in-causing" cases: situations in which a nonvoluntary act is preceded by a culpable voluntary act that causes it.[21] Consider, for example, a defendant whose car swerves out of control and kills several pedestrians during an epileptic seizure.[22] Unquestionably, the seizure itself is involuntary. Still, liability under a negligent driving statute might be reconciled with this second formulation of the act requirement if the offense is construed to *include* the prior failure to take prescribed medication that would have prevented the subsequent seizure. Respondents report varying intuitions about whether and under what conditions liability is appropriate in such cases. Some go so far as to doubt that these cases admit of a principled solution at all,[23] especially when a statute imposes strict liability for the injury.[24] For present purposes, however, the important point is that the latter sense of "includes" is almost certainly *not* the sense involved in the foregoing prizefight or brake cases. Culpability-in-causing cases often invoke a sense of *includes* that is neither temporal nor spatial. Unlike the fighters or the driver who fails to brake, the epileptic omits to take his medication *prior* to the time he begins to drive, and he omits to take his medication at a place *other than* where he is driving. To impose liability on the epileptic, the sense of "includes" in this formulation of the act requirement must be construed differently from the familiar sense in which the act of fighting includes the acts of punching and the omission of resting, or the act of driving includes the acts of steering and the omission of failing to brake. I admit that I have little idea how to explicate this different (nontemporal and nonspatial) sense of "includes,"[25] and thus I do not understand how the act of driving *includes* the failure to take medication.

Although the "includes" relation is unclear, what about the "based on" relation that must obtain between liability and act to satisfy this second formulation of the act requirement? Regardless of how this relation might be construed in other contexts, it should help to explain how the drafters of the Code believed that crimes of possession could be reconciled with the act requirement. As we have seen, when liability is imposed for a state of possession, the act requirement is said to be satisfied when the possessor either (1) knowingly procured or received the thing possessed, or (2) was aware of his control thereof for a sufficient period of time to have been able to terminate his possession. Let me hazard an interpretation. The possession section contains two disjunctive clauses, each describing an act on which liability for possession might be based. The first of these clauses, (1), refers to procurement or receipt. Procurement and receipt, I assume, are typically acts. When either of these acts is performed knowingly, it provides the act on which liability for possession can be based. Liability is *for* possession, which is *not* an act, but such liability satisfies the act requirement nonetheless, because it is *based on* something that *is* an act: procurement or receipt. So far, my interpretation seems sensible.[26] Matters become a bit more complex, however, when we turn to the second clause in the possession section—the alternative description of the act on which liability for a crime of possession might be based. Liability for a crime of possession may satisfy the act requirement when (2) the possessor is aware of his control over the thing possessed for a sufficient period of time to be able to terminate his possession. The referent of this latter clause—the failure to terminate possession—is, I assume, an omission. When this omission takes place over a suitable period of time, with awareness of the nature of the thing possessed, it constitutes the omission on which liability for possession can be based. Again, liability is *for* possession, which is *not* an act, but such liability satisfies the act requirement nonetheless, because it is *based on* prior conduct (that is, an act or omission).[27]

Of course, we still need to know *why* the particular acts or omissions described by the Code provide the conduct on which liability for a crime of possession may be based. The Code simply stipulates that an act of knowingly procuring a thing, for example, stands in the appropriate relation to the state of possession to render liability for the latter compatible with the act requirement. But why should this be so? An example (or even two examples) of when the requirement is satisfied is a far cry from a general analysis of the *based on* relation. We still lack an understanding of this relation, and thus of the act requirement itself. Let me provide two examples to illustrate what I take to be the central difficulty.

Suppose the state enacted a statute that punished a defendant for a given evil thought—say, the wish that the Statue of Liberty should be destroyed by a terrorist attack. This statute, I assume, would violate the act requirement as anyone purports to construe it. Suppose, however, that a clever commentator argued that the statute did not violate the act requirement after all. Admittedly, the object of liability is a thought, which is not an act. But the act requirement is not violated by this statute, according to this train of thought, because liability could be *based on* conduct that *is* an act. Liability might be based on participation in a terrorist training program in which the thought occurred, for example—which unquestionably is a voluntary act the person had the power not to perform. I assume that the argument of this commentator is unsound. But what exactly is wrong with it? The only way to demonstrate the error in his reasoning is to explicate the *based on* relation to show that the act of participating in a terrorist training program at which the thought occurred does not stand in the appropriate relation to the object of liability (the thought itself) to satisfy the act requirement. Without an explication of the *based on* relation, the act requirement may be compatible with punishment for thoughts.

A second example reveals a related difficulty. Consider two persons—Dave and Eric—in possession of cocaine. Dave's acquisition of cocaine was performed knowingly; Eric's was not. Dave deliberately bought a substance he knew to be cocaine; Eric bought a substance he reasonably believed to be sugar, which, much to his surprise, turned out to be cocaine. The state seeks to impose liability for possessing a controlled substance on both Dave and Eric, and the question is whether liability would be compatible with the act requirement. I assume that the second formulation of the act requirement would allow liability to be imposed on Dave, but not on Eric. As we have seen, possession offenses are said to be compatible with the act requirement when the possessor knowingly procured or received the thing possessed. Despite the important difference between Dave and Eric, however, the mode of acquisition performed by Eric is no less of an act than that performed by Dave. *Both* Dave and Eric came in possession of cocaine by the act of buying it. Clearly, it would be unfair to impose liability on Eric. But our willingness to punish Dave but not Eric has nothing to do with a difference in whether they acted. The obvious objection to punishing Eric is his lack of culpability, not his lack of action. But what does the presence or absence of culpability have to do with the presence or absence of action? Does anyone believe that a purchase can become an act only when the purchaser knows what he is purchasing? In short, the Model Penal Code provision governing possession is really about culpability and does not tell us *why* liability satisfies the *act* requirement when it is based on some acts but not on others. Thus I do not believe that the Model Penal Code provision about possession goes very far in explaining the nature of the appropriate relation that must obtain between the object of liability and the act that is needed to satisfy the act requirement. It simply offers the name of a relation—the "based on" relation—without telling us what it means or how it should be interpreted.

Return to (2), the second disjunctive clause in the Code's possession provision. This clause is a bit more complex because it makes clear that liability for a crime of possession need *not* be based on an act in order to satisfy the act requirement. The act requirement may be satisfied when liability for a crime of possession is based on an *omission*. According to the Code, an omission is not an act, but a "failure to act."[28] Thus it is somewhat misleading to say that the Model Penal Code contains an *act requirement*. It is more accurate to say that the Model Penal Code contains a *conduct* requirement, that is, an *act or omission requirement*. Liability for a crime of possession satisfies the conduct requirement when it is based on an act or omission. Although I believe this conclusion is of crucial importance for any theorist who hopes to gain a deep understanding of the nature of the (so-called) act requirement, I will neglect it in my subsequent discussions. I will continue to suppose we are trying to formulate and justify something that should simply be called the *act requirement*.

I have made only modest progress in suggesting how to understand the concept of action and how to formulate the act requirement in criminal law. Perhaps it is rash to move to normative controversies when so many basic issues remain unsettled. Nonetheless, I propose to do so. Perhaps an investigation of the normative issues surrounding the act requirement will assist us in understanding these unresolved issues. In other words, we might gain insight into how to construe the act requirement by attending to the reasons for believing that the criminal law ought to include it.

II Is the Act Requirement Defensible?

Despite the many foregoing confusions, theorists who accept the act requirement ultimately must *defend* it, that is, support the normative proposition that the criminal law *should* include it. They must show why we should be critical of (real or imaginary) cases in which penal liability is imposed in violation of the act requirement. If I am correct about (some or all of) the kinds of liability that would violate this requirement—liability for omissions, nonvoluntary conduct, status offenses, or thoughts—the normative task is to explain why liability in (some or all of) these categories is (or would be) unjustified.

This task is formidable. Return to the case of omissions. If there is anything that is morally problematic about liability for an omission—as many theorists believe—it is doubtful that the basis of this problem is that omissions are not acts. It is more plausible to suppose that liability for omissions is worrisome on some other ground—because, for example, it typically involves more onerous infringements of liberty, leaving persons with fewer options than cases in which liability is imposed for an act. In any event, there may be *no* single principle that underlies our reservations about the several kinds of liability that seem inconsistent with the act requirement. Although the search for a single unifying principle may be fruitless, in what follows I will suggest that the justification that appears to underlie the act requirement actually supports a competitive principle—an alternative that is more defensible than the act requirement. The normative work thought to be done by the act requirement may be accomplished more effectively by supposing that criminal liability requires *control*. Or so I will argue.

Why do so many theorists accept the act requirement? To his credit, Michael Moore is among those few criminal theorists who attempt to explain "why those, and only those, who act are deserving of punishment."[29] I will examine his argument closely, since efforts to defend the act requirement are few and far between. Moore's reply begins by contrasting two "views of morality." He describes the first as the "classical view" or the "virtue-based conception."[30] According to this view, "morality is primarily concerned with the virtue of individual persons."[31] Actions are important on this conception, but "only as subsidiary means of promoting persons' virtue."[32] Moore describes the second view of morality as the "nonclassical" view.[33] According to this view, "morality is fundamentally a matter of norms. Such norms do not have as their subjects virtuous character."[34] Instead, these norms prohibit or permit actions. In contrast to the classical conception, "the sufficiency of action for responsibility falls out easily from this nonclassical view of morality."[35]

Moore invokes this distinction between these two "views of morality" to conclude that "desert must be such that we deserve punishment for violations of morality's norms of obligation, but we do not deserve punishment for violation of morality's ideals of virtuous character."[36] His argument, as I understand it, has two parts—one negative, the other positive. The negative part of his argument attempts to show that persons do *not* deserve punishment under the classical view. Moore contends that although we "rightly judge people morally by their characters in non-legal contexts,"[37] the *law* should not punish persons pursuant to such judgments. He maintains that

> no one deserves to be punished for lacking grace—or for lacking any other virtue. Those who lack virtue, but do not exhibit it through bad actions, have done no wrong. They have wronged themselves, by being less worthy persons than they should be; but they have not wronged anyone else.... Without wrongdoing, what is there to exact retribution for?[38]

Thus Moore concludes that a person should *not* be punished *for* her lack of virtue or bad *character*. But why *should* a person be punished *for* her bad *acts*? Moore's positive argument is that actions alone exhibit the feature in virtue of which persons deserve to be punished. That feature is *choice*. According to Moore, "it is the choice to do evil on a particular occasion that makes a person morally responsible for any wrong that flows from such choice, irrespective of whether such choice expresses bad character or not."[39] Surely, however, this dichotomy is incomplete. The claim that punishment is justifiable for acts is not made more plausible by discrediting the claim that punishment is justifiable for the lack of virtue. These are not the only two alternatives; bad acts and the lack of virtue do not exhaust the many possible objects of moral evaluation. Moral philosophers might evaluate a wide range of diverse objects and states of affairs. Perhaps persons deserve punishment for a number of such objects of evaluation, even if they do not merit liability for the lack of virtue.

Moreover, Moore's negative argument for concluding that punishment cannot be deserved for nonacts (in particular, the lack of virtue) appears circular. He contends that those who lack virtue but do not exhibit it through bad actions do not deserve punishment because "they have done no wrong."[40] Of course, persons who have not performed a bad action have *done* no wrong. Since they have not acted, they cannot have engaged in wrong*doing*. But why should criminal liability require a wrong *doing*? Perhaps Moore's reply is that only a *doing* can *be* wrong. Or perhaps his answer is that only a *doing* can *wrong* anyone. On Moore's own account, however, these replies cannot be correct. Moore allows that one can wrong *oneself* without acting,[41] even though he believes that one cannot wrong anyone *else* without acting. Apparently, then, nondoings *can* be wrong, and one *can* wrong someone without acting. Moore contends only that one cannot wrong *others* without acting. Why this should be so is mysterious. I see no reason to believe that the conditions for wronging others are unlike the conditions for wronging oneself. Thus I find no noncircular reason to conclude that criminal liability requires a wrong *doing*. If other states of a person can be wrongful, why should criminal liability be withheld because these other states do not consist in a *doing*?[42]

In the absence of alternative attempts to defend the act requirement, we might begin our normative inquiry by starting with propositions that all commentators should concede. The act requirement is designed to serve as a constraint on justified impositions of penal liability. It serves this function because it purports to confine the punitive sanction to those matters over which it is fair to hold persons responsible. The challenge for commentators is to specify the necessary conditions for criminal responsibility. This is a tall order. I assume that a defendant is not responsible for criminal conduct unless it bears the appropriate connection to his practical agency. Thus Vincent Chiao rejects the act requirement in favor of what he calls the "practical agency condition."[43] I believe, however, that his principle merely restates the problem rather than solves it. Exactly how must practical agency be implicated in criminal behavior in order for penal responsibility to be warranted? What is important to our theory of criminal responsibility, I submit, is not action itself but something that actions typically presuppose. The identity of this elusive "something" must relate to practical agency, our ability as autonomous beings to guide our behavior by reasons.

As we have seen, Moore identifies *choice* as the crucial feature that separates appropriate from inappropriate objects of deserved punishment and liability. Why does he believe that choice is so fundamental, and that blame and retribution are unjustifiable for states of affairs that are *not* objects of choice? The answer, I believe, is that persons typically have *control* over their choices, and persons are responsible and deserve punishment only for those states of affairs over which they have control. I submit that the absence of control, and not the absence of action, establishes the outer boundary of deserved punishment and responsibility. I claim, in other words, that what I will call the *control requirement* should be substituted for the act requirement as a necessary condition of criminal liability and deserved punishment.[44]

If I am correct that control is crucial for criminal responsibility, it is easy to see why we might be led (or misled) into believing that an act should be required.

Paradigmatically, our acts are under our control, while our nonacts are not under our control. The question of whether our theory of criminal responsibility should lead us to abandon the act requirement in favor of the control requirement is best decided by attending to two types of possible cases:

> *Type A:* Cases in which liability is imposed for something over which the agent has control, even though it is not an act.
> *Type B:* Cases in which liability is imposed for an act, even though the agent lacks control over it.

If criminal responsibility is justifiable in type (A) but not in (B), we are entitled to conclude that a control requirement does a better job promoting the normative function of the act requirement than the act requirement itself. Unfortunately, my suggestion will prove hard to confirm. Since both the concepts of action and that of control are vague and imprecise, it will not be easy to describe cases that clearly qualify as examples of type (A) or (B). We should not expect a definitive demonstration of the superiority (or inferiority) of the control requirement to the act requirement. Nonetheless, I hope the following considerations are suggestive.

Let us begin with type (B). Examples are (real or imaginary) cases in which liability is imposed for a nonvoluntary act. An action is nonvoluntary, it seems plausible to believe, when an agent lacks control over it. The performance of such an act is not guided by reasons and thus does not bear the appropriate relation to practical agency to make a defendant responsible for it. If nonvoluntary acts exist, the voluntariness and act requirements must be distinct. This view *appears* to conform to that adopted in the Model Penal Code. The Code seemingly requires an action and then, as a distinct condition, requires that that action be voluntary. An *act* is defined as a "bodily movement whether voluntary or involuntary,"[45] and a separate provision requires voluntariness.[46] The Code does not *define* voluntariness or nonvoluntariness; it simply lists several examples of nonvoluntary actions, characterizing all remaining cases as those that are "not a product of the effort or determination of the actor."[47] Thus the Code appears to contemplate the existence of nonvoluntary actions; voluntariness is an independent condition added to the act requirement. But this view of the relation between the act and voluntariness requirements is problematic, even as an interpretation of the Code. Suppose that James pushes Steve's body into contact with Carl, causing Carl to fall off a cliff and die. Of course, the imposition of liability on Steve would violate the voluntariness requirement. Admittedly would the imposition of liability violate the act requirement as well, as something independent of the voluntariness requirement? At first blush, the answer would seem to be no. According to the Code's definition of action, it would appear that Steve has acted. After all, there has been a bodily movement, and the body that has moved is that of Steve. Yet it seems wrong to say that Steve has acted (albeit nonvoluntarily). Steve's body has moved, but Steve has not moved his body. If Steve's *acts* are those events in which not only Steve's body moves but also Steve moves his body, then Steve has not acted at all. Thus, even the Code might be interpreted so that the voluntariness requirement is redundant with the act requirement. Although the locution "nonvoluntary action" is not transparently incoherent, I am inclined to believe that so-called nonvoluntary actions are not actions at all.[48] If I am correct, real or imaginary cases in which liability is imposed for a nonvoluntary action cannot be examples of type (B)—because no such actions exist.

Suppose, however, that nonvoluntary actions *do* exist. As I have said, it seems plausible to suppose that agents lack control over such actions. The reason to deny that defendants should be liable for their nonvoluntary actions is the absence of control. The lack of control explains why liability should not be imposed when defendants lose control over their vehicles in warding off a swarm of bees—the kind of case with which I began. If control somehow were present despite the absence of voluntariness, however, our intuitive resistance to liability would evaporate. Control might be present although voluntariness is absent when defendants are able to exercise *indirect* rather than *direct* control over what they do. We exercise *indirect* control over what we do when we cause ourselves to perform or not to perform some action by performing some *other* action. I might prevent myself from sleepwalking, for example, by tying myself to the bed. The realization that we exert indirect control over some of our actions helps to explain our intuitions in the "culpability-in-causing" cases to which I referred: those situations in which a nonvoluntary act is preceded by a culpable voluntary act that causes it. When an agent performs a voluntary act, intending, knowing, or consciously disregarding the risk that it will cause her to perform a subsequent nonvoluntary criminal act, we are likely to allow liability because the criminal act was under the control of the agent. It is reasonable to expect her to refrain from performing the prior voluntary act that caused her to perform the subsequent nonvoluntary criminal act—and to punish her if she fails to refrain.

Clear type (B) cases are very hard to find; perhaps none exist. What about type (A)? Perhaps some criminal *omissions* are examples of type (A): liability is imposed for something over which the agent has control, but is not an act. Return to the example of the guards at Buckingham Palace. I am unsure whether they act. Perhaps such examples should be treated as borderline cases—cases in which reasonable minds may disagree about whether an action has been performed. My point, however, is that the presence or absence of action seems irrelevant to the fairness of imposing liability. Trying to resolve these cases by deciding whether the defendant has *acted* is misguided. The presence or absence of control, however, seems crucial.[49] As long as the guards exercise control over their failure to move, liability should not be precluded by whatever normative considerations underlie the act requirement. The same analysis applies to bystanders who fail to rescue their victims. If the bystander has no control over whether a child drowns, why would anyone think it fair to convict him for the death? A consequence one cannot control is an inappropriate basis of liability.[50] Control without action, however, is seemingly a fair basis for punishment. If we do not want to hold bystanders criminally responsible when they have control over the deaths of drowning children, we will need to appeal to a different principle from that which underlies the act requirement.

Perhaps omissions are not the best examples of type (A); a better candidate is presented by R. A. Duff. He invites us to imagine a case in which "I am standing, innocently, by your valuable vase. A child playfully grabs my arm, and moves it toward the vase in such a way that it will clearly knock the vase over. I could easily resist the child, and withdraw my arm, but do not; the vase is broken."[51] Would liability for the offense of criminal damage be compatible with the act requirement? Here again we have a borderline case of action; there may be no right answer to whether the breaking of the vase is accomplished by my act. The important point, however, is that the determination of whether I act in this scenario seems irrelevant to the justifiability of convicting me of the offense. The crucial question is not whether I did or did not *act*, but whether I had or lacked the degree of control over the breaking of the vase that would make it fair to be held responsible for it. If resisting the child is easy, as Duff stipulates, I see no reason not to impose responsibility for breaking the vase. At the very least, liability in this case should not be regarded as problematic because of something called the act requirement. Instead, liability is unproblematic because the values that underlie the (so-called) act requirement are served. Liability is consistent with ensuring that people are convicted only for events (in this case, the breaking of the vase) over which they are responsible, and they are responsible for these events that bear the appropriate relation to their practical reasoning when they have a sufficient degree of control over their occurrence.

But several central questions remain, and I do not pretend to have precise answers to them. First, what exactly *is* control? Second, control admits of degrees. *What* amount of control over a state of affairs is sufficient to satisfy the requirement I am tempted to substitute for the act requirement? Third, how exactly should the control requirement be formulated? In particular, can some version provide a plausible solution to the notorious culpability-in–causing cases? Is it sensible simply to ask whether there ever was a time in which the defendant had sufficient control over the occurrence of the harm (e.g., the deaths of the pedestrians) that he should have taken prior steps to prevent it (e.g., by taking medication to prevent a seizure) so that it is fair to hold him liable when he fails to do so? Notice that this question does not ask for a factual determination. Whatever may be true of the concept of action, the question of whether the agent had control over a state of affairs is not solely empirical. Issues surrounding control are largely normative. It may have been misguided to think that a purely factual concept like action could play the role in a theory of criminal responsibility typically assigned to the act requirement.

Beyond this simple observation, however, I will not hazard answers to these difficult questions. Admittedly, nothing is achieved merely by replacing one set of mysteries with another. Like many philosophers, I must be content with the modest progress that is made by asking the right questions. I conclude that we should not be confident about whether criminal law contains an act requirement unless and until we gain a better understanding of the basic issues I have discussed here. Once we gain this understanding, we may find that an alternative requirement—the requirement of *control* or possibly some other dimension of practical agency—does a better job serving the normative objectives of the act requirement than the act requirement itself.

NOTES

1. Few American commentators express reservations about the act requirement. See, for example, Michael Moore, *Act and Crime* (Oxford: Clarendon Press, 1993); Paul Robinson, *Fundamentals of Criminal Law* (Boston: Little, Brown, 2d ed., 1995), p. 250; Wayne LaFave, *Criminal Law* (St. Paul: West, 3d ed., 2000), pp. 195–202; and Joshua Dressler, *Understanding Criminal Law* (New York: Lexis, 4th ed., 2006), p. 93.

2. See Douglas Husak, *The Philosophy of Criminal Law* (Totowa, N.J.: Rowman & Littlefield, 1987); A. P. Simester, "On the So-Called Requirement for Voluntary Action," 1 *Buffalo Criminal Law Review* 403 (1998); Antony Duff, "Action, the Act Requirement and Criminal Liability," in J. Hyman and H. C. Stewart, eds., Agency and Action (Cambridge: Cambridge University Press, 2004), p. 69.

3. 370 U.S. 660 (1962).

4. See *Hill v. Baxter* [1958] 1 Q.B. 277.

5. This result is controversial as a matter of positive law if traffic offenses are construed as "violations" to which the requirement of a voluntary act does not apply. See the discussion in Dressler, *supra*, note 1, pp. 108–109.

6. John Austin, *Lectures on Jurisprudence* (R. Campbell ed., 1979), p. 424.

7. Devastating criticisms were thought to be provided by H.L.A. Hart: "Acts of Will and Responsibility," in H. L. A. Hart, *Punishment and Responsibility* (Oxford: Oxford University Press).

8. Michael Moore, *Act and Crime: The Philosophy of Action and Its Implications for Criminal Law* (Oxford: Clarendon Press, 1993).

9. Michael Moore: "Renewed Questions about the Causal Theory of Action," in Andrei Buckareff and Jesus Aguilar, eds., *Causing Human Action: New Perspectives on the Causal Theory of Action* (Cambridge, Mass.: MIT Press, Bradford Book, 2010).

10. See the symposia in 142 *University of Pennsylvania Law Review* (1994), pp. 1443–1890.

11. See George Fletcher, "On the Moral Irrelevance of Bodily Movements," 142 *University of Pennsylvania Law Review*, 1443, 1445 (1994).

12. See, for example, the suggestion in Donald Davidson, *Essays on Actions and Events* (Oxford: Oxford University Press, 1980), p. 49.

13. See Duff, *supra*, note 2.

14. *Id.* To be fair, the actions that Duff believes criminal law should presume are "not of the kind that legal theorists have sought, but action as an exercise of our capacity for rational agency" (102). Thus Duff's position is very similar to the conclusion I defend here.

15. For further thoughts, see Douglas Husak, "Rethinking the Act Requirement," 28 *Cardozo Law Review* 2437 (2007).

16. According to one commentator, the requirement should be formulated as follows: "A person is not guilty of an offense unless her conduct, which must include a voluntary act, and which must be accompanied by a culpable state of mind (the mens rea of the offense), is the actual and proximate cause of the social harm, as proscribed by the offense." Dressler, *supra*, note 1, p. 101.

17. See Markus Dirk Dubber, "The Possession Paradigm: The Special Part and the Police Power Model of the Criminal Process," in Antony Duff and Stuart Green, eds.,

Defining Crimes: Essays on the Special Part of the Criminal Law (Oxford: Oxford University Press, 2005), pp. 91, 96–97.

18. Drug offenses are perhaps the most controversial examples. See Douglas Husak, *Overcriminalization* (New York: Oxford University Press, 2008).

19. § 2.01(4).

20. § 2.01(1).

21. See Paul Robinson: "Causing the Conditions of One's Own Defense: A Study of the Limits of Theory in Criminal Law Doctrine," 71 *Virginia Law Review* 1 (1985).

22. The most celebrated such case, applying a statute proscribing the negligent operation of a vehicle resulting in death, is *People v. Decina*, 138 N.E.2d 799 (1956). A closely related but slightly distinct problem arises in trying to hold Dr. Jekyll liable for the subsequent nonvoluntary homicidal acts of the monstrous Mr. Hyde.

23. See Mark Kelman: "Interpretive Reconstruction in the Substantive Criminal Law," 33 *Stanford Law Review* 591 (1981).

24. Efforts to base liability on a prior *culpable* act strike some theorists as especially problematic when the offense is an instance of strict liability. See Larry Alexander, "Reconsidering the Relation among Voluntary Acts, Strict Liability, and Negligence in Criminal Law," 7 *Social Philosophy and Policy* 84 (1990).

25. For further thoughts about this question, see Douglas Husak and Brian McLaughlin, "Time Frames, Voluntary Acts, and Strict Liability," 12 *Law and Philosophy* 95 (1992).

26. Still, one should wonder why the act requirement is satisfied when the act of procurement is performed culpably (in this case, knowingly) but not otherwise. What does culpability have to do with action?

27. *Conduct* is the generic term the Code employs for acts and omissions. See § 1.13(5).

28. § 1.13(4).

29. Moore, *supra*, note 1, p. 48.

30. *Id.*, pp. 49–50.

31. *Id.*, p. 49.

32. *Id.*, pp. 49–50.

33. *Id.*, p. 51.

34. *Id.*, p. 51.

35. *Id.*, p. 51.

36. *Id.*, p. 53. Notice Moore's use of the "for" relation here and elsewhere.

37. *Id.*, p. 54.

38. *Id.*, p. 53.

39. *Id.*, p. 51.

40. *Id.*, p. 53.

41. *Id.*, p. 53.

42. I explore Moore's views further in Douglas Husak, "The Relevance of the Concept of Action to the Criminal Law: Michael Moore's *Act and Crime*," 6 *Criminal Law Forum* 327 (1995).

43. Vincent Chiao, "Action and Agency in the Criminal Law," 15 *Legal Theory* 1 (2009).

44. See Douglas Husak: "Does Criminal Liability Require an Act?," in R. A. Duff, ed., *Philosophy and the Criminal Law: Principle and Critique* (Cambridge: Cambridge University Press, 1998), p. 60.

45. § 1.13(2).

46. § 2.01(2).

47. § 2.01(2)(d).

48. Some courts have held that an involuntary act "is in reality no act at all. It is merely a physical event." *State v. Utter,* 479 P.2d 946, 950 (1971). For scholarly support, see Jeffrie Murphy, "Involuntary Acts and Criminal Liability," in his *Retribution, Justice, and Therapy* (Dordrecht: Reidel, 1979), p. 116.

49. In a class of cases popularly known as Frankfurt-style counterexamples, Harry Frankfurt famously argues that a person may do x freely (and thus be responsible for x-ing) even though he lacked the ability to do otherwise. I take no position on the principle of alternative possibilities or whether Frankfurt-style counterexamples show that moral responsibility for x does not imply the ability to do otherwise.

50. Some theorists believe that consequences are *never* under the control of agents, and thus hold that the occurrence or nonoccurrence of harm should be irrelevant to criminal responsibility. I believe agents generally *do* have control over the consequences of their actions, although I will not defend that claim here. For an impressive defense, see Michael S. Moore, *Causation and Responsibility* (New York: Oxford University Press, 2009), chapter 2.

51. Duff, *supra,* note 2, pp. 90–91.

SELECTED BIBLIOGRAPHY

Austin, John. *Lectures on Jurisprudence.* Ed. R. Campbell. London, 1879.

Chiao, Vincent. "Action and Agency in the Criminal Law." 15 *Legal Theory* 1 (2009).

Corrado, Michael. "Is There an Act Requirement in the Criminal Law?" 142 *University of Pennsylvania Law Review* 1529 (1994).

Dan-Cohen, Meir. *Harmful Thoughts: Essays on Law, Self, and Morality.* Princeton: Princeton University Press, 2002.

Davidson, Donald. *Essays on Actions and Events.* Oxford: Oxford University Press, 1980.

Duff, Antony. "Action, the Act Requirement, and Criminal Liability." In J. Hyman and H. C. Stewart, eds., *Agency and Action,* 2004.

Fletcher, George. "On the Moral Irrelevance of Bodily Movements." 142 *University of Pennsylvania Law Review* 1443 1994.

Hart, H. L. A. "Acts of Will and Responsibility." In *Punishment and Responsibility.* Oxford: Oxford University Press, 1968.

Holmes, Oliver Wendell. *The Common Law.* 1881.

Husak, Douglas. "Does Criminal Liability Require an Act?" In R. A. Duff, ed., *Philosophy and the Criminal Law,* 1998.

———. *The Philosophy of Criminal Law.* Totowa, N.J.: Rowman and Littlefield, 1987.

———. "Rethinking the Act Requirement." 28 *Cardozo Law Review* 2437 (2007).

Moore, Michael. *Act and Crime: The Philosophy of Action and Its Implications for Criminal Law.* Oxford: Clarendon Press, 1993.

———. "Renewed Questions about the Causal Theory of Action." In Andrei Buckareff and Jesus Aguilar, eds., *Causing Human Action: New Perspectives on the Causal Theory of Action.* Cambridge, Mass.: MIT Press, 2010.

Morris, Herbert. "Punishment for Thoughts." 49 *Monist* 342 (1965).

Murphy, Jeffrie. "Involuntary Acts and Criminal Liability." In *Retribution, Justice, and Therapy.* Dordrecht: Reidel, 1979.

Simester, A. P. "On the So-called Requirement for Voluntary Action." 1 *Buffalo Criminal Law Review* 403 (1998).

CHAPTER 5

ATTEMPTS

ANDREW ASHWORTH

CRIMINAL attempt is one of a small group of inchoate offenses that have an established place in most systems of criminal law. Full study of the law of attempts would lead into the depths of the philosophy of action and the controversies in moral philosophy about the role of "moral luck."[1] Even without endeavoring to resolve those issues, there is an abundance of contentious issues in the theory of attempts liability. Why are attempts punishable? What exactly is the "preventive" rationale to which some people tend to resort in answering that question, and what is its relation to the purposes of the criminal law? What principles are relevant to fixing the conduct requirement in criminal attempts? Is it helpful to distinguish a "subjectivist" from an "objectivist" position? Why has there been a tendency to assume that only intention should suffice for attempts liability, when lesser forms of culpability are thought appropriate for substantive crimes? When, if at all, is it relevant that a particular attempt was impossible of consummation? Should (all) attempts be punished less than the corresponding substantive crimes? These are some of the issues that have puzzled scholars, judges, law reformers, and students over the years, and that have contributed to the irrepressible attraction of this part of the criminal law to philosophers and lawyers alike.

This chapter begins by considering the "criminal-law context" of attempts, placing them within the category of inchoate offenses and then situating those offenses within a wider group of nonconsummate offenses. From there we move toward the three major elements of the crime of attempt—the fault element, the minimum conduct requirement, and the relevance of impossibility.

1 Inchoate Offenses

The Model Penal Code has three inchoate offenses—attempt, conspiracy, and solicitation. The crime of attempt deals with cases where an individual tries to commit a substantive offense; conspiracy with cases where two or more people agree to commit a crime; and solicitation with cases where an individual encourages another person to commit a crime. English law has traditionally had three inchoate offenses of attempt, conspiracy, and incitement, but the offense of incitement has recently been abolished and replaced by the somewhat broader offense of "encouraging and assisting a crime."[2]

Where a wrong justifies criminalization, does it follow that there is an equally strong case for creating inchoate offenses around that substantive crime? Most legal systems seem to operate on this premise, insofar as their general inchoate offenses attach automatically to every new crime. Thus the Model Penal Code treats inchoate offenses as being of general applicability, so that offenses of attempt, conspiracy, and solicitation attach to every substantive crime. Similarly, English law has operated for many years on a presumption that its inchoate offenses apply to every substantive crime. In other words, inchoate liability belongs to the general part of the criminal law.

Without attempting to uncover the historical roots of this presumption, it may fairly be assumed that it developed at a time when the paradigmatic form of a criminal offense was the "harm plus culpability" model. In other words, the presumption seems to be most appropriate in relation to traditional result-crimes such as murder, wounding, sex crimes, causing damage, stealing property, and so forth. More recently, various different forms of criminal offense have developed, notably the (growing) group of substantive crimes defined in the inchoate mode. The Model Penal Code contains a number of offenses defined so as to penalize conduct before any consequence occurs, for example, offenses of bribery that criminalize anyone who "solicits, accepts or agrees to accept" a benefit in given circumstances.[3] A recent English example is the Fraud Act 2006, section 2 of which criminalizes the dishonest making of a false representation with intent to make a gain or cause a loss. This replaced the traditional result-crime of obtaining property by deception, and the distinguishing feature of the new offense is that there is no need for the prosecutor to prove any "obtaining": no gain or loss needs to be made, no result achieved. Simply the dishonest making of a false representation, with the intention to cause loss or gain, is sufficient. Such a formulation has advantages for the prosecution (less has to be proved),[4] but the style of drafting, in the inchoate mode, means that the substantive offense already occupies the space that the offense of attempt would have occupied in relation to the former offense of obtaining property by deception. Yet the striking point is that, in accordance with the general presumption, the law of inchoate offenses applies automatically to substantive offenses defined in this mode, as in other modes. The effect is that, just as the law of inchoate offenses casts a "preventive circle" around all result crimes, here the law of inchoate offenses casts a preventive circle around offenses that have already been defined in such a way as to extend the ambit of the criminal law, thereby producing a much broader and more extensive preventive circle.

Thus, by operation of the general presumption, the criminal law expands beyond its normal boundary so as to extend to some fairly remote conduct, penalizing an early preparatory act such as attempting to make a false representation (e.g., by composing a false e-mail and trying unsuccessfully to send it to a mail-list). Yet the rationale for the general presumption of inchoate liability does not apply where the substantive offense is already defined in the inchoate mode, since an offense so defined has already increased the preventive circle. However, this obvious counterargument has not been adopted: it seems to have little purchase with law reform bodies or legislatures (it is rarely mentioned), and there appear to be no particular conventions about drafting offenses in one way or the other. It may be true that attempts to commit substantive offenses defined in the inchoate mode are likely to be prosecuted rarely, but that is no more than a practical prediction. In theory, the effect of combining the presumption of inchoate liability with the drafting of substantive offenses in the inchoate mode is to produce doubly inchoate and doubly preventive extensions of the criminal law, perhaps randomly (given the absence of drafting conventions) and usually without offering any special justification for extending criminalization further back into the early stages of preparation.

2 NONCONSUMMATE CRIMES

The inchoate offenses are perhaps the central example of nonconsummate crimes, but they belong to the general part of the criminal law and therefore apply automatically. Legislatures have been creating a raft of specific offenses that are nonconsummate, in the sense that they penalize conduct without the need to prove that a particular harm occurred.[5] They are essentially preparatory or preinchoate offenses, criminalizing conduct that may be seen as preparation for doing a wrong or causing a prohibited harm.

Thus, whereas the offense of attempt penalizes a person who takes a substantial step toward the substantive crime or does a more than merely preparatory act, there are now offenses that criminalize conduct much more remote from the harm of the substantive offense. An example is section 5 of the Terrorism Act 2006 (UK), which makes it an offense for a person, with intent to commit an act of terrorism or to assist another to do so, to engage in "any conduct in preparation for giving effect to" that intention. The conduct may therefore be perfectly normal and nondangerous of itself: buying a map or a railway timetable or obtaining a price list for chemicals may fulfill the actus reus.[6] The essence of the offense is the intention, coupled with a preparatory act of some kind.[7]

Another prominent form of nonconsummate crime is the offense of possession. Two categories of possession offense are particularly relevant here. First, there are offenses of possessing ordinarily nonincriminating articles with a further intention of committing a wrong, such as a crime or terrorist act. An example is provided by section 16(2) of the Terrorism Act 2000 (UK), which makes it an offense for a person to possess money or other property where the person "intends that it be used, or has reasonable cause to suspect that it may be used, for the purposes of terrorism."[8] The property possessed may be neutral (e.g., money), and so the focus of the offense is on the fault element. Where the requirement is of a further intention (the intention to use the money for the purposes of terrorism), that aligns these possession offenses with crimes defined in the inchoate mode: doing an act with a prohibited intent. However, this particular possession offense includes the alternative fault requirement of merely having "reasonable cause to suspect" that the money would ultimately be used for terrorist purposes, presumably by someone else. Given that the article possessed may be wholly neutral, this objective ground of liability marks a significant departure from the normal approach, and is objectionable in point of principle.[9]

The second category consist of offenses of possessing articles that are regarded as dangerous in themselves, in the sense that they are taken to indicate a criminal use (counterfeiting articles, burglary tools, and unlicensed guns) and so are typically criminalized without the need for the prosecutor to prove an intention to carry out that criminal use. This is a major difference from the inchoate and preparatory offenses discussed so far, for which intention must usually be proved, and it raises deep questions of principle. Moore calls these "proxy crimes," in the sense that possession is criminalized "either as a proxy for past acts (which we can't prove) or as a proxy for propensities (which we can't punish because they haven't yet happened)."[10] Proxy crimes of the first type had been termed "presumed or evidentiary offenses" by Bentham,[11] on the ground that they "furnish a presumption of an offense committed"; Bentham regarded them as a necessary part of the preventive function of the criminal law, whereas modern liberals would object to the presumption, or at least to the inability of a defendant to argue that the presumption is inapplicable to the present case. Proxy crimes of the second type include simple prohibitions on possessing burglary tools, counterfeiting instruments, unlicensed guns, knives, and other weapons of offense, crimes that abound in contemporary criminal law. Not only do such crimes contain no intent requirement, but they also criminalize a person before any step has been taken to use the article unlawfully. In that respect, they are objectionable on the same ground as some standards for the conduct element in attempts, for not respecting the individual's autonomy and opportunity for a change of mind.[12] Insofar as they criminalize the possessor on the basis of what others might do with the article(s), Simester and von Hirsch argue that such offenses violate ordinary principles of imputation, unless there is evidence that the possessor has some kind of "normative involvement" in that other's subsequent choice to (mis)use the possessed article. To what extent it would be appropriate to go beyond the boundaries of the law of complicity in this respect remains for debate.[13]

A third form of nonconsummate offense is risk based: this includes the growing number of crimes that penalize conduct on the ground of the risk it creates, typically requiring a fault element of recklessness or negligence but sometimes imposing strict liability. Within this category are offenses of explicit risk such as careless driving and dangerous driving and the endangerment of air travelers, and offenses of implicit risk such as speeding and drunk driving (both of which are penalized because of the risk they create and are essentially offenses of strict liability). These offenses raise questions of principle—particularly relating to the nature of the link between the conduct penalized and the risk it actually presents—which cannot be pursued here.[14] The Model Penal Code contains an offense of "recklessly engag[ing] in conduct which places or may place another person in danger of death or serious bodily injury,"[15] confined to such serious cases. English law has no general endangerment offense.

We will keep those three forms of nonconsummate criminal liability in view as we reflect on the law of criminal attempts, and will return to them in the concluding section of the essay.

3 Rationale of Attempts Liability

The rationale for having inchoate offenses must be closely connected to the rationale for the criminal law itself. Let us begin with the proposition that the rationale for the criminal law is to provide for the conviction and punishment of those who culpably do serious public wrongs, the distinctive technique being to declare those wrongs, to provide for the public censure of those who commit them (by means of conviction under a procedure that satisfies due process or human rights principles), and to provide for punishment up to a proportionate maximum. This recognizes the criminal law's declaratory purpose, and a preventive purpose that is fulfilled by providing a disincentive in the form of state punishment of those who are convicted. In view of this rationale, and given that the criminal law is the state's most condemnatory response (which may involve deprivation of liberty), the decision to criminalize certain conduct should only be taken for strong reasons and with assurance that no restraining principle applies.[16] Once the justifications for creating a crime have been met, the form of the offense should be such as to comply with the general "rule of law" principles (notably fair warning and certainty of definition), and the protections of criminal procedure (including the presumption of innocence and the right to a fair trial) should apply.

But would a system of criminal law that provided only for the conviction and punishment of those who did serious wrongs be adequate? The further question is "Adequate for what?" One answer to this is to refer back to the preventive purpose of the criminal law. Attaching the prospect of punishment to the conviction is intended to act as a deterrent, thereby reducing the frequency with which the wrong is done and the harm caused. If there were no law of attempts, this would weaken the preventive force of the criminal law, as Hart argued:

First, there must be many who are not completely confident that they will succeed in their criminal objective, but will be prepared to run the risk of punishment if they can be assured that they have to pay nothing for attempts which fail; whereas if unsuccessful attempts were also punished the price might appear to them to be too high. Again, there must be many cases where men might with good or bad reason believe that if they succeed in committing some crime they will escape, but if they fail they may be caught. Treason is only the most obvious of such cases, and unless attempts were punished, there would, in such cases, be no deterrent force in the law's threat attached to the main crime.[17]

These are consequentialist reasons for having a law of attempts, to underpin and reinforce the substantive offenses. They can be supported by arguing that the law of attempts strengthens the preventive function by enabling the police and others to intervene in situations where a person is on the way to perpetrating the wrong itself, thereby preventing the (full) harm from occurring. There are also good retributive reasons for creating a "preventive circle" around each substantive offense through a law of attempts. On this view, the conclusion that those who culpably commit serious public wrongs deserve the censure of criminal conviction and punishment should apply also to people who have sufficiently committed themselves to the wrong, even though they have not yet caused it: they are equally/substantially/sufficiently culpable and are therefore deserving of censure and punishment. As Duff argues:

Whether or not the fact of resulting harm should make any difference to the agent's criminal fate, we must surely agree that if it is wrong to cause a harm intentionally or recklessly, it is also (and not much less) wrong to attempt to cause such a harm, or to take an unreasonable risk of causing such harm. A law that condemned and punished actually harm-causing conduct as wrong, but was utterly silent on attempts to cause such harms, and on reckless risk-taking with respect to such harms, would speak with a strange moral voice.[18]

Duff's argument is intended to capture risk-taking as well, but its application to criminal attempts is clear and persuasive. Just as the retributive rationale for substantive offenses makes little sense without a commitment to prevention, in terms of dissuading people from doing the wrong, so it makes little sense for the criminal law to wait until the wrong has been done before defining the conduct as an offense. Thus there are good consequentialist and retributive reasons for having a law of attempts.

The justification for attempts liability is sometimes couched in terms of the attempter's dangerousness. Thus the commentary to the Model Penal Code provisions on attempts, still savoring of 1960s positivism, focuses on the dangerousness of the individual:

Conduct designed to cause or culminate in the commission of a crime obviously yields an indication that the actor is disposed toward such activity, not alone on this occasion but on others. There is a need, therefore, subject again to proper safeguards, for the legal basis on which the special danger that such individuals present may be assessed and dealt with. They must be made amenable to the corrective process that the law provides.[19]

It should be noted that part of the rationale here is that the attempter represents a danger of committing future crimes, as well as having manifested danger on the particular occasion of the failed attempt. However, it is not clear how one can assess the likelihood of an unsuccessful attempter repeating the conduct, and this future-regarding aspect of the preventive rationale will not be taken further here. Without that aspect, references to dangerousness may be regarded merely as describing the probability that the attempter would have gone on to commit the substantive crime.

Both on consequentialist and on retributive grounds, therefore, it has been argued that a criminal law confined to substantive offenses would not make sense. If a wrong is serious enough to criminalize, then the law should also penalize attempts to commit it. Although we shall return to these matters in the concluding section, two points should be made at this stage. The first is that this is often abbreviated to a "preventive" rationale, but we should note that in this context "prevention" cannot practically mean the total elimination of the wrongdoing or harm-causing activities. The realistic aim is the reduction of those activities to a tolerable level, and so references to the preventive rationale must be understood in this attenuated sense. The second point recalls the growth of substantive offenses defined in the inchoate mode: it might be argued that the criminal law, instead of having a general law of attempts, should only penalize an attempt or other preparatory act where a strong justification for doing so in connection with a particular crime is made out. This would, for example, cut out the rather random extensions of the criminal sanction that result from the inchoate mode of drafting and the general presumption of inchoate liability. We should keep an open mind on whether a general law of attempts is justifiable or dispensable.[20]

4 THE FAULT ELEMENT IN ATTEMPTS

The orthodox approach is to state that liability for a criminal attempt requires proof of intention, and that anything less (notably, recklessness) will not suffice. But why should this be so, when recklessness is a sufficient *mens rea* element for many serious crimes? In particular, why should it be so when the crime that is being attempted is defined as requiring either intent or recklessness? The best answer to this question appears to be that the crime of attempt extends liability beyond its normal boundaries (i.e., beyond the bounds of substantive offenses) and that the further away from the causation of harm we criminalize people, the more we should insist on proof of intent rather than mere recklessness.[21] This remoteness argument may appear to be a good liberal principle, well grounded in the seriousness with which we should treat censure and punishment and in the restrictive principles of criminalization that flow from that.[22] One problem with it is that it may be considered overbroad, since it would require a radical revision of the many possession offenses that do not require intent; as noted earlier, there are strong principled arguments for possession offenses to be narrowed in that way, but others would reject this as unpractical in the world in which we find ourselves. If it is unpractical for possession offenses, should it be regarded as such an incontrovertible principle for attempts?

Another argument advanced in support of the proposition that attempts liability should require intention is the "ordinary language" argument: attempt connotes trying, and one can only try intentionally, so it follows that intent must be required for criminal attempts. However, the issues of principle here should be determined by rational argument rather than by linguistic conventions that might have other origins.[23] In particular, it remains to be decided why liability for an inchoate offense should not require the same fault element as liability for the substantive offense, if the remoteness argument is not considered conclusive. Those subjectivists who maintain that the role of chance and outcome-luck should be kept to a minimum in the criminal law would be content, in principle, with a law of inchoate liability whose fault requirements matched those for the substantive offense that was the object of the attempt, conspiracy, or solicitation. This would mean that the fault element for attempted damage to property should be the same as for the substantive offense of damaging property; and insofar as the substantive offense may be committed by someone who is reckless as to causing damage, so a person who acts recklessly in a way that creates a risk of causing damage should be liable to conviction. This does not commit these subjectivists to advocating liability in such cases, since they may well subscribe to a number of restraining principles (not just the remoteness principle stated above but also a principle of not extending police power over individuals without evidence of substantial risk,[24] for example). But it does mean that, in principle, that is the direction in which "full subjectivism" points,[25] even though it may be questioned whether such an offense would be better termed "endangerment" than attempt.

For those who are persuaded that only intent should be a sufficient fault element for attempt, either on the remoteness argument or on a version of full subjectivism that takes account of restraining principles, there are still two questions to be answered. What do we mean by "intention"? And could a lesser fault element suffice in relation to other requirements of the substantive offense? The meaning of intention could be confined to purpose (as the ordinary language argument might indicate) or could be extended to cover foresight (as is more normal for substantive offenses). The latter, wider approach is preferred in the Model Penal Code, which requires the attempter to act "with the purpose of causing or with the belief that [the act] will cause" the prohibited result.[26] The justification for going beyond purpose is that "in both instances a deliberate choice is made to bring about the consequence forbidden by the criminal law, and the actor has done all within his power to cause this result to occur."[27] English law likewise favors the inclusion of "foresight of virtual certainty" within the meaning of intent here.[28] It seems that this is not supported by reasoning particular to the law of attempts. It is rather that, generally speaking, the criminal law defines intention in terms of these two alternative forms, purpose or foresight—although the requirement in English law, "foresight of virtual certainty," may be narrower than the test of foresight included in the Model Penal Code: that the act "will cause" the prohibited result. It is sometimes stated that purpose and foresight are properly regarded as indicating the same level of culpability, but no such assertion is necessary in order to support the inclusion of foresight within the definition of intention. All that is required is a judgment that it is fairer to classify foresight with purpose, as a species of intention, than to treat it as simply a form of recklessness; and that judgment of fairness depends on an assessment of the moral attitude toward the prohibited consequence that the foresight implies, and of its closeness to other strains of culpability that we classify as intention.

What about combining intention with a lesser degree of fault in relation to other elements of the substantive offense? If the crime of rape is committed by a man who has sex with another person reckless as to whether that other consents or not, does it not make sense to convict of attempted rape a man who tries to have sex with another person reckless as to whether the other consents or not?[29] It would surely be perverse to acquit that man of attempted rape on the basis that full intention should be required as to all elements of the offense, with the implication that for a conviction of attempted rape the man must intend to have sex with the other *knowing* that the other does not consent. Duff refers to the "common intuition" that recklessness as to the relevant circumstance (here, absence of consent) should be sufficient when combined with an intent to do the act,[30] but recognizes that there is no satisfactory distinction between consequences and circumstances when analyzing the elements of criminal offenses. His proposal is to resolve this difficulty by requiring "an intention such that the agent would necessarily commit an offense in carrying it out,"[31] a formulation that satisfies the "common intuition" while eschewing the difficulties over consequences and circumstances. The Model Penal Code achieves a similar result through its phrase "acting with the kind of culpability otherwise required for commission of the crime."[32]

5 The Conduct Element in Attempts

Without yet concluding the question of the fault element in attempts, we should go on to consider some of the problems surrounding the conduct element. In principle, there is a whole spectrum of possible conduct requirements, with "any overt act" as the least demanding and the "last act" as the most demanding, and a number of intermediate possibilities such as the "substantial step" test of the Model Penal Code, the "more than merely preparatory" test of English law, the "unequivocal act" test favored by some, and so on.[33] On what basis should the selection be made?

In a liberal system of criminal law, there must be respect for each individual as a rational agent, and this militates against a wide law of attempts that criminalizes conduct at an early stage. It is generally accepted that punishment for mere thoughts is objectionable: that would be to invade the individual's private world, and to allow liability to turn on ideas unlikely to be executed rather than ideas that the individual has manifestly brought forward into the external world. More generally, Duff argues that we should treat an individual as capable of desisting (or capable of being persuaded to desist), "because this is what it is to respect him as a responsible agent."[34] This is taken to rule out any conduct requirement that impinges at an early stage in the course of preparation, such as "any overt act" or a merely preparatory act. Indeed, it may also argue against the Model Penal Code's "substantial step" test, which criminalizes some merely preparatory conduct as an attempt. Those tests are objectionable, on Duff's view, because they criminalize the individual as an attempter at a time when there is still the possibility of a change of mind—they "deny him the freedom to decide for himself whether to desist" and "pre-empt his future actions by force, and thus infringe his autonomy."[35] Similarly, Alexander and Ferzan insist that an attempter should not be criminalized so long as she retains complete control, and so may respond to the law's injunction not to commit the substantive wrong.[36] Now some may take the view that this reasoning places too much emphasis on the individual's freedom as a moral agent: where there is clear evidence of an intention to commit the substantive crime, should it not be sufficient for the law to regard the individual as having crossed the threshold when an overt or preparatory act is done in pursuance of that intent? If, moreover, the law also provides a defense of voluntary abandonment or voluntary renunciation of criminal purpose, does that not make adequate provision for a change of mind by a responsible agent? Duff thinks not, as do Alexander and Ferzan, and they therefore move further along the spectrum of steps toward committing the crime. Before assessing those views, let us examine some of the other plausible reasons for requiring more than an overt act.

A second argument would be that, since the crime is called an attempt, ordinary language requires that the conduct look like an attempt and not like something patently short of an attempt. This would favor those conduct requirements lying close to the substantive offense, such as the "last act" test and a few others, on the basis that it is only when the actor reaches that late stage that he can be said to be actually trying or attempting to commit the offense. Merely satisfying the "substantial step" requirement of the Model Penal Code, for example, would not necessarily be sufficient to enable a court to say that the actor was trying to commit the full offense at that stage, for example, by reconnoitering a house with a view to burglary. But before this line of argument is taken too far, its premise must be questioned. Why should the law be bound by linguistic convention? The law can draw its own boundaries, based on rational argument and judgments of degree. It is one thing to argue that in a system that uses jury trial, there are practical dangers of miscarriages of justice if the law diverges too greatly and inexplicably from ordinary language. It is quite another to assume that the law has to adhere to whatever linguistic conventions have developed, rather than expanding (or possibly contracting) the ordinary meaning for the purpose of legal usage. So long as the legal meaning can be explained clearly, why should it not differ?

This brings us to a third argument, that some of the most-used conduct requirements for attempt fail to satisfy the principle of legality, and particularly the "fair
warning" principle. English law requires the attempter's conduct to have been a
"more than merely preparatory act."[37] Text-writers make much of the divergent
interpretations of this phrase by the courts, and apparent inconsistencies in its
application to different sets of facts.[38] There are two issues here. One is that the law
of attempts should be clear enough to give citizens fair warning of when their conduct is likely to constitute an attempt. The second and more important issue is that
it is unacceptable if the law's test is so opaque as to generate inconsistent decisions
from the courts. One way of reducing inconsistency might be to introduce legislative examples: this is the approach taken by the Model Penal Code, which specifies
seven forms of conduct that, "if strongly corroborative of the actor's criminal purpose, shall not be held insufficient as a matter of law."[39] There may be a problem
with some of the examples given there (e.g., reconnoitering the place, possessing
materials for subsequent use), in that they may seem too remote from an attempt to
justify intervention on those grounds at that time,[40] but as a legislative technique
this has the potential to remove much of the vagueness that leads to inconsistent
decision-making.

A further argument is that conduct requirements that include any overt or preparatory act give too much power to the police and other enforcement agents, and
create the risk of decisions taken on unreliable evidence. Those who have argued in
favor of a requirement such as an "unequivocal" or "noninnocent" act[41] seek to avoid
the dangers of evidential manipulation by the agents of the state. Where the conduct
proved is not of itself compromising, there is an enhanced danger that confessions
will be forced or fabricated, that other evidence will be "planted" on suspects, and so
forth. The danger may be particularly great in a legal system like the English, where
adverse inferences may be drawn in court from a failure to answer police questions
earlier in the investigation.[42] These possibilities cannot be dismissed as insignificant,
particularly since they resonate with the importance of respecting individuals as
responsible agents. The question is how strongly the arguments sound against a reasonably broad law of attempts. If, for example, it were to be argued that the Model
Penal Code's formulation of the "substantial step" test is the appropriate conduct
requirement, how much weight should be given to the possibility of police abuses as
a counterargument? One response is that these possible dangers should be handled
in an entirely different way. The issues relate to the supervision and accountability of
the relevant government agents: if codes of conduct and their enforcement need to
be sharpened in order to strengthen the defenses against these kinds of official abuse,
that is the proper approach rather than distorting the law of attempts. There may be
an empirical rebuttal of that, demonstrating that all efforts to regulate or "rein in" the
relevant enforcement agents in a given jurisdiction have failed in the past; but all
those steps must be proved before this is treated as a clinching argument in the law
of attempts. In principle, evidential difficulties should be resolved separately.

Where does consideration of these four possible objections leave the search for
an acceptable test of the conduct requirement in attempts? Some subjectivists may

wish to insist that once there is evidence of a firm intention to commit the substantive crime, any overt act should suffice, or at least anything that constitutes a "substantial step" (in the Model Penal Code's formulation) since a firm intention evidenced by external acts is sufficient to justify conviction and punishment for an attempt—possibly subject to a defense of voluntary abandonment, where the evidence supports it. Some subjectivists and many objectivists would prefer to wait until the actor has progressed further: mere preparation for committing a crime, as by reconnoitering a house (one of the Model Penal Code examples), is not sufficiently close to the substantive crime to justify labeling it as an attempt. Alexander and Ferzan go so far as to support a "last act" test, on the basis that only at this late stage is it possible to be sufficiently sure that the attempter has made an irrevocable decision to perpetrate the substantive wrong.[43] For them, the availability of a defense of voluntary renunciation appears insufficient. Duff takes a less stringent view, arguing that what we must seek is a test that ensures that the actor can already be said to be "in the process of" committing the substantive offense: the actor has embarked on the offense, she is "on the job" (to use an English colloquialism), and she is not merely getting ready to commit it.[44] When the actor is already engaged on the commission of the offense, it does not show lack of respect for her as a responsible agent to label that conduct as an attempt and to enable the enforcement authorities to arrest for attempt. The actor is sufficiently committed in the external world (in addition to the intention to commit the substantive crime) to justify conviction and punishment for attempt, at least so long as the defense of renunciation of criminal purpose or voluntary abandonment is kept open for those who change their minds. Whether one can go so far as to say that this resonates with the popular meaning of an attempt, bringing about a "desirable coincidence of social policy and ordinary language,"[45] is less important, since it was argued above that ordinary language should not be the touchstone. Any such general test does leave the problem of inconsistent interpretations, however, and this should be tackled through the legislative technique of illustrative but nonexhaustive examples, following the approach (not the details) of the Model Penal Code provisions.

6 Impossible Attempts

Fundamental questions about the rationale for attempts liability, and indeed about the purpose of the criminal law itself, become all the more pressing when we turn to attempts to do the impossible. The Model Penal Code adopts the view that, in general, impossible attempts should be punishable in the same way as other attempts: the actor is to be judged "under the circumstances as he believes them to be" if those circumstances diverge from the true facts.[46] The English Law Commission took the same view,[47] although the poorly drafted provisions of the Criminal Attempts Act 1981 were only interpreted that way after a false start.[48] There is also similarity in the approaches to two related issues. If what the actor tries to do is legally impossible, that is, it would not be a crime on the facts as the actor believes them to be, there should be no criminal liability—a person cannot be convicted of attempting to commit a nonexistent crime. If what the actor is trying to do is a crime, but the means adopted are so extraordinary that reasonable people would regard them as too far removed from reality to produce the prohibited harm (e.g., trying to kill a person by witchcraft or by sticking pins into a wax doll), there should also be no criminal liability for attempting that crime.

The close similarity of the Code and English law on this topic does not reflect a scholarly consensus. There are deep divisions here, with subjectivists of various hues supporting the prevailing Anglo-American legal approach of having no impossibility defense, contrasting with objectivists who maintain that the logic of the subjectivist stance is flawed and its social implications unacceptable. Let us move toward these conflicting positions by examining the distinction between complete and incomplete attempts, then reviewing the subjectivist position, assessing the objectivist challenge, applying the different approaches to cases of factual and legal impossibility, and finally revisiting subjectivism as a general approach to the criminal law.

Analysis of the problems of the law of attempts may be assisted by drawing a distinction between incomplete and complete attempts. Most of the discussion in sections 4 and 5 above has revolved around incomplete attempts, that is, cases in which the actor has been stopped or has desisted before doing everything that he intended to do in order to bring about the substantive offense. Indeed, in section 5 the very issue was the minimum conduct requirement for a (necessarily incomplete) attempt. However, there are also attempts in which the actor has done everything that he intended but has failed to cause the prohibited harm that constitutes the full offense—smuggling into the country a substance believed to be cannabis but which is dried lettuce, putting a form of sweetener into someone's coffee in the belief that it is cyanide, putting one's hand in a pocket in order to steal money when the pocket is empty, and so forth. Complete attempts bring the disagreement between subjectivists and objectivists to a head, since it can be said that the complete attempter has caused no harm in the external world, and that may be used as an argument against criminal liability in such cases. Why would anyone want to convict and punish a person who has failed to injure any of the interests and values that the criminal law is designed to protect, and who was not even (like the incomplete attempter) on a realistic path to doing so?

This is the point at which the subjectivists step forward. The term "subjectivist" is used here to designate those who subscribe to two basic principles—the intent principle, that actors should be held liable according to what they intended to do, and not according to what actually did or did not occur; and the belief principle, that actors should be judged on the basis of what they believed they were doing, not on the basis of actual facts or circumstances that were not known to them at the time.[49] In support of these principles, it is argued that a person should only be held criminally liable for matters that lie within that person's control or can be regarded as that person's choice. From time to time our endeavors do not turn out as we wanted: we can rarely be certain that a particular result will follow our effort to produce it. In a system of official censure such as the criminal law, the aim should be to draw a straight line through the vagaries of fortune and the vicissitudes of life, minimizing the influence of chance and keeping as close as possible to the actor's choice and control. The focus of the criminal law should be on the defendant's culpable trying, and what happens after that (i.e., whether or not the substantive offense results) is of subordinate importance.[50]

This emphasis on removing outcome-luck from a significant role in the criminal law opens up the wider debate on moral luck, which cannot be reviewed here.[51] Clearly there are other forms of moral luck, such as the abilities and temperament with which each of us is endowed, and the situations in which we find ourselves. The tendency of subjectivists is to accept that those other forms of luck exist but to maintain that they are not such as to deprive individuals of a sufficient amount of freedom of choice and control (defenses to criminal liability should cater for cases where there is such deprivation), and to treat them as setting the scene for the choice that the actor makes.[52] On this argument, the person who tries unsuccessfully to open a security box or to kill another by shooting is just as culpable as the person who succeeds in opening the security box or in shooting the other dead. In pulling the trigger or trying to pick the lock, the actor has made the significant choice of committing herself to producing the prohibited harm. What happens thereafter is a matter of chance, to the actor, and should not affect criminal liability. It will properly affect whether the actor is liable to pay compensation, of course, because compensation is due only for harm done. But the focus of the criminal law is on culpable actions, and there is no relevant moral difference in terms of culpability between a completed attempt and the substantive crime.

Objectivists disagree. Duff argues that the subjectivist assertion that all that an individual can be accountable for is the "trying" is based on an untenable theory of human action.[53] A proper assessment of actions, on his view, inevitably involves taking account of the impact of what we do in the material and social world. But it is questionable whether conceding these criticisms from the philosophy of action undermines the subjectivist argument: it weakens one supporting pillar yet leaves the argument that luck plays a major role in whether an attempt succeeds or not, and that a system of public censure such as the criminal law should try to minimize the effect of luck on its assessments when the level of culpability is the same. To this, Duff replies that our understanding of human action is inevitably objective, in the sense that we cannot properly separate actions from their impacts in the external world. He shows that our typical responses differ greatly according to whether an action caused the intended harm or failed to do so. To the subjectivist's insistence that typical emotional responses or demands for compensation are very different from the interests of the criminal law, he replies that we simply cannot (and do not) separate actions from their results.[54] A person who has tried to kill and has succeeded is a murderer, whereas one who has tried to kill and has failed is not, and is merely an attempted murderer. This difference reflects the material and social world as we find it: objectivists such as Duff do not deny the central role of culpability in justifying the imposition of criminal liability, but they disagree with the subjectivist view that assessments of culpability can be detached from that material world.

The objectivist engagement with the material world leads to the exclusion of certain forms of impossible attempt from the criminal law. While there is general agreement that those whose understanding of the world is radically different should not be convicted of attempt (e.g., an attempt to kill by sticking pins in a wax effigy), Duff goes further and suggests that any alleged attempt that "fails to engage with the world as an attempt to commit the offense" should not amount to an attempted crime. Excluded on this ground would be actions that are "not directed toward a victim or object of a kind whose existence is required for commission of the offense,"[55] such as handling goods in the belief that they are stolen when they are not, or trying to obtain money by altering a check for $9 to $697,000,000. Such actions, according to Duff, simply lie too far from any menace. They are unlikely to generate alarm, and might even provoke amusement. The objectivist sees insufficient reason to criminalize them as attempts, whereas the subjectivist adheres to the view that there is sufficient culpability to justify their inclusion—although in the case of the altered check, which is pitched halfway toward the manifestly unreal case of the wax effigy, any punishment might well be reduced in order to reflect the degree of disengagement apparent in such an amateurish effort.

The subjectivist, wishing to focus on culpable actions and to reduce the impact of outcome-luck on criminal justice, would support the criminalization of all impossible attempts except for two. The "manifestly unreal" cases, such as the wax effigy, have already been mentioned. The other type of excluded case is the legally impossible attempt:[56] an example is the man who believed that the package he was smuggling into the United Kingdom contained currency and admitted that he was attempting to smuggle it in, when in law there is no offense of importing currency.[57] Subjectivists would favor nonliability because the offense attempted does not exist; on the objectivist test developed by Duff, these cases would mostly be excluded, since there is no "intention such that the agent would necessarily commit an offense in carrying it out."[58] For the subjectivist, the exception for "legally impossible" attempts[59] brings into play a tempting symmetry between the doctrines of mistake and impossible attempts. Taking the belief principle as the starting point—that a person should be judged on the facts as he believed them to be—this indicates that the belief can exculpate if those facts would disclose no offense (mistake of fact) and inculpate if the facts disclose an offense (factually impossible attempt); and that if the belief concerns the criminal law, a belief that conduct is not an offense when it is does not exculpate (mistake of law), whereas a belief that conduct is an offense when it is not does not inculpate (legally impossible attempt). Those who reject the possibility of a satisfactory distinction between factual and legal mistakes are unimpressed by the symmetry argument.[60] However, even those who regard the symmetry as a useful insight and as an in-principle starting point rarely pursue its logic without qualifications. Is it not plausible to regard the symmetry as helpful in general, while arguing in favor of, say, requiring reasonable grounds for certain mistakes of fact or allowing a defense of mistake of law in cases of reliance on official advice? In the debate between subjectivist and objectivist perspectives on criminal liability, there should be no insistence that each approach must remain "pure" if it is to be philosophically respectable. There may be good arguments for recognizing certain limiting principles, qualifications and exceptions, and those arguments should not be dismissed merely on the ground that they are inconsistent with the general principle (exceptions usually are).

7 Punishing for Criminal Attempts

Once a person is convicted of a criminal attempt, on what principles should the sentence be based? In particular, should the starting-point for sentencing be less than, or the same as, that for the substantive offense? In answering these questions, we should return to the distinction between incomplete and complete attempts. If we are dealing with a legal system that imposes liability for an attempt before the attempter has done the last act—for example, the Model Penal Code's "substantial step" test, or English law's "more than merely preparatory" test—then the starting point for the sentence ought surely to be below that of the full offense. Consequentialists would point to the need to keep back a portion of the punishment so as to give the attempter a disincentive against going further with the attempt;[61] retributivists would argue that the incomplete attempter has manifested less wickedness and therefore deserves less punishment than a person who commits the full offense, not least because there is still time for renunciation.

Where the attempt is complete—where the attempter has done all that was intended but has failed to cause the full offense to happen—there is no relevant moral difference between the complete attempter and the substantive offender. They deserve the same punishment: the only difference between their cases lies in the result, and that is a matter of chance or luck.[62] The result is relevant for issues such as compensation, but should not go to sentence. Thus, although this conclusion runs counter to popular feelings,[63] the starting point for sentencing the complete attempter should be the same as that for the substantive offender, on the principle that "an actor who acts culpably has his blameworthiness and punishability—his desert—fixed by that culpable act alone, regardless of whether it produces a harmful result."[64] However, objectivists such as Duff regard it as important to mark the difference between the (unsuccessful) complete attempter and the (successful) substantive offender by lowering the sentence of the former, since on a communicative theory of punishment, the sentence "should not be utterly divorced from our extra-legal moral understandings of, and responses to, the wrongs that people do."[65]

8 THE FUTURE OF ATTEMPTS

The second half of this chapter has shown that the essential elements of any doctrine of criminal attempts are strongly contested. While everyone accepts that an attempt requires intention, there is disagreement about the relevant meaning of intention, whether it can be combined with recklessness as to other elements of the offense, and so forth. How the conduct element should be defined is open to debate, and even if the problems of uncertainty can be reduced by the use of legislative examples, there is disagreement over the stage at which conduct should be criminalized as an attempt and over the limiting principles or policies that should be given weight. In relation to attempts to do the impossible, there is a strong disagreement between subjectivists, who (largely because they emphasize culpability and wish to minimize the role of chance) would criminalize almost all factually impossible attempts, and objectivists, who adopt a narrower view based on the requirement that the conduct must engage with the material world in order to qualify as an attempt. And when it comes to sentencing attempters, there is disagreement between those who would select the same starting point for sentencing the complete attempter as for the substantive offender and those who would insist on taking account of "popular understanding" and of results as objective facts.

Assessing the different views on these issues leads into the depths of the philosophy of action and the debates in moral philosophy over "moral luck." For the criminal law, these different views also raise practical problems about the most appropriate way to approach such a troubled and contested realm of liability. It is assumed here that the justifications for casting a "preventive circle" around each substantive wrong are accepted, but there are problems of policy and practice involved in implementing this. In these concluding paragraphs, three of those problems are briefly discussed—whether a law of attempts is necessary and desirable, how the answer to that question relates to broader issues of liability for nonconsummate offenses, and whether a large-scale re-labeling of offenses is called for.

Is a law of attempts necessary and desirable? In section 1 above, a distinct malfunction was pointed out: because the law of attempts is conceived as belonging to the general part of the criminal law, it applies to every substantive offense so as to extend the reach of the criminal sanction. Since there are no firm drafting conventions, some offenses are drafted as traditional result-crimes and others are drafted in the inchoate mode, so as to criminalize the doing of a preparatory act with intent; but the inchoate offenses (such as attempt) apply to them both in the same way. Nobody in the legislature or law reform agencies, it seems, has a grip on the extent to which behavior is criminalized because of the automatic operation of this doctrine of the general part. Interestingly, that is not the case with offenses of reckless endangerment: there is no such general offense that attaches to all substantive offenses, so there has to be a conscious decision to create such an offense in respect of risks of a particular type of harm: the Model Penal Code, as we noted,[66] has a general offense of reckless endangerment in relation to the danger of causing death or serious bodily injury, but not otherwise. So the key question, posed in a classic article by Glazebrook,[67] is why we do not proceed in the same way with attempts. In other words, why do we not instruct our law reformers to consider on each occasion what they think should justifiably be criminalized, rather than relying on the rather capricious operation of the general presumption of inchoate liability? In that way we could abolish the law of attempt, avoid the vagueness of its conduct requirement, and state exactly which preparatory acts should be criminalized whenever a revising the criminal law or creating a new offense. That might not dispense with the impossibility issue (surely a general provision on that would be appropriate), but it would be a vastly improved approach for those who believe that the limits of the criminal law should be scrutinized and justified to a higher degree than currently.[68] Some offenses might properly be drafted in the inchoate mode,[69] but this would be done deliberately and would not then be subject to further expansion through the operation of the presumption of inchoate liability. Sadly, the prospects for such a principled approach are rather dim in this age of rapidly drafted new offenses to address alleged social evils, although permanent law reform agencies might be persuaded of its merits.[70]

What about the broader issue of liability for nonconsummate offenses, raised in section 2 above? First, this may be an area of greater practical importance than the law of attempts, since many offenses of possession or of doing a preparatory act are more remote from the substantive offense. At present, it seems that the restraining principles identified in section 5 above in relation to the conduct element in attempts do not receive adequate weight in decisions to create new preparatory or possession offenses.[71] Not only do these "proxy" offenses bestow considerable practical power on law enforcement agencies and leave no opportunity for a person to decide whether or not to use the article, but they base criminalization on a presumption of future wrongdoing. As argued earlier, this is wrong in principle; but it is unlikely that governments will abolish such offenses, because of what they believe to be the preventive effect of possession laws.[72] Second, an increasing number of nonconsummate offenses seem to be concerned with risk-creation and forms of endangerment. Although this topic falls outside this chapter, it is relevant to mention that there appears to be no principled framework that specifies how far the law ought to go in criminalizing risk-creation and what limiting principles ought to apply.[73]

Finally, do the arguments in this chapter suggest that the whole shape of the criminal law ought to be reconsidered? One argument would be that subjectivism, in some of its versions, suggests that basic principles of culpability and of equality of treatment militate in favor of liability not just for the intentional attempter but also for the reckless endangerer and (where the law criminalizes negligence) for the negligent harm-doer. However, those who adopt this general approach tend to subscribe to limiting principles (need for strong reasons for criminalization, danger of oppressive policing) that are taken to defeat the "basic principles" in this instance.[74] A more sweeping argument would be that all substantive offenses ought to be relabeled, if the subjectivist approach is followed, to reflect the argument that there is no relevant moral difference between one who attempts and fails and one who attempts and succeeds. Murder would be relabeled attempted murder, robbery attempted robbery, and so forth. The obvious response to this suggestion is that, logical as it may appear, it would be so unacceptable to victims (who might see it as denying their victimization), to the public, and, no doubt, to the media, that for pragmatic reasons it deserves little attention. Objectivists would regard this as strengthening their position, but subjectivists would say that they are merely yielding to political expediency without conceding their "no relevant moral difference" thesis.

NOTES

1. The fullest study is the masterly monograph by R. A. Duff, *Criminal Attempts* (Oxford: Oxford University Press, 1996).

2. The change was effected by Part 2 of the Serious Crime Act 2007. For a brief assessment, see A. Ashworth, *Principles of Criminal Law* (Oxford: Oxford University Press, 6th ed., 2009), pp. 458–463.

3. American Law Institute, *Model Penal Code*, s. 224.8; for discussion, see A. Ashworth, "Criminal Attempts and the Role of Resulting Harm under the Code, and in the Common Law," (1988) 19 *Rutgers Law Journal* 725, at pp. 765–766. See also the U.S. federal bribery statute, 18 U.S.C. para. 201, discussed by S. P. Green, *Lying, Cheating and Stealing: A Moral Theory of White-Collar Crime* (Oxford: Oxford University Press, 2006), ch. 16.

4. See Duff (above, n. 1), p. 56; also A. Ashworth, "Defining Criminal Offenses without Harm," in P. Smith (ed.), *Criminal Law: Essays in Honour of J. C. Smith* (London: Butterworths, 1987); I. P. Robbins, "Doubly Inchoate Crimes" (1989) 26 *Harvard Journal on Legislation* 1.

5. See generally D. Husak, "The Nature and Justifiability of Nonconsummate Offenses," (1995) 37 *Arizona L.R.* 151.

6. See V. Tadros, "Justice and Terrorism," (2007) 10 *New Criminal Law Review* 658, at p. 672, discussing a similar offense in s. 58 of the Terrorism Act 2000 (U.K.); and, more generally, D. Ohana, "Desert and Punishment for Acts Preparatory to the Commission of a Crime," (2007) 10 *Canadian Journal of Law and Jurisprudence* 113, and B. McSherry, "Expanding the Boundaries of Inchoate Crimes: The Growing Reliance on Preparatory Offenses," in B. McSherry, A. Norrie, and S. Bronitt (eds.), *Regulating Deviance* (Oxford: Hart, 2009).

7. Note that, by virtue of the presumption of inchoate liability, all the inchoate offenses would also apply to this offense—penalizing, for example, an attempt to do an act "in preparation for giving effect to…"

8. See the offense contrary to s. 5 of the Terrorism Act 2006 (above), and also n. 6.

9. See further M. D. Dubber, "The Possession Paradigm: The Special Part and the Police Power Model of the Criminal Process," in R. A. Duff and S. P. Green (eds.), *Defining Crimes: Essays on the Special Part of the Criminal Law* (Oxford: Oxford University Press, 2005).

10. M. Moore, *Act and Crime* (Oxford: Oxford University Press, 1993), 22.

11. J. Bentham, *Principles of the Penal Code* (ed. C.K. Ogden, 1931), 425.

12. See the discussion of Duff's views in part 5 below; cf. F. Schauer and R. Zeckhauser, "Regulation by Generalization," (2007) 1 *Regulation and Governance* 68.

13. A. P. Simester and A. von Hirsch, "Remote Harms and NonConstitutive Crimes," (2009) 28 *Criminal Justice Ethics* 89, at p. 99.

14. See further R. A. Duff, *Answering for Crime* (Oxford: Hart, 2007), pp. 161–172, and J. Oberdiek, "Toward a Right against Risking," (2009) 28 *Law and Philosophy* 367.

15. American Law Institute, *Model Penal Code*, s. 211.2.

16. See D. Husak, *Overcriminalization* (Oxford: Oxford University Press, 2008).

17. H. L. A. Hart, *Punishment and Responsibility* (Oxford: Oxford University Press, 2nd ed., 2008), p. 129.

18. Duff (above, n. 1), p. 134.

19. Commentary to Article 5 of American Law Institute, *Model Penal Code* (1985), p. 294.

20. This point is taken further in section 8 below.

21. For a slightly different version of this argument, see J. Stannard, "Making Up for the Missing Element: A Sideways Look at Attempts," (1987) 7 *Legal Studies* 194.

22. See generally Husak (above, n. 16).

23. Accord: Duff (above, n. 1), 30–31.

24. For a similar restraining principle, see Husak (above, n. 16), 162.

25. See Duff's critique of this "radical subjectivism," above n. 1, 171–172.

26. Article 5.01(b).

27. Model Penal Code, Commentary, 305. The commentary also states that "the actor's dangerousness" is very nearly as great as in the case of purposive conduct; a better argument is that based on the level of culpability.

28. The relevant case-law is discussed by Ashworth (above, n. 2), at 441.

29. It should be noted that rape in English law is no longer defined in this way since the Sexual Offenses Act 2003: for a summary of the new law, see Ashworth (above, n. 2), at 327–354.

30. Duff (above, n. 1), 12.

31. Ibid., 22.

32. Model Penal Code, s. 5.01(1).

33. For a sensitive review of the various tests, see D. R. Stuart, *Canadian Criminal Law*, 4th ed. 2001 (Toronto: Carswell), ch. 10A.3.

34. Duff (above, n. 1), 389.

35. Ibid.

36. L. Alexander and K. K. Ferzan (with S. J. Morse), *Crime and Culpability* (Cambridge: Cambridge University Press, 2009), ch. 6.

37. Criminal Attempts Act (U.K.) 1981, s. 1.

38. For example, A. P. Simester and G. R. Sullivan, *Criminal Law: Theory and Doctrine* (Oxford: Hart, 4th ed., 2010), 330–332.

39. American Law Institute, *Model Penal Code*, s. 5.01(2).

40. In other words, there may be grounds for arresting someone found reconnoitering a house or possessing certain articles, but that does not mean that such acts should be classified and punished as attempts to commit a particular substantive offense.

41. See Salmond J. In *R. v. Barker* [1924] N.Z.L.R. 865, at 869; and A. Enker, "Impossibility in Criminal Attempts: Legality and the Legal Process" (1969) 53 *Minnesota L.R.* 665.

42. On this, see Cross and Tapper's *Evidence*, 11th ed. 2007 by C. Tapper (Oxford: Oxford University Press), 689–699.

43. Alexander and Ferzan (above, n. 36), 216.

44. Duff (above, n. 1), 58 and 390.

45. Law Commission of England and Wales, *Attempt, Conspiracy and Impossibility in Relation to Attempt, Conspiracy and Incitement* (London: Her Majesty's Stationery Office, Law Com No. 102, 1980), para. 2.8, cited with agreement by Duff (above, n. 1), 390.

46. *Model Penal Code* (above, n. 39), s. 5.01(1)(c).

47. Law Commission of England and Wales (above, n. 45), No. 102.

48. Criminal Attempts Act (U.K.) 1981, s. 1(4), interpreted by the House of Lords as preserving a version of the impossibility defense in *Anderton v. Ryan* [1985] A.C. 560, a decision strongly criticized by G. Williams, "The Lords and Impossible Attempts," (1986) 45 *Cambridge Law Journal* 33, and overruled by the House of Lords in *R. v. Shivpuri* [1987] A.C. 1.

49. A. Ashworth, "Belief, Intent and Criminal Liability," in J. Eekelaar and J. Bell (eds.), *Oxford Essays in Jurisprudence: Third Series* (Oxford: Oxford University Press, 1987); see also Duff (above, n. 1), ch. 6, explicating the subjectivist approach as a prelude to criticizing it; and S. J. Morse, "Reasons, Results and Criminal Responsibility" (2004) 24 *University of Illinois Law Review* 363.

50. Accord: Alexander and Ferzan (above, n. 36), ch. 5.

51. The most influential essays are those of T. Nagel, "Moral Luck," in his *Mortal Questions* (Cambridge: Cambridge University Press, 1979), and B. Williams, "Moral Luck," in his *Moral Luck* (Cambridge: Cambridge University Press, 1981); the subsequent literature is voluminous.

52. Accord: Alexander and Ferzan (above, n. 36), 188–190.

53. Duff (above, n. 1), chs. 9 and 10.

54. Ibid., chs. 11 and 12.

55. Ibid., 384; cf. Alexander and Ferzan (above, n. 36), 223, for a different view.

56. I use this term only to denote cases where the defendant was mistaken as to the law (although cf. note 59 below).

57. *R. v. Taaffe* [1984] 1 A.C. 539; in fact the package (unbeknown to the would-be smuggler) contained cannabis, which it is illegal to import.

58. Duff (above, n. 1), 363.

59. A category that depends, of course, on the ability to craft a satisfactory distinction between mistakes of law and of fact; it was partly this difficulty that led Duff (ibid.) to propose a formula that does not rely on this distinction.

60. E.g., J. Hasnas, "Once More unto the Breach: The Inherent Liberalism of the Criminal Law and Liability for Attempting the Impossible," (2002) 54 *Hastings Law Journal* 1, at 21–23.

61. J. Bentham, *Theory of Legislation* (ed. C. K. Ogden, 1931), 427.

62. For elaboration, see Ashworth (above, n. 3), 738–750.

63. P. Robinson and J. Darley, *Justice, Liability and Blame: Community Views and the Criminal Law* (Boulder, Colo.: Westview Press, 1995), 23.

64. Alexander and Ferzan (above, n. 36), 192.

65. Duff (above, n. 1), 353.

66. Above, n. 14 and accompanying text.

67. P. R. Glazebrook, "Should We Have a Law of Attempted Crime?," (1969) 85 *Law Quarterly Review* 28.

68. See the arguments of Husak, above n. 16.

69. For suggestions, see Duff (above, n. 1), 141.

70. It must be said that recent reports from the Law Commission of England and Wales seem to be headed in the opposite direction, since they deal generally with inchoate offenses and complicity.

71. See further A. Ashworth, "The Unfairness of Risk-Based Possession Offences," (2011) 5 *Criminal Law and Philosophy* (forthcoming).

72. For creative suggestions on how to reconfigure "proxy crimes" see Alexander and Ferzan (above, n. 36), 306–313.

73. See, however, Duff (above, n. 14), chs. 6 and 7.

74. See the discussion by Duff (above, n. 1), 171–172.

CHAPTER 6

....

THE PHILOSOPHICAL FOUNDATIONS OF COMPLICITY LAW

....

CHRISTOPHER KUTZ

THE standard model of criminal liability is beautiful in its simplicity. Take homicide and imagine a crowd outside a nightclub. The proverbial shot rings out, a person falls, and a suspect is identified and charged with the killing. The law of homicide prohibits the taking of life without excuse or justification. A jury must answer two questions as a result: First, a question about conduct and causation, or actus reus: did the suspect cause the victim's death, by firing a shot that hit the victim and ended his life? Second, a question about the defendant's mental state, or mens rea: did the suspect cause this death intentionally, or was he aware of the risk he was imposing, or—at the least—would a reasonable person have been aware of that risk? If the answer to both questions is yes, then the defendant will be convicted of some form of homicide, depending on his degree of deliberateness or awareness.

Saying that these are easy questions does not imply that their answers are easily forthcoming. The basic facts will be in dispute, and coincidences may complicate the answer. Perhaps the suspect genuinely believed it was a toy gun, or cigarette lighter, that he was demonstrating; if so, no mens rea, and no liability. Or perhaps the victim had collapsed from a drug overdose moments before he was shot; if so, then no causation. Nonetheless, the basic liability package is clear: a responsible defendant (i.e., capable of rational self-regulation) who acts intentionally or otherwise culpably to cause social harm, and in fact does so.

Moral philosophy and the philosophy of punishment are clear about the wrong as well. No Kantian could reasonably universalize a maxim of doing deliberate or indifferent lethal harm in a world in which we must expect reciprocal concern from others. Hence we may call for retribution, in the form of a social principle of deliberately harming those who deliberately harm others. No utilitarian could think such behavior socially worthwhile, in the absence of any special justification. We must inflict suffering, lest this defendant or others be emboldened by the success of his antisocial behavior. (Perhaps we should add some rehabilitation, for further behavioral benefit.) And with the deliberateness or other form of culpability established, no liberal could object to the infliction of punishment on someone who so chose to flout the norms of criminal law.[1] While skepticism is possible, for example about the role of moral luck or freedom of the will, the basic conceptual questions of moral culpability and liability to punishment are basically overdetermined in the single actor case.

Inchoate liability, for attempted acts of social harms, represents the first form of complication. Doctrinally, inchoate liability appears simple at first blush: it merely peels away from the basic liability package the causation element, so we are left with the causally inert package of intentional (or otherwise culpable) conduct by a responsible agent. In fact, doctrinal questions complicate quickly, as soon as we move away from an insistence on tying liability to the final stage of conduct that would otherwise have caused harm—to the pull of the trigger or the lighting of the match, for example. Once a criminal "attempt" may be found to lie in some course of conduct short of that last step, criminal law must settle a range of difficult boundary questions about the sufficiency of the actus reus: what extent of conduct suffices to warrant punishment, and is necessary to prove the existence of criminal intent?

Return to the nightclub fight and stop the action earlier, with a patron pulling a gun from his waistband, but now wrestled to the ground by a bouncer. Can such an act, accompanied by further evidence of intent, be enough to ground a charge of attempted murder?[2] Framed normatively, the question is yet more contested: given that no harm actually occurred, is the attempt to impose harm sufficient to legitimate punishment? Retributivist theories, based in occurrent harms, would seem to have no clear answer whether nonharmful conduct can warrant suffering in return. Instrumentalist theories must weigh the benefits of deterring socially risky behavior against the costs of punishing conduct that might not have been consummated in a final act.

But the complexities of inchoate liability pale in contrast to accomplice liability. Return one last time to the nightclub: two patrons are squared off and angry, when a third person in the crowd hands a gun to one of them, saying, "Give him what he deserves." The fighter who has been handed the gun shoots and kills. Clearly, he is guilty of some form of homicide, and morally responsible for that act. But both morality and law insist that the fact that only he pulled the trigger does not exhaust the question of responsibility. The onlooker with the gun also contributed to the death—notwithstanding that it was the shooter's decision whether to pull the trigger, and independent of whether the shooter might have killed with a knife instead. The act of handing a gun itself causes no harm and violates no legal norm.[3] But this basic principle, that indirect contribution to someone else's bad act can render one responsible for that act, is subject to a vast range of challenges and questions. Consider now some casebook chestnuts and real variations:

1. Judge Tally has learned that his sister-in-law has been seduced by a cad, Ross, and that his brothers-in-law, the Skeltons, are planning to kill Ross. Tally also learns that a friend of Ross has just sent a warning telegram to be delivered to Ross, in the town where he has fled. Acting quickly, Tally sends a second message to the telegraph operator in that town, instructing him not to warn Ross. As a consequence, the warning telegram is not delivered. However, since the Skeltons are already hot on Ross' trail, there is little reason to think the warning would have had effect in any event. The Skeltons catch up with Ross and gun him down. Query: Is Judge Tally also guilty of Ross's murder?[4]

2. Iago, seeking to frame an innocent, persuades his jealous commander, Othello, that his wife has been unfaithful. Iago plants evidence, insinuates Desdemona's betrayal, and then, as Othello's jealousy rises to fever pitch, suggests that Othello strangle her. Othello does and is charged with murder, but is convicted only of manslaughter, on the ground that most people, in the circumstances, might have behaved in similar fashion, and so is not fully responsible for his acts. Query: Is Iago guilty of a more serious crime?[5]

3. Nahimana, a producer at a Rwandan radio station, set editorial policy and wrote editorial scripts for a radio station urging members of the Hutu tribe to take up arms against Tutsi tribe members, both in general and in specific cases, who were accused of planning to assassinate Hutu political figures. Query: Is Nahimana guilty not only of "incitement to produce genocide," but of the resulting genocide itself?[6]

4. Maxwell, a member of a Protestant Irish militant organization, was asked to drive his car to an inn owned and frequented by Catholics, thus leading a car containing four strangers to the inn. Maxwell did not know what specific crime was intended, although he knew it was a "military operation" of some sort. Query: Is Maxwell guilty of the pipe-bombing of the inn conducted by the four strangers?

These cases raise a number of extraordinarily difficult questions about the ascription of responsibility within both morality and criminal law. The Judge Tally case asks whether a defendant must have made a clear difference to an outcome, in order to be judged culpable for that outcome. Iago challenges us to distinguish the culpability of the coolheaded instigator from that of the hot-blooded perpetrator. Nahimana poses the question whether rhetoric can be the attributable cause of another's crime. The scale of the act of genocide also raises the question whether complicity, amplified by technology, can result in too great a scope of liability. And Maxwell asks whether foresight of another's crime can be treated as the equivalent of an intention to commit that crime.

These questions arise within criminal law, in relation to the formal concepts of intent and cause. They also reflect a specific dialectic within criminal law, between its backward-looking, retributive structure and the forward-looking, risk-reducing aims that have become an increasing part of its modern justification. A retributive view of criminal law puts pressure precisely on the difficult points of interpersonal causation and joint activity, while an instrumentalist conception, like that embodied in the U.S. Model Penal Code, rests on vaguer grounds, such as whether a given defendant has manifested some form of social dangerousness, independent of the causal efficacy of the particular role he played.

These problems of criminal law are equally philosophical challenges. While ascriptions of interpersonal causation are part of the bread and butter of daily life—"He made me do it!" is a defense often heard at home—and while talk of complicity permeates politics and social life, the subject demands a philosophically rigorous investigation. Criminal law, as a systematic body of law in which questions of causation are resolved and attributions of responsibility are made, provides a nearly ideal forum for working out the lines of such an investigation.

My aim in this chapter is to explore the philosophical interest of the problems raised by accomplice liability, and then to make my own case for several propositions, some specific to complicity law, and some to theories of responsibility generally:

1. The normative justification for accomplice liability generally is the risk-enhancing character of aiding or encouraging another's criminal efforts. That is, accomplice liability is best conceived as a form of inchoate liability at the level of act-type criminalization.

2. The basis of accomplice liability for a particular defendant is an analytically distinctive intent to further a shared goal (what I have called elsewhere a "participatory intent") whether or not the perpetrator knows the goal is shared, not the specific conduct of the accomplice or its consequences. Such an intent satisfies a range of theories of legitimate punishment, including liberal harm-based and liberty-maximizing theories.

3. Three consequences for complicity doctrine follow:
   i. Causation, at the level of the token contribution, need not be shown, nor need one adopt a particular theory of causation in order to make sense of complicity doctrine. One need only show that the act of assistance or encouragement was of the right type to make a difference.
   ii. Criminal liability, and retrospective responsibility generally, must be understood pluralistically, not reductively: a range of bases can establish a warrant for sanction, including intentional participation, affiliation, causation, and risk-imposition.
   iii. Knowing facilitation may be a useful category for criminalization, but it is analytically distinct from the participatory intent characteristic of complicity law.

I do not propose to demonstrate these conclusively, although I will present my own views of their merits. The plan is as follows: first, I set out briefly the basic legal elements of complicity law, concentrating on Anglo-American law. Next, I will examine the key notions of philosophical interest: causation, joint action, and intentionality. I then consider the different valences of responsibility, as between accomplices and direct perpetrators. Last, I look to the outer limits of accomplice liability, as reflected primarily in liability for mass atrocities.

II Basic Elements of Complicity Law

Complicity doctrine renders one person liable for the criminal act of another when the accomplice (usually called the "secondary" party, whom I will call S) intentionally aids, encourages, or both, the direct perpetrator (whom I will call P) in the commission of that act. The most basic point about complicity liability is that complicity is not itself a crime, but rather a mode of individual liability cantilevered out from the basic model of individual criminal liability. Thus, accomplice liability is part of the system of ancillary liability models that include inchoate (attempt) liability and vicarious liability (liability in virtue of a preexisting relationship). Its distinctive doctrinal elements and liability scheme must be understood in relation to that basic model. The hornbook phrase is that accomplice liability is derivative, grounded in the liability of the principal. This is true, in the limited sense that at common law, there can be no accomplice liability unless a principal has at least attempted a crime. But the elements of accomplice liability are defined independently, not derivatively, in terms of the more basic concepts of individual direct liability.

With jurisdictional and analytical caveats and exceptions to follow, we can sketch out the hornbook elements of accomplice liability as follows: Someone is liable for the conduct of another as an accomplice if, prior to the other's attempt at or commission of a criminal act, the first person does or says something that could assist or encourage the second in the commission of the act, intending that the second in fact engage in the criminal act. The physical conduct, or actus reus, element of complicity is evidently broad, and defined only in relation to acts of assistance or encouragement (including inducement); the mental, or mens rea, element is accordingly narrower, and requires that the accomplice have an intent closely analogous to that of the principal. Thus, one does not become an accomplice to another's burglary merely by pointing out, to someone loitering on the street, that a house has a window open. Rather, one needs to point out the vulnerable window with the specific intent that the addressee enter with the aim of permanently depriving the owners of property.

We can take a first schematic cut at the modes of direct and indirect individual liability in the table:

The table reveals straightaway the most striking feature of accomplice liability: the asymmetry, or one-way dependence, between S's and P's liability. P's liability turns strictly on whether P has performed the actus reus with the requisite intent. If so, and regardless of the outcome, P is liable for at least an attempt. And when P does so, if S has incited, encouraged, or aided P (with or without knowledge by P), then S is liable, too—in most jurisdictions, moreover, liable as if S had himself performed P's act. But if P does not make at least a culpable attempt, S bears no liability at all—even though every other basis for S's liability remains the same. Imagine, for example, that S hopes to aid P's plan to murder a common enemy, by mailing P a more effective poison than the one at P's disposal. If P receives the poison and doses V's coffee with it, S has become a murderer or attempted murderer (as has P, of course). But if P decides at the last minute not to dose the coffee, or is otherwise

	P acts/attempts?	S liable?
S encourages	✓	[Check]
S acts via innocent P	✓	✓
S & P jointly act	✓	✓
S instigates/solicits	✓	✓
S instigates/solicits		✓ (for solicitation)[7]
S gives aid	✓	✓
S gives aid (known to P)		
S attempts to aid/encourage		

prevented from getting far enough down the path to the poisoning for P's act to constitute an attempt, then S's potential liability has shifted from murderer to nothing, even though he acted with murderous intent and despite no change in his conduct.

This anomaly, which has been the object of reform attempts in both the United States and United Kingdom, reflects a conceptual gap at the heart of complicity law, and it is difficult to justify under any plausible penal theory that includes inchoate liability. If S's moral culpability is equivalent under both scenarios, as well as the riskiness of S's behavior in mailing a more dangerous poison, then it is hard to find a normatively persuasive basis for distinguishing liability. The anomaly represents a substantial moral luck effect within criminal law.

There is another anomaly as well, revealed in another table. The previous table focused only on cases of deliberate complicity, where S has the purpose of encouraging or assisting P's commission of the crime. But an important range of cases involve holding S to a weaker standard of culpability: knowledge, foresight, or recklessness as to P's commission of a crime.

Generally speaking, English and civil (including international criminal) law make knowing or foreseen provision of aid or encouragement a basis for criminal liability, while most U.S. jurisdictions do not.[8] (Some U.S. jurisdictions, notably New York, have a lesser penalty for knowing facilitation.) To take a standard example: S works in a gun shop and serves a customer seeking to purchase a handgun that can be easily modified to accommodate a silencer. S strongly suspects that the customer intends a murder, but does not himself intend to facilitate a murder, only a gun sale. In the United Kingdom, the seller might well be liable for the resulting murder, unless shopkeepers are given a specific safe haven from liability.[9] In France, in the famous case of Vichy collaborator Maurice Papon, Papon was held liable for crimes against humanity when he transported French Jews to the Nazis, knowing of their eventual fate though without any interest in bringing it about. By contrast, in the United States most courts have held to the requirement announced by Judge Learned Hand that an accomplice have "a stake" in the criminal venture, seeking for

S's intent	P's act	S is liable as accomplice?
S knows that P will engage in criminal act C	P does C	Yes in U.K., no in U.S.
S has agreed that P will engage in criminal act C	P does C	Yes in U.K., mostly in U.S.
S has agreed that P will engage in criminal act C	P does C and different criminal act C'	Yes, mostly, so long as C' is within scope of C
S believes P may engage in criminal act C	P does different and more serious act C'	Unclear

it to succeed, and that mere knowledge is not enough.[10] But the requirements of that state can be satisfied rather easily. The so-called *Pinkerton* doctrine in federal criminal law, for example, which makes conspirators liable as accomplices for foreseeable acts committed by coconspirators within the scope of the conspiracy, has the effect of extending accomplice liability for intentional crimes to defendants who merely foresee the crime. Thus, with the addition of facilitation or co-conspirator liability, complicity doctrine involves a second significant anomaly: P must satisfy a stricter culpability standard than S for the same crime. A major task for a philosophical reconstruction is determining whether this disparity can be given a principled basis in complicity law, for instance in a claim that the affiliative character of complicity makes room for a looser mens rea standard, under principles of vicarious, principal-agent liability, or whether it is an undesirable inconsistency better handled through a separate form of criminalization.[11]

The final, striking feature of complicity doctrine does not appear within these tables at all, and this is the peculiar equivalence of accomplice and direct liability. Within Anglo-American and much civil (but not German) law, accomplices are treated as liable to the same punishment as direct perpetrators.[12] This is a long-standing principle in the Anglo-American common law, codified uniformly by statute, and true as well in most other jurisdictions. The notable exception is Germany, where aiding accomplices are given a significant discount from their principals' sentencing, although inducing accomplices are given no such discount.[13] The equivalence of accomplice and principal liability is peculiar because, in the case of attempt liability—arguably the closest analogue to accomplice liability—by far the dominant pattern is a systematic reduction in punishment. While neither the attempt discount nor the accomplice non-discount might be justifiable in the end, one might think there is a substantial argumentative burden to be met for a principle of punishment that does not distinguish between offenders who do, and do not, complete the actus reus of the target offense. A bank clerk who provides a surveillance schedule, endorsing a robbery plan that includes killing a guard, has done something terrible. But the position that the clerk should be treated as a killer of the guard requires argument, to say the least.

There remain a number of puzzles within complicity doctrine that do not generate so much philosophical as simple policy interest, such as whether one can become an accomplice to a crime of strict liability—for example, by urging another to have sexual relations with a partner who, unbeknownst to both, is underage—or whether, if liability is extended, it extends to foreseeable as opposed to actually foreseen harms. There are equally questions about the role of aid or encouragement that cannot possibly make a difference, whose blameworthiness (like other forms of inherent impossibility) will turn ultimately on a balancing of antisocial animus against the conservation of penal resources. I turn instead to the chief philosophical puzzles.

III Puzzle : Causation and the Accomplice

The beginning of philosophical wisdom about complicity lies in Sanford Kadish's classic article "Complicity, Cause and Blame: A Study in Doctrine." Kadish argues that complicity doctrine functions as a complement to direct perpetrator liability, providing a form of culpability when ordinary notions of physical causation cannot supply a sufficient ground. Sometimes, the difficulty is said to lie in the legal maxim of novus actus interveniens—the idea that causal chains, hence ascriptions of moral and legal responsibility, are cut by others' freely chosen acts. The maxim indeed states a general normative principle that an individual's voluntary choice provides a basis for imputing responsibility to that individual—as evidenced in the lameness of the excuse "Everyone's doing it." But this maxim, most obviously found in criminal-law cases involving suicide, is more honored in the breach outside the suicide context.[14] In fact, we routinely recognize both causation and responsibility to flow along interpersonal channels as well, as when one person instigates another to commit a crime.

Contrast two examples, where claims of interpersonal causation might, and might not, go through. In the first, S, intent on murdering P's spouse, V, puts poison in the sugar that he knows P will give her, but without telling P. In such a case, S will be charged as the perpetrator of the murder and deemed to have used P as an "innocent agent," an instrument of S's will.[15] "P was not the real killer, S was!" we might say—and the law will draw a comparable conclusion, treating P as the "innocent instrument" of S's "procuring of the crime." Even if P is later pleased at V's death, S is deemed in both law and ordinary morality to have been the principal cause and perpetrator of the death, while P is excused from liability. Causation, running through P's voluntary but ignorant acts, connects S directly to the proscribed harm, such that P's actions are seen merely as an instrument for S to realize his goals.

In a second case, S and P discuss V's shoddy treatment of P. S agrees that V's behavior toward P has been disgraceful, and suggests that P punish V. S gives P poison to put in V's coffee, disguised as sugar, and P does so, poisoning V. Now, it may have been the case that P would not have acted but for S's encouragement and assistance. Ordinary language reflects this: we might say that S's persuasion was *a* cause of V's death, or even its instigation. But it would take matters a step further to identify S as *the* cause of V's death, even if, but for S's intervention, V would still be alive. This is so not just because P's acts contribute to V's death, but because the proposal became, once accepted by P, a project of P's own will. This internal, subjective element of will formation, according to Kadish, is what resists incorporation into the external, objective notion of causation in criminal law. Criminal law marks the distinction in the form of liability by treating S as the accomplice to rather than perpetrator of V's death, and excusing the prosecution from the need to prove causation in this instance.[16] Whereas P's liability lies in the causing of V's death without justification or excuse, S's liability lies in assisting or encouraging P, with the intent of furthering the murder. Complicitous encouragement, not causation, provides the linchpin of liability.

One must bear in mind that Kadish's point is not that complicity in every case fills a causal gap, or that direct perpetration is in every case causal—or, more important, that causation is well defined in criminal law:

> I do not mean to say that the language of causation is inappropriate when dealing with one person's influence on the actions of another even when the latter's actions are entirely volitional. We commonly speak of one person occasioning the actions of another or of one person's action being the result of what another person says or does. This is appropriate because causation, broadly conceived, concerns the relationship between successive phenomena, whether they have the character of events or happenings, or of another person's volitional actions. The point I mean to stress is that in dealing with the influence of one person upon the actions of another, we refer to a different kind of causal concept than that involved in physical causation. However philosophers may dispute the point, as far as the law is concerned, the way in which a person's acts produce results in the physical world is significantly different from the way in which a person's acts produce results that take the form of the volitional actions of others. The difference derives from the special view we take of the nature of a human action.[17]

This point is well taken. Legal theorists, making use of philosophical discussions, divide on the best metaphysical account of causation: whether it is a matter of counterfactual dependence ("c caused e" is true if and only if, if c hadn't occurred, e would not have occurred); conditional dependence ("c caused e" is true if and only if c is a nonredundant element of a set of other nonredundant conditions sufficient for the occurrence of e); probabilistic relations ("c caused e" is true if and only if the occurrence of c raised the probability of e's occurrence); or a brute, singular physical relation involving the transferal of forces.[18] And there is room for further debate whether criminal law's (or tort's) distinctive use of the term "causation" means anything more than "the sort of relation for which liability is appropriately imposed," and for which a normatively constrained sine qua non relation is the best approximation.[19]

In fact, descriptive metaphysics is less the issue than normative significance. We might agree that the cause of the house burning down was both the faulty circuit and the failure of the fire department to turn up in time to douse the flames—even though the metaphysically parsimonious would not recognize the omission as a genuine cause. While fire investigators and tort lawyers might further disagree about which is to count as the cause, that disagreement lies in policy, not philosophy. The issues of overdetermination and interagent causation presented by complicity are similar. The central issue of causation lies in the attribution of relative degrees of significance, more than in the resolution of the puzzles of overdetermination. Overdetermination cases present a verbal puzzle, choosing the appropriate formulation of a causal condition that respects the way in which energies or productive efficacies (in whatever Molièresque formulation one prefers) flow into a jointly realized event. But once we have a formulation, for example the strong "NESS" (Necessary Element of a Set of Sufficient Conditions) test, according to which each contributor to an overdetermined event can count nonetheless as a part cause of the event—in this case, because each might be deemed a nonredundant element of a set of conditions jointly sufficient for the event—then the verbal problem of overdetermination is solved. Not so the normative problem, which requires establishing the punitive (or normative) significance of an overdetermined contribution, so that a treatment for the contribution can be established.

A classic example by Jonathan Glover illustrates well the question of normative significance, and brings out some of the difficulties in assigning normative weight to complicitous behavior. Glover offers two variants of a situation in which a group of thieves descends on a group of hungry villagers. In variant A, thirty thieves working separately descend on thirty hungry villagers, each with a bowl of thirty beans. Each thief takes all the beans from a villager's bowl, resulting in thirty hungry villagers. Clearly each thief is guilty of a serious theft, causing a villager to go hungry. In variant B, the thieves again descend, but with a common plan that each now take a single bean from each villager. There are still thirty hungry villagers, but no thief has individually made a significant difference to any one of them.

We might render matters more salient by assuming that each villager dies of starvation as a result of the theft of his or her beans. The question is whether the difference in individual causal agency adds up to a moral difference, such that we can regard the thieves in variant A, but not in variant B, as murderers.[20] Following the route of causal efficacy, however, leads to many puzzles. On the one hand, each thief in A directly causes the death of a particular villager, and so each might be accountable for a single death. In B, no thief directly causes any death, so none might be counted a direct murderer. But if we take seriously the fact that each acted according to a plan, then each thief in B might well be regarded as worse, for each has causally contributed to each death. Indeed, to stretch the example further, we might even treat each as a necessary part of an unnecessary but sufficient condition of each death, if leaving a single bean might have extended a villager's life.[21] So, in variant B, we seem to have a situation in which each acts thirty times worse, even though it is only in A that a thief's acts are individually sufficient for death.

It is, of course, difficult to discuss the example without presupposing the moral category under discussion: complicity.[22] But the example does help us see the smoothing effect of complicity, as it irons out otherwise sharp gradations in causal contribution.

As I have written before, moral responsibility in such situations is best understood not separably, in terms of individual causal relations, but collectively, in terms of what the gang has done.[23] The thieves' responsibility must be understood *inclusively*: each is included in the group that did the wrong, and bears responsibility qua member of that group. The basis of responsibility in such a case is not the difference an individual contributor makes, but the common plan, mediated by each individual's intention to participate in that plan. The anomaly in the responsibility between individually acting thieves in A and collectively acting thieves in B stems from the different intentions with which each group acts. In A, the basic subject of the act is the individual thief, whereas in B it is "we thieves," from which an individual role is derived. The different, individual vs. collective, bases of responsibility, then, explains the different scope of responsibility. By contrast, if the thieves in A were to have agreed that each would steal all the beans from a single villager, then the basis of their responsibility would be the same as that of the thieves in B, rendering them, too, responsible for all thirty deaths.

Complicity doctrine functions in law as it does in morality—eliding individual inquiries into causation by treating the harm intended (what I intend to do as part of our act) as the basis for criminal liability. A further virtue of the category of complicity is that it avoids not just the problem of establishing the normative significance of individual causal responsibility but also the epistemic problem of determining ostensible causal contributions in the first place. The standard example is the robbery-shootout, where neither robber is willing to identify the other as the triggerman. With a criminal complicity doctrine, the state need only show a common plan to threaten violence in order to render each liable for the death.[24]

Now, one might still insist, against the overall shape of the doctrine, that causal responsibility lies at the root of complicity, both in the tendency of each accomplice to fortify the will of the others (and so to contribute horizontally, as it were, as well as vertically, toward the harm) and in the difference each contributes to the realization of the harm. English criminal law scholar K. J. M. Smith takes such a line, noting that while the case law is contradictory, and while administrative ease often makes determination of causation impossible, nonetheless the basically causal structure of complicity can be discerned in its derivative nature.[25] On this argument, the historic form of accomplice liability, which treated the "causing" principal as the basic site of liability, as well as the now-abrogated distinction between accessories and principals more broadly, points to the causal core.

Perhaps. But one might equally find that legal doctrine is shifting philosophically as well as doctrinally away from a focus on objective causation to subjective intent, and so moving from causation to participation. This is, fundamentally, to shift accomplice liability from a harm to a risk, or inchoate, basis. The doctrinal argument for the inchoate nature of accomplice liability was nicely stated by the UK Law Commission:

> An accessory's legal fault is complete as soon as his act of assistance is done, and acts thereafter by the *principal*, in particular in committing or not committing the crime assisted, cannot therefore add to or detract from that fault. Moreover, it is not the present law, and it is logically impossible that it should become the law, that the accessory must *cause* the commission of the principal crime; and for that reason also the actual occurrence of the principal crime is not taken into account in assessing the accessory's culpability. Even under the present law, therefore, where the principal crime has to be committed before accessory liability can attach, the conditions for the liability of the accessory should be, indeed can only be, assessed at the time of, and in relation to, that act of assistance.[26]

The issue here is not just whether accomplice liability is best conceived as a way of bringing about (causing) another's crime, but whether it is conceived as derivative in any robust sense—that is, with the principal's acts forming part of the basis of the accomplice's crime. As the Law Commission points out, as a conceptual matter accomplice liability forms a complete package in its own terms: the mental element is defined in terms of a subjective intent to assist another's crime, while the physical element is defined in terms of acts that further that subjective intent. Whether there actually is an act by a principal furthered by the accomplice's doings is immaterial to an assessment of their purpose, and so should be immaterial to an assessment of the accomplice's liability.

This is an argument from doctrine, not philosophical principle. And it comes into conflict with other pieces of doctrine, notably the rule cited by Smith: the derivative character of complicity. But if one treats that rule as a mistaken conclusion, then a new scheme of accomplice liability falls into place, one better aligned with both the actual elements of liability as well as the conceptual and normative reasons grounding that liability. Hence, the Model Penal Code's treatment of Judge Tally as equivalently liable whether or not he has actually contributed to a killing or merely tried. The vexed relationship between luck and causality loses importance under this view.

IV The Bases of Accomplice Liability

Once we see participatory intentions rather than causal contributions as at the root of complicity, then we can broaden the philosophical views we take of the normative basis of liability. Causal significance can still count as one factor in determining an appropriate social or legal response, but only as one factor. In some cases, a focus on participatory intentions means that we shift from backward-looking to forward-looking theories of liability. In other cases, we can look to dimensions of character and moral valence that cut across the harm-done/harm-threatened division. In short, recognizing the distinctive basis of liability renders intelligible the plurality of bases for punishment.

Two examples, mentioned at the beginning of the chapter, will help to make this case. The first is Iago's machinations, setting the stage for the tightly wound Othello to explode into jealous (if unfounded) rage. The second is Nahimana, whose responsibility for the Rwandan genocide lay in his contribution to a climate of hatred and violence, rather than his use of a physical weapon himself. Both played on the prejudices and sentiments of others, influencing but not causing their behavior. In both cases, the responsibility is serious enough—indeed perhaps graver than that of the direct killers—that it confirms the range of normative factors at root.

Iago, recall, is furious at Othello for promoting Cassio above him and plots revenge against them both. By insinuating a romance between Cassio and Desdemona (Othello's wife), Iago is able to prompt Othello to a murderous rage, triggered finally by a piece of evidence planted by Iago's wife, Emilia. Othello strangles Desdemona in her bed, only to realize quickly he has been set up by Iago. This is of course no excuse, in Shakespeare's time or our own: Othello is guilty of at least voluntary manslaughter, and perhaps even second-degree murder, depending on a jury's sympathies for the torments of misplaced sexual jealousy or the reasonableness of his suspicions. But Iago's case is more complicated. On a derivative theory of accomplice liability, his own guilt cannot be greater than that of his principal. If Othello is guilty of manslaughter, to which Iago casually contributed, then Iago's liability must be similarly limited. No antecedent cause can be responsible for a greater effect than its intermediary, after all.

But such an outcome is at odds with the force of the tragedy and moral common sense. Othello is too strong to be considered a victim, and Shakespeare is clear that honor alone does not compel him to kill—the murder arises more from his own insecurities, and proceeds with fair deliberation.[27] But he is still essentially moved by a world of false clues Iago constructs around him. Iago, meanwhile, is not subject to the specific irrationality of sexual jealousy; Desdemona's killing is the object of his plot, not an outbreak of passion. He is a deliberate murderer, without question. While Othello is more than a mere instrument of Iago's will, Iago's greater culpability is supported by the distinctive nature of his plan—the way it incorporates Othello's agency.

In a less literary vein, the distinction between the manipulative secondary party and the principal of mitigated accountability arises whenever roles are differentiated and control (or power in some form) lies with the accomplice. The nurse who follows a doctor's bidding to inject a euthanizing solution into a patient's intravenous line is the direct instrument of killing, but primary responsibility for the killing lies with the doctor who gives the order.[28] Similarly, a gang leader who sends foot soldiers into a neighborhood where violence is likely to erupt may be guilty of murder, though the factual killers are guilty of manslaughter. And it is of course possible that a secondary party might ask another to break into a house in order to seize property said (falsely) to belong to him. The accomplice would, in such a case, satisfy the intent requirement for burglary, while the principal might satisfy only the requirement for illegal entry.[29] More striking yet is the German case reported by George Fletcher in which a KGB assassin was deemed to bear minimal responsibility relative to his controller, on the grounds that he was "alienated" from his act, regarding it as not fully his own. In all these cases, the distinction between the accomplice's liability and the perpetrator's is found in a range of subjective factors: capacity for self-governance, identification with the act, and incorporation of another's agency into one's own plan.[30]

The lesson of *Othello* is that, in morality, indirect participation can be more serious than direct action. Alas, this lesson has been learned in a nonliterary way again and again, in the field of international criminal law. The issues of causation and accomplice liability that lie on the margin of individual cases come to the forefront in the cases of genocide and mass atrocity of recent decades. Such crimes are important not only because of their moral and political significance but also because of the complicated chains of influence through which they arise and are perpetuated. Return to the case of Nahimana, whose Rwandan radio station (RTLM) contributed to the fear and hatred at the root of the Tutsi massacre. Nahimana was charged with, among other things, both incitement to genocide and direct responsibility for that crime; he was convicted at trial.[31] The prosecutor's theory of the case rested on Nahimana's authorship of a widely-distributed article, "Rwanda: Current Problems and Solutions"; RTLM's advertisements for the hatred-spewing Hutu Power newspaper, *Kangura*; a number of radio editorials broadcast early in 1994; and a radio interview on April 25, 1994, in which Nahimana referred to Tutsis as "enemies."

The connections between Nahimana and the genocide may seem stunningly weak, given the gravity of the crime charged. No direct causation could be shown, only a pervasive possibility of influence. This is inevitable: few cases of mass atrocity have at their roots a well-defined command structure, an arch-génocidaire giving orders to a few subcommandants. And even in those rare and well-defined cases, the mass aspect of the atrocity will still owe much to the less coordinated efforts of individuals like Nahimana, who share an ideology—and may even be significant contributors to its propagation—but nonetheless cannot be easily located within a causal chain.

Yet, as with Iago, if we abjure such cases of complicity and focus only on causation, we lose the broader moral canvas. We need not minimize the direct responsibility of the direct perpetrators, those carrying the machetes, if we at the same time recognize the indirect yet more extensive liabilities of the contributors. International criminal law struggles with this burden of justifying liability for those able to keep their hands clean of the immediate killing and even to avoid leaving a paper trail of direct orders. In international criminal law, the doctrine of joint criminal enterprise serves the same purpose as the conjunction of conspiracy and complicity doctrine within Anglo-American criminal law. This doctrine allows for liability despite less specified forms of direct contribution to the underlying criminal acts. Nonetheless, an overall causal connection between the activities of the participants in the enterprise and the direct perpetrators must still be found.[32] In Nahimana's case, this meant showing that his earlier influence on RTLM continued into the period of the active killing. On appeal, he was able to convince the court that the connections between his contributions to the station's ideology and the unfolding massacre did not, in fact, meet the rather ill-defined causal threshold of actual commission of the crime, although his conviction for instigating the crime of genocide remained, on the basis of those contributions.[33]

The wayward path of Nahimana's trial and appeal reveal the inherent instabilities of complicity, as much a matter of doctrine as of concept. These instabilities arise because in fact the bases for accomplice liability vary, relying here on direct causation, there on atmospheric conditioning, given focus by the specificity of intent and capacity for self-control, and always leavened by a background consideration of the magnitude of the evil. Within the well-defined binaries of accomplices keeping watch while the triggermen rob, these instabilities are well managed: mens rea can be shown to be shared, and the intersection of roles is tightly bound enough that specific causal inquiries can be put aside. But in more diffuse organizational or ideological contexts, the several bases of complicity verge on unmanageability, leading to divergent judgments about whether any causal condition is or needs to be met.

V Participatory Intent versus Knowledge

We have seen that the conduct component of accomplice liability is not easily understood in terms of causal difference-making, given the range of ways an accomplice can contribute to a principal's outcome—from the marginal contribution of attendance at an illegal jazz concert,[34] to the attempted interception of a warning telegram, to the amplification of a climate of collective mistrust and dehumanization. A corollary of the widely varying act requirement in complicity doctrine has been greater doctrinal focus on the question of the intent required for liability. The hornbook rule, as I mentioned above, is that the accomplice must have an intent to further the commission of the crime by the principal: a lookout offers his surveillance with the aim of enhancing his partner's chance to break in, a Mob accountant keeps the books in order to help the usury business profit.[35] I have elsewhere described the requirement as involving a "participatory intent"—an intent or purpose to do one's part in a collective act, such that one's own personal efforts are directed at achieving the collective aim.[36] Thus, for example, we consider the lookout in the burglary an accomplice not just because he is standing at the door but because he sees himself as standing at the door in order to help achieve the shared goal of a successful liberation of the store's goods. The accountant, likewise, tailors her accounting to the aim of understanding the profits and losses of the (illegal) business. Were the situation to change—say it became clear that a lookout would be more useful on another side of the building—then an accomplice who genuinely aims at enabling the burglary would move. Such counterfactual dependence, between the instrumental act of the secondary party and the aim of the group (or the principal), reflects the intentional structure of complicity.

Attention to the ways individuals intentionally cooperate, and so build and live social lives, has become an exceedingly rich area of philosophical inquiry. Work by Margaret Gilbert, Michael Bratman, Seumas Miller, John Searle, and Raimo Tuomela, among others, has transformed our understanding of human social agency.[37] Many philosophers now understand cooperation not as constructed from ordinary, first personal intentions ("I'll do this, if you'll do that") but as reflecting a more radically social form of agency ("I'll do this as part of our doing that").

Much of this scholarship raises questions that go beyond issues of accomplice liability, such as the difference between bare coordination and full cooperation, the ethical obligations that arise from (and may be constitutive of) cooperation, the ontology of social groups, and the reducibility of participatory intentions to ordinary individual intentions. But there is important carryover, and potential cross-fertilization, between law and philosophy in this area. The first site of convergence concerns the basic structure of the accomplice's intent, whose distinctive character is illuminated by the philosophical concepts of joint action and intentionality. But the real value may lie in the contributions of philosophy of action to two other standard questions within complicity law: the alienated accomplice, and the knowing facilitator.

Take first the alienated accomplice—the person who is indifferent to the success of the venture as a whole (perhaps because he does not profit from it) but nonetheless deliberately contributes to the venture. Individuals participate in collective ventures for a variety of reasons, including desire to profit and fear of repercussions if they refuse. In any of these cases, an accomplice put to trial might say, "I didn't intend to help the principal succeed—I was just doing my job."

A powerful example of this is the case of James Maxwell, who was tapped by the Ulster Volunteer Force to lead a car of men he knew were up to no good to the location they requested, where they subsequently planted a bomb. In his defense, he said he neither shared their mission nor knew the plan they meant to carry out; hence he lacked the intent to further their pipe-bombing of an inn.[38] Under a certain understanding of participation, that would be correct. Indeed, the language of American complicity law suggests that one needs "a stake in the venture," something more than mere association, to be an accomplice.[39] But the language is misleading if it suggests that the accomplice must be subjectively attached to the mission of the principal. The actual standard in law is functional, not subjective: one is deemed to satisfy the standard if one's acts are guided counterfactually by the principal's aim—however one feels about that aim. In the *Peoni* case, the issue of intent arose because Peoni had sold counterfeit bills to one Regno, who then sold them on again; the question was whether Peoni was Regno's accomplice in the second sale. Peoni was acquitted, not because of his attitude toward Regno's sale but because once he had sold Regno the bills, he did nothing to further Regno's subsequent sale, hence there was no reason to conclude that Peoni had an intent to participate in Regno's crime, only an intent to commit his own individual crime of selling the false notes. It would have been a different matter if Regno had been a regular customer of Peoni, such that Peoni was dependent on Regno's success in passing on the bills, thus generating further business; then it could have been said of Peoni that "he [sought] by his action to make it succeed."

So a subjective attitude of identification is not necessary so long as other evidence can show the integration of the accomplice's act into a plan of the principal. This makes sense within law, given the difficulty of proving something as introspective as identification. But it makes sense philosophically as well. Once we see joint action as both pervasive in our environment and constitutive of our social world, we realize that the constraints on participation must be very weak, to accommodate this pervasiveness. A functional understanding of joint action, manifest in the counterfactual dependence of the accomplice's act on the principal's aim, covers the territory of social action from the behavior of animals, to children, to interdependent conventions of trust and reciprocity underlying more complex social behavior.[40]

A functional understanding of complicity does, however, leave open another question: whether knowing but otherwise indifferent facilitation constitutes complicity. These cases typically arise where the secondary party provides a routine good or service to another actor, aware that the principal will make use of the good or service to commit another crime. Standard examples include Internet services that permit posting ads for prostitution services, gun sellers who have reason to believe the gun will be used in a crime, or laborers performing basic chores (such as cooking or field-clearing) that play a role in a criminal enterprise. Courts and legislatures have struggled with the policy question of whether to burden providers of these goods with the risk of criminal implication. But an analytical, philosophical question is prior: is there really a difference between the alienated accomplice, mentioned above, and the mere knowing facilitator? Can the notion of participatory intent make the distinction?

Lessons from more basic philosophy of action serve well here: the distinction between intentional (purposive) action and action done with the awareness of side effects is real, and crucial to understanding how we integrate specific aims into our more general plans.[41] As both Bratman and Antony Duff have argued, while our decisions to act incorporate our awareness of the consequences of those acts, there remains a difference between, say, acting with the intent to cross a lawn, knowing it will track the snow, and acting with the intent to track the snow.[42] In the second case, but not the first, failure to produce the tracks will result in a shift in plans, perhaps a redoubling of the path. The difference, in other words, goes to the core of intentional agency.

Now, having the analytical distinction in hand does not resolve the moral or legal treatment of someone who acts knowing that effects will be produced. While the distinction may not be relevant to the permissibility of the action, it will bear on the character of the agent, contributing to both a retributive assessment and a calculation of the risk posed by him.[43] As T. M. Scanlon notes, it would be mistaken to think, for example, that the permissibility of an act might vary, simply in virtue of the attitude taken by the actor—for example, a bombing raid might be deemed permissible if done by a pilot who seeks a military target, knowing of civilian collateral casualties, but be impermissible if done by a pilot seeking civilian casualties, aware that a military target will be taken out. Nonetheless, we might decide that a distinction between the two cases is relevant to our treatment of the pilots, for one might pose a greater risk of escalating violations of the law of war.

Similarly, in the context of complicity, we might also decide that the deterrence advantages of treating nonintending facilitators outweigh the risk of chilling their legal behavior. Or we might decide that the implicit moral condemnation of a criminal conviction requires the specific wicked purpose of violating the law or harming another, rather than simple indifference to normative constraints. Such a judgment is contextual and complex, reflecting an understanding of the policy goals and meaning of criminal punishment. But it must not be seen as a direct function of complicity doctrine. Efforts at law reform have in fact recognized this, by seeking to carve out criminal facilitation as a distinct and lesser offense, as in the Model Penal Code's proposals for a new offense.[44] The weaker criterion in international criminal law, which requires only recklessness on the secondary party's part as to the principal's commission of the crime, represents a substantial, even dangerous, weakening of the standard, and so confuses complicity law as well.

VI From Doctrine to Philosophy, and Back Again

The philosophical lesson we might derive from these doctrinal investigations is that our systems, attitudes, and institutions of responsibility respond to a variety of intuitions, instrumental goals, and epistemic constraints. These appear in the guise of formal requirements, for example of causation—requirements honored as much in the breach as in the observance. Within a project of philosophical reform of complicity law, there is therefore ample room to move doctrine in the direction suggested by the Model Penal Code and the Law Reform Commission: toward an inchoate theory of complicity, which predicates liability on the attempt to aid rather than on what is actually done. I favor such an approach to doctrine myself, and have written that it offers the best interpretation of the causal requirement we find in doctrine: causation is necessary as a type- and not a token-requirement.[45] That is, while the accomplice's act must be of the sort that could have made a difference to the commission of the principal's crime, it need not be shown to have actually made a difference.

A virtue of such an approach is that it makes it possible to square complicity doctrine with a more circumscribed theory of punishment, one aiming forward at risk-reduction, whether through deterrence, treatment, or incapacitation. Once we realize that a Judge Tally who tries and fails to intercept a warning telegram is as dangerous as a Judge Tally who succeeds, an inchoate theory of complicity becomes compelling. But outside the conversation of the reformers, in the messier world of real penal and social institutions, the inchoate theory of accomplice liability also seems incomplete. The issue is not just one of reconciling an instrumental approach to punishment with atavistic elements of retributivism in our moral intuitions— and the belief that punishment ought to track harm produced, not merely harm intended. The argument about the significance of resulting harm is familiar.[46] But what we may learn by looking specifically at complicity is the way these other bases of accomplice liability, including motive and role, form of contribution, and specificity of intent, all play a role in judgments not just of threshold liability but of the appropriate penal response. If a more realistic picture of accomplice liability leaves us, as Michael Moore suggests, with a doctrine more mosaic than linear, that doctrine reflects the real polyvocal and polyvalent system of moral judgment in which we live.[47]

NOTES

1. These theories of responsibility and punishment are put forward as caricatures here; they will be elaborated below.

2. Many jurisdictions hold that possession or display of a loaded gun can, with other evidence, suffice for attempted murder. See, e.g., State v. Walker, 705 So. 2d 589 (Fla. Dist. Ct. App. 4th Dist. 1997) (prima facie case for attempted murder in case of a student who brought a loaded gun to school, having told witnesses that he was going to kill the assistant principal); Cohen v. Wyoming, 191 P.3d 956 (Wyoming 2008) (attempted murder could be found in case of defendant reaching for a gun when stopped by a police officer).

3. Assume, for the sake of the example, that the gun is properly licensed.

4. State ex rel. Martin v. Tally, 102 Ala. 25 (1894). This is a rough and opportunistic adaptation.

5. William Shakespeare, *Othello* [1604].

6. Prosecutor v. Ferdinand Nahimana, Jean-Bosco Baraygwiza, Hassan Ngeze, Case No. ICTR-99–52-T, Trial Chamber Summary [2003].

7. If S's instigation goes beyond "mere" encouragement, S can be liable as a perpetrator of an attempt. See, e.g., U.S. v. Church, 29 Mil. J. Rptr. 679 (Ct. Milit. Rev. 1989) (S liable for attempted murder, having provided government agent posing as hitman with weapon, photos, and detailed plans).

8. *Powel and Daniels, English* [1999] 1 AC 1.

9. At the least, there would be uncertainty in the UK treatment of the case.

10. U.S. v. Peoni, 100 F.2d 401 (2nd Cir. 1938).

11. See A. P. Simester, "The Mental Element in Complicity," *Law Quarterly Review* 122: 592–600 (2006), and Law Commission, *Participating in Crime*, Par. 3.53ff. (2007).

12. The exception to the uniform treatment of accomplices and principals is Germany, where secondary liability is formally distinguished. For example, the U.K. Aiding and Abetting Act directs that liability be equivalent, as does the Model Penal Code. In France, e.g., Art. 121–6 of the Criminal Code directs that the *complice* be punished as a principal

offender. In the United States, capital liability for nontriggermen actors has been disfavored since Tison v. Arizona, 481 U.S. 137 (1987), absent a specific finding of reckless indifference to human life by the accomplice.

13. StrafgesetzBuch Secs. 27, 49(1). Instigators receive the same penalty as principals. See Markus Dubber, "Criminalizing Complicity," *Journal of International Criminal Justice* 5: 977–1001 (2007).

14. See, e.g., People v. Campbell, 124 Mich. App. 333 (1983) (homicide conviction of defendant who suggested suicide reversed because victim's use of gun negated defendant's liability; see also the discussion in H. L. A. Hart and Tony Honoré, *Causation in the Law* (New York: Oxford, 2nd ed. 1985), pp. 73–75.

15. Model Penal Code, Sec. 2.06(2)(a).

16. The absence of a causation requirement will receive a later defense.

17. Sanford Kadish, "Complicity, Cause and Blame: A Study in the Interpretation of Doctrine," *California Law Review* 73: 329–410, 335 (1985).

18. These positions are associated, respectively, with Lewis, "Causation," *Journal of Philosophy*, 70: 556–567; J. L. Mackie, *The Cement of the Universe* (New York: Oxford University Press 1980), and Richard Wright, "Once More Into the Bramble Bush: Duty, Causal Contribution, and the Extent of Legal Responsibility," *Vanderbilt Law Review* 54: 1071–1132 (2001); and Michael Moore, *Causation and Responsibility* (New York: Oxford University Press, 2009).

19. See chapter 7 here, as well as Hart & Honoré, *Causation and the Law,* Ch. 1.

20. Assuming the thieves knew or should have known death would result; felony murder would also result in murder.

21. This is a so-called inus condition: an insufficient but nonredundant part of an unnecessary but sufficient condition, in that the death could have been produced in many ways, but happened to be produced by this very configuration of elements. See Mackie, *Cement of the Universe,* pp. 62–63.

22. Strictly speaking, each is a co-perpetrator rather than an accomplice.

23. See my *Complicity: Ethics and Law for a Collective Age* (New York: Cambridge University Press, 2001), Ch. 3.

24. Under felony-murder doctrine, only the common plan to rob must be shown, since murder liability will flow from the underlying felony.

25. K. J. M. Smith, *A Modern Treatise on the Law of Complicity* (London: Cambridge, 1991), pp. 88ff.

26. "Assisting and Encouraging Crime," U.K. Law Commission Consultation Paper No. 131 (1993), para. 4.24 (quoted in Law Commission, *Participating in Crime* [2007], para. 1.33.

27. "Ah, balmy breath, that doth almost persuade Justice to break her sword," Othello says while kissing the sleeping Desdemona farewell. *Othello,* Act 5, Scene 2.

28. On the other hand, as Fletcher notes, if the doctor knows that the patient has asked for assistance while the nurse does not, the nurse may lack an excuse or mitigation that the doctor has. George Fletcher, *Rethinking Criminal Law* (Boston: Little Brown, 1978), Sec. 8.6.1.

29. Glanville Williams, *Criminal Law: The General Part* (London: Stevens and Sons, 2d ed. 1961), Sec. 130 (Parties to the same act guilty of different degrees of crime).

30. Fletcher, *Rethinking,* Sec. 8.7.1.

31. Nahimana, Barayagwiza & Ngeze v. The Prosecutor, Case No. ICTR-99-52-A (ICTR Appeals Chamber 28 November 2007). The massacres took place mainly between April 6 and mid-July 1994.

32. Allison Danner and Jenny Martinez, "Guilty Associations: Joint Criminal Enterprise, Command Responsibility, and the Development of International Criminal Law," *California Law Review* 93: 75–170 (2005).

33. Nahimana, Appeal, p. 513. On appeal, the standard of proximate causation could not be met for the earlier broadcasts, but could for the later ones.

34. Wilcox v. Jeffery [1951] 1 All ER 464.

35. Matters are slightly different for co-perpetrators, where each aims to do part of the completed crime, but does not necessarily aim to assist the other's commission of that crime.

36. See my *Complicity*, Ch. 3.

37. See, e.g., in a large corpus, Margaret Gilbert, *On Social Facts* (Princeton: Princeton University Press, 1992); Michael Bratman, *Faces of Intention* (New York: Oxford University Press, 1999), Chs. 5–8; John Searle, *The Construction of Social Reality* (New York: Free Press, 1995), Seumas Miller, *Social Action: A Teleological Account* (New York: Cambridge University Press, 2001); and Raimo Tuomela, *Cooperation: A Philosophical Study* (Dordrecht: Springer, 2000). I have also contributed to this discussion in my "Acting Together," *Philosophy and Phenomenological Research* 61: 1–31 (2000).

38. Director of Public Prosecutions for Northern Ireland v. Maxwell [1978] 1 W.L.R. 1350.

39. The words are Judge Learned Hand's, from U.S. v. Peoni, 100 F.2d 401 (2d Cir. 1938).

40. This point is powerfully made by John Searle, in *The Construction of Social Reality* (New York: Free Press, 1997).

41. The language of intentions and plans comes from Michael Bratman's germinal treatment of the issue, in his *Intentions, Plans, and Practical Reason* (Cambridge: Harvard University Press, 1987).

42. R. A. Duff, *Intention, Agency, and Criminal Liability* (Oxford: Blackwell, 1990), Sec. 4.1.

43. This distinction between act-assessment and agent-assessment in double effect cases is well explored by T. M. Scanlon, *Moral Dimensions: Permissibility, Meaning, Blame* (Cambridge: Harvard University Press, 2008).

44. See the Model Penal Code, Comment 2.06, p. 318 (restricting facilitation liability to rendering of substantial aid).

45. Christopher Kutz, "Causeless Complicity," *Criminal Law and Philosophy* 1: 289–305 (2007).

46. Still one of the best expositions is Stephen Schulhofer, "Harm and Punishment: A Critique of Emphasis on the Results of Conduct in the Criminal Law," *University of Pennsylvania Law Review* 122: 1497–1607 (1974).

47. Michael Moore, "Causing, Aiding, and the Superfluity of Accomplice Liability," *University of Pennsylvania Law Review* 156: 395–452. For Moore, the many bases of complicity suggest that the doctrine itself can and should be replaced by existing doctrines tailored to, variously, risk, direct causation, and vicarious liability. In my view, the doctrine is best understood in terms of the range of underlying factors, with risk playing a unifying role. But this is an issue of doctrinal taxonomy, not philosophy.

CHAPTER 7

CAUSATION IN THE CRIMINAL LAW

MICHAEL MOORE

I THE USE OF CAUSATION IN CRIMINAL LAW DOCTRINES

The special part of the substantive criminal law consists of several thousand prohibitions and requirements. Criminal codes typically *prohibit* citizens from doing certain types of action and sometimes (but less frequently) *require* citizens to do certain types of actions. Causation enters into both the prohibitions and the requirements of a typical criminal code, for such statutes either prohibit citizens from *causing* certain results or require them to *cause* certain results. Sometimes this use of causation is explicit, as when the law prohibits one from *causing* the death of another; more typically the causal requirement is implicit in the law's use of causative verbs of action, as when the law prohibits *killings*. In either case, causation is crucial to criminal liability.

In this, criminal law mirrors morality. For the injunctions of morality are also "causation-drenched." Causing a harm matters to the degree of our moral blameworthiness, along with intention and other factors. It is thus no accident that liability in the criminal law also turns on causation.

Given the prolixity of liability doctrines having causation as an element in criminal law, one might think there would be as many tests of causation as there are causal requirements in such prolix doctrines. Yet what is commonly called the "general part" of the criminal law is built on a contrary insight: the elements of liability do *not* vary with each different rule in which they appear. There are general notions of intention, voluntariness, excuse, and the like, and the law seeks a similarly general notion of causation. These are *general*, in the sense that these notions apply to give a uniform meaning to each doctrinal requirement framed in terms of these concepts.[1] They together form what is known as the "general part" of the criminal law.

That at least is the promise held out by the doctrines of the general part of criminal law. This promise is blunted somewhat vis-à-vis causation by the fact that there are so many different doctrines about causation competing for dominance within criminal law. Despite their differences, such doctrines purport to be about the same thing: the causal relation. It has been a perennial puzzle which of such doctrines accurately captures the causal requirement for liability that courts are actually applying in criminal cases. Just bringing some order to this tournament field of competing doctrines, as I shall undertake to do in this essay, is a challenging task.

I often focus as much on tort law theories of causation as on criminal law. This is because many of the leading cases on causation, most of the causal doctrines finding some acceptance in the law, and most of the theorizing about causation, originate in the law of tort and not in the criminal law. The reasons for this are not hard to discern. Unlike the thousands of specific actions prohibited or required by the criminal law, a large part of tort law consists of but one injunction: do not unreasonably act so as to cause harm to another. Such an injunction pretty obviously places great weight on causation. It leaves open a full range of causal questions, much more than do injunctions of criminal law such as "Do not intentionally hit another."

Criminal law thus has been a borrower from torts on the issue of causation. Such borrowing has not been uniform or without reservations. Aside from the greater demands of directness of causation implicit in specific criminal prohibitions, the criminal sanction of punishment is sometimes said to demand greater stringency of causation than is demanded by the less severe tort sanction of compensation. Still, the usual form such reservations take is for criminal law to modify causation doctrines in tort by a matter of degree only.[2] Foreseeability, for example, is a test of causation in both fields, but what must be foreseeable, and to what extent, is sometimes thought to be greater in criminal law than in torts. Such variation by degree but not in kind has allowed causation in criminal law and in torts to be discussed via the same tests, which I shall now do.

II The Dominant Conception of Causation in Extant Theories of the Criminal Law

The conventional wisdom about the causation requirement in both criminal law and torts is that it in reality consists of two very different requirements. The first requirement is that of "cause in fact." This is said to be the truly *causal* component of the law's two requirements framed in causal terms, because this doctrine adopts what is thought of as the "scientific" notion of causation. Whether cigarette smoking causes cancer, whether the presence of hydrogen or helium caused an explosion, are factual questions to be resolved by the best science the courts can muster. By contrast, the second requirement, that of "proximate" or "legal" cause, is said to be an evaluative issue, to be resolved by arguments of policy and not arguments of scientific fact. Suppose a defendant knifes his victim, who then dies because her religious convictions are such that she refuses medical treatment.[3] Has such a defendant (legally) caused her death? The answer to such questions, it is said, depends on the policies behind liability, not on any factual issues; factually, it is thought, the knifing surely caused her death.

By far the dominant test for cause in fact is the common-law and Model Penal Code "sine qua non" or "but-for" test.[4] Such a test asks a counterfactual question: "but for the defendant's action, would the victim have been harmed?" This test is also sometimes called the necessary condition test, because it requires the defendant's action to have been necessary to the victim's harm. The appeal of this test stems from this fact. The test seems to isolate something we seem to care a lot about, both in explaining events and in assessing responsibility for them: did the defendant's act make a difference? Insofar as we increase moral blameworthiness and legal punishment for actors who *cause* bad results (and not just try to), we seemingly should care whether a particular bad result would have happened anyway, even without the defendant.

There is no equivalently dominant test of legal or proximate cause. There are in fact seven distinguishable sorts of tests having some authority within the legal literature. I shall defer description of these until after I have described the variations in the dominant legal test for cause in fact.

III Problems with the Dominant Analysis of Cause in Fact, Motivating Modified Cause-in-Fact Tests

The best way to approach the various tests for cause in fact in law is by examining problems for the dominant, counterfactual test. For it is these problems that motivate alternative tests of cause in fact. Very generally, there are four sorts of problems with the counterfactual test for causation in fact that are raised in the legal literature. One set of these problems has to do with proof and evidence. As an element of the prima facie case, causation in fact must be proven by the party with the burden of proof. In criminal cases, that is the prosecution, who must prove beyond a reasonable doubt what would have happened absent the defendant's act. Counterfactuals by their nature are difficult to prove with any degree of certainty, for they require the fact finder to speculate what would have happened if the defendant had not done what she did. Suppose a defendant culpably destroys a life preserver on a sea-going tug.[5] When a crewman falls overboard and drowns, was a necessary condition of his death the act of the defendant in destroying the life preserver? If the life preserver had been there, would anyone have thought to use it? thrown it in time? thrown it far enough? gotten it near enough to the victim that he would have reached it? We often lack the kind of precise information that could verify whether the culpable act of the defendant made any difference in this way.[6]

A second set of problems stems from an indeterminacy of meaning in the test, not from difficulties of factual verification. There is a great vagueness in counterfactual judgments. The vagueness lies in specifying the possible world in which we are to test the counterfactual.[7] When we say "But for the defendant's act of destroying the life preserver," what world are we imagining? We know we are to eliminate the defendant's act, but what are we to replace it with? A life preserver that was, alternatively, destroyed by the heavy seas? A defendant who didn't destroy the life preserver because she had already pushed the victim overboard when no one else was around to throw the life preserver to the victim? and so on and on. To make the counterfactual test determinate enough to yield one answer rather than another, we have to assume that those applying this test share an ability to specify some definite possible world that is "similar" to our actual world, and that it is in *this* possible world that we ask our counterfactual question.

The third and fourth sets of problems stem from the inability of the counterfactual test to match what for most of us are firm causal intuitions. The third set of problems arises because the counterfactual test seems too lenient in what it counts as a cause. The criticism is that the test is thus overinclusive. The fourth set of problems arises because the counterfactual test seems too stringent in what it counts as a cause. The criticism here is that the test is underinclusive.

The overinclusiveness of the test is mostly raised by legal theoreticians in cases of coincidence. Suppose a defendant culpably delays his train at t^1; much, much later at t^2, and much further down the track, the train is hit by a flood.[8] Had the delay at t^1 not occurred, there would have been no damage or loss of life at t^2. In this case, the counterfactual test yields the unwelcome result that the defendant's delaying caused the harm. Such cases of overt coincidences are rare, but they are the tip of the iceberg here, in that innumerable remote conditions are necessary to the production of any event. Oxygen in the air over England, timber in Scotland, Henry VIII's obesity, and Sir Francis Drake's perspicacity, were all probably necessary for England's defeat of the Spanish Armada;[9] but we should be loath to say that each of these was a cause of that defeat. The problem is greatly exacerbated by the admission of omissions as causes: the Spanish Armada was also defeated because Martian spaceships didn't show up to help them, and that failed to happen because there are no Martians.

The fourth set of problems for the counterfactual test has to do with the test's underinclusiveness, mostly exhibited in legal theory in the well-known overdetermination cases,[10] in which each of two events c^1 and c^2 is independently sufficient for some third event e. Logically, this entails that neither c^1 nor c^2 is necessary for e, and thus, on the counterfactual analysis of causation, neither of them can be the cause of e. Just about everybody rejects this conclusion, so such cases pose a real problem for the counterfactual analysis of causation.[11]

Legal theorists have long distinguished two distinct kinds of overdetermination cases. The first are the concurrent cause cases: two fires, two shotgun blasts, two noisy motorcycles are each sufficient to burn, kill, or scare some victim. The defendant is responsible for only one fire, shot, or motorcycle. Yet his fire, shot, or noise joins the other one, and both simultaneously cause their various harms. On the counterfactual analysis, the defendant's fire, shot, or noise was not the cause of any harm because it was not necessary to the production of the harms—after all, the other fire, shot, or noise was by itself *sufficient*. Yet the same can be said about the second fire, shot, or noise. So on the but-for test, neither was the cause! And this is absurd.

The preemptive kind of overdetermination cases are different. Here the two putative causes are not simultaneous but are temporally ordered. The defendant's fire arrives first and burns down the victim's building; the second fire arrives shortly thereafter and would have been sufficient to burn down the building, only there was no building to burn down. Here our intuitions are just as clear as in the concurrent overdetermination cases, but the result is here different: the defendant's fire did cause the harm, and the second fire did not. Yet the counterfactual analysis again yields the counterintuitive implication that neither fire caused the harm because neither fire was necessary (each being sufficient) for the harm.

Situated rather nicely between these two sorts of overdetermination cases are what I have called the asymmetrical overdetermination cases.[12] Suppose one defendant nonmortally stabs the victim at the same time that another defendant mortally stabs the same victim; the victim dies of loss of blood, most of the blood gushing out of the mortal wound. Has the nonmortally wounding defendant caused the death of the victim? Not according to the counterfactual analysis: given the sufficiency of the mortal would, the nonmortal wound was not necessary for, and thus not a cause of, death. This conclusion is contrary to common intuition as well as some legal authority.[13]

Defenders of the counterfactual analysis are not bereft of replies to these objections;[14] for present purposes, however, I shall not discuss these replies but move on to present other tests that have been substituted for the counterfactual test in an attempt to avoid these problems. With regard to the problem posed by the overdetermination cases, the best known alternative is to propose an "INUS" (an Insufficient but Necessary element of an Unnecessary but Sufficient set) or "NESS" (Necessary Element of a Sufficient Set) test: an event c causes an event e if and only if c is a necessary element in a set of conditions sufficient for e.[15] It is the stress on *sufficiency* that is supposed to end-run the overdetermination problems. In the concurrent cause cases—the two fires joining to burn the victim's house—each fire is said to be a necessary element of its own sufficient set, so each fire is a cause. In the preemptive case—the fires do not join and one arrives first—the first fire is a necessary element of a sufficient set, and so is the cause; the second fire is not, because it is not thought to be part of a sufficient set (absent from its set is the existence of a house to be burned).

Other modifications of the counterfactual test have also been adopted. One of these is the "fine-grained effect" approach of the Commentary to the Model Penal Code.[16] On this test, one does not ask whether *the harm* would have occurred but for the defendant's act; rather, one asks whether a more particularly described harm would have happened without the defendant's act. So in the concurrent cause case of the two independently sufficient fires that join to burn down the victim's house, we do not ask, "Was the defendant's fire necessary to a *destruction* of plaintiff's house?" Rather, we ask, "Was the defendant's act necessary to the destruction of the victim's house where, when, and in the manner that it was destroyed?" It is much more likely that the defendant's fire *was* necessary to the destruction of the victim's house in just the way it was destroyed, so the counterfactual test seems to do better in the concurrent overdetermination cases with this fine-grained approach.[17]

For the preemptive overdetermination cases, the problem is easier for the counterfactual test. Here one introduces a stipulation about the time of the event: if the defendant's act was necessary to the house destruction being earlier than it otherwise would have been, then he was the cause, but if his act was only necessary to the house destruction happening at some time or other (including later), his act is not necessarily the cause. As the cases put this point,[18] causes must *accelerate* their effects; if they fail to accelerate them (either by making no change in temporal location or by retarding them), then such factors are not causes even though necessary to when the putative effect happened. This helps with the preemptive cause cases because a preempting fire is necessary to a house's destruction at t^1, even if (given that there is a preempted fire right behind it at t^2) that first fire is not necessary either to a house destruction later (at t^2) or to a house destruction sometime (t^1 or t^2). This stipulation regarding temporally asymmetrical necessity should be regarded as a third modification of the law's counterfactual test.

The coincidence objection to the counterfactual test yields a fourth modification to that test. In cases like that of the negligently speeding train that, because of its speed, arrives at just the place where a falling tree hits it,[19] one should not ask, "But for the act of driving would the train have been hit?" Rather, one should isolate that aspect of the act that made it negligent. Thus: "but for the fact that the driving was over the speed limit, would the train have been hit?" To this modified counterfactual question, the answer is yes. If the train had been going even faster it would not have been hit either (just as if it had been going slower).[20] So the fact that the act was one of *speeding* was not necessary to the harm, even if the act (which was an act of speeding, among other things) was necessary to the harm. This in law is called the "aspect cause" version of the counterfactual test.[21]

A fifth modification to the counterfactual test of cause in fact is more by way of substitution than of amendment. This is the First and Second *Restatement of Torts* "substantial factor" test.[22] Motivated mostly by worries about overdetermination cases, the American Law Institute in both of its first two *Restatements* urged that a "substantial factor" test be substituted for sine qua non as the test of cause in fact in torts. The test asks only whether a defendant's action was a substantial factor in the production of the harm complained of. This admittedly circular and vague test was thought to help in overdetermination cases like that of the joint fires, because so long as each fire was quite substantial (in comparison to the other fire) each was a cause of the harm, even though neither fire was a necessary condition of the harm.

Notice that the substantial factor test "solves" the overdetermination problem mostly because it does not say enough to get itself into trouble in the overdetermination cases. It thus allows our clear causal intuitions full play in these cases. The ad hoc nature of this solution is evident when one sees how the First and Second *Restatement of Torts* managed to salvage what they could of the sine qua non test: if a putative causal factor is a necessary condition of some harm, then (under the *Restatements*) it is per se substantial.[23] Necessary condition–hood, in other words, is sufficient for cause in fact. But necessary condition–hood is not necessary for cause in fact, so that a factor can be substantial even if it is not a necessary condition. This amounts to saying that one should use the necessary condition test when it works, but when it yields counterintuitive results (as in the overdetermination cases) one shouldn't use it but should rely on naked causal intuition.

The sixth and final modification of the counterfactual test of cause in fact is motivated by the proof problem. Particularly in criminal cases (where one has to prove causation "beyond a reasonable doubt") it is often impossible to prove that the harm would not have happened but for the defendant's act. What courts in effect adopt is a "lost chance" approach to counterfactuals.[24] On this modified test, one does not ask whether the act was necessary to the harm actually occurring; rather, one asks only whether the act was necessary to the harm having the chance of occurring that it did. This is a "necessary to chance (of harm)" sort of test, not a "necessary to harm" test.[25]

What courts and legal theorists have actually done in "modifying" the counterfactual test in these six ways is to propose quite different theories about the nature of causation. The INUS and NESS tests, for example, are in reality nomic sufficiency tests, a version of a generalist theory of causation that reduces singular causal relations to general causal laws and does not make essential use of counterfactuals (except insofar as counterfactuals are part of the analysis of the idea of a scientific law.)[26] The substantial factor test, to take another example, is really the law's version of a primitivist approach to singular causation, a version of singularist theories examined elsewhere.[27] The necessary-to-chance modification is in reality the substitution of a probabilistic theory of causation for a purely counterfactual theory.[28] It is thus a mistake to think that the law's dominant statement of what is its test for cause in fact—sine qua non—in fact evidences any deep or univocal commitment of the law to a theory of causation that is truly counterfactual in its nature.

IV SKEPTICAL APPROACHES TO THE CAUSE-IN-FACT REQUIREMENT

Legal theory, like philosophy, has had its share of skeptics about causation. Most of such legally located skepticism has been directed at the proximate cause half of the dominant analysis of causation in the law. Such skepticism there considers "proximate *cause*" a misnomer and reinterprets the proximate cause requirement in noncausal, policy terms (as we shall see later). More radical is the skepticism here considered. Some legal theorists are skeptical of there being any natural relation in the world named by "causation." This skepticism includes what the law names "cause in fact" as well as "proximate cause."

Before we describe such skepticisms in legal theory, we do well to be sure we have a firm grasp on what skepticism about causation is. Take David Hume, often listed as a skeptic about causation.[29] Hume famously identified singular causal relations as spatiotemporally located instances of causal laws, and he identified causal laws as no more than uniformity in sequence between types of events.[30] Hume was thus doubly a reductionist about the causal relation, reducing it ultimately to regular concurrence. In this, he is commonly said to be a skeptic.

Because Hume's analysis takes "the glue" out of the causal relation—a cause doesn't *make* its effect occur, it is only regularly followed by its effect—it is commonly classified as skeptical. And in a sense it is, if one treats the making-things-happen "glue" to be essential to any relation properly called "causal." But Hume's views are not radical enough to count as skeptical in the sense intended by legal theoreticians. For Hume gives what Saul Kripke calls a "skeptical solution"[31] to the problem of causation: he doesn't deny that causation exists, but he reduces it to something less ontologically queer than "glue."

A better model of the radical skepticism here considered is the "ascriptivist" views that Herbert Hart once held (later repudiated).[32] In a famous analysis of causative verbs such as "A hit B," Hart urged that we *describe* no natural relations (e.g., A caused there to be contact on B's body) but rather *ascribe* responsibility to A for the contact on B's body. If this bit of pre-Austin speech act analysis were true, then causatives (and analogously, words of causation) would only be the labels used to express conclusions about responsibility. Such words would not name real relations that could be the justifying grounds for attributing responsibility to someone.

Such are the views of the legal skeptics here considered. Such skeptics appear to deny that causation exists as any kind of natural relation, be it a "glue-like" natural relation, regular concurrence in nature, or something else. Because it is easiest to approach such skepticism historically, I shall begin with the American legal realists (with whom almost all of the skepticisms about proximate causation also originated).

Most of Henry Edgarton's much-cited work details his skepticism about *proximate* causation.[33] Some of it, however, reveals him to have been a skeptic about the cause-in-fact requirement as well. He notes, for example, that the symmetrically concurrent overdetermination cases were divided into two camps by the cause-in-fact doctrines of his day: where there were two culpable actors starting fires (where the fires joined to produce a larger fire burning down the plaintiff's house), either actor was a cause of the destruction; but when only one of the fires was of culpable origin, the other being either natural or of *innocent* human origin, then the culpable actor was not a cause of the destruction. From such examples, Edgarton suggested that the cause-in-fact requirement was (like the proximate cause requirement) all a matter of policy, a matter, that is, depending on "our free and independent sense of justice and—perhaps—the interests of society."[34]

A late blooming of this legal realist conclusion was the well-known work of Wex Malone.[35] Malone largely focused on an issue that preoccupied philosophers in the 1950s:[36] the pragmatic features by which we pick out "*the* cause" of some event. Malone found, unsurprisingly, only context-specific, practical interests guiding such locutions of causal emphasis, and skeptically concluded that that was all there was to causation. To be said to be "the cause" of some harm was just another way of saying one was responsible for the harm.

The skepticism of American legal realism has had two intellectual descendants in legal theory. One of these consists of the self-styled "critical" theorists—the critical legal studies movement (or "Crits") whose heyday was in the 1970s and 1980s in America.[37] Much of this movement's skepticism is simply warmed-over postmodernism, a passing fashion in many disciplines besides law.[38] Much more interesting intellectually were criticisms that were not based on postmodernist platitudes but were specific to causation.

Mark Kelman's skepticism was of this kind.[39] Kelman urged that all causal requirements in the law were part of the "liberal myth" of objective criteria for liability, but rather than reciting (yet again) the platitude of the historically situated knower, Kelman actually directed arguments against the law's cause-in-fact tests mirroring anything in natural fact. Kelman accurately perceived that the NESS variation of the counterfactual theory was one of the most accepted versions of it within contemporary legal theory, and he produced some of the criticisms of that variation that I myself pursue.[40] From the perceived failure of the counterfactual theory of cause in fact, Kelman concluded that cause in fact itself cannot be a matter of fact. (Whether this is correct, of course, depends on whether there are no other, *non-counterfactual* theories of causation that fit the demands of a cause-in-fact requirement in the law.)[41]

The general, positive prescription that is supposed to flow from the skepticisms of the legal realists and the Crits is not so clear. One gathers that once skepticism (about causation being a matter of objective fact) has removed the blinders, we can see that it is only interests and policies that lead us to conclusions about moral responsibility and legal liability. Presumably, then, the positive prescription is for us to do this openly, balancing all relevant considerations, in arriving at our conclusions of what was the cause of what.

The other intellectual descendant of the American legal realists on causation is the "law and economics" movement in contemporary legal theory. These theorists are seeking to show that legal rules and institutions either are or should be *efficient*, in the post-Pareto sense of that word.

Like the Crits, legal economists tend to be radical skeptics about causation. The leading early papers on causation[42] all express skepticism about "causation" picking out any real relation in the world.[43] Lawyers are just doing intuitive economics or some other policy balancing, in their use of causal idioms, because that is all they *can be* doing. Shavell, Landes, and Posner explicitly rely on Edgarton,[44] picking up precisely where Edgarton began his skepticism, in the liability rules for symmetrically concurrent overdetermination cases.

The positive, reconstructive prescriptions of the law and economics types differ from those of the Crits and the legal realists in that the policy favored is much more specific: liability (including the supposedly causal requirements for liability) should give incentives for efficient behavior. Yet unnoticed by the economists was that this monistic policy focus on efficiency made their causal skepticism unnecessary and beside the point.

This is because if efficiency is the normative polestar for both tort and criminal law, then there is a nonskeptical basis for denying the relevance of the metaphysics of causation to the interpretation of legal usages of "cause." Such a basis begins with the quite correct insight that legal texts are to be interpreted in light of the purposes (values, functions, "spirit," "mischief," etc.) such texts serve.[45] Often such purposes will justify an interpreter in holding the legal meaning of a term to be quite different from its ordinary meaning in nonlegal English. "Malice," for example, means roughly "recklessness" in Anglo-American criminal law, whereas it means spiteful or otherwise bad motive in ordinary English.[46]

It is certainly possible that "cause" is like "malice" in this regard. Whether this is so depends on what one takes to be the purpose of those legal texts that use "cause." Consider American tort law by way of example. Following the welfare economics of A. C. Pigou, it was for a time fashionable to think that the purpose of liability rules in tort law was to force each enterprise or activity within an economy to pay its "true costs."[47] Those costs included damage caused to others by the activity as much as they included traditional items of cost like labor, raw materials, capital, and so on. The thought was that only if each enterprise paid its true costs would the goods or services produced by that enterprise be correctly priced, and only if such correct pricing occurred would markets achieve an efficient allocation of resources. This came to be known as "enterprise liability" in the tort law theory of 1950s America.

If the point of tort law were to achieve an efficient allocation of resources, and if such efficiency could be achieved only by discovering the "true costs" of each activity in terms of that activity's harmful effects, then "cause" as used in tort liability rules should mean whatever the metaphysics of causation tells us the word means. For on this theory it is the harmful effects that an activity really causes that are the true costs for that activity; and this rationale thus demands a robust use of some metaphysical view about causation.

Contrast this Pigouvian view of tort law with the post-1960 view of Ronald Coase: tort law indeed exists in order to achieve an efficient allocation of resources, yet such efficiency will be achieved whether tort liability tracks causal responsibility or not.[48] Coase's essential insight was that opportunity costs are real costs, too, to economically rational actors, so that a forgone opportunity to accept a payment in lieu of causing another person some harm already forces the harm-causer to "internalize" all costs of his activities. Such a harm-causer need not be liable for such harms in order to have him pay for the "true costs" of his activity; he already "pays" by forgoing the opportunity to be bought off by the sufferer of the harm. As each harm-causer and harm-sufferer decides on the desired level of his activity, he will thus take into account all effects of his interaction without tort liability forcing him to do so.[49]

On this Coasean analysis of tort law, there is simply no need for liability to turn on causation. Rather, either tort liability is irrelevant to efficient resource allocation (in a world of low transaction costs), or tort liability should be placed on the cheapest cost-avoider (in a world where transaction costs are high) in order to induce that person to take the cost-effective precautions. In either case, legal liability should not track causal responsibility, for even when there are high transaction costs the causer need not be the cheapest cost-avoider.

The irrelevance of causation to the giving of efficient incentives has left economists struggling to make sense of the cause-in-fact requirement of criminal law and tort liability rules. Since no metaphysical reading of "cause" is appropriate to the goal of efficiency, some policy calculus is given as the legal meaning of "cause." Such policy calculus typically generates a probabilistic interpretation of "cause," so that any activity that raises the conditional probability of some harm that has occurred is said to have "caused" that harm.[50] For any theory seeking to use the law to give incentives to efficient behavior in a world of high transaction costs, this probabilistic interpretation is seemingly just what is required. To criticize such probabilistic interpretation of legal cause on the ground that probability is a poor metaphysical account of what causation is would thus be beside the point...if efficiency were the point of tort and criminal law.[51]

My own view, undefended here, is that it is not. If the point of criminal law were the utilitarian point of deterring crime, then a constructed idea of legal cause perhaps could be justified; such a functional definition would take into account the incentive effects of various liability rules. But the function of criminal law is not utilitarian; it is retributive. Criminal law serves the exclusive function of achieving retributive justice.[52] This requires that its liability rules track closely the moral criteria for blameworthiness. One of those criteria is causation of morally prohibited states of affairs.[53] Thus, again, "cause" as used in criminal law must mean what is means in morality, and what it means in morality is to name a relation that is natural and *not* of the law's creation.

For those with non-justice-oriented theories of criminal law, it remains true that the cause in fact requirement of criminal law will have a probabilistic or other policy-based interpretation. Such an interpretation is also motivated by skepticism about there being any natural relation properly labeled "causal," but as we have seen, such skepticism is but icing on the cake for such non-justice-oriented views of the criminal law.

V Taxonomizing the Various Tests of Proximate Causation

It was useful in taxonomizing the seven variations of the counterfactual test to show how such variations were produced in response to problems perceived to exist for the first variation, which was the pure, unmodified counterfactual test. While there is no test of proximate causation that is comparably dominant (even if only in lip service) to the counterfactual test of cause in fact, it is nonetheless useful to display the various proximate cause tests as they react to problems in other tests of proximate causation. I thus include some discussions of standard problems with each version of the tests within legal theory as I describe what motivates others of the tests.

The basic taxonomizing principle here is to separate tests that do not view proximate causation as having anything to do with real causal relations (the conventional view within legal theory) from tests that are motivated by the contrary thought. I shall begin with the former kind of test, what I shall call policy-based proximate cause tests. Policy-based proximate cause tests are themselves usefully divided into two camps. Some—general policy tests—are justified by their service of a wide range of policies, indeed as wide as the policies that justify liability at all in torts or criminal law. By contrast, other tests are in the service of only one policy: the measurement of the culpability of the actor in terms of the mental state she had or should have had as she acted.

Beginning with the general policy-based proximate cause tests: the first of these are what we may call "ad hoc policy tests."[54] The idea is that courts balance a range of policies in each case that they adjudicate where a defendant has been found to have caused-in-fact a legally prohibited harm. They may balance certain "social interests," like the need for deterrence, with certain "individual interests," like the unfairness of surprising a defendant with liability. Courts then decide wherever such balance leads. Whatever decision is reached on such case-by-case policy balancing is then cast in terms of "proximate" or "legal" cause. Such labels are simply the conclusions of policy balances; the labels have nothing to do with causation in any ordinary or scientific sense.

The second sort of test here is one that adopts general rules of legal causation. Such rules are adopted for various policy reasons also having nothing to do with causation, but this test differs from the last by its eschewal of case-by-case balancing; rather, per se rules of legal causation are adopted for policy reasons. Thus, the common-law rule for homicide was that death must occur within a year and a day of the defendant's harmful action, else he could not be said to have legally caused the death.[55] Analogously, the "last wrongdoer rule" held that when a single victim is mortally wounded by two or more assailants, acting not in concert and acting seriatim over time, only the last wrongdoer could be said to be the legal cause of the death.[56] Such sorts of tests also found a temporary home in tort law with its "first house rule," according to which a railroad whose negligently emitted sparks burned an entire town was only liable for the house or houses directly ignited by its sparks, not for other houses ignited by the burning of those first burnt houses.[57] There is no pretense in such rules of making truly causal discriminations; rather, such rules were adopted for explicit reasons of legal policy. The first house rule, for example, was said to be justified by the policy of subsidizing the then developing railroad industry.

The main problem with both ad hoc and the rule-based policy tests is that they seek to maximize the wrong policies. The general "functionalist" approach[58] of such tests to legal concepts is correct: we should always ask after the purpose of the rule or institution in which the concept figures in order to ascertain its legal meaning. Yet the dominant purpose of the criminal law's concept of causation is to grade punishment proportionately to moral blameworthiness.[59] One who intentionally or recklessly causes a harm that another only tries to cause or risks causing is more blameworthy.[60] Proximate cause tests thus should serve the function of grading offenders, placing them either with the more blameworthy causers of harm or with the less blameworthy riskers or intenders of such harm.

We must thus not seek the meaning of causation in extrinsic policies; rather, the legal concept of causation will serve its function in criminal law only if the concept names some factual state of affairs that determines degrees of moral blameworthiness. By ignoring the dominant function of causation in criminal law, the legal realists' explicit policy tests constructed an artificial concept of legal cause that is unusable in any just punishment scheme.

This problem does not infect the next two policy-based proximate cause tests, the foreseeability and the harm-within-the-risk tests. For those tests do seek to describe a factual state of affairs that plausibly determines both moral blameworthiness and connects a defendant's culpability to particular harms. These tests are thus serving the dominant policies that must be served by the concept of causation in justice-oriented theories of criminal law. Their novelty lies in their relocation of the locus of blame. On these theories, "legal cause" is not a refinement of an admitted desert-determiner, true causation; it is rather a refinement of another admitted desert-determiner: mens rea (or "culpability" in the narrow sense with which I use that term).

Consider first the well-known foreseeability test.[61] As is not the case with the rule-based policy tests, here there is no multiplicity of rules for specific situations (like homicide, intervening wrongdoers, railroad fires, etc.). Rather, there is one rule universally applicable to all criminal and tort cases: was the harm that the defendant's act in fact caused foreseeable to her at the time she acted? This purportedly universal test for legal causation is usually justified by one of two policies: either the unfairness of punishing (or extracting compensation from) someone for harms that they could not foresee, or the inability to gain any deterrence by sanctioning such actors (since the threat value of tort or criminal law sanctions is nonexistent for unforeseeable violations of liability rules).

Some jurisdictions restrict the foreseeability test to one kind of situation. When some human action or natural event intervenes between the defendant's action and the harm, the restricted test asks not whether the ultimate harm to the victim was foreseeable but whether that intervening action or event was foreseeable to the defendant when he acted.[62] This restricted foreseeability test is like the restricted rules we saw before and is unlike the universal test of legal causation the foreseeability test usually purports to be.

Precisely because it is a culpability test, the foreseeability test becomes subject to its own policy-based objection, that of redundancy.[63] Why should we ask *two* culpability questions in determining blameworthiness? After we have satisfied ourselves that a defendant is culpable—either because she intended or foresaw some harm, or because she was unreasonable in not foreseeing some harm (the unreasonableness being judged in light of the degree of that harm's seriousness, the magnitude of its risk, and the lack of justification for taking such a risk), the foreseeability test bids us to ask, "Was the harm foreseeable?" This is redundant, because any harm intended or foreseen is foreseeable, and any harm foreseeable enough to render an actor unreasonable for not foreseeing, it is also foreseeable.

The only way the foreseeability test avoids redundancy is by moving toward the other alternative here, the harm-within-the-risk test. That is, in situations where the defendant was culpable in intending, foreseeing, or risking some harm type H, but what his act in fact caused was an instance of harm type J, the foreseeability test of legal cause becomes nonredundant the moment one restricts it to asking whether J was foreseeable, a different question than the one asked and answered as a matter of mens rea about H. Yet this is to do the work of the harm-within-the-risk test: solving what I shall shortly call the "fit problem" of mens rea. Moreover, it is to do such work badly. Foreseeability is not the right question to ask in order to fit the harm in fact caused by a defendant to the type of harm she either intended to achieve, or foresaw that she would cause, or risked. If the foreseeability test is to be restricted to this nonredundant work, it is better abandoned for the harm-within-the-risk test.

Let us examine, then, this fourth policy-based proximate cause test, the rather badly labeled "harm-within-the-risk" test.[64] Like the foreseeability test, this test purports to be a test of legal cause that is universally applicable to all tort and criminal cases. This test, too, is justified on policy grounds and does not pretend to have anything to do with factual or scientific causation. Doctrinally, however, the test differs from a simple foreseeability test.

Consider first the arena from which the test takes its name, crimes or torts of risk creation. If the defendant is charged with negligent homicide (or wrongful death in torts), for example, this test requires that the death of the victim be within the risk that made the actor's action negligent. If it was negligent to drop a can of nitroglycerine because it might explode and kill the victim, but instead it kills him by cutting his toe and causing him to bleed to death, then the harm that happened (bleeding) was not within the risk of harm (explosion) that made it negligent to drop the can. Similarly, if the charge is manslaughter (for which consciousness of the risk is required in some jurisdictions), this test requires that the death of the victim be within the risk the awareness of which made the defendant's action reckless.

Extension of this test to non-risk-creation crimes or torts requires some modification. For crimes or torts of strict liability, where no mens rea is required, the test requires that the harm that happened be one of the types of harms the risk of which motivated the lawmaker to prohibit the behavior. For torts or crimes requiring knowledge (or "general intention") for their mens rea, the test asks whether the harm that happened was an instance of the type of harm foreseen by the defendant as she acted. For torts or crimes requiring purpose (or "specific intent") for their mens rea, the test asks whether the harm that happened was an instance of the type of harm the defendant intended to achieve by her action.[65]

What motivates all of these variations of the harm-within-the-risk test is the following insight: when assessing culpable mens rea, there is always a "fit problem."[66] Suppose a defendant intends to hit his victim in the face with a stick; suppose further he intends the hit to put out the victim's left eye. As it happens, the victim turns suddenly as she is being hit, and loses her right ear to the blow. Whether the harm that happened is an instance of the type of harm intended is what I call the fit problem. Fact finders have to fit the mental state the defendant had to the actual result he achieved and ask whether it is close enough for him to be punished for a crime of intent like mayhem. (If it is not close enough, then he may yet be found guilty of some lesser tort or crime of battery or reckless endangerment.)

The essential claim behind the harm-within-the-risk test is that "legal cause" is the label lawyers should put on a problem of culpability, the problem I call the fit problem. Proponents of this test urge that legal cause, properly understood, is really a mens rea doctrine, not a doctrine of causation at all.

The main problem for the harm-within-the-risk test itself does not lie in any of the directions we have just explored with respect to foreseeability as a test. The harm-within-the-risk test is in the service of a justice-oriented policy in its seeking of a true desert-determiner and does not ask a redundant question. To grade culpability by the mental states of intention, foresight, and risk, we do have to solve the aforementioned fit problem. The real question for the harm-within-the-risk test is whether this grading by culpable mental states is all that is or should be going on under the rubric of "legal cause."

Consider in this regard two well-known sorts of legal cause cases. It is a time-honored maxim of criminal and tort law that "you take your victim as you find him." Standard translation: no matter how abnormal may be the victim's susceptibilities to injury, and no matter how unforeseeable such injuries may therefore be, a defendant is held to legally cause such injuries. Hit the proverbial thin-skulled man or cut the proverbial hemophiliac, and you have legally caused their deaths if they die, no matter how rare these conditions might be. This is hard to square with the harm-within-the-risk test. A defendant who intends to hit or to cut does not necessarily (or even usually) intend to kill. A defendant who foresees that his acts will cause the victim to be struck or cut, does not necessarily (or even usually) foresee that the victim will die. A defendant who negligently risks that his acts will cause a victim to be struck or cut is not necessarily (or even usually) negligent because he also risked death.

The second sort of case involves what are often called "intervening" or "superseding" causes.[67] Suppose the defendant sets explosives next to a prison wall intending to blow the wall and to get certain inmates out. He foresees to a practical certainty that the explosion will kill the guard on the other side of the wall. He lights the fuse to the bomb and leaves. As it happens, the fuse goes out. However, a stranger passes by the wall, sees the bomb, and relights the fuse for the pleasure of seeing an explosion; or a thief comes by, sees the bomb and tries to steal it, dropping it in the process and thereby exploding it; or lightning hits the fuse, reigniting it and setting off the bomb; and so on. In all variations, the guard on the other side of the wall is killed by the blast. Standard doctrines of intervening causation hold that the defendant did not legally cause the death of the guard.[68] Yet this is hard to square with the harm-within-the-risk test. After all, did not the defendant foresee just the type of harm an instance of which did occur? Because the harm-within-the-risk question asks a simple type-to-token question—was the particular harm that happened an instance of the type of harm whose foresight by the defendant made him culpable—the test is blind to freakishness of causal route.[69]

The American Law Institute's Model Penal Code modifies its adoption of the harm-within-the-risk test in section 2.03 by denying liability for a harm within the risk that is "too remote or accidental in its occurrence to have a [just] bearing on the actor's liability or on the gravity of his offense."[70] Such a caveat is an explicit recognition of the inability of the harm-within-the-risk test to accommodate the issues commonly adjudicated as intervening cause issues.

Such a recognition is not nearly broad enough to cover the inadequacy of the harm-within-the-risk approach. The basic problem with the test is that it ignores *all* the issues traditionally adjudicated under the concept of legal cause. The test is blind not only to freakishness of causal route in the intervening cause situations, blind not only to the distinction between antecedent versus after-arising abnormalities so crucial to resolution of the thin-skulled man kind of issue, but the test also ignores all those issues of remoteness sought to be captured by Sir Francis Bacon's coinage, "proximate causation."[71] Even where there is no sudden "break" in the chain of causation as in the intervening cause cases, there is a strong sense that causation peters out over space and time. Caesar's crossing the Rubicon may well be a necessary condition for my writing this essay, but so many other events have also contributed that Caesar's causal responsibility has long since petered out. The logical relationship at the heart of the harm-within-the-risk test—"was the particular harm that happened an instance of the type of harm whose risk, foresight, or intention made the defendant culpable?"—is incapable of capturing this sensitivity to remoteness. As such, the harm-within-the-risk test is blind to the basic issue adjudicated under "legal cause." The harm-within-the-risk test may well ask a good question, at least with regard to crimes of intent, knowledge, or recklessness, but it asks it in the wrong place.[72]

I turn now from the policy-based tests of proximate causation to those tests based on the view that proximate causation, like cause in fact, has to do with real causal relations in the world. The oldest of these tests is that suggested by Sir Francis Bacon's coinage, "causa proxima." The simple idea behind such a remoteness test is that causation is a scalar relation—a more-or-less sort of thing, not an all-or-nothing sort of thing—and that it peters out over time.

A criticism of the remoteness test, often voiced in the legal literature,[73] is that distance in space and remoteness in time are irrelevant to degrees of causal contribution. Examples like *People v. Botkin*,[74] where poisoned candy went a great distance (from California to the victim in New Jersey), or an undetonated bomb left buried for many years before it explodes and injures a victim, are trotted out in support of the criticism.[75] Justice Cardozo rejoined that such criticism surely ran counter to strong community sentiment that spatiotemporal distance does matter to degrees of causal contribution,[76] but one would hope that one could do better than that. Spatiotemporal distance is a serviceable proxy for the number of events or states of affairs through which a cause exerts its influence on its effects, and the number of events is relevant to the degree of causal contribution. This is the metaphysical view that causation "tires" through its links.[77]

A second and quite distinct kind of cause-based proximate cause test is the "direct cause" test. Despite the name, this test does *not* require that there be a complete absence of any event or state of affairs intervening between a cause and its effect, for that cause to be legally "proximate." Not even the ancient direct/indirect distinction between the writs of trespass and trespass-on-the-case in torts was this stringent in its requirement of directness (for trespass).[78] On the contrary, chains can be sufficiently *direct* for the direct cause test even though they are quite long chains extending over considerable space and time. It is only if a special kind of event—an "intervening" (aka "superseding," "extraneous") cause—intervenes that the chain is insufficiently direct. The heart of the direct cause test is thus the idea of these chain-breaking, intervening causes.

Beginning with a series of articles in the 1950s and culminating in their massive book, *Causation in the Law* in 1959, Herbert Hart and Tony Honoré sought to describe the idea of intervening causation that they saw as implicit both in the law and in everyday causal idioms.[79] One can see their concept most easily in three steps. First, presuppose some version of the counterfactual analysis: a cause is at least a necessary condition for its effect (or perhaps a NESS condition, as it was for Hart and Honoré).[80] Second, a cause is not just *any* necessary condition; rather, out of the plethora of conditions necessary for the happening of any event, only two sorts are eligible to be causes. Free, informed, voluntary human actions and those abnormal conjunctions of natural events we colloquially refer to as "coincidences" are the two kinds of necessary conditions we find salient and honor as "causes" (versus mere "background conditions"). Third, such voluntary human action and abnormal natural events cause a given effect only if some other voluntary human action or abnormal natural event does not intervene between the first such event and its putative effect. Such salient events, in other words, are breakers of causal chains ("intervening causes") as much as they are initiators of causal chains, so if they do intervene they relegate all earlier such events to the status of mere background conditions.

Hart and Honoré built on considerable case-law support for their two candidates for intervening causes.[81] Indeed, it is arguable that the basic distinction between principal and accomplice liability in criminal law depends in large part on this conceptualization of causation, as does the tort law distinction between "in concert" and "concurrent causer" kinds of joint tort-feasors.[82] One worry for this view of causation, nonetheless, is that it is incomplete with respect to the remoteness range of issues usually dealt with under the rubric of "legal cause" in the law. Causation in the law fades out gradually as much it breaks off suddenly, and the direct cause analysis ignores this.

VI UNIFIED APPROACHES TO CAUSATION
IN THE LAW

The problems with the conventional legal analysis of causation—in terms of a bifurcation into cause in fact and proximate causation—have tempted some legal theorists to abandon the conventional analysis root and branch. This generates a search for a unitary notion of causation that is much more discriminating (in what it allows as a cause) than the hopelessly promiscuous counterfactual cause-in-fact test of the conventional analysis. Indeed, the search is for a unitary concept of causation that is so discriminating that it can do the work that on the conventional analysis is done by both cause-in-fact and proximate cause doctrines. It is far from obvious that causation is in fact a sufficiently discriminating relation that it can do this much work in assigning responsibility. Nonetheless, there are three such proposals in the legal literature, each having some doctrinal support in the law.

One we have seen already: the fourth variation in the counterfactual test for cause in fact. If one does not ask whether the defendant's act was necessary for the occurrence of the harm—if one instead asks whether that aspect of her act that made her negligent or otherwise culpable caused the harm—then one has a causal test almost as discriminating as the simple counterfactual test coupled with a harm-within-the-risk version of the proximate cause test.[83] This is not surprising, because both tests rule ineligible any aspects of the defendant's act that does *not* make her culpable. For the aspect-causation view, such culpability-irrelevant aspects of the defendant's action are not (relevantly) the cause of the harm; for the harm-within-the-risk test, such culpability-irrelevant aspects of the defendant's action do not fit the culpable mental states of the defendant. Whether one puts it as causation (the aspect-cause view), or as culpability (the harm-within-the-risk view), the discriminating power is roughly the same.

A second unified view of causation in the law is the oldest of these kinds of proposal. It conceives of causation as a metaphysical primitive. Causation is not reducible to any other sort of thing or things, so there is little by way of an *analysis* that one can say about it. However, the one thing we can say is that the causal relation is a scalar relation, which is to say, a matter of degree. One thing can be *more* of a cause of a certain event than another thing. Given the scalarity of causation, all the law need do is draw the line for liability somewhere on the scale marking degrees of causal contribution. On matters that vary on a smooth continuum, it is notoriously arbitrary to pick a precise break-point; where is the line between middle age and old age, red and pink, bald and not-bald, or caused and not-caused? This approach thus picks an *appropriately* vague line below which one's causal contribution to a given harm will be ignored for purposes of assessing responsibility. Let the defendant be responsible and liable for some harm only when the degree of his causal contribution to that harm has reached some non de minimis, or "substantial," magnitude. This is the original "substantial factor" test, as articulated by Jeremiah Smith in 1911.[84] To the common objection that the test tells us little, its defenders reply that that is a virtue, not a vice, for there is little to be said about causation. Like hard-core pornography, causation is something we can "know when we see it,"[85] without need of general definitions and tests.

The third and last of these unified notions of causation is physicalist in its ambitions. Some theorists have thought that we can say more about the nature of the causal relation than that it is scalar and that a substantial amount of it is required for responsibility. On this third view, the nature of causation is to be found in the mechanistic concepts of physics: matter in motion, energy, force.[86] This test is similar to the substantial factor view in its conceiving the causal relation to be scalar but differs in its reductionist ambitions: causation is not a primitive but can be reduced to some kind of physical phenomena.

This view handles easily the overdetermination cases that are such a problem for the conventional analysis. When two fires join, two bullets strike simultaneously, two motorcycles scare the same horse, each is a cause of the harm because each is doing its physical work. When one nonmortal wound is inflicted together with a larger, mortal wound and the victim dies of loss of blood, each is a cause of death because each did some of the physical work (loss of blood) leading to death.

Such a mechanistic conception of causation is mostly a suggestion in the legal literature because of the elusive and seemingly mysterious use of "energy" and "force" by legal theorists. One suspects that some such view is often applied by jurors, but unless theorists can spell out the general nature of the relation being intuitively applied by jurors, this test tends to collapse to the metaphysically sparer primitivist substantial factor test.

VII Conclusion

The law, as we have seen, has a bafflingly large number of legal tests for causation. There is no universally accepted theory in the general part of the law of crimes. We have thousands of separate usages of "cause" in the thousands of liability rules of criminal law; and we have nine variations of cause-in-fact tests, seven varieties of proximate cause tests, and three proposals supposing that a unified test should supplant any of the sixty-three possible combinations of the bifurcated tests. Despite this prolixity and disagreement about the proper test of causation to be given to juries, such juries often seem unperplexed at making findings of causation in particular cases. This may be because causation, like some other elements of liability such as intention and insanity, may be known better by common intuition in particular instances than by the abstract tests legal theorists have devised to "guide" such intuitions.

Be that as it may, the number of competing tests behooves one to organize them at least into distinct groupings. This has been my limited ambition in this essay. The following outline of the criminal law tests for causation may provide a helpful summary of the taxonomic conclusions.

I. Bifurcated tests
   A. Cause-in-fact tests
      1. Simple counterfactual test (the legal test of "sine qua non")
      2. Modified counterfactual tests in law
         a. Necessary element of a sufficient set
         b. Necessary to the time, place, and manner of an effect's occurrence
         c. Asymmetrically temporal test: necessary to accelerations (but not retardings) as cause
         d. The necessity of culpable aspects of acts (versus acts that are culpable) as causes
         e. Necessity as a usually present and always sufficient criterion of "substantial factor" causation
         f. Causation as necessity to chance
      3. Tests for causal skeptics: cause in fact as a matter of policy
         a. Ad hoc balancing of all policies (Crits and legal realists)
         b. Incentive-based policies and probabilistic tests (legal economists)
   B. Proximate cause tests
      1. Tests regarding proximate causation to be a matter of policy
         a. Tests based on a wide range of policies
            i. Ad hoc policy balancing test
            ii. Rule-based policy tests
               (1) Year and a day rule
               (2) First house rule
               (3) Last wrongdoer rule

      b. Tests based on the policy of gauging culpability (mental state) of the actor
        i. Foreseeability test
        ii. Harm-within-the-risk test
   2. Tests regarding proximate causation to be a matter of fact (about real causal relations)
      a. Space-time proximity tests and the sheer number of events in the chain between cause and effect
      b. Direct cause tests
   3. Tests regarding proximate causation to be partly causal and partly policy: direct cause with foreseeability (of the intervening cause)

II. Unified tests
   A. Aspects cause revisited (see item I.A.2.d)
   B. Cause as a scalar primitive: the original substantial factor test
   C. Physically reductionist tests: cause as physical force

NOTES

1. On the general part of the criminal law, see Michael Moore, "A Theory of Criminal Law Theories," *Tel Aviv University Studies in Law*, 10 (1990), 115–185, reprinted as chapter 1 of Michael Moore, *Placing Blame: A General Theory of the Criminal Law* (Oxford: Clarendon Press, 1997).

2. Moore, *Placing Blame*, 363 n. 1.

3. As in *Regina v. Blaue*, [1975] 3 All Eng. Rep. 446 (Ct. App. 1975).

4. American Law Institute, *Model Penal Code* § 2.03(1) (Proposed Official Draft, 1962).

5. A variation on the facts of *New York Central R. R. v. Grimstad*, 264 F. 2d 334 (2d Cir. 1920).

6. Eric Johnson nicely details how courts often impose liability in both torts and criminal law by simply sweeping under the rug these uncertainties in verifying counterfactuals. Johnson, "Lost Chance in Criminal Cases," *Iowa Law Review* 91 (2005), 66–71.

7. I explored this problem in *Placing Blame*, 345–347, and in chapter 16 of Moore, *Causation and Responsibility: An Essay in Law, Morals, and Metaphysics* (Oxford: Oxford University Press, 2009), relying on the philosophical literature on counterfactuals. In the legal literature this indeterminacy was earliest explored in Robert Cole, "Windfall and Probability: A Study of 'Cause' in Negligence Law," *California Law Review* 52 (1964), 459–512, 764–821.

8. *Denny v. N.Y. Central R.R.*, 13 Gray (Mass.) 481 (1859).

9. Moore, *Placing Blame*, 268–269.

10. Richard Wright, "Causation in Tort Law," *California Law Review* 73 (1985), 1775–1798.

11. See Moore, *Causation and Responsibility*, chapter 17.

12. See *id.*, chapters 5 and 17.

13. *People v. Lewis*, 124 Cal. 551, 57 P. 470 (1899).

14. See chapter 17 of Moore, *Causation and Responsibility*.

15. J. L. Mackie, *The Cement of the Universe* (Oxford: Oxford University Press, 1980); Wright, "Causation in Tort Law." I have paraphrased Wright's shortened version of Mackie's longer stated test. I discuss such tests in Moore, *Causation and Responsibility*, chapter 19.

16. American Law Institute, *Commentaries on the Model Penal Code* § 2.03(1) (1985).

17. That it only *seems* to do better is argued persuasively in Wright, "Causation in Tort Law," 1777–1780. I also reject this "fragile" events approach in *Causation and Responsibility*, chapter 17.

18. *Oxendine v. State*, 528 A. 2d 870, 872–873 (Del. 1987).

19. *Berry v. Borough of Sugar Notch*, 43 A. 240 (Pa. 1899).

20. As the Pennsylvania court noted in *id.*

21. Wright, "Causation in Tort Law."

22. American Law Institute, *Restatement of Torts* §§ 431–435 (1934); *Restatement (Second) of Torts* §§ 431–433 (1965).

23. The *Restatements* hold that a but for factor is a cause in fact of a harm. *Restatement of Torts* §§ 431–433 (1934).

24. Eric Johnson, "Criminal Liability for Loss of a Chance."

25. "Necessary to Chance" is explored in chapter 13 of Moore, *Causation and Responsibility*.

26. *Id.*, chapters 16, 19.

27. Moore, "Introduction: The Nature of Singularist Theories of Causation," *Monist* 92 (2009), 3–22, reprinted in Moore, *Causation and Responsibility*, chapter 20.

28. Moore, *Causation and Responsibility*, chapter 13.

29. I am unconcerned with whether the regularity theory sketched below was really believed by Hume. On this, see, e.g., Barry Stroud, *Hume* (London: Routledge and Kegan Paul, 1977), chapters 3 and 4; and Galen Strawson, *The Secret Connexion* (Oxford: Clarendon Press, 1989). The Humean theory is an interesting and an influential one even if it turns out that Hume never held it.

30. Moore, *Causation and Responsibility*, chapter 19.

31. Saul Kripke, *Wittgenstein on Rules and Private Language* (Cambridge, Mass.: Harvard University Press, 1982), 66–68.

32. H. L. A. Hart, "The Ascription of Responsibility and Rights," *Proceedings of the Aristotelian Society* 49 (1949), 171–194. A like skepticism is directed specifically at causation in Meir Dan-Cohen, "Causation," in S. Kadish, ed., *Encyclopedia of Crime and Justice* I (New York: MacMillan, 1983), 165–166 ("the question of causation (namely, 'Is there a causal relation between A's conduct and B's death?') amounts to asking whether punishing A is necessary"). Citing Peter Geach's damning criticism (in Geach's "Ascriptivism," *Philosophical Review* 69 [1960], 221–225), Hart came to reject the speech-act semantics that lead him to his ascriptivism about causative verbs. H. L. A. Hart, *Punishment and Responsibility* (Oxford: Oxford University Press, 1968), v.

33. Henry Edgarton, "Legal Cause," *University of Pennsylvania Law Review*, 72 (1924), 211–244, 343–375.

34. Edgarton, "Legal Cause," 347. See also Leon Green, "Are There Dependable Rules of Causation?," *University of Pennsylvania Law Review*, 77 (1929), 604–606. ("The inquiry while stated in what seems to be in terms of *cause* is in fact whether the defendant should be held responsible.")

35. Wex Malone, "Ruminations on Cause-in-Fact," *Stanford Law Review* 9 (1956), 60–99.

36. Joel Feinberg nicely summarized much of this literature of 1950s philosophy (such as Morton White and R. G. Collingwood) in his "Action and Responsibility," in Feinberg, *Doing and Deserving* (Princeton: Princeton University Press, 1970), 143–147. The usual response of contemporary philosophy to this older literature is the same as the proper response to Malone: concede that "*the* cause" designations depend on a host of pragmatic factors, some of them evaluative, but deny that this affects the objectivity of causation judgments generally. See, e.g., David Lewis, "Causation," *Journal of Philosophy* 70 (1973), 556–567, reprinted in Ernest Sosa and Michael Tooley, eds., *Causation* (Oxford: Oxford University Press, 1993), 195–196. Richard Wright does a good job of demolishing Malone on this point. Wright, "Causation in Tort Law," 1743–1745.

37. See generally Mark Kelman, *A Guide to Critical Legal Studies* (Cambridge, Mass.: Harvard University Press, 1987).

38. Explored in Moore, "The Interpretive Turn in Modern Theory: A Turn for the Worse?," *Stanford Law Review* 41 (1989), 871–957, reprinted as chapter 10 of my *Educating Oneself in Public: Critical Essays in Jurisprudence* (Oxford: Oxford University Press, 2000).

39. Mark Kelman, "The Necessary Myth of Objective Causation Judgments in Liberal Political Theory," *Chicago-Kent Law Review* 63 (1987), 579–637.

40. Moore, *Causation and Responsibility*, chapter 19.

41. As I noted in my early response to Kelman. See Moore, "Thompson's Preliminaries About Causation and Rights," *Chicago-Kent Law Review* 63 (1987), 497–521, reprinted as chapter 7 of Moore, *Placing Blame*.

42. See, e.g., Guido Calabresi, "Concerning Cause and the Law of Torts: An Essay for Harry Kalven, Jr.," *University of Chicago Law Review* 43 (1975), 69–108; Steven Shavell, "Analysis of Causation and the Scope of Liability," *Journal of Legal Studies* 9 (1980), 463–503; and William Landes and Richard Posner, "Causation in Tort Law: An Economic Approach," *Journal of Legal Studies* 12 (1983), 109–134.

43. The influence of the American Legal Realists (Malone, Edgerton, and Green) is quite evident in the law and economics literature on causation. Thus, Guido Calabresi concludes to his satisfaction that "in the law "cause in fact" … is in the end a functional concept designed to achieve human goals." Calabresi, "Concerning Cause and the Law of Torts," 107. There, he reached this conclusion on just the grounds Malone used in reaching a like conclusion. See 105–106. Similarly skeptical of causation are Landes and Posner, "Causation in Tort Law." Landes and Posner, in their rush to replace causation with probability theory, feel entitled to deride the philosophical attempt to define causation as "fruitless," totally context-dependent in its meaning, and in any event irrelevant to the purposes for which tort law should use the concept; 109–111, 119. Steve Shavell explicitly adopts Edgerton's and Calabresi's "instrumentalist" approach to causation, defining the concept so as to serve "well-specified social goals." Shavell, "Analysis of Causation and the Scope of Liability," 502. Shavell recognizes that there exists a common-sense notion of cause that antedates the law, but in such a common-sense concept, "questions about causation are to an important extent resolved by resort to intuitions about the justness of applying a rule of liability." *Id.* Calibresi, Landes, Posner, and Shavell are not fully aware of how truly skeptical they are about causation, because often they seek to rescue the concept by giving it a probabilistic definition. If they clearly saw the difference between ex ante probability theory, which deals with *types* of acts, and ex post causation theory, which deals with particular actions ("act-tokens"), they would see that they are not in any sense analyzing causation but are replacing it with something else. On this, see Richard Wright,

"Actual Causation vs. Probabilistic Linkage: The Bane of Economic Analysis," *Journal of Legal Studies* 14 (1985), 435–456.

44. See Shavell, "Analysis of Causation and the Scope of Liability," 495; and Landes and Posner, "Causation in Tort Law," 110.

45. On purposive interpretation of legal texts, see Michael S. Moore, "The Semantics of Judging," *Southern California Law Review* 54 (1981), 279–281; and Moore, "A Natural Law Theory of Interpretation," *Southern California Law Review* 58 (1985), 383–88.

46. On the criminal-law meaning of "malice" in the law of homicide, see Moore, "Natural Law Theory on Interpretation," 332–336.

47. A late expression of this view of tort law is to be found in Guido Calabresi, "Some Thoughts on Risk Distribution and the Law of Torts," *Yale Law Journal* 70 (1961), 499–553.

48. Ronald Coase, "The Problem of Social Cost," *Journal of Law and Economics* 3 (1960), 1–44.

49. I thus put aside those who interpret Coase to be a causal skeptic. (See, e.g., Richard Epstein, "A Theory of Strict Liability," *Journal of Legal Studies* 2 [1973], 164–165, for an interpretation of Coase according to which the Coasean insight was that we cannot say what is the cause of what.) Although Coase, like many other economists, does evince some skepticism about causation, he made a much better point than this "interactive effects" interpretation gives him credit for: it is that causation does not matter for the efficient allocation of resources.

50. Calibresi, "Concerning Cause and the Law of Torts"; Shavell, "Analysis of Causation and the Scope of Liability"; Landes and Posner, "Causation in Tort Law."

51. For a good discussion of the economists" misuse of "cause" to name an increase in conditional probability, see Richard Wright, "Actual Causation versus Probabilistic Linkage: The Bane of Economic Analysis"; and Wright, "The Efficiency Theory of Causation and Responsibility: Unscientific Formalism and False Semantics," *Chicago-Kent Law Review* 63 (1987), 553–578.

52. Or so I argue in Moore, *Placing Blame*, chapters 2–4.

53. Argued for in *id.*, chapter 5; Moore, *Causation and Responsibility*, chapters 2–3.

54. The most influential example of ad hoc policy tests is Henry Edgarton, "Legal Cause."

55. Joshua Dressler, *Understanding Criminal Law*, 2d ed. (New York: Matthew-Bender, 1995), 466–467.

56. Jeremiah Smith, "Legal Cause in Actions in Tort," *Harvard Law Review* 25 (1911–12), 111. See also Lawrence Eldredge, "Culpable Intervention as Superseding Cause," *University of Pennsylvania Law Review* 86 (1938), 121–135.

57. *Ryan v. New York Center R.R.*, 35 N.Y. 210, 91 Am. Dec. 49 (1866).

58. Felix Cohen, "Transcendental Nonsense and the Functional Approach," *Columbia Law Review* 35 (1935), 809–849; Cohen, "The Problems of a Functional Jurisprudence," *Modern Law Review* 1 (1937), 5–26.

59. Moore, *Placing Blame*, chapter 5.

60. *Id.*; Moore, *Causation and Responsibility*, chapter 2.

61. Discussed in detail in Moore, *Placing Blame*, 363–399.

62. *Id.*, 363 n. 1.

63. An old but still unanswered and cogent objection to the foreseeability test of proximate causation. See, e.g., Leon Green, "The Wagon Mound No. 2: Foreseeability Revised," *Utah Law Review*, [1967], 197–206.

64. Explored in detail in Moore, *Causation and Responsibility*, chapters 7–10.

65. American Law Institute, Model Penal Code §§ 2.03(2), 2.03(3), 2.03(4).

66. Moore, *Placing Blame*, 469–476. See also Moore, "Intention as a Marker of Serious Culpability," in R. A. Duff and S. Green, eds., *Philosophical Foundations of Criminal Law* (Oxford: Oxford University Press, 2010).

67. Explored in detail in Moore, *Causation and Responsibility*, chapter 11.

68. *Id.*, chapter 11.

69. *Id.*, chapter 10.

70. American Law Institute, Model Penal Code § 2.03(2)(b) (Proposed Official Draft, 1962).

71. Bacon's first maxim was "Injura non remota causa sed proxima spectator." Bacon, "Maxims of the Law," in Bacon, *The Elements of the Common Law of England* (London: Assigns of I. Moore, 1630), 1. See the discussion of Bacon's "causa proxima" in Joseph Beale, "The Proximate Consequences of an Act," *Harvard Law Review* 33 (1920), 633–658. Beale (unsurprisingly, since this was also Beale's own view) concludes that "Bacon's idea of the remote cause … was a purely physical idea," 634 n. 4.

72. The place to ask and answer these questions of fit is with respect to mental states, not causation. With respect to negligence, which is not a mental state, I have urged that we should not ask the fit question at all, anywhere. Moore, *Causation and Responsibility*, chapters 8–9.

73. See, e.g., Beale, "Proximate Consequences of an Act," 642–643.

74. *People v. Botkin*, 132 Cal. 231, 64 P. 286 (1901).

75. Beale, "Proximate Consequences of an Act," 642.

76. "There is no use in arguing that distance ought not to count, if life and experience tells us that it does." *Bird v. St. Paul F. and Minneapolis Ins. Co.*, 224 N. Y. 47, 120 N.E. 86 (1918). See also Edgarton, "Legal Cause," 367–372.

77. Moore, *Causation and Responsibility*, chapter 5.

78. Despite Bacon telling us that the law "contenteth it selfe with the immediate cause and judgeth of acts by that, without looking to any further degree" (Bacon, "Maxims," 1), even the ancient distinction between the writ of trespass (for directly caused harms) and trespass on the case (for indirectly caused harms) was not so strict about directness. A famous example is the "squib case," *Scott v. Shepard*, 96 Eng. Rep. 525 (K.B. 1773), in which a lighted squib containing gunpowder was thrown by the defendant near one person, who threw it near another, who threw it near the victim, where the squib exploded. The court held that "the injury is the direct and immediate act of the defendant," so that the writ of trespass was appropriate.

79. H. L. A. Hart and A. M. Honoré, "Causation in the Law," *Law Quarterly Review* 72 (1956), 58–90, 260–281, 398–417. H. L. A. Hart and A. M. Honoré, *Causation in the Law* (Oxford: Clarendon Press, 1959).

80. H. L. A. Hart and Tony Honoré, *Causation in the Law*, 2d ed. (Oxford: Clarendon Press, 1985). The second edition works a number of changes, almost all of them at the behest of Tony Honoré. One might doubt whether Herbert Hart ever fully shared the NESS view. Honoré certainly did. See his "Necessary and Sufficient Conditions in Tort Law," in David Owen, ed., *Philosophical Foundations of Tort Law* (Oxford: Oxford University Press, 1995).

81. The early case law is summarized in Charles Carpenter, "Workable Rules for Determining Proximate Cause," *California Law Review* 20 (1932), 229–259, 396–419, 471–539. Even more exhaustive is Carpenter, "Proximate Cause," *Southern California Law Review* 14 (1940), 1–34, 115–153, 416–451; 15 (1942), 187–213, 304–321, 427–468; 16 (1943), 1–23, 61–92, 275–313.

82. See Sanford Kadish, "Complicity, Cause and Blame: A Study in the Interpretation of Doctrine," *California Law Review* 73 (1985), 323–410. Also explored in detail in Moore, *Causation and Responsibility*, chapter 13.

83. The fit is not perfect. For some counterexamples, see Carpenter, "Workable Rules for Determining Proximate Cause," 408; see also Wright, "Causation in Tort Law," 1759–1766.

84. Smith, "Legal Cause in Actions of Tort." Primitivist theories of causation outside the law are examined in Moore, *Causation and Responsibility*, chapter 20.

85. Justice Potter Stewart's famous "test," in *Jacobellis v. Ohio*, 378 U.S. 184, 197 (1961).

86. Beale, "Proximate Consequences of an Act"; Beale, "Recovery for Consequences of an Act," *Harvard Law Review* 9 (1895), 80–89; Epstein, "Theory of Strict Liability." Physical reductionist theories of causation outside the law are explored in Moore, *Causation and Responsibility*, chapter 20.

CHAPTER 8

RESPONSIBILITY

JOHN DEIGH

THE criminal law regulates conduct by threatening and imposing punishment for its violation. In a perfectly just system of criminal law, punishment is imposed only on people who are and have been found guilty of doing some action that the law proscribes. Guilt implies responsibility for such actions, and therefore, in a just system, punishment is imposed on those who violate the law only if they are responsible for the acts they do that violate it. This requirement is a bedrock principle of justice in the criminal law. It holds regardless of whether punishment is imposed for reasons of retribution or deterrence. At the same time, these different views of the general rationale for punishment entail different ways of understanding being responsible for a criminal offense. They correspond, then, to two different ways of conceiving of responsibility in the criminal law. And as retribution and deterrence are the two major rationales for punishment, the study of responsibility in the criminal law chiefly focuses on these two conceptions.

The conception entailed by the retributive rationale for punishment is modeled on the idea of moral responsibility for wrongdoing. That is, legal guilt, on this conception, is modeled on moral guilt. Punishment is then seen as a just desert for crime. The conception entailed by the deterrence rationale, by contrast, does not reflect an understanding of punishment as a just desert for crime. Rather, it reflects an understanding of punishment as a means of preventing crime. Accordingly, the conditions of responsibility, on this conception, are fixed by law with an eye toward efficiency in the use of punishment to reduce the frequency of crime in the population the law governs. Some theorists of the criminal law who take deterrence as the general rationale for punishment treat efficiency as the sole factor that determines these conditions. They hold a pure deterrence theory. Others, however, maintain that considerations of fairness ought to constrain the pursuit of efficiency in the use of punishment to prevent crime, and they, therefore, take these considerations as an additional factor that determines the conditions of criminal responsibility.

This second group of deterrence theorists holds what is sometimes called a mixed theory. They too, however, reject the understanding of punishment as a just desert for crime. The considerations of fairness that they invoke as constraints on the pursuit of efficiency in the use of punishment to prevent crime have to do with giving those whose conduct the law regulates fair opportunity to avoid liability to punishment and not with protecting those who do not *deserve* punishment from being punished.

Let us call the first conception of criminal responsibility *desert-based* and the second *consequence-based.*[1] The former, as I noted, is modeled on the idea of moral responsibility. Typically, when we attribute moral responsibility for an action, we do so in virtue of the action's being either morally blameworthy or morally praiseworthy, and to be either morally blameworthy or morally praiseworthy, the action must spring from a state of mind that is itself morally blameworthy or morally praiseworthy. By the same token, then, criminal responsibility for an offense, on this first conception, is attributed in virtue of the blameworthiness of the action—that is, that it is a culpable act, and for an action that the law proscribes to be done culpably, it must spring from a blameworthy state of mind. By contrast, on the second conception, criminal responsibility for an offense entails that the offender exercised or could have exercised certain powers in committing the offense. Specifically, it entails that the offender exercised or could have exercised those deliberative and executive powers that enable people to adjust their conduct in response to offers and threats. They are those powers, that is, that enable people first to determine which, among the different actions open to them in the circumstances they face, is the best one to do and then to act accordingly. Alternatively, they are those powers that enable people first to determine which action, among the different actions open to them in the circumstances they face, they have most reason to do and then to act accordingly. In either case, it is not essential to a person's being criminally responsible for his action, on this conception, that he act from a morally blameworthy state of mind.

One evident consequence of the distinction between these two conceptions is that the mental element, or mens rea, of a crime is characterized differently according as responsibility in the criminal law is conceived as desert-based or consequence-based. Thus, on the desert-based conception, one can take *mens rea* literally to mean a guilty or wicked mind., For on this conception, the mental state with which an offender must act to act criminally is a morally blameworthy state. By contrast, on the consequence-based conception, *mens rea* becomes a technical term for whatever state of mind is the mental state with which the offender must have acted for his conduct to count as criminal. Hence, on this conception, one looks to how the crime is defined and particularly to what its mental elements are to determine the mens rea, and those mental elements need not be morally blameworthy. Not surprisingly, then, those who favor the desert-based conception regard any crime for which no mental element is necessary for someone to be guilty of committing it as an aberration if not a perversion of the criminal law, whereas those who favor the consequence-based conception typically regard such crimes as merely exceptions to a general rule about the conditions of guilt in the criminal law. Or if, instead, they object to such crimes on principle, the principle on which they base their objection is independent of any concern with the law's inflicting punishment on people who have acted blamelessly.

As these last remarks suggest, desert-based and consequence-based conceptions of criminal responsibility represent different ideals. They do not purport to reflect the actual practice in the criminal law of determining an offender's responsibility for his or her offense. The actual practice, being an amalgam of different ideas and programs that have prevailed at different times in the history of the practice, lacks the coherence necessary for a single ideal to be realized in it. Consequently, it would be a mistake to suppose that the theories incorporating these conceptions are meant to describe or explain this practice. They are not. Rather, they, and more particularly, the conceptions they incorporate, are used as standards for criticizing the practice and for guiding efforts to reform it. In short, for those who use them, they represent how the practice ought to be and not how it actually is. They are thus tools of legal criticism and legal reform and not of legal exegesis. In this chapter, I will explicate both conceptions of criminal responsibility. Since the desert-based conception is the more traditional of the two, I will begin with it.

1. Desert-Based Conceptions of Responsibility in the Criminal Law: The Model of Moral Responsibility

A. The Traditional Account

The traditional account of moral responsibility in philosophy makes freedom of the will a necessary condition of being responsible. That is, on this account, people are morally responsible for their actions only if their actions issue from their will and only if that will is free. Further, on the traditional account, for a person's will to be free, it must be true that the person could have willed to act differently from the way he has in fact willed to act. And while some philosophers continue to debate whether this latter condition can obtain in a deterministic universe, a universe, that is, in which every event (or at least every event after that which produced the universe) is completely caused by the events that precede it, the arguments that it cannot are sufficiently powerful to have put those who believe it in retreat. In particular, the once popular idea for how to understand the possibility of this condition's obtaining in a deterministic universe, G. E. Moore's idea that the condition is completely definable by a set of conditional statements that could be true in a deterministic universe, no longer seems viable.[2] The objection, due to J. L. Austin, that the relevant sense of *could* in the statement of the condition resists being so defined has never been satisfactorily answered.[3] Consequently, on the strongest version of the traditional account, for an agent's action to issue from a will that is free, it must not be completely caused by external events that precede it. On this version of the traditional account, in other words, people are capable of initiating actions on their own volition, where "on their own volition" means that the circumstances in which they find themselves, the events and conditions that define those circumstances, do not determine their decision or choice as to how to act in those circumstances. Nor do they determine their actions. Whatever influence prior events and conditions have on how people exercise their will, they may still will to do a certain action, and that they have so willed is never merely the direct consequence of those events and conditions.

Because on this version of the traditional account, no one and nothing else causes the actions a person does of his own free will, to attribute to him responsibility for the action is similar to common attributions of responsibility for an event (e.g., a disaster) to things in virtue of their being the principal cause of that event. It is similar, that is, to saying that Mrs. O'Leary's cow was responsible for the Great Chicago Fire or that a defective O-ring was responsible for the Challenger Disaster of 1986. The difference is that, unlike these common attributions of causal responsibility, one cannot shift the responsibility onto prior events and conditions. The person alone is the original and thus ultimate cause of his or her actions and therefore of its consequences. Hence, when those consequences include harms and injustices, injuries and insults, some of which are intended, foreseen, or wantonly risked, then the agent becomes through his will an author and promoter of evil, unless of course the good that he intends to bring about by his actions would justify, were it realized, his causing those harms and injustices, injuries and insults, that he intends or foresees. The point is that the state of mind with which he acts is morally blameworthy. When criminal responsibility is modeled on moral responsibility in accordance with this version of the traditional account of moral responsibility, mens rea is essential to an offender's being responsible for his or her offense. Indeed, we can see directly from this modeling why the defenders of retributive theories of punishment are among the severest critics of strict liability offenses in the criminal law. Moreover, because what, on this version of the account, makes the state of mind with which the guilty offender acts morally blameworthy is a will allied with evil (either through intention, foresight, or wanton indifference), we can also see why defenders of retributive theories of punishment are among the strongest skeptics of allowing inadvertent negligence to be a sufficient mental element in the definition of some crimes.

The obvious drawback to this way of conceiving of criminal responsibility is that it entails a metaphysical view of human action that is hard to maintain within secular thought. The trend in secular thought is against treating human beings as having powers that remove them from the natural world and likewise against treating human actions as exceptions to the general rule that events and states of affairs that occur in the natural world are the effects of natural forces and processes. And the account of free will, on the strongest version of the traditional account, is plainly one that attributes to human beings such powers and that entails seeing voluntary human actions as exceptions to this rule. At the same time, endorsing a weaker version of the traditional account is problematic as well, since it requires holding to a view that is in retreat. Consequently, lacking arguments to rebut the powerful arguments that support the strongest version over the others, those who hold that criminal responsibility is modeled on moral responsibility need to look for a different account of moral responsibility from the traditional one to maintain their view.

B. Moral Responsibility without Free Will

One possibility is to deny that moral responsibility for an action requires that the action issue from the exercise of a free will. This possibility is suggested in Harry Frankfurt's influential essays on moral responsibility and freedom of the will.[4] Frankfurt, in one of those essays, "Alternate Possibilities and Moral Responsibility," attacks the thesis that a person is morally responsible for an action he does only if he could have acted differently.[5] To the contrary, Frankfurt argues, someone who willingly does some action in circumstances in which, unbeknownst to him, he could not have acted differently is still morally responsible for doing the action. Since the action issued from his will in exactly the same way as it would have issued from his will if he were in circumstances in which he could have acted differently, he is no less at fault for doing it and no less appropriately credited with doing it. As we observed earlier, what makes a person's actions blameworthy or praiseworthy is that they spring from a blameworthy or praiseworthy state of mind, and a person who willingly acts in circumstances in which, unbeknownst to him, he could not have acted differently may very well act with the same state of mind as he would have had if he had done that action in circumstances in which he was able to act differently. Hence, he may act with a blameworthy or praiseworthy state of mind and thus his action may be blameworthy or praiseworthy even though he acts in circumstances in which he could not act differently. And if his action is either blameworthy or praiseworthy, then he is morally responsible for it.

This argument, moreover, applies mutatis mutandis to acts of will. That is, just as the argument yields the conclusion that one can be morally responsible for an action even when one acts in circumstances in which one could not have acted differently, so too a parallel argument about willed actions yields the conclusion that one can be morally responsible for an action one does willingly even when one wills to do the action in circumstances in which one could not have willed differently. In either case, it is sufficient that one is ignorant of that feature of one's circumstances in virtue of which one cannot either act differently or will differently. Admittedly, the latter case is stranger than the former: the well-known example that Frankfurt uses to illustrate it is one of someone whose decision-making capacity is subject to manipulation by a manipulator who is remarkably perceptive—he intervenes with the decision making of the person he's manipulating only when the latter begins to form a will contrary to what he, the manipulator, wants him to will. Nonetheless, the example illustrates the intelligibility of the relevant circumstances, and their intelligibility is sufficient for the argument to yield the conclusion that people are morally responsible for actions they do in such circumstances. Consequently, on this parallel argument, a person can be morally responsible for an action he does even if, as in this example, the action does not issue from his exercising a free will.

What, then, is the alternative account of moral responsibility that Frankfurt and others who defend the separation of moral responsibility from freedom of the will put forward in place of the traditional account? And how does it explain people's being morally responsible for their actions in a deterministic universe? On either the traditional account or this alternative, the decisive factor that determines whether someone is morally responsible for an action is how the will from which his action issues is formed. On the traditional account, its formation must consist in an exercise of free will. Having a free will is what qualifies a person as a moral agent, and its exercise in performing an action is essential to the person's being morally responsible for that action. On the alternative account, the possession of certain capacities for action that do not necessarily imply the possession of a free will is what qualifies a person as a moral agent, and their exercise in forming and executing a will is essential to the person's being morally responsible for the action that issues from that will. The capacities for action whose possession qualifies a person as a moral agent, on this account, are certain cognitive, affective, and volitional capacities. Specifically, the person must have mature and unimpaired rational faculties, be free of severe emotional disturbances, and have the self-control necessary for suppressing desires and urges that conflict with his will. The description of these capacities so far is rather general. Specific descriptions of them differ with different versions of the alternative account. On Frankfurt's version, for instance, a capacity for reflecting critically and evaluating one's desires and a capacity to form, in response to those evaluations, desires to have and be moved to act by certain desires are the capacities that qualify someone as a moral agent.[6] On a version advanced by Gary Watson, the capacity to have values, conceived as a different capacity from that of having desires and understood to include the capacity to be moved to act in accordance with one's values, is what qualifies someone as a moral agent.[7] On versions held by John M. Fischer and R. Jay Wallace, being capable of recognizing the reasons for action presented by one's circumstances and responding appropriately are the capacities that qualify one as a moral agent.[8]

In all of these versions the capacities are such that their possession is explicable by the causal processes by which human beings acquire a personality, and their exercise is explicable by the causal forces that impinge on human beings in the circumstances in which they act. Hence, each gives an account of moral responsibility for an action that is compatible with the action's occurring in a deterministic universe. At the same time, because the different versions represent competing theories of moral agency, they bring new questions to the study of moral responsibility. Because the different theories give different answers to the question what cognitive, affective, and volitional capacities qualify a person as a moral agent, not all versions of this alternative account agree about who qualifies as one. Thus versions like Frankfurt's exclude from the class of moral agents any person who is unreflective about his own desires and, consequently, can form no attitudes toward any of them that move him either to act on or to suppress it, whereas versions like Fischer's and Wallace's identify such persons as moral agents as long as they can recognize and respond appropriately to the reasons for action that their circumstances present. And contrarily, the latter versions exclude from the class of moral agents people who are consistently unresponsive to features of their circumstances that give reason for action, whereas the former identify such persons as moral agents as long as they are reflective about their desires and can form attitudes toward some of those desires that move them either to act on them or to suppress them. Hence, unlike the traditional account, which relies on indicia of possessing a free will to determine who qualifies as a moral agent, any version of this alternative account relies on a theory of moral agency to determine who qualifies as one, and since no such theory has emerged as the soundest, all versions of this account are to some extent promissory. They provide a program for making sense of attributions of moral responsibility in a deterministic universe but leave unsettled at the margins of human conduct, so to speak, whether someone is morally responsible for his actions.[9]

The problem is especially clear in the case of psychopaths. A psychopath is not just a career criminal or a constant troublemaker. He is also someone whose persistent wrongdoing is the result of certain emotional deficits. Specifically, psychopaths are incapable of empathy and lack the capacity for feeling guilt, shame, or remorse. Their disorder, however, does not reflect a lack of intelligence. Psychopaths are not morons. Indeed, many are highly intelligent and have powerful cognitive abilities. They are sufficiently socialized to understand the norms of their society and to anticipate the blame and condemnation that result from violations of those norms, and accordingly they can use their cognitive abilities to make and carry out plans that reflect their interest in avoiding those sanctions. The question, then, is whether, given this combination of cognitive abilities and emotional deficits, they qualify as moral agents. The two elements in this mix, taken separately, yield opposing answers. Not surprisingly, then, there are persuasive theories of moral agency on either side.

On the one hand, theories that identify moral agency with having developed powers of reason and self-control classify psychopaths as moral agents. On such theories, it is sufficient to be a moral agent that a person is capable of making and acting on choices that reflect his values and interests and that are not the products of either delusional thoughts or overpowering desires and urges. That the person lacks the ability to empathize with others or is insusceptible to moral feelings does not disqualify him. On these theories, psychopaths qualify as moral agents as long as they know what actions morality prohibits and what actions it requires and are able to conform their conduct to those prohibitions and requirements. Accordingly, they are responsible for their violation whenever they meet the conditions of responsibility that generally apply. On the other hand, theories of moral agency like those that Fischer's and Wallace's views represent exclude psychopaths from being moral agents. They exclude them because psychopaths, being incapable of empathy and being insusceptible to moral feelings, are incapable of recognizing and responding appropriately to moral reasons for action. With respect to such reasons, they are dumb. While they know that kiting checks, say, is wrong in the sense that, if caught, they will suffer social sanctions, they do not understand their actions as wrong in the sense of being hurtful to others or society. That is, because they do not experience empathically the pain and distress that their actions cause others to feel, they do not recognize the hurtfulness of their actions as reasons to forbear doing them. Thus, on theories according to which the capacity to recognize and respond to such reasons is essential to being a moral agent, they do not qualify as such and are therefore not responsible for the wrongs they do. How to resolve the dispute between these theories is the central problem on this first alternative to the traditional account of moral responsibility.

C. Strawson's Account

A second alternative that has significantly influenced recent philosophical work on moral responsibility is the account P. F. Strawson puts forward in his essay "Freedom and Resentment."[10] In this essay, Strawson takes up the question of whether determinism implies that human beings lack the freedom necessary to be morally responsible for their actions. But rather than consider what it means to have a free will or under what conditions an action issues from one, Strawson examines what the conditions are under which moral responsibility for an action is justly attributed. More exactly, since such attributions are implicit in our praising good deeds and punishing bad ones, Strawson considers what the conditions are under which a person is justly praised or punished for his actions. Accordingly, he replaces the initial question with the question of whether the truth of determinism threatens the sustainability and justifiability of our practices of praising good deeds and punishing bad ones. The question, then, on which Strawson concentrates is how to understand these practices as justified on the assumption that determinism is true. For seeing how they would be justified on this assumption would remove the threat to them that the truth of determinism poses, and if the practices can thus be sustained, one can then both draw out of their workings the relevant idea of the freedom that human beings must have to be morally responsible for their actions and safely attribute such freedom to them.

To answer the question, Strawson starts with certain facts about human psychology and human behavior that appear to be completely consistent with determinism. Specifically, he starts with what appear to him to be plain, natural facts about human interpersonal relations and certain attitudes that are integral to these relations. Strawson's aim is to draw from these facts a rich description of the dynamics of these relations and therefore, given that the practices of praising good deeds and punishing bad ones are mirrored in this description, to show how our practices of praising good and punishing bad deeds could emerge from these facts. Accordingly, if one can understand the dynamics of our interpersonal relations as defined by these facts consistently with determinism, then a similar understanding will hold of those practices. Hence, if we are justified in maintaining interpersonal relations as defined by these facts, we will be justified in sustaining the practices as well. What recommends proceeding in this way, Strawson observes, is that while the study of interpersonal relations he undertakes parallels that of our practices of praise and punishment, it is less fraught than the latter with uncertainties about the consistency of what is being studied with determinism.

The plain, natural facts about men and women with which Strawson starts—what he calls commonplaces—are these.[11] A central concern of people who live together in communities is what their intentions and attitudes are toward each other. They place great importance on these intentions and attitudes, and they interact with each other with an expectation that generally their fellows behave with goodwill toward them. The goodwill each expects of others consists in the others' keeping, as best they can, from harming one in their conduct toward or interactions with one and in their being responsive to harm they may nonetheless cause by being solicitous of one's injury and feelings. Such goodwill may be basic to human personality generally (though not universally), or it may derive from more basic emotions and primitive attachments. Either is compatible with the general fact that Strawson means to emphasize: that people are highly sensitive to and greatly concerned with whether others are well- or ill-disposed toward them. This sensitivity and concern gives rise in a person to certain attitudes and feelings when others—particularly certain others—behave in ways that manifest good or ill will toward him. Thus, while one naturally takes pleasure in benefits that come one's way on account of another's behavior, one responds, not just with pleasure, but with gratitude too, when one sees that the other intended to benefit one through his actions and because of his affection, esteem, or goodwill toward one. Likewise, while the harm inflicted on one by another's actions is disagreeable, one will feel not just displeasure, but also resentment if one recognizes in his actions malice or ill will toward one. Gratitude and resentment are Strawson's initial examples of attitudes that result from one's seeing in another's actions evident good or ill will toward one. Other examples are love, forgiveness, and hurt feelings. He calls these attitudes "personal reactive attitudes."

The personal reactive attitudes arise, then, in the context of interpersonal relations in which each of the parties expects and indeed demands of the others that they act with goodwill toward him or her. The attitudes and the responses they elicit in turn are evidence of these expectations and demands. Resentment is Strawson's prime example. Thus, when one party in a relationship of mutual goodwill injures another and the injured party feels resentment in response, the offender may try to remove these feelings with expressions of regret or apologies and such explanations as "It was an accident," "I didn't mean to," "I didn't see you coming" or similarly "I couldn't help it," "I slipped," or "I had no choice." Each of these explanations is typically offered to assuage resentment by denying that the offending action manifested ill will. They are meant, that is, to restore the relationship to the prior state of mutual goodwill by giving the injured reason to abandon his belief that the offender acted with indifference or malice toward him. The offender in making such pleas is in effect saying that he did not, despite his having caused injury, lack the goodwill toward the person he injured that is expected of him. He is saying, in other words, that while he is an appropriate object of reactive attitudes particularly at the time he caused the injury, the resentment the injured feels is misplaced in this case.

Strawson compares such pleas with pleas that are offered to assuage resentment by denying that one was even, at the time one injured another, an appropriate object of reactive attitudes: "I lost my head," "I was only a child," "It happened during a psychotic breakdown," "I was in a complete trance," and so on. Each of these explanations is meant to exempt the offender, at least at the time of the offense, from the class of people of whom one expects some degree of goodwill in their dealings with one. It is in effect a plea to look on the offender, not as a fellow participant in the kind of friendly or cooperative relations that presuppose mutual goodwill, but rather objectively as someone to be managed, controlled, or handled. In taking this outlook toward someone, one ceases to see his actions as manifesting good or ill will toward one and consequently one loses one's disposition to feel resentment, gratitude, or any of the other reactive attitudes toward him. One may of course still be liable to some feelings toward him. That one looks on the offender objectively does not mean that one becomes incapable of feeling sympathy, fear, or irritation toward him. What it means, though, is that one no longer engages with him with an attitude of goodwill and an expectation of its being reciprocated. While his actions can, then, provoke emotional responses in one, these responses do not belong to the class Strawson defines as that of the reactive attitudes. Hence, the objective view of someone that pleas of this second type invite is sharply opposed to the view one takes of another with whom one participates in an interpersonal relationship.

Strawson's idea of drawing from certain plain, natural facts about human interpersonal relations a description of the dynamics of those relations that mirrors the practices of praise and punishment is already evident in this account of how resentment arises in the context of such relations and of the responses it in turn elicits. Specifically, one can see in this account reflection of the concerns with innocence and guilt at the heart of the practice of punishment. At the same time, resentment is not an exact correlate of punishment since it is a personal attitude, an attitude one has in response to being injured by another, and punishment reflects an impersonal attitude toward the act to which it is a response. And in view of this disparity, Strawson adds to his description two classes of reactive attitudes, which are analogues of the personal reactive attitudes. These are the vicarious and the reflexive reactive attitudes. The first class consists of attitudes one takes toward the goodwill or ill will of another, not in reaction to the manifestation of that will in the person's actions toward oneself, but in reaction to its manifestation in his actions toward others. They include indignation, moral approval, and moral disapproval. The second consists of attitudes one takes toward oneself in virtue of one's recognizing that others expect one to act with goodwill toward them and in reaction to the goodwill or ill will with which one acts toward others. They include compunctions of conscience, a sense of obligation, and feelings of guilt and remorse.

The vicarious reactive attitudes are, then, the correlates to the practices of praise and punishment that Strawson needs for his description to mirror these practices. Accordingly, he characterizes the vicarious reactive attitudes as moral attitudes. He does so in virtue of their being impersonal or disinterested. He does not, therefore, in conceiving of indignation as a third-party analogue of resentment, suppose that to feel it in response to someone's injuring another in a way that shows lack of due regard for the victim one must have a special attachment to or specially identify with the victim. Rather, he supposes that one comes, by generalizing from one's own expectation of goodwill toward oneself from others, to expect goodwill from each toward everyone else, and this general expectation naturally disposes one to respond with indignation or disapproval when, say, one witnesses an injury done to someone to whom one has no special attachment by another, who manifests attitudes toward the injured that fall short of the goodwill toward others that one has come to expect of people in their transactions with others. Similarly, one becomes disposed to respond with approval when one witnesses a beneficent action toward someone to whom one has no special attachment by another who manifests goodwill toward the beneficiary in so acting. In either case, being the correlates of praise and punishment they too imply the attribution of moral responsibility for the actions to which they are responses.

Indignation, being the impersonal analogue of resentment, elicits from those who are its objects the same two types of plea as resentment. That is, like resentment, it elicits, on the one hand, pleas of mistake, accident, inadvertence, or loss of control, intended to persuade those to whom the pleas are offered that one did not manifest ill will toward the person one injured and, on the other, pleas of moral incompetency due to immaturity, a psychotic breakdown, somnambulism, or the like, intended to persuade them that one was not, when one acted, an appropriate object of reactive attitudes. The difference between these two types of plea show, Strawson then argues, that the truth of determinism does not threaten the attributions of moral responsibility implicit in indignation.

Specifically, he argues that there is a significant difference between viewing someone as a participant in an interpersonal relationship with you and viewing him as an object whose behavior is the product of the external forces and conditions to which he is subject and who is to be managed or controlled accordingly. The latter is consistent with the view we would take of people and their actions if we were to accept the thesis of determinism and regard them in its light. It is the view we are disposed to take of someone when we see him as immature or dysfunctional in a way that incapacitates him for normal interpersonal relationships. In that case, we abandon the view of him as a participant with us in such relationships and regard him, instead, with detachment of a sort that an objective view of him entails. Nor is this the only occasion on which we would view someone objectively. We also, typically, take such a view of people generally when we are making social policy or designing a program to provide certain services to a given population. And we sometimes take such a view when, because of the strain of our relations with someone, we need to put distance between him and us of the sort that a detached attitude toward him creates. In each of these cases, we maintain an objective view only temporarily or only toward certain individuals. We could not, Strawson maintains, permanently hold such a view of all people, for doing so would require our doing something we cannot in fact do, namely, cease to have interpersonal relationships. Nor, to continue Strawson's argument, would it be wise permanently to adopt the objective view even if we could, for to do so would mean our giving up human life as we know it, and abandoning our humanity is an unreasonable sacrifice. Determinism, Strawson concludes, is thus no threat to any of the reactive attitudes. We would not cease to be liable to them even if we did accept its truth, nor would we have good reason to suppress them. It is, therefore, no threat to the attributions of moral responsibility implicit in them, in particular, in the vicarious ones.

Strawson's argument, if sound, shows the futility and imprudence of our trying to suppress attitudes toward the actions of others that entail our attributing to them moral responsibility for those actions. Presumably, Strawson thinks, too (for he does not say), either that the argument also shows the futility and imprudence of our trying to abandon the practices of praise and punishment that mirror these attitudes or that it shows that abandoning them would be pointless since we would continue, through the expression of these attitudes, to attribute moral responsibility to people for their actions. The question remains, however, whether the argument thereby shows that these practices are justified. As a practical matter, we may be stuck with them, and it may be a good thing that we are, but neither of these points establishes that we are justified in making the attributions of moral responsibility that the practices require. Critics of Strawson's argument have pressed just this point in objecting to it. To be justified, they argue, the beliefs that the attributions represent must be true, and for a belief that someone is morally responsible for something he did to be true, there must be facts about him and about what he did in virtue of which it is true. But if there could be no such facts in a deterministic universe, then the belief must be false if determinism is true. In other words, the truth of determinism, if it is true, would falsify these beliefs, and hence the attributions of moral responsibility that represent them are all unjustified. Strawson's attempt to remove the threat of determinism by making the question of justification a practical one therefore fails. Or so his critics have argued.

To maintain Strawson's account in the face of this objection requires a more radical position than Strawson appears to hold. It requires denying the validity of asking whether beliefs about a person's being morally responsible for his actions are true if determinism is true. It requires, in other words, denying that the question has an answer, either yes or no. The basis for this position is Strawson's distinction between the two views of the world, participant and objective. That is, on this position, because questions about the implications of determinism presuppose the objective view, one cannot, given that view of the world, verify or falsify beliefs about a person's being morally responsible for his actions. Accordingly, determinism cannot imply the falsity of those beliefs. By the same token, asking whether such beliefs are true presupposes the participant view, which means that one conceives actions for which people are morally responsible as originating in their doers' will regardless of whether one can explain their origination in the will as the effect of prior events stretching back to the beginnings of time. Accordingly, the truth conditions of these beliefs are independent of determinism. On this position, then, to ask whether attributions of moral responsibility are justified if determinism is true is to ask a misplaced question.[12] And though this position incorporates Strawson's distinction between the two views, objective and participant, it is nonetheless more radical than the position that Strawson appears to hold, for its fundamental premisses are (1) that any reference to facts or truths about the world presupposes a specific frame of reference or way of viewing the world and (2) for every frame of reference or way of viewing the world, there is some fact or truth about the world that does not presuppose it. From these premisses it follows that sometimes, at least, questions whose constituent concepts imply different frames of reference or ways of viewing the world cannot be answered.

Of course, if these two ways of viewing the world, participant and objective, are not equally sound as bases of true beliefs, then this defense of Strawson's account fails. In particular, if the only sound basis on which to form true beliefs about the world is the objective view, as some have argued, then beliefs that one forms on the basis of the participant view are false if the objective view cannot also serve as a basis for them. Consequently, if beliefs about people's being morally responsible for their actions are products of the participant view, as Strawson's account implies, then they are all false, since the objective view of the world provides no basis on which to form them. The debate, then, between critics and defenders of Strawson's account, once the latter appeal to this more radical position, turns on whether we would be justified in taking the participant view to be as sound a basis of true belief as the objective view. Those who maintain that beliefs about people's being morally responsible for their actions are illusory or fictitious deny that we would be. Those who maintain that there is no single standpoint from which all facts and truths can be grasped and that therefore a belief about someone's being morally responsible for an action may be true even though the objective view provides no basis for it hold that we would.

Strawson's account of moral responsibility, then, if defensible, offers a model for a desert-based conception of responsibility in the criminal law. On this conception, the infliction of punishment on offenders corresponds to indignation, and accordingly criminal offenses correspond to failures to meet the expectations of goodwill toward others that those who share interpersonal relationships have of each other, failures that excite indignation. These offenses thus consist not only in actions that the law proscribes but also in states of mind with which those actions are done and by virtue of which punishment for them is deserved. Pleas of both types that Strawson distinguishes have obvious correlates in criminal law. These are the excuses and exemptions by which those who have done some legally proscribed action may be either acquitted or, alternatively, immunized—owing to immaturity, for instance—from prosecution in a criminal court. At the same time, there is no division in the criminal law between, say, excuses and exemptions that maps onto Strawson's distinction between the two types of plea. His distinction of two views, the participant and the objective, is not systematically represented in the criminal law. Rather, some excuses that the law recognizes, such as accident and mistake, reflect the participant view and some, such as insanity, reflect the objective.[13]

What is represented, however, is the extent to which the criteria for being regarded as someone toward whom it is appropriate to take the participant view is a matter of social convention. That is, because on Strawson's account, one can always take the objective view toward others, even if only selectively or temporarily, one can sometimes take it toward people who have manifested ill will toward others or oneself. It is possible, then, on Strawson's account, for people who can manifest ill will toward others to be nonetheless conventionally excluded from the class of people toward whom taking the participant view is appropriate. After all, not every type of derangement prevents those who suffer from it from acting maliciously, and in many cases treating such people humanely may require responding to them with sympathy rather than resentment or indignation. The humane response, in that event, entails viewing them objectively, and thus their condition becomes a basis for the second type of plea that Strawson distinguishes. Whether psychopathy is such a condition is an open question. But in any case the question of whether psychopaths are morally responsible for their actions is not problematic on Strawson's account, for the answer depends on considerations that fall outside of his account. Similarly, in the criminal law, questions of whether to excuse from responsibility or to exempt from prosecution people who intentionally break the law but whose lawbreaking is due to some mental disorder or disease may be treated as questions of social policy. In other words, because the objective view is always available to lawmakers, they may adopt, with regard to these questions and consistently with a desert-based conception of responsibility that is modeled on Strawson's account, such laws as considerations of the public good recommend.

II. Consequence-Based Conception of Responsibility in the Criminal Law

A. The Account of Classical Utilitarianism

Strawson introduced his distinction between participant and objective views to show how one could understand our attributions of moral responsibility in the same way as they are understood on the strongest version of the traditional account of moral responsibility and still accept the possibility of determinism. Strawson's argument, as we have seen, requires explaining our attributions of moral responsibility as implicit in the vicarious reactive attitudes to which, by virtue of our social nature, we are susceptible. They thus presuppose the participant view but not the objective view, the view that acceptance of the truth of determinism presupposes. If the criminal law likewise presupposed the participant view and not the objective view, then it its conception of responsibility would have to be modeled on moral responsibility to be coherent. But because the relationship between government and those whom it governs is not an interpersonal one, it is possible, and perhaps even wise, for public officials to resist adopting the participant view when exercising their office. In any event, the objective view is one that they, and particularly those officials who make and administer the criminal law, may take, not merely occasionally, but rather as part of the normal conduct of their duties. A conception of responsibility that is not modeled on moral responsibility—that is, one that is consequence-based rather than desert-based—is therefore suitable as a coherent conception of responsibility in the criminal law. Indeed, legal philosophers, especially legal positivists, who maintain that morality is not essential to law favor such a conception.

Philosophers of this stripe criticize and evaluate law by applying ethical standards that are separate from legal standards. Foremost among these is the Principle of Utility, the principle that, on the utilitarian theory of ethics, is the fundamental standard of right and wrong. It is the principle according to which an act, policy, law, practice, and so on is right if it brings about as much happiness in the world as any of the alternative acts, policies, and so on that could be performed or implemented and wrong otherwise. Jeremy Bentham is generally regarded as the prime mover in the development of utilitarianism in modern moral and political philosophy, and it is no accident that he is also the prime mover in the development of legal positivism. Bentham dismissed all major theories of ethics opposed to utilitarianism as merely intellectual vehicles for the expression of warm and cold feelings toward the objects of ethical judgment.[14] Ethical judgments that consist, instead, in applying the Principle of Utility to the acts, policies, laws, practices, and so on that are being judged are alone, Bentham argued, objective judgments, and accordingly this principle's application proceeds from the objective view of the world. The criminal law, Bentham held, is properly concerned with preventing actions that cause harm and therefore unhappiness, and it does so by inflicting punishment on those who commit such actions. Legal punishment, because it serves as a threat to those who contemplate committing such actions, though its infliction makes its recipients less happy and creates some unpleasant anxiety in those who may be tempted to commit these actions, nonetheless, if effective, brings about through its effect as a deterrent to harmful conduct less unhappiness in the world than would result if no punishment were inflicted for such conduct. On the classical utilitarian theory, then, as expounded by Bentham, questions of whom the law should punish and how severe their punishment should be are answered by applying the Principle of Utility to the norms and practices that constitute the criminal law. For convenience I will call this application of utilitarianism to the criminal law *pure deterrence theory*.

A major challenge for pure deterrence theory is to justify the requirement in the criminal law, which I identified at the outset of this chapter as one of its bedrock principles of justice, that to receive punishment for a criminal offense, one must be responsible for committing it. Offhand, the principle appears to be at odds with pure deterrence theory since it seems likely that with some offenses at least punishment that is inflicted on offenders without regard to whether or not they are responsible for committing these offenses would prove to be a more effective deterrent than punishment whose infliction conformed to this principle. To show that the principle is not at odds with the theory, so it seems, one would have to show that the increase in the frequency of punishment and in the unpleasant anxiety across the population that would occur if the principle were abandoned would more than offset the decrease in unpleasantness that would result from the reduction in the frequency of offenses that abandoning the principle would bring about, and it is hard to see how one could convincingly show this. Bentham, however, took a different tack. Rather than justify the principle by showing that its abandonment would lead to more unhappiness than its preservation, he argued that, in effect, one could conceive of responsibility as a necessary condition of an offender's being liable to punishment in a way that enabled one to derive the principle as a consequence of pure deterrence theory.

Bentham's argument was roughly as follows. Paradigmatically, one is responsible for one's actions when the actions are the result of one's having chosen to do them. A choice, when it is rational, results from one's determining which of the different actions available to one in the circumstances has the most expected utility, where the expected utility of an action is the extent to which the agent's desires would be satisfied by achieving its end multiplied by the likelihood of the agent's achieving it. The law, by threatening punishment for an action, thereby decreases the expected utility of doing it for those who are aware of the threat and whose choices of action are rational. Hence, a person who is unaware that he has chosen to do an action of a kind that the law punishes or whose choice of action or its subsequent execution results from some impairment to his capacity for making and acting on rational choices does not act on a rational choice that he makes in light of the law's threat of punishment for such actions. The threat of punishment in these cases is, to use Bentham's term, inefficacious.[15] Similarly, the threat is inefficacious in the case of someone who, though aware that the law threatens punishment for the action he chooses and though fully capable of making and acting on rational choices, cannot, in view of the magnitude of the harm he would incur if he were to forbear doing it, reasonably be expected to forbear. Consequently, the Principle of Utility, Bentham inferred, requires that the offenders in all of these cases be spared liability to punishment, since punishing them would cause unhappiness to no good effect. Accordingly, Bentham supposed, on pure deterrence theory, an offender should not be held liable to punishment for an offense unless the offender is responsible for committing it in the sense of its being the product of his having rationally chosen to do it in circumstances in which he could reasonably be expected to forbear. So it follows, on this argument, that one can derive, as a consequence of pure deterrence theory, the principle in the criminal law requiring responsibility for an offense as a condition of liability to punishment for that offense.

The argument, however, is flawed. It contains a non sequitur, a point that was forcefully made by H. L. A. Hart in several of his essays on responsibility and excuses in the criminal law.[16] Hart observed that punishment is effective as a threat when it deters people who would otherwise commit an offense from committing it, and such people will be deterred even by punishment that is inflicted on offenders whose commission of the offense was due to ignorance, mistake, accident, or one of the other factors that are commonly taken to negate attributions of responsibility. For the threat of such punishment is likely to move people to be even more cautious and careful about how they act when they are in circumstances in which they recognize some risk of their breaking the law.[17] It would deter, in particular, those who break the law in the belief that they will be able to escape punishment by pleading ignorance, mistake, and so on. The threat therefore has the potential of reducing the frequency with which the relevant offenses are committed, since it has the potential of increasing the measures and care people take to avoid committing them. If the punishment is sufficiently severe, rational agents, in calculating the expected utility of the different actions open to them, will see that these more cautious and careful actions have greater expected utility. Bentham's error, then, was to focus too narrowly on the class of actual offenders and omit considering the class of potential offenders, people who may be tempted to break the law but have not yet broken it. Hence, while Bentham's observations about the inefficaciousness of the threat of punishment on offenders whose offenses are due to ignorance, mistake, accident, or the like are correct, they are irrelevant to the question of whether the threat would be efficacious in deterring potential offenders. That it may well be is sufficient to show that one cannot derive, as a consequence of pure deterrence theory, the principle requiring responsibility for a criminal offense as a condition of liability to punishment for that offense.

To justify the principle within pure deterrence theory, then, one must show that abandoning the principle as a requirement of the criminal law would bring greater unhappiness to society (or make the population less happy overall) than preserving it as a requirement of the law. The prospects of such a utilitarian justification, however, as I noted above, are not bright. Yet abandoning the principle as a general requirement of the criminal law on utilitarian grounds does not mean that one could not justify on such grounds applying the principle to some parts of the criminal law. That is, while wholesale justification of the principle on utilitarian grounds may appear very unlikely, piecemeal justification with respect to different parts of the criminal law may be more promising.[18] In any case, it is open to pure deterrence theory to support making the offender's being responsible for the offense a requirement of liability to punishment for some offenses and not for others. The question for the theory, then, is not whether it supports making all offenses in the criminal law strict liability offenses but rather for which offenses it supports doing so. Consequently, the theory may turn out not to support as radical a reform of the criminal law as it first appears to.

B. The Account of Mixed Theories

Still, even if pure deterrence theory turns out not to support radical reform of the criminal law, it plainly denies that requiring responsibility for an offense as a condition of liability to punishment is grounded on a principle of justice that is independent of the Principle of Utility and constrains its application. For this reason alone, the theory is hard to defend. Common opinion, at least in modern democratic societies, holds that justice is a value that matters independently of the contribution its promotion makes to bringing about aggregatively more happiness in society. Specifically, it holds that the value of justice matters in virtue of the special value each person has in his or her own right, respect for which requires that the benefits and burdens the law confers and imposes be distributed fairly among the persons it governs. This special value that each person has is not recognized on pure deterrence theory. Efficiency in promoting the general happiness of those whom the law governs being the only thing that determines how benefits and burdens should be distributed, fairness in their distribution is not a factor. Such a theory would make sense if human beings were, like bees, social animals without individual personalities. But in view of our individuality and the value we attach to it, the theory simply seems out of touch.

There are, though, other theories of responsibility in the criminal law that, like pure deterrence theory, incorporate a consequence-based conception.[19] These alternative theories treat the requirement of responsibility as an independent principle of justice. As such, the principle constrains how the criminal law operates as an institution designed to prevent crime through the deterrent effect on potential offenders of punishing actual ones. The theories thus combine the value of deterrence and the value of justice, with the latter serving as a constraint on the pursuit of the former. On these mixed theories, the constraint, if observed, ensures that the conditions of liability to punishment are fair with respect to who, among offenders, qualifies for it. The burden of liability, in other words, is fairly imposed on offenders when the principle of justice is observed, so not everyone who breaks the law and is found to have done so has to bear this burden. In particular, it is fairly imposed if people have ample and reasonable opportunity to avoid the imposition. The opportunity is ample if the threat of imposition is made public with enough advance notice to enable people to change their plans so as to avoid it and if the threat is well-publicized. And it is reasonable if the loss or cost that one must incur to avoid the imposition of the burden is itself reasonable. For short, let us say that the burden is fairly imposed if people have a fair opportunity to avoid its imposition.

The theme of the law's providing fair opportunity to avoid liability to punishment is the key to how these mixed theories explain the requirement of responsibility as an independent principle of justice. Their explanation relies on the leading idea in Bentham's attempted derivation of the principle as a consequence of pure deterrence theory: that for a person to be responsible for an action he did in violation of the law, the action must be the result of a rational choice that the person makes in the light of the law's threat to punish those who so violate the law. While Bentham erred in arguing for restricting punishment to those lawbreakers whose violation of the law resulted from such choices on the grounds that punishment was efficacious only when imposed on them, it is a different matter to argue for so restricting punishment on the grounds that only when punishment is imposed on such lawbreakers is it fair. In general, people value having options and being able to choose among them when deciding how to live their lives. Under such conditions, if the options are real and not merely hypothetical as is the case with an option no one could reasonably be expected to choose, then people have some measure of control over how their lives go, and people generally value having such control. They value, that is, both being treated as people who are masters of their own fate and being able to predict the consequences they incur as the result of the choices they make. Accordingly, they will accept as fair the outcomes of their choices when those outcomes are foreseeable. The outcomes are, to use a familiar metaphor, what they bargained for.

Hence, when punishment is a foreseeable outcome of an action one rationally chooses to do knowing one has the option of forbearing, the imposition of punishment is fair. By contrast, if the action is the only real option open to one or one reasonably believes it to be, then one is not in a position to choose to act differently or cannot, because of one's belief, be expected to choose to act differently. In this case the imposition of punishment would be unfair, for one lacks fair opportunity to choose to avoid the imposition. Or at least that is how things will appear to one given one's reasonable belief that one had no other option. Similarly, if the action is the result of an accident or a choice made under an ignorant or mistaken understanding (for which one is not at fault) of one's circumstances or is the product of impairment of one's capacities to make and act on rational choices, then the imposition of punishment for the act would be unfair. It is unfair, after all, to punish someone for something he could not help doing. Here, too, the person lacks the opportunity to choose to avoid the imposition, either because he is disabled from making and acting on a rational choice or because he already and faultlessly believes he is acting in a way that avoids punishment. Accordingly, one can understand responsibility for actions done in violation of the law to attach to those violations that result from a rational choice made in the light of the law's threat of punishment and take its being a requirement for liability to punishment as a matter of justice, not because only violations of law committed by those who rationally choose to break the law in light of the threat of punishment are blameworthy and therefore deserving of punishment, but because making those who break the law liable to punishment for their actions is fair only if they have had fair opportunity to avoid liability. Only under these conditions can one say that the punishment they receive is what they bargained for.

The standard of a fair opportunity to choose to avoid liability to punishment that mixed theories use to determine the conditions of criminal responsibility creates a strong presumption against including strict liability offenses in the criminal law. For to include them is to admit some injustice (i.e., unfairness due to the imposition of punishment for action the individual could not help doing) into the criminal law by design and not merely as the inevitable result of just but fallible procedures, and this is surely unwelcome. A mixed theory might, then, categorically exclude strict liability offenses from the criminal law. On such a theory, the standards of justice that constrain how the law works to deter crime always have priority in the sense that the law, however it works to deter crime, must first meet these standards. Alternatively, though, a mixed theory might allow some strict liability offenses as exceptions to the general rule that the justice of the law cannot be compromised to further its aim of deterrence. That is, on such a theory, standards of justice do not have priority in the way they constrain how the criminal law works to deter crime. Rather, they have such great weight in comparison to that of increasing the deterrent effect of punishment that they become subordinate to the law's aim of deterring crime only when, for example, the level of due care a person is expected to take when engaging in certain actions is high in view of the public harm that is risked by such actions and the likelihood that a person who engages in these actions will take greater care to avoid causing this harm will increase if the liability to punishment for causing it is strict. Further, to mitigate the injustice of making liability to punishment strict in these cases, some would argue that the punishment itself must not carry the stigma that, say, incarceration brings. It must instead be limited to fines, and the crime for which it is imposed must be classified as a misdemeanor.[20]

A more difficult issue for mixed theories is how their account of criminal responsibility as depending on there being a fair opportunity to choose to avoid liability to punishment is compatible with the law's taking negligence in the performance of certain harmful actions as sufficient for criminal responsibility.[21] Can their account of criminal responsibility accommodate offenses in which negligence in the performance of some harmful action is sufficient for responsibility? This issue does not arise on desert-based conceptions of responsibility since negligent wrongdoing of this sort is unquestionably blameworthy. Drivers who, because they are attending to their eye makeup, say, rather than to the conditions of the traffic around them, fail to stop their vehicle before hitting the car ahead of them and killing its driver, act culpably, and desert-based conceptions of criminal responsibility have no difficulty accounting for this. On mixed theories, by contrast, the question arises whether such drivers have a fair opportunity to avoid liability to punishment given that their actions are not the result of a rational choice made in light of the threat of punishment. Consequently, understanding negligence in the performance of certain harmful actions as a sufficient condition of responsibility is problematic on these theories. Someone, for example, whose action, owing to his negligence, causes death is not obviously, on these theories, responsible for homicide given that he did not foresee that what he was doing would have such fatal consequences. It is open, therefore, to ask whether he had a fair opportunity to choose to avoid liability to punishment since he was not aware at the time of his action that the law threatened punishment for his doing it. To avoid this result, defenders of mixed theories must put forward a standard of fair opportunity to choose to avoid liability to punishment that applies to those who, because they act carelessly, do not foresee the harms their actions risk at the time that they do those actions.

Hart offered the following standard to keep his theory from excluding negligence from ever being a sufficient condition of responsibility.[22] To have a fair opportunity to choose to avoid liability, Hart argued, the offender, in cases in which he is unaware at the time of acting that his action risks harm, must, first, be acting in circumstances in which a reasonable person would take care not to cause harm and, second, have the normal adult capacities for taking such care. Negligence, Hart observed, is not the same as inattention or inadvertence. It implies a failure to take the precautions against causing harm that a reasonable person would take. By contrast, to act inattentively or inadvertently is to act without paying attention or adverting to what one is doing regardless of whether harm is in the offing and regardless of whether one has capacities that enable people to take reasonable precautions against causing harm. These are the capacities of understanding, memory, attention, and self-control by virtue of which a person knows in general the risks entailed by engaging in certain actions and is able, when engaging in any of them, to monitor himself and take precautions against the harms his action risks. Because negligence implies a failure to exercise these capacities, one can, when one's actions risk harm and when negligence is sufficient for liability to punishment for causing such harm, choose to avoid liability by exercising them as a reasonable person would. After all, Hart points out, a person who didn't exercise them because he "just didn't think" and as a result causes harm—a driver who without thinking or looking in his rearview mirror backs his car into a pedestrian—is not someone who couldn't help doing what he did.[23] Hence, Hart concludes, to take negligence in the performance of harmful actions as sufficient for criminal responsibility is not to impose liability on offenders in the absence of a fair opportunity to choose to avoid liability.

Yet whether Hart has succeeded in showing how negligence may, on a mixed theory, sometimes be a sufficient condition for criminal responsibility is still open to question. While no doubt a plea by a negligent offender that he couldn't help doing what he did would fall flat, the same would be true of a person who caused harm as a result of making an innocent mistake about his circumstances. He too is not someone who couldn't help doing what he did. If he has the capacities to avoid or to correct his mistake and it is within his power to exercise them, then he could have helped doing what he did by exercising them. Nothing prevented him from doing so.[24] Still, he is excused from responsibility because, though he did not exercise the capacities he has that would have enabled him to avoid or correct his mistake, he is not at fault for not exercising them. Because it is an innocent mistake, neither his making the mistake nor his causing harm as a result is blameworthy. What distinguishes him from someone who negligently causes harm is that the latter's omitting to exercise his capacities for taking precautions against causing harm is blameworthy. His omission is a sign of indifference or at least insufficient concern for the well-being of others, and too little concern for the well-being of others, when one fails to take care not to harm others because of it, deserves blame. To use this distinction, however, to explain why negligence in the performance of harmful actions may be sufficient for responsibility but an innocent error in judgment is not is to invoke a desert-based conception of responsibility as the conception underlying the attachment of criminal responsibility to failures to take reasonable care, and such a conception is not available on a mixed theory. Hart, in other words, still owes us an explanation of why on his theory a negligent offender has a fair opportunity to *choose* to avoid liability to punishment.

To give such an explanation would require offering different grounds from those entailing a desert-based conception of responsibility for distinguishing harmful action due to an innocent mistake from harmful conduct due to inadvertence that fails to meet a standard of reasonable care. But since the latter need not be willful to count as negligence, since Hart understands it just to consist in not exercising certain capacities as a reasonable person would when one has those capacities, it is hard to see what grounds Hart could offer. It is hard to see, that is, why, on this understanding of negligence and on a mixed theory's consequence based conception of responsibility, taking negligence in the performance of harmful actions as sometimes sufficient for criminal responsibility does not simply turn some criminal acts of homicide, arson, battery, and property damage into strict liability offenses.

NOTES

I thank the participants at the roundtable discussion sponsored by the Law and Philosophy Program of the University of Illinois College of Law for their many helpful comments on an earlier draft of this chapter. I am particularly grateful to Stephen Morse for his written comments on that draft and to David Dolinko for his written comments on a later draft.

1. The distinction roughly corresponds to T. M. Scanlon's distinction between responsibility as attributability and substantive responsibility. See Scanlon, *What We Owe to Each Other* (Cambridge, Mass.: Harvard University Press, 1998), pp. 248–294. Gary Watson's distinction between responsibility in the sense of attributability and responsibility in the sense of accountability is different. See Gary Watson, "Two Faces of Responsibility" in his *Agency and Answerability: Selected Essays* (Oxford: Clarendon Press, 2007), pp. 260–288.

2. G. E. Moore, *Ethics* (Oxford: Oxford University Press, 1912).

3. J. L. Austin, "Ifs and Cans" in *Philosophical Papers,* 2nd ed., J. O. Urmson and G. J. Warnock, eds. (Oxford: Oxford University Press, 1970), pp. 205–232—reprinted from *Proceedings of the British Academy.*

4. Harry Frankfurt, *The Importance of What We Care About: Philosophical Essays* (Cambridge: Cambridge University Press, 1988).

5. *Journal of Philosophy,* 66 (1969): 829–839. Reprinted in *The Importance of What We Care About,* pp. 1–10.

6. "Freedom of the Will and the Concept of a Person," *Journal of Philosophy* 68 (1971): 5–20. Reprinted in *The Importance of What We Care About,* pp. 11–25.

7. Gary Watson, "Free Agency," *Journal of Philosophy* 72 (1975): 205–220.

8. John M. Fischer, *The Metaphysics of Free Will: An Essay on Control* (Oxford: Blackwell, 1994), and John M. Fischer and Mark Ravizza, *Responsibility and Control: A Theory of Moral Responsibility* (Cambridge: Cambridge University Press, 1998). R. Jay Wallace, *Responsibility and the Moral Sentiments* (Cambridge, Mass.: Harvard University Press, 1996).

9. See my "Moral Agency and Criminal Insanity," in John Deigh, *Emotions, Values, and the Law* (New York: Oxford University Press, 2008), pp. 196–219.

10. P. F. Strawson, "Freedom and Resentment," *Proceedings of the British Academy* 48 (1962): 1–25. Reprinted in *Free Will,* 2nd ed., Gary Watson, ed. (Oxford: Oxford University Press, 2003), pp. 72–93.

11. Ibid. (reprint), pp. 75–77.

12. And more generally, one cannot coherently consider the justifiability of attributions of moral responsibility from an objective view of the world. Indeed, one might conjecture that the strong account of freedom of the will results from the tacit assumption that moral responsibility is a condition that is comprehensible from the objective view.

13. Moreover, some exemptions, such as those that arise from statutes of limitations, reflect neither view.

14. See Jeremy Bentham, *An Introduction to the Principles of Morals and Legislation*, chapter 2, section 1. London: Methuen.

15. Ibid., chapter 13, section 3.

16. See, for example, "Legal Responsibility and Excuses," in H. L. A. Hart, *Punishment and Responsibility: Essays in the Philosophy of Law* (Oxford: Oxford University Press, 1968), pp. 28–53, esp. pp. 41–43.

17. See, on this point, Richard A. Wasserstrom, "Strict Liability in the Criminal Law," *Stanford Law Review* 12 (1960): 731–745. Hart emphasizes the way strict liability can deter those who would otherwise commit the crime because they were confident of the state's being unable to prove that they acted intentionally.

18. See Richard Posner, "An Economic Theory of the Criminal Law," *Columbia Law Review* 85 (1985): 1193–1231.

19. See H. L. A. Hart, "Prolegomena to the Principles of Punishment," "Legal Responsibility and Excuses," and "Punishment and the Elimination of Responsibility," all reprinted in Hart, *Punishment and Responsibility*. See also T. M. Scanlon, "The Significance of Choice," in *The Tanner Lectures on Human Values*, Stirling M. McMurrin, ed. (Salt Lake City: Utah University Press, 1988), 151–200, and *What We Owe to Each Other*, pp. 248–294.

20. One exception, of course, might be felony murder statutes. If a mixed theory allowed these, it would do so presumably because they do not bring any significantly greater stigma to the offender than he already suffers in being convicted of the underlying felony, and because the injustice of incarcerating him for murder has, in view of the underlying felony, significantly less weight when balanced against the effect of such statutes in deterring offenders from carrying lethal weapons or using violence in committing their crimes.

21. See Richard A. Wasserstrom, "H. L. A. Hart and the Doctrine of *Mens Rea* and Criminal Responsibility," *University of Chicago Law Review* 92 (1967): 92–126.

22. "Negligence, *Mens Rea* and Criminal Responsibility," in Hart, *Punishment and Responsibility*, pp. 136–157.

23. Ibid., p. 150.

24. The pleas we should expect him to make are "I didn't mean to do it" and "If I had known, I wouldn't have." But then the negligent offender could, with equal appropriateness, make the same pleas.

BIBLIOGRAPHY

Austin, J. L. (1970). *Philosophical Papers Philosophical Papers*, 2nd ed., J. O. Urmson and G. J. Warnock, eds. (Oxford: Oxford University Press).

Bentham, Jeremy (1789/1970). *An Introduction to the Principles of Morals and Legislation*, J. H. Burns and H. L. A. Hart, eds. (London: Methuen).

Deigh, John (2008). *Emotions, Values and the Law* (New York: Oxford University Press).

Fischer, John M. (1994). *The Metaphysics of Free Will: An Essay on Control* (Oxford: Blackwell).

Fischer, John. M., and Ravizza, Mark (1998). *Responsibility and Control: A Theory of Moral Responsibility* (Cambridge: Cambridge University Press).

Frankfurt, Harry (1988). *The Importance of What We Care About: Philosophical Essays* (Cambridge: Cambridge University Press).

Hart, H. L. A. (1968). *Punishment and Responsibility: Essays in the Philosophy of Law* (Oxford: Oxford University Press).

Moore, G. E. (1912). *Ethics* (Oxford: Oxford University Press).

Posner, Richard (1985). "An Economic Theory of the Criminal Law," *Columbia Law Review* 85: 1193–1231.

Scanlon, T. M. (1988). "The Significance of Choice," in *The Tanner Lectures on Human Values*, Stirling M. McMurrin, ed. (Salt Lake City: Utah University Press), pp. 149–216.

——— (1998). *What We Owe to Each Other* (Cambridge, Mass.: Harvard University Press).

Strawson, P. F. (1962). "Freedom and Resentment," *Proceedings of the British Academy* 48: 1–25.

Wallace, R. Jay (1996). *Responsibility and the Moral Sentiments* (Cambridge, Mass.: Harvard University Press).

Wasserstrom, Richard (1960). "Strict Liability in the Criminal Law," *Stanford Law Review* 12: 731–745.

——— (1967). "H. L. A. Hart and the Doctrine of *Mens Rea* and Criminal Responsibility," *University of Chicago Law Review* 92: 92–126.

Watson, Gary (2007). *Agency and Answerability: Selected Essays* (Oxford: Clarendon Press).

CHAPTER 9

CULPABILITY

LARRY ALEXANDER

I⊤ is a working assumption of this essay that the criminal law should necessarily be concerned with culpability. That is because of two other working assumptions of this essay: that criminal law should be primarily concerned with retributive desert, and that retributive desert is strongly connected to culpability. (Although I shall not defend this point here—I have done so elsewhere—I regard retributive desert as resting exclusively on culpability and not at all on whether or not harm is caused; if retributive desert were based in part on outcomes, then one would have to both embrace "moral luck" and produce a defensible theory of "proximate causation."[1] I believe moral luck is oxymoronic, and I have yet to see a defensible theory of proximate causation.)[2]

I Is the Locus of Culpability One's Acts or One's Character?

Culpability theorists divide over what one is culpable *for*. Although it is natural to think that one is culpable for one's acts—a view I myself subscribe to—there is a tenable case that can be made for one's character being the true target of culpability claims.[3] After all, when we punish culpable actors, we punish *them*, not their acts. And we punish them sometimes years after they acted. Is it not, therefore, plausible to conclude that what they did is not constitutive of their desert but evidence of who they are—a window on their character—and that it is the latter that engages our reactive emotions and is the true basis of retributive desert? This would explain why character evidence is frequently admitted for sentencing purposes, and why repeat offenders are regarded by many as more culpable for their last offense than one for whom the same offense is his first.

Although I cannot satisfactorily refute the character account of culpability in these pages, I can summarize my reasons for rejecting it and going with the more orthodox account that ties culpability to acts. Here, I quote from my recent book coauthored with Kim Ferzan (with contributions by Stephen Morse), language we took from an earlier article by Stephen:

> In our view, we should not punish because of someone's character, nor should we exculpate someone because his action is somehow "out" of his character. One is not to blame for one's character because—even assuming that one could provide a precise definition of character—it is clear that one's character per se does not cause harm to others and that much of one's character is beyond rational control. [Moreover, given that one can only change one's character slowly and indirectly, at the moment one acts, one's character is completely beyond one's control.] Only actions cause harm to others, and only actions are potentially fully guidable by reason. Conversely, one should not be excused because his conduct was "out of character." Such an approach gets things exactly backwards—action must be conceptually prior to character. Actions can be judged morally without knowing anything about the agent's character; character can only be judged morally in light of the agent's actions. Moreover, whatever action an agent performs is in a real sense "in character" for the agent. After all, the agent did it, and presumably others with apparently similar characters placed in similar circumstances would not do it. Even if the action was statistically unlikely for the agent and was not the type of thing this type of agent seems predisposed to do by her character, or even if the agent was subject to unusually stressful or tempting circumstances, it is still the case that every agent is capable of statistically unlikely behavior that she is not usually disposed to do, and not everyone subject to unusual stresses or temptations responds by offending. The criminal law fairly expects all rational agents to act properly even in the face of unusual circumstances for which the agent bears no responsibility. In summary, to punish for character would be unjust; and to fail to punish merely because a wrongdoer otherwise has good character would be to neglect the positive value of retributive desert.[4]

II What Makes a Culpable Act Culpable?

Culpable acts are culpable in that they manifest insufficient concern for the interests of others. They manifest insufficient concern when the actor wills an action that he believes unleashes a risk of harm to others' morally protected interests, and he does so for reasons that do not justify the risk he believes he has unleashed.

A The Willed Action

There are several things packed into this account of culpability that require explanation. By "wills an action," I mean, in most instances, that the actor wills a bodily movement, such as squeezing a trigger, depressing an accelerator, or placing a lit match on a fuse. If, however, the actor believes that a mental act—such as multiplying two numbers in her head—can cause harm to others, then her willing that mental act can be culpable as well. Moreover, if the actor believes that by willing her finger to squeeze a trigger, she will do so, she is culpable for so willing even if her hand is paralyzed and her finger fails to respond. (I take up separately the matter of culpable omissions.)

B Unleashed Risk

By "unleashes a risk," I mean creates a risk that the actor believes is then beyond his control to affect. Thus, if I do not believe I am Superman and capable of traveling "faster than a speeding bullet," then when I squeeze the trigger of a gun I believe to be loaded and aimed at another person, I will believe that I have created a risk of harm that is beyond my ability to affect. When, on the other hand, I light a long dynamite fuse, at that moment I would ordinarily calculate the "unleashed" risk of an explosion to be quite low. I can still snuff it out if I choose to do so because, until the fuse burns too far, I will in most cases remain conscious and ambulatory. Because, however, there is some chance that were I to have a change of heart and wish to snuff the fuse out, I would be unable to—perhaps because something renders me unconscious or otherwise prevents me from snuffing it out—I have at the moment of lighting the fuse "unleashed" a small risk of an explosion, and one that increases over time. (Indeed, given the possibility that kryptonite might appear and negate his powers, even Superman might be culpable were he to fire a bullet at another; the firing of a gun by Superman is thus like the lit fuse for us mere humans.)

C Risk

A term in the formula for culpability that also needs unpacking is "risk." I take risk to be an epistemic, perspectival notion, not an ontic one. (I leave aside quantum events, for which probabilities may be ontic.) That is, risk refers to the odds that the actor gives that his act will eventuate in harm. It is thoroughly subjective. Objective risk is a chimera.

> Risk is an essentially epistemic concept [because] [r]isk is always relative to
> someone's perspective, a perspective that is defined by possession of certain
> information but not other information. In law, when we say that there is a "risk"
> of x's occurrence, we are using "risk" in the sense of relative frequency. That is,
> any given reference class will yield a relative frequency for an event's occurrence.
> However, one may formulate the reference class widely or narrowly, thus
> changing the relative frequency. To ask what the risk is that John will be hit by
> lightning, we can give accurate answers if we say that there is a one in a billion
> chance that a person gets hit by lightning, a one in a million chance that a person
> gets hit by lightning in the area in which John lives, a one in a thousand chance
> that a person gets hit by lightning on a golf course in the area where John lives, a

one in one hundred chance that a person gets hit by lightning on a golf course during a rain storm in the area where John lives, and a one in one chance that John got hit by lightning on a golf course during a rain storm this Tuesday in the area where John lives. All of these probability assessments are correct within their given reference classes. In contrast, with full information, there is no need to resort to a probability. For God—who possesses complete information about everything—risk does not exist. For God, all events have a probability of either one or zero (leaving aside quantum events). So even though Albert was playing golf with John—and thus all the relative frequency accounts (except the last one) applied—in actuality, Albert did not get hit by lightning, and thus, though he was "risked" to different degrees depending upon the reference class, there was no harm at all.

The "objective" approach thus creates the following quandary. We must be able to assign a risk to an activity that is different from both whatever risk the actor perceives and the risk God perceives (one or zero). Therefore, this approach requires that we construct an artificial perspective containing some but not all information. There [are] obviously an indefinite number of such possible perspectives, each one generating a different risk. Depending upon how narrowly or widely one defines the reference class, the relative frequency will change. But there is simply no nonarbitrary way for us to select among reference classes. Nor does it make any sense to [me] why the culpability of an actor should hinge not upon what the actor knows, or what God would know, but upon what some other individual's perspective might be. One who drops a bowling ball from the top of a building to measure the force of gravity for himself, and who believes there are people below whom he's putting in extreme danger, is [culpable]....This is true despite the fact that his companion believes the risk is greater than he does; the building's doorman would have estimated the risk to be slightly lower; and a window washer, with a better view below, knows that there are very few people below so that dropping the ball is unlikely to injure anyone. It simply makes no sense to allow the actor's liability to hinge, not upon what he knows, or God knows, but upon the arbitrary selection among the friend, doorman, and window washer for the correct perspective for assessing "objective risk."

Or, to take a different example, suppose A and B are each driving cars on a two-lane highway and are approaching a blind curve. They both believe that if they stay on their side of the highway, the probability of causing injury or death when they go around the curve is very small. Likewise, they both believe that if they veer over into the left lane when rounding the curve, the probability of causing injury or death (by striking an oncoming vehicle) is quite high. Moreover, actuarial tables support their beliefs—very often an oncoming car will be entering the curve from the opposite direction, but rarely will there be a stalled vehicle or pedestrian in the right hand lane. Nonetheless, C, a bystander situated at a good vantage point, can see that this time there are *no* vehicles approaching from the opposite direction, but there *is* a small child just around the curve in the right lane. Thus, C estimates the risk of injury or death of veering into the left lane to be zero but the risk of remaining in the right lane to be virtually one. If A were to remain in the right lane, we would not deem him culpable. On the other hand, if B were to veer into the left lane, we *would* deem him ...[culpable]—not attempting to be…[culpable], but…[culpable] full stop. Yet, from C's perspective, A would be creating a huge risk and B none. If any risk is "objective" then, it is the risk C assesses. Yet C's assessment, like God's, should be immaterial.

There is no gap between the actor's subjective estimate of the risk and the "true" or "objective" risk because the latter is either illusory (other than as a referent to the one or zero "probability" of whether harm occurs) or arbitrary (as there is no principled way to select among relative frequency accounts). For the very same reasons, as…[I shall later] discuss, [I] believe that negligence is not an appropriate basis of criminal responsibility.[5]

D The Holism of Risk and Risked Harms

I have spoken up to this point of a culpable act as one that unleashes a risk of harm to others' morally protected interests. To be precise, however, I should speak not of *a* risk of *a* harm but of *risks* of *harms*. For any given culpable act will almost always create risks of different harms, risks that will vary in magnitude. Firing a bullet may create a risk of magnitude W of causing death, a risk of magnitude X of causing injury, a risk of magnitude Y of causing property damage, and a risk of magnitude Z of causing fright. Indeed, when the harm itself is a matter of degree—as are bodily injury and property damage but not death—the different degrees of those harms will be risked differentially. Thus, firing the bullet may create a risk of magnitude A of serious bodily injury, a risk of magnitude B of slight bodily injury, a risk of magnitude C of a large property loss, a risk of magnitude D of a smaller property loss, and so on. The culpability of a given act of risk creation will be a function of the sum of those various risked outcomes discounted by the magnitudes of the risks. (To be clear, as stated earlier, it is not the actual outcomes that matter but the outcomes risked.)

E Duration of Risk

Some acts are discrete unleashings of risks. Firing a gun is an example. Each firing unleashes risks, and each firing may or may not be culpable, depending on the actor's assessment of those risks and the reasons she believes exist that might justify unleashing such risks. Firing five shots at an intended victim is, holding the risks constant, five culpable acts, and five times as culpable as firing once. Moreover, this is true whether the five shots occur over a thirty-second interval or over five weeks.

Other acts are continuous rather than discrete. Speeding through traffic is an example. Transporting a kidnap victim is another. Such acts create different levels of risks (of different harms) over time. Their overall riskiness is their average momentary riskiness times their duration. Holding the environment constant, speeding for ten minutes is riskier than speeding for thirty seconds.

F Reasons

1 *How Reasons Justify Risk Impositions Generally*

We impose risks of harms to morally protected interests all the time, whether we are driving a car, walking down the street, starting a fire in the barbecue grill, or engaging in an endless number of other activities. We are usually not culpable for doing so, however, because we usually have reasons for doing so that are weighty enough to justify imposing whatever risks we impose. A life free from putting others at risk would be an impossible one, and surely not a human one. And the question for culpability is not only how great are the risks we are unleashing but also what reasons we have for doing so.

In general, acts imposing risks of harm are justified by their likely consequences. A simple utilitarian would weigh an act's expected good consequences, discounted by their probabilities, against its expected bad consequences, discounted by their probabilities. As one moves away from simple utilitarianism, whether of a preference-satisfaction or hedonic variety, to more complex forms of consequentialism—where the Good to be maximized might be satisfaction of idealized preferences or "cleansed" preferences, or production of an objective list of goods, and where the maximization of that Good might be constrained by egalitarian, maximin, prioritarian, or welfare-floor distributive principles—the question of what consequences will justify what risk impositions becomes more complex. Still, no matter the complexity of the consequentialist theory in play, the culpability of unleashing risks is a function of that consequentialist theory.

2 *Deontological Constraints*

Having said that, however, I do not want to deny the relevance of deontological principles to the culpability of risk imposition. Deontological principles are constraints on the consequentialist considerations that might otherwise justify risk impositions. And I believe the most plausible deontological principles are those that prohibit producing good consequences through *using* others—their bodies, labors, and talents—without their consent. Using refers not to whether the actor "intends" harm to another, as opposed to foresees it. Rather, it refers to *how* the actor expects the otherwise justifying consequences to be brought about by the act in question.

Take, for instance, the usual examples, Trolley and Transplant.[6] In Trolley, one can switch a runaway trolley from a track on which there are five trapped workers to one on which there is one trapped worker. In Transplant, one can remove five vital organs from one healthy patient to save the lives of five dying ones. Most people believe the net saving of four lives justifies switching the trolley but not harvesting the organs. The most plausible deontological account of this distinction rests not on the actor's intention—as I shall argue, in Trolley he can be justified even if he intends to kill the one worker—but on the causal structure underlying the production of the justifying consequences. The one worker is not "used" to save the five.

They would be saved were he absent. But the one patient in Transplant *is* used. Were she absent, the five would have died.[7]

3 *Reasons, Motivations, and Belief*

I said it does not matter why the person switches the trolley. His act is not culpable even if he acts only because he wishes to kill the one worker. Let me explain and qualify that statement.

First, the explanation: So long as it is better according to our consequentialist theory that one worker die and five workers are saved than that five workers die and one is saved, then we want the actor to switch the trolley. Even if he has no moral obligation to do so—such an obligation would violate the deontological constraint against using *him*—if he does switch the trolley, he does what we want him to do: he produces the best consequences. What motivated him to do so is immaterial because it does not negate the consequentialist benefits of the act. If the only thing that will induce him to produce the best consequences is ill will toward the one worker, then although it reveals an ugly character, that ill will is, on this occasion at least, useful in producing good consequences. Or put differently, if an act would be morally permissible if engaged in by a properly motivated actor, it remains morally permissible even if engaged in for vile reasons.

Now, the qualification: The act that is permissible is only nonculpable if the actor believes the facts that count as the justifying reasons actually exist. He does not have to be motivated by them; but he does have to believe they are present. Thus, if the actor in Trolley were unaware of the five trapped workers, and aware only of the one worker he wanted to kill, then he would be culpable for switching the trolley. The act would still be a permissible one in this sense, namely, that an actor aware of the five trapped workers would be nonculpable were *he* to switch the trolley. But if the actor is unaware of the five, then his act is culpable. Motivation because of the justifying reasons is immaterial to culpability, but awareness of them is not.

4 *The Deontological Constraint and Measurement of Culpability*

Introducing deontological constraints into the picture complicates assessments of culpability. If culpability were merely a matter of comparing the risks to others against the actor's reasons for imposing them—again, reasons referring not to what motivates him but to what good consequences of his act he perceives are possible, discounted by their perceived likelihood—then the degree of culpability of an act would be determined by the gap between the possible bad consequences and the possible good consequences the actor perceived. In Trolley, holding the likelihood of deaths constant and assuming no other relevant consequences, the actor who switches the trolley would be praiseworthy. If, however, he were to switch the trolley from the one worker to the five, risking a net four deaths, then he would be culpable to the same extent as he would have been praiseworthy in the original case.

Transplant, however, and its invocation of a deontological constraint on producing the best consequences—a saving of net four lives—throws a wrench into the assessment of culpability. Thus, suppose the actor violates the constraint and saves the five dying patients by sacrificing the one healthy patient. He has acted wrongly because he has violated the healthy patient's right not to be "used." But just how *culpable* is he? Violating deontological constraints because one wishes to produce the overall best consequences is wrong, so presumably doing so is culpable. But if the question is how culpable, the answer cannot be supplied in the same way as when the imposition of risk is wrong solely because of a negative balance of likely consequences. The "using" of another shows insufficient concern for others' rights, but not necessarily insufficient concern for others' well-being.

I have no answer to this problem. It is one produced by deontological constraints, and it can be "solved" only by jettisoning such constraints. To jettison them and become thoroughgoing consequentialists, however, would "solve" this problem only by eliminating any role for culpability assessments and the assessments of retributive desert that turn on them insofar as they are supposed to place a ceiling on justifiable punishment. For that ceiling is itself a deontological constraint.

5 *Reasons That Justify and Reasons That Excuse*

The types of reasons that can negate culpability for imposing risks of harm fall into two principal categories. They can be labeled either "justifying" and "excusing" or "agent-neutral" and "agent-relative" (or perhaps "social" and "personal"). Justifying or agent-neutral reasons are those that are reasons for anyone to impose the risks in question. Thus, in Trolley, anyone aware of the consequences at stake could switch the trolley or urge or assist others in switching the trolley. (Again, one need not be motivated by the justifying reasons to escape culpability, but need only believe that they exist.)

Excusing or agent-relative reasons are reasons that negate the actor's culpability but do not justify others' assistance of the actor. Threats to an actor or her loved ones, whether from human or nonhuman sources, and whether lawful or not, can, depending on their magnitude, excuse her imposing risks on others.[8] Of course, often a threat of harm to the actor or her loved ones will justify her risk imposition because the risks she imposes on others are of a lesser magnitude in terms of the harms risked or their likelihood than the risk(s) the actor confronts if she does not impose risks on others. A threat to shoot a driver unless she drives ten miles per hour over the speed limit might be such a case. However, if the actor's risk imposition constitutes the using of another and thus violates the deontological constraint defining the other's rights, the actor cannot be justified. She can only be excused, and no one not subject to the same threat can assist her. Moreover, her victim(s) can justifiably resist her risk imposition, whereas they could not do so justifiably were she justified in imposing the risk. (They could be excused for resisting her, of course.)

Because excusing reasons are personal to the actor, unlike justifying reasons, then to excuse, they must be the reasons for which the actor acts, in contrast to justifying reasons. When one is threatened with death or severe bodily injury unless one steals from a third party—unjustifiable because it entails using the third party for one's own benefit—one will be excused and thus nonculpable only if one steals *because* of the threat.[9] In Trolley, as I have said, the switching is justifiable and is nonculpable so long as the actor is aware that he is probably saving the five, even if he is not switching it for that reason. But the "hard choices" that potentially excuse do so only if they are in fact hard choices. If the actor does not care about his own safety or that of his children, then threats to the actor or his children will not excuse otherwise unjustifiable risk impositions.

G Culpability and the Quality of Deliberation: Of Impulse, Insanity, and Altered Consciousness

An actor can impose risks of harm for insufficient reasons yet not be fully culpable or culpable at all. First, the actor may not have sufficient *capacity* for weighing risks and reasons. For example, the actor may be too young to be deemed a morally responsible agent—too young to fully comprehend the reasons against imposing various risks. Or the actor may be mentally disabled by retardation or similar conditions so as to not be morally responsible. And, of course, the actor may be mentally ill in a way that renders her incapable of appreciating the reasons against risk impositions to the degree required for moral responsibility.

Second, the actor may be in a condition of altered consciousness, such as automatism, somnambulism, or hypnotic trance, and incapable of consciously accessing the full panoply of reasons that he can access under normal conditions. Most courts and commentators regard actors in such conditions as lacking moral responsibility and thus culpability for the risks they impose.

Third, an actor may be acting in a state of severe agitation or acting impulsively. Such an actor acts in a degraded condition for deliberating about risks and reasons. Although she may appreciate the risks she is imposing and may lack sufficient reasons for imposing them, the degraded quality of her deliberative circumstances reduces her culpability to some extent even if it does not entirely eliminate it.

H Culpability for Omissions

To this point, I have assumed an act—a willed bodily movement—to be that for which an actor is potentially culpable. Occasionally, however, we deem moral agents culpable for not acting—for omitting to act. Although Anglo-American criminal law does not criminalize bad samaritanism in general, it does criminalize breaches of some specific duties to act. In general, those duties arise as a result of voluntary undertakings. When one signs up to be a policeman, fireman, or lifeguard, for example, one undertakes obligations to act, the breach of which may render one criminally liable. The same is true when one marries: one acquires a duty to rescue one's spouse from peril, breach of which may render one criminally liable. Or when one causes another's peril in any of a number of ways, one acquires a duty to attempt to remove that peril, breach of which may again render one criminally liable. Sometimes one acquires duties to rescue others merely because of a status relation, even if that is not entered into voluntarily. Parents have obligations to rescue their children from peril, even if those children resulted from rape.

If one has an affirmative duty to act in order to prevent harm to another, how is culpability for omitting so to act assessed? The answer is that culpability for omissions is, like culpability for acts, a function of risks and reasons. But the risks/reasons calculus is somewhat more complicated for omissions than it is for acts. It is more complicated in two respects: First, there is an extra dimension of risk involved in omissions: the probability that the grounds for the duty to act do or do not exist. Al has a duty to rescue his child, Ben, if Ben is drowning, but Al may not know with certainty that the apparently drowning boy is Ben and not someone else.

Second, the risks and reasons in play in omitting to act are actually the perceived risks and reasons of any of an indefinite number of courses of action. If that is Ben, is he really drowning, or will he survive if Al does nothing? If he will drown unless Al acts, should Al dive in himself—which may reduce Ben's risk of drowning by x amount but increase Al's risk of drowning by y amount, increase Al's risk of heart attack by z amount, and almost certainly ruin Al's new suit. Or should Al call the lifeguard, which will be less risky to Al but perhaps more risky for Ben because of the time involved. Or should Al try to throw a life preserver to Ben, an act with different risks and reasons at stake?

Third, the risks associated with omissions vary over time. At T_1, if Al does nothing, he may perceive the risk to Ben to be low, as he knows that, barring his sudden unconsciousness, paralysis, or other unlikely obstacle, he still has time to rescue Ben. At T_2, if Al does nothing, he will perceive the risk to Ben to have increased. And at some point, the risk Al perceives from his inaction may render him culpable *even if he later successfully rescues Ben*. (The same analysis applies to someone who lights a fuse to burn down a building but who believes for some period of time that he can probably put it out before it ignites the fire.)

Omissions are culpable based on the risks and reasons perceived by the actor, but the analysis is far more complex than it is for acts.

III THE RISK AND REASONS ANALYSIS OF CULPABILITY COMPARED WITH CURRENT DOCTRINE

Orthodox criminal law doctrine analyzes culpability by reference to the actor's mental state at the time of acting, just as I have done. (The culpability type deemed "negligence" is an exception; I discuss negligence in section V.) But instead of treating culpability in a unitary manner, as I have done, orthodox criminal law doctrine, as rationalized by the Model Penal Code, divides culpable mental states accompanying acts into three types: purpose, knowledge, and recklessness.[10]

When someone acts with the culpable mental state of "purpose," she has as her conscious object that she bring about the harmful result in question, engage in the harmful conduct in question, or act in the proscribed circumstances in question.[11] When someone acts with the culpable mental state of "knowledge," she believes to a practical certainty that her act will cause the harmful result, that her act is of the proscribed type, or that she is acting in the proscribed circumstances.[12] (The Model Penal Code assimilates belief that one is acting in certain circumstances to the hope or desire that one is so acting, but those mental states are no more similar than are purpose and knowledge with respect to results and conduct.)[13] When someone acts recklessly, she believes her act will create a substantial risk of harm, a risk so substantial as to be unjustifiable.[14] (The actor need only believe the risk is of a certain magnitude; whether that magnitude is "substantial," and whether it is "unjustifiable" given the actor's reasons, are objective matters of law about which the actor's beliefs are immaterial.)

Knowledge and recklessness are really on a continuum of belief regarding probabilities, with knowledge occupying the endpoint and recklessness occupying the space between "substantial" and "practical certainty." The unjustifiability of the perceived risk is built into the definition of recklessness, whereas it is external to the definition of knowledge. Nevertheless, there are always justifications available for acting with belief to a practical certainty that harm will result from one's act, even if the accused must raise them (whereas with recklessness, their negation is part of the prosecutor's case).

Purpose, on the other hand, deals not with the actor's assessment of risk but with his reasons. One can act with purpose even if one believes one's chances of success are remote. If the Jackal hopes to collect the OAS's bounty for assassinating de Gaulle, then he acts with the purpose to kill even if he takes what he believes to be a one in a hundred shot at him.

On my analysis of culpability, the degree of perceived risks and the reasons for taking such risks, discounted by the perceived probabilities of their obtaining, are two components of a unified analysis. The greater the perceived the risk of harm, and the worse those harms are, the more culpable the actor, reasons remaining constant. That is why knowledge will be more culpable than recklessness when the actor's reasons are the same. And the purpose to cause harm is typically a very bad reason for imposing even the slightest increase in the harm's likelihood. Within a range of perceived risk of harm, the purposeful actor will be more culpable than the actor who creates the same perceived risk for more benign reasons. But it is not at all clear that one who imposes a very tiny risk for the purpose of causing harm is more culpable than one who imposes a very high risk but is indifferent toward whether it occurs.

What this shows is that perceived risks and reasons do all the work in culpability analysis, but that the unified account is capable of capturing the many degrees of culpability, whereas the traditional view has room only for three levels, with purpose overlapping the other two. The perceived risk continuum runs from zero to certainty. The reasons continuum runs from the saintly to the demonic. Culpability is highly variable, a variability captured by my account but not the traditional one.

IV Culpability and the Traditional Account of Recklessness

One might fairly assess my account of culpability as having reduced all culpable mental states to that described by the traditional account of recklessness. After all, the latter focuses entirely on risks and reasons, as do I in analyzing culpability. Nevertheless, there are some differences between my account of culpability and the traditional definition of recklessness.

To begin with, I have claimed that risk is subjective and perspectival, the actor's estimate of the probabilities of various harms that her act increases. Leaving aside quantum theory, which is quite irrelevant to the probabilities in question, there is no such thing as an objective risk. The only "objective risks" are one or zero. Yet when recklessness is defined, it is not clear whether the risk to which the actor adverts is supposed to be an objective risk or is instead—and correctly—a risk that is nothing more than the actor's own estimate. For example, the Model Penal Code's definition of recklessness speaks of the actor's consciously disregarding a substantial and unjustifiable risk.[15] That formulation is ambiguous as between a totally subjective view of risk and a view that posits risk as an objective fact, one that is independent of anyone's perspective and information. If the latter is the correct interpretation, then my account of culpability is at odds with it.

A second and clear difference between my analysis of culpability and the traditional account of recklessness is that the latter requires the risk to which the actor adverts to be both substantial and unjustifiable, whereas I require only that the risk be unjustifiable.[16] I do so because imposing what one perceives to be a very tiny risk can nevertheless be culpable if one's reasons for doing so do not justify imposing it. If Deborah wishes to play involuntary Russian roulette on passersby just for the thrill of putting others at risk, her pulling the trigger is culpable irrespective of the ratio of empty chambers to loaded ones in her gun. It is difficult to see how she could justify imposing on others even a one in a million risk of getting shot if her only reason for doing so was the thrill she received from imposing that risk.

If I am right about this, then the substantiality prong of traditional recklessness should be jettisoned. The unjustifiability prong does all the work necessary for distinguishing culpable from nonculpable risk impositions.

Finally, as is true of the traditional view of recklessness, my view of culpability makes justifiability a purely objective matter. The actor's beliefs regarding the justifiability of his risk impositions are immaterial. Deborah cannot justify and render nonculpable her playing involuntary Russian roulette merely by believing that the thrill she receives justifies it. Conversely, one who believes she creates the ordinary level of risks to others in driving to the grocery store to buy food is not culpable for doing so even if she believes she is.

I should point out some difficult problems that this view of risk and justification creates. On the one hand, it entails that certain dangerous fanatics will not be culpable for committing acts that greatly risk serious harms. For if they believe, erroneously, that great benefits will flow from their acts, benefits that would indeed justify those acts, then they have not acted culpably in committing them. Erroneous but sincere beliefs, no matter how addled, can potentially justify almost any act, even if deontological constraints are thrown into the mix. This makes misguided fanatics regarding the facts quite dangerous but not necessarily culpable.

On the other hand, the objective view of justification entails that the so-called cultural defense should not be available to exculpate risk imposers.[17] If a daughter's promiscuity is believed to justify killing her to preserve family honor, that cannot make it so. Almost everyone agrees with that. Disagreement surfaces, however, over whether such an erroneous belief can mitigate or eliminate culpability.

My view is that it is conceivable that some erroneous views about justifications can mitigate or eliminate culpability, but that those erroneous views must be of the kind that do not evince cruelty, extreme selfishness, indifference to human suffering, and the like. Views evincing such traits are incapable of justifying risk impositions, and in that sense, the justification prong of culpability is objective and unrelated to the actor's own views of justification.

V Negligence and Strict Liability

If criminal punishment is only justified if the criminal is deserving of it, and if his deserving punishment depends on his having acted culpably, then criminal punishment should never be premised on negligence or be a matter of strict liability.[18] The exclusion of strict liability follows as a matter of definition: strict liability is liability in the absence of culpability. (Culpability can also be absent, even when mens rea *is* required, if the underlying conduct, even when engaged in purposely, is not wrongful.) If, therefore, culpability is necessary for punishment, strict liability is logically precluded.

Of course, if the mere occurrence of some event X entailed an actor's culpability to degree Y with a probability of Z no matter the evidence negating culpability—and Z were high enough to satisfy the requisite standard of proof of culpability—then holding a defendant criminally liable on the mere occurrence of X would be consistent with punishment premised on culpability. Notice, however, how stringent and unlikely is that set of conditions. We can safely conclude, I believe, that strict liability should be off the table if punishment is to be based on desert.

Negligence, however, has seemed to most people to be a type of culpability. As I said, negligence does not refer to a mental state of the actor at the time she acts. Rather, it refers to the absence of a mental state, the failure of the actor to advert to the riskiness of her act. The negligent actor is one who estimates the risks of harm from her act to be lower than a reasonable person would estimate those risks to be.[19] The negligent actor is culpable, it is claimed, because she should have estimated the risk to be higher, the "should" being a moral one.

There are two related objections to deeming negligence a form of culpability. First, the "reasonable person" standard by which the negligent actor is judged cannot be constructed nonarbitrarily. The "objective" riskiness of the negligent actor's act is, as I earlier asserted, either one or zero, depending on whether it did or did not cause the harms it allegedly risked. And because acts can presumably be negligent whether or not they cause harm, when the negligent act causes no harm, the negligent actor will have overestimated the "objective" risk. If the reasonable person would have estimated the act to be riskier than the negligent actor estimated it to be, the reasonable person would have misjudged the "objective" riskiness of the act more than the negligent actor did.

Therefore, the reasonable person is reasonable not because his estimate of risk would have been closer to the "objective" risk than was the negligent actor's but because his estimate would exemplify a better perspective on the risk than did the negligent actor's. In what sense would it have been better, if not in the sense that it would have come closer to the actual risk? It would have been better presumably because the reasonable person would have had more relevant information about the risks, or would have adverted to information to which the negligent actor did not advert, or would have made inferences from shared information that the negligent actor failed to make; and on the basis of this added information, this advertence to information, or these inferences from information, the reasonable person would have estimated the risk of harms to be sufficiently high to render the negligent actor's act culpable given the latter's reasons for acting.

However, the reasonable person is not supposed to have total information. Nor, presumably, is the reasonable person one who never fails to advert to information he does in some sense possess—never fails to notice things within his field of vision, and never fails to remember anything. And the reasonable person is surely not perfect in making proper inferences from facts in his possession. If the reasonable person lacked any of these failings, much less all of them, he would be godlike, not human.

So the reasonable person has failings—in information, attention, and reasoning. Only he does not have the negligent actor's failings in these regards. How, then, can the reasonable person's failing be specified other than arbitrarily?

Consider one representative example. The actor drops a bowling ball from the top of the Empire State Building to test the effects of air pressure on a sphere. She believes, for some reason, that it has so little chance of hitting someone below that this minute risk is justified by her scientific reasons. And assume it would be if only her estimate of the risk were correct. She is not culpable on my account of culpability. But she is presumably a perfect example of the negligent actor.

Let us suppose the actor is negligent because of her beliefs about the number and location of people on the street below. She believes there are no people in the vicinity of the landing zone.

Now consider three other individuals whose estimates of the risk might differ from hers. There is the person at her office window on the eightieth floor who believes the street below is filled with people, and that therefore the act is likely to kill or injure someone. There is the window washer on the twenty-third floor, who thinks there are only a few people on the street below, and who estimates the risk lower than does the woman on the eightieth floor, but higher than does the negligent actor. And there's the janitor looking out a second-floor window, who sees no one in the vicinity of the bowling ball and therefore estimates the risk to be virtually zero—even lower than the negligent actor's estimate.

Which one of these three, each of whom has a different vantage point and therefore different information, is the reasonable person? Is the reasonable person on the eightieth floor, the twenty-third floor, or the second floor? How can any answer be other than arbitrary?

My second argument against negligence as a form of culpability is this: We are not morally blameworthy for not knowing certain things, failing to notice or remember things, or failing to reason perfectly. In other words, we are not morally blameworthy for not being godlike. And at the times we act, we can do nothing other than act on the information that at the time we possess, remember, advert to, and reason from, given whatever reasoning ability we have at the moment. Any sense of "could have done otherwise" requires that we assume some change in information, attention, or reasoning ability from what the actor actually possessed at the time of the act.

The belief that the negligent actor is morally blameworthy despite his being in the grip of whatever information, attentiveness, and reasoning ability he possesses at the time he acts is due, I suggest, to one of two errors. One error is to confuse culpability for acts with moral criticism of character. The other is to confuse culpability for negligent acts with culpability for acts that lead to negligent acts.

The first error is exemplified by moral criticism of this sort: "If you were more considerate of others, less self-absorbed, or more conscious of your responsibilities, you would not have failed to notice, forgotten, or failed to draw the proper inferences." It is no doubt the case that some negligent acts reflect character flaws, and that the counterfactuals invoked in the quoted criticism are sometimes true, if any counterfactuals can be said to be true. Nevertheless, as I said at the outset, a person cannot be deemed culpable for her character—though she may be culpable for failing to take steps to improve her character if she is aware that her character flaws create an unjustifiable risk that she will harm others either inadvertently or advertently. And if she cannot be deemed culpable for her character traits, then it is immaterial to her culpability that had she had better character traits, there was less chance that she would have failed to advert to a risky feature of her act, forgotten it, or failed to draw the inference that some perceived feature of her act and circumstances betokened risk.

The second error is exemplified by this criticism: "If you had not blown off the parenting class on symptoms of serious childhood illnesses, you would have recognized your child's symptoms as betokening a life-threatening disease." Again, it is no doubt the case that a negligent act is sometimes (often?) causally traceable to an earlier culpably risky act, such as failing to read the warnings on medicine labels, failing to leave reminders of an important risk-reducing task (such as fixing one's brakes or inspecting one's furnace), and other like failures while being aware that failing to do so would increase the risk of harming others by increasing the risk of crucial ignorance or forgetting. Nevertheless, although negligence may sometimes be traceable to an upstream culpable act, that does not render the negligent act or omission itself culpable.

To conclude, when an actor *does not* perceive a feature of what he is doing as highly risky, even though the so-called reasonable person would, whether because of ignorance, forgetfulness, or defective inferences, he *cannot*, at that moment, perceive that feature as risky. Perhaps he could have done so had he earlier undertaken some action that he did not undertake. And perhaps that earlier course of action was culpable. But at the time of the time negligent act or omission, he *cannot* perceive the risk that he *does not* perceive. And he cannot be deemed culpable for what he cannot do. Negligence is not a form of culpability.

VI Inchoate Crimes and Culpability

How does my analysis of culpability bear on the criminal-law doctrines regarding attempts, solicitation, conspiracy, and complicity—the so-called inchoate crimes? In short, it suggests that some substantial modifications of those doctrines is in order.

First, with respect to attempts, we must distinguish between completed and incomplete attempts. Completed attempts are those where the actor believes he has engaged in the forbidden conduct or believes that the forbidden result will occur without further conduct on his part. An example of the first disjunct is conduct that the actor believes is sexual penetration without consent—rape—but where it turns out the actor is mistaken about the conduct. (He either does *not* achieve sexual penetration or he *has* received the victim's consent to it.) An example of the second disjunct is firing a bullet at a victim intending to kill him or believing that he will be killed, but where the bullet does not in fact kill him.

Because I reject the view that causing harm adds to a culpable actor's negative desert, I have no use for the attempt/success distinction. So completed attempts, when they are culpable, are culpable for the same reasons that mere recklessness regarding risks of harm is culpable: they represent the conscious imposition of risks of harm for reasons that do not justify such risk impositions.

Incomplete attempts are a different story. An incomplete or substantial step attempt is one where the actor intends to engage in a completed attempt in the future and has taken some steps toward that end. Although I am certain to encounter fierce opposition on this point, I deny that incomplete attempts are culpable acts.

First, the "substantial steps" element of incomplete attempts has only an evidentiary role; it is not itself constitutive of the culpability that incomplete attempts are alleged to exemplify. The substantial steps are supposed to corroborate the actor's intention to proceed to a completed attempt. They are supposed to show that the actor's intention is real. It is the intention itself that is supposed to be what makes the actor culpable, not the steps that merely evidence its existence.

So the question becomes, is intending to commit an act in the future that may be culpable when committed itself a culpable act? In other words, is intending to impose an unjustifiable risk itself the imposition of an unjustifiable risk?

I will assume for purpose of argument that intending is an act and that it is different from desiring, wishing, fantasizing, and like mental states. It is the (mental) act of deciding what one will do in the future. Still, it must be pointed out that it will not be clear, even to the actor, whether she has really intended, as opposed to desired, wished, and so on. (That is why the substantial steps are required—to separate intendings from these other mental states.)

Even if intendings are acts, do they unleash an increased risk of harm? The important point here is that the actor is aware that no matter how firm his intention, he can always reconsider up to the point when he does what he intends and completes the attempt. All the risks of harm that the latter will impose are within his ability to nullify up to the time he takes the intended act. He has not yet unleashed those risks. Moreover, it is always rational for him to reconsider and withdraw an intent to act wrongly. Even if there are some intentions that it would be irrational for actors to reconsider, an intention to act wrongly is surely not one of them. And this is true no matter how many steps the actor has taken in pursuance of executing that intention. (No matter how great the sunk costs in a wrongful endeavor, it will always be rational to decide not to recover them.)

So I deny that intending a possibly culpable future act is itself a culpable imposition of unjustifiable risks of harms. Intending to act culpably is therefore not itself a culpable act, though it does evince a flawed character.

Notice that if I am wrong about this, and intending to act culpably is culpable, then there will be some quite vexing problems that the culpability theorist will have to solve. Those problems arise from the conditionality of intentions, the unknown circumstances of the future intended act, and difficulties relating to individuating acts of intending.

With respect to the conditionality of intentions, it is difficult to imagine an intention to commit a possibly culpable act that is not either expressly or implicitly conditional. Consider Jack, who intends to kill Jill, but only if she has been unfaithful, there are no police present, he has not received love letters from a beautiful actress, and so on. Jack may deem the possibilities of various conditions obtaining as ranging from very slight to very likely. He may not, for example, believe that Jill has been unfaithful. On the other hand, he may not believe that there is much chance that he will receive amorous missives from a gorgeous actress. Still, if the defeating conditions do not obtain and the promoting conditions do, Jack does firmly intend to kill Jill, or so he believes—though he also believes he could change his mind.

If Jack's intending to kill Jill is a culpable act, how is its culpability affected by Jack's estimate of the probabilities of the various promoting and defeating conditions? Is its culpability discounted by them, or is it impervious to them? Is the robber who threatens "Your money or your life" and is not bluffing (or so he believes) as culpable as one who intends an assassination, even if the robber believes he is almost certain to get the money and not have to follow through on the threatened killing? If one is culpable for intending a culpable act, these questions will need to be resolved. On my view of culpable acts, they are immaterial.

The culpability of an act depends on the risks of harms the actor believes she has unleashed. Those risks will depend on the circumstances in which the act takes place as perceived by the actor. An actor will believe driving at one hundred miles per hour is less risky if she believes there is little traffic on the road, the road condition is good, and her reflexes are sound than if she believes the opposite.

However, if intending a future culpable act were itself a culpable act, then the circumstances that would bear on the culpability of that future act will be opaque. If Roger now intends to drive one hundred miles per hour at ten o'clock tomorrow morning, does he intend a culpable act, and if so, how culpable will it be? Perhaps the road will be deserted then. Perhaps he will be rushing a seriously ill passenger to the hospital. Given some circumstances, his intended act will be quite culpable. Given still others, it will not be culpable at all. Indeed, even Jim's intention on Monday to kill Joan on Tuesday will not be culpable if it turns out that Jim believes on Tuesday that Joan is a terrorist and about to blow up a stadium full of people. If the culpability of an act depends on its perceived circumstances, and those circumstances do not exist at the time the intention to act is formed, then if the culpability of the intention is a function of the culpability of the intended act, it cannot be ascertained prior to the act in question.

One response to this difficulty might be to base the culpability of the intended act on the actor's own prediction of the relevant circumstances. If, for example, Roger believes that when he drives at one hundred miles per hour tomorrow, as he presently intends, the road will be dry and free of traffic, then he intends an act of low or no culpability, even if his intent is not conditional on the road's being dry and traffic free. Conversely, if Roger believes the road will be wet and congested, then he presently intends a highly culpable act.

This solution to the opacity of future circumstances creates more difficulties even as it eliminates some. For if Roger's culpability for intending to drive one hundred miles per hour depends on his current estimate of future road conditions, then his culpability for so intending will vary from time to time as he revises his estimate of those conditions. If he believes when he forms the intention that the road will be dry and traffic-free but later, still retaining the intention, he believes the road will be wet and congested, and still later, he believes the road will be wet but less congested, his culpability will vary over time with his varying perception of the culpability of the act he intends. If, say, Roger is arrested for an incomplete attempt to drive dangerously, his culpability will turn on the time he is arrested, which seems to make his culpability a matter of luck. ("If you had arrested me earlier [or later], I would have been less culpable, despite my intention's remaining constant.") And this is true regardless whether Roger's culpability is based on his estimate of the future circumstances at the time he is arrested or on his average culpability from the inception of his intention to the time of his arrest.

The problem of opaque future circumstances segues nicely into the problem of duration. Suppose that while Roger continues all Monday to intend to drive one hundred miles per hour on Tuesday, Richard intends at eight o'clock Monday morning to drive one hundred miles per hour on Tuesday, revokes that intent at nine o'clock, revives it at ten o'clock, and on and on. Is each fresh intention of Richard a separate culpable act? If so, then his total culpability is much higher than Roger's, even if, come Tuesday, Roger retains his intention and Richard has permanently eradicated his. That result is counterintuitive.

On the other hand, suppose Roger has the intention in question all day Monday but revokes it permanently Tuesday morning, whereas Richard forms his similar intention on Tuesday only moments before he intends to drive. If the duration of Roger's intention increases his culpability, then Roger should be more culpable than Richard even though he, but not Richard, has now renounced the intention. Moreover, if the duration of the intention contributes to its culpability, that will not be for the same reason that the duration of ordinary acts of risk imposition increases their culpability. In the latter case, the longer one engages in risk creation, the more risk one creates. Driving recklessly for an hour creates a greater risk of harm than driving recklessly for thirty seconds. But intending a future possibly risky act for a longer time does not seem to create a risk of harm that is greater than intending that act for a shorter time. Richard's plan to drive one hundred miles per hour does not seem to create less risk than Roger's, even though Roger formed it a day earlier than Richard did.

Although I do not claim to have provided here a knockdown argument or set of arguments against the proposition that intending a (possibly) culpable act is itself a culpable act, I do believe I have raised some serious theoretical problems that proponents of that view must resolve. My doubts about the prospects for this lead me to reject the proposition.

Moving now from attempts to solicitation, conspiracy, and complicity, my view of culpability entails some doctrinal revision here as well. In current doctrinal formulations, liability for solicitation, conspiracy, and complicity turns on some act—encouragement, agreement, or aid—committed with the purpose of promoting a crime or crimes.[20] Solicitation and conspiracy are completed crimes in their own right, and liability for them does not depend on whether the crime that the solicitor or conspirator intended to promote ever occurs. The liability of an accomplice, on the other hand, depends on a crime having been committed by the principal. However, under many codes and the Model Penal Code, one who acts in a way that would make her an accomplice were the principal to commit the crime is guilty of an attempt to commit that crime even if the principal does not act.[21]

It appears, therefore, that the liability of the solicitor, the conspirator, and the would-be accomplice (for attempt) is inchoate liability—just as is the liability for incomplete attempts. And as I have rejected culpability in the case of the latter, it might appear that I should reject the culpability of the solicitor, conspirator, and would-be accomplice.

I would, indeed, reject their culpability were it predicated on their purpose to promote future crimes. Unlike the incomplete attempter, however, whose nefarious purposes relates only to *his own* future conduct, the solicitor, conspirator, and would-be accomplice are creating or increasing risks of *others'* culpable conduct. And once unleashed, that risk is frequently beyond the solicitor's, conspirator's, or would-be accomplice's ability to recall.[22] If, therefore, his reasons do not justify his increasing this risk of harm due to others' conduct, then his encouraging, agreeing to, or aiding the commission of that conduct is culpable in its own right, and is so regardless of whether the conduct ever occurs. Put differently, the culpability of solicitation, conspiracy, and complicity can be analyzed exactly the same way as the culpability of all acts that the actor perceives as imposing risks of harms, except that in the case of solicitation, conspiracy, and complicity, those perceived risks flow from the conduct of persons other than the actor, conduct that the actor by his act has rendered more likely.

Culpability is a function of the risks of harms to others' legitimate interests that the actor believes his act has unleashed beyond his control and his reasons for so acting. It also is a function of the duration of those risks to the extent that duration affects the risks' overall magnitude. And it is a function of the actor's capacity to access and assess moral reasons and the quality of his deliberative circumstances. It is not, however, affected by results. Nor does it attach to negligent acts, or to intentions regarding future ones. If criminal punishment should be responsive to negative desert, and negative desert is solely a function of culpability, then criminal law doctrines need to be revised accordingly.

Thanks, as always, to my various collaborators and critics, particularly Kim Ferzan, Stephen Morse, Mitch Berman, Michael Moore, and Heidi Hurd.

NOTES

1. *See* generally Larry Alexander and Kimberly K. Ferzan (with contributions by Stephen J. Morse), *Crime and Culpability: A Theory of Criminal Law* (2009).

2. *See id.* at Ch. 5. I should add that Michael S. Moore's magisterial *Causation and Responsibility* (2009) ultimately abandons the attempt to come up with a theory of proximate causation and opts instead for a scalar notion of causation. Nothing in Moore's almost six hundred pages on the topic persuades me that causation, scalar or otherwise, bears on retributive desert.

3. *See, e.g.,* George P. Fletcher, *Rethinking Criminal Law* (1978), 799–802; R. B. Brandt, "A Motivational Theory of Excuses," in *Nomos 27: Criminal Justice* (J. R. Pennock &

J. W. Chapman, eds., 1985), 165–98; Michael D. Bayles, "Character, Purpose, and Criminal Responsibility," 1 *Law & Phil.* 5 (1982).

4. Alexander and Ferzan (with Morse), *supra* note 1, at 16–17. The principal source for the quoted material was Stephen J. Morse, "Reason, Results and Criminal Responsibility," 2004 *U. Ill. L. Rev.* 363.

5. Alexander and Ferzan (with Morse), *supra* note 1, at 29–30.

6. *See* Judith Jarvis Thomson, "The Trolley Problem," 94 *Yale. L.J.* 1395 (1965).

7. I believe the notion of using people as involuntary resources for the production of good consequences better captures the intuitions behind the so-called Doctrine of Double Effect than the intention-foresight distinction. *See* Alexander and Ferzan (with Morse), *supra* note 1, at 96–103. *See also* Kimberly K. Ferzan, "Beyond Intention," 29 *Cardozo L. Rev.* 1147 (2008).

8. There is a live question, which I cannot pursue here, whether extremely tempting *offers* can excuse. If a threat to injure the actor's child can excuse the actor's violating others' rights, can an offer to heal the actor's child do the same?

9. If the actor has a preexisting intention to steal and is then threatened with severe harm if he does not do so, the threat can still excuse the actor's stealing by rendering nonoptional his reconsidering the intention to steal.

10. *See* Model Penal Code, § 2.02 (1985).

11. *See* Model Penal Code, § 2.02(2)(a) (1985).

12. *See* Model Penal Code, § 2.02(2)(b) (1985).

13. *See* Model Penal Code, § 2.02(2)(a)(ii) (1985).

14. *See* Model Penal Code, § 2.02(2)(c) (1985).

15. Id.

16. Id.

17. *See, e.g.,* Diana C. Chu, "The Cultural Defense: Beyond Exclusion, Assimilation, and Guilty Liberalism," 82 *Cal. L. Rev.* 1053 (1994); Note, "The Cultural Defense in the Criminal Law," 99 *Harvard L. Rev.* 1293 (1986).

18. This position is, of course, quite controversial. On the culpability of negligence, see, e.g., Alexander and Ferzan (with Morse), *supra* note 1, at Ch. 3; Kenneth W. Simons, "Culpability and Retributive Theory: The Problem of Criminal Negligence," 5 *J. Contemp. Leg. Issues* 365 (1994); A. P. Simester, "Can Negligence Be Culpable?," in *Oxford Essays in Jurisprudence* (J. Horder, ed., 4th Series, 2000). On strict liability, see *Appraising Strict Liability* (A. P. Simester ed., 2005).

19. *See* Model Penal Code, § 2.02(2)(d) (1985).

20. *See* Model Penal Code, §§ 5.02(1), 5.03(1), and 2.06(3)(a) (1985).

21. *See* Model Penal Code, § 5.01(3) (1985).

22. Sometimes, however, the success of the culpable act that is the object of the solicitation, conspiracy, or aid will require the actor himself to act culpably in the future. In those cases, the actor who solicits, conspires, or aids is no more culpable than one who has committed an incomplete attempt—that is, not at all.

CHAPTER 10

JUSTIFICATION AND EXCUSE

KIMBERLY KESSLER FERZAN

J. L. Austin famously distinguished justification from excuse:

> In general, the situation is one where someone is *accused* of having done
> something.... Thereupon he ... will try to defend his conduct....
>
> One way of going about this is to admit flatly that he, X, did do that very
> thing, A, but to argue that it was a good thing, or the right or sensible thing, or a
> permissible thing to do, either in general or at least in the special circumstances of
> the occasion. To take this line is to *justify* the action, to give reason for doing it:
> not to say, to brazen it out, to glory in it, or the like.
>
> A different way of going about it is to admit that it wasn't a good thing to
> have done, but to argue that it is not quite fair or correct to say *baldly* "X did A."
> We may say it isn't fair just to say X did it; perhaps he was under somebody's
> influence, or was nudged. Or, it isn't fair to say baldly he *did* A; it may have been
> partly accidental, or an unintentional slip. Or, it isn't fair to say he did simply
> A—he was really doing something quite different and A was only incidental, or he
> was looking at the whole thing quite differently. Naturally these arguments can be
> combined or overlap or run into each other.
>
> In the one defence, briefly, we accept responsibility but deny that it was bad:
> in the other, we admit that it was bad but don't accept full, or even any,
> responsibility.[1]

This distinction between justification and excuse appears to be both clear and
perspicuous. It appears that justifications entail accepting responsibility but denying
the conduct was wrongful or impermissible, whereas excuses admit the conduct was
wrongful but deny the defendant was responsible. The distinction enables us to categorize different sorts of defenses, which arguably could have different legal implications.

But first appearances can be deceiving. The articulation of the distinction,
and its usefulness, are subjects of significant debate. Does justification include

only the right or also the permissible? Does it depend on the actor's beliefs or just the objective facts? What is the basis for excusing the actor? That it does not reflect his character or that his choice was undermined? And the questions continue.

One preliminary question is why we attend to this distinction at all. To the average lawyer, this may seem to be an intellectual exercise in taxonomy, having little to do with the everyday practice of law. However, there may be both theoretical and practical reasons to employ this distinction. As Joshua Dressler summarizes the arguments, the distinction matters if we are to send clear moral messages, to provide theoretical consistency in the criminal law, to potentially determine the liability of accomplices, to potentially determine the appropriateness of third-party aid, to determine the retroactive applicability of a change in a defense, and to determine the constitutionality of the allocation of the burden of proof.[2] And, as Stephen Morse notes, excused defendants may also be subject to preventive detention, whereas justified defendants are simply acquitted.[3]

Consider one example. Take the view that justifications are action guiding, that whether an act is justified determines whether the putative victim of the actor's conduct may defend against him, and that justifications determine whom third parties may aid. Now, consider the question of whether it is appropriate to instruct the jury that the "reasonable person" for self-defense law is a person who shares the defendant's battered woman syndrome (assume the defendant misperceived the nature of a threat because of the syndrome). If one believes that justifications indicate right actions, against which the "victim" cannot defend and with which third parties should assist (and one believes that self-defense should be exclusively a justification), then one might not want to say that such a case is an instance of justified self-defense. Rather, one might argue that the defendant's diminished rationality entitles her to an excuse. A theorist might then rely on jury verdict reform to communicate this difference beyond the jury to the community at large.

That is, because we would not want others to assist someone who misperceives a threat, we would not want this to be a case of "justifiable self-defense."[4] Moreover, correctly classifying the case will prevent further corruption of self-defense, as calling a wrongful act "justified" might serve as a poor analogy in a later case. For instance, would the paranoid schizophrenic be entitled to a "reasonable paranoid schizophrenic" instruction, as well?[5] And if not, why not? In other words, understanding the parameters of *justifiable self-defense* is necessary to determine the parameters of that reasonable person standard.[6] As described below, the conflicting theories have conflicting implications.

I SOME PRELIMINARIES

A Types of Defenses

Justifications and excuses are types of defenses. They should be distinguished from two other defense types—what Paul Robinson calls "absence of an element defenses" and "nonexculpatory defenses."[7] An absence of an element defense is not a true defense. Rather, it constitutes a denial of one or more of the elements of the crime—for example, alibi. Nonexculpatory defenses do not deny that the defendant has committed the crime and is deserving of punishment but relieve the defendant of punishment to serve extrinsic policies. For instance, a claim of diplomatic immunity does not deny that a diplomat might have committed a crime, but immunizes the diplomat from criminal liability in exchange for similar treatment of U.S. diplomats abroad. In serving the goal of protecting a U.S. citizen, the United States sacrifices the ability to punish the foreign diplomat.

In contrast, justifications and excuses follow an admission or finding that the defendant has committed the underlying offense, but offer an argument for why the defendant should nevertheless not receive criminal punishment. A claim of self-defense, for instance, does not deny the underlying assault but rather gives a reason why the defendant's action was nevertheless permissible. Unlike nonexculpatory defenses, these defenses serve to negate the wrongfulness or criminality of the act or the punishability or blameworthiness of the actor, thus speaking directly to the purposes of punishment in the first instance.[8]

B Definitions versus Theories

In dividing defenses into these two categories, we should be aware of the distinction between the "definition" of justification (or excuse) and a "theory" of justification (or excuse).[9] Interestingly, although most theorists correctly parse the theory of excuse from its definition, theorists often conflate definition and theory with respect to justifications. That is, for excuses, theorists define excuses as indicating that the defendant is not blameworthy. They then proceed to explain, substantively, why the defendant is not blameworthy, arguing, for example, that the defendant's choice was undermined by a rationality impairment. On the other hand, theorists often argue that the substantive theory of justification—as, for example, the lesser evil—just is the definition.

As Doug Husak points out, Paul Robinson falls into this trap by arguing that justifications just are those instances of engaging in the lesser evil. Thus, Robinson would find unintelligible someone having a justification even when committing greater evil, or not having a justification when engaging in the lesser evil.[10] But the claims are coherent once one attends to the distinction between what a justification is and, then, what the best underlying theory is.

As to the definitions, many theorists argue that justifications concern the act, whereas excuses concern the actor.[11] A *justification* renders an action "right," "permissible," "not wrongful," or "not punishable." An *excuse* means that the offender is not blameworthy or, at least, not punishable. And because justifications apply to the rightness of the act, they universalize, that is, they apply to any actor, whereas excuses are said to be "personal" because the excusing circumstances apply solely to the defendant.[12]

Whether justification entails "right" conduct or simply permissible conduct has immediate implications. Conduct may be permissible—because of, say, an agent-relative permission—without being all things considered right. What should we say of such an action? Because criminal law only prohibits wrongful conduct, there seems to be room for justification to include permissions. In fact, the criminal law would then be divided into a binary world of justified conduct and prohibited conduct. On the other hand, those theorists who wish to reserve the label, "justified," for right conduct—either to stay consistent with the etymology of justification, to allow more moral nuance, or to ensure justification serves the function of guiding third parties—will want some other category for merely permissible conduct. Depending on the theorist's motivations, he will propose either that we add additional categories beyond justification and excuse or that we relegate the permissible to excuses.

In addition, even the preliminary division between act for justifications and actor for excuses raises questions. One might wonder whether using the act/actor distinction is simply a shift in focus from one elusive distinction to another.[13] The most troublesome group is agent-relative permissions—is the mother who kills to save her child simply less blameworthy or does she engage in permissible conduct? Yet many instances are clear. If Alice kills Bob because she mistakes him for an attacker, we can separate the act (killing someone who was not an aggressor) from the actor (Alice's lack of blameworthiness in making this mistake).

Another possible way to put the justification/excuse distinction is that justifications are part of the rules of conduct, whereas excuses are part of the principles of adjudication.[14] Justifications set forth norms that tell the actor when she may engage in an action that would otherwise be prohibited by the criminal law. Excuses articulate the principles by which we determine ex post that a defendant should not be punished.

Of course, even put this way, there are questions about the distinction. For instance, the duress defense requires a person to exhibit the firmness of a "reasonable person." It seems, then, that the evaluation of whether the defendant has lived up to this standard is action guiding—"I can steal the Monet to prevent the death of my mother but not to prevent being beaten with a wet noodle"—and if this is the case, then either duress is *not* an excuse or excuses *can* have action-guiding norms.[15]

C Priority

Another question is the priority of justification to excuse.[16] Some theorists argue that a defendant would prefer to be justified rather than excused. Of course, this view both oversimplifies and overcomplicates matters. A defendant prefers an acquittal to a conviction. And because offense elements may build in a justification or an excuse—that is, a legislature can construct an offense with elements that would otherwise constitute a justification or excuse—there may be no natural priority between them.

There are two questions here, one of logical priority and one of normative. As to logical priority, one question is whether our definitions of justification and excuse *should* be constructed to entail priority or whether we should first construct our definitions and then determine whether there is such a priority. To consider one way this might matter, if one conceives of excuses as negating the blameworthiness of an actor for committing a wrong, then a justification, which denies wrongfulness, seems prior to excuse.[17] However, if excuses are simply questions of whether an *act* is attributable to an actor, then justifications need not be prior. For instance, creating a magnificent painting (which needs no justification) may not be attributable to (and therefore reflect on the praiseworthiness of) an actor if that actor is completely insane. (It may seem odd to think of the painter as "excused" for creating a magnificent painting. However, if one finds the example odd, then one is implicitly presupposing that an actor is excused for *wrongdoing*.)

As for the normative priority, once again, whether it is better to be justified than excused may depend on one's definitions and theories. But here, too, priority may not be an issue around which to construct one's definitions of justification and excuse. We might define and theorize them first and then see what they say about which one a defendant might prefer. More important, however, this appears to be a bit of a category mistake, as the very question assumes that justifications and excuses are commensurable along the same continuum. However, if justifications speak to the quality of the act, and excuses speak to the blameworthiness of the actor, then there is no reason to believe that there is a natural hierarchy among evaluations of acts and evaluations of actors.

In sum, there are preliminary questions about the definitions of justification and excuse as well as the logical and normative relationships between the two. These preliminary structures then have bearing on the substantive theories of justification, as we will see below.

II Justifications in Greater Detail

A The Theory of Justification: An Overview of the Debate

The central debate surrounding justifications is whether justifications are based on the objective assessment of the act alone or are partially or wholly an objective assessment of the act *from the actor's perspective*. The nomenclature here has run a bit amuck.[18] When theorists refer to the state of affairs from an omniscient point of view, they call this the "objective" view, the "deeds" view, and the "guiding reasons" perspective. When theorists refer to the assessment of the actor's point of view, they refer to it as the "subjective" view, the "reasons" view, and the "explanatory reasons" perspective. Importantly, the latter is usually assessed against a normative standard. That is, subjectivists typically claim that it is not sufficient that the actor believe the justifying facts exist; rather, subjectivists require both that the actor honestly hold the belief and that the belief is reasonable.

It is perhaps best to begin with an example. Assume that while driving, Alfred comes to believe that his passenger, Betty, is very sick. On the basis of appearances, Alfred believes she is going to die, so he speeds and runs through red lights. As it turns out, Betty was just hung over, and her life was not the least bit imperiled. If a police officer wants to give Alfred myriad tickets for his driving offenses, would Alfred have a claim of justification, excuse, or neither?

Consider three different views of justification: objective, subjective, and dual. According to the objective view, the bottom line is that Betty was not sick, and an omniscient actor would not have sped and ran the lights. Alfred got it wrong. He would be excused if his mistake was reasonable, but not justified. The subjective view would focus on what Alfred believed and assess the reasonableness of his conduct based on that belief. Under such a theory, Alfred would be justified, not excused. A dual approach would require both that the conduct be objectively right and that the agent acted for this reason. Under this view as well, Alfred would not be justified, as his act was not objectively right.

The most significant differences between these views are their treatment of mistakes and unknowing justifications. Alfred's is a "mistake" case. Alfred acts on the basis of his beliefs, but he is mistaken as to the actual facts. Unknowing justifications are those instances in which the actor lacks the so-called justifying beliefs, but the facts support a justification. For instance, consider the actual case where someone stole a backpack from a crowded Israeli square and brought it to a secluded area, only to discover the backpack contained a bomb.[19] The backpack thief violated the criminal law rule against stealing, yet by so doing he saved many, many lives. A purely objective view about justification would claim that the defendant was justified (but would hold him guilty of an attempt), whereas the subjective and dual views would say that the defendant was guilty of theft, as he lacked the justifying belief or intent (or "explanatory reasons").

B Assessing the Theories

1 *The Objective View*

According to objectivists, whether the defender does the "right" thing is a function of the world as it is, not the world as it seems.[20] Objectivists do not care what is in the actor's mind. They only care about the value of the act itself. The theory about this value that predominates the literature is consequentalist: to be justified, the act must be the lesser evil. That is, this view of justification is embodied in the necessity defense wherein a defendant may cause some harm to prevent greater harm.

Because justification entails right action, objectivists adopt incompatibility and universality theses.[21] The incompatibility thesis claims that two people cannot have incompatible justifications. Justification is about right action, and only one person can be right. Moral law does not allow for "moral combat," where two opposing actors may both be right.[22] In addition, the universality thesis maintains that if one person is justified, then another individual is justified in helping her. Right action is the type of action that generalizes to all. If one person is entitled to use force, then others may aid her. This universality is another way to distinguish justification from excuse: excuses are personal to the actor—others may not commit that very act; whereas justifications generalize to all, such that anyone may perform that act.

A functional account of justification derives from the universality and incompatibility theses.[23] That is, the moral corollaries of right action provide guidance to other actors as to how they should behave. This functional account is the view often cited in treatises to distinguish justification from excuse. If the actor is justified in using force, it follows that others may come to her aid, and the "defender" is not likewise justified in using force. Moreover, an acquittal premised on justification "sends the message" that this conduct is the right thing to do. The functional implications—that justifications tell third parties what to do—are best understood as merely a logical corollary of what a "right" action entails.[24] However, this third-party implication is sometimes stated as though it were its own theory or definition of justification. But as Mitch Berman points out, the third-party conception of justification, standing on its own, appears "entirely stipulative."[25]

The final aspect of the objective theory is conceptual. These theorists maintain that the justification/excuse distinction is symmetrical with the criminal law's wrongdoing/culpability distinction. Assume, for example, that Carla leaves a restaurant with Dan's very similar looking umbrella. When Carla takes Dan's umbrella, we might say that that Carla's belief, that Dan's umbrella is her own, is a reasonable one. But the fact remains that Carla has taken someone else's umbrella. Thus, Carla has committed the actus reus of an offense.

Of course, the fact that Carla's belief is reasonable speaks to her culpability.[26] In addition to being concerned with individuals who take the property of another, criminal law cares about the actor's culpability. If the crime required that Carla intended to take the property of another, then by mere logic her mistaken belief negates the required element of culpability. From the opposite angle, we might argue that criminal law should require subjective awareness of wrongdoing, and that it would be unfair to punish Carla, whose mistaken belief was reasonable. But when we make such an argument, we grant that Carla has done something impermissible; we simply argue that she should not be subject to criminal law's sanctions.

Thus, argue objectivists, an actor is justified when her action is the right thing to do. Her belief may render her action culpable or nonculpable, but the rightness or wrongfulness of action is derived from the way the world actually is, not the way it seems to the actor.

In light of these views, objectivists maintain that the reasonably mistaken actor is not justified, but simply excused. Albert is excused.[27] Just as Carla may mistake her umbrella for Dan's, thus doing the wrong thing nonculpably, an actor, like Albert, may make a mistake as to whether he needs to act. In such cases, we excuse the actor—we understand the root of his epistemic error—but there is still a truth of the matter that renders the conduct unjustified. An objectivist maintains that Albert has not done the right or permissible thing. A third party—aware of the actual facts ("epistemically privileged")—cannot help Albert (after all, Betty is not sick) and would be an accessory to any crime committed by Albert.

Objectivists also stake out a position on the importance of justificatory intent. Objectivists argue that just as a wrong deed is not justified when done for the right reason, a right deed is not unjustified when done for the wrong reason. Thus, the bomb thief acts justifiably when he believes he is stealing a backpack in a crowded square and in so doing unknowingly moves a bomb. The objectivist wants an epistemically privileged third party to aid the bomb thief and wants to acknowledge that saving the people in the crowded square is the "right" thing to do.

Just because the backpack thief's conduct is justified does not mean that he completely escapes punishment, however. Rather, according to the objectivist, the unknowingly justified actor is guilty of an impossible attempt.[28] Robinson argues that this treatment is in accord with our treatment of attempts generally. When a person attempts a crime but fails, his subjective culpability makes him liable for the attempt offense, not for the completed crime. It thus follows, according to Robinson, that justifications should likewise follow the result (no net harm done) and not the actor's culpability.[29]

One substantial problem for a pure objectivist view is reconciling this view of justification with the concept of justified risks.[30] The objectivist view has no room for best guesses, and no guidance for actors either. That is, if the criminal law should always measure the quality of an act by whether it in fact causes the best result, it is then committed to claiming that reasonable conduct may often be wrongful.

The problem, however, is that objectivists seem to want it both ways. They want room for "reasonable risks" while simultaneously maintaining that reasonable mistakes about justification are excused. For instance, the leading objectivist Paul Robinson has argued that the Model Penal Code's definitions of recklessness and negligence conflate ex ante rules of conduct with ex post rules of adjudication.[31] The Model Penal Code, according to Robinson, only defines the culpability terms of recklessness and negligence, but does not define the ex ante conduct rule—that is, it does not define what constitutes a prohibited risk, the disregard of which would be culpable. In light of this omission, Robinson argues that to articulate a rule of conduct, a criminal code should contain a definition of a prohibited risk.[32] He offers, as one example, that an "actor creates a 'prohibited risk' when he creates a substantial and unjustified risk that a prohibited result will occur. A risk is substantial and unjustified if, given its nature, degree, and circumstances, its creation is a deviation from the standard of care of a reasonable person."[33] There must be a "prohibited risk" for the defender to fail to be aware of or to consciously disregard.[34] Thus, if the risk is not substantial or unjustifiable, the actor has not violated society's rules of conduct.

Thus, consider the conflicts in Robinson's position. Robinson privileges an epistemically limited point of view for risks, in contrast to the omniscient view at work within his theory of justification. He then claims that risks are unjustified if, given the nature, degree, and circumstances, the action is a deviation from that which a *reasonable* person would take. Now consider Albert. On the one hand,

Robinson claims that Albert is not justified because he does not achieve a "net social benefit." Albert unnecessarily runs the red lights. Thus, because justifications are ex ante conduct rules, Albert should be told not to act. On the other hand, Albert takes a justifiable risk and does so because his behavior is *reasonable*. Now, the ex ante conduct rules regarding "prohibited risks" tell Albert that it is permissible to act, and ironically, do so on the subjectivists' rationale—the risk's reasonableness (given the nature, degree, and circumstances, a reasonable person would do the same thing Albert did). Albert is at once taking a justified risk and acting unjustifiably. Robinson is not employing two different senses of "justified" here. Rather, he is reaching contradictory conclusions about the very same case.[35]

Ultimately, the objective view itself is not incoherent. It merely requires the commitment to the claim that in instances of risk taking, we cannot create action-guiding norms for that risk. Rather, we can only create action-guiding norms for results and relegate risks to the realm of culpability.

2 *The Subjectivist Account*

The subjectivist account takes a different view of criminal law norms. It essentially makes room for reasonable error in exactly the way the objective view does not. The subjective view holds that the defendant *is complying* with a criminal law norm when she acts "reasonably." Thus, this account still holds that justifications are rules of conduct but, unlike the objective view, includes reasonable behavior within the criminal law's *conduct* rules.

The subjectivist view is attractive for a number of reasons. First, some argue that it is consistent with the ordinary language argument for the meaning of justification, in which one is justified if one has "sound, good reasons" for what one does.[36] It is also in accord with the use of "justified" in epistemology, which means a well-founded belief about facts.

Second, unlike the objective view, the subjective view makes room for *permissible* as well as right actions.[37] If one's theory of justification is patently consequentialist, then one has no need for a concept of permissible actions because actions will either cause more good than harm, or vice versa.[38] (Perhaps one must resolve ties. The criminal law currently does not regard ties as justified actions.)

On the other hand, if one believes that morality is richer than mere consequentialism, then one must confront agent-relative permissions. If the law grants the individual permission to do something that would otherwise be wrongful, the question is what the appropriate label is for the conduct. Notice that the conduct is now permissible (thus, a universal rule of conduct, pointing toward a justification) but the permission is given only to the actor (thus, the agent-specific aspect that leans toward excuse).[39] Agent-relative permissions, therefore, exist in an odd limbo. They do not perform some of the functions of justifications, as they do not forbid "victim" resistance or permit third-party assistance, but neither do they serve merely to excuse as, they render not only the actor less blameworthy but also the act permissible for that actor. A subjective account arguably allows more room for this realm of permissibility, a feature of our rich morality for which the objective approach does not have an account.

Subjectivists do not have a "functional" account of justification. Because subjectivists maintain that the actor's reasons are the root of justification, they reject the universality and incompatibility theses. That is, they reject that the fact that A is justified has any bearing on whether B is justified—A and B with conflicting interests may nevertheless both be justified in acting in opposite ways. For example, Kent Greenawalt applies the subjective view to the facts in *People v. Young*,[40] wherein the defendant saw two middle-aged men assaulting a young man. Young intervened to help the young man. As it turned out, the two middle-aged men were plainclothes detectives attempting to arrest the young man. Greenawalt argues against the incompatibility thesis, maintaining that Young was justified in intervening and that the police officers were justified in repelling Young.

The subjective view thus conflicts with the objectivist position as to reasonably mistaken actors and justificatory intent. To the subjectivist, the reasonably mistaken actor is justified. When Albert believes that Betty is dying and runs the red light, his reasons for action—"saving Betty's life"—are good reasons for action. Thus, Albert is justified. The reasons theorist also maintains that justificatory intent is required. The bomb thief is guilty of theft.[41]

One question for the subjective view is whether the defender must be motivated by, or simply believe, that the justifying circumstances exist.[42] Particularly in those circumstances in which the actor believes that he will produce a net societal benefit, should the criminal law be concerned with whether the defendant is properly motivated by those beliefs so long as he believes they exist? In other words, is there a reason not to justify the speed-devil ambulance driver or the bloodthirsty executioner if they act, knowing that the law endorses their conduct, for less than commendable reasons? If the criminal law does not care why we do not violate the law, should the criminal law care whether we are properly motivated by justifying circumstances so long as we are aware of them? (Notably, if one need not be aware of justifying circumstances, then the view is objectivist, not subjectivist.)

Thus, the subjective view eviscerates any functional use of the justification label vis-à-vis the conduct of second and third parties. That is, it does not follow from the fact that one actor is justified that another actor may aid him. If one believes that justifications merely set forth rules of conduct for the one actor, this is not a troubling implication. However, for those who endorse the view that justifications have implications for third parties—and indeed, that this is the raison d'être for justifications—this is a damning implication.

There are significant puzzles for the subjective view. First, it creates a conceptual asymmetry between offenses and defenses. As objectivists point out, Alfred is indistinguishable from Carla, who takes an umbrella reasonably believing it to be her own. While a subjectivist must also maintain that Carla has good reason to take "her own umbrella," such an assessment fails to capture the full situation. Carla does not do the right thing when she takes someone else's umbrella; she simply lacks culpability.[43]

Kent Greenawalt, a subjectivist, does seek to distinguish these cases.[44] He claims that the man who reasonably, but mistakenly, believes that a woman is consenting to sexual intercourse is neither justified nor excused, while the reasonably mistaken self-defender is justified. Yet Greenawalt's basis for this distinction is unconvincing. He claims that "[a]s to some elements of some crimes, we may think one should not proceed on less than virtual certainty that the element is absent."[45] In addition, "[t]he rape example does suggest the broader point that the circumstances of victims should matter for classification."[46] However, neither of these statements provides a principled distinction between the two cases. Both the reasonably mistaken rapist and Alfred may be virtually certain that there is consent, or a real danger, respectively.

The second problem with the subjectivist position is that we typically treat excused actors, whether insane, immature, or acting under duress, as *innocent aggressors*. This is so despite the fact that a reasonable child may believe a real gun to be a fake, and a person of reasonable firmness may succumb to a threat. That is, actors can behave both reasonably and wrongly.[47] Indeed, a reasonable adult may mistakenly believe a loaded gun to be unloaded. Still, this person is an innocent aggressor.[48]

Notably, there is an equivocation at work with the use of reasonableness, the ubiquitous standard under the subjective view.[49] Take Albert. We could assess the justifiability of his behavior given the risks and reasons as he perceives them (this is the inquiry of justifiability within the mens rea of recklessness.) If we think that one should run through a red light to save a dying passenger, then Albert is acting reasonably or justifiably. On the other hand, one might question whether Albert's belief that Betty is ill is "reasonable." For this inquiry, we compare Albert to the so-called reasonable person. This person is not omniscient (for then there could never be a mistake) nor is this person identical to Albert (for then he would make the same mistake). The reasonable person standard is more problematic than the use of reasonable as a justification.[50] The question of justification reasonableness is simply a weighing of values, whereas the question of the reasonable person requires some principled way to determine which characteristics of Albert are included in the calculation and which are not.[51] For our purposes, importantly, the subjectivists often seek to use the latter, reasonable person evaluation for reasonableness.

A problem for the subjectivist, then, is to specify when reasonableness is permissible and when it is nevertheless excused. In so doing, the subjectivist should take care to distinguish those reasonableness standards that stand in for a balance of interests from those that compare the defendant to some idealized standard. For instance, the reasonable person in self-defense is typically an idealized standard. But what about the reasonable person in duress, a defense typically characterized as an excuse? Of course, in resolving this issue, the subjectivist may conclude that all reasonable conduct is justified, thereby shifting some excuses into the realm of justifications. The claim can be coherent, but unfortunately, it is far too often inconsistently argued.

3 Dual Theories

Dual theorists argue that the actor must not only perform the objectively right deed but also be motivated by that reason. Dual theorists see the concept of justification as inextricably intertwined with the conceptual distinction between offenses and defenses. To consider one such argument, George Fletcher argues that the distinction between offenses and defenses is substantive, not formal. The prima facie norm tells people "Do not kill," and then a defense allows people "to kill only when threatened with deadly force by another." Collapsing these two, Fletcher contends, is equivalent to treating the killing of an unlawful aggressor like the swatting of a "fly" because we eliminate the prima facie norm against killing other people.[52]

In Fletcher's view, the justified actor violates a prohibitory norm. That is, the criminal law says that it is wrongful to kill another human being. Fletcher argues that our prohibitory norms contain objective and subjective elements: the actor must not only engage in the conduct but do so with the requisite mental state. Now, when the actor claims to have acted in self-defense, the prohibitory norm is still violated, but, maintains Fletcher, the defendant offers a justification. Because these norms are ontologically on par with prohibitory norms, they likewise require objective and subjective elements.[53]

Another dual theorist, John Gardner, argues that "justification is called for only when one also has some reason *not* to act, believe, etc. as one does."[54] Gardner views an offense as setting forth a guiding reason against an action, which the criminal law then translates into a rule. Gardner does not believe this rule is a mere "rule of thumb" but he claims that a criminal offense is a protected reason that is itself immune from being weighed. An actor is not permitted to weigh the value of committing the offense because the law's authority protects (and outweighs) all reasons in favor of committing the offense. However, the law does create justifications that give an individual a canceling permission to commit the offense. This cancels the value of the rule. Then, the underlying action must still be morally justified by the balance of reasons. To serve as a justification, then, the reasons for acting must defeat the guiding reason and must *cancel* the value of the rule. That is, if the backpack thief does not know of the bomb, the reasons for acting (saving many people) defeat the guiding reason against (taking property of another), but because the backpack thief does not know of this reason, he is not given permission to ignore the rule against theft. The thief thus lacks a justification.

Hence, the theory of justification, as right deed for right reason, derives from a theory about the relationship between offenses and defenses.[55] The ultimate claim is that a defendant cannot violate a prohibited norm of the criminal law without being guided by an actual justification for violating that norm (and, for Gardner, canceling the value of the prohibitory rule). In these cases, the unknowingly justified actor cannot take advantage of a justificatory reason because his reasoning was not directed at the interests that outweigh the norm. And the mistaken actor likewise cannot take advantage of a justification because his conduct ultimately did inflict the very wrong that the prohibitory norm spoke to, even though his belief that he was acting justifiably may entitle him to an excuse.[56]

Because this view requires both an objective and a subjective element, it offers conflicting messages about what follows from when an actor is or is not justified. When justified, and thus the right deed for the right reason, the implications for the victim and third parties are the same as under the objective view.[57] But it does not follow that when an actor is not justified, third parties would not be justified in assisting. For instance, even if the defendant is not acting for the right reason, and therefore not acting justifiably, a third party—aware of the right reason—may want to encourage the action. Hence, a potential worry about this view is that it cannot separate act from actor and therefore does not distinguish between whether an action ought to be performed and whether a particular actor ought to have a defense for performing it.

The other more general question for dual theories is whether they can be squared with risk creation offenses.[58] A significant number of laws are risk creation offenses, in which we tell people that it is permissible to risk harm for certain reasons but not for others. These risk creation offenses, because they require that the risk be unjustifiable, implicitly build the defense into the offense elements themselves. That is, compare Edgar, who knows he is killing Frieda, with George, who knows he is risking the death of Harriet. Edgar may offer a defense, whereas George will merely claim that the risk is justifiable. But the nature of the inquiry, as to whether Edgar and George are "justified," is the same. The question for the dual theorist, then, is why one's theory of justification should rely on the distinction between offenses and defenses, when many offenses of risk creation incorporate justifications into the offense themselves.[59] For his part, Fletcher recasts risks as part of the offense definition, but the justifiability of the risk as part of the offense "justification." The problem is that this approach improperly reifies risk. That is, risks can't and don't harm others—they are merely epistemic constructs, and thus according to Fletcher's own views, have no place in the language of offense definition.[60]

C From Theory to Practice

There are several issues with translating a theory of justification to the practice of criminal law, and indeed, the imperfections of the practice of criminal law may lead to distortions of the underlying justification.

First, there is the obvious problem of moral disagreement. If some legislators believe that it is "right" for a person to stand his ground rather than retreat, and others believe that one should not take life needlessly, it may be that the legislature cannot agree ex ante as to whether a particular case is justified or excused, but the legislators may nevertheless agree that providing a defense (of some sort) is appropriate.[61] Conversely, as a matter of positive law, the legislature may choose not to follow morality: a legislature can also choose not to provide a defense, even when there is a lesser evil, and indeed, the Model Penal Code specifically requires that the legislature not have considered a defense.[62]

Second, there is the problem of jury disagreement.[63] Paul Robinson proposes jury verdict reform as a way of sending messages about when conduct is right (and therefore acquittal is warranted) as opposed to when the offender is simply not blameworthy.[64] But if jury verdicts are to send moral messages, what should the system do about verdicts in which all jurors agree that acquittal is appropriate but disagree as to why? Indeed, one might worry that the cost of achieving clear messages will somehow ultimately be borne by criminal defendants, as this may be a way for prosecutors to argue that the jury has not reached a unanimous verdict.

More fundamentally, however, anytime a legislature seeks to draft a rule, it will have to take into account that citizens may very likely err. Thus, what may be justified in one case may not be justified overall, given the likelihood of error (and abuse). A rational legislature may decide to draft a rule that gets most, but not all, cases right. This means that there will be a gap between the morally justified in an individual case and the legally justified as an overall rule.[65]

As one example, consider the imminence requirement in self-defense. The imminence requirement has received significant scholarly attention because battered women have claimed that the imminence requirement places them at a significant disadvantage vis-à-vis their abusers. Many theorists argue that imminence is simply a proxy for necessity, thus the standard should be changed to one of "immediate necessity." Irrespective of whether imminence merely serves this proxy function (and I have my doubts),[66] the fact that imminence serves a proxy function does not mean that it serves no function at all. Rather, by crafting the imminence rule, legislatures seek to prevent actors from making errors and inappropriately taking the law into their own hands.[67]

Moreover, legislatures may seek to draft rules for when individuals are uncertain about the facts. This issue circles us back to the question of whether there should be action-guiding norms in cases of risk. For instance, if killing a culpable aggressor can be justified, but killing an innocent aggressor is viewed as excused, the legislature might want to create a law the gives guidance to the defender and third parties as to what to do when one only suspects that she is being attacked by a culpable aggressor. Indeed, although the defender herself will ultimately escape liability in either event (she will either be justified for killing a culpable attacker or excused for acting as a person of reasonable firmness would), the same is not true of a third-party intervener. Ostensibly, society does not want a third party to intervene if the defender would be only excused. But what should a third party do if he does not know whether the attacker is innocent or culpable? In such circumstances, a legislature might wish to create a rule that resolves how the party should act in instances of epistemic uncertainty. This rule will authorize conduct even in cases in which the underlying facts—were the actor to know them—would not. Thus, justifications, as a matter of positive criminal law, may not reflect what morality would otherwise dictate simply as a matter of concession to the practicalities of the real world.

In light of the gap between morality and positive criminal law, Mitchell Berman has argued that conceptually legal justifications do not entail that the conduct is the morally right thing to do.[68] Although theorists can engage in substantive arguments about whether law should follow morality, as a matter of positive law, the two can

depart. Thus, Berman argues, when we argue about the conceptual nature of justification, we cannot say anything more than that the conduct is not criminal, as it is
conceptually possible to have conduct that is wrongful but not criminal or criminal
but not wrongful.

D Analyzing Individual Defenses as Justifications

Depending on one's theory of justification, one might analyze different defenses *as*
justifications. Some defenses appear to be analyzed from a top-down perspective,
whereas others are analyzed from a bottom-up approach. So, for instance, theorists
who analyze self-defense often reason (1) that self-defense is a justification, (2) that
justifications fall within one of the theories above, and therefore (3) that the elements of self-defense must be of a certain sort.[69] On the other hand, a claim that
duress is a justification begins with the analysis of the elements and shows how
those elements conform to a particular normative theory.[70] Notably, at least one
theorist has argued that the proper inquiry should not be types of defenses but
tokens.[71] Such an approach would hold the structure of the defense constant, but
depending on the net social benefit (or some other such calculation), the defense
may or may not fit within the theory of justification. This would allow some
instances of self-defense to be viewed as justified, while other instances of self-
defense would be seen as excused. Either way, there are often two questions at work:
the theory of justification and the theory of the defense.

Although a direct analysis of the various defenses is beyond the scope of this
chapter, some of the issues directly intersect with the theory of justifications themselves. I will thus detail two puzzles about how self-defense relates to the broader
questions of the theory justifications.

Although theories of self-defense appear throughout the literature, one significant worry about the theory of justification debate is that it pays little attention to
the defenses that supposedly fall within the theory, and simply assumes that all justifications are alike. The necessity, choice-of-evils defense appears to be patently
consequentialist, authorizing one harm to prevent another greater harm.

Yet self-defense appears to be difficult to explain as a matter of best consequences.[72] First, why is the defender's life discounted? And indeed, what if in all
other respects, the culpable aggressor is a more worthwhile person (a doctor curing
cancer) than his intended victim (a criminal law theorist)? Second, if discounted,
there must be a point at which the aggregation of multiple culpable aggressors outweighs the defender's interests. Finally, even if theorists seek to add the general value
of deterrence into the mix, the ultimate result is that the defender's right is contingent on these calculations. This impersonal balancing of interests differs sharply
from viewing self-defense as a matter of one person responding to another's attack,
and seems to lose the fundamentally personal nature of the defense.

Another point about the self-defense/necessity distinction is in order. It may be
that our theory of necessity does not require justificatory belief but our theory of
self-defense does. The backpack thief discussed earlier committed the lesser evil, so

we would want third parties to help him, and we would not want anyone to stop him. But this distinction does not necessarily hold in the case of self-defensive action. Assume that Alfred wants to kill Betty and points a gun at her (that is hidden under a table). Betty, enraged at Alfred over another matter, throws a knife at him. A purely objective view has to tell us who is the offender and who is the defender. It appears to be a first in time principle.[73] But the question is why either party should have the privilege of being deemed the "defender" simply because he or she was slower on the draw. Indeed, why would it be "right" for third parties to assist either person here? We do not have a lesser evil; we do not have an aggressor and a defender; what we have is two bad guys trying to kill each other. The difference between self-defense and necessity is that the actor's belief that she is in danger changes the quality of the act from aggression to self-defense. Hence, justificatory belief may be required for self-defense, but not necessity.[74]

E Assessment

From the perspective of extant criminal law, Mitchell Berman is certainly correct that the state of the law does not mirror morality, though one may wonder whether we cannot say *anything* more about those defenses that serve as action guiding than that they are not criminal, or whether we cannot say *anything* more about excuses than that the actor is not punishable. From the perspective of criminal law theory and how criminal law should be understood, we may want a tighter connection between law and morality. That is, the fact that an actor is not blameworthy seems to be a good reason to excuse, and the fact that an action is right seems to be a good reason for a legislature to offer that action a justification.

The question, then, though, is what service this scholars' distinction between justification and excuse can be put to in the context of laws of the real world. There is no clear winner here.

If justifications serve the purpose of announcing right conduct or of giving information to second and third parties, subjective substantive theories will always have "perplexing borders," as these theories define justification in such a way that they do not entail these implications.[75] However, to those who see these implications as the tail wagging the dog, one may simply want to examine whether these implications obtain in any given case without claiming that justifications must entail implications for third parties.[76]

Indeed, Antony Duff claims that we ought to abandon the binary distinction of justification and excuse for "right/wrong," "warranted/unwarranted," and "excused/unexcused."[77] Duff seeks to follow objectivists about justification in noting that right conduct is viewed objectively, but he also seeks to make room for the subjectivist's recognition that conduct that is right from the actor's point of view is more than merely excused.

Ultimately, the problem is that there is broad disagreement about why we would want these terms in the first place. Many objectivists are attracted to the functional aspects of justifications. Subjectivists, for their part, believe actions need only be permissible to be justified, and they also seek to fairly label the good faith actions of the defendant (and built into this view is that excuses are somehow "lesser" defenses). The dual theorist approaches this from a broader conceptual view as to the relationship of justification to offenses and defenses. With these three competing reasons for seeking to employ the label "justification," it is doubtful that theorists can or will reach a consensus on the theory of justification. Nevertheless, it is doubtful that the debate will end, particularly because the top-down analysis of most defenses requires theorists to stake out positions on the nature of justifications themselves. Moreover, the top-down nature of most of this theorizing means that our understandings of particular defenses will ultimately be hostage to the theorist's underlying theory of justification.

III Excuses

A Some Preliminaries

Unlike justifications, excuses are generally understood as assessing the *actor's* blameworthiness. Whereas justifications most naturally speak to consequentialist concerns, excuses are more at home within retributive theory. After all, even if an insane actor cannot be deterred, punishing him might still prevent fabricated claims from others and might nevertheless instill respect for the underlying conduct rule.[78]

One significant question within the excuse literature is how much ground excuses should cover. For some, excuses cover any claim that negates the actor's blameworthiness. For other theorists, excuses, like justifications, assess the actor's reasons; thus, claims of irrationality are not excuses at all. We must therefore once again encounter the question of how many categories we need, a question that can only be answered by determining at the outset the purpose of the label "excuse."

B Excuses versus Exemptions

One distinction within the excuse literature is that between excuses and exemptions. Consider trees, animals, and young children. At one time, a tree that fell on someone was chopped up, and dogs and horses that caused injury were destroyed.[79] But punishing such things and creatures seems wrong because they lack the capacity to reason about causing harm. They are not rational. Small children who display minimal rationality still lack a full appreciation of the nature and quality of their acts.

When something or someone lacks the capacity to comply with moral and legal norms, some theorists propose considering such individuals to be *exempt* rather than *excused*. The theory behind exemptions is often stated as the view that these entities are not the appropriate addressees of moral norms. This exempt status is reserved for those creatures that lack practical reasoning skills at such a significant level that they generally cannot comply with moral norms.[80] Or, as Antony Duff puts it, "The difference between an excusable agent and a seriously disordered agent is analogous to that between someone who makes an understandable mistake in playing a game and someone who is not playing the game at all."[81]

Even within the core of exemptions there are some questions. First, in some respects it seems odd to say that children are not the proper addressees of moral norms. Part of what moral education is, and part of what parents try to do, is to enable children to grasp these norms. Moreover, some sort of watered-down version of these norms certainly applies—norms against hitting, kicking, and biting are seen as sufficiently graspable that children are held accountable for their behavior. Of course, these educative punishments are intended to inform the child's later moral reasoning. For our purposes, it is simply worth noting that the relationship between children and moral norms is somewhat complicated.

There are other borderlines. Consider psychopathy. According to the traditional understanding, the psychopath is an individual who fails to understand moral norms because he lacks the capacity to form emotional attachments to others.[82] Viewed this way, one might imagine the psychopath to be akin to the *Star Trek* character Data, an android. Data does not form any emotional attachments. He can only act logically and rationally. Applied to the psychopath, all criminal laws appear to the psychopath as malum prohibitum laws appear to us—the only reason we have to follow these laws is because we will otherwise be punished. If this is the case, and these individuals lack any capacity to care about others and their ends, it may be that the psychopath's lack of the capacity to reason is of such a nature that we may view him to be exempt. Interestingly, at least one scholar has questioned the empirical picture of the psychopath, arguing that the psychopath is not even rational.[83] Paul Litton claims that a requirement for rational self-governance is the capacity to reflect on, to evaluate, and to further one's ends. This requires an ability to give and assess the *value* of one's ends. Because psychopaths cannot assign value and act in accordance with the weight of these values, the psychopath is not simply morally blind—he is irrational. If this is the case, the psychopath clearly falls within the category of exempt actors.

The insane also raise the question of excuse or exemption. In most cases, the insane are not exempt. Even a paranoid schizophrenic who kills because of divine command may still be expected not to run through red lights or rob a bank. That is, many instances of insanity are time and situation specific. Of course, there may be instances where the insane have become completely out of contact with reality. At that point, exemption, rather than excuse, may be the more appropriate category.[84]

C Theories of Excuse

Recall that excuses focus on the actor. On the basis of some underlying normative considerations, we determine that the actor is not blameworthy. These excuses do not guide action but serve as principles of adjudication that tell the decision-maker that this particular defendant is not deserving of punishment.[85]

By virtue of what is the defendant not blameworthy? According to one theory—the "choice" theory—the defendant must either lack the capacity or fair opportunity to conform her conduct to the requirements of law. According to another theory—the "character" theory—the criminal act does not sufficiently reflect on the defendant's settled character to demonstrate that *she* is worthy of punishment. Finally, another family of theories—"reasons" theories (not to be confused with subjectivist theories of justification!)—maintains that the defendant's reasons demonstrate that the defendant is not blameworthy because she has lived up to our expectations or because her reasons place her act in a more favorable light.

To briefly illustrate, assume that a terrorist kidnaps Margo's son and threatens to kill him unless Margo kills five people. Margo kills the five. Conceptually, this is a case of duress. A choice theorist would claim that we should excuse Margo because she lacked a fair opportunity to comply with the law: a person of reasonable firmness in the actor's situation would do what Margo did—act to save her child. A character theorist might argue that the act of killing the five people does not show Margo to be a bad person deserving of punishment. This act does not reflect who *she* is. Finally, under one reason theorist's account, Margo did all that we would expect of her. She has conformed with societal expectations even when she kills the five. (This would not be the case had Margo killed five to prevent her child from being beaten with a wet noodle.) These three theories are elucidated below.

1 *Choice, Reasoning, and Attitude*

The choice theory flows from the law's concept of a person as practical reasoner.[86] Just as the law presupposes that individuals act for reasons and thus can be guided by criminal-law rules, excuses set forth those conditions under which the defendant cannot be so guided. Choice theorists argue that the grounds for excusing an actor are that she lacked the rationality to appreciate the criminality of her conduct or the volitional ability to conform her conduct to the requirements of law. Notably, to the choice theorist, the fact that an action is *caused* is not sufficient to excuse it.[87]

The choice theorist therefore seeks to explain insanity (as either a volitional or rationality impairment), duress (as a volitional, "hard choice" impairment), and extreme involuntary intoxication (as a volitional or rationality impairment), as well as potentially covering (depending on one's theory of justifications) mistakes as to justification. Yet the choice theorists typically do not seek to explain mistakes with respect to elements of the offense. The Model Penal Code view, and arguably the correct view, is that mistakes are not excuses. If the defendant makes a mistake that negates the required mens rea for the offense, then he is not offering a defense. Rather, his claim is that the prosecution has not met its burden of proving every element beyond a reasonable doubt.

Choice theories are broad. They cover even those cases that might otherwise be treated as exemptions, such as infancy or complete irrationality. Moreover, because the quality of one's reasoning may be seen as a continuum concept, there is also room in choice theory for diminished responsibility claims, according to which a defendant is entitled to mitigation but not acquittal.[88]

The attitudinal theory of excuse advanced by Peter Westen is akin to choice theories.[89] Westen looks to those sorts of claims that do not trigger our reactive emotions of blame and resentment. One might say this is just the other side of the reasoning coin. Culpability, choosing to harm others, reflects that an individual lacks sufficient concern for the interests of others. Thus, knowingly killing someone is culpable because it manifests insufficient concern. Excuse, in turn, negates this inference of insufficient concern. Hence, an actor who lacks the rational capacity to appreciate that her conduct is wrong, for example, does not display such insufficient concern. Just as criminal law culpability may be framed either mechanistically or normatively, so can choice theories of excuse.[90]

One debate within the choice theory of excuse is the proper treatment of insanity based on volitional impairments. What is the difference between an irresistible impulse and an impulse that is not resisted? This concern is both theoretical and practical. The theoretical concern is whether there are true impairments of volition (that do not collapse into rationality impairments). Most significant, the volitional impairment must be articulated within criminal law's folk psychological framework; otherwise, if framed mechanistically, the impairment conflates causation with excuse.[91] The practical concern is how we would measure them. As Westen argues, "no choice" is just metaphorical for that for which we lack a scientific explanation.[92] Notably, some theorists argue that the volitional prong can be collapsed into the rationality prong.[93]

One critique of at least some forms of choice theory is that it is overinclusive, as it would arguably excuse the negligent who do not make choices.[94] There are two general responses to this objection. First, Michael Moore has argued that there is a different culpability at work for negligence—the culpability of unexercised capacity. A prerequisite to negligence liability would then be having the rational capacity to understand that one's conduct could cause harm.[95] Second, one might embrace this implication, and then argue that negligence should not be a basis for criminal liability.[96] Of course, the latter path is the more radical, and requires the theorist to depart significantly from the extant criminal law.

2 Character Theories

Character theorists argue that an individual cannot be punished for a crime if it does not reflect the defendant's underlying character, motivation, or agency.[97] In other words, people should not be punished for those actions that are "out of character." Underlying this theory is the view that one is ultimately responsible for one's character, and actions are just proxies for character.

As summarized by Peter Westen, the character theories would excuse a defendant if:

(1) he made a reasonable and good-faith mistake that is consistent with his being of good character, (2) he was compelled by pressures over which he had no control (other that [*sic*] the pressures of settled character), (3) he was too young to have developed a settled character, (4) he acted from insanity rather than any settled character on his part, or (5) his conduct was out of character for him.[98]

Hence, like choice theorists, character theorists seek to theorize a broad range of reasons why a defendant is not criminally blameworthy.

There are significant problems with character theories. First, it seems that even if an action is "out of character," that should not be sufficient to exculpate the defendant.[99] Second, character theorists make the commission of a criminal act merely evidentiary, as opposed to providing the primary basis for responsibility. Not only does this shift radically refocus the criminal law but also this view of the relationship of character and action is utterly at odds with evidence law, which prohibits the use of character evidence to show that an action was or was not in conformity with the actor's character.[100] Third, character theorists seem to get the relationship between character and action exactly backward—action is prior to, and constitutive of, character.[101] To put the matter bluntly, one act of theft *makes* you a thief.

Finally, character theories are not immune from the charge that they fail to explain negligence liability. As Michael Moore points out, negligence liability requires only an isolated act, and a negligent act may be due to clumsiness or stupidity rather than a vicious character.[102] Hence, even character theorists cannot square their theories of excuse with the current law of negligence.[103]

Still, there seems to be some grain of truth to character theories. An agent is not simply a choosing machine. As Antony Duff says, "[a] 'character' conception expresses a significant truth about *who* can be held criminally liable: that only moral agents, whose actions exhibit the structures of thought, attitude, and motivation that constitute 'character,' should be held liable."[104] This sort of argument aligns itself with a theory of exemptions. That is, moral agency is a prerequisite to moral responsibility.

In light of critiques of character theories, two theorists have proposed a different version of character theory, one that might best be described as a "personal identity" claim.[105] G. R. Sullivan and Victor Tadros both contend that the defendant is entitled to an excuse because his "unity of the self" was "destabilized." As Tadros puts it, "[w]here the agent has undergone a fundamental shift in character for which he is not responsible, the actions performed as a consequence of that shift do not reflect on that agent *qua* agent in the appropriate way." Thus, they argue that, in one infamous case, an involuntarily intoxicated (drugged) pedophile was entitled to an excuse, despite testimony that he did not lack substantial capacity to control his conduct.

There are a couple of concerns with this approach. First, as an empirical matter, "destabilized" seems metaphorical. The agent will perceive herself as experiencing the situation. A person who acts at the point of a gun experiences the situation as something happening to *her*. In some circumstances, we may realign our priorities, and feel the pull of some otherwise suppressed desires, but we do not suffer a destabilization of our *selves* in a deep sense.

In addition, such stressful situations rarely change an individual's beliefs or desires as much as they reveal preexisting features of his character. To illustrate, consider Albert, who walks in on his wife committing adultery. Now, when Albert gets angry and kills his wife, are we to say that he *changed* his identity? Rather, it seems that Albert reacts out of preexisting feelings that he has for his wife and preexisting tendencies to react in a violent way. As Jeremy Horder says, "D's reaction is likely to stem from the influence of a perfectly ordinary and reasonable, more or less 'settled,' aspect of D's character, namely his tendency to feel wounded or indignant at what was perceived to be a serious attack on his or her self-image and self-esteem, a feeling that then generated what is in such instances an all-too-common desire, the desire to 'get even' by some means or another."[106] Ultimately, when Albert is tried for killing his wife, he is the same person who killed his wife; moreover, his action, in the face of his wife's adultery, revealed what Albert's values were before, during, and after the act of killing.

Finally, this view makes personal identity far too fragile. Even if involuntary intoxication creates a reordering of one's desires, or gives rise to some new beliefs or desires, our daily encounters create the same pressures. Are we all "destabilized" by every odd encounter? Indeed, just as we may be destabilized by an intoxicant, we can then seemingly be destabilized by viewing beautiful ruby earrings, but the fact that the latter creates an intense desire does not undermine one's responsibility for theft.[107] It cannot be that every pressure on our character challenges who we are. And indeed, by the time these character theorists specify the types of situations in which we normatively judge the challenge as *unfairly* destabilizing character, it is likely that the theory collapses into the "hard choice" account offered by choice theorists.

3 *Reasons and Excuses*

Just as one theory of justification analyzes the reasons for which the actor violates the prohibitory norm, so do some theories of excuse. These theorists essentially view the act of offering an excuse as one of *accepting responsibility* for the act but *denying liability* for it.[108] Excuses look to the actor's reasons that thereby reveal him not to be blameworthy for the act. Notably, various theorists offer quite disparate views of how these reasons are said undermine blameworthiness. Three leading views are set forth below.

John Gardner's view is that the gist of excuses is *living up to societal expectations*.[109] This view departs from other character theories by claiming that a defendant is not excused for acting out of character but precisely because she meets our normative expectations of her. For example, one is not entitled to an excuse for duress if one does not act with the proper reasonable firmness. Gardner also claims that this normative expectation may vary for differing roles.

Jeremy Horder also seeks to analyze excuses in terms of reasons. Like Gardner, Horder distinguishes excuses in terms of reasons from denials of responsibility, which fall within the category of exemptions, although Horder does make room for a partial excuse of diminished capacity. Although Horder's rather complicated views cannot be easily summarized here, Horder's general view is that excuses place the defendant's act in a more favorable light, when the "morally active" reasons for his conduct are scrutinized.[110] Notably, unlike most excuse theories, Horder claims that the actor's reasons reflect on the *act*, not simply the *actor*.

A third theorist, Claire Finkelstein, does not expect reasons-based theories to fully exhaust our theory of excuse, but she offers one conceptual category—that of rational excuses.[111] Finkelstein argues that both self-defense and duress are rational excuses. She claims that they are not justification because the actor acts for personal reasons and not for the societal good. The "adaptive disposition" on which the actor acts enhances her welfare. Society excuses these actors because these dispositions are ones that it is beneficial for societal members to possess.

Importantly, these views leave many defenses to the realm of exemptions, offering theories only of the rationally intelligible.[112] Moreover, the remaining excuses come very close to being personal justifications, as they serve as individualized rules of conduct. Beyond these category concerns, one may question the explanatory force of Gardner's view, as it seems hard to say that when one seeks an excuse one is saying that one *has* lived up to expectations, rather than hoping for an exception from those expectations.[113] One final and critical question for the reasons theorist is how to draw the boundary between exemptions (denials of responsibility) and excuses (denials of liability). Because capacity is a continuum concept but these theorists see a stark contrast between denying responsibility and offering rationally intelligible reasons, they must offer an account of what to do with a battered woman who claims that her battered woman syndrome *slightly* modifies what can be reasonably expected of her in a coercive (duress-type) situation.[114]

D Implementation Questions

Because excuses (arguably) fall within retributive theory, there are inevitable conflicts about the recognition of particular excuses. That is, consequentialists may justly fear that, for example, recognizing an "ignorance of the law" excuse will lead to false claims, clog the courts, and undermine citizens' knowledge of the law. Indeed, Jeremy Horder argues that while the necessary conditions negate blameworthiness, there are further "sufficient" conditions, which require an assessment of the law's "strategic" or "common good" concerns.[115] On the other hand, if criminal law seeks to punish only the blameworthy and deserving, then the defendant must be entitled to raise this excuse. Notably, this sort of conflict between goals may partially justify shifting the burden of proof for excuses, but not for justifications, although this burden shifting is constitutionally permissible for all defenses.

IV Revisiting the Relationships between Justification and Excuse, Law and Morality, and Individual Defenses

As this discussion hopefully reveals, the relationship between justification and excuse, law and morality, and the conceptual structure of individual defenses leads to a complex interplay of moving parts. To briefly summarize this complexity, let us focus on the defense of duress.

Should duress be viewed as a justification or an excuse? To an objectivist who endorses a consequentialist theory of justifications, the answer is that duress is an excuse, as the defendant commits the greater evil, but does so under significant pressure. On the other hand, one might seek to justify duress in two ways. First, one might argue that complying with the standard of the person of reasonable firmness is complying with law's conduct rule. Second, one might argue that duress should at least be seen as a personal justification. It is a conduct rule that allows a mother to favor her own child; it is not simply a rule that says that an actor is less blameworthy. Either way, a subjective theory of justification has room for duress.

Of course, there are separate theories for duress if one is inclined to characterize it as an excuse. Choice theorists might argue that this is "too hard" a choice for a defendant to be deemed blameworthy. Character theorists will claim that this situation destabilizes the mother's self, such that her actions do not reflect on her settled character—the mother is not a bad person. And those who assess her reasons will find that she acted for reasons that excuse her; indeed, Gardner will argue that she *lived up* to societal expectations, and Horder will claim that her reasons place her act in a more favorable light.

Consider now how these questions about duress put pressure back on the act/actor distinction and on the rule of conduct/rule of adjudication distinction. If a mother commits the greater evil to save her children, one might think that this is the greater evil, and a wrongful act. Yet it does not seem sufficient to simply say that the mother is less blameworthy. Rather, it seems that under some description, "saving one's child" is a commendable *act*. Moreover, as mentioned previously, when a mother questions the amount of resolve she should have—*reasonable* firmness, not extraordinary or superhuman—the law in a sense *guides* her conduct. She does indeed live up to societal expectations.

Let us take one final round and explore duress through the prism of criminal rule implementation. Recall Claire Finkelstein's argument that duress is a rational excuse. Once again, we see the agent-relative but action-guiding nature of these defenses. But Finkelstein's next move introduces an additional wrinkle. She argues that the disposition to protect one's child in the case of duress, for instance, is adaptive, and "maximizes society's overall welfare."[116] Notice, though, that this move shifts duress from an excuse to a justification, as it is in society's best interest to encourage this adaptive response. Thus, though the individual case appears to present the greater evil, the overall situation is one of justification.[117] This argument thus presents the reverse of cases in which, although an individual act (say, escaping from prison to avoid being raped) appears justified, because the defense will be abused, miscalculated, or misunderstood, the consequentialist calculus comes out negative and/or a rational legislature will enact a rule barring the behavior. Hence, how the rule will affect the conduct of later actors can both make a seemingly justified act excused and make a seemingly excused act justified. In sum, the relationship individual defenses, conceptions of justification and excuse, and their implementation in the real world is a complex one.

I wish to thank the participants in the roundtable on this handbook for the fruitful discussion of this manuscript, and especially Michael Moore for organizing the roundtable and Mitch Berman for serving as my commentator.

I would also like to thank Marcia Baron, Steve Garvey, Doug Husak, and Dennis Patterson for their comments on the manuscript.

NOTES

1. J.L. Austin, "A Plea for Excuses," *Proceedings of the Aristotelian Society* 57 (1956–57): 1–30. Reprinted in *The Philosophy of Action*, Allan R. White, ed. (Oxford: Oxford University Press, 1968), pp. 19–20.

2. Joshua Dressler, *Understanding Criminal Law*, 4th ed. (Matthew Bender, 2006), § 17.05.

3. Stephen J. Morse, "Excusing and the New Excuse Defenses: A Legal and Conceptual Review," *Crime & Justice* 23 (Nov. 1998): 329–406, p. 334.

4. There are two ways to solve the puzzle. One way is to deny that the reasonable person can be modified with a rationality impairment (the view that the irrational reasonable person is simply a contradiction in terms). A second method is to deny more broadly that any sort of misperception is justified (the view that all reasonable mistakes are excuses).

5. As noted by Morse, "Excusing and the New Excuse Defenses," p. 382.

6. I would do away with the reasonable person standard in self-defense altogether, but that argument is beyond the scope of this chapter. *See* Kimberly Kessler Ferzan, "Justifying Self-Defense," *Law and Philosophy* 24 (2005): 711–749.

7. Paul H. Robinson, *Structure and Function in Criminal Law* (Oxford: Clarendon Press, 1997), pp. 68–70. For the argument that nonexculpatory defenses are not "defenses" but claims that trials are barred, see R.A. Duff, *Answering for Crime* (Oxford: Hart, 2007), ch. 8.

8. One open question is whether justifications and excuses fully exhaust the terrain of defenses based on desert. Of course, this depends on how one defines justification and excuse.

9. Douglas N. Husak, "Justifications and the Criminal Liability of Accessories," *Journal of Criminal Law & Criminology* 80 (1989): 491–520, p. 495.

10. Ibid., p. 499.

11. Ibid., p. 496; Michael Moore, *Placing Blame: A General Theory of the Criminal Law* (Oxford: Clarendon Press 1997), pp. 482–483. But see Marcia Baron, "Justifications and Excuses," *Ohio State Journal of Criminal Law* 2 (2005): 387–406, p. 393.

12. Although this is the typical formulation—that justifications universalize whereas excuses are personal—this formulation is not exactly apt. Perhaps it would be better to say that a justification allows anyone to commit the act whereas an excuse only excuses the actor's commission of the *act*. After all, the conditions relevant for an excuse are equally applicable to all; it is simply that the excuse does not render anyone other than the actor "not punishable" for committing that action. (Squeezing someone's neck while believing one is making lemonade does not render the neck squeezing permissible for other individuals; it just renders the one insane actor not punishable for that action. But the condition of being insane *universally* excuses.) I thank Doug Husak for urging me to clarify this point.

13. Douglas N. Husak, "The Costs to Criminal Theory of Supposing That Intentions Are Irrelevant to Permissibility," *Criminal Law and Philosophy* 3 (2009): 51–70.

14. Robinson, *Structure and Function*, p. 138; Mitchell N. Berman, "Justification and Excuse, Law and Morality," *Duke Law Journal* 53 (2003): 1–77, p. 33.

15. R.A. Duff, "Rule-Violations and Wrongdoings," in *Criminal Law Theory: Doctrines of the General Part*, Stephen Shute & A.P. Simester, eds. (Oxford: Oxford University Press, 2002), 47–74.

16. *See* Douglas Husak, "On the Supposed Priority of Justification to Excuse," *Law and Philosophy* 24 (2005): 557–594; Marcia Baron, "Is Justification (Somehow) Prior to Excuse? A Reply to Douglas Husak," *Law and Philosophy* 24 (2005): 595–609.

17. *See* George P. Fletcher, "The Right and the Reasonable," *Harvard Law Review* 48 (1985): 949–982, p. 960.

18. Cf. John Gardner, "Justifications and Reasons," in *Harm and Culpability*, A.P. Simester & A.T.H. Smith, eds. (Oxford: Clarendon Press, 1996): 103–129 (employing guiding and explanatory reasons) with Robinson, *Structure and Function*, p. 101 (deeds versus reasons).

19. Paul H. Robinson, "The Bomb Thief and the Theory of Justification Defenses," *Criminal Law Forum* 8 (1997): 387–409.

20. Robinson, *Structure and Function*, p. 101; Heidi M. Hurd, "Justification and Excuse, Wrongdoing and Culpability," *Notre Dame Law Review* 74 (1999): 1551–1573, p. 1571.

21. *See* George P. Fletcher, "Should Intolerable Prison Conditions Generate a Justification or an Excuse for Escape?" *UCLA Law Review* 26 (1979): 1355–1369, p. 1358.

22. *See generally* Heidi M. Hurd, *Moral Combat* (Cambridge: Cambridge University Press, 1999). On the other hand, if justifications include conduct that is not right, but is nevertheless permissible, then conflicts are possible. *See* Douglas N. Husak, "Conflicts of Justifications," *Law and Philosophy* 18 (1999): 41–68.

23. B. Sharon Byrd, "Wrongdoing and Attribution: Implications beyond the Justification-Excuse Distinction," *Wayne Law Review* 33 (1987): 1289–1342, p. 1292 ("the decisive characteristic distinguishing justifications from excuses is the *function* rather than the content of these norms").

24. Hurd, *Moral Combat*, p. 8.

25. Mitchell N. Berman, "Lesser Evils and Justification: A Less Close Look," *Law and Philosophy* 24 (2005): 681–709, p. 692.

26. *See* Hurd, "Justification and Excuse," pp. 1558–59.

27. Ibid., pp. 1563–1564.

28. Byrd, "Wrongdoing and Attribution," p. 1311; Hurd, "Justification and Excuse," pp. 1566–1567; Robinson, "Bomb Thief," p. 398.

29. Of course for those theorists (like myself) who do not believe that results matter, the same result is reached in either event.

30. Husak, "Accessories," p. 506 (medieval doctor using best medical evidence of the times); Victor Tadros, *Criminal Responsibility* (Oxford: Oxford University Press, 2005), pp. 286–98.

31. Paul H. Robinson, "Prohibited Risks and Culpable Disregard or Inattentiveness: Challenge and Confusion in the Formulation of Risk-Creation Offenses," *Theoretical Inquiries in Law* 4 (2002): 367–396, p. 377.

32. Ibid., p. 372 ("modern American codes typically have no provision that describes, even in such general terms, the kinds of risks that are prohibited or even the factors that are relevant to defining a prohibited risk").

33. Ibid., p. 377.

34. Ibid., pp. 385–388.

35. This problem is pervasive for Robinson. He also introduces epistemic elements into self-defense. *See* Ferzan, "Justifying Self-Defense." He is also not alone in encountering this difficulty. For a critique of Heidi Hurd's position, see ibid.

36. Kent Greenawalt, "The Perplexing Borders of Justification and Excuse," *Columbia Law Review* 84 (1984): 1897–1927, p. 1903.

37. Ibid., pp. 1903–1907; Joshua Dressler, "New Thoughts about the Concept of Justification in the Criminal Law: A Critique of Fletcher's Thinking and Rethinking," *UCLA Law Review* 32 (1984): 61–99.

38. For one significant attempt to understand permissibility beyond the consequentalist view of lesser-evils, see Husak, "Accessories."

39. *See* Larry Alexander & Kimberly Kessler Ferzan, with Stephen J. Morse, *Crime and Culpability: A Theory of Criminal Law* (Cambridge: Cambridge University Press, 2009), ch. 4.

40. 11 NY 2d 274 (1962); Greenawalt, "Perplexing Borders," pp. 1919–1920.

41. This is putting aside the question of whether the thief stole the "property of another."

42. Alexander & Ferzan with Morse, *Crime and Culpability*, chs. 2 & 4; Anthony M. Dillof, "Unraveling Unknowing Justification," *Notre Dame Law Review* 77 (2002): 1547–1600. For a nuanced argument that justification must turn on the actor's reasons and not his beliefs, see Duff, *Answering*, pp. 277–284.

43. *See* Hurd, "Justification and Excuse," pp. 1563–1564.

44. Kent Greenawalt, "Justifications, Excuses, and a Model Penal Code for Democratic Societies," *Criminal Justice Ethics* 17 (1998): 14–28, p. 22.

45. Ibid.

46. Ibid.

47. Cf. John Gardner, "The Gist of Excuses," *Buffalo Criminal Law Review* 1 (1998): 575–598.

48. H.L.A. Hart, *Punishment and Responsibility: Essays in Philosophy of Law* (New York: Oxford University Press, 1968; reprint, 1995), p. 14 ("the most prominent of these excusing conditions are those forms of lack of knowledge which make action unintentional").

49. Peter Westen, "Individualizing the Reasonable Person in Criminal Law," *Criminal Law and Philosophy* 2 (2008): 137–162. For a critical view of the use of reasonableness in American criminal law, see Fletcher, "Right and Reasonable."

50. Alexander & Ferzan with Morse, *Crime and Culpability*, ch. 3.

51. Westen, "Individualizing."

52. *See* George P. Fletcher, "The Nature of Justification," in *Action and Value in Criminal Law*, Stephen Shute et al., eds. (Oxford: Oxford University Press, 1993): 175–186.

53. Ibid.

54. Gardner, "Justifications and Reasons," p. 107.

55. For Gardner this structure is not necessary. One could have broader offenses. However, he does believe that this dual requirement is constitutive of justifications when our law is structured as it is.

56. For another dual theory, see Duff, *Answering*, pp. 277–284.

57. Fletcher, "Right and Reasonable," p. 954 ("No one is entitled to defend against a justified act, and third parties are permitted, indeed encouraged, to assist the justified actor.").

58. For a fuller discussion of this problem with Fletcher's view, see Kimberly Kessler Ferzan, "Holistic Culpability," *Cardozo Law Review* 28 (2007): 2523–2543. For a critique of Gardner, see Tadros, *Criminal Responsibility*, p. 286.

59. Nevertheless, whether a substantive or merely formal distinction, the categorization of offense versus defense does have practical implications. The state may constitutionally require the defendant to prove a defense, but not an offense element. And, the state is bound by the principle of legality—that is, giving fair notice—in a way that leads to offenses being interpreted narrowly, but the same restriction does not apply to defenses, which can be extended or even created judicially. *See generally* George P. Fletcher, *Rethinking Criminal Law* (Boston: Little, Brown, 1978), pp. 572–573.

60. For Gardner's attempt to resolve the problem by arguing that risk-creation offenses are "fault-anticipating wrongs" that are parasitic on some underlying simpler norms, see John Gardner, *Offences and Defences: Selected Essays in the Philosophy of Criminal Law* (Oxford: Oxford University Press 2007): 151–153, 258–259.

61. Greenawalt, "Perplexing Borders," p. 1906.

62. Berman, "Justification and Excuse," p. 11; Larry Alexander, "Lesser Evils: A Closer Look at the Paradigmatic Justification," *Law and Philosophy* 24 (2005): 611–643.

63. Greenawalt, "Perplexing Borders," pp. 1901–1902.

64. Robinson, *Structure and Function*, pp. 204–207.

65. *See* Alexander & Ferzan with Morse, *Crime and Culpability*, ch. 8.

66. Kimberly Kessler Ferzan, "Defending Imminence: From Battered Women to Iraq," *Arizona Law Review* 46 (2004): 213–262.

67. Kimberly Kessler Ferzan, "Self-defense and the State," *Ohio State Journal of Criminal Law* 5 (2008): 449–478.

68. Berman, "Justification and Excuse."

69. E.g., Fiona Leverick, *Killing in Self-Defence* (Oxford: Oxford University Press, 2006); Suzanne Uniacke, *Permissible Killing: The Self-Defence Justification of Homicide* (Cambridge: Cambridge University Press 1994).

70. Peter Westen and James Mangiafico, "The Criminal Defense of Duress: A Justification, Not an Excuse—And Why It Matters," *Buffalo Criminal Law Review* 6 (2003): 833–950.

71. Tadros, *Criminal Responsibility*, p. 117.

72. Berman, "Lesser Evils," p. 694; Ferzan, "Self-Defense and the State"; Sanford H. Kadish, "Respect for Life and Regard for Rights in Criminal Law," *California Law Review* 64 (1976): 871–901.

73. For the problems created with contemporaneous attacks, see Russell L. Christopher, "Unknowing Justification and the Logical Necessity of the Dadson Principle in Self-Defence," *Oxford Journal of Legal Studies* 15 (1995): 229–251.

74. Larry Alexander, "Unknowingly Justified Actors and the Attempt/Success Distinction," *Tulsa Law Review* 39 (2004): 851–859; Ferzan, "Justifying Self-Defense."

75. *See* Greenawalt, "Perplexing Borders."

76. Baron, "Justifications and Excuses," p. 404; Tadros, *Criminal Responsibility*, p. 119.

77. Duff, *Answering*, pp. 271–77.

78. Hart, *Punishment and Responsibility*, p. 19.

79. Oliver Wendell Holmes, Jr., *The Common Law* (Boston: Little, Brown, 1923), ch. 1.

80. *See* ibid., pp. 38–43.

81. Duff, *Answering*, p. 287.

82. *See, e.g.*, Peter Arenella, "Convicting the Morally Blameless: Reassessing the Relationship between Legal and Moral Accountability," *UCLA Law Review* 39 (1992): 1511–1622; Jeffrie G. Murphy, "Moral Death: A Kantian Essay on Psychopathy," *Ethics* 82 (1972): 284–298.

83. Paul Litton, "Responsibility Status of the Psychopath: On Moral Reasoning and Rational Self-Governance," *Rutgers Law Journal* 39 (2008): 349–392.

84. Tadros, *Criminal Responsibility*, p. 124.

85. Robinson, *Structure and Function*, p. 138; Berman, "Justification and Excuse," p. 33; George P. Fletcher, "Rights and Excuses," *Criminal Justice Ethics* 3(2) (1984): 17–27.

86. Hart, *Punishment and Responsibility*, p. 152; Sanford H. Kadish, *Blame and Punishment: Essays in the Criminal Law* (New York: MacMillan, 1987), pp. 81–106; Moore, *Placing Blame*, pp. 549–562; Morse, "Excusing and the New Excuse Defenses," pp. 337–342.

87. Moore, *Placing Blame*, ch. 12; Morse, "Excusing and the New Excuse Defenses," pp. 349–353. Compare Michael Corrado, "Notes on the Structure of a Theory of Excuses," *Journal of Criminal Law and Criminology* 82 (1992): 465–497.

88. Stephen J. Morse, "Diminished Rationality, Diminished Responsibility," *Ohio State Journal of Criminal Law* 1 (2003): 289–308.

89. Peter Westen, "An Attitudinal Theory of Excuse," *Law and Philosophy* 25 (2006): 289–375.

90. Cf. Ferzan, "Holistic Culpability."

91. *See* Stephen J. Morse, "Against Control Tests for Criminal Responsibility," and the comments thereon in *Criminal Law Conversations*, Paul H. Robinson, Stephen Garvey, and Kimberly Kessler Ferzan, eds. (Oxford University Press, 2009).

92. Westen, "Attitudinal Theory," p. 338.

93. Morse, "Against Control Tests"; Stephen J. Morse, "Culpability and Control," *University of Pennsylvania Law Review* 142 (1994): 1587–1660.

94. Jeremy Horder, "Criminal Culpability: The Possibility of a General Theory," *Law and Philosophy* 12 (1993): 193–215; Westen, "Attitudinal Theory," p. 336.

95. Moore, *Placing Blame*, pp. 417–418.

96. Alexander and Ferzan with Morse, *Crime and Culpability*, ch. 3.

97. *See generally* Richard R. Brandt, *Morality, Utilitarianism, and Rights* (Cambridge: Cambridge University Press 1992), pp. 196–288; Fletcher, *Rethinking*, pp. 799–802; Moore, *Placing Blame*, pp. 548, 562–574 (critique).

98. Westen, "Attitudinal Theory, p. 332.

99. Jeremy Horder, *Excusing Crime* (Oxford: Oxford University Press, 2004), p. 118; Stephen J. Morse, "Reason, Results, and Criminal Responsibility," *University of Illinois Law Review* 2004 (2004): 363–444.

100. Federal Rule of Evidence 404(a); Benjamin B. Sendor, "The Relevance of Conduct and Character to Guilt and Punishment," *Notre Dame Journal of Law, Ethics & Public Policy* 10 (1996): 99–136.

101. Morse, "Reasons, Results"; R.A. Duff, *Criminal Attempts* (Oxford: Oxford University Press 1997), p. 188.

102. Moore, *Placing Blame*, pp. 590–591.

103. For a discussion of some theorists' attempts to narrow the reach of negligence so as to only capture those acts that manifest indifference, see Alexander and Ferzan with Morse, *Crime and Culpability*, ch. 3.

104. Duff, *Attempts*, p. 191.

105. G.R. Sullivan, "Making Excuses," in *Harm and Culpability*, A.P. Simester and A.T.H. Smith, eds. (Oxford: Oxford University Press, 1996), 131–152; Tadros, *Criminal Responsibility*,§ 11.2; *see also Criminal Law: Theory and Doctrine* A. P. Simester and G. R. Sullivan, eds. (Oxford: Hart, 2000), pp. 646–47.

106. Horder, *Excusing Crime*, p. 123.

107. Ibid., p. 120.

108. Duff, *Answering*, pp. 19–23.

109. Gardner, "Gist of Excuses."

110. Horder, *Excusing Crime*.

111. Claire Finkelstein, "Excuses and Dispositions in Criminal Law," *Buffalo Criminal Law Review* 6 (2002): 317–359.

112. Westen, "Attitudinal Theory," p. 349.

113. Horder, *Excusing Crime*, pp. 116–117.

114. Compare Horder, *Excusing Crime*, ch. 4, with Gardner, *Offences and Defences*, chs. 8 and 9, and with Duff, *Answering*, pp. 290–291.

115. Horder, *Excusing Crime*, pp. 15–20.

116. Finkelstein, "Excuses and Dispositions," p. 357 n. 50.

117. Westen, "Attitudinal Theory," p. 353.

CHAPTER 11

DURESS

JOSHUA DRESSLER

SOCIETY has conflicting feelings about persons who commit crimes under duress.[1] People are likely to view them as both victims and villains. They feel compassion for the coerced actor (imagine a mother who is told that her beloved child will be killed unless she does as she is ordered) and yet also, perhaps, some contempt for her decision to accede to the threat by harming an innocent person (imagine that she is ordered to maim another parent's little child). And, even though it may be true, as Hyman Gross has observed, that the exculpatory claim "I couldn't help it," "appeals...urgently to our moral intuitions,"[2] there is something odd about the defense: The coerced actor is asking to be acquitted although she suffers from no mental disorder, knew precisely what she was doing, and chose to avoid harm to herself or others close to her by causing considerable harm to an innocent stranger.

Why would the law exculpate a person for such a self-interested act? This chapter, after a brief survey of existing duress law, considers this question, as well as other issues relating to the outer edges of duress law.

1. LAW OF DURESS

1.1 Traditional Law

The defense of duress has been described as being of "venerable antiquity,"[3] but this is misleading. Early scholars, and some more modern ones, have opposed recognition of the duress defense or have favored such limited application of it (e.g., only for minor offenses) as to render it nearly useless as an exculpatory claim. Nonetheless, courts and now legislatures do recognize the defense, although it is rarely invoked. More than a century ago, James Fitzjames Stephen wrote that "hardly any branch of the law…is more meager or less satisfactory"[4] than the doctrine of duress. This statement is only slightly less true today. Although the defense is often defined with imprecision, its general parameters can be summarized.

The traditional duress defense is exceptionally narrow. Subject to clarification below, the defense in the United States and in England may be described as follows: A person who is not at fault for placing himself in the coercive situation will be exculpated if he commits an offense as a result of a coercer's unlawful threat to imminently kill or grievously injure him or a family member. In the paradigmatic case, the coercer threatens to kill or grievously injure the defendant or the relevant third person unless the victim commits a particular crime. This defense is unavailable in murder prosecutions.[5]

Innocence of Defendant.

A person may not successfully plead duress if he is responsible for his coercive predicament. The fault factor may be evaluated in various ways. The law may simply state that the defendant must not have been "at fault," or it may specify that the defense is unavailable if the actor's fault is of a specified level (e.g., negligence or recklessness), or the law may be more specific, as is a New Zealand statute that provides that the defense is unavailable to "a party to any association or conspiracy whereby he is subject to compulsion."[6]

Requirement of a Threat, as Distinguished from an Offer.

Threats coerce, but offers, it is said, do not. A person threatens another if, with the intention of changing another person's behavior, she proposes to render the other person (or a third party) worse off relative to some baseline. ("Unless you rob the bank, I will gouge your eyes out.") Ordinarily the baseline will be the conditions that existed immediately preceding the proposal along with the normal course of events that could be expected to follow but for the intervention of the proposal. In contrast, an offer will make the other person better off relative to the identical baseline. ("If you rob the bank, I will give you half of the proceeds.")[7] A person, of course, may issue both a threat and offer. ("Unless you rob the bank, I will gouge your eyes out; but if you do as I say, I will give you half of the proceeds.") As a matter of criminal law doctrine, the principle that offers do not coerce is unexceptionable, although the urge to act in response to an offer may be stronger than the urge to avoid threatened harm. What matters is that threats limit a person's freedom while offers expand it. There is more to be said on this point, but in the typical coercive situation the assumption is that one who commits a crime as a result of an extreme threat typically acts "out of character" due to fear; people who commit crimes as a result of a temptation (offer) are thought to be acting "in character" as the result of greed or some other vice.

Nature of the Threat.

Not all threats coerce. First, only unlawful threats have legally exculpatory effect. Threats to impose lawful injury do not threaten legitimate interests of the "coerced" person. Occasionally scholars will suggest that a lawful threat can exculpate,[8] but they misuse the term "lawful" to make such a point. For example, assume A, an insane person, threatens to kill B unless B commits a robbery. A's mental condition does not render her threat any less unlawful. For purposes of the criminal law, a threat is unlawful if it is wrongful, even if the person issuing the wrongful threat can avoid legal responsibility for it, as here by pleading legal insanity.

The "unlawful threat" component of the defense leads by implication to a second, controversial feature of traditional duress law: The threat must flow from a human agency rather than a force of nature. Danger arising from a tornado, flood, or starvation, for example, may cause a person to commit a crime, but the threat of harm from such a condition—if "threat" is even the proper word—is not an "unlawful" one, as the latter term presupposes a human actor capable of wrongful thoughts and conduct.

Third, the threatened harm must be imminent. The "imminency" requirement—sometimes phrased in terms of whether the threat can be immediately carried out, or is "present, imminent and impending"[9]—is often treated as a surrogate for a related concern: that the threatened harm is genuine or, at least, is one that would cause a person to have a well-grounded (reasonable) fear that it will be carried out. The imminency requirement also serves two other purposes: it enhances the likelihood that the fear caused by the threat is operating on the mind of the actor at the time of the criminal conduct, thereby satisfying the requirement of a causal connection between the threat and the criminal act; it also serves as a proxy for the sometimes separately stated requirement that, to exculpate, there must be no reasonable opportunity to escape from the threatened harm except by compliance.

Fourth, the traditional rule is that unlawful threats to cause nonphysical harm, for example, economic or reputational injury, and unlawful threats of physical harm to property do not qualify. The only threat of physical harm that legally coerces is what is characterized as a "deadly threat" to another person. Sometimes the defense is limited to "do-as-I-say-or-I-will-kill-you" threats, but it is more often expanded to include unlawful threats to cause grievous bodily (life-threatening) harm, which falls within the broad definition of "deadly force" used by many courts and statutes.[10]

The "No Murder" Limitation.

It is frequently stated that the duress defense is unavailable in murder prosecutions, although some court opinions that have so asserted also found other reasons to deny the defense (e.g., insufficient evidence of an imminent threat). As late as the 1980s in the United States it was claimed that "no case has been found in which the defendant was held entitled to a duress charge in a murder case."[11] In

1975, the English House of Lords held that a coerced accomplice to a murder could claim the defense, but the same tribunal overruled itself twelve years later.[12]

The no-defense-to-murder rule is subject to exceptions or, at least, technicalities. In a U.S. jurisdiction in which murder is divided into degrees, a coerced murder may constitute second-degree, rather than first-degree, murder on the ground that the killing, although intentional and perhaps even premeditated, lacked the calm deliberation that is frequently required for first-degree murder. And some courts have suggested that because duress can exculpate a person for felonies other than murder, the effect is that the duress plea can exculpate a person prosecuted for felony-murder.[13]

1.2 Modern Reform

Perhaps the most significant reform proposal regarding duress comes from the influential drafters of the Model Penal Code.[14] The Model Penal Code provides:

> It is an affirmative defense that the actor engaged in the conduct charged to constitute an offense because he was coerced to do so by the use of, or a threat to use, unlawful force against his person or the person of another, that a person of reasonable firmness would be unable to resist.[15]

The defense is unavailable if the actor "recklessly placed himself in a situation in which it was probable that he would be subjected to duress." As with traditional duress doctrine, the defense does not apply to nonhuman coercive conditions.

The Model Penal Code duress defense differs from traditional law in significant regards. First, it is not limited to criminal conduct motivated by threats, but also applies to situations in which the defendant acts because of prior use of unlawful force by the coercer. Second, in regard to threats, there is no imminency requirement.

Third, the defense applies to threats (or force) directed at any person, and not simply the defendant or a family member.

Fourth, the defense applies broadly to *any* physical force or threat of force—not simply deadly force—that "a person of reasonable firmness in his situation would have been unable to resist." If accepted literally, however, the defense only applies if the "person of reasonable firmness" would be rendered completely devoid of self-control ("*unable* to resist") by the unlawful actor's force or threat of force.

Fifth, the defense may be asserted in murder prosecutions. According to research in 2008, twelve American states by statute, and one state by case law, follow the Model Penal Code approach in this regard. Two other states by case law recognize a partial defense (permitting duress to reduce the offense from murder to manslaughter). Nonetheless, seventeen states by statute, and fourteen states by case law, continue to apply the no-defense rule.[16]

Finally, although it is not evident from the language of the defense, the drafters have indicated that the defense is broad enough to permit its use in the nonparadigmatic case in which "force or threats are employed to get the actor to perform one act; to avoid performing that act, [the defendant] performs a different, and criminal, act."[17] Thus, the defense potentially applies if a coercer demands that the defendant commit crime X, but the coerced person commits crime Y instead to avoid committing X.

2 EXCULPATORY THEORIES: INVOLUNTARY ACT AND MENS REA

There is considerable uncertainty as to the reason why coercion exculpates, when it does. Two explanations seek to show that a person who acts under duress lacks one of the essential elements of the crime for which he has been charged.

2.1 Actus Reus

One exculpatory explanation could be characterized as an actus reus claim. It may be argued that a person who acts under duress has not performed a voluntary act, which is a general requirement of the criminal law. This argument fails. First, one who is coerced to act does just that—acts—unlike a person whose body is moved by an external force, as when a person is shoved by X into Y, or when his arm is grabbed by X and used to commit an offense on Y. In the latter circumstances, the victim of the external force contributes nothing personally to the harm; a coerced individual, however, *does* act.

It is also incorrect to state that duress exculpates because the actor's conduct is physically involuntary in the sense that, although there is no *external* force involved, there is some *internal* malfunction, such as an epileptic seizure, that renders the defendant's conduct unchosen. The coerced actor's conduct is voluntary in the fundamental sense that he *chooses*—in the language of earlier centuries, "wills"—his physical actions. He chooses to commit the offense rather than accept the consequences of the coercer's threat. The coerced person's actions in committing an offense are controlled by his mind and not simply by his brain: that is, the coerced actor makes a conscious decision to accede to the threat, whereas a truly involuntary actor is the victim of nonconscious impulses from the brain directed to other parts of the body.

2.2 Mens Rea

Another prima facie exculpatory claim is that a coerced actor is not guilty of the offense he commits because he does not possess the culpable state of mind—mens rea—that is required in the definition of the offense charged. This argument is usually, but not always, false.

A coerced actor acts with a generally culpable state of mind. As stated in *Director of Public Prosecutions for Northern Ireland v. Lynch*,[18] "the decision of the threatened man whose constancy is overborne so that he yields to the threat, is a calculated decision to do what he knows to be wrong, and is therefore that of a man with…a 'guilty mind.'"

Today, however, the criminal law often uses the concept of mens rea in a more specific way to require proof that the defendant committed the harm prohibited by the offense with a specific mental state. Even in this situation, however, one who acts under duress usually possesses the requisite mens rea for conviction. The coerced person who kills or rapes a victim, smuggles contraband into a foreign country, or receives stolen property, ordinarily does so with the requisite mens rea: she intends to kill to avoid harm to herself; he intentionally has nonconsensual intercourse; she purposely hides contraband as she crosses a border in order to avoid detection; or he knowingly receives stolen property.

Some offenses as defined, however, require proof that the actor possessed a specific motive when he committed the actus reus of the offense, and this state of mind might be absent in coercive circumstances. For example, consider a mother whose child is kidnapped and informed by the malefactor, "I will kill your boy unless you steal the original Picasso from the local museum. I will release him as soon as you hand over the painting." The mother takes the painting, hands it to the kidnappers, takes her son back into her custody, immediately thereafter reports her actions to the police, and informs them where they can find the painting and kidnapper. If the mother were charged with larceny, defined as the trespassory (nonconsensual) taking and carrying away of the personal property of another with the purpose of permanently depriving the owner of the property, she ought to be acquitted for lack of mens rea: the coercive circumstances and her actions immediately following the return of her child unequivocally demonstrate that her conscious objective in taking the Picasso was not to *permanently* deprive the museum of its property but rather to save her son.[19] In this relatively rare situation, the defendant does not need to plead a justification or excuse defense but can avoid conviction by introducing evidence of duress to negate the government's required proof of an element of the offense.

3. Justification and Excuse

3.1 Preliminaries

Once one puts aside the exceedingly limited mens rea argument for exculpation of a coerced actor, the central descriptive and normative questions of this chapter are implicated: Why does, and should, the criminal law acquit an actor who, fully aware of his conduct, intentionally commits a wrongful act as a result of duress? Put differently: Is duress properly characterized as a justification defense, excuse defense, or some combination of the two? Second, in light of the answer(s) to the preceding question(s), are the narrow contours of traditional duress law appropriate and philosophically coherent, or should the defense be broadened?

To determine whether duress is a "justification" or "excuse" defense, one must settle on the meaning of these terms. Semantics matter. As has been nicely pointed out, an atheist can accept the truth of the sentence "God exists" if she understands "God" to mean "my wristwatch."[20] Unfortunately, the twentieth-century trend of courts was to pay little regard to the distinction between the concepts of justification and excuse and, consequently, to use the terms interchangeably, despite substantial philosophical attention to the subject in the last quarter of the twentieth century and since.[21]

3.2 "Justification"

According to one definition, conduct is "justifiable" if, but only if, it is proper, good, desirable, or morally right conduct. A justification defense, in this sense, is recognized when society ultimately approves of the actor's conduct (or, in utilitarian terms, seeks to encourage such conduct), even though the prima facie elements of the offense have been proven. Thus, the intentional taking of the life of another human being ordinarily is a crime (murder); however, if a law enforcement officer intentionally kills a bank robber who is threatening the life of a customer, this homicide is justifiable in the sense stated here: The officer's actions, motivated by public interest, are morally right; we characterize his conduct as right, proper, or societally desirable.

This conception of justification is too narrow. Consider a killing in self-defense of a deadly aggressor. Such self-defensive actions, unlike the officer's, are motivated by self-preservation rather than the public good. Moreover, what if the defendant could have avoided killing the aggressor by retreating from his home, even though the law may not require this? Or what if the aggressor who must be killed is a child dangerously firing a loaded gun? Many people might feel more comfortable describing the actor's genuine self-defensive conduct in one of these scenarios as "permissible, tolerable, not wrongful" conduct, rather than "right, proper, or desirable."

Although no consensus exists, the broader definition of "justification" is more commonly accepted.[22] That is, justified conduct is conduct that under ordinary circumstances is criminal, but that under the special circumstances encompassed by the defense is affirmatively desirable or, at the least, not wrongful. A working definition, therefore—the one that will be used in this chapter—is that justified conduct is conduct that, at best, is morally right and socially desirable, but that, at a minimum, is tolerable, nonwrongful behavior.

What converts a crime, for example murder, into tolerable, nonwrongful, or even morally or socially desirable conduct? In Blackstone's time, the concept of justification largely took on a public-interest cast, that is, the actor needed to be motivated by more than self-interest to claim justifiable homicide. Today, other moral theories of justification abound, among the most significant being (1) moral forfeiture, (2) moral rights, and (3) lesser harm.

According to the moral forfeiture theory, a person may forfeit her moral and legal interest in her bodily integrity or property by wrongfully threatening the interests of an innocent person. Consider self-defense. A person of sound mind and capacity who wrongfully threatens the life of another can be said to forfeit her right to life; thus, her death does not constitute legally recognized harm. In these circumstances, it is more accurate to say that the justified actor's conduct was not wrongful—no societal harm has occurred—than to assert that the defender's conduct necessarily was morally desirable or right.

A second account of justification is the moral rights principle. Rather than focus on the lost (forfeited) right of the wrongdoer, this principle focuses on the rights of the innocent person. Here, for example, self-defense can be justified on the ground that A has a right to protect her bodily integrity and autonomy from a wrongful attack by B. So understood, self-defensive actions are affirmatively proper.

The third and most common way to justify conduct is to show that the actor's conduct resulted in a lesser harm or evil than if she had not so acted. To turn again to self-defense, when A is threatened by imminent wrongful aggression by B, A's choices are stark—kill or be killed—so B's death is a lesser harm or evil than the alternative. One can reach that conclusion on the ground that the aggressor, but not the innocent person, forfeited her right to life; that the person attacked was asserting her moral right of autonomy but the aggressor was not; or that we want to deter aggression and that this is promoted by encouraging self-defense.

In considering whether the defense of duress is based on justification principles, the focus in this chapter will be on the latter—the choice-of-evils account of justification.

3.3 "Excuse"

According to J. L. Austin, in justification defenses the defendant accepts responsibility for his actions but denies that he has done anything wrong, whereas with excuses he admits that his conduct was wrong but does not accept responsibility, in full or in part, for it.[23] Alternatively, as George Fletcher explains the distinction, "a justification negates an assertion of wrongful conduct. An excuse negates a charge that the particular defendant is personally to blame for the wrongful conduct."[24] The intriguing challenge with excuses is to provide a persuasive account of why society and the law are willing to consider an actor blameless, and not criminally responsible, even though he has committed a wrongful act.

It is now well recognized that Jeremy Bentham's explanation for excuses—that they are recognized in circumstances in which the actor is nondeterrable—will not do. First, a legal system without excuses would prevent deterrable offenders from harboring the belief that they could commit a crime and falsely convince the jury of their nondeterrability. Moreover, a strict liability system would be less expensive and would render the overall deterrent threat more credible. Modern utilitarians, most notably H. L. A. Hart, have developed more sophisticated arguments for recognizing excuses. Hart has argued that a legal system that maximizes personal choices within the context of coercive law—a system that accordingly excuses people who cannot freely choose—will result in maximizing personal freedom by ensuring citizens that they can avoid the pain of punishment by choosing obedience to the law.[25] Sanford Kadish puts it best, however, when he argues that what any non-desert-based argument for excuses, including Hart's, "is missing is an account of the concern for the innocent person who is the object of a criminal prosecution.... To blame a person is to express a moral criticism, and if the person's action does not deserve criticism, blaming him is a kind of falsehood and is, to the extent the person is injured by being blamed, unjust to him."[26] In short, excuse defenses are required as a matter of simple justice to the blameless wrongdoer. Three nonconsequentialist excuse theories, therefore, predominate: (1) causation, (2) character, and (3) choice.

First, the causation account of excuses asserts that a person is not responsible for criminal conduct caused by some condition for which the actor is also not to blame.[27] If I am not to blame for condition C (e.g., mental illness), and C causes me to commit W, a wrongful act (e.g., rape), then I am not to blame for W. This explanation fails to accurately describe current Anglo-American excuse law. For example, even if Albert's hatred, fear, or repugnance of gay persons is the result of a pathology, he will not be excused for killing a gay person in the absence of some cognitive or volitional incapacity, even though it may be that, but for the mental illness, he would not have committed the crime. And, on a fundamental level, for those who believe that all effects have causes (determinism), whether those causes are "biological, psychological, sociological, astrological, or some combination of the above,"[28] moral responsibility is an illusion,[29] and the causation theory is useless; and it is a false theory if one rejects determinism and asserts that effects exist without causes. Few people seriously defend the causal theory. As Stephen Morse has observed, "[m]ost often, those arguing for the causal theory are simply advocates for excusing one type of defendant or another."[30]

A second explanation for the recognition of excuses is character-based. Although accounts in this area differ in certain respects, the essence is that a person does not deserve to be punished unless her conduct is a manifestation of her bad character, of the fact that she is "antilinked"[31] to the moral values of the community. According to this account, a person should not be held responsible for her wrongful conduct if it is "out of character," that is, the crime was not "determined by (or in some other way expressive of) those enduring attributes of ourselves we call our characters."[32]

Advocates of this account must first explain what is meant by "character." Does "enduring attributes of ourselves" mean anything more than the synthesis of all of our prior actions? Beyond this, how is character (however defined) to be evaluated in a courtroom? As Jeffrie Murphy has observed, "there are staggering obstacles in the way of making [character] judgments about others." Do jurors (or any of us) possess "the knowledge required to impute deep character depravity to others with any degree of reliability"?[33] Indeed, in a liberal polity do we even want jurors engaged in such character attribution? Descriptively as well, character theories diverge from existing punishment practices. The law frequently holds a person responsible for conduct that may be loosely characterized as "out of character,"[34] and people with bad character who commit crimes are not, as a consequence of their character, denied the application of excuse law.

Most fundamentally, the character theory requires its adherents to explain why we are responsible for our (bad) character. Certainly few today would doubt the claim that genetics and early childhood conditions—factors over which we have no control—deeply shape a person's character and, therefore, behavior (notice the faulty causation theory cropping up again). Given this reality, one must ask why, and if so when, a person may be held responsible for her character so as to be blamed for it and the resulting conduct. The answer to the "why," but not to the "when," may be that "[i]n life, as in cards, being dealt a bad hand requires us to develop and exploit our skills and virtues rather than capitulate to circumstances or resort [to one's bad character]."[35] This statement, however, assumes that people possess the capacity to fundamentally change their character. Even if we have this capacity in general, surely there are those who lack it (perhaps again for genetic reasons). Assuming the requisite capacity, *when* can we attribute a person's responsibility to her? Is it when she should be aware of her antisocial character but perhaps isn't? as soon as she *is* aware? or only when she is aware and subsequently can be described as having *chosen* affirmatively to identify with it (or, at least, to "capitulate" to her bad character)? These questions, which lack good answers, demonstrate that the character explanation of excuses will not do.

By far the dominant modern explanation of excuses, and the one that comes closest to explaining Anglo-American law, is the choice theory. This account is thinner than the first two: it looks at the actor at the time of the crime and does not seek to resolve the perplexing and perhaps humanly unresolvable questions of an actor's fundamental character. According to this theory's advocates, a person is responsible for her conduct and, therefore, deserves to be blamed for wrongful conduct if, at the time of the crime, she possessed the capacity and fair opportunity "to function in a uniquely human way, i.e., freely to choose whether to violate the moral/legal norms of society."[36] Such free choice is absent when a person lacks the substantial capacity or fair opportunity to (1) understand the factual circumstances relating to her conduct; (2) appreciate that her conduct violates societal norms; or (3) conform her conduct to the dictates of the law.[37] This account of blaming practices takes into consideration claims of internal disabilities of the actor ("substantial incapacity" claims), which call into question the person's ability to function as a moral agent, as well as external conditions or events that constrain the actor's choices ("no-fair-opportunity" claims), which do not call into question the person's moral agency but still render her, in these unique circumstances, not a fair candidate for blame.[38] The choice account of responsibility, like the other excuse theories, is subject to potential criticism by determinists: if a person is "caused" to behave in a certain way, can we truly say that the person possessed the "capacity" or "fair opportunity" to do otherwise?[39]

In considering whether the defense of duress is based on excuse principles, the primary focus in this chapter will be on the choice account of excuses.

3.4 Why the Distinction Matters

The question of whether duress is a justification defense or an excuse (or, perhaps, can be shown to be either, depending on particular circumstances) is a matter of more than philosophical interest (although surely it is that, which itself is sufficient reason for interest). First, the criminal law is intended to express society's evaluations of right and wrong conduct. There is a distinct difference between a community stating that particular conduct is proper (or, at least, tolerable) and stating that it is wrongful conduct but that, for specific reasons, the actor should not be held criminally accountable for it. The law should accurately express its moral sentiment.

Second, any effort to develop theoretical consistency in the criminal law—for example, to be sure the law relating to such full or partial defenses as duress, necessity, and provocation make sense in relationship with each other—requires consideration of the justification/excuse distinction.

Third, the characterization of duress as a justification or, instead, as an excuse, might have practical significance in individual cases. According to some scholars, a justification defense is universizable: if act X is justifiable, anyone may justifiably assist the actor to do X; and it is unjustifiable to resist X (i.e., there cannot be incompatible justifications). Thus, if a coerced actor is justified, for example, in raping a woman, it would follow according to this view that the coerced actor may call on others, *including persons in no way implicated by the coercion*, to assist in the rape and such persons would also be exculpated;[40] and this would also mean that a police officer or the husband of the victim would not be justified in preventing the rape. These seemingly unacceptable conclusions need not follow if the rape is merely excused. There is considerable dispute in regard to this understanding of the concept of justification,[41] a dispute that necessarily goes beyond the scope of this chapter, so some or all of these practical implications are disputable, but the earlier reasons for caring about the distinction, as well as other concerns,[42] remain valid.

4. DURESS AS A JUSTIFICATION

The most straightforward argument for the view that duress is a justification defense is a lesser-harm one: that the harm or evil of breaking the law because of coercion is less than the harm or evil that was unlawfully threatened against the defendant. One who, with no realistic option, steals a car because his child is held at gunpoint *is* justified in doing so on a lesser-harm basis. As R. A. Duff has put it, "[w]e might indeed sometimes commend such an agent for doing 'the right thing' in that situation, and for being clear-headed enough to see what she should do."[43] Understood this way, duress is nothing more than a variant of the justification defense of necessity. The latter defense typically applies when a person reacts to a *natural*, that is, nonhuman, imminent threat of an extremely serious nature by committing a crime less serious than the harm threatened. Duress, in contrast, deals with unlawful *human* threats. Thus, according to this view, duress and necessity should fall under the broad umbrella of a single choice-of-evils justification plea.

On its face, this understanding of duress seems to work if the defense is limited to the narrow common-law version of the defense. If the only exculpatory threat the law recognizes is an imminent deadly one, and the defense is unavailable in murder prosecutions, then a coerced actor seemingly is always committing the lesser of two evils when he accedes to the deadly threat.

This analysis, however, is descriptively inadequate. First, it cannot fully explain the duress defense in any jurisdiction that recognizes the defense in murder prosecutions and/or if the defense is broadly defined to permit exculpation when a person accedes to a nondeadly threat, for example, any threat that would cause "a person of reasonable firmness" to commit the offense. Unless one concludes that the defense should not be available in such circumstances, a more sophisticated and broader explanation of the defense is required.

Second, it is not true that the defense always applies when the coercer threatens to cause greater harm than the harm demanded by him. If my family and I will be killed unless I kill my neighbor, the traditional duress defense does not apply, even though a utilitarian lesser-harm calculus could support the homicide. This suggests that the no-homicide rule is based on Kantian, nonconsequentialist principles and so calls into question the conclusion that the duress defense itself is simply a lesser-harm, utilitarian-based justification defense. Consider, as well, the rule that a person is never justified in acceding to a *non*imminent threat of death or grievous injury (or, for that matter, a lesser threat). To an act-utilitarian, and even a rule-utilitarian, the defense should apply to nonimminent threats of greater harm, if the threat is sufficiently likely to occur, and reasonably reliable cost-benefit calculations are possible.[44]

Third, the duress defense *does* apply in cases in which the coerced actor may cause equal or greater social harm than that threatened. If vengeful Albert threatens to gouge my son's eye out unless I rape Albert's ex-girlfriend, Carla, the duress defense applies if I accede to the threat. Yet it is hardly clear that Carla's rape is a lesser harm than that threatened by Albert. Indeed, most juries, required to balance the harms, would probably reach the opposite conclusion.

In short, the lesser-social-harm explanation explains some, but not all, cases in which duress exculpates and fails to explain some coercive circumstances that are denied. It is also an uninteresting explanation in that a sensibly constructed justification defense (one that incorporates both unlawful human threats as well as natural forces) would incorporate lesser-harm duress claims, yet this still leaves other cases of coercion that require explanation. This lesser-social-harm account of duress "lacks the right intuitive feel. If one should be acquitted [in coercive circumstances] it does not seem to be because, or at least not primarily because, acquiescence promotes greater *social* utility."[45]

Now consider this hypothetical. A coercer threatens to cut off my child's left arm unless I do the same to another innocent child. The duress defense applies here, yet if I accede to the threat, I have not committed a lesser harm and thus have not acted justifiably.[46] Or have I? Perhaps the lesser-harm justification conception of duress can be saved by applying a different conception of "lesser harm." Rather than (or in addition to) focusing on what actions result in greater societal utility, some philosophers[47] advocate "agent-relative" (as distinguished from agent-neutral) teleology or defend "agent-centered prerogatives," that is, the harm to the person threatened is considered from his perspective and not from the neutral perspective of the law or society as a whole.

According to this perspective, the standard approach to lesser-harms analysis, which calculates the costs and benefits of conduct exclusively from the standpoint of the law's general aims, is too narrow. Instead, a person is entitled to prefer her own and her family's welfare over that of strangers. According to Gary Watson,[48] it is not unreasonable for an individual in a coercive predicament to refuse to subordinate her own or her family's interests to that of the public; the defense of duress, so understood, recognizes "a space in which compliance with the law is optional." Coerced actors have a prerogative—an agent-centered one—to value their own well-being (and that of loved ones) above that of strangers. Watson argues that the criminal law's legitimacy in a liberal democracy (which does not use the criminal justice system to compel virtue from its citizens) is in jeopardy unless the law acknowledges "the limits of its own moral jurisdiction." Otherwise, good citizens will not respect the law.

Watson concedes that this agent-relative principle is not "explicitly and unequivocally endorsed" by the law. Indeed, the principle of an agent-centered prerogative is flatly inconsistent with the view held by some scholars that justification defenses are universizable,[49] and limited to conduct characterized as "right, desirable, or proper." On the other hand, for those who reject the universizability thesis, and those who contend that a justification defense can involve merely tolerable or permissible conduct, agent-relative valuation cannot be so quickly rejected.

This conception of cost-benefit calculation is plausible. There is little doubt that most people *do* value themselves over others, their families over strangers, and members of their religious, racial, ethnic, or national community over "outsiders." In addition, the agent-relative approach *is* consistent with the traditional rule that the duress defense is limited to threats to the coerced person or family. According to this approach, when a coerced actor accedes to a threat, what might appear to the law as a greater-harm choice (and thus unjustified) will actually result in a lesser-harm outcome because the coerced actor is entitled to place a higher value on his own interests than society would. But how much? May I cause severe harm to another innocent person to protect myself from minor injury? Does the answer to that question change if, instead, I am trying to protect my spouse or my child? What if I, a lonely person, feel as deeply attached to my dog as you are to your spouse or sibling? Assuming the defense applies to homicides and I am justified in killing an innocent person to save my own life, what about killing two people, or three? How far should agent-relativity go?

Practicalities aside, there are principled objections to agent-centered prerogatives. The moral principle that innocent human life should be valued equally is a deeply held one. Yes, people typically *do* act in their own self-interest, but most people probably endorse Hyman Gross's observation that "we have a right to require [of a person] more than a bare showing that self-interest prompted what he did."[50] The claim that it is not unreasonable for an individual to refuse to subordinate her own or her family's interests to the goals of the community would be more accurate if it were stated that it is *understandable* when an individual behaves in this manner. Perhaps some people understand why I might rape an innocent woman in order to avoid having my eye gouged out by a coercer, or even why I might kill an innocent person to avoid being maimed, but to understand this is not necessarily to excuse, and far less to justify the conduct.

All of this may be true and even acknowledged by advocates of agent-centered prerogatives, but trumped in their view on political theory grounds. But here, too, Watson overstates his claim that the legitimacy of the system is jeopardized if it compels compliance with the law. He is right that a democratic system should demonstrate respect for its citizens, but respect is shown by treating people justly, not necessarily by tolerating self-interested behavior. In a liberal society, a genuinely coerced actor who commits greater societal harm in order to protect himself or his family quite plausibly should not be punished for his conduct. But that only demonstrates (or at least claims) that duress should *excuse,* not that a person has a prerogative to ignore societal goals and deeply held (and important) moral beliefs about the equal value of human life.

In conclusion, some cases of duress involve a coerced actor committing the lesser of two *societal* evils or harms. In any jurisdiction that defines the defense of necessity (or choice-of-evils) broadly, encompassing conduct motivated by human as well as nonhuman sources, these cases of duress can be resolved in this manner, leaving the remainder of exculpatory duress cases in need of further explanation. Alternatively, some coerced actors, while causing greater societal harm by acceding to a threat, cause lesser harm if one accepts the principle of agent-relative contextualization, a conception of a "personal justification" that strangers may not assert. Even here, however, not all cases can be justified in this manner; even among its advocates the agent-centered prerogative to act in a self-interested manner is not unlimited. In addition, this rationale has nothing to say about the potential exculpation of actors who respond in a disinterested manner to threats to strangers. In short, the duress-as-justification claim is neither a sufficient explanation of the criminal law duress doctrine as it has developed, nor broad enough to satisfactorily resolve many normative issues relating to coercion.

5. Duress as an Excuse

Although coerced conduct may sometimes be justifiable, duress is better—and sometimes can only be—understood as an excuse. As noted earlier, utilitarian theories have little place in excuse analysis (and can be critiqued anyway), but the duress defense (or, at least, a version of it) may be explained in admittedly discredited Benthamite excuse terms. Punishment is unjustifiable if it will produce no benefit in the form of crime reduction, and it is at least empirically plausible that the legal threat of punishment will not deter criminal conduct that is the result of certain threats, particularly imminent deadly ones. Nor, it might be added, is there likely to be reason to consider most coerced actors dangerous or in need of rehabilitation. Following Hart's approach to excuses, as well, our quality of life is improved if we know that the law will excuse us if we accede to extreme threats. A rule-utilitarian, therefore, should be prepared to recognize the defense in those circumstances in which the cost-benefit calculation favors an excuse, presumably when the threat is especially great (an imminent deadly threat being the most salient). As already pointed out, however, the core of any excuse claim is going to be nonconsequentialist in nature, so these arguments are largely makeweight.

Once one turns away from utilitarianism, one may try simply to explain the recognition of the defense of duress in terms of the emotion of compassion that we, as observers, ordinarily feel about the coerced wrongdoer: "We feel a close connection to [him]. He is perceived as a normal person in an abnormal situation. His weakness is our weakness. We find it impossible to separate him from ourselves; there, but for the grace of God or good fortune, go the rest of us."[51] All of these observations are important to understanding duress, but the emotions that we feel about the coerced actor are not and should not be the key to understanding the defense. Descriptively, people sometimes feel compassion for wrongdoers whom the law does not excuse, such as a criminal born into and shaped by a dysfunctional home life or social environment that makes it exceptionally difficult to be law-abiding. And just as the emotion of compassion can result in false positives, it can lead to false negatives: a legally insane wrongdoer sometimes evokes fear rather than compassion, yet the law properly excuses such a person. Ultimately, what we feel about others is not the key to whether and when we should excuse. Wrongdoers should be excused when it is unjust to blame and punish them. It is their right to be excused and is not dependent on our feelings of compassion.

Why is it just to excuse a coerced actor in certain circumstances? Consider, first, the coerced actor who seeks to explain his actions this way: "I am a good person. I would not have committed this crime if I had not been threatened." This understandable explanation triggers two separate but related false excuse accounts, one based on causation ("But for the threat I would never have committed this crime; since I am not to blame for the former, I am also blameless for the latter"), and one on character ("I am a good person, so I should not be punished").

The causation claim cannot explain the existing defense. Although this account of the defense is consistent with the requirement that the actor be free of fault for finding himself in the coercive situation, it does not explain the requirement that the coercive threat be a deadly one, or even that it be one that would cause a person of reasonable firmness to commit the crime. The causation theory, if taken seriously, would require the exculpation of any person, including one born weak-willed, who could convince the fact finder that he would not have committed the crime in question but for the threat, even if it was merely a minor physical threat or merely a threat to property, reputation, or the like. Indeed, the causation theory would justify exculpation of an actor who could show that, but for an exceedingly attractive unlawful *offer*, he would not have committed the crime. This demonstrates why causation is an unacceptable explanation for any excuse claim. Causation is not the same as compulsion.[52]

The character explanation suggests that the duress defense should be recognized when a threat "would motivate a person with the proper character to perform an (otherwise) evil act."[53] According to this account, the will of the coercer—and, thus, *his* bad character—is directed through the "passive mediating structure"[54] of the coerced party. This explanation fatally suffers from all of the difficulties of the character theory generally. It also is descriptively imperfect: Even if jurors were provided (which they are not) with the facts necessary to determine the character of a defendant, the law does not, in itself, deny a "bad" person the duress defense. What can be said in descriptive defense of the character explanation is that when the elements of the defense are satisfied there is a distinct possibility that a person of good character, *whether or not the defendant is such a person*, would accede to the threat and commit the crime. The assumption is that even good people commit bad acts when threatened (or when a loved one is threatened) by death, grievous injury, or perhaps certain other threats. The defendant gets the benefit of the excuse without consideration of his own character. Understood this way, the character explanation of duress is really a proxy for a different excuse account: Any person, regardless of character, should not be held accountable for actions that are the result of pressures that no person may fairly be expected to overcome. The choice theory, therefore, best fits the duress defense.

As examined earlier, the choice explanation of excuses focuses on whether the person, at the time of the offense, had the *capacity* and *fair opportunity* to understand the facts relating to his conduct, to appreciate that his actions violate society's mores, and to conform his conduct to those mores. It is theoretically possible, but implausible, that a coerced person would find himself so fearful that he does not know what he is doing, or that he knows what he is doing but lacks the capacity to know it is wrong. The fundamental basis for excusing the coerced actor instead involves the third element of free choice: Although he knew what he was doing and realized it was wrong, he lacked the capacity or fair opportunity to conform his conduct to the law.

Some assert that coerced wrongdoers should be excused because the effect of a deadly threat is to overwhelm the actor's *capacity* to control his conduct; essentially he cannot conform to the law's dictates because his will has been overborne.[55] This explanation is descriptively false. The defense does not excuse those, and only those, who can demonstrate volitional incapacity. A person genuinely threatened with death who calmly deliberates his choices and who chooses to accede to the threat is not denied the defense on that ground; and a weak-willed person or one who is peculiarly susceptible to a certain type of minor threat is denied the excuse even if he could somehow prove that his fear had a disabling effect on him.

Even if there were a way to identify the point at which a particular person's "will" is overborne, this would not be an acceptable standard for excusing a person because it would permit the weak-willed person to avoid criminal responsibility. At some point in one's life a person becomes (or should become) aware of his strengths and weaknesses. One who is (or should be) aware that he too easily accedes to others' unlawful entreaties or demands has the responsibility to attempt to strengthen his resolve; one who fails to make that effort should be held accountable even if his will was (in this unrealistic hypothesis) truly overborne. The exception to this would be if he could prove the existence of some verifiable disability that prevented him from acting otherwise, but this would (or should) establish an independent ground for irresponsibility (e.g., insanity) or reduced responsibility (e.g., diminished capacity), not duress.

This is not to say that fear does not make self-control more difficult, for it does (a matter considered in subsection 6.2). The most that can be said in support of a *total*-incapacity explanation of duress, however, is that it is based on "the incapacity of *men in general* to resist the coercive pressures to which the individual succumbed,"[56] but this is simply another way of saying that we believe that all people have a breaking point and that the law should not punish those who experience threats that would cause "men in general" to break. This explanation suggests that the basis for the duress claim has less to do with an empirical judgment about a person's *capacity* (or incapacity) to obey the law—the statement "I couldn't help it" is metaphorical—and more to do with the *opportunity* to conform to the law.

The best explanation of duress is that coercion excuses when a person lacks a fair opportunity to act lawfully. The basis for the excuse is not that there is something wrong with the internal "machinery" of the actor (as with insanity), but with external circumstances (the threat) acting on a normal person. One who claims duress says, in essence, "I am only human. You can't fairly expect more of me than what I did." When the choices confronting a person, through no fault of her own, are so great—when a person finds herself in such a "dark place[]"[57]—that it is too much to expect (predictively) and demand (normatively) that she make the "right" (most socially desirable) choice, the law properly excuses that individual. Thus, the defense is not founded on the ground that the coerced person lacks the inherent attributes of a moral agent, but rather on the ground that she is not a fair candidate for the stigmatization and punishment that flow from a conviction.

Understood this way, duress is a normative, or moralized, theory of excuse. The question, quite simply, is "what we can fairly expect of each other in a civilized society"?[58] The basis is not that the actor encountered an unfair choice, for one who is subjected to an unlawful threat, even a trivial one, by definition is placed in an unfair position, yet that is insufficient basis for an excuse. Nor is it enough that the choice the actor encountered was a hard one. We are all confronted by hard choices in life. Nor is the issue simply whether the person standing in judgment of the actor, for example a juror, believes that she would have done the same thing in similar circumstances, although this effort to put oneself in the shoes of the actor is a feature of the excusing process. A person, in honest reflection, might say, "I probably would have done what the defendant did in his situation, but I would expect to be punished for it." The more apt question to ask in the duress context is whether the juror believes it is unfair to punish the person, given the threatening circumstances, for having chosen the wrong option.

The Model Penal Code language—whether the threat was such that a person of reasonable firmness would be "unable to resist" committing a crime—is faulty to the extent that it implies that the basis for the defense is (at least as to the hypothetical person of reasonable firmness) the notion of incapacity. The person-of-reasonable-firmness standard, however, gets at the essence of the doctrine. This language properly suggests that the criminal law does not require virtue and should not require, at the risk of punishment, saintly moral strength from its citizenry; but neither should it deprive individuals of the respect they deserve by assuming that they cannot act as responsible moral agents in difficult circumstances.

Is the person of "reasonable firmness," then, a person with no more than an ordinary degree of moral fortitude? The term "reasonable" sometimes has a different purpose or meaning in the context of an excuse, as distinguished from justification, defense.[59] For example, the provocation doctrine generally provides that a person is partially excused for killing another as the result of provocation if a "reasonable person"—in reality, an "ordinary" person of average disposition, as some courts expressly provide[60]—might have been liable to lose self-control in the same circumstances. An application of an ordinary-person standard in the duress context, although empirical in the sense that it would seek to identify what level of moral strength is typical of human beings, would still represent a normative standard because the decision not to punish such a person constitutes a normative judgment.[61]

One should be careful, however, about such an interpretation. This understanding of the person of reasonable firmness ought to require the law and the fact finder to ask "whether a person with the kind of commitment to the values protected by the law (and violated by this action), *and with the kind and degree of courage we can properly demand of citizens*, would have been thus affected by such a threat."[62] As long as jurors are not hypocritical—as long as they would demand as much of themselves as they demand of others—then the duress defense justly accords an excuse to wrongful-but-coerced actors while still treating them with respect as responsible moral agents.

6. Duress and Homicide

6.1 Full Defense

The traditional rule that duress cannot be asserted as a defense to murder is probably based on the faulty premise that the defense is meant to justify a criminal
homicide on lesser-harm grounds or, alternatively, on the deontological moral pos-
tulate that the killing of an innocent person, even to save a greater number of lives,
is always wrong. At the least, the no-defense rule is a function of a lack of serious
focus on the justification/excuse distinction, as evidenced by the fact that some
courts, in a single opinion, will describe duress claims, and the reasons for rejecting
the defense in homicide cases, in both "justification" and "excuse" terms.[63]

Blackstone wrote that a coerced person "ought rather to die himself than escape
by the murder of an innocent,"[64] a quotation frequently repeated in modern case
law. To state what one *ought* (or not) to do is to speak of what is (or is not) justifiable. It says nothing about what ought-not conduct might be excusable. Thus, too,
the English House of Lords in the coerced homicide context has espoused the "principle" that the "overriding objects of the criminal law must be to protect innocent
lives and to set a standard of conduct which ordinary men and women are expected
to observe if they are to avoid criminal responsibility."[65] As a justificatory principle,
this is a plausible assertion; as a statement about excuses, it is confused. Taken as an
assertion about excuses, it would suggest that the law should not recognize any
excuse defense. Similarly, a U.S. court explicitly defended retention of the common-
law duress rule (at least in one-life-for-one-life situations) on the explicit ground
that the duress defense is a choice-of-lesser-evils defense and, therefore, that the
plea must be denied because "[w]hen the defendant commits murder under duress,
the resulting harm—i.e. the death of an innocent person—is at least as great as the
threatened harm—i.e. the death of the defendant."[66] That this justificatory analysis
may even extend to duress claims when a defendant seeks to protect more than one
life by killing one innocent—thus, a situation in which a utilitarian calculation of
evils could justify the taking of an innocent life, but a nonconsequentialist moral
argument against killing innocent people would still prevail—is seen in Lord
Hailsham's citation in *Regina v. Howe*, a duress case, of the famous "necessity" ruling of *Dudley and Stephens*,[67] a decision frequently cited for the authority that one
may not *justifiably* kill an innocent person even to save a greater number of lives
threatened by starvation.

Once one understands duress as an excuse claim, the no-defense rule loses
almost all of its intellectual authority. Although it could be argued that one who
chooses her own life (or, perhaps, that of a family member) over that of a stranger
demonstrates the character flaw of self-centeredness and, therefore, should be
denied an excuse, this argument has no place in a choice-oriented explanation of
duress. Self-preservation, although not an instinctual reaction, as is evidenced by
acts of heroism in wars and emergencies, is nonetheless a very strong urge that

argues against a categorical no-defense rule. The statement by Lord Coleridge that he and the other members of the House of Lords "are often compelled to set up standards we cannot reach ourselves, and to lay down rules which we could not ourselves satisfy,"[68] has validity in a justification-based, Kantian-like environment but should be attacked as hypocritical and unjust in an excuse context. No person has a *fair* opportunity to comply with a law with which the highest judicial authorities admit that they, themselves, *could* not comply.

This is not to say that the nature of a coercer's demand—whether to assault an innocent person, steal a Picasso painting, rob a bank, rape a child, kill an innocent person, or kill ten innocent people—is irrelevant to the question whether a person should be excused for his actions. If the duress defense were properly understood exclusively in personal incapacity-oriented terms, then the nature of the coercer's threat would be irrelevant: Once one concludes that fear of death or grievous injury destroys one's capacity for choice, it follows that a person should be excused any crime he commits as a result of the capacity-destroying threat. However, the duress defense is a moralized excuse. The issue is whether the coerced actor had a *fair* opportunity to avoid committing a crime,[69] so it follows that the options confronting the coerced party are relevant. The duress defense *does* include a balancing-of-harms aspect, but it is one that does not reach the conclusion that acceding to the threat is a lesser harm than the alternative. The nature of the threat is relevant, however, in determining whether it is *unfair* to expect the person to choose the lesser of two evils or to choose self-sacrifice among equal harms—in short, the question is whether the coerced actor is a fair candidate for blame and punishment. Given the chance, it is possible to imagine fair-minded persons sitting on a jury concluding that a defendant lacked a fair opportunity to comply with the law if he was forced to choose between the rape or death of his child at the coercer's hands and the death of an innocent stranger at his own hands; the moral calculus might very well be different if the same person must choose to give up his own life or that of his child (or, at least, try to resist the coercer even if chances of success are tiny) rather than kill a classroom filled with children.

However one resolves the moral issues, a categorical no-excuse rule is indefensible, which is the position taken by U.S. jurisdictions that apply the Model Penal Code version of duress, and is the view expressed by England's Law Commission in 2006, which recommended that duress be made a full defense to murder committed in response to a threat of death or life-threatening harm.[70]

6.2 Partial Defense: Duress versus Provocation

The no-defense homicide rule is anomalous in light of other criminal law doctrines. For example, the duress defense generally applies if a coerced person tries to kill another, fails, and is charged instead with an offense such as assault with intent to kill or to commit grievous bodily injury. Even more perplexing, however, is the law's recognition of the provocation partial defense to murder with the simultaneous denial of even a partial defense to coerced murder.

Two explanations may be offered for this distinction, but neither withstands scrutiny. The first explanation relates to self-control. The provocation defense is recognized because some provocative acts are so egregious that the provoked party is likely to find self-control much more difficult;[71] one who kills as a result of serious provocation is less culpable than one whose control mechanisms are undiminished by external circumstances. In contrast, the duress defense is not an incapacity-oriented defense. That is why the defense remains available to a person, threatened with great harm, who consciously and in full control of his faculties commits a crime. Granting this distinction, however, there is no reason to assume that fear, induced by a deadly threat, cannot affect control mechanisms in much the same way and to the same degree as anger, induced by provocative actions or words, does. Although the *full* defense of duress is not based on the ground that coerced actors *fully* lose self-control (and the defense should not be justified on the related ground that some threats will cause the hypothetical person of reasonable firmness to be *unable* to resist committing a crime), there is no reason based on considerations of self-control simultaneously to recognize a partial defense to killing caused by righteously provoked anger while denying a partial defense to a person whose fear for himself or a loved one has undermined his self-control to the same degree.

A second purported justification for the distinction between the law's treatment of provocation and that of coercion relates to the homicide victim: The provoked killer ordinarily kills the provoker, whereas the coerced actor kills an innocent third person. This distinction makes sense under some theories of justification: If one accepts the forfeiture doctrine of justification, for example, it can be claimed that there is greater social harm in the death of an innocent person than in that of one who wrongfully triggered the incident by acting provocatively. But this distinction loses most or all of its authority once one understands that the two defenses are excuses rather than justifications. Moreover, there is a competing argument in favor of a duress defense, at least of a partial nature, when one understands that whereas a provoked defendant acts in an excessive, punitive, retaliatory manner, a coerced defendant is responding, albeit often unjustifiably, in order to prevent future harm to himself or others.

In short, even if a full defense is not recognized, a person who is coerced to kill an innocent person is entitled to a partial defense as long as the law recognizes a partial defense in provocation cases.

7. NECESSITY VERSUS DURESS

7.1 Necessity

The "necessity" defense is often treated as a justification defense that applies when a person responds to a naturally caused (more accurately put, nonhuman) dangerous condition or threat—for example, a tornado raging toward the individual, an aggressive rabid dog, or death by starvation on a lifeboat—by committing a crime less serious than the danger confronting the individual.[72] In contrast, the duress defense is traditionally limited to persons who act in response to a human do-X-or-I-will-do-Y threat, where X is a crime and Y is serious physical harm to the person threatened or someone related to him. If duress were simply and always a justification defense—if X were always a lesser harm than Y—there would exist no more than an arbitrary distinction between necessity (natural) threats and duress (human) threats that could sensibly be avoided by merging the two defenses into one.

Consider the situation once duress is understood to be an excuse defense. Some critical gaps in the law then occur, the most notable of which is that one who is threatened by a natural force (thus taking the case outside the realm of the human-threat duress defense) has no exculpatory defense if she commits a greater harm than was threatened (thus taking it outside the realm of the justificatory necessity defense). In addition, if the necessity defense is limited to nonhuman threats, a person who commits a lesser harm as a result of a human do-this-or-else threat would not have a justification-necessity defense. Finally, consider a humanly caused danger, but one that does not involve a "do-this-or-else" threat. For example, suppose I see two thugs running toward a parked car in which I am a passenger waiting for the driver to return from an errand. I have good reason to fear that the thugs will cause serious harm to me. Therefore, I drive the car away although I have no driver's license.[73] The crime I have committed is certainly less than the harm I reasonably feared, but will the justificatory defense of necessity be available to me in this case of a humanly caused danger? Or what if the harm I fear from the thugs is *less* than the harm I cause (for example, I fear a robbery, so I drive my vehicle into their bodies, permanently disabling them or even killing them). Is the duress excuse defense available to me in this situation, since the thugs did not order me to commit the crime of seriously harming them?

Some of these concerns are resolved in jurisdictions (for example, those that have followed the direction of the Model Penal Code) that recognize a justification-necessity defense that applies to human and nonhuman threats alike. But there has been much greater hesitancy to similarly expand duress to nonhuman threats. The same Model Penal Code drafters who expanded necessity to include human threats persist in limiting the duress excuse defense to "unlawful" threats, which by this language excludes nonhuman threats or dangerous conditions.

Why is there resistance to broadening the conception of duress to include nonhuman threats? Advocates of the traditional approach suggest that the concept of coercion involves an interpersonal relationship,[74] and that victimization implies a victim wronged by another.[75] According to this view of duress, the reason why the source of the threat is critical is that when the threat emanates from a human source, the idea of the crime belongs to the threatener—it is another person's will in operation—whereas when the danger comes from a natural source, the idea of the crime arises entirely from the mind and will of the defendant. In the former case, the law can excuse the coerced actor and still hold someone responsible for the crime; in the latter, if the law excuses the defendant there is no one responsible for the resulting harm. The latter distinction should not matter, however. The law already recognizes that social harm cannot always be redressed through punishment, as when an insane person commits a crime. If there is reason to believe that the defendant, confronted by a nonhuman threat, lacked a fair opportunity to comply with the law, that should be sufficient basis to excuse her wrongdoing. It is unjust to hold a person criminally accountable for harm she has caused simply because there is no other person to whom to attach criminal responsibility. It is submitted, therefore, that the excuse of duress should apply to nonhuman forces to the same extent as human threats.

7.2 Duress of Circumstances

The traditional limitation of duress to human threats notwithstanding, there is limited case law, especially in the United Kingdom, recognizing what is sometimes characterized as "duress of circumstances," a defense that applies when a person commits a crime as a result of a threat (in England, limited to one of death or life-threatening harm) that does not fit the paradigmatic "commit-this-crime-or-else" form.[76] This version of duress can encompass a natural threat (and thus is in consonance with the position taken in subsection 7.1), and it may also involve an unlawful *human* threat that does not fall within the usual parameters of a duress claim. For example, suppose that an inmate in a penal institution, threatened with sexual attack or some other serious injury, flees the prison and is later returned to custody and charged with prison escape. American courts have struggled to determine whether the prisoner should be allowed to claim any defense and, if so, whether it is better understood as a (justification) necessity or (excuse) duress claim.[77] Some courts have determined that it cannot be duress because the inmate who threatened the safety of the defendant did not order him to escape, which then leaves only a justificatory claim of necessity (and, then, only if the defense is broad enough to include human actors), which might not apply depending on the balancing of harms. "Duress of circumstances" offers another option. This result is consistent with the no-fair-opportunity conception of duress.

Without so denominating it (and perhaps without realizing it), American jurisdictions that have enacted the Model Penal Code version of duress have also accepted the human-threat version of "duress of circumstances." The language of the Code's duress provision permits a person to assert the excuse if, as a result of prior violence or present unlawful threats of violence, he commits any crime, *even one not ordered by the threatening party*, that a person of reasonable firmness would have been unable to resist committing. This model of the defense would allow the escaping prisoner to assert duress. Intriguingly, it would also seem to allow a person to seek an excuse for harm committed *against the coercer* that is not otherwise covered by a justification defense. For example, a woman who has been beaten and degraded regularly by her partner and who kills him while he is asleep might not be able to claim self-defense (for lack of imminency or immediate necessity) or even lesser-harm necessity but would seemingly have the right to have a jury consider a claim of duress on the ground that the abuser's prior violence would cause a person of reasonable firmness to act as she did.[78] Thus, this version of duress allows the law to find a way to provide justice to the battered woman without justifying vengeance or preemptive strikes; it also allows her to be excused without having to claim insanity, opening herself to the implication that she is not a moral agent, not to mention that she would be subject to civil commitment as a result of her supposed mental illness. As with any duress claim, the battered woman claiming duress would be seeking exculpation on the ground that she responded as any other normal person might in similar unfair circumstances.

7.3 "Rotten Social Background"

Consider a person born into a broken home, or with parents deeply involved in a life of crime, who lives in deep poverty, where the only people "succeeding" are drug pushers, gang members, and other criminals. Should a person shaped by these experiences—by what one judge has called a "rotten social background"[79] (RSB)—who turns to crime be excused for his criminal activities? Various scholars, most notably, Richard Delgado, think so.[80]

Of course, a person living in these conditions might have a traditional duress defense in some circumstances if, for example, he seeks to avoid involvement in criminal activities rampant in the community but is forced by a gang member to participate in a crime. But advocates of an RSB defense are making a far more expansive argument: that people who live in these circumstances and who turn to crime as a result should be excused, even in the absence of any specific imminent (or nonimminent) human threat. Must one who accepts the validity of "duress by circumstances" also recognize a duress excuse for RSB defendants?[81]

One can offer a predictable, straightforward causation explanation for excusing RSB defendants: they are not to blame for the conditions in which they were born and brought up; those conditions caused them to develop an antisocial belief structure; that belief system caused them to commit crime. If one were to accept the causation theory of excuses, the RSB defendant would have a valid claim, but that is only because the causation theory, taken seriously, nullifies everyone's criminal responsibility. As noted earlier, causation is not the same as compulsion.

There *is* an initially plausible duress claim. The claim would be that a person brought up and living in horrible social conditions lacks a fair opportunity to conform his conduct to the law. A person who grows up in a seriously deprived environment will, through no fault of his own, almost inevitably identify with the surrounding antisocial culture. The pressures to conform to that criminal culture, especially in the absence of counter-influences in the home environment, are sufficiently great that it may fairly be argued that the RSB actor was not "given the opportunities that promote responsible attitudes."[82]

Notice, however, how such a claim turns the duress defense on its head. Duress by circumstances typically involves an actor who commits a crime against his will, coerced by some extreme event, such as those confronting Dudley and Stephens in a lifeboat, starving to death, who killed another to eat the remains.[83] The RSB defendant, however, is committing crimes consistent with his will. What the RSB defendant *really* is arguing is that he is not to blame for his criminally inclined character because of the conditions in which he was brought up—he did not have a fair opportunity to incorporate lawful values.

Even if one accepts this assertion as factually accurate, it does not follow that the law must recognize an RSB duress claim. It can readily be conceded that it is very difficult (although not impossible) for a person who grows up in a terrible environment to develop socially acceptable values, but that is not the point of a duress-based excuse. The issue is not whether a person had a fair opportunity to live a better life or develop a better character but whether the person (given those background realities) had a fair opportunity not to commit the particular crime on the particular occasion.[84] That is, the question that must be asked is whether, given the RSB defendant's antisocial values, he had a fair opportunity not to rob the particular liquor store, rape the particular woman, or kill the particular person who stood in the way of his antisocial goals.

The duress defense cannot go so far as to allow exculpation on this basis. The duress defense represents a very limited exception to the general rule that a person who possesses normal adult practical reasoning skills is morally and legally accountable for his intentional conduct. To claim that a person of "reasonable moral firmness" would be unable to resist robbing, raping, or murdering on a particular occasion, where there is no specific threat being imposed, runs counter to the law's and society's requirement of personal responsibility. As has been written, "the difference between the person who acts with a gun at his head, sharks in the sea, or starvation on the immediate horizon, on the one hand, and the RSB actor, on the other, is too basic to ignore."[85]

NOTES

1. Joshua Dressler, "Exegesis of the Law of Duress: Justifying the Excuse and Searching for Its Proper Limits," 62 *S. Cal. L. Rev.* 1331, 1331 (1989).

2. Hyman Gross, *A Theory of Criminal Justice* 276 (1979).

3. Regina v. Howe [1987] 1 AC 417, 428.

4. James Fitzjames Stephen, *A History of the Criminal Law of England* 105 (1883).

5. For sources that summarize the traditional elements of duress, see Glanville Williams, *Criminal Law: The General Part*, §§ 242–247 (2d ed. 1961) (English law); Dressler, *supra* note 1, at 1135–1343 (U.S. law); Claire O. Finkelstein, "Duress: A Philosophical Account of the Defense in Law," 37 *Ariz. L. Rev.* 251, 253–257 (1995) (U.S. law).

6. N.Z. Crimes Act 1961, § 24(1).

7. Alan Wertheimer, *Coercion* 204–206 (1987).

8. E.g., Stanley M. H. Yeo, *Compulsion in the Criminal Law* 98 (1990).

9. E.g., State v. Scott, 827 P.2d 733, 740 (Kan. 1992).

10. E.g., State v. Clay, 256 S.E.2d 176 182 (N.C. 1979) (defining "deadly force" in the context of self-defense as "force likely to cause death or great bodily injury").

11. Model Penal Code and Commentaries, § 2.09 at 371 n 24 (Revised Comments 1985).

12. Regina v. Howe [1987] 1 AC 417, *overruling* Lynch v. Director of Public Prosecutions for Northern Ireland [1975] AC 653.

13. People v. Anderson, 50 P.3d 368, 379 (Cal. 2002) (dictum); *contra* State v. Moretti, 120 Pac. 102. 104 (Wash. 1912) (denying defense in accidental killing during a robbery).

14. The Model Penal Code is the product of the American Law Institute, a prestigious organization composed of criminal law scholars, jurists, and practitioners in the United States. The Model Penal Code as a whole, adopted by the Institute in 1962, has significantly influenced American law.

15. Model Penal Code § 2.09(1).

16. The law in unclear in the remaining American states. I thank Susan Landrum (Ohio State University–Moritz Law School '09), for her research on this subject.

17. Model Penal Code and Commentaries, *supra* note 11, at 377.

18. [1975] A.C. 653, 703 (Lord Kilbrandon).

19. See also Regina v. Steane [1947] K.B. 997 (C.A.) (Defendant, who broadcast pro-German messages on the radio, was charged with doing an act likely to assist the enemy "with the intent to assist the enemy"; held: he was entitled to argue to the jury that, due to coercion, he did not intend to assist the enemy).

20. Mark Schroeder, "Teleology, Agent-Relative Value, and 'Good,'" 117 *Ethics* 265, 281 (2007).

21. Joshua Dressler, "Justifications and Excuses: A Brief Review of the Concepts and the Literature," 33 *Wayne L. Rev.* 1155, 1158 (1987).

22. For discussion of the debate regarding the two interpretations of "justification," see Joshua Dressler, "New Thoughts about the Concept of Justification in the Criminal Law: A Critique of Fletcher's Thinking and Rethinking," 32 *UCLA L. Rev.* 61 (1984); Kent Greenawalt, "The Perplexing Borders of Justification and Excuse," 84 *Colum. L. Rev.* 1897 (1984).

23. John L. Austin, "A Plea for Excuses," in *Philosophical Papers* 175, 176 (3d ed. 1979).

24. George P. Fletcher, "The Right and the Reasonable," 98 *Harv. L. Rev.* 949, 958 (1985).

25. H.L.A. Hart, *Punishment and Responsibility* 17–24 (1968); Sanford H. Kadish, "Excusing Crime", 65 *Cal. L. Rev.* 257, 263–264 (1987) (criticizing Bentham's explanations and summarizing the Hart position).

26. Kadish, *supra* note 25, at 264.

27. For the most complete explanation and rejection of this theory, see Michael S. Moore, "Causation and the Excuses," 73 *Cal. L. Rev.* 1091 (1985).

28. Stephen J. Morse, "Thoroughly Modern: Sir James Fitzjames Stephen on Criminal Responsibility," 5 *Ohio St. J. Crim. L.* 505, 507 (2008).

29. There have been efforts by philosophers, lawyers, and others to accommodate the "truth" of determinism with the deeply held view that people can properly be blamed and held morally responsible for their actions. Some "compatibilists" seek to draw distinctions between "hard" and "soft" determinism (the former of which seemingly renders moral responsibility impossibile, but the latter of which allows for moral responsibility). This debate goes beyond the scope of this chapter.

30. Morse, *supra* note 28, at 508.

31. Robert Nozick, *Philosophical Explanations* 382 (1981).

32. Michael S. Moore, "Choice, Character, and Excuse," 7 *Social Phil & Pol'y* 29, 29 (1990).

33. Jeffrie G. Murphy, "Moral Epistemology, the Retributive Emotions, and the 'Clumsy Moral Philosophy' of Jesus Christ," in *The Passions of Law* 149, 157–158 (Susan A. Bandes ed. 1999).

34. E.g., a person of "good character" with too little sleep or worrying about conditions in her life might push someone down in a moment of pique. If serious harm results, a prosecutor might choose to bring criminal battery charges, and the person's good character would not excuse.

35. William Wilson, "The Structure of Criminal Defences," 2005 *Crim L. Rev.* 108, 110–111.

36. Joshua Dressler, "Reflections on Excusing Wrongdoers: Moral Theory, New Excuses, and the Model Penal Code," 19 *Rutgers L.J.* 671, 701 (1988).

37. See Joshua Dressler, *Understanding Criminal Law* § 17.03[E] (4th ed. 2006); Hart, *supra* note 25, at 181; Andrew Ashworth, *Principles of Criminal Law* 254–256 (3rd ed. 1999).

38. Kyron Huigens, "Duress Is Not a Justification," 2 *Ohio State J. Crim. L.* 303, 306–311 (2004).

39. See *supra* note 29.

40. E.g., United States v. Lopez, 662 F. Supp. 1083 (N.D. Cal. 1987) (trial court stating that the question of whether alleged perpetrator D1's claimed defense is characterized as a justification or, instead, excuse defense, is critical to the determination of whether alleged accomplice D2 can assert D1's defense in his own case).

41. George Fletcher may be the most consistent advocate of the universizability doctrine. For a summary and critique of Fletcher's views, see the sources cited in note 22.

42. The proper allocations of burdens of proof, and the moral legitimacy of retroactive application of changes in duress law, arguably depend on consideration of the justification/excuse distinction. Dressler, *supra* note 37, at 17.05[F]–[G].

43. R. A. Duff, "Rule-Violations and Wrongdoings," in *Criminal Law Theory: Doctrines of the General* Part 63 (S. Shute & A.P. Simester eds. 2002).

44. Finkelstein, *supra* note 5, at 257–265.

45. Wertheimer, *supra* note 7, at 166.

46. This is the position, for example, of the Model Penal Code, which denies the defense of justification in equal-harm circumstances. Quite arguably, however, the law should justify any action that is not a greater harm. If I am put in a position in which I must choose between two equal harms, the law should be indifferent to my choice. Peter Westen & James Mangiafico, "The Criminal Defense of Duress: A Justification, Not an Excuse—And Why It Matters," 6 *Buffalo Crim. L. Rev.* 833, 885 (2003). As long as one understands "justification" as meaning that the conduct in question is not wrong, rather than that it is affirmatively right or desirable, any justification defense should apply in equal-harm circumstances. On the other hand, if one of the two "equal" paths requires me (presumptively) to violate the law and the other does not require a law violation, then the harms are *not* equal, since there is additional social harm from the act of violating society's laws.

47. E.g., Gary Watson, "Excusing Addiction," 18 *Law & Phil.* 589, 608–611 (1999); Wertheimer, *supra* note 7, at 165–169; see generally Schroeder, *supra* note 20.

48. See the pages cited in note 47.

49. See section 3.4, *supra*.

50. Gross, *supra* note 2, at 281.

51. Dressler, *supra* note 36, at 683.

52. Morse, *supra* note 28, at 516.

53. Wertheimer, *supra* note 7, at 294 (describing this as Aristotle's "ambivalent" argument for an involuntariness conception of duress).

54. John Lawrence Hill, "A Utilitarian Theory of Duress," 84 *Iowa L. Rev.* 275, 289 (1999).

55. Regina v. Hudson 2 All E.R. 244, 246 (CA 1971); see 2 Paul H. Robinson, *Criminal Law Defenses*, § 177(b) (1984).

56. Model Penal Code and Commentaries, *supra* note 11, at 374 (emphasis added).

57. Rosa Ehrenreich Brooks, "Law in the Heart of Darkness: Atrocity and Duress," 43 *Va. J. Intl. L.* 861, 862 (2003).

58. George P. Fletcher, *Basic Concepts of Criminal Law* 83 (1998).

59. Yeo, *supra* note 8, at 17.

60. E.g., Maher v. People, 10 Mich. 212, 220 (1862) (providing that provocation is sufficient to reduce the offense to manslaughter if "reason should...be disturbed or obscured by passion, to an extent that might render ordinary men, of fair average disposition, liable to act rashly") (emphasis omitted).

61. Huigens, *supra* note 38, at 311.

62. Duff, *supra* note 43, at 64 (emphasis added).

63. E.g., People v. Anderson, 50 P.3d 368, 369 (Cal. 2002) (citing Blackstone for the view that "duress is no *excuse* for killing an innocent person" and in the next paragraph stating that "[w]e conclude that, as in Blackstone's England, so today...fear for one's own life does not *justify* killing an innocent person.") (emphasis added).

64. 4 Blackstone, *Commentaries on the Law of England* 30 (1769).

65. Regina v. Howe [1987] 1 AC 417, 430.

66. People v. Anderson, 50 P.3d 368, 371 (Cal. 2002).

67. (1884) QBD 273.

68. Id. at 288.

69. This is not to say that a coerced person does not have some basis for making an incapacity-based volitional claim, as explained in section 6.2 *infra*.

70. The Law Commission, "Murder, Manslaughter and Infanticide," § 6.21 (Nov. 26, 2006), at 116.

71. See Joshua Dressler, "Why Keep the Provocation Defense: Some Reflections on a Difficult Subject," 86 *Minn. L. Rev.* 959 (2002).

72. But see Perka v. The Queen (1985) 13 D.L.R. (4th) 1 (permitting the defense in context of natural threats, apparently only as an excuse, when instinct "overwhelmingly impel[s] disobedience" with the law).

73. See Regina v. Conway [1988] 3 All ER 1025 (C claimed that he violated traffic laws because he believed that two men, actually nonuniformed police officers, were assassins intending to harm a passenger in his vehicle; held: C entitled to "duress by circumstances" [discussed in section 7.2 *infra*] instruction).

74. J. Roland Pennock, "Coercion: An Overview," in *Coercion* 3 (*Nomos XIV*, J. Pennock & J. Chapman eds. 1972).

75. Herbert Fingarette, "Victimization: A Legalist Analysis of Coercion, Deception, Undue Influence, and Excusable Prison Escape,"42 *Wash. & Lee L. Rev.* 65, 106 (1985).

76. Law Commission, *supra* note 70, § 6.7 at 112.

77. For example, People v. Unger, 362 N.E.2d 319 (Ill. 1977).

78. A fair reading of the Model Penal Code duress provision would permit a jury instruction on duress: she would argue that, as a result of prior "use of...unlawful force" on the battered woman, a "person of reasonable firmness" would have been unable to resist engaging in her conduct (killing her abuser). This, of course, does not fit the paradigm of

duress, which assumes the coerced actor commits a crime against an innocent third person, but the language of the Code is broad enough to allow this claim to be made. For a defense of this claim, see Joshua Dressler, "Battered Women and Sleeping Abusers: Some Reflections," 3 *Ohio St. J. Crim. L.* 457 (2006); Joshua Dressler, "Battered Women Who Kill Their Sleeping Tormenters: Reflections on Maintaining Respect for Human Life While Killing Moral Monsters," in *Criminal Law Theory: Doctrines of the General Part* 259 (S. Shute & A. P. Simesters eds. 2002).

79. United States v. Alexander, 471 F.2d 923, 961 (D.C. Cir. 1973) (Bazelon, J., dissenting) ("rotten social background" coined by the trial judge and then used in the Bazelon opinion).

80. For example, Richard Delgado, "'Rotten Social Background': Should the Criminal Law Recognize a Defense of Severe Environmental Deprivation?," 3 *Law & Inequality* 9 (1985).

81. Delgado, in a scatter-gun approach, provides various nonduress grounds for exculpation, including justification theories, and excuse theories based on insanity, cultural defense, and so on. Those approaches go beyond the scope of this chapter. For a brief summary of his positions in *id.*, and a critique of them, see Dressler, *supra* note 1, at 1377–1379.

82. Ferdinand Schoeman, "Statistical Norms and Moral Attributions," in *Responsibility, Character, and the Emotions* 311 (F. Schoeman ed. 1987).

83. Dudley & Stephens, (1884) QBD 273.

84. A different exculpatory argument might be made: A society so unjust as to permit such dehumanizing character-harming conditions lacks moral authority to blame and punish the criminal actor. (Interestingly, however, some observers have noted that juries composed of persons living in the same "rotten" conditions seem at least as willing as others to blame RSB wrongdoers.) Such a no-standing-to-blame-and-punish argument is not a duress claim, but rather a political-theory explanation that falls outside the scope of this chapter.

85. Dressler, *supra* note 1, at 1384.

SELECTED BIBLIOGRAPHY

Listed here are sources of value to those researching the criminal law topic of duress, as considered in this chapter. (Many of the works cited in the notes are not included here.)

Alexander, Larry. 1999. "A Unified Excuse of Preemptive Self-Protection." *Notre Dame Law Review* 74: 1475–1505.

Ashworth, Andrew. 2007. "Principles, Pragmatism and the Law Commission's Recommendations on Homicide Law Reform." *Criminal Law Review* 2007: 333–344.

Berman, Mitchell N. 2002. "The Normative Function of Coercion Claims." *Legal Theory* 8: 45–89.

Brooks, Rosa Ehrenreich. 2003. "Law in the Heart of Darkness: Atrocity and Duress." *Virginia Journal of International Law* 43: 861–888.

Brudner, Alan. 1987. "A Theory of Necessity." *Oxford Journal of Legal Studies* 7: 339–368.

Carr, Craig L. 1991. "Duress and Criminal Responsibility." *Law and Philosophy* 10: 161–188.

Dressler, Joshua. 1989. "Exegesis of the Law of Duress: Justifying the Excuse and Searching for Its Proper Limits." *Southern California Law Review* 62: 1331–1386.

Fingarette, Herbert. 1985. "Victimization: A Legalist Analysis of Coercion, Deception, Undue Influence, and Excusable Prison Escape." *Washington and Lee Law Review* 42: 65–118.

Finkelstein, Claire O. 1995. "Duress: A Philosophical Account of the Defense in Law." *Arizona Law Review* 37: 251–283.

Hill, John Lawrence. 1999. "A Utilitarian Theory of Duress." *Iowa Law Review* 84: 275–338.

Hitchler, Walter Harrison. 1917. "Duress as a Defense in Criminal Cases." *Virginia Law Review* 4: 519–545.

Huigens, Kyron. 2004. "Duress Is Not a Justification." *Ohio State Journal of Criminal Law* 2: 303–314.

Morgan, Edward M. 1984. "The Defense of Necessity: Justification or Excuse?." *University of Toronto Faculty Law Review* 42: 165–183.

Nozick, Robert. "Coercion." 1969. In *Philosophy, Science and Method: Essays in Honor of Ernest Nagel,* ed. Sidney Morgenbesser, Patrick Suppes, and Morton White, 440–472. New York: St. Martin's Press.

Pennock, J. Roland, and John W. Chapman, eds. 1972. *Coercion.* Chicago: Aldine Atherton.

Reed, Alan. 1996. "Duress and Provocation as Excuses to Murder: Salutary Lessons from Recent Anglo-American Jurisprudence." *Journal of Transnational Law and Policy* 6: 51–92.

Wertheimer, Alan. 1987. *Coercion.* Princeton: Princeton University Press.

Westen, Peter, and James Mangiafico. 2003. "The Criminal Defense of Duress: A Justification, Not an Excuse—And Why It Matters." *Buffalo Criminal Law Review* 6: 833–950.

Uniacke, Suzanne. 1989. "Killing under Duress." *Journal of Applied Philosophy* 6: 53–69.

———. 2007. "Emotional Excuses." *Law and Philosophy* 26: 95–117.

Yeo, Stanley M. H. 1990. *Compulsion in the Criminal Law.* Sydney: Law Book.

CHAPTER 12

··

INSANITY DEFENSES

··

WALTER SINNOTT-ARMSTRONG
AND KEN LEVY

In 1843, Daniel M'Naghten believed that the Tories, including prime minister Robert Peel, were plotting to destroy him and that the only way to defend himself was to kill the prime minister first. M'Naghten shot into the prime minister's carriage and killed the passenger, who turned out to be the prime minister's private secretary, Edward Drummond. M'Naghten's act clearly qualified as murder; he intentionally killed a human being with malice aforethought. M'Naghten did think that his act was justified as self-defense, but the threat was both imagined and not immediate, so he could not cite self-defense as a defense. Nonetheless, the jury did not find him guilty. They instead found him not guilty by reason of insanity. He was committed for the rest of his life to a mental institution, but he did not have to go to prison at all.[1]

This verdict outraged many people in 1843, just as happened when John Hinckley was found not guilty by reason of insanity after shooting President Reagan in 1981.[2] Such (in)famous cases create the impression that political assassins can get off just by pleading insanity. That impression, however, is inaccurate because many insanity pleas are not successful. In 1963, Jack Ruby pleaded insanity but was convicted of murdering Lee Harvey Oswald, the presumed assassin of John Fitzgerald Kennedy. In 1968, Sirhan Sirhan pleaded diminished responsibility but was convicted of murdering Robert Kennedy. In 1972, Arthur Bremer pleaded insanity but was convicted of attempting to assassinate Alabama governor George Wallace. So the insanity defense is hardly a free ticket home.

Another reason why the insanity defense is not a free ticket home is that people who are found not guilty by reason of insanity are not sent home. They are locked up in mental institutions, and they sometimes spend more time in these mental institutions than they would have spent in prison if they had been found guilty.

In 1983, the Supreme Court held that someone who was found not guilty by reason of insanity could be held indefinitely even though he had been charged only with attempted shoplifting, which called for a maximum sentence of one year.[3] Thus, the verdict "not guilty by reason of insanity" should not always be welcomed by defendants or feared by citizens.

Still, successful insanity defenses are often controversial. On the one hand, when a defendant is known to have intentionally caused a death, it strikes many as unjust to find that person not guilty. On the other hand, it strikes many as unfair to find someone guilty of committing an offense for which he was not morally responsible. This conflict between intuitions lies at the heart of the insanity defense.

Is Insanity Medical or Legal?

To understand this controversy, it is crucial to ask what kind of concept insanity is. It is common to think that insanity is a medical condition. Psychiatrists, however, almost never describe their patients as "insane" or "sane." It would not help them in diagnosis or treatment to employ this dichotomy. Instead, they use such diagnostic categories as schizophrenia, paranoid delusion, kleptomania, and borderline personality disorder to decide what is wrong with their patients and how to treat them. It is the *judges and lawyers* who have to decide who is insane and which mental conditions make someone insane. The law classifies some people as sane and others as insane in order to determine who should be held criminally responsible, competent to stand trial, capable of handling their own financial affairs, or capable of living without supervision. In this way, insanity is a legal concept.[4]

Compare vision.[5] Optometrists determine whether one's eyesight is 20/20, 20/40, 20/80, or 20/200 (corrected or uncorrected, in bright or low light); whether one is nearsighted or farsighted; and which colors one is able to detect. But even with the most detailed diagnosis of an individual, lawmakers still need to decide how good someone's vision needs to be in order to obtain a license to drive a car or a bus or to fly a plane or how bad vision must be in order to qualify for disability benefits or insurance payments—and so on for other legal purposes.

Similarly, although psychiatrists are best qualified to determine a person's mental condition, lawmakers still need to decide whether that mental condition removes legal responsibility or some other legal status. Where the law draws the line between sanity and insanity depends on particular contexts and purposes. The law might draw one line between those who are competent to stand trial and those who are not and a different line between those who need to be civilly committed to mental institutions and those who do not.

Because the insanity defense is concerned with criminal responsibility and punishment, the crucial question here is which kinds of mental conditions do or should remove criminal responsibility. Different formulations of the insanity defense specify different mental conditions for this role.

THE M'NAGHTEN RULE

"Madness" became a complete defense to criminal charges as early as the time of Edward III in fourteenth-century England.[6] In the sixteenth century, a prominent legal treatise specified "knowledge of good or evil" as the test of sanity and responsibility.[7] Courts proceeded to adopt a variety of insanity defenses until most courts settled on the rule in M'Naghten's case in 1843:

> To establish a defense on the grounds of insanity, it must be clearly proved that, at the time of committing the act, the party accused was labouring under such a defect of reason, from disease of the mind, as not to know the nature and quality of the act he was doing; or, if he did know it, that he did not know that what he was doing was wrong.[8]

This rule places a heavy burden of proof on the defense, distinguishes between two kinds of knowledge, and requires a mental disease to cause a defect of reason.

Although this rule refers to knowledge, what really matters here seems to be true belief rather than knowledge. If knowledge is defined as justified true belief plus some Gettier condition,[9] then agents can lack knowledge by (1) lacking any belief, (2) having false beliefs, (3) lacking justification, or (4) failing a Gettier condition. It would be inappropriate to excuse someone with true beliefs simply because those beliefs are not justified or fail some Gettier condition. Thus, it is (1) and (2) rather than (3) or (4) that make defendants lack knowledge in the way that removes responsibility under the M'Naghten rule.

The M'Naghten rule's distinction between knowing the nature and quality of the act and knowing that it is wrong also needs to be clarified. A classic example of not knowing "the nature and quality of the act" is a husband's strangling his wife while believing that he is squeezing juice from a lemon. This agent does not know that he is killing anyone. Other examples are harder to classify. Consider Joy Baker, who shot and killed her aunt while deluded into thinking that her aunt was the devil and had come to hurt her.[10] Baker seems to have known that she was shooting a person,[11] but she did not know that her act was not necessary to prevent harm to herself.[12] Thus, Baker knew part, but not all, of "the nature and quality of her act."

Of course, no agent knows every quality of any act, so courts need to decide which qualities of an act are essential. In order to limit which qualities of an act must be known for responsibility and therefore which delusions excuse, the judges in M'Naghten's case proposed a counterfactual test:

> [If] he labours under such partial delusion only, and is not in other respects insane, we think he must be considered in the same situation as to responsibility

as if the facts with respect to which the delusion exists were real. For example, if under the influence of his delusion, he supposes another man to be in the act of attempting to take away his life, and he kills that man, as he supposes, in self-defense, he would be exempt from punishment. If his delusion was that the deceased had inflicted a serious injury to his character and fortune, and he killed him in revenge for such supposed injury, he would be liable to punishment.[13]

In the former case, the defendant is honestly motivated by self-preservation, the motivation that is required for self-defense. In the latter case, the defendant's motivation is not self-preservation but revenge, which has never been a recognized defense. So even if he were not deluded but correct in his beliefs, his act still would not be justified.

This counterfactual test, however, might seem to rule out too much. Consider Howard Barton Unruh, who killed thirteen people in Camden, New Jersey, on September 6, 1949, because he was convinced that his neighbors "ha[d] been making derogatory remarks about [his] character." He even imagined that actress Barbara Stanwyck was one of his hated neighbors. What finally set him off was his discovery that someone had stolen the gate to his fence. Unruh was never tried for the massacre. Instead, he was diagnosed as a paranoid schizophrenic, pronounced insane, and put in a unit for the criminally insane. While Unruh's delusion seems to be the very kind of mental illness that is supposed to remove responsibility, at least according to many people at the time and many proponents of the insanity defense, he still seems to be responsible under the counterfactual test because his acts would not have been justified even if his beliefs about his neighbors had been true. In this case, then, that added clause seems to yield the wrong verdict.[14] Thus, it remains controversial and difficult to specify precisely which parts of the nature and quality of the act the defendant must know in order to remain responsible for her actions under the M'Naghten rule.

When we turn our attention to the other kind of knowledge mentioned in the M'Naghten rule—knowledge that the act was wrong—it becomes crucial to determine which kind of wrongness the agent needs to know in order to be criminally responsible under the M'Naghten rule. There are four main possibilities.

The first possibility is that a responsible agent needs to know that the act is illegal or criminal—that is, *legally* wrong. To know this is to know something about the laws in the particular jurisdiction and how they apply to the act.

The second possibility is that a responsible agent needs to know that the act is contrary to the moral beliefs of most people in the particular society—that is, *socially wrong*. To call an act socially wrong in this sense is to refer not merely to custom or etiquette but, instead, to moral beliefs and principles generally accepted in that community. In order for a defendant to know that an act is socially wrong, then, she must know something about what people in a given society generally believe about morality.

A third possibility is that a responsible agent needs to know that the act violates that particular agent's own moral principles or moral beliefs—that is, that it is *personally wrong*. In order for a defendant to know what is personally wrong, she must be aware of her own moral beliefs and how to apply them.

Finally, a responsible agent might need to know that the act is just plain *morally* wrong. For a defendant to know this is not for the defendant to know what other people do or would say or believe about the act or about its moral status.[15] Instead, it is to know something about the act itself—namely, that there is at least one property of the act that gives it the moral status of being wrong. For example, a defendant cannot know that rape is just plain morally wrong unless the defendant knows that rape has some property that makes it morally wrong—for example, that it causes severe and unjustifiable harm to the victim. If the defendant believes that rape is wrong only because it happens to violate laws in a certain legal system or only because other people believe that it is wrong, then that defendant does not really understand what makes rape morally wrong and therefore does not know that rape is just plain morally wrong.

Knowing that an act is morally wrong in this fourth sense does not require knowing the law or the moral beliefs of society or of the agent. These beliefs are all distinct from the moral status of an act because the law, society, and the agent can all be incorrect. That is shown by cases like slavery, which can be seen as morally wrong even at times when it did not violate the law or the moral beliefs of society or of many individuals. Although many acts that are morally wrong will also be legally, socially, and personally wrong, these notions of wrongness come apart when individuals or societies hold deviant moral beliefs.

This fourth notion of moral wrongness might seem inappropriate for a legal test of insanity because it cannot be applied without making or assuming a moral judgment. To apply the first three tests, judges and juries need only do empirical research to determine what the law is or which moral standards are accepted by society or by this defendant. They do not need to make any normative judgments about whether or not those laws or standards are justified or correct. In contrast, in order to apply the fourth test to a particular defendant, juries or judges would have to ask (1) whether or not the defendant's act was immoral, (2) what makes it immoral, and (3) whether or not the defendant knew (or was able to know) that the act was immoral on that basis. These questions are normative, but the answer is usually not controversial, at least in cases involving core offenses, such as murder, rape, kidnapping, and theft. In any case, the judge or jury's decision will rest on its own moral principles rather than on its understanding of the moral principles of society or of the defendant.

Opponents might object that it would be unfair for a judge or jury to condemn a defendant merely because the defendant did not happen to share the judge's or jury's own beliefs about what is morally wrong. But if the law explicitly or implicitly directs the jury or judge to determine whether or not the defendant knows that an act is morally wrong, then, because knowledge implies truth,[16] the jury or judge cannot apply the law as stated without determining whether or not the act is *in fact* morally wrong. The law, unless redefined explicitly, then seems to authorize the jury or judge to apply her own views about what counts as moral knowledge and truth.[17]

M'Naghten jurisdictions do not agree about which kind of wrongness must be known in order for an agent to be responsible. Most seem to have remained silent, and at least two have explicitly refrained from adopting a position, on this issue.[18] Regarding the jurisdictions that have taken a position, some of them maintain that defendants may generally be found not guilty by reason of insanity only if, as a result of mental illness, they did not know that their acts were *legally* wrong.[19] Other jurisdictions explicitly specify that legal knowledge is not enough for responsibility; that even if defendants knew that their acts were illegal, they might still be eligible for a verdict of not guilty by reason of insanity if they did not know that their acts were *socially wrong*.[20] No jurisdiction seems to accept the view that a defendant may be found not guilty by reason of insanity simply because he failed to know that his act violated his own personal moral beliefs.[21] In contrast, some jurisdictions that allow the insanity defense when the defendant did not know that the act was wrong do specify that they mean moral wrongness as opposed to legal wrongness and then do not say that they mean social wrongness or social morality. Since they refer to moral wrongness and do not redefine moral wrongness as social wrongness, it seems reasonable to interpret their test as requiring knowledge of plain moral wrongness.[22]

The differences among these interpretations are illuminated by deific-decree delusions. A classic example is *Hadfield*.[23] Hadfield reportedly believed himself to be a modern Christ sent by God to be crucified in order to save the world. In order to get the crucifixion process going, he shot in the king's direction. Hadfield seems to have believed (1) that his act was illegal, (2) that society would judge his act morally wrong if they heard about it, given their current beliefs, yet (3) that his act was not in fact morally wrong. Suppose, then, that Hadfield were a modern-day defendant in a M'Naghten jurisdiction. Given (1)–(3), Hadfield is eligible for the insanity defense under the M'Naghten rule if that rule is interpreted so that it applies to those who did not know that their acts were personally wrong or morally wrong (the third and fourth interpretations), but not if that rule is interpreted so that it applies only to those who did not know that their acts were legally or socially wrong (the first and second interpretations).

In contrast, imagine that, while Hadfield still believed (1) and (3), he was deluded about society's beliefs, so he thought that society shared his beliefs that he was Christ, that his shooting would save the world, and therefore that it was not morally wrong. In this case, Hadfield would have been eligible for the insanity defense under the social, personal, and moral wrongness interpretations but still not under the legal wrongness interpretation of the M'Naghten rule.

When combined with M'Naghten's counterfactual test,[24] delusions like these reveal the need for further distinctions. Contrast two variations on Hadfield's story. In both variations, Hadfield knows that society does not actually share his delusions and does actually judge his act to be morally wrong. These cases vary in Hadfield's beliefs about what society counterfactually would believe if his society did share his beliefs that he is Christ and that his act would save the world. "Hadfield I" believes correctly that, if society shared these beliefs, then it would not judge his act to be morally wrong. So Hadfield I knows that his act is contrary to society's actual moral beliefs not because they subscribe to different moral principles but because they apply the same moral principles to what they take to be a very different factual situation. Hadfield I, then, knows that his act is socially wrong on the basis of a factual disagreement rather than on the basis of a disagreement about moral principles.

In contrast, "Hadfield II" believes correctly that his society would still judge his act to be morally wrong even if they came to share his beliefs that he is Christ and that his act would save the world (perhaps because they hold absolute principles against ever endangering innocent lives, as Hadfield did). Hadfield II, then, knows that his act is socially wrong not so much on the basis of a factual disagreement as on the basis of a disagreement about moral principles.

Given this distinction, the M'Naghten rule could be interpreted as excusing those who do not know that their acts are socially wrong on the basis of a factual disagreement or as excusing those who do not know that their acts are socially wrong on the basis of a disagreement about moral principles. Hadfield II would be excused under both interpretations, but Hadfield I would be excused under only the former and not the latter interpretation. Applying these interpretations to cases would require determinations not only of what the defendant believes about actual society but also of what the defendant believes about what society would conclude in counterfactual situations.

A parallel distinction can be drawn for the moral wrongness interpretation. Let's assume that Hadfield's act would not have been morally wrong if it really would save the world, as he believed. In contrast, Unruh's killing would still have been morally wrong, even if all of Unruh's beliefs were correct about his neighbor's derogatory comments. Let's further assume (going beyond the reports) that Unruh believed that his act was not morally wrong because he believed that it is morally permissible to kill people for making derogatory remarks. If so, Unruh lacked a kind of moral knowledge that Hadfield did not lack. Hadfield might have held defensible moral principles (such as that saving the world is an adequate justification for shooting in the king's direction) even though he misapplied those principles because he wrongly believed that he was Christ and that his plan would help to save the world. In contrast, Unruh (under our supposition) did not know either the situation (because he was not in fact being insulted) or the appropriate moral principles (because derogatory comments do not justify killing). In other words, Unruh (under our supposition) lacked moral knowledge of both the facts and the relevant moral principles, whereas Hadfield lacked only knowledge of the facts and not of the relevant moral principles. If the M'Naghten rule were interpreted as excusing only those who are ignorant of the relevant moral principles, then only Unruh, not Hadfield, would be excused on this basis. But if the M'Naghten rule were interpreted as excusing those who are ignorant of the facts and therefore of the morally correct course of action, then both Unruh and Hadfield would be excused.

Courts do not draw all of these fine distinctions when they apply the M'Naghten rule, but they do express various attitudes toward cases like these. Some jurisdictions hold that deific delusions do not excuse and therefore that defendants who claim that they were following God's commands should still be found guilty. This reaction might be motivated either by skepticism that the defendant really did believe in a divine command or by fears of practical problems if all such defendants were found not guilty.[25]

Other jurisdictions, however, reach the opposite conclusion: that such deific delusions do remove responsibility when defendants thought that following God's commands was the morally right thing to do.[26] Some of these jurisdictions excuse only those defendants who believed that society would not have morally condemned their acts if society had shared their factual beliefs, as with Hadfield I.[27] On such tests, responsibility depends on knowledge of what can be called counterfactual social wrongness. Other jurisdictions excuse defendants if their acts would not have been morally wrong if their delusional beliefs had been true—a kind of counterfactual moral wrongness test.[28]

Whichever kind of knowledge is required for responsibility, the M'Naghten rule requires that lack of knowledge to be related to "a defect of reason, from disease of the mind." Bare lack of knowledge does not remove responsibility, especially if the agent should know what he is doing. Someone who does not know that there is poison in a drink that he serves still might be responsible if he was negligent—that is, if he should have known or should have checked to see whether there was poison in the drink. In contrast, it seems inappropriate to say that the agent ought to have known better when his lack of knowledge was due to "a defect of reason, from disease of the mind."

It is still not clear what counts either as a disease of the mind or as a defect of reason. One plausible interpretation is that a lack of knowledge results from a defect of reason when it does not respond to reasons to the contrary. This absence of reasons-responsiveness constitutes (or is evidence of) an inability to know what one is doing or that it is wrong.[29] M'Naghten's belief that the prime minister was out to get him was probably resistant to reason in this way. No matter how much one argued with him, he would still believe this falsehood. People who suffer from paranoia are often like that. They are not able to correct their beliefs in light of evidence or reason. That might explain why they are said to labor under "a defect of reason."

IRRESISTIBLE IMPULSE AND LOSS OF CONTROL

The exclusive focus on knowledge in the M'Naghten rule motivated revisions in many jurisdictions. The original formulation covers only mental diseases that affect cognition, but it fails to cover other mental diseases, including volitional or emotional diseases that disrupt or undermine people's abilities to choose and act in certain ways.[30] For example, Lorena Bobbitt was found not guilty by reason of (temporary) insanity after she cut off her husband's penis with a kitchen knife while he slept on June 23, 1993. "The defense argued—and the jury, after slightly more than six hours of deliberation, apparently agreed—that Mrs. Bobbitt, flooded with nightmarish images of her husband's abuse and suffering from a variety of mental illnesses, snapped psychologically after her husband raped her, and yielded to an 'irresistible impulse' to strike back."[31] Mrs. Bobbitt knew what she was doing and presumably knew that it was wrong, since her husband was no threat to her while he was sleeping, and her act would not, and was not intended, to make her safe. So she would seem to have no excuse under the purely cognitive M'Naghten rule. Yet she still might seem not guilty by reason of insanity for attacking her husband.

Consider also kleptomaniacs who steal items even though they know that they could easily afford the items, there is a significant danger that they will be caught, and the punishment that they are likely to receive if caught is many times worse than any pleasure or profit that they might gain from stealing.[32] Why, then, do they continue to steal even if it is not in their self-interest? They claim that they just can't help themselves. If so, their mental diseases are much like being addicted to a drug, except that they usually did nothing to create their mental diseases.

This kind of disease can be seen as a kind of "defect of reason," but here the defect is in what is called practical reason rather than theoretical reason. The judges might have intended their reference to a defect of reason in the M'Naghten rule to cover this kind of practical or volitional defect.[33] Later generations, however, saw reason as more narrowly cognitive. Given this restrictive interpretation and our advancing knowledge of mental diseases that are not purely cognitive, many experts thought that some special clause needed to be added to the M'Naghten rule in order for it to excuse these volitional impairments, and many states expanded the M'Naghten rule by incorporating some reference to volition.

The most common way in which states expanded the M'Naghten rule was by adding an "irresistible impulse" test. According to one formulation of the irresistible impulse test, a person is not criminally responsible if he is

> impelled to do the act by an irresistible impulse, which means before it will justify a verdict of acquittal that his reasoning powers were so dethroned by his diseased mental condition as to deprive him of the will power to resist the insane impulse to perpetrate the deed, though knowing it to be wrong.[34]

This test seems to view mental disease as a kind of force that overcomes the agent's ability to resist because either the force of the impulse is too strong or the agent's willpower is too weak(ened) or both.[35]

It is not clear what it means for an impulse to be irresistible. One possibility is that an impulse is irresistible when the particular agent is unable to resist it in the actual circumstances of the offense. Another possibility, which counts fewer impulses as irresistible, is that the particular agent must be unable to resist it in any circumstances. And there might be an objective standard built into the defense as well: an impulse does not count as irresistible unless it is too strong to be resisted by any normal or reasonable person.

The notion of an impulse is also problematic because it suggests suddenness. In contrast, many volitional diseases do not operate quickly. Just as people can be addicted to cigarettes for a long period of time without feeling any sudden impulses to smoke immediately (especially if they smoke before any impulses arise), so some volitional diseases display themselves in long-term patterns of behavior rather than in quick impulses. While a kleptomaniac might not feel any sudden rush to steal, she still might be unable to stop herself from stealing for any extended period of time.

One reason why she might be unable to stop herself is that the tension mounts until it is too great to resist. A second reason for her inability to stop herself might be that the tension does not increase but her willpower weakens, so her ability to resist the continuous tension diminishes. On a recent view, willpower is like a muscle that can get tired when it is used.[36] Yet a third possible reason why she might be unable to avoid misconduct is that the pressure is unrelenting for long periods and fighting it requires more attention and hope than she can keep up for long enough. After all, I can raise ten pounds easily, but I cannot keep it raised for an hour. The weight does not get heavier, and I might not get so tired that I literally cannot hold it up any more, but I always eventually let it down because my attention lapses or I lose hope and become resigned to the inevitable. Likewise, some forms of mental illness might create persistent urges that can be resisted for a while but not forever. Such mental diseases might make people unable to avoid certain acts without either weakening the will or causing any irresistible urge.

These kinds of cases are excused from criminal responsibility under some "loss of control" tests. One leading case, *Parsons v. State*, held that a person who knows what he is doing and that it is wrong

> may nevertheless not be legally responsible, if the following two conditions concur: (1) if, by reason of the duress or such mental disease, he had so far lost the power to choose between the right and wrong, and to avoid doing the act in question, as that his free agency was at the time destroyed; (2) and if, at the same time, the alleged crime was so connected with such mental disease, in the relation of cause and effect, as to have been the product of it solely.[37]

This rule (the "Parsons rule") is broader than an irresistible impulse rule, which applies only when there is sudden impulse or weakened will power, because the Parsons rule does not mention either impulse or resistance, so it covers any loss of "the power to choose" regardless of what causes that loss.

The Parsons rule also requires causation. This requirement was probably implicit when the M'Naghten rule referred to "a defect of reason, *from* disease of the mind,"[38] but the Parsons rule makes this requirement explicit in its clause (2). The point is to ensure that the mental disease is causally relevant to the crime. For example, even if someone suffers from kleptomania at the time of his crime, this mental disease hardly helps to remove his legal responsibility if his crime was rape. In order to remove responsibility, the mental disease must not merely be present at the time of the crime but must also actually cause the crime in an appropriate way.

The term "solely" at the end of the Parsons rule might seem too strong because acts almost never have one lone cause, especially if causes are understood as necessary ("but for") conditions. More likely, the Parsons rule uses the term "solely" to refer not to necessary conditions but to the "triggering" or "proximate" cause of the alleged crime. On this view, the term "solely" in the Parsons rule really means *primarily*. It is meant to exclude certain kinds of causal overdetermination: namely, situations in which the defendant's mental disease is not the primary cause of, or motivation behind, her crime. Suppose, for example, that a patient with kleptomania murders her psychiatrist in order to avoid having to pay her psychiatry bills. To be sure, she would not have committed the murder but for her mental illness; for, without the illness, she never would have met her psychiatrist in the first place. But she is still responsible for this murder because her mental defect, kleptomania, is not the *primary* cause of her action. Instead, her act is primarily caused by a factor that is *not* either identical with or the product of her kleptomania: greed.

THE PRODUCT TEST

Although loss-of-control tests are broader than cognitive tests, they still do not cover all kinds of mental illness. For example, some mental illnesses affect emotion more than they affect will or cognition. One example might be depression, including the extreme postpartum depression that is reported to lead some mothers to kill their children shortly after birth.

Moreover, many psychiatrists object to the artificiality of dividing our mental worlds into cognition, volition, and emotion. According to these psychiatrists, these categories are vague and intertwined. For these reasons, they suggest that an insanity defense should refer to mental disease generally, without any commitment to subdivisions.

Some legal authorities who accepted this view adopted the "Durham rule," which is also known as the Product Test:

> [A]n accused is not criminally responsible if his unlawful conduct was the product of mental disease or mental defect.[39]

This simple test requires only two elements: (1) mental disease or defect, and (2) a causal connection between the mental disease or defect and the act.

The main problem with the Durham rule stems from its very point. While it is simpler than the M'Naghten and Parsons rules, and while it also gives psychiatrists the freedom to testify as they want and juries the freedom to consider what they want, the Durham rule fails to give psychiatrists or juries much, if any, guidance on how to testify or decide cases.

When tough decisions have had to be made, courts have felt forced to come up with their own ways of answering questions about the Durham rule. The first question is whether a mental disease causes an act when it is only a necessary and not a sufficient condition of the act. It might seem that a mental disease would not excuse in such cases because to say that the mental disease is not sufficient for the act is just to say that it did not necessitate or compel the act, in which case the act could have been avoided. Still, courts tended to follow general theories of legal causation, according to which the main decision on the causal prong of the Durham test was whether or not the mental disease was a necessary condition of the act. If "the accused would not have committed the act he did commit if he had not been diseased as he was,"[40] then the act was seen as a product of the disease.

The next question is what counts as a mental disease. While it might seem tempting just to say that "mental disease" in the Durham rule has the same meaning as the medical term "psychosis," this interpretation gives too much legal power to psychiatrists, since psychiatrists decide which conditions to label "psychosis." Critics accordingly charged the Durham rule with imposing "trial by label."[41] Moreover, when psychiatrists classify mental illnesses, they typically have in mind the treatments that they administer. The classifications that work for treatment might not work for criminal justice or other legal purposes.[42] Partly for this reason, a leading decision in the Durham tradition defined "mental disease" in legal terms:

> [A] mental disease or defect includes any abnormal condition of the mind which substantially affects mental or emotional processes and substantially impairs behavior controls.[43]

The goal of this definition was to provide the guidance to witnesses and juries that the original Durham rule by itself had failed to provide.

There are three things to notice about this definition of mental disease. First, unlike the M'Naghten rule (as it is commonly interpreted), this definition does not give priority to cognition but rather refers to "emotional" and broadly "mental" processes. Second, the conjunction "and" implies that a condition does not count as a mental disease unless behavioral controls are impaired. Third, the term "substantially" has been added, presumably because mental diseases are rarely, if ever, completely overwhelming.

This recognition of partial mental illness is crucial. A kleptomaniac might be able to keep himself from stealing when he knows that a policeman is standing at his elbow but still not able to stop himself when he knows only that a policeman is likely to be watching from the other side of the room or that nobody is watching. Or he might be able to go for a week without stealing but not for a whole month. It is not clear whether a kleptomaniac who steals once a week even though he is compelled to steal only at least once a month is morally or legally responsible. Such incomplete incapacities do not guarantee that the person will steal under all circumstances, but they still affect the person's behavior in many circumstances of everyday life, where cues and temptations abound. Whether or not an individual defendant retains enough capacity for responsibility is, in effect, left up to the jury to determine, possibly in light of community standards.[44]

THE MODEL PENAL CODE

Many of these modifications were brought together by the American Law Institute in its popular Model Penal Code (MPC) formulation of the insanity defense, which said:

> A person is not responsible for criminal conduct if at the time of such conduct as a result of mental disease or defect he lacks substantial capacity either to appreciate the criminality (wrongfulness) of his conduct or to conform his conduct to the requirements of the law.[45]

The American Legal Institute included the parenthetical "wrongfulness" after "criminality" because it wanted to leave states free to choose either term. The MPC also added a restriction:

> The terms "mental disease or defect" do not include an abnormality manifested only by repeated criminal or otherwise anti-social conduct.[46]

This restriction was intended to keep contract killers, serial killers, sociopaths, and psychopaths from being found not guilty by reason of insanity just because they committed so many crimes. It is not clear, however, that it still applies to psychopaths today, since contemporary science has found many manifestations of psychopathy beyond criminal or otherwise antisocial conduct.[47] In any case, despite this clarification, the MPC never provides any positive definition of mental disease.

The MPC rule is still clearly broad. It refers to appreciation rather than knowledge, does not require complete loss of capacity, and covers volitional as well as cognitive defects. In this way, the MPC rule seems to excuse acts resulting from all of the kinds of mental disease discussed above, with the possible exception of purely emotional impairments.

This MPC rule was a great hit. By 1980, the MPC rule or some close relative was adopted in twenty-eight states as well as by every federal court of appeals that had addressed the issue. In the majority of states, the rule was adopted legislatively.[48] (The M'Naghten rule was used in every other state except New Hampshire and the District of Columbia, which stuck with their versions of the Durham rule.) The popularity of the MPC rule at that time might have been due in part to its flexibility. States could interpret this rule in various ways to fit their preferences.

To understand the MPC rule, we need to ask, first, what the phrase "he lacks substantial capacity" means. The need to refer to *capacities* should be clear. Although the M'Naghten rule hinged on actual knowledge rather than ability to know, the criminal law clearly should not excuse agents who do not happen to know that their acts are wrong if those agents could be reasonably expected to know that their acts are wrong. Such agents can be held responsible for their failure to exercise their ability to know the wrongfulness of their conduct. In contrast, agents who lack the capacity to know that their acts are wrong obviously cannot be held responsible for failing to exercise this capacity, a capacity that they don't have. This point helps to explain why the MPC is formulated in terms of a capacity to appreciate rather than in terms of actual appreciation.

Capacities clearly come in degrees. The MPC rule highlights this point by referring to *substantial* capacity. Still, this MPC clause is ambiguous between a relative measure and an absolute measure. It might seem to say either that agents are not responsible if their capacity falls substantially below what is normal or that agents should be excused only when the capacity that they retain, if any, is not substantial. To see the difference, imagine that degrees of capacity can be located on a scale from one to ten, any decrease of three or more points counts as substantial, and most people are at capacity level nine. Then someone with capacity level five lacks substantial capacity in the former, relative sense (he is more than three below the normal nine) but retains a substantial capacity in the latter, absolute sense (he is more than three above the bottom). What is important here is that even if an agent retains some capacity to appreciate wrongfulness, she still might be eligible for the insanity defense under the MPC clause if her retained capacity is either substantially below what is normal or too minimal to count as substantial.[49]

Next we need to ask which capacity matters. The MPC rule refers to two specific capacities: the capacity to conform one's conduct to the law and the capacity to appreciate the wrongfulness of one's act. The conformity clause, also known as the *volitional prong*, seems to be intended to capture the point of irresistible impulse and loss of control tests like those discussed above. If agents lack substantial capacity to control their conduct, and if they (like most of us) run into situations where they need to exercise control in order to conform to the law, then they lack capacity to conform to the law. Certain compulsions, possibly including kleptomania, are believed to fall under this clause.[50]

The other clause refers instead to appreciation of wrongfulness. This part of the MPC rule, often called the *cognitive prong*, is supposed to correspond to both parts of the M'Naghten rule, since an agent cannot appreciate the wrongfulness or criminality of an act if she cannot appreciate the nature and quality of the act, especially if the relevant parts of the nature and quality of an act are those that matter to criminality and wrongfulness. In the examples discussed above, if a husband cannot know that he is squeezing a lemon instead of his wife's neck, or if Joy Baker cannot know that she is shooting her aunt rather than the devil, then they both lack substantial capacity to appreciate the wrongfulness of the act.

In contrast, when an agent does know the relevant nature and quality of the act, then it is less clear what it means to say that she lacks substantial capacity to appreciate its wrongfulness. The term "wrongfulness" in the MPC rule is subject to the same interpretations as the term "wrong" in the M'Naghten rule discussed above. Four kinds of wrongfulness were distinguished: legal, social, personal, and moral. Many jurisdictions do not clearly distinguish these interpretations, but courts could interpret the MPC rule so that it requires substantial appreciation of any of these kinds of wrongfulness (or any combination of them).

One alternative for jurisdictions that use the MPC rule is to hold that it is enough for criminal responsibility that an agent appreciates that her act is illegal or criminal—that is, *legally* wrong. The MPC explicitly allowed this option by including the word "criminality" in addition to "wrongfulness" in its proposed insanity defense. Some jurisdictions adopt this interpretation explicitly.[51] The rationale behind this view is presumably either retributive (because agents who can know the law are rational enough to be morally responsible for not obeying it) or deterrent (because threats of criminal punishment can deter criminal behavior if the agent can know which acts risk punishment). On this view, the defendant need not also understand the moral basis for the law.

In contrast, the MPC rule also allows states to refer to wrongfulness instead of criminality, and some states explicitly adopt this option.[52] Within this group, several jurisdictions specify that by "wrongfulness" they mean *social* wrongfulness, so that defendants are eligible for the insanity defense if and only if they lack substantial capacity to appreciate that their acts violate the moral code in the relevant society— that is, that people in that society do or would see the act as immoral.[53] The rationale is presumably that it would not be fair to hold people morally responsible for violating the prevailing social morality if they cannot appreciate what the prevailing social morality forbids. A defendant might, for example, personally believe that wife-beating is not immoral. Nonetheless, on this approach, it would still be legitimate to punish him for wife-beating as long as he can appreciate the fact that most of his society believes that wife-beating is immoral.

The third possible interpretation of "wrongfulness" in the MPC is that an agent is not criminally responsible for an act unless she has substantial capacity to appreciate that the act is *personally* wrong in the sense that it violates her personal moral beliefs. As with the corresponding interpretation of the M'Naghten rule, no jurisdiction adopts this interpretation of the MPC rule.[54]

Finally, the MPC could be interpreted as suggesting that an agent is not criminally responsible for an act unless she has substantial capacity to appreciate that the act is just plain *morally* wrong. On this interpretation, it is not enough that the agent can appreciate that the act is contrary to law or contrary to social or personal moral beliefs. To be criminally responsible, the agent must be able to appreciate the facts about the act that make it morally wrong and also that these facts do make it morally wrong. Some jurisdictions seem to adopt or allow this moral interpretation at least implicitly insofar as they specify that the relevant kind of wrongfulness is moral rather than legal wrongfulness or criminality and do not add that the relevant kind of wrongfulness is only social wrongfulness.[55]

A rationale for this moral wrongfulness interpretation might come from an expressive theory of punishment, according to which a major, if not *the* major, purpose of punishment is to express moral condemnation of criminal acts.[56] A penalty such as a parking fine merely inflicts a loss as a way of controlling behavior. We usually do not morally condemn people who get parking tickets, as long as they pay their fines. Criminal punishments also inflict losses, but that is not all they do. They also typically express moral condemnation of acts and agents. We condemn rapists as bad people even if they suffer losses for what they do. Fines would not be enough for rape even if they worked to prevent it. We also wish to proclaim to society that rape is morally wrong and, ideally, to make rapists understand its wrongness and feel remorse for their crimes.

Given such an expressivist purpose for punishment, it seems inappropriate to punish agents who lack the capacity to understand why their acts are immoral because they cannot understand what is being expressed. We can fine people for parking illegally even if they cannot understand the reasons why this parking space is reserved, but moral condemnation seems inappropriate if a person lacks the capacity to understand any moral reason why the violated law is a law in the first place. Insofar as criminal punishment goes beyond behavior control by penalties and is supposed to express moral condemnation, it seems appropriate to excuse those who cannot understand any moral reasons behind the criminal laws that they break because they cannot understand what would be expressed by the punishment.

After specifying the kind of wrongfulness that needs to be appreciated, a separate question of interpretation still needs to be answered. Jurisdictions need to specify what it means to *appreciate* that kind of wrongfulness. The term "appreciate" is the MPC's replacement for the term "know" in the M'Naghten rule, so it helps to begin by asking what counts as knowing wrongfulness.

One possibility is that the relevant kind of knowledge or appreciation is no more than the ability to answer questions correctly. We do, after all, say that someone knew the answer when he got it right on a game show or a standardized test. This abstract and isolated kind of knowledge, however, hardly seems sufficient for moral or criminal responsibility. Giving the correct answer is compatible with failing to *understand* the answer or its meaning. Such a thin mental state might be enough for awarding a prize on a quiz show, but it seems inadequate to warrant criminal punishment.

A few courts have explicitly adopted a similar view, usually in dicta, that even if a person possesses a bare "theoretical," abstract, or cognitive understanding of wrongfulness, she may still be found legally insane if she lacks a deeper emotional or affective understanding of wrongfulness.[57] The change from "know" in the M'Naghten rule to "appreciate" in the MPC rule is arguably an attempt to move beyond a purely abstract account of knowledge. Appreciation requires the person not only to know the right answers to questions but also to understand those answers. What, then, is this understanding?

Understanding might be shown, among other ways, by drawing appropriate inferences from answers. Thus, if a person says not only that his act is wrong but also that its wrongfulness implies that he ought to feel bad about it, that he deserves punishment for it, and so on, then he knows and appreciates its wrongfulness at a deeper level than someone who calls it wrong but cannot say what this answer implies. This deeper level of knowledge or appreciation still remains purely cognitive insofar as drawing out implications is a cognitive skill.

One problem with this "inferential" view of understanding is that a person might be able to draw out implications without understanding what the implications mean any more than she understood what implied them. Such abstract inferences without understanding are exemplified by psychopaths, who often make normal moral judgments and draw normal inferences from them but still do not emotionally appreciate what they say. For example, when asked if he experienced remorse for a murder that he had committed, one psychopath said, "Yeah, sure, I feel remorse." Pressed further, he said that he didn't "feel bad inside about it." Similarly, when asked whether he had ever committed a violent offense, a man serving time for theft answered, "No, but I once had to kill someone."[58] Hence, real appreciation requires more than merely drawing out abstract inferences.

Another interpretation of understanding solves this problem by requiring not only cognition and inference but also "affective knowledge" or "emotional appreciation."[59] On this view, a defendant does not appreciate the wrongfulness of an act if, for example, she does not "internalize the enormity" of the criminal act.[60] Someone who announces that an act is wrong and mimics common inferences about the need for remorse and punishment still might not have appropriate feelings or motivations.

Consider, by analogy, a person on a roof who says that it would be stupid to jump off because it would cause him great pain and disability. But then he jumps off anyway, and he gives no reason other than that he thought it would be fun. This act seems to be strong evidence that the jumper did not really know or appreciate just how stupid jumping was, even if he called it "stupid" and drew appropriate inferences. What he lacked was appropriate emotions or feelings, especially fear, and motivations, such as desire to avoid to pain and disability. His cognitive abilities did not connect to his decision-making, and this disconnection is grounds for saying that he did not fully know or appreciate how stupid his act was.

This point still holds if the jumper does not regret his jump after it breaks his legs. That would be even more evidence that he does not fully appreciate what is wrong with his act, since what is wrong is that he lost much more than he gained by jumping.

Now extend these points to appreciation of moral wrongfulness as opposed to imprudence. Imagine that instead of jumping, someone pushes a victim off the roof. Just as the jumper could not be thought to fully appreciate the stupidity of jumping off the roof when he lacked the appropriate emotions and motivations (fear and self-protection), the pusher does not seem to fully appreciate the immorality of pushing another person off the roof if he equally lacks the appropriate emotional concern for this other person's well-being. This concern seems necessary to fully appreciate why it is morally wrong to push the victim off the roof.

Law has often underestimated the importance of emotion, but contemporary psychology calls for correcting this oversight.[61] There are several reasons to think that emotion is necessary for the kind of capacity to appreciate that is required for moral responsibility and therefore should be required for criminal responsibility. First, emotions and cognition are hard to separate because emotions are necessary for normal cognition even apart from morality. Antonio Damasio, among others, has argued that people whose emotions are reduced or destroyed by frontal lobe damage, for example, cannot properly assess risks and benefits.[62] Second, emotions are necessary for triggering inhibitions and therefore for consistent law-abiding action and for deterrability in the long run.[63] Third, emotions help us pick out what is salient, and a sense of salience is necessary for consistent decision-making in the face of overwhelming amounts of information.

More generally, the same basic argument for excusing insane defendants applies as well to defendants whose mental illnesses affect emotions: to blame people for acts that result from mental illness, even when that mental illness manifests itself only or primarily in an emotional deficit, is like blaming a sick person for blowing his nose in a library. Of course, not all emotional deficits excuse all crimes, but some emotional deficits still might excuse some crimes at least partially. That is why most jurisdictions provide for the defense of extreme emotional disturbance, a condition that reduces a higher degree crime to a lesser degree crime of the same kind (e.g., first-degree homicide to second-degree homicide).

The point can also be brought out by analogy to children and animals. Imagine that your five-year-old son yells, "I hate you!" He is angry but not so angry as to be out of control. He knows that these words will hurt you deeply, and that is exactly why he utters them. Still, we do not hold him fully morally responsible. The reason for excusing him seems to be that he lacks certain relevant emotions. He does not fully appreciate what he is doing or why it is wrong. If that is why we (partially) excuse this child, then similar lacks in adults that result from mental disease or defect should excuse them as well. If lack of substantial capacity to emotionally appreciate wrongfulness explains why children are not (fully) responsible for their actions, then it should also remove or at least reduce responsibility in adults.

A FEDERAL RULE

Despite its flexibility and popularity, the MPC rule ran into problems. First, it turned out to be hard to apply to actual cases. Many commentators blamed the MPC rule for the *Hinckley* decision, which they saw as misguided. As a result, in reaction to this decision, several states abandoned or weakened the MPC rule by avoiding or dropping the volitional prong and returning to a formulation closer to the old M'Naghten rule.[64] (See below on these reforms.) Second, other critics complained that the notion of "substantial" capacity was too vague and favored, in the interest of clarity and easy application, requiring total incapacity for an insanity defense.

For these reasons, the U.S. Congress in 1984 adopted the following statutory definition of insanity:

> It is an affirmative defense to a prosecution under any Federal statute that, at the time of the commission of the acts constituting the offense, the defendant as a result of a severe mental disease or defect, was unable to appreciate the nature and quality or the wrongfulness of his acts. Mental disease or defect does not otherwise constitute a defense.[65]

The restriction to "severe" mental illness, the deletion of the volitional prong, and the last sentence were all intended to reduce the number of defendants who would be eligible for the insanity defense and thereby to avoid future decisions like that in *Hinckley*.

Insanity as Irrationality

In addition to these developments in law, some legal theorists have proposed a novel way to understand insanity. They emphasize that mentally ill people typically act irrationally, and they claim that this irrationality is the basis on which the insane lack responsibility and should be excused.[66] Different proponents of this general approach disagree about the nature of irrationality, but they agree that insanity should be understood in terms of irrationality of some kind.

Still, we need to look carefully at the kind of irrationality that is supposed to remove responsibility. Consider someone who kicks a computer out of anger. This act of kicking is irrational insofar as it hurts his foot and the computer for no good reason. Nonetheless, the kicker seems responsible for any damage to the computer. Indeed, he also seems just as responsible if what he kicks is not his computer but rather a child. As long as he has (1) the ability to think things through and realize that he has no reason to kick the child and many reasons not to, and (2) the ability to act on his reasons, we can reasonably expect him to exercise these abilities and hold him fully responsible if he fails to exercise them, regardless of the irrationality of his act. Since irrationality does not remove responsibility in cases like this, irrationality by itself cannot be what removes responsibility in cases of insanity.[67]

What removes responsibility, if anything, is a lack of the *capacity* to be rational. People lack this capacity if they cannot form rational beliefs or rationally consider the criminality or wrongfulness of their acts (a defect in theoretical rationality) or if they cannot act according to the reasons that they have (a defect in practical rationality). These are exactly the lacks that remove responsibility according to the MPC rule. So it is not clear that these theoretical revisionists are so far from the MPC rule after all.

The notion of irrationality might give us additional insight into the MPC approach by revealing an underlying unity among defenses involving mental incapacities such as insanity, mental retardation, intoxication, somnambulism, and hypnosis.[68] Still, no jurisdiction has officially adopted this suggestion or defined insanity directly in terms of irrationality. This omission might be because the term "rational" is vague and controversial. Still, it might be possible for the rationality approach to be developed in fruitful ways.

Arguments for an Insanity Defense

Partly because of the difficulties in defining "insanity," there are serious doubts about whether or not our laws should recognize insanity as a separate defense at all. People whose criminal acts are due to mental disease can sometimes be found not guilty on the basis of other, less controversial conditions of responsibility, such as that the agent lacked the specific mens rea for the crime. That finding makes a big difference with regard to how the legal system treats defendants. If they are found to lack mens rea, then they are acquitted and released. In contrast, if they are found not guilty by reason of insanity, then they are committed to a secure mental facility, possibly for longer than they would have spent in prison.[69] This difference makes it important to ask whether, and why, we should have a separate defense for insane people who would not be excused on any other ground, including lack of mens rea.

The main argument for an insanity defense is simple:

> If the insanity defense were abolished, the law would not take adequate account of the incapacitating effects of severe mental illness. Some mentally ill defendants who were psychotic and grossly out of touch with reality may be said to have "intended" to do what they did but nonetheless may have been so severely disturbed that they were unable to understand or appreciate the significance of their actions. These cases do not arise frequently, but when they do a criminal conviction, which signifies the societal judgment that the defendant deserves to be punished, would offend the basic moral intuitions of the community. Judges and juries would be forced either to return a verdict of conviction, which they would regard as morally obtuse, or to acquit the defendant in defiance of the law. They should be spared that moral embarrassment.[70]

Insanity removes moral responsibility, and criminal punishment without moral responsibility is both morally and practically problematic. If the (main) purpose of punishment is either to repay moral wrongs or to express moral condemnation, then punishment seems inappropriate when the punished person was not morally responsible. Still, this conclusion is controversial because it is not clear that the (main) purpose of punishment is retribution or expression of moral condemnation rather than more consequentialist goals like rehabilitation, incapacitation, specific deterrence, general deterrence, victim healing, or protection of society.

But why does insanity remove moral responsibility? One answer is that moral responsibility requires the ability to do otherwise (or control) and insanity negates the ability to do otherwise.[71]

This requirement of the power to do otherwise for moral responsibility seems to stand behind the voluntary act requirement. For example, an epileptic is not responsible for hitting someone during an unforeseeable seizure. There is no voluntary act in this case, but why not? Our criminal law does not count bodily movements as voluntary acts in certain cases, such as seizures, reflexes, hypnosis, and sleepwalking, because they do not result from conscious will. But why should those conditions remove responsibility? The reason seems to be that we cannot avoid doing what does not result from conscious will, which is what enables us to control what we do. This rationale for the voluntary act requirement applies also to acts that result from mental illnesses if their agents could not avoid having the illness and then acting as the illness dictates.

Similarly, consider cognitive excuses. Reasonable mistakes excuse in a way that unreasonable mistakes do not. Why? A natural answer is that we can avoid unreasonable mistakes by being careful, but we cannot avoid making mistakes that are reasonable unless we exercise more caution than it is reasonable to expect of us. Likewise, if mental diseases make people unable to avoid breaking the law, we cannot reasonably expect them to have done otherwise and therefore should not hold such people responsible or punish them for their illegal actions.

This point seems to motivate formulations of the insanity defense that hinge on capacity, control, or what is irresistible, but it also extends to cognitive insanity defenses or cognitive prongs of insanity defenses. If a person is so deluded that she cannot know whether what she is cutting is a steak or a person, then she cannot avoid cutting people who sit next to her while she eats steak. And if she cannot know that it is morally wrong to cut people, then we cannot reasonably expect her to choose her actions according to appropriate moral reasons.

Moreover, even if she knows both that she is cutting a person and that this is wrong, she still might lack the capacity to refrain from cutting others (perhaps because of alien-hand syndrome or some other psychological compulsion). The clauses in insanity defenses that refer to capacity, control, or resistibility seem tailored to capture such conditions, conditions under which a person cannot avoid performing illegal acts. So if both (1) the ability to do otherwise is necessary for moral responsibility and (2) moral responsibility is necessary for justified criminal punishment, then we should not criminally punish people who lack the requisite abilities because of insanity.

Of course, abilities come in degrees. It is harder for some people than others to obey the law. Circumstances also matter. Some insane people can avoid breaking the law by seeking treatment during their lucid periods or by avoiding situations in which they will end up doing harm. Still, if insane people lack the degree of ability or control that is needed in order for them to be morally responsible on some occasions, then they should be excused from criminal punishment for acts that they perform on these occasions (assuming that these conditions can be proved by the applicable standards of evidence).

It might be argued that even insane people who *can* conform their conduct to the law still might be excused for some of their bad acts. Sometimes a person is capable of refraining from acting, but it is still unreasonable to expect that person to refrain from acting. Consider coercion. If a robber says, "Your money or your life," then you are still capable of refusing to hand over the money. You might even have a chance of escaping with the money. Still, you cannot reasonably be expected to take such a chance, which is why we do not blame you for handing over the money. Likewise, this reasonable-expectations excuse constitutes another rationale for an insanity defense. When people are insane in such a way that they are unable to respond to reasons (as discussed above). it seems unreasonable to expect them to act on different reasons and thereby to avoid the acts that their mental illnesses cause them to perform.

A separate set of arguments for the insanity defense comes from consequentialists. If someone really is insane in a way that removes the ability to avoid doing illegal acts, then threats of punishment will not deter this person from breaking the law. He will continue to commit the illegal acts regardless, in which case punishment would be pointless.[72] Similarly, if the purpose of punishment is moral education of criminals or rehabilitation more generally, then these purposes cannot be served by punishing insane people who simply cannot learn or come to know right from wrong.[73] Indeed, punishment and confinement might even exacerbate some mental illnesses, perhaps by removing support networks.

ARGUMENTS AGAINST AN INSANITY DEFENSE

Other consequentialists argue on the opposite side of the issue that even if punishment cannot specifically deter, morally educate, or rehabilitate certain insane people, punishing the insane can still promote other benefits. These other benefits are sometimes claimed to justify abolishing or severely restricting the insanity defense.

One benefit is supposed to be general deterrence—that is, deterring people in society other than the specific individual who is punished.[74] Punishing the insane can promote general deterrence in at least two ways. First, threats of punishment can deter *some* insane criminals. Even if fully insane people cannot be deterred or taught moral lessons, those who are only partially incapacitated can be affected by threats of punishment. Such threats can provide incentives that are strong enough to counteract their insane inclinations. The above consequentialist arguments *for* the insanity defense arguably seem to forget that people have various degrees of control (as discussed above), and threats of punishment can affect probabilities and rates of misbehavior by those who still have some vestige of control.

The second way in which punishing the insane might promote general deterrence is by preventing sane criminals from hoping (usually mistakenly) that they might be able to avoid punishment by faking insanity. A few criminals have reported that they considered in advance the possibility of faking insanity if they were caught.[75] There is no reliable evidence of how often this happens, but the insanity defense arguably interferes with deterrence to some extent if there are any criminals who commit crimes that they would not otherwise have committed if they had not thought that they could avoid punishment by faking insanity. This is just one instance of the general point that whenever the law allows yet another way to avoid punishment, this extra avenue of impunity increases the perceived chances of escaping punishment and thereby decreases the power of general deterrence.

A second consequentialist argument against the insanity defense is that a verdict of not guilty by reason of insanity arguably creates the impression that the criminal "got away with it." After millions of television viewers watched Hinckley shoot President Reagan in 1981 and then be found not guilty by reason of insanity, many people thought that he got off at least partly because he was rich and had tricky lawyers and psychiatrists on his side. Whether or not this widespread belief was true, the impression that rich, devious people get away with crimes can decrease people's respect for the law and thereby their motivation to obey the law.

Third, many critics of the insanity defense fear that dangerous people are incapacitated for less time in mental institutions than in jails and, therefore, that the insanity defense might end up putting dangerous people back out on the street. This belief was not true in the nineteenth century, when people committed to mental institutions often stayed there for the rest of their lives. Today, in contrast, new drugs and new requirements for involuntary commitment combine to make release seem easier and quicker, and people who are safe while on their medications can become very dangerous when they go off them.

Fourth, there is the fundamental problem of determining whether or not a particular defendant really is insane. In many cases, psychiatrists testify on both sides, and juries don't know which experts to believe. In addition, psychiatrists themselves often admit that even if they can determine what a person actually believed and intended to do, they cannot determine whether or not a particular defendant had the ability to do what she did not actually do or to believe what she did not actually believe. It is not even clear what kind of evidence could support claims about such abilities and counterfactuals. These evidentiary difficulties and difficult judgment calls make some results seem arbitrary. Indeed, some convicted criminals in prisons have more serious psychiatric problems than others who were found not guilty by reason of insanity.

All of these practical problems are often presented as additional reasons to restrict the insanity defense as well as to change the procedures surrounding it. Can scientific progress, like that in neuroscience for example, help solve these problems? Some hope so, but it is not at all clear yet. While we wait for better diagnoses and treatments, we face a difficult choice between narrowing the insanity defense so as to increase crime prevention and widening the insanity defense so as to ensure that we do not punish anyone who is not really morally responsible.

PROPOSED REFORMS

When such powerful arguments conflict, it is reasonable to try to give each side its due. The main goals are to minimize the risk of punishing people who are not morally responsible and also to maximize the prevention of crime through deterrence, moral education, and the incapacitation of dangerous people. These goals are supposed to be furthered in varying degrees by the various reforms that have been proposed.

The most radical proposal is to abolish the insanity defense entirely. Many prominent scholars have advocated abolition.[76] Even if the insanity defense is abolished, however, defendants can still be found not guilty if they lack a mental condition (such as intent or knowledge) that is required for a crime. Insanity also might reduce a crime, say, from first-degree or second-degree murder to manslaughter under doctrines of diminished responsibility. Still, the end result of abolition is that people who commit crimes because of insanity will more often be punished.[77]

There are at least three less radical approaches to reforming the insanity defense. First is to reduce its scope by reducing the number of mental conditions that preclude guilt. A proposal of this kind was advocated by the American Bar Association and the American Psychiatric Association.[78] The proposal is to drop the volitional prong of the MPC rule, which (as we have seen) excuses defendants who lack substantial capacity to conform their conduct to the law.[79] Without this clause, the only people who would be found not guilty by reason of insanity would be those who lack substantial capacity to appreciate either what they are doing or that it is wrong, which is closer to the original M'Naghten rule. This proposal is motivated not only by a desire to reduce the number of insanity verdicts but also by supposedly special difficulties in determining whether an individual who *did not* conform to the law still *could have* conformed to the law.

The main problem with this proposal is that even people who know right from wrong do not seem to be morally responsible or, therefore, justly punishable for their actions if they truly could not have avoided performing them. If the reason why cognitive incapacities remove responsibility is that they render one unable to avoid breaking the law, then it is hard to see why volitional or emotional incapacities would not also remove responsibility for the same reason.

A second proposal for reforming the insanity defense is to model it after another feature of the federal rule discussed above. Model Penal Code jurisdictions could drop the word "substantial" so that only a complete lack of capacity to appreciate or conform would remove responsibility. They could also change the word "appreciate" back to "know" in order to ensure that lack of emotional appreciation of the wrongfulness would not remove responsibility. Unfortunately, it is not clear how much difference such wording changes would make to decisions by juries or judges.

A third proposal for reforming the insanity defense is to adopt a new verdict, usually called "guilty but mentally ill." The exact difference between the verdicts of guilty but mentally ill and not guilty by reason of insanity varies, and the former might either replace or be allowed in addition to the latter so that juries could decide between these two verdicts.[80] Separate rules would then have to be formulated for the different verdicts. There might even be separate trials with different procedures for determining guilt and insanity. But however this new verdict is formulated and handled, the point is to allow juries to label defendants as "guilty." The continued use of this key term is supposed to reduce the impression that a criminal "got away with it" and thereby promote respect for the criminal justice system. In addition, people who would be found guilty but mentally ill would sometimes be required to serve out their sentence in prison if they were released from a mental institution before a certain period. This verdict would reduce the chances that dangerous people would return to the streets too soon and would take away much of the incentive to try to fake insanity.

Still, as always, opponents of such proposals argue that if someone really was insane when she committed the crime, then she was not morally responsible. In that case, sending her to prison after she is cured amounts to punishing an innocent person.[81]

Finally, those who fear that the insanity defense lets too many dangerous people back on the streets often propose stricter requirements for release from mental institutions. While the government is now usually required to show that involuntary mental patients are dangerous to themselves or to others, some reformers want people who are found not guilty by reason of insanity to be confined until the patients themselves prove that they are no longer dangerous. Jurisdictions could also require approval by a judge or a panel before release, and some even suggest that the victim or her relatives be reserved a place on the panel. All of these steps would create longer stays for those found not guilty by reason of insanity.

This proposal has its own problems. First, it might lead to inequities insofar as defendants who harmed wealthy victims would probably be confined longer than those who harmed poor victims simply because wealthy victims tend to have more friends who are better able to attend meetings of release panels and to speak at them more articulately and forcefully against release. Second, opponents object, as before, that these people are not guilty in the first place. And if the government cannot show that they are dangerous, as in other cases of involuntary confinement, then it should not be allowed to restrict their freedom. Third, it will be extremely hard for anyone in prison for a crime to prove that she is no longer dangerous at all. What kind of evidence could one cite for such a negative claim?

Restrictions on courtroom evidence have also been proposed. One possibility is to limit defense testimony about the background and emotional history of the defendant. Some critics claim that sad stories of a defendant's childhood can stir up emotions that distort verdicts. If all that is relevant is the defendant's mental condition at the time of the crime, then it might seem irrelevant to talk about his life at other times, much less how his parents treated him when he was young.

Psychiatrists, however, often respond that a person's mental condition cannot be understood properly in isolation from circumstances that gave rise to it. If so, juries need to know the defendant's background in order to reach a justified verdict. Informing the jury of the defendant's past crazy behavior can also help to dispel fears that the defendant might now be faking insanity.

Other restrictions on evidence are also possible. If problems arise when psychiatrists are forced to use legal language, then the law could prohibit psychiatric experts from saying anything directly about the legal issues. Or if insanity trials are ruined by battles between defense and prosecution experts, then the court could assign its own impartial panel of experts. This panel might testify in addition to, or instead of, the experts of both sides.

Such restrictions on evidence, however, fly in the face of a strong tradition of allowing great leeway to defendants in presenting their cases. Without such leeway, defendants will be at the mercy of judges who are not always inclined to select experts sympathetic to defendants and thereby give defendants the fairest possible trials.

Possibly the most popular reform is to shift the burden of proof. Before *Hinckley*, most state and federal courts required the prosecutor to prove the defendant's sanity beyond a reasonable doubt.[82] This burden was often hard to carry because insanity is obscure and experts conflict. It also seems natural to presume that people are sane in the absence of any evidence to the contrary.[83] For these reasons, revisionists proposed either to lighten the burden of proof on the prosecution or to shift the burden to defendants to prove their *insanity*, as in the original M'Naghten rule.

Since *Hinckley*, most states and the federal system have required the defense to prove that the defendant is insane, usually either by a preponderance of evidence or by clear and convincing evidence, as in the federal rule discussed above. To critics, such shifts seem to conflict with the traditional view that every element necessary for someone to be guilty must be proven by the prosecution beyond a reasonable doubt. This stringent requirement is usually justified by the dangers of convicting innocent people who cannot prove their innocence. Reducing the burden on the prosecution or shifting the burden to the defense might increase the chance of punishing people who are not guilty, if insane people really are not guilty. Of course, defenders of this proposal respond that the insanity defense should be seen as an affirmative defense, comparable to entrapment, and the defense always bears the burden of proof for affirmative defenses.[84]

All of these reforms are contentious, partly because each brings dangers as well as promises of improvement. The proper course, then, seems to depend on how many mistakes of various kinds are likely to be made and also on the relative importance of the different kinds of mistakes. Any balancing act will be difficult and debatable.

NOTES

We happily thank Larry Crocker, John Deigh, and David Dolinko for very helpful comments on previous drafts.

1. *Regina v. M'Naghten*, 10 Cl. & Fin. 200, 9 Eng. Rep. 718 (1843).

2. *U.S. v. Hinckley*, 1:81cr00306 (D.D.C., Aug. 24, 1981).

3. *Jones v. U.S.*, 463 U.S. 354 (1983). Given the risks, it might seem surprising that anyone would plead not guilty by reason of insanity to a minor criminal charge. Experts estimate, however, that as many as 86 percent of insanity pleas are for nonviolent felonies and misdemeanors (National Mental Health Association, *Myths and Realities: A Report of the National Commission on the Insanity Defense* [1963], pp. 20–21). Even for serious crimes, the insanity defense is rarely invoked, though its rate might be underestimated because prosecutors frequently dismiss charges against defendants who plead insanity if they agree to civil confinement in a mental institution. *See* Joshua Dressler, *Understanding Criminal Law*, 4th ed. (LexisNexis, 2006), p. 367.

4. *See U.S. v. Freeman*, 357 F.2d 606, 619–620 (2d Cir. 1966) ("At bottom, the determination whether a man is or is not held responsible for his conduct is not a medical

but a legal, social or moral judgment. Ideally, psychiatrists—much like experts in other fields—should…furnish the raw data upon which the legal judgment is based. It is the psychiatrist who informs as to the mental state of the accused—his characteristics, his potentialities, his capabilities. But once this information is disclosed, it is society as a whole, represented by judge or jury, which decides whether a man with the characteristics described should or should not be held accountable for his acts."). For a more compromising view, see *State v. Worlock*, 117 N.J. 596, 606 (1990) ("The insanity defense is a legal standard incorporating moral considerations often established by medical testimony. Notwithstanding advances in psychiatry, mental states remain inscrutable, especially when an abnormal state is in issue. Generally, the determination of a defendant's ability to distinguish between right and wrong depends on psychiatric testimony. Such testimony provides insight into a defendant's mental condition and enables the fact-finder to differentiate defendants who can choose between right and wrong from those who cannot. Ultimately, the insanity defense requires satisfaction of a legal, not a medical, standard. As applied, the 'right and wrong' test blends legal, medical, and ethical concepts. Perhaps for this reason, courts have generally admitted any credible medical testimony on the insanity defense."). Some courts do refer to "medical insanity," but then they distinguish it from legal insanity (though this is misleading for reasons given in the text). *See, e.g., Epps v. State*, 984 So. 2d 1042, 1048 (Miss. Ct. App. 2008) ("It is well established in Mississippi law that just because a criminal defendant is considered medically insane does not mean that he is M'Naghten insane."); *People v. Irwin*, 4 N.Y.S.2d 548, 550 (N.Y. 1938) ("In New York State insanity, to constitute a defense to crime, must be legal insanity as distinguished from what might be loosely or colloquially termed medical insanity."); *Fuller v. State*, 423 S.W.2d 924, 925 (Tex.Cr.App. 1968) ("[M]ere mental deficiency or derangement, though it may constitute a form of insanity known to and recognized by medical science, does not excuse one for crime."); *State v. Crenshaw*, 98 Wash.2d 789, 793 (1983) ("The insanity defense is not available to all who are mentally deficient or deranged; legal insanity has a different meaning and a different purpose than the concept of medical insanity."); *Simecek v. State*, 243 Wis. 439, 447 (1943) ("[U]nder the settled law of this state insanity from a medical standpoint does not necessarily constitute legal insanity in the sense that it constitutes a defense in prosecutions for crime. One may be medically insane and yet be criminally responsible for his acts.").

5. This analogy comes from Herbert Fingarette, *The Meaning of Criminal Insanity* (Berkeley: University of California Press, 1972), pp. 38–39.

6. *See* Dressler, *supra* n. 3, at 363.

7. William Lambard, *Eirenarcha, or the Offices of the Justices of Peace* (London: Newbery and Binneham, 1581).

8. *Regina v. M'Naghten*, *supra* n. 1, at 722.

9. On Gettier conditions, see Robert K. Shope, *The Analysis of Knowing: A Decade of Research* (Princeton: Princeton University Press, 1983).

10. This case is described by Richard Bonnie, "The Moral Basis of the Insanity Defense," 69 *ABA Journal* 194 (Feb. 1983).

11. Baker might have thought either that her aunt was the devil or that her aunt was a human person "possessed" by the devil. In the former but not the latter case, Baker might not know that she was shooting a human person.

12. Her act did not meet the legal requirements for self-defense because, although her motive was self-preservation, it was unreasonable for her to think that her life was in immediate danger. Still, her act might have been justified self-defense if her beliefs had been reasonable and true.

13. *Regina v. M'Naghten, supra* n. 1. *See also Webb v. State*, 270 Ga. 556, 557 (1999) ("[I]t has long been recognized that 'if the delusion is as to a fact which would not excuse the act with which the prisoner is charged, the delusion does not authorize an acquittal of the defendant.'") (citations omitted); *Finger v. State*, 117 Nev. 548, 576 (2001) ("[I]f a jury believes [that the defendant] was suffering from a delusional state, and if the facts as he believed them to be in his delusional state would justify his actions, he is insane and entitled to acquittal. If, however, the delusional facts would not amount to a legal defense, then he is not insane. Persons suffering from a delusion that someone is shooting at them, so they shoot back in self-defense are insane under M'Naghten. Persons who are paranoid and believe that the victim is going to get them some time in the future, so they hunt down the victim first, are not."); *Overton v. State*, 56 S.W.2d 740, 741 (Tenn. 1933) ("Overton, being possessed by an insane delusion that Scott was seeking his life, should be judged as if Scott was actually seeking his life; that, believing Scott was attempting his life, Overton was justified, according to this belief, in cutting up Scott by way of defense.... 'Under [the M'Naghten case] and those following it a homicide committed under an insane delusion is excusable, if the notion embodied in the delusion and believed to be a fact, if a fact indeed, would have excused the defendant.'") (citation omitted);

14. Consider also a contemporary murderer who has an insane delusion such as that he is Jack the Ripper. *See Fingarette, supra* n. 5.

15. Notice that this point does not rule out moral testimony. Just as we can know the temperature on the basis of testimony, even though to know the temperature is not to know what anyone believes about the temperature, so too we can know that an act is wrong on the basis of testimony, when we are justified in trusting the person who gives the testimony, even though knowing that the act is wrong is distinct from knowing that anyone believes that it is wrong.

16. *See* Shope, *supra* n. 9.

17. In applying their own moral standards, judges and juries need not claim that their moral beliefs are objective, much less universal or infallible. The issue here is only about *whose* moral standards—society's, the defendant's, or the legal decision-maker's—are used to determine whether the defendant's moral beliefs count as moral knowledge. To hold that juries and judges may or should use their own moral standards in this way is not to assume that their moral standards are true or objective, although this approach is sometimes (mis)understood in this way. *See, e.g., State v. Bott*, 310 Minn. 331, 336 (1976) ("The instruction used, although it employed the phrase 'contrary to law,' was clearly directed to the issue whether defendant appreciated his act was wrong in a moral sense. The trial court's use of this phrase was clarified by its explanation that '(k)nowledge that the act was wrong refers to the moral side.' The court apparently accepted the philosophic concept of a natural law under which certain rules of conduct—moral rules—inhere throughout the very fabric of the universe and which legislatures and courts have undertaken to reflect. An act which contravenes a properly enacted criminal statute, in the view of the naturalist, contravenes the moral law as well. While we are persuaded that the jury understood the instruction in this way, we think the better practice is to instruct the jury in the terms of the statute but with the explanation that the word 'wrong' is used in the moral sense and does not refer simply to a violation of statute.").

18. For the two courts that have explicitly refrained, see *Ivery v. State*, 686 So.2d 495, 501 (Ala. Crim. App. 1996); and *State v. Abercrombie*, 375 So.2d 1170, 1178–79 (La. 1979).

19. *See, e.g., State v. Hamann*, 285 N.W.2d 180, 183–184 (Iowa 1979); *Finger v. State*, *supra* n. 13, at 576; *State v. Hodgen*, 47 N.C. App. 329, 334 (1980); *Ruffin v. State*, 270 S.W.3d 586, 592 (Tex. Cr. App. 2008); *State v. Crenshaw, supra* n. 4, at 793–796.

20. *See, e.g., U.S. v. Ewing*, 494 F.3d 607, 620 (7th Cir. 2007) ("'[C]riminality' or 'contrary to law' is too narrow a definition of wrongfulness, and 'subjective personal morality' is too broad. The second of the alternative definitions of wrongfulness—contrary to objective societal or public morality—best comports with the rules established in M'Naghten's case."); *State v. Tamplin*, 986 P.2d 914 (Ariz. Ct. App. 1999); *People v. Stress*, 205 Cal.App.3d 1259, 1274 (Cal. Ct. App. 1989) ("Although seldom addressed by the courts, which have generally left the word 'wrong' undefined in jury instructions, the question is whether moral wrong is to be judged by society's generally accepted standards of moral obligation or whether the subjective moral precepts of the accused are to be employed. While the inherent 'slipperiness' of the terminology in this area may leave some doubt, it appears most courts mean that the defendant is sane if he knows his act violates generally accepted standards of moral obligation whatever his own moral evaluation may be."); *People v. Serravo*, 823 P.2d 128, 134–37 (Colo. 1992); *State v. Worlock, supra* n. 4, at 609–11; *People v. Wood*, 12 N.Y.2d 69, 76 (1962); *People v. Adams*, 26 N.Y.2d 129, 135–136 (1970).

21. Some retributivists might argue that the purpose of punishment is to restore justice by counterbalancing what Kant calls "inner viciousness" in *The Metaphysical Elements of Justice*, trans. John Ladd (Indianapolis: Bobbs-Merrill, 1965), p. 103. On this view, people are not morally responsible or, therefore, criminally punishable for doing what they did not or could not personally believe to be morally wrong. But this position would produce practical problems. *See, e.g., People v. Coddington*, 23 Cal.4th 529, 608–609 (Cal. 2000), *rev'd on other grounds* by *Price v. Superior Court*, 25 Cal.4th 1046 (2001) ("'[M]oral obligation in the context of the insanity defense means generally accepted moral standards and not those standards peculiar to the accused.'...'The fact that a defendant claims and believes that his acts are justifiable according to his own distorted standards does not compel a finding of legal insanity.' As we explained in [a previous case], this aspect of the M'Naghten test...is necessary 'if organized society is to formulate standards of conduct and responsibility deemed essential to its preservation or welfare, and to require compliance, within tolerances, with those standards.'") (citations omitted); *People v. Wood*, 12 N.Y.2d 69, 77 (1962) ("[T]he jury...could reasonably have found that defendant was operating under a standard of morality he had set up for himself and which applied only to him. The law does not excuse for such moral depravity.")

22. *See, e.g., State v. Ulm*, 326 N. W. 2d 159, 161 (Minn. 1982) ("To convict a defendant who raises mental illness defense, defendant must know that his act was wrong in a moral sense and not merely know that he has violated a statute."); S.C. Code Ann. § 17-24-10(A) (2009) ("It is an affirmative defense to a prosecution for a crime that, at the time of the commission of the act constituting the offense, the defendant, as a result of mental disease or defect, lacked the capacity to distinguish moral or legal right from moral or legal wrong or to recognize the particular act charged as morally or legally wrong.").

23. *Rex v. Hadfield*, 27 How. St. Tr. 1281 (K.B. 1800).

24. *See supra* n. 13 and surrounding text.

25. *See, e.g., McElroy v. State*, 242 S.W. 883, 884 (Tenn. 1922) ("It is no new thing for criminals to attempt to justify their conduct upon the excuse that they acted on the command of God. They have frequently claimed to have seen visions and to have gotten instructions from the Almighty to do wicked things.... Such excuses were not taken into account in olden times, nor do we think they can now be allowed to avail. Men cannot put themselves beyond the reach of the law by the indulgence of such vain imaginations. To permit this would impair the practical administration of justice.").

26. *See, e.g., People v. Skinner*, 39 Cal. 3d 765, 778–81 (1985) ("Where defendant, who killed his wife, clearly could not distinguish right and wrong with regard to his act, believing that marriage vow 'till death do us part' bestowed on marital partner God-given right to kill other partner if he or she was inclined to violate marital vows, defendant was entitled to judgment of not guilty by reason of insanity, without any further hearing to determine whether he was capable of knowing or understanding nature and quality of his act."); *People v. Schmidt*, 216 N.Y. 324, 340 (N.Y. 1915) ("Obedience to the law is itself a moral duty. If, however, there is an insane delusion that God has appeared to the defendant and ordained the commission of a crime, we think it cannot be said of the offender that he knows the act to be wrong."); *State v. Potter*, 68 Wash. App. 134, 149 (1992) ("[T]he trial court properly instructed the jury that if the deific decree overcame the defendant's cognitive ability to know that his act was 'wrong,' the jury could find him not guilty by reason of insanity."); *State v. Cameron*, 100 Wash.2d 520, 526–27 (1983) ("[O]ne who believes that he is acting under the direct command of God is no less insane because he nevertheless knows murder is prohibited by the laws of man. Indeed, it may actually emphasize his insanity. In the instant case, there is considerable evidence (although not unanimous) from which the jury could have concluded that petitioner suffered from a mental disease; that he believed his stepmother was satan's angel or a sorceress; that he believed God directed him to kill his stepmother; that because of the mental disease it was impossible for him to understand that what he was doing was wrong; and…that his free will had 'been subsumed by [his] belief in the deific decree.'") (citations omitted)

27. *See, e.g., State v. Wilson*, 242 Conn. 605, 616 (1997) ("[A] defendant may establish that he lacked substantial capacity to appreciate the 'wrongfulness' of his conduct if he can prove that, at the time of his criminal act, as a result of mental disease or defect, he substantially misperceived reality and harbored a delusional belief that society, *under the circumstances as the defendant honestly but mistakenly understood them,* would not have morally condemned his actions.") (emphasis in text); *People v. Serravo, supra* n. 20, at 139 ("In our view, the 'deific-decree' delusion is not so much an exception to the right-wrong test measured by the existing societal standards of morality as it is an integral factor in assessing a person's cognitive ability to distinguish right from wrong with respect to the act charged as a crime.").

28. *See, e.g., State v. Worlock, supra* n. 4, at 611 ("In the exceptional case, such as the deific exception in which the defendant claims that he or she acted under a command from God, the court should instruct the jury that 'wrong' encompasses both legal and moral wrong."); *Cunningham v. State*, 1879 WL 3956, at *6 (Miss. 1879) ("If a crazed enthusiast violates the law, impelled by a madness which makes him deem it the inspired act of God, he has only done that which his diseased and deluded imagination taught him was right; and if the act would be proper in one so divinely inspired, and was the direct and necessary consequence of the delusion, there can be no punishment, because, however rational on other subjects, he was on that subject incapable of having a criminal intent."). *See also supra* n. 13.

29. On the relationship between reasons-responsiveness and ability, capacity, and control, see John Martin Fischer and Mark Ravizza, *Responsibility and Control: A Theory of Moral Responsibility* (Cambridge: Cambridge University Press, 1998); and Philip Pettit, *A Theory of Freedom: From the Psychology to the Politics of Agency* (Cambridge: Polity Press, 2001). Of course, reasons-responsiveness comes in degrees, and someone might respond to certain reasons but not others. We will ignore such complications here.

30. *See U.S. v. Freeman, supra* n. 4, at 624 ("[T]he gravamen of psychiatric objections to the M'Naghten Rules…was not that they looked to the cognitive feature of the

personality, undeniably a significant aspect of the total man, but that they looked to this element exclusively.") (citation omitted); *State v. Gardner*, 616 A.2d 1124, 1126 (R.I. 1992) ("M'Naghten was predicated upon an outdated psychological concept. As we stated, '[i]nsanity affects the whole personality of the defendant, including will and emotions,' not just cognitive capacity.") (citation omitted); *State v. Colby*, 6 Ohio Misc. 19, 22 (1966) ("The Court has reached the conclusion that the present 'right and wrong' test, the M'Naghten rules, for deciding criminal responsibility is 'based on an entirely obsolete and misleading conception of the nature of insanity, since insanity does not only, or primarily, affect the cognitive or intellectual faculties, but affects the whole personality of the patient, including both the will and the emotions. An insane person may therefore know the nature and quality of his act and that it is wrong and forbidden by law, and yet commit it as a result of the mental disease.'") (citation omitted).

31. David Margolick, "Lorena Bobbitt Acquitted in Mutilation of Husband," *New York Times* (January 22, 1994), pp. 1, 7. Cognitive disease might also have been present because "[i]n testimony, Mrs. Bobbitt said she had not realized what she had done until later when she fled their home and was in her car." There was no evidence, however, that any cognitive deficit contributed to her act.

32. *See* Joel Feinberg, "What Is So Special about Mental Illness?" in *Doing and Deserving* (Princeton: Princeton, 1970), pp. 272–292.

33. *See* John Deigh, "Moral Agency and Criminal Insanity," in his *Emotions, Values, and the Law* (New York: Oxford University Press, 2008), pp. 196–219.

34. *Smith v. U.S.*, 36 F.2d 548, 549 (D.C. 1929).

35. Some tests in this tradition refer only to weakening of resistance rather than to increase of impulse. *See, e.g., Davis v. U.S.*, 165 U.S. 373, 378 (1897) (holding that a defendant is not responsible if his will "has been otherwise than voluntarily so completely destroyed that his actions are not subject to it, but are beyond his control.").

36. *See* M. T. Gailliot, N. L. Mead, and R. F. Baumeister, "Self-Regulation," in *Handbook of Personality: Theory and Research, 3d ed.*, O. P. John, R. W. Robbins, and L. A. Pervin eds. (New York: Guilford Press, 2008), pp. 472–491.

37. *Parsons v. State*, 81 Ala. 577, 597 (1887).

38. Our emphasis.

39. *Durham v. U.S.*, 214 F.2d 862, 874–875 (1954). There was precedent for this proposition in *State v. Pike*, 49 N.H. 399, 402 (1969); *see also Royal Commission on Capital Punishment 1949–53, Report 131* (Cmd. 8932) (London: HMSO, 1953).

40. *Carter v. U.S.*, 252 F.2d 608, 617 (D.C. 1957). This decision raises the problem of deviant causal chains, discussed above.

41. *See, e.g., U.S. v. Brawner*, 471 F.2d 969, 977–78 (D.C. 1972).

42. *See supra* n. 4 on the issue of whether insanity is a legal or medical classification.

43. *McDonald v. U.S.*, 312 F.2d 847, 851 (D.C. 1962).

44. *See, e.g., State v. Johnson*, 121 R.I. 254, 268 (1979).

45. American Law Institute, *Model Penal Code* (Philadelphia; The American Law Institute, Final Draft, 1962), § 4.01(1).

46. American Law Institute, *Model Penal Code* § 4.01(2). As noted in *State v. Johnson, supra* n. 44, at 269 n. 10, seventeen states that adopted the Model Penal Code rule added this clause by 1979: Alaska, Arkansas, Connecticut, Hawaii, Illinois, Indiana, Maine, Maryland, Missouri, Montana, Oregon, Tennessee, Texas, Utah, Vermont, Wisconsin, and Wyoming. Still, this clause remains controversial.

47. On nonbehavioral manifestations of psychopathy, see *The Psychopath: Emotion and the Brain*, by James Blair, Derek Mitchell, and Karina Blair (Oxford: Wiley-Blackwell,

2005). Whether or not psychopaths should be found not guilty by reason of insanity is discussed and debated in a special issue of *Neuroethics* 1, 3 (2008), pp. 149–212.

48. *See State v. Johnson, supra* n. 44, at 262 n. 4.

49. What counts as substantial is not clear, but it is illuminating that a minority of the American Law Institute proposed alternative wording: "A person is not responsible for criminal conduct if at the time of such conduct as a result of mental disease or defect, his capacity either to appreciate the wrongfulness of his conduct or to conform his conduct to the requirements of the law is so substantially impaired that he cannot justly be held responsible." This alternative wording might have helped to clear up the ambiguity between absolute and relative measures (discussed in the text).

50. For more detail on volitional incapacity, see Michael Corrado, "Responsibility and Control," 34 *Hofstra L. Rev.* 59 (2005); and "The Case for a Purely Volitional Insanity Defense," 42 *Tex. Tech L. Rev.* 481 (2009).

51. Arkansas, Iowa, Maryland, Nevada, Oregon, and Virginia. *See* Ark. Code Ann. § 5-2-312(a)(1)(B) (2009) ((a)(1) "It is an affirmative defense to a prosecution that at the time the defendant engaged in the conduct charged he or she lacked capacity as a result of mental disease or defect to: (A) Conform his or her conduct to the requirements of law; or (B) Appreciate the criminality of his or her conduct."); *State v. Dye*, No. 08–0887, 2009 WL 3337617, at *4 (Iowa Ct. App., Oct. 7, 2009) ("The words 'right' and 'wrong' in [Iowa Code Ann. §] 701.4 refer to legal right and wrong, not moral right and wrong."); Md. Code Ann., [Criminal Procedure] § 3-109(a)(1) (2009) ((a) "A defendant is not criminally responsible for criminal conduct if, at the time of that conduct, the defendant, because of a mental disorder or mental retardation, lacks substantial capacity to: (1) appreciate the criminality of that conduct"); Nev. Rev. Stat. Ann. § 174.035(5)(b)(2) (2009) ((5) "Under [a plea or defense of not guilty by reason of insanity], the burden of proof is upon the defendant to establish by a preponderance of the evidence that: (a) Due to a disease or defect of the mind, he was in a delusional state at the time of the alleged offense; and (b) Due to the delusional state, he either did not: (1) Know or understand the nature and capacity of his act; or (2) Appreciate that his conduct was wrong, meaning not authorized by law."); Or. Rev. Stat. Ann. § 161.295(1) (2009) ("A person is guilty except for insanity if, as a result of mental disease or defect at the time of engaging in criminal conduct, the person lacks substantial capacity either to appreciate the criminality of the conduct or to conform the conduct to the requirements of law."); Va. Code Ann. § 4801(a)(1) (2009) ("(a) The test when used as a defense in criminal cases shall be as follows: (1) A person is not responsible for criminal conduct if at the time of such conduct as a result of mental disease or defect he lacks adequate capacity either to appreciate the criminality of his conduct or to conform his conduct to the requirements of law.").

52. As noted in *State v. Johnson, supra* n. 44, at 269 n. 9, seventeen states that adopted the Model Penal Code rule chose the term "wrongfulness": Alaska, Connecticut, Delaware, Hawaii, Idaho, Indiana, Maine, Michigan, Missouri, New York, Ohio, Tennessee, Texas, Utah, Wyoming, West Virginia, and Wisconsin.

53. States that interpret "wrongfulness" in the Model Penal Code rule in terms of the community's or society's sense of morality include Arizona, California, Colorado, Connecticut, Indiana, New York (which provides for an insanity *defense* that is a hybrid of M'Naghten and Model Penal Code), Rhode Island, South Carolina, and Washington. *See, e.g., State v. Wilson*, 242 Conn. 605, 616 (1997) ("[W]e conclude that a defendant may establish that he lacked substantial capacity to appreciate the 'wrongfulness' of his conduct if he can prove that, at the time of his criminal act, as a result of mental disease or defect, he substantially misperceived reality and harbored a delusional belief that society, under

the circumstances as the defendant honestly but mistakenly understood them, would not have morally condemned his actions.").

54. *See supra* n. 21 for possible reasons.

55. *See, e.g., U.S. v. Freeman, supra* n. 4, at 622 n. 52 ("We have adopted the word 'wrongfulness' in Section 4.01 as the American Law Institute's suggested alternative to 'criminality' because we wish to include the case where the perpetrator appreciates that his conduct is criminal, but, because of a delusion, believes it to be morally justified."). Failure to appreciate moral wrongness would also be enough in jurisdictions that excuse those who lack capacity to appreciate either moral or legal wrongness. *See, e.g.,* S.C. Code Ann. § 17-24-10(A) (2009) ("It is an affirmative defense to a prosecution for a crime that, at the time of the commission of the act constituting the offense, the defendant, as a result of mental disease or defect, lacked the capacity to distinguish moral or legal right from moral or legal wrong or to recognize the particular act charged as morally or legally wrong.").

56. *See* Antony Duff, *Punishment, Communication, and Community* (New York: Oxford University Press, 2000). Of course, neither moral condemnation nor retributive motives are always perfectly sensitive to the mental problems that afflict perpetrators. We often are so angry or devastated that we want to hold killers responsible even when they are not actually morally responsible and even when we know that they are not morally responsible. This natural psychological tendency, however, conflicts with our moral belief that just punishment requires moral responsibility.

57. *See, e.g., State v. Wilson, supra* n. 27, at 614 ("As Herbert Wechsler, chief reporter for the Model Penal Code, stated in his model jury charge: 'To appreciate the wrongfulness of conduct is, in short, to realize that it is wrong; to understand the idea as a matter of importance and reality; to grasp it in a way that makes it meaningful in the life of the individual, not as a bare abstraction put in words.'") (citation omitted); *People v. Adams,* 26 N.Y.2d 129, 135 (1970) ("'A new dimension is accorded the word 'know' by following it with 'or appreciate.' This is designed to permit the defendant possessed of mere surface knowledge or cognition to be excused, and to require that he have some understanding of the legal and moral import of the conduct involved if he is to be held criminally responsible.'") (citation omitted); *State v. Dyer,* 16 Or. App. 247, 258 (1974) ("The effect of the word 'understand' in the [State v.] Gilmore[, 242 Or. 463 (1996)] formulation is to allow a full range of testimony as to emotional as well as intellectual cognition of the act, a practice which the drafters wished to continue by using 'appreciate.'"); *State v. Johnson, supra* n. 44, at 268 (1979) ("Our [new] test [of the insanity defense] consciously employs the more expansive term 'appreciate' rather than 'know.' Implicit in this choice is the recognition that mere theoretical awareness that a certain course of conduct is wrong, when divorced from appreciation or understanding of the moral or legal impact of behavior, is of little import.").

58. Robert Hare, *Without Conscience* (New York: Atria, 1993), p. 125.

59. American Law Institute, *Model Penal Code and Commentaries* (1985), § 4.01(1), p. 166; *see also State v. Wilson, supra* n. 27, at 614 ("The drafters of the Model Penal Code purposefully adopted the term 'appreciate' in order to account for the defendant whose 'detached or abstract awareness' of the wrongfulness of his conduct 'does not penetrate to the affective level.'").

60. *See* Christopher Slobogin, "The Integrationist Alternative to the Insanity Defense," 30 *Am. J. Crim. L.* 315 (2003).

61. *See supra* n. 30 on emotional mental illness, and Terry Maroney, "Emotional Competence, 'Rational Understanding,' and the Criminal Defendant," 43 *Am. Crim. L. Rev.* 1375 (2006).

62. *See, e.g.,* Antonio Damasio, *Descartes' Error: Emotion, Reason, and the Human Brain* (New York: Avon Books, 1994), pp. 212–217.

63. *See* Christopher Slobogin's arguments that deterrability is essential for responsibility in "A Jurisprudence of Dangerousness," 98 *Nw. U. L. Rev.* 1 (2003).

64. States whose insanity defenses contain only a cognitive prong, usually M'Naghten, and lack a volitional prong include California, Louisiana, Minnesota, Nebraska, New York, North Carolina, Ohio, Oklahoma, South Dakota, Texas, and Washington. *See* Ohio Rev. Code Ann. § 2945.391 (2009) ("Proof that a person's reason, at the time of the commission of an offense, was so impaired that the person did not have the ability to refrain from doing the person's act or acts, does not constitute a defense."); Okla. Stat. Ann. tit. 21, § 154 (2009) ("A morbid propensity to commit prohibited acts existing in the mind of a person who is not shown to have been incapable of knowing the wrongfulness of such acts forms no defense to a prosecution therefor."); S.D. Codified Laws § 22-5-7 (2009) ("A morbid propensity to commit prohibited acts existing in the mind of a person who is not shown to have been incapable of knowing the wrongfulness of such acts forms no defense to a prosecution therefor."); *People v. Severance,* 138 Cal.App.4th 305, 324 (2006) ("The irresistible impulse test...has long been discredited in California as a test for legal insanity."); *State v. George,* 768 So.2d 748, 757 (La. Ct. App. 2000) ("[U]nder the law and jurisprudence of this state, the defendant cannot claim the defense of irresistible impulse."); *State v. LaTourelle,* 343 N.W.2d 277, 282 (Minn. 1984) ("This court has rejected the 'irresistible impulse' definition."); *State v. Canbaz,* 270 Neb. 559, 574 (2005) ("the theory of 'irresistible impulse'...is a defense not recognized in Nebraska."); *People v. Hakner,* 34 N.Y.2d 822, 823 (1974) (noting that New York Legislature rejected irresistible-impulse defense); *State v. Helms* 284 N.C. 508, 514–515 (1974) ("Under the law of this State there is no halfway house on the road to insanity which affords sanctuary to those who know the right and still the wrong pursue.... '[T]he law is far from excusing criminal acts committed under the impulse of [irresistible] passions.'") (citation omitted); *Saenz v. State,* 879 S.W.2d 301, 308 (Tex. Crim. App. 1994) (irresistible impulse is "doctrine that is no longer recognized in Texas."); *State v. Edmon,* 621 P.2d 1310, 1314 (Wash. Ct. App. 1981) ("This 'irresistible impulse' defense is not accepted in Washington.").

65. 18 U.S.C. § 20. This move was anticipated in *U.S. v. Lyons,* 731 F.2d 243, 15 Fed. R. Evid. Serv. 859 (5th Cir. 1984) (en banc).

66. *See* Feinberg, *supra* n. 32; Fingarette, *supra* n. 5; Michael Moore, *Law and Psychiatry* (Cambridge: Cambridge University Press, 1974); Charles Culver and Bernard Gert, *Philosophy and Medicine* (New York: Oxford University Press, 1982); Jennifer Radden, *Madness and Reason* (London: Allen and Unwin, 1985); and Stephen Morse, "Diminished Rationality, Diminished Responsibility," 1 *Ohio St. J. Crim. L.* 289 (2003).

67. For more arguments against assimilating insanity and irrationality, see Walter Sinnott-Armstrong, "Insanity vs. Irrationality," 1 *Public Affairs Quarterly* 1 (1987); and Slobogin, n. 60.

68. *See* Herbert Fingarette and Ann Fingarette Hasse, *Mental Disabilities and Criminal Responsibility* (Berkeley: University of California Press, 1979).

69. *See Jones v. U.S., supra* n. 3. Prosecutors could be authorized or even required to bring civil commitment proceedings in parallel with criminal proceedings whenever the defendant's mental condition poses a danger to others. This proposal, however, would hardly be free of practical problems.

70. Bonnie, *supra* n. 10.

71. *See* Fischer and Ravizza and Pettit, *supra* n. 29. Harry Frankfurt ("Alternate Possibilities and Moral Responsibility," 66 *Journal of Philosophy* 829 [1969]) and his followers have proposed various counterexamples to the proposition that moral responsibility entails the power to do otherwise, but they need not detain us here because they are not directly relevant to mental illness or conditions of legal responsibility.

72. Jeremy Bentham, *An Introduction to the Principles of Morals and Legislation* (Garden City, N.Y.: Doubleday, 1961, originally published 1789) and Slobogin, "A Jurisprudence of Dangerousness," n. 63.

73. *See* Jean Hampton, "The Moral Education Theory of Punishment," 13 *Philosophy and Public Affairs* 208 (1984).

74. *See* H. L. A. Hart, "Principles of Punishment," in *Punishment and Responsibility* (Oxford: Oxford University Press, 1968), pp. 18–20.

75. Fakers or malingerers were cited often after Hinckley as reasons to abolish the insanity defense. *See, e.g.,* Orrin Hatch, "The Insanity Defense Is Insane," *Reader's Digest* (Oct. 1982).

76. Pre-Hinckley abolitionists include Thomas Szasz, *Law, Liberty, and Psychiatry* (New York: Collier-Macmillan, 1963); Goldstein and Katz, "Abolish the Insanity Defense, Why Not?" 72 *Yale L.J.* 853 (1963); Alan Dershowitz, "Abolish the Insanity Defense," 9 *Crim. L. Bull.* 434 (1973); and Norval Morris, *Madness and the Criminal Law* (Chicago: University of Chicago Press, 1982). Morris and Bonnie criticize each other's views in "Debate: Should the Insanity Defense Be Abolished?" 1 *Journal of Law and Medicine* 117 (1986–87).

77. Three states have abolished the insanity defense: Idaho, Kansas, and Montana. Defendants in these states may still use mental illness to show "diminished capacity" to form the specific intent that is required for the offense being charged.

78. *See American Bar Association Policy on the Insanity Defense,* Approved by the ABA House of Delegates, February 9, 1983; American Psychiatric Association, *Statement on the Insanity Defense* (Washington, D.C.; American Psychiatric Association, 1982).

79. To date, the only state that seems to have adopted the Model Penal Code's version of the insanity defense but without the volitional prong is New York. *See also U.S. v. Lyons,* n. 65.

80. States that allow a verdict of guilty but mentally ill include Alaska, Delaware, Georgia, Illinois, Indiana, Kentucky, Maryland, Michigan, Mississippi, Nevada, New Mexico, Oregon, Pennsylvania, South Carolina, South Dakota, Utah, and Washington. Most of these states allow not guilty by reason of insanity as well. *See* "'Guilty but Mentally Ill' Statutes: Validity and Construction," 71 A.L.R. 4th 702; "Mental Illness Not Amounting to Insanity; 'Guilty but Mentally Ill' Verdict," 21 Am. Jur. 2d, Criminal Law § 38; "Guilty but Mentally Ill or Mentally Retarded," 22 C.J.S., Criminal Law § 130.

81. *See, e.g., Kansas v. Crane,* 534 U. S. 407 (2002); and *Kansas v. Hendricks,* 521 U. S. 346 (1997).

82. Dressler, *supra* n. 3, at 369. Recall that the burden was on the defense in the original M'Naghten rule.

83. *But see* Eule, "The Presumption of Sanity: Bursting the Bubble," 25 *UCLA L. Rev.* 637 (1978).

84. In *Leland v. Oregon,* 343 U.S. 790 (1952), the Supreme Court held that Oregon may require a defendant raising an insanity defense to prove insanity beyond a reasonable doubt. *See also* James M. Varga, "Due Process and the Insanity Defense; Examining Shifts in the Burden of Persuasion," 53 *Notre Dame Lawyer* 123 (1977). Of the forty-seven states that provide for an insanity defense, most of them explicitly designate it as an affirmative defense, a defense that the defendant has the affirmative burden of proving, whether

beyond a reasonable doubt, by clear and convincing evidence, or by a preponderance of the evidence. Only two states, Nevada and Utah, tend to treat the insanity defense not so much as an affirmative defense but more, like the three abolitionist states (Idaho, Kansas, and Montana), as a diminished capacity defense. The difference is that the diminished capacity defense does not impose an affirmative burden on the defendant but rather constitutes a means by which the defendant can try to establish that the prosecutor has not met *her* affirmative burden of proving that defendant had, at the time of the alleged offense, the specific intent required to be guilty of the offense.

CHAPTER 13

....

GENDER ISSUES IN THE CRIMINAL LAW

....

MARCIA BARON

I. INTRODUCTION

....

In keeping with this volume's theme of philosophical issues in criminal law, this essay will focus on philosophical questions in criminal law that have a significant gender component rather than on gender issues more generally. Due to space limitations, it will focus on just three areas: two defenses, namely, self-defense and the provocation defense, and rape.

It is important to keep in mind a fact that is such a familiar feature of the landscape that it easily escapes notice. The law reaches back many centuries, many centuries before women attained citizenship. Not only have women had the vote for less than one hundred years, but in a number of small but significant ways, women have even much more recently not been treated as full citizens and, arguably, in some ways are still not so treated.[1] It is important to be alert to these "small but significant ways" and to take notice of such details as the following, mentioned in a 1998 ruling by the High Court of Australia rejecting the appeal of a woman convicted of the murder of her abusive husband: in 1981 she applied for a mortgage, but the bank refused to grant one unless a male was also liable to repay the loan.[2] Given how very recent, tenuous and arguably incomplete women's status as full citizens is, and given the continuity between criminal law as it is now, and criminal law as it was long before women were citizens, we should not be surprised to find that our laws and legal system are only gradually accommodating the fact (if indeed it is a fact) that women are now full citizens. (Related points worth bearing in mind are that it was not long ago that juries were all male, and only very recently have we begun to have a sizeable number of female lawyers, prosecutors, judges and legislators.) Progress in this direction is of course not the same in all areas of the law, and in all areas of the criminal law, so the mere fact that one can point to very impressive changes in some areas should not be taken to show that in fact the problems have by now all been adequately addressed.

II. Provocation

> The presence or absence of the heat of passion on sudden provocation...has been, almost from the inception of the common law of homicide, the single most important factor in determining the degree of culpability attaching to an unlawful homicide.
>
> <div align="right">U.S. Supreme Court Justice Lewis F. Powell Jr. in
<i>Mullaney v. Wilbur</i> (1975)</div>

> The vast majority of killers are male. Even in the domestic context, men are much more likely to have been the serious aggressors whether they are ultimately killers or victims. These grim facts might at one time have been regarded as part of the natural order of things which it is the function of the law to reflect. One must now ask whether the doctrine of provocation, under the cover of an alleged compassion for human infirmity, simply reinforces the conditions in which men are perceived and perceive themselves as natural aggressors, and in particular *women's* natural aggressors. Unfortunately, the answer to that question is yes.
>
> <div align="right">Jeremy Horder, <i>Provocation and Responsibility</i></div>

A. Introduction

The provocation, or heat of passion, defense has gained notoriety in recent years as a defense that allows male homicidal violence against women to be regarded as understandable, and partially excusable.[3] Not that the defense is restricted to male violence, or to male violence against women; anyone who kills in a "sudden heat of passion" that results from "adequate provocation" is guilty only of manslaughter, not murder. But, as Donna Coker emphasizes, "English and American jurists and legal scholars repeatedly refer to adultery as *the* paradigm example" of adequate provocation.[4] And although the defense (at least officially) is now as available to a woman who kills her adulterous husband or his partner as to a man who does so,[5] it is far less common for women to kill in such a situation.[6] Contrary to the popular view, reflected in so many films, that hell hath no fury like a woman scorned,[7] a man scorned, or a man who believes himself cuckolded, is far more dangerous to others than is a woman in a comparable situation.[8]

The heat of passion defense, moreover, lends itself less well to some cases that would seem far more meritorious than adultery cases, for example, cases where the killer was the victim of chronic violence and psychological abuse at the hands of the deceased and after years of trying to placate or flee from the abuser, finally snapped and killed him. *That* provocation seems more extreme than infidelity, yet the defense is shaped in such a way that it is a stretch for it to cover such cases.[9]

Is the provocation defense hopelessly tainted by sexism, so much so that it is not worth retaining? Or is it seriously tainted but fixable? Or is the sexism simply the sexism one finds in many places, in the criminal law and in the world in general, and thus arguably not a reason to abandon or modify the defense? I will offer reasons for thinking that the answer to the last question is "no" and suggest ways in which the provocation defense might be improved to address the problems. Whether it is better to improve on the defense or to abandon it altogether, however, I will leave open.[10]

My task is complicated by two related facts: the provocation defense differs considerably from one jurisdiction to the next, and the underlying doctrine of provocation is itself murky and contested. I will not try to cover all the variations in the law of provocation; and I cannot address all the complexities about exactly what the doctrine of provocation is, though I will touch on a few salient issues. Unless I indicate otherwise, by "the defense" I mean the traditional Anglo-American heat of passion defense and not the American Law Institute's Model Penal Code (MPC) version of it (adopted, sometimes in modified form, in several states in the United States). I begin with an overview in which I try to bring out what seems right about the defense. It is all too easy just to attack it.

B. Overview of the Defense

As noted above, one who commits what would otherwise be a murder is guilty only of manslaughter if he or she kills in a "sudden heat of passion" as the result of "adequate provocation." The underlying idea is similar to that behind deeming premeditated (i.e., cold-blooded) murders more heinous than other murders and differentiating first-degree from second-degree murder accordingly: other things being equal, the "cooler" the homicide, the more culpable the killer.

Intuitively, there seems to be something right in this idea. Someone who plans and carries out a murder with cool detachment seems more culpable than someone who kills in the heat of the moment. One who kills because very upset about something, though not about something that it was reasonable to be so upset about, may well deserve to be convicted of murder but perhaps not punished as harshly as someone who kills "in cold blood." And if what the defendant was upset about is something that would upset most of us—or more to the point, something that would upset a reasonable person—and indeed upset him or her so much that "the control of reason is disturbed,"[11] then, the thought is, perhaps the crime should not be seen as murder at all, but only as manslaughter. The defendant is still culpable, but not as culpable as a murderer.[12]

This fundamental idea and the standard that emerges from it are elaborated in the 1862 case of *Maher v. People*. For a homicide to count as a murder, it

> must, in all ordinary cases, have been committed with some degree of coolness and deliberation, or, at least, under circumstances in which ordinary men, or the average of men recognized as peaceable citizens, would not be liable to have their reason clouded or obscured by passion; and the act must be prompted by, or the circumstances indicate that it sprung from, a wicked, depraved or malignant mind—a mind which, even in its habitual condition, and when excited by no provocation which would be liable to give undue control to passion in ordinary men, is cruel, wanton or malignant, reckless of human life, or regardless of social duty.[13]

By contrast, a killing in the heat of passion "is the result of…temporary excitement, by which the control of reason was disturbed, rather than of any wickedness of heart or cruelty or recklessness of disposition."[14] If the killing was "committed under the influence of passion or in heat of blood, produced by an adequate or reasonable provocation, and before a reasonable time…elapsed for the blood to cool and reason to resume its habitual control" and is the result of temporary excitement, "then the law, out of indulgence to the frailty of human nature, or rather, in recognition of the laws upon which human nature is constituted, very properly regards the offense as of a less heinous character than murder, and gives it the designation of manslaughter."[15]

The general principle put forward in *Maher* is that a killing should be considered manslaughter, not murder, if it

(a) was the result of temporary excitement, by which the control of reason was disturbed;

(b) was committed while the defendant was "in the heat of passion," i.e., before he or she had cooled off;

(c) was provoked by "adequate or reasonable" provocation, i.e., "provocation which would be liable to give undue control to passion in ordinary men"; and

(d) took place before "ordinary men, or the average of men recognized as peaceable citizens," would have cooled off.

C. A Dubious History

Maher reflects a shift toward a general, abstract standard for deciding whether the provocation was adequate. Previously, only certain event types were regarded as adequate provocation. In early English common law, the following provoking incidents were held to be sufficiently grave to warrant the reduction from murder to

manslaughter: a "grossly insulting assault"; the sight of "a friend, relative, or kins-
man being attacked"; "seeing an Englishman unlawfully deprived of his liberty";
and "seeing a man in the act of adultery with one's wife."[16] As Celia Wells remarks,
it "does not require a rabid feminist to spot the gendered tenor" of these prototypes
of provocation.[17] There is, first of all, the fact that a wife's adultery was legally adequate provocation[18] while a husband's was not. In addition—and not unrelated—
male honor figures prominently in all four prototypes.

But, it will be pointed out, things have changed. The rigid categories are no
more; a husband's adultery can constitute adequate provocation; and male honor
has gradually figured less prominently as the defense ceased to be defined by reference to specific types of provoking events. This provides some basis for thinking
that the gendered tenor of the defense would have disappeared. To that in due
course. First, a more detailed historical sketch is in order.[19]

Whereas in the seventeenth and eighteenth centuries the (implicit) reason for
thinking that mitigation was called for seems to have been that honor called for
retaliation, so that it was not entirely wrong[20] to kill in such circumstances, the
defense gradually became more an excuse than a justification. The idea remained
that to kill in the heat of passion was to kill out of anger brought on by adequate
provocation, but whereas the earlier idea was clearly that this was righteous anger,
and that mitigation was in order largely for that reason, over time more emphasis
was placed on anger's power to obscure reason. That the anger was righteous was
not central; what mattered was its effect on the individual (qua rational agent). The
rationale for the provocation defense thus shifted into what we see in *Maher*: mitigation is in order as a concession to human frailty.

Contrast the rationales for mitigation in the following two passages:

> If one man upon angry words shall make an assault upon another, either by
> pulling him by the nose, or filliping upon the forehead, and he that is so assaulted
> shall draw his sword, and immediately run the other through, that is but
> manslaughter; for the peace is broken by the person killed, and with an indignity
> to him that received the assault. [Lord Chief Justice John Holt in *R. v. Mawgridge*
> (1707)][21]

> You will have to say, consulting your own natures, whether the prisoner was not
> under such a state of excitement as to be totally unconscious of what he was
> about....The more a father brooded over a case like this, the more likely he would
> be to be goaded into desperation and madness....At least it is reducible to the
> offence of manslaughter, if reason had not had time to resume her seat. [Defense
> counsel to jury in *R. v. Fisher* (1837)][22]

For Justice Holt, what matters most is that it was the deceased, not the defendant, who broke the peace (and not with mere words). Although he does not explicitly state that the defendant is not entirely in the wrong, that seems to be the
implication, given the suggestion that the deceased bears a considerable share of
responsibility for what transpired. Fisher's counsel, by contrast, apparently sees the
most significant feature of the provocation to be the state of mind it induces. And

what a state of mind! The picture here seems to be of someone who is barely an agent, whose actions are more like those of someone under hypnosis, or sleepwalking ("totally unconscious of what he is about") than of someone who has intentionally, or even just knowingly, killed another.[23]

This shift toward seeing provocation as an excuse rather than a justification might be considered an improvement. Although I agree that the decline in the part played by male honor—indeed, honor in general—is salutary, the metamorphosis into an excuse is less so. As I see it, it is important that the violence was a reaction to a serious wrong; that component of the defense can be retained without a conflation of serious wrong with attack on one's honor. More on this below.[24]

D. The Provocation Defense Today

1. So, just what is so bad about the defense (setting to one side its dubious history)? I begin by distancing myself from one way of answering that question. As I see it, the following is *not* the problem: the provocation defense far more often provides a defense for men than for women. I mention this because even leading criminal law scholars sometimes speak as if it is, or as if that is the main objection that feminists have to it.

Consider Joshua Dressler's discussion of feminist challenges to the provocation defense. It opens with a well-chosen quotation: "Nowhere except perhaps in rape cases [...] is the gendered—or more accurately 'sexed'—nature of law more apparent than in so-called domestic homicide cases in which men kill women and then claim provocation."[25] He proceeds to offer a helpful gloss of the "abolitionist argument": "Although the defense is supposedly founded on compassion for ordinary human infirmity, it is really a legal disguise to partially excuse male aggression by treating men 'as natural aggressors, and in particular *women's* natural aggressors.'"[26] "Legal disguise" is probably too strong either for truth or as a representation of the feminist objection, insofar as "disguise" implies intent, but his synopsis captures the core idea. I would add that the defense is gendered in the following way: it purports to be a concession to human frailty, when it is in fact a concession only to certain sorts of frailties, those often thought to be part and parcel of masculinity. More on this shortly. The problem I wish to highlight is that in his critique of the argument, Dressler treats it as if it were saying something quite different, viz., that because men benefit from the defense more than women do, the defense should be abolished. "That the provocation defense is primarily invoked by males is an insufficient reason to repeal it."[27] I certainly agree, but nothing in the quotations from those to whom he attributes the argument assert or even hint at that. It trivializes feminist challenges to suggest that this is the key feminist claim.[28]

2. Enough on what the problem is not. What is the problem? One problem is indicated in the quotation from Jeremy Horder at the beginning of section II, above: the defense "reinforces the conditions in which men are perceived and perceive themselves as natural aggressors, and in particular *women's* natural aggressors." But, it

will be asked, what reason is there to think that the defense still does this today? A related problem, one which I noted above, forms part of the answer to that question: although the provocation defense purports to be a concession to human frailty, it is a concession primarily just to certain sorts of frailties, those often thought to be part and parcel of masculinity.[29] The connection between the two problems is as follows: insofar as the defense provides (under cover of "concession to human frailty") a concession to male aggression, jealousy, a sense of entitlement to the devotion and affection of the woman he wants to make "his," and (hinted at by that last) a sense of ownership toward his wife or girlfriend, the defense partially excuses male aggression (at least, aggression toward his (insufficiently loyal) female partner and any man who looks to be luring her away). It treats it as, in effect, "just human nature."

Evidence that the concession is not to human frailty (or frailties) in general, is found in the fact that the law does not generally show lenience toward those who kill in circumstances in which it is difficult for them to conform their conduct to the law. Lenience is not extended toward those who, enraged by U.S. foreign policy, (seek to) kill a high-ranking official responsible for leading the country into war against Iraq. Of course this might be dismissed as a special case; there is, for policy reasons, little lenience shown toward those who assassinate political leaders. But if we are going to allow ourselves to appeal to policy considerations, the seriousness of the problem of domestic violence should render this too a "special case." Lenience toward those who blow up too easily and kill their loved ones when angered by some (alleged) misconduct would not seem to be good policy, particularly when domestic violence is so very common, so underreported, and so difficult to prosecute.[30]

The claim that the concession is not to human frailty in general can be supported by examining actual cases to get a sense of where lenience is shown and where it is not.[31] What is puzzling, as one peruses provocation cases, are the many instances in which the provocation is violence or threatened violence, and where mitigation clearly does seem to be in order, but where the defendant is convicted of murder (and the conviction, if challenged, upheld). This is all the more startling given the many cases where mitigation seems far less deserved, yet is granted. One reads a 1987 Tennessee case where a murder conviction is set aside because *D* (Thornton), whose wife had told him that she wanted to end the marriage, killed his wife's lover upon "discovering" them in bed together (discovering this after spying on them through her window for hours, then driving home to get a camera and a gun, though not without first letting the air out of *V*'s tires).[32] Then one reads a 1993 Tennessee case where *D* (Furlough) awoke one morning to find her husband "standing over their daughter with her diaper off, his pants down and his penis erect."[33] He "told her to forget what she had seen" but later that day[34] told her (according to her testimony) that "he was going to 'have [the child]' when they got home and was going to 'make [her] watch.'"[35] *D* killed him minutes later.[36] This appellant was shown less sympathy: the court affirmed her first-degree murder conviction and life sentence.[37] In each instance we understand why someone in such a situation might react as the defendants did, and we understand it in a way different from the "understanding" (i.e., basic comprehension) of why someone might murder another for money or to eliminate the sole witness to a crime. Both Furlough and Thornton are deeply upset, and understandably so, at what they see as (and what in Furlough's case unquestionably is) the egregiously wrongful conduct of an intimate. If a concession to Thornton is in order because we understand how easily one could react with lethal violence upon the discovery that one's wife—even an estranged wife, if one were eager to be reconciled—was having an affair with another man, surely such lenience is even more in order concerning Furlough, given the enormity of the crime her husband was about to commit that morning and now vowing to commit when he got home.[38] It is hard to imagine that a concession to human frailty could be in order for Thornton but not for Furlough.

It is instructive, too, to look beyond provocation to consider what concessions the criminal law makes to human frailty. With some notable exceptions, lenience is rarely shown (at least in gradations of crimes) toward those whose circumstances are such that they found it very difficult to conform their conduct to the law. (By "circumstances are such that" I mean to indicate that I am not speaking here of cases of insanity and diminished capacity.) The exceptions, interestingly enough, are (a) cases where the difficulty is due to the serious misconduct[39] of another and (b) lesser-of-two-evils cases. Provocation cases fit neatly into the category of exceptions *only insofar as the difficulty is indeed due to another's serious misconduct.*[40] That this is so lends support to a proposal that the provocation defense be limited by a requirement that the provocation be serious misconduct, perhaps to be specified as misconduct of a type and magnitude that merit imprisonment.[41] If this proposal is rejected as too restrictive, and the argument is made that lenience is indeed in order simply as a concession to human frailty, the question resurfaces: which frailties, and why are they so typically qualities associated with masculinity? And why should lenience be shown here when it is not generally the case that the fact that the circumstances rendered it very difficult to conform one's conduct to the law is regarded as warranting mitigation? We do not mitigate robbery upon discovery that the defendant was an addict, desperate for money to buy his next fix. There is no partial defense for those who, desperate to avoid eviction, steal from the cash register in order to have enough money to pay the rent rather than have to live, with their young children, on the streets.

These considerations strongly suggest that while purporting to be a concession to human frailty, the provocation defense is a concession only to certain frailties, generally those seen as at worst a necessary, albeit unfortunate, part of masculinity (and, at times, as something at least a little more positive).[42]

3. Some of the above may elicit the following reaction: that the provocation defense is better suited for killings in a state of passion caused by the discovery that one is being cuckolded than for killings in a state of desperation, anger, and fear brought on by years of abuse, combined with the very likely prospect of further abuse, is not a serious problem as long as the latter killings can qualify for *some* defense. In cases

where the defendant kills her abusive partner to prevent further serious bodily harm to herself or to her children, shouldn't the killing qualify as self-defense? If so, why worry about whether the provocation defense can cover it?

I share the view that many such killings should qualify as killings committed in self-defense. But not all should, and many that probably should not so qualify seem clearly to be killings in response to extreme provocation. (Also worth mentioning here, though it will be elaborated on in section III, is that the law of self-defense is not very well suited to cover many of the killings by battered women of their batterers that arguably should qualify as killings committed in self-defense.) There is something amiss if ongoing violence either does not qualify as adequate provocation or does so only by stretching the defense—and in a way that requires the good (nonsexist) will of judges. So in addition to the pragmatic problem—there should be *some* defense that mitigates in cases where an acquittal, on grounds of self-defense, either is really not warranted, or is warranted morally (and arguably should be warranted legally) but is not warranted by the law in its current form—there is a question that would remain even if *every* case of battered women killing their batterers could be handled by some defense but not by provocation. To wit, why should there be a concession to human frailty when the provocation is adultery yet not when the provocation is ongoing, violent abuse? Surely conduct that is (and should be) illegal would be a better candidate for adequate provocation than conduct that is not illegal (and should not be).[43]

E. The Legal Barriers

1. In this section I trace some of the problems discussed above to their sources in the law. I begin, though, by addressing a deflationary reaction, to the effect that the source of the problems is not the law, but simply an insidious sexism in such forms as the following: whereas in males, aggression is admired (as well as viewed as inevitable), it is not admired in women; so aggression in males that goes too far is, not surprisingly, viewed less negatively than aggression in females. (Another source, one that would dovetail well with the last, might be acceptance of the sociobiological story according to which it is only rational for a man to be deeply upset by his wife's infidelity, because he needs to feel certain that any offspring he views as his really are his; she, by contrast, has little reason to doubt that those she regards as her offspring really are hers. Yet another source is the view of battered women as so very different from the rest of us, and so accustomed to violence and brutality, that what would provoke most of us is not thought to provoke—to provoke sufficiently, anyway—a battered woman.[44] It is as if she is ineligible to plead provocation because she endures so much that she is, in effect, beyond provocation.) This or a similar attitude probably is part of the story, and my discussion will in fact lend some support to the position that it plays a very large part. But it would be a mistake to chalk the problems up to sexism (or even, more helpfully, to pinpoint various underlying sexist views) and leave it at that. Instead, we need to locate in the provocation defense

and in the doctrine of provocation sources that, no doubt in part because they tap into the sexism noted, generate the problems.

2. Earlier I mentioned the usual requirements for the heat of passion defense. At this point, elaboration is needed to explain more fully how it is that women who kill their abusive partners often run afoul of one or more of the requirements. As noted before, the heat of passion defense traditionally requires: (a) absence of premeditation and (b) sudden heat. Related to (b) is (c): the passion has, in the United Kingdom, traditionally been expected to be anger.[45] In the United States, courts vary as to whether they insist that the passion be anger, or allow a wider range of passions, but the paradigm seems to be something explosive, something that erupts suddenly, overpowering or obscuring reason.[46] Simmering resentment that boils over or an ongoing sense of desperation (very likely blended with fear and perhaps anger) that reaches a breaking point, is while not ruled out, at some distance from the paradigm.[47]

In addition, there is (d): the heat is supposed to be due to a provoking incident, not to a series of provocations that build up gradually.[48] (This is closely related to (b) but somewhat different, since one could require that the passion itself erupt suddenly, without thereby ruling out the possibility that this could happen as the result of a series of provocations.)

Also, (e): the killing, as noted earlier, has to have taken place before the defendant "cooled off"; thus, one who kills immediately is more apt to get the defense than is one who initially controlled his rage but later, reflecting on the wrongdoing, became increasingly agitated. Unless an incident can be pointed to that, at least against the background of what happened already, is sufficient to reignite the passion so that the agent "reheats" and can therefore be said to have killed in the heat of passion, the lapse of time, if long enough that the agent either did cool off or should have cooled off, precludes the defense.[49]

And, finally, (f): the provocation has to be "adequate." This (along with the requirement that it not be the case that the agent cooled off or should have cooled off by then) is the "objective" component, designed to ensure that the provoking incident was not trivial.

Consider *Furlough* once again. Furlough killed her husband hours after finding him on the verge of raping their baby, and minutes after he threatened to do so when they got home. She appealed her first-degree murder conviction on grounds of defense of another and provocation (among others). Since at the time of the killing, the danger to their daughter was not imminent, the appeal on the first ground was dismissed. Her provocation claim was dismissed for a similar reason: "assuming that the incident about which the appellant testified occurred, it occurred early that morning and the victim was not at the time of the shooting attempting to engage in any sort of sexual act with their daughter."[50] Her case for either defense would have been stronger had she killed him at the moment she found him standing over their daughter, apparently about to rape her. It was later, some minutes after he threatened to rape the baby when they got home and flipped open his switchblade "in her face," that she shot him.[51]

Furlough ran afoul of a number of the traditional requirements for provoca-tion: according to the court, she acted with premeditation and deliberation;[52] she did not act in a sudden heat, since she did not kill him upon, or very soon after, witnessing him about to rape their daughter (and it seems to have been thought either that the "heat" had subsided or that whether or not she remained deeply upset, a reasonable person would have cooled off by then). While there is a hint that perhaps the later incident of threatening to rape their baby when they returned home might be adequate provocation, the fact that she killed him not at that moment, but some minutes later seems to have been regarded as evidence that she did not kill in a "sudden heat."[53] It therefore strikes some as a premeditated killing committed in revenge, or perhaps simply out of a desire to be rid of him.

This is illustrative of a general problem for women who kill their abusive part-ners: they kill at the wrong time—the wrong time, that is, for purposes of having the usual defenses to homicide available to them, but the right time if they wish to avoid being killed while attempting to kill. Of course, not all such killings merit mitigation, but many do, and that self-defense and the heat of passion defense are compara-tively out of reach for women who kill their batterers signals a problem with these defenses.

More generally, it is a problem that both defenses are harder to come by for those who, because they are less experienced at combat or because they are physi-cally much weaker than their provoker/attacker, attack at a time when the pro-voker/attacker is off guard. As Horder writes, the provocation defense is not very able to accommodate "the morally significant claims of those—perhaps typically, women—whose reaction to provocation is not…usually a more-or-less immedi-ate, violent explosion of temper."[54] Horder speaks of the "privileged access to the defence" on the part of "those—perhaps, mainly men—who have a 'shoot from the hip mentality' (and hence only fore-arm themselves by picking up a knife if it is more-or-less immediately to hand), as compared with those—perhaps, mainly women—whose response to provocation needs to be more measured because they are confronting someone known to be stronger and more aggressive."[55]

Those who suspect that the problem lies not in the requirements themselves, but in the attitudes of (among others) judges, can draw support for their view from *Furlough*. The requirements in no way forced the ruling that either she must have cooled off or that a reasonable person would have cooled off in the time that elapsed (either from the initial provocation that morning or the subsequent provocation). The ruling suggests an inability to comprehend why, if she really killed in the heat of passion, she did not kill him at the very moment when he flipped his knife at her while saying he would rape the baby when they returned home; the conclusion reached seems to have been that the killing must not have been committed in the heat of passion. So it is not implausible to claim that in this instance, anyway, the problem was not so much the requirements listed above as the judges' interpreta-tion of them with respect to this case. The plausibility of the claim is all the more evident when we compare it to the other Tennessee case cited above, *Thornton*, where there was considerably stronger evidence of premeditation and where the provocation was adultery (on the part of a wife who had already said she wanted to end the marriage) rather than an attempted rape of the defendant's baby. Further evidence that the problem lies more with the judges than with the requirements of the traditional heat of passion defense can be found in the court's peculiar description of the provocation as the deceased's "desire to have sexual relations with their baby"[56] (as if the provocation were a confessional statement, "I don't understand it, and I hate myself for it, but I feel some sexual desire towards our baby!") and the fact that they treat the provocation as evidence of motive, hence of premeditation: "In this case there was ample evidence of premeditation....By her own testimony, the appellant admitted that she was distressed by what she believed was her husband's desire to have sexual relations with their baby."[57] It is noteworthy that what one would think should count as provocation—the (credible)[58] threat to rape the baby—and thus tend to mitigate, is instead used against her. Also remarkable is the assumption that her mind was "free from the influence of excitement, or passion"[59] at the time that she killed him.

But setting aside the fact that the judges did not *need* to rule that she premeditated, or that the elapsed time was too long, we can see that the requirements themselves tend to render it difficult for an abused woman who kills the abuser to plead provocation.

3. Is there any reason for the requirements? That premeditation is thought to be inconsistent with the defense is not surprising, given the underlying idea that the cooler the homicide, the more culpable the killer. Premeditation is often assumed to be "cold"; yet must it be? Can I not plan a killing while in the grip of desperation and fear? (The fear and desperation may make me less able to plan *well*, but I can at least plan.) Perhaps the assumption that a premeditated killing could not possibly warrant a heat of passion defense should be reconsidered.

The requirement that the heat be sudden; the expectation that it will be provoked by a single incident, rather than the cumulative effect of ongoing abuse; the "no cooling off" requirement together with the assumption that a reasonable person will quickly cool off; and the requirement that there was no premeditation—what do these reflect? A lack of imagination, perhaps, but what else? One very understandable concern they reflect is that the heat of passion defense *not* serve as a defense for revenge killings. To obviate that, an effort is made to limit the defense to instances in which one suddenly "explodes."

Certainly we do not want to mitigate in cases of revenge, but the requirement that the heat be sudden[60] may be excessive. Now, on one very common picture of what it is to kill in the heat of passion, a picture that aims both to make sense of the mitigation and to differentiate heat of passion killings from revenge killings, the requirement is not unduly restrictive: on that picture, the killer "lost control." That the killer lost control is, on that view, the main reason why mitigation is in order as well as a highly appropriate necessary condition for a killing to qualify for the defense. If you believe that mitigation is in order because the killer had lost control at the time of the killing, you have a reply to a challenge posed above (see penultimate paragraph of II.D.2) questioning why concession is given in some instances where it was very difficult for the defendant to conform his conduct to the law but not in others. Only if the defendant had lost control is a concession in order.

The language and imagery of "loss of self-control" are tempting, but caution is needed. It is not a helpful concept if it explains mitigation only by depicting killings in the heat of passion as involuntary. The provocation defense is not a defense that aims to deny that there was a voluntary act; killing in the heat of passion is not similar to killing under hypnosis (much less to an accidental killing committed during a seizure). Yet the language used by those who rely on this model of what it is to kill in the heat of passion is often remarkable for its suggestion that the defendant was not even acting voluntarily when he killed. Recall the defense counsel's remark to the jury in *R. v. Fisher*: "you will have to say…whether the prisoner was not under such a state of excitement as to be totally unconscious of what he was about." Language suggesting that the conduct was involuntary can easily be found in more recent cases as well. Consider the definition of heat of passion used in the following 1964 Wisconsin case of *State v. Hoyt*:

> "Heat of passion" which will reduce murder to manslaughter is such mental disturbance, caused by reasonable, adequate provocation, as would ordinarily so overcome and dominate or suspend exercise of judgment of an ordinary man as to render his mind for the time being deaf to the voice of reason;…and cause him, uncontrollably, to act from impelling force of the disturbing cause rather than from any real wickedness of heart or cruelty or recklessness of disposition.[61]

"Cause him, uncontrollably"? One wonders why, if this is what killing in the heat of passion is, it is not a complete defense rather than a partial one. If even a reasonable (or ordinary) man would have been caused, uncontrollably, to so act (and if the defendant was so impelled), why hold the defendant responsible? The only possible explanation would seem to be that the defendant placed himself in a situation where he should have known he would be "overcome," incapacitated from acting reasonably. But no such explanation is hinted at in *Hoyt*.

Just what it is to lose self-control, what it is to regain it, whether one can partially lose self-control, and to what extent loss of self-control simply befalls one rather than being (partially) allowed by the agent are questions that, though philosophically fascinating, are beyond the scope of this essay. If we are going to continue to rely on loss of self-control in either the law of provocation or the underlying provocation doctrine, however, more work is needed to try to make sense of the notion.[62] But it should not be assumed that we need to rely on it. My suspicion is that the language of loss of self-control is not doing any real work other than creating a convenient but perhaps illusory impression, viz., that something happens to the agent who kills in the heat of passion that is similar to, but not as extreme as, what happens to someone who really does act involuntarily and that, therefore, warrants mitigation.

In its 2006 report on partial defenses to murder, the English Law Commission reaffirmed the position taken in its 2004 report that "a positive requirement of loss of self-control" is "unnecessary and undesirable."[63] The requirement privileges "men's typical reactions to provocation over women's typical reactions." "Women's reactions to provocation are less likely to involve a 'loss of self-control,' as such, and more likely to be comprised of a combination of anger, fear, frustration and a sense of desperation."[64] Of course, one might argue that is just bad luck for women who kill from a combination of anger, fear, frustration and a sense of desperation; the defense simply is not intended to cover that. But unless there really is some partially disabling experience for which the agent is not culpable—that is, an experience aptly captured by the phrase "loss of self-control"—and unless we can determine (as well as we can with respect to other mental states crucial for the criminal law) whether or not the agent was in this state at the time of the killing, there is no justification for a requirement of loss of self-control.

If we abandon the requirement, is there anything left of the defense? To some leading scholars writing on provocation, loss of control is at the very core of the provocation doctrine.[65] To see how the defense might be retained without requiring a loss of self-control, consider the Law Commission's proposal. I quote it in its entirety, both because it is helpful to see how the various pieces fit together, and because it encompasses other reforms, in addition to dropping the requirement of loss of control, that are relevant to my discussion.

1. Unlawful homicide that would otherwise be first degree murder should instead be second degree murder if:
   (a) the defendant acted in response to:
      (i) gross provocation (meaning words or conduct or a combination of words and conduct) which caused the defendant to have a justifiable sense of being seriously wronged; or
      (ii) fear of serious violence towards the defendant or another; or
      (iii) a combination of both (i) and (ii); and
   (b) a person of the defendant's age and of ordinary temperament, i.e., ordinary tolerance and self-restraint, in the circumstances of the defendant might have reacted in the same or in a similar way.[66]
2. In deciding whether a person of the defendant's age and of ordinary temperament, i.e., ordinary tolerance and self-restraint, in the circumstances of the defendant, might have reacted in the same or in a similar way, the court should take into account the defendant's age and all the circumstances of the defendant other than matters whose only relevance to the defendant's conduct is that they bear simply on his or her general capacity for self-control.[67]
3. The partial defence should not apply where:
   (a) the provocation was incited by the defendant for the purpose of providing an excuse to use violence; or
   (b) the defendant acted in considered desire for revenge.
4. A person should not be treated as having acted in considered desire for revenge if he or she acted in fear of serious violence, merely because he or

she was also angry towards the deceased for the conduct which engendered that fear.

5. A judge should not be required to leave the defence to the jury unless there is evidence on which a reasonable jury, properly directed, could conclude that it might apply.[68]

The proposed reform favors allowing the defense to mitigate only from first-degree murder to second-degree murder. I will not address that particular proposal. Of greater interest, for my purposes, are the following changes. Instead of requiring (or even relying on a picture of) loss of self-control, the proposed defense requires only that the defendant "acted in response to" X. The requirement that this be something more than a minor annoyance is handled by having a more robust "objective" requirement.[69] That is, the constraints on X are robust, whereas there is not a very robust subjective requirement. The subjective requirements are mainly in (3) and concern not so much D's emotional state as D's intentions, for they work to rule out instances where the defendant sought revenge or incited the provocation in order to have an excuse to kill the provoker.

The constraints on X are themselves of interest: X need not be provocation, but if it is, it has to be *gross* provocation; and if it is not provocation, the defense is available only if D acted out of fear of serious violence toward the defendant (or another). The defense is also available if D acted out of a combination of fear of serious violence and a justifiable sense of having been seriously wronged. It is not required that there was no cooling off period; it is not required that the provocation was sudden or even that the killing was done without premeditation. The danger that vengeful killings would qualify for mitigation is handled directly by (3)(b); such killings are simply excluded. At the same time, that one's fear of serious violence is mixed with anger toward the deceased for the conduct which engendered the fear does not entail that the defendant "acted in considered desire for revenge" and thus does not preclude the defense. Also noteworthy is that the provocation, as explained in (1)(a)(i), must have caused the defendant to have a justifiable sense of being seriously wronged. This is part of the strong objective requirement I mentioned above. I fully endorse this, but those who prefer to weaken the "adequacy" requirement, as the MPC has, will of course oppose it.[70]

Finally, note that what is required by way of a reasonable person requirement is that a person of the defendant's age and of ordinary tolerance and self-restraint might have reacted in the same or in a similar way. There is no mention of sex; the standard varies only relative to age.[71] There is no mention of reasonableness per se; this too seems salutary. The content of the objective standard—that is, what we want when we require that a "reasonable" or "ordinary" person might also have so (re)acted—may vary depending on the defense (or offense) in question, and here what matters is not, say, being mindful of one's environment, but tolerance and self-restraint. Circumstances other than the defendant's age do not enter in if they bear only on the defendant's capacity for self-control. But when we ask "Might a person of ordinary tolerance and self-restraint have acted as *D* did were he or she in *D*'s situation?" we may take into account, in thinking about what *D*'s situation was, any circumstances, including *D*'s history as a battered woman. Such circumstances, or history, would enter in to explain why she was fearful,[72] why she felt seriously wronged, and why it was justifiable to feel seriously wronged.

4. More needs to be said about the requirement of loss of self-control and the arguably problematic role it has played in the provocation defense. Relating to the philosophical puzzle of just what it is to lose self-control and yet still be sufficiently an agent that it makes sense to hold one somewhat responsible for one's actions is an issue noted by the Law Commission in *Partial Defenses to Murder*.

> A noteworthy issue which emerged from our discussions with psychiatrists was that those who give vent to anger by "losing self-control" to the point of killing another person generally do so in circumstances in which they can afford to do so. An angry strong man can afford to lose his self-control with someone who provokes him, if that person is physically smaller and weaker. An angry person is much less likely to "lose self control" and attack another person in circumstances in which he or she is likely to come off worse by doing so. For this reason many successful attacks by an abused woman on a physically stronger abuser take place when that person is off-guard.[73]

As the passage suggests, there is something suspect about the claim that one lost self-control if one does so only vis-à-vis one's female partner, never one's buddies or one's boss, even though the provocation itself is quite severe in the latter cases.[74] If one "loses" self-control only when one can (in one's view) afford to do so, that suggests that one is allowing oneself to lose self-control. Going a bit beyond the passage quoted, I want to emphasize the following. Whether we regard loss of self-control as something that just befalls one, or as compatible with allowing oneself to lose self-control,[75] this much is clear: the exculpatory potential of the explanation of S's violence in terms of S having lost self-control is significantly weakened if S allowed himself to lose self-control.

Loss of self-control is a dangerously slippery notion. The suggestion is that because one lost control, one is not responsible for what one has done; at the same time, we also use "lost control" rather metaphorically, in a way that is compatible with allowing oneself to lose control and that leaves up in the air whether the "loss" should exculpate at all. Treating loss of self-control as the conceptual core of the provocation defense thus has its dangers. Unless we spell out just what we mean, for the purposes of the provocation defense, by "loss of self-control," we may be granting exculpatory force where, once we reflect on what in fact happened, it becomes clear that excusing conditions do not apply.

The second point to extract from the quotation is that the person who, relative to the victim, is physically weaker or less experienced and skilled at combat is less likely than the physically stronger or physically more aggressive person to fit our picture of what it is to lose self-control (and indeed to be able to fit any plausible picture of what it is to lose self-control). Thus if the crucial point of differentiation between intentional killings for which mitigation is in order and those for which it is not is that the former are committed by someone who is out of control, then those who are more aggressive and kill those who are relatively unlikely to put up serious resistance (or to retaliate later with lethal violence if the attack ends up for whatever reason not being lethal) are more likely to benefit from a defense based on this "concession to human frailty." This seems clearly unjust, whoever the parties are; it just so happens that the beneficiaries, under such a scheme, are far more often male.

A further point is that lurking in the background of many discussions of the heat of passion defense is an assumption that loss of self-control entails (if not conceptually, as a matter of human nature) acting violently. Consider the following statement from Dressler, "Why Keep the Provocation Defense?" "The provocation must be so serious that we are prepared to say that an ordinary person in the actor's circumstances, even an ordinarily law-abiding person of reasonable temperament, might become sufficiently upset by the provocation to experience substantial impairment of his capacity for self-control and, as a consequence, to act violently."[76] As a consequence? Why would loss of self-control have as its consequence acting violently? (Is there a default we revert to when we lose self-control, and if so, is that default one of acting violently?) Dressler may mean only that in this particular situation the consequence of the loss of self-control was to act violently, such violence being one of many potential consequences of the loss of self-control. But then the same problem arises in a different place: if the consequence need not be violence and is often—happily, more often—that one screams at the provoker, writes an angry, intemperate letter, or, more dramatically,[77] hurls one's unfaithful partner's clothing out the window, we cannot explain the violence by reference to the loss of self-control. It is one of several ways one might act when one's capacity for self-control is impaired. Violence—especially homicidal violence—is in no way entailed by loss of self-control. We know this, of course, but discussions of the provocation defense that rely on loss of self-control frequently present the violence as simply flowing from, or entailed by, a loss of self-control.

That loss of self-control is viewed as entailing violence is related to the point that the "concession to human frailty" is really only a concession to certain frailties. Think about the defenses we do not have (and the mitigation that is rarely available at sentencing). We do not have a defense for child neglect based on emotional trauma from (say) one's lover having left one. Yet emotional trauma certainly can issue in severe depression, and that can involve a failure to fulfill basic duties. The concession, rather, is to a certain type of upset, one issuing in a certain type of reaction, viz., violence.

This is not to deny that the provocation defense has a historical explanation; it developed in large part as a way to limit the reach of the death penalty and as part of a gradual reform of homicide law. Given that historical explanation, it might seem unfair to suggest that there is something peculiar about there not being a provocation defense, or something similar, for other felonious misconduct traceable to emotional trauma. (After all, we do not have a provocation defense for all violent conduct but only for murder and sometimes attempted murder.) Nonetheless, insofar as the justification for retaining the defense is a concession to human frailty, we need to look closely at whether the law normally does show such concessions; whether it should (and if so, with respect to which crimes); and if so, what reforms are in order to bring it about that the concessions do not favor the frailties and emotional distress (and the felonious misconduct that arises there from) of men over those of women (or, for that matter, of women over those of men).

F. The Reasonable Person

Not only in the provocation defense, but throughout the criminal law the reasonable person standard plays a central role. In part because it was until recently called "the reasonable man" standard, the standard itself has been viewed by many with suspicion. There is indeed reason to worry that only the name has changed and that by employing a "reasonable person" standard we in effect judge everyone by reference to a reasonable man. But what should be done about it? Some have thought that because of the danger that the standard remains that of the reasonable man we need either to abandon the standard altogether or to employ a dual standard: a reasonable woman standard and a reasonable man standard. That the latter is a bad idea is evident from the fact that specifying gender will have the effect of enshrining in law the inequality in traditional expectations of men and of women.[78] Women are not expected to be quick to resort to violence, so evaluating a woman's claim to have killed in the heat of passion by reference to a reasonable woman standard would mean holding women to a higher standard.[79] A man deeply upset by x might unfairly be thought not to meet a reasonable man test if it is commonly thought that such things upset reasonable women but not reasonable men. Not only on these pragmatic grounds, but also normatively, it makes far more sense (at least on the assumption that we do not regard gender polarization as desirable)[80] to ask of everyone that they comport themselves as reasonable people than to ask them to comport themselves as reasonable women and reasonable men.[81]

The above suggestion, however, does not address the question of whether the standard should be abandoned altogether. Why retain it? The answer (tying it now to the provocation defense) is that some such standard is needed lest the defense be granted whenever the jurors or judges are convinced that D really was very, very upset when he (or she) killed, so upset that... (and here one has to fill in the "subjective" requirement—D lost self-control). Not that a reasonable person standard is the only way to block that. We could revert to the old custom of enumerating those situations that count as adequate provocation, or we could specify constraints on what the provocation can be, (1) specifying that it has to be something illegal or (2) specifying via a list what it cannot be, for example, a baby crying, or suspected but unconfirmed adultery, or perhaps any adultery, confirmed or not. I'll assume we do not want to consider a return to the old custom; but what about (1) and (2)? They would work better as constraints that would supplement a general standard (and in the case of (2), also as signposts to guide jurors) than as a substitute for the standard. Regarding (1): clearly not everything that is illegal would be adequate provocation. Regarding (2): because it is not feasible to come up with a complete list of incidents that deeply upset some people but would not be adequate provocation, enumerating "inadequate" provocation would be helpful only as a way of shedding some light on the guiding principle.[82] It would not remove the need for a guiding principle.[83]

Supposing we agree that a guiding principle is needed, there might still be disagreement as to whether it should be couched in terms of reasonableness. Indeed, in legal scholarship, rulings, and statutes, various terms are used as if they were interchangeable with "reasonable person," among them, "ordinary person," "average person," and "ordinarily prudent person." The terms just mentioned are not equivalent, and many of the problems raised, including those concerning gender, arise because "ordinary" is used in place of "reasonable" or "reasonable" is interpreted as if it meant "ordinary."[84] The mention of prudence complicates things further, since prudence has to do with being cautious and not taking risks; it may be a fairly decent stand-in for "reasonable" in certain contexts (for example, in tort law, and marginally in criminal law in connection with negligent homicide), but it is not at all suited to replace "reasonable" in other contexts. I suspect that one reason why the reasonable person standard has gotten a lot of bad press is that nonequivalent terms are substituted for "reasonable."

A guiding principle keyed to reasonableness makes much more sense than one that is keyed to what is "average," and this holds true throughout the criminal law. That the "average" person in D's situation might well embezzle, as D did, neither justifies nor excuses D. But that a reasonable person in D's situation might well do as D did carries considerably more normative weight.[85] Likewise, substituting "ordinary" or "average" for "reasonable" is at best misleading. That something is ordinarily done does not make it reasonable; that the average, or ordinary, person views a situation as an X-type situation does not mean that it is reasonable to do so. The view of the "ordinary person" is likely to reflect common prejudices or misconceptions; part of the point of choosing the word "reasonable" is to indicate that we are supposed to try to rise above such prejudices (though of course the law cannot require heroism, only modest effort).

Supposing we agree that "reasonable" is preferable to "prudent" and to less normatively charged terms, such as "ordinary," and that these terms should not be treated as interchangeable with "reasonable," we still should fine-tune the standard to reflect the fact that what is called for, while fitting under a general umbrella of "reasonableness," varies depending on the defense (or offense) in question. "Reasonable" needs to be elaborated (or at least understood) at times in terms of self-control in the face of intense emotion and at other times in terms of reasonable belief (where this in turn reflects several concerns that may need to be elaborated, among them, that one apportion one's belief to the evidence, that one take appropriate steps to guard against error, and that one take note of one's environment, including the words and demeanor of those with whom one is interacting).[86]

Clarifying both what is meant by "reasonable" in general, in the reasonable person standard, and what more specifically is called for in the defense in question will go a long way toward meeting the objections raised against the reasonable person standard. To be sure, the suspicion that the reasonable person standard to some extent remains a reasonable man standard has some validity, and the measures just described will only partially address that issue. An additional measure is to have some benchmarks to guide jurors as to what sorts of things count as reasonable. With provocation, this is best done by indicating (among other things) that infidelity (marital or not) and a partner's decision to end the relationship are not adequate provocation (either alone or conjoined) and that homosexual advances constitute adequate provocation to no greater extent than do heterosexual advances.

Many other objections to the reasonable person standard could be mentioned here, some of them instantiations of objections to the use of objective standards for self-defense and the heat of passion defense.[87] I have little sympathy with these objections,[88] and since I am short on space will not discuss them at length. But worth explaining is an unfortunate development, an error that helped to give objectivity—and the reasonable person—a bad name.

The error was this: it was supposed by some that objectivity required ignoring all details of the defendant's situation. (The same error arises in connection with self-defense; see III.B, below.) Thus, when it was asked whether a reasonable person in the defendant's situation might have acted as the defendant did, "situation" was understood so narrowly that features of the defendant obviously relevant to understanding why the defendant was enraged were regarded as among those from which we must abstract when considering how a reasonable person might have reacted.[89] Obviously, if we are to ask how a reasonable person might react to being called a filthy Jew and to being told "Too bad Hitler didn't kill them all," it helps to know whether we are to imagine a reasonable person who is Jewish. If the defendant were, in addition to being Jewish, a Holocaust survivor or the child of a survivor, this too would be relevant. It is no way at odds with objectivity to understand the question to be, "Might a reasonable person—Jewish, and the son or daughter of a Holocaust survivor [etc.]—have reacted as the defendant did if called a filthy Jew?"

More generally, having one standard for all does not mean that in applying the standard we may not attend to the context of the attack or insult or to features of the person in virtue of which the insult is (particularly) stinging. But it does mean that the standard is not calibrated to reflect the notion that, say, people from one ethnic group, or geographical region, are less tolerant, or more hotheaded, than those from another.[90] Everyone is held to the same standard—that of the reasonable person, where "reasonable" may be cashed out differently depending on the defense in question. Does this mean that everyone who fails to meet the standard is blameworthy? No; as H. L. A. Hart stressed, an invariant standard is quite compatible with recognizing excusing conditions, so if there are some who, despite their best efforts, fail to meet the standard of the reasonable person, we might opt to excuse them.[91] This is arguably the best way to handle the problems that are often cited as reasons why an invariant (or "objective") standard is problematic.[92]

As we'll see in the next section, some of the same issues arise in connection with self-defense. Here, too, there is wariness concerning an "objective" standard, though it plays out a little differently, the focus being on whether "reasonable" should be understood "subjectively" or "objectively."

III. Self-Defense

A. Introduction

The serious issue involving gender in the law of self-defense is best stated first without reference to gender. The law is well-equipped to handle situations where the attacker and defendant are in a one-time conflict and are roughly comparable in combat readiness but is less suited to situations involving ongoing violence, a determination on the part of one person to control, subjugate, and terrorize another, and a relative lack of power on the part of the latter.[93] It is particularly unsuited to handle killing in self-defense when the danger is not imminent, for example, when the attacker/victim is asleep. The general implications for the self-defense claims of battered women who kill their batterers are obvious; the specifics will be explained in due course.

It is worth bearing in mind that it is not only battered women's self-defense claims that pose a challenge to self-defense laws but, also, the self-defense claims of others who are likewise in a relatively powerless position and are the victims of ongoing violence. Also worth noting is that though my discussion is limited to self-defense, many of the same issues arise in connection with defense of others, and the conditions required to justify defense of others parallel those required for self-defense.[94] This is important for two reasons. First, the lives of the battered woman's relatives may also be endangered, and the battered woman who kills may be acting both in self-defense and in the defense of her children or other relatives. She may opt for killing her abuser rather than attempt to flee, in part because of a concern that in the event that she does manage to flee safely, he will retaliate by killing one or more of her relatives. Second, there may be, in addition to the self-defense and defense-of-other claims of the battered woman, defense-of-other claims of, say, a mother who kills her son-in-law to protect her daughter, whom he has battered and threatened to kill.[95]

There is disagreement over how best to modify the law to address the problems—and indeed about what the problems are, or even whether there is a problem. Some think (as I do) that a change in the law of self-defense is called for. Some deny that anyone could be justified in killing an abuser while he is asleep or otherwise off guard, and on that basis hold either that a murder conviction is not inappropriate, or that a conviction of manslaughter is in order (on grounds either of provocation or imperfect self-defense), or that an acquittal may be in order but not on self-defense grounds, since self-defense is a justification.[96] Others agree that an acquittal may be in order, and on self-defense grounds, but only if self-defense (or at least "mistaken" self-defense) is construed as an excuse rather than a justification.[97] Others share my view that one can be justified in killing one's batterer in his sleep, but for a somewhat different reason: because he subjects her to a regime of tyranny from which she has no escape.[98] My focus here will be on cases that I think warrant acquittal on self-defense grounds, where self-defense is understood as a justification (and understanding justification as tied—as indeed it is in the law of self-defense—to reasonable belief rather than to truth).[99]

Complicating the issue is the fact that some—perhaps a great many—failures to do justice to battered women's self-defense claims do not point to a problem in the statutes themselves, or the underlying doctrines, but only to problems in their application. This suggests that the precarious status of women's self-defense claims is due in considerable part to residual views from the days, not long past, when domestic violence was generally tolerated in the law—views reflected in resistance to taking seriously women's reports of abuse, despite ample corroboration; in a belief that domestic violence is usually just mutual combat; and in resistance to regarding violence inflicted on a woman by her husband or boyfriend as just as bad as violence inflicted by another man. This is definitely the case in instances where the batterer was killed when awake and aggressive; see, for example, *State v. Hundley*.[100] Nonetheless, there are other cases, such as *State v. Norman*,[101] where the failure to acquit on self-defense grounds or to overturn the conviction shows a flaw in the law itself, and flaws in the law itself—the statutes and especially the underlying doctrine—are my concern here.

B. The Reasonable Belief Requirement

1. Before focusing on battered women's self-defense claims, we need to take a close look at self-defense law and, in particular, the reasonable belief requirement. What is the requirement and why have it?

The law of self-defense does not require that that it actually *was* necessary to act as the defendant did. Perhaps the victim's gun was not loaded. Perhaps the victim was only joking. What matters is how it seemed to D and (though this part is a bit more controversial) whether it was reasonable to believe that V was going to attack D[102] (and, we might add, reasonable to act accordingly, using force to do so).[103] This seems to me clearly right. The defense should *not* be limited to those who really did need to use physical force. (Indeed, this would be a difficult requirement to implement, for we may not know what would have happened had the victim not killed or otherwise disabled the attacker.) At the same time, fear should not suffice for an acquittal on self-defense grounds. We hold people responsible for not being so trigger-happy as to shoot whenever they feel afraid or sense danger. This is part of the management of one's emotions—fear, anger, desperation, jealousy—that we ask of each other and of ourselves. The requirement, then, is that one have believed it was necessary to use self-defensive force and that one have believed it on reasonable grounds.[104]

Clearly, it is important to attach to the defense some constraints so as to discourage violence against another when one has insufficient reason for thinking that the use of violence is necessary to thwart an attack. The reasonable belief requirement is (obviously!) one such constraint.[105] Among the other constraints are the imminence and the retreat requirements. I'll discuss these shortly and will suggest that, in the United States, the imminence requirement bears far too much of the burden of limiting the defense and the retreat requirement far too little. But let's first take a closer look at the reasonable belief requirement.

In the United States, self-defense is generally understood as follows (with some variation from one jurisdiction to another): "a non-aggressor is justified in using force upon another if he reasonably believes that such force is necessary to protect himself from imminent use of unlawful force by the other person." In addition, "*deadly* force is only justified in self-protection if the actor reasonably believes that its use is necessary to prevent imminent and unlawful use of *deadly* force by the aggressor,"[106] where deadly force is generally understood to mean "force intended or likely to cause death or grievous bodily injury."[107]

How should "reasonably" be understood in this context? The answers given are usually divided into those that understand it "objectively" and those that understand it "subjectively," with the former being more standard. The terms used are not entirely apt, and indeed the answers themselves are generally not very clear, but the key difference between these answers is that "objectively reasonable" insists on an invariant standard. Application of the invariant standard can (contrary to what "subjectivists" sometimes claim) take into account many aspects of the defendant's situation (including relevant history between the defendant and the victim and experiences that provide a rational basis for a belief that it is necessary to use self-defensive force). But it cannot take into account experiences (e.g., a previous assault by someone other than the victim) that, while helping to explain why the defendant acted as he or she did, do not provide a rational basis for the belief. This differentiates it from a subjective understanding of "reasonable." More generally, a subjective reading of "reasonable" allows reasonableness to be relativized to the defendant. Bernhard Goetz, the (in)famous "subway vigilante," advocated a subjective reading when he objected to a jury instruction to consider the circumstances of the incident and determine "whether the defendant's conduct was that of a reasonable man in the defendant's situation" and claimed that a proper instruction would be to consider "whether a defendant's beliefs and reactions were 'reasonable to *him*.'"[108]

Given the reasons for requiring reasonableness, a subjective reading seems inadequate, particularly if understood as Goetz understood it. Yet many people have thought that the best way to address the problem that battered women who killed their batterers all too often fail to receive a jury instruction on self-defense is to embrace a subjective reading.[109] The approach taken usually involves a twist that distinguishes it from Goetz's understanding of "reasonable." The idea seems[110] to be to relativize "reasonable" to the[111] relevant group of which the defendant was a member, for example, battered women suffering from battered woman syndrome. The defense could then argue that to the battered woman, killing the batterer was reasonable, indeed the only possible option other than being seriously injured or killed. Expert witnesses explained that from the vantage point of those suffering from battered woman syndrome, the batterer is omnipotent and the danger he poses to her omnipresent; a psychiatrist who examined the defendant would (the defense hoped) testify that she suffered from the syndrome. The subjective reading of "reasonable" thus allowed the defense to sidestep the question of whether a reasonable person simpliciter might have acted as she did—that is, have believed that the victim posed a lethal threat and that lethal force was needed to thwart the attack, and have acted accordingly. Moreover, the requirement that the threat be, or be reasonably believed to be, imminent is met if "reasonably" is understood subjectively. We see this approach in the claim of the dissent in *Norman* that "'from the perspective of the battered wife, the danger is constantly 'immediate'" and that in "the context of the doctrine of self-defense, 'imminent' is a term the meaning of which must be grasped from the defendant's point of view."[112]

One obvious objection to this approach (and to Goetz's) is that an acquittal on self-defense grounds is then far too easy to obtain. "Reasonable" is doing very little work. On Goetz's version, the reasonableness requirement is met as long as the defendant's beliefs and reactions were reasonable to him, and though it is not entirely clear what that means, the idea seems to be simply that the defendant sees his beliefs and reactions as reasonable. On the second subjective reading, the idea seems to be that the reasonableness requirement is met if and only if there is a relevant group of which the defendant is a member, such that it is common, and very understandable, for members of that group to view the situation (and other situations of the same sort) as the defendant did (where, we might add, those in that group are not to blame for so viewing it). Although I have framed the second subjective reading in a way that provides something of a shield against the objection, there are nonetheless problems, one being that it seems to conflate excuses with justifications. That it is understandable for D to so view the situation and that D should not be blamed for so viewing it support excusing D, obviously, but do not support a justification (and do not support a claim that D acted reasonably or on a reasonable belief).[113]

Another objection to this "subjective" approach is that it "pathologizes" battered women. The worry takes different forms. One is a concern about image, in particular, pernicious stereotyping.[114] Without denying that reinforcing pernicious stereotypes is undesirable, I have a somewhat different concern. The approach that appeals to battered woman syndrome—where the syndrome is viewed as a pathology—does not merely contribute to an unfortunate stereotype of women as helpless or as victims. It treats the battered woman who kills her batterer as if she is supposing there is danger where there isn't or grave danger where there is only minor danger. It treats her as if her judgment that she (or her loved ones) is in grave danger is mistaken, indeed, unreasonably so. Yet the details of the cases that seem to merit acquittal on self-defense grounds[115] support acquittal *not* because the woman is understandably deluded—deluded as a result of the syndrome she suffers—but because a reasonable person in her situation might well judge, as does she, that the danger is real, serious, and not safely averted without resort to lethal force. By contrast, the subjective approach explains her conduct by pointing not to the repeated violence inflicted on her by the batterer, his threats to kill her, and her unsuccessful attempts to flee, but to a "syndrome" caused by the violence, a syndrome that impairs her judgment.[116]

The much-discussed case of Judith Norman is a good illustration of how a focus on battered woman syndrome, where the syndrome is viewed as a pathology,[117] occludes the fact that often the defendant's circumstances are such that a reasonable person in her situation might well judge it necessary, for reasons of self-defense, to kill the batterer. Norman's husband, J. T., had been abusing her for about twenty years at the time she killed him. He forced her to engage in prostitution and beat her, sometimes with a baseball bat, if she resisted doing so or if he was dissatisfied with the amounts of money she made. Shortly before she killed him, he was jailed on a charge of driving while impaired. After his release, he was angrier and more abusive than ever. The sheriff's deputies were called to the home, but informing her (incorrectly)[118] that they needed a warrant before they could arrest him, they left the scene. They were called back less than an hour later, after she had taken a bottle of pills. As she was attended by paramedics, J. T. told the paramedics to let her die[119] and told her she would "pay for taking those pills" and more specifically that he would kill her, her mother, and her grandmother.[120] While Judith was being treated in the hospital for her drug overdose, a therapist persuaded her to go to the mental health center to look into having J. T. committed for treatment for alcoholism. Upon learning of the plan, J. T. told her "he would 'see them coming' and would cut her throat before they got to him." She also went to the social services office to seek welfare benefits, but he followed her there, interrupted her interview, and insisted that she go home with him. At home he slapped and kicked her, threw objects at her, put a cigarette out on her torso, and refused to let her eat or bring food into the house for their children.[121] Using a gun her mother had in her possession, Judith shot him in the head that night while he was asleep.

Norman's manslaughter conviction was overturned by the court of appeals (holding that the trial court judge erred in refusing to provide a jury instruction on self-defense) but was later reinstated by the North Carolina Supreme Court. Consider the following excerpt from the dissent to the latter ruling:

> In his expert testimony a clinical psychologist concluded that defendant fit "and exceed[ed]" the profile of an abused or battered spouse, analogizing this treatment to the dehumanization process suffered by prisoners of war…during the Second World War and the brainwashing techniques of the Korean War. The psychologist described the defendant as a woman incarcerated by abuse, by fear, and by her conviction that her husband was invincible and inescapable:

> Mrs. Norman didn't leave because she believed, fully believed that escape was totally impossible. There was no place to go. He, she had left before; he had come and gotten her. She had gone to the Department of Social Services. He had come and gotten her. The law, she believed the law could not protect her; no one could protect her, and I must admit, looking over the records, that there was nothing done that would contradict that belief. She fully believed that he was invulnerable to the law and to all social agencies that were available; that nobody could withstand his power.[122]

While the psychologist's testimony in fact lends a good deal of support to the position that a reasonable person who knew everything Norman knew about her husband and about what happened when she attempted to flee or to get help might well have judged that it was necessary to kill him to prevent him from killing her (or her relatives), the testimony is enlisted to show that Norman believed she had no choice other than to kill him *because* as someone who suffered from battered woman syndrome, she was "incarcerated by...her conviction that her husband was invincible and inescapable."[123] It is as if the problem were mainly her own inability (thanks to damage done to her by the years of violence and emotional abuse) to see clearly a solution that the rest of us can see.

The "pathologizing" that concerns me is the treatment of Norman as in effect deluded, when there is good reason to believe that a reasonable person in her situation might well have judged that she was in serious danger of being killed or seriously injured and could safely thwart the threat only by killing the attacker.

2. Thus far I have primarily presented reasons against a subjective reading of "reasonable." I turn now to reasons in favor of it. First, as noted above, a subjective reading provides a significant tactical advantage. It circumvents the barrier posed by the imminence requirement, since, according to experts on battered woman syndrome, the danger seems to a battered woman suffering from this syndrome omnipresent and indeed always imminent. On an objective reading of "reasonable," the imminence requirement is a formidable obstacle. My view is that the problem is the imminence requirement, and we need to challenge that rather than weaken the constraints on self-defense by reading "reasonable" "subjectively." More on that shortly.

A subjective reading is also favored for a reason put forward by Goetz: an objective standard for "reasonable," it is claimed, is unduly limiting in that it requires ignoring the features of the situation (at least, ignoring as many as possible). Recall the basis for Goetz's appeal: the prosecutor had instructed the grand jurors that "they were to consider the circumstances of the incident and determine 'whether the defendant's conduct was that of a reasonable man in the defendant's situation.'"[124] Goetz argued that this standard precludes a jury from considering such factors as the defendant's prior experiences.[125] The appellate division agreed. But the New York Court of Appeals rejected the claim that "an objective standard means that the background and other relevant characteristics of a particular actor must be ignored." The appellate court explained:

To the contrary, we have frequently noted that a determination of reasonableness must be based on the "circumstances" facing a defendant or his "situation." Such terms encompass more than the physical movements of the potential assailant.... [T]hese terms include any relevant knowledge the defendant had about that person—including, for example, any information the defendant had concerning the assailant's prior acts of violence or reputation for violence. They also necessarily bring in the physical attributes of all persons involved, including the defendant. Furthermore, the defendant's circumstances encompass any prior experiences he had which could provide a reasonable basis for a belief that another person's intentions were to injure or rob him or that the use of deadly force was necessary under the circumstances.[126]

I think this is exactly right. If an "objective" standard means one that is independent of the defendant's attitudes, beliefs, and values, there is no incompatibility between applying an objective standard and taking into account, in applying it, various features of the defendant's situation. Not just any features, of course; but the court of appeals counted as relevant only prior experiences and knowledge about the putative aggressor that could provide a reasonable basis for a belief that person intended to injure or rob him or her. In addition, the physical attributes of all parties involved may be taken into account, presumably just insofar as these are relevant to the assessment that (lethal) force is necessary to thwart the attack. It is noteworthy that more facts about the assailant than about the defendant are treated as potentially relevant. This is as it should be: a wide array of attributes of the assailant is relevant to a judgment that the presumed assailant indeed does aim to injure the defendant, a sense of the gravity of the injury threatened and the degree of force that needs to be used to thwart it, and a judgment of whether it is safe to flee rather than to use force. Fewer attributes of the defendant are relevant to that judgment.

At least one distinguished legal scholar has taken the view of objectivity rejected in *People v. Goetz*. Claire Finkelstein writes that a "thoroughly objective approach to [the question of reasonableness] will leave out the particular characteristics that might require a defendant who is much smaller and weaker than the aggressor to use force earlier than the hypothetical reasonable person."[127] This conception shapes many other discussions, as well, such as the following explanation in *State v. Leidholm*: "An objective standard of reasonableness requires the fact-finder to view the circumstances surrounding the accused at the time he used force from the standpoint of a hypothetical reasonable and prudent person....Ordinarily, under such a view, the unique physical and psychological characteristics of the accused are not taken into consideration in judging the reasonableness of the accused's belief."[128]

If one understands "objective standard" as Finkelstein and *Leidholm* do, a subjective standard of reasonableness is clearly preferable. No standard that ignores the physical characteristics of the accused would be a good standard for assessing the reasonableness of a belief concerning the need to use (lethal) force to repel a threat. But why suppose that an objective standard would ignore such characteristics? Surely hypothetical reasonable persons would take into account their own physical characteristics in judging how much danger they are in and whether they need to use force—perhaps lethal force—in self-defense. Suppose I know I am little more than half the weight of the man who threatens me and that he is far more practiced in physical attacks on, and combat with, other humans than I am. That would be a strong reason for judging that I will not be able to defend against an attack unless I do so when he is asleep or off guard. There is no reason to exclude such facts as these from the "circumstances" and no reason to think that if we count them as part of the circumstances we no longer have an objective test. Inclusion of them no more diminishes the objectivity of the test than does inclusion of the fact that the (alleged) aggressor had a gun in his hand.

C. The Imminence Requirement

There is no question but that a subjective construal of "reasonable" provides a tactical advantage for battered women who kill their batterers. To those who, like me, think that justification should continue to be understood as a justification, a subjective construal of "reasonable" seems a bad idea. But if we set that aside, leaving open the possibility of reconceiving it as an excuse, there remains the problem of working out the details: coming up with a plausible formulation of a subjective standard. It does not need to be construed as crudely as Bernhard Goetz advocated, as "is reasonable to the defendant"; an alternative that I suggested is implicit in some discussions of battered women relativizes reasonableness to a particular group of which the defendant is a member. But that has its own problems. We would need to decide what count as groups to which "reasonable" can be relativized. Would we count as a group of the relevant sort those who believe in demonic possession? Those who are bigoted? Those who are poorly educated, narrow-minded, or both?[129] If we do not want to count some of those putative groups as groups of the relevant sort, what basis would we have for excluding them? Although it might be possible to address the problems of deciding—and deciding in a principled way—what counts as a group for this purpose and of determining which (of those groups of which one is a member) is the relevant group, doing so does not look promising.

If we do not avail ourselves of the tactical advantage of a subjective standard, the imminence requirement is a serious obstacle. Indeed, that requirement is the fundamental reason (apart from unfair application of the law) why battered women who kill their batterers are often not able to plead self-defense. The problem is evident in *Norman*. The violence had escalated, giving Judith good reason to fear that it would soon turn lethal, but J.T. had not said (nor had Judith claimed that she believed) that he would kill her the next morning. Even if he had, in most U.S. jurisdictions that would not count as imminent danger. That he was asleep at the time is a significant barrier to a self-defense claim.[130] In this section, I argue that although adopting a subjective standard of "reasonable" is one way to fix the problem—since it allows us to say that to a battered woman, the danger is always imminent—it is preferable to address the problem head-on by dropping or weakening the imminence requirement. To be sure, there are reasons for retaining an imminence requirement. It is, as noted above, important to attach to the defense of self-defense (and defense of others) some constraints so as to discourage using violence against another when one has insufficient reason for thinking that the use of violence is necessary. The reasonable belief requirement speaks to this, and an objective standard of reasonableness of course entails a more robust constraint than does a subjective standard. But the imminence requirement provides an additional limitation on the use of violence, and we need to reflect on whether a dilution of the imminence requirement excessively weakens the constraints on using self-defense.

The imminence requirement provides a safeguard of sorts: in insisting that self-defensive killing be limited to thwarting an imminent attack, we reduce the risk that a life will be taken needlessly. If the attack is not imminent, there is always the hope that even without the (presumedly) intended victim taking steps to thwart it, it will not happen. Maybe the aggressor will change his or her mind; maybe he or she was not really intending to inflict harm but just to scare or intimidate; or perhaps the whole thing was intended as a harmless prank.

The problem, though, is that waiting until the danger is imminent before using self-defensive force is sometimes quite dangerous; occasionally it virtually ensures that one will be unable to defend oneself when the attack occurs. Consider the following hypothetical, courtesy of Paul Robinson: "A kidnaps and confines D with the announced intention of killing him one week later. D has an opportunity to kill A and escape each morning as A brings him his daily ration." The imminence requirement, would, as Robinson writes, "prevent D from using deadly force in self-defense until A is standing over him with a knife." Surely D should not be required to wait until the attack is imminent. In Robinson's words, "If a threatened harm is such that it cannot be avoided if the intended victim waits until the last moment, the principle of self-defense must permit him to act earlier."[131] I would go further: if a threatened harm is such that the chances of avoiding it are slim if the intended victim waits until the last moment, the principle of self-defense must permit him to act earlier. (It is important to be clear, though, that "threatened harm" does not mean simply "a harm that the actor fears will befall him"; there has to be some aggression, or threat of aggression conveyed by the aggressor, before the use of self-defense is warranted.)[132]

The hypothetical not only brings out what is so problematic about the imminence requirement; it also helps us see why imminence may initially seem crucial. It is important insofar as it is a marker for necessity, and if we don't look closely—don't pay attention to situations of long-term battering by a partner who is determined not to let one leave and (other) hostage situations—it might seem to track necessity very closely. Indeed, imminence is often spoken of as if it tracks necessity perfectly: as if it is both necessary and sufficient for the necessity of using self-defense against an aggressor.

Let's examine both tacit assumptions, that is, that it is necessary for the necessity of using self-defense and that it is sufficient for it. That it is not necessary is evident from Robinson's hypothetical (unless one holds that it is the fact that D is kidnapped rather than A's announced plan to kill D that justifies D in killing A at a time when there is no immediate danger).[133] That imminence is not sufficient for the necessity of using force in self-defense is evident from the fact, noted above, that the assailant might be joking, or only aiming to intimidate, with no intention of really carrying out his or her threats.[134]

It is striking how often imminence is spoken of as if "the danger was imminent" entailed "self-defensive force was absolutely necessary." I suspect that an ambiguity in the word "imminent" may be to blame, leading many to hear or read "the danger is imminent" as entailing that it is (virtually) certain to happen and thus conferring on the imminence requirement a spurious air of unimpeachability. "The danger is imminent" can mean simply what it literally does mean, viz., that the danger, such as it is, is an immediate danger. But it can also convey a high degree of certainty that the dreaded thing will happen unless it is stopped. The mistake is to conflate these two ways we use "imminence" and to construe imminence in such a way that we tacitly assume that the mere fact that the risk is a risk of immediate attack entails that there is a very high risk that such an attack will happen.

This mistake may seem too unlikely to merit mention. But it is quite common. Here is one example of the conflation of the two senses of "imminent."[135] When Justice Mitchell reinstated Judith Norman's conviction, he stressed that she "was not faced with an instantaneous choice between killing her husband or [sic] being killed or seriously injured."[136] The implication (for why mention it otherwise?) is that in cases that warrant acquittal on self-defense grounds—cases where the imminence requirement is met—the defendant *is* faced with that choice.[137] But often that is not the case. Frequently (indeed, typically) the choice, when properly spelled out, was not between killing and being killed or seriously injured; it wasn't *that* certain that he would be killed or seriously injured if he had not killed the (apparent) aggressor. The choice, rather, is typically between killing and *risking the possibility of being killed or seriously injured* (a possibility the agent thinks, with good reason, is very likely).

If a stranger drives up to me in a parking lot as I walk to my car and says, pointing a gun at my head, "I am going to kill you unless you get into this car with me," and I happen to have a gun on my person and manage quickly to draw it and shoot him, the imminence requirement is met. But I could not have known for sure at the time that I shot him that if I did not do so, he would kill me.[138] Maybe he only looked to be a stranger (and one with criminal intent) but actually was a well-intentioned acquaintance from twenty years ago whom I didn't recognize, someone with an unfortunate sense of humor, dangerously good theatrical skills, and a realistic looking fake gun. Or perhaps the apparent assailant really was an assailant but though serious about intimidating me into getting into the car with him (and with sinister plans of what he would do when I did), had no intention of shooting me if his effort to force me to get in the car failed and I darted off. It could also be that, though serious at the time he issued the threat to kill me, he would have changed his mind as I ran away. Or, alternatively it could be that he would have shot but missed me. Or perhaps the gun would have jammed.

In short, that the risk—perhaps a moderate risk, perhaps a very high risk—is imminent does not necessarily mean that unless one uses force against the aggressor to thwart that risk, the dreaded thing will happen. Whether or not the attack is imminent, in the sense that the danger, such as it is, is immediate, it may well be the case that the defendant could not have known for sure that if she did not use lethal force against the aggressor that she or someone else would have been killed or seriously injured by him.

To be sure, imminence reduces some of the risk that the use of (lethal) force was in fact unnecessary (whether or not it ever comes to light that it was unnecessary). When there is very little time, there is less of a chance that someone will come to the rescue (or that the attacker will die of natural causes or undergo a personal transformation). But we have to balance that against the consideration that in the cases of many battered women under attack by their batterers, they have been attacked repeatedly already, often very recently, and often with escalating violence; the would-be rescuers have declined to help or proven to be unavailable; attempts to flee (or obtain assistance) have met with increased violence and threats to kill family members if the attempt is repeated. They may thus in some instances have more reason (more than some in prototypical "self-defense situations") to think that a lethal attack (or another infliction of serious bodily harm) is inevitable unless they use force before the next (or more serious) attack becomes imminent.[139]

The considerations in the previous eight paragraphs militate in favor of dropping the imminence requirement, either by treating imminence (as in Canada)[140] as one of several factors to be weighed in considering whether the use of force was necessary (or at least reasonably believed to be so) or by replacing the requirement with a rebuttable presumption that if the danger was not imminent, self-defensive force was not permissible. Why is it thought by many that the imminence requirement should be retained?

D. Imminence and Retreat

Those who defend the imminence requirement (in either its current form or one that allows only slightly more latitude) emphasize the importance of limiting self-defense, especially lethal self-defense.[141] But we can agree that that is important yet not agree that the imminence requirement is necessary for properly constraining the defense or the best way to do so. It is often forgotten in discussions of the imminence requirement that there are other ways to reduce the risk that force will be used unnecessarily. An obvious way to constrain the use of self-defensive force is by imposing a retreat requirement. In marked contrast to the imminence requirement, the retreat requirement is rejected altogether by the majority of U.S. jurisdictions, and even in jurisdictions where it is in place, it is quite limited. There is, in addition to the qualification that retreat from one's home is not required (apart from those jurisdictions that, curiously enough, do require retreat from one's home if it is also the assailant's home), this constraint: retreat is never required unless the person knows that she or he can retreat in complete safety. Note that it is not just that the person thinks she or he can probably retreat in complete safety; retreat is required only if the person in question knows it is safe and, moreover, completely safe.

Given that the whole point of constraints on the use of self-defense is to try to prevent the unnecessary use of self-defensive force (especially lethal force), the retreat requirement is more to the point than is an imminence requirement. After all, as Dressler notes, "If a person can safely retreat and, therefore, avoid killing the aggressor, deadly force is, objectively speaking, unnecessary."[142] By contrast, the fact that a danger is not imminent does not entail that one can safely avoid using lethal force (though an explanation is owed as to why, if the danger was not imminent, one could not avoid it). The retreat requirement gives a clear and eminently sensible instruction: flee if you safely can rather than kill (or harm). The imminence requirement gives an instruction that is less sensible: no matter how dangerous it is for you to do so, refrain from using (lethal) self-defensive force until the danger is imminent. The first is a demand we should expect reasonable beings to endorse; the second is not.

Now one might argue that the retreat requirement as it stands is too weak to constrain self-defense sufficiently and that therefore we need an imminence requirement to do justice to the fact that even the life of an aggressor should not be taken unless absolutely necessary. It may indeed be the case that the effect of the strong constraints built into the retreat requirement is that the intended victim is rarely required to retreat.[143] But the solution, if we think that self-defense needs more constraining than is provided by the retreat requirement with its various qualifications, need not to be retain a very robust imminence requirement. We might instead modify some of the qualifications built into the retreat requirement, perhaps holding that one who believes unreasonably that retreat in complete safety is not possible would have a self-defense claim only against a charge of murder, not against a charge of reckless or negligent homicide.[144]

Placing some of the burden of restricting self-defense on the retreat requirement seems so obvious a solution that the question naturally arises: why is it that the imminence requirement has been expected to bear almost the entire burden? I suggested earlier that there may be an unwitting conflation of two distinct senses of "imminent" and that this conflation creates the illusion that satisfying the imminence requirement guarantees that the use of lethal force really was necessary; but another factor needs to be mentioned as well. Here is a clue: the traditional name for the approach that is the majority rule in the United States—the "no retreat rule"—is "the true man rule." A true man stands his ground; the law—or so was the sentiment as the retreat requirement inherited from English law came to be rejected in much of the United States in the late nineteenth century—should not force a "true man who is without fault" to "fly from an assailant."[145] The imminence requirement is not at odds with traditional conceptions of masculinity and masculine virtue; the retreat requirement is.

One might retort that ideals of masculinity have only a little to do with it; there is also the consideration that when the danger is imminent, less can be expected of the person under attack. Someone under attack cannot be expected to think about whether he or she can avoid inflicting violence; if able to fight back, he or she should be permitted to do so. By contrast, more should be expected of someone who is not in imminent danger.

This makes some sense; but notice again the assumption that the heat of the moment has excusatory force and that desperation, and the physical and emotional pain of recent blows, against the backdrop of years of abuse, somehow do not. That more should be asked of someone not in imminent danger makes sense if we insert a *caeteris paribus* clause, but if the person not in imminent danger has repeatedly been the victim of the attacker's violence, perhaps also seen her children beaten (and her cat or dog killed) by this man, is it reasonable to expect from her the calm reflection not expected of the person in imminent danger?

E. Concluding Remarks on Self-Defense

I have been suggesting in this section that the law of self-defense is flawed if it cannot treat cases such as Judith Norman's as self-defensive killings. The sticking point is the imminence requirement, and serious consideration should be given to weakening it so that there is at most a rebuttable presumption that if the danger was not imminent the killing was unnecessary (and not reasonably believed to be necessary). The imminence requirement has borne too much of the burden of constraining self-defense. The retreat requirement is more closely tied to the necessity of using self-defensive force and—if we can get past the notion that it is a matter of honor to attack rather than flee from a bad guy—appears a better way to constrain self-defense.

IV. RAPE[146]

A. Introduction

The law of rape, unlike that of self-defense and provocation, has for some time been recognized to be seriously tainted by sexism and over the past few decades has been significantly revised in an effort to address the problems.[146] Rape shield laws now restrict the admissibility of evidence that the complainant was promiscuous; the corroboration requirement (required only for rape, not for any other crimes) is gone; there is no longer a requirement that the complainant have resisted "to the utmost"; the Hale instruction admonishing jurors that a claim to have been raped is easily fabricated has been abolished; and the law has generally been rendered gender-neutral, acknowledging both that men can be victims of sexual assaults and that women can be perpetrators.[147]

Despite these reforms, the prosecution and conviction rates for rape remain low. It is likely that the most serious underlying issues are attitudinal, encompassing suspicions that women who claim to have been raped are likely to be lying, at least more likely to be lying than are those who claim to be the victim of another crime,[148] along with the sense that rape by an acquaintance, especially one with whom one has had any intimacy, is not very serious and probably does not warrant prosecution unless it also involves some serious battering. One sees signs of these attitudes in a multitude of places;[149] for example, in the blogs in my local newspaper reacting to a report of a sexual assault ("What was the 14-year-old girl who claims to have been raped at 2 p.m. Tuesday doing out of school anyway? She probably is in trouble for truancy and so made up a story of being raped.") The fact (as reported in the *New York Times*) that there is an enormous backlog of untested rape kits containing physical evidence obtained from sexual assault victims also suggests that rape is not taken very seriously.[150]

Nonetheless, there are aspects of current sexual assault law that are cause for concern and that indeed may be part of the explanation of the tenacity of such attitudes as those reported. Until recently, some of these attitudes were firmly entrenched in the law; a residue of earlier law may send a message that the views are indeed warranted. The continued requirement of force,[151] a holdover from the recently jettisoned resistance requirement, lends legitimacy to the idea that a woman's "no" may safely—as far as the law is concerned—be disregarded. One consideration in reflecting on what reforms are in order is whether the current law, albeit inadvertently, serves as a stamp of approval to such attitudes as those mentioned above.[152]

Rape is essentially nonconsensual sex.[153] Just what that means, and whether rape requires more than nonconsent and sex, will be the subject of the rest of section IV. Although it matters just what counts as sex, I will skip over that in favor of the more philosophically rich question of what counts as nonconsensual. Since in most U.S. jurisdictions not only nonconsent but also force is required, that requirement merits discussion.[154] Finally, there is the *mens rea* component, more easily understood via the MPC categories of culpability (purposely, knowingly, recklessly, and negligently) or, perhaps more helpful still for purposes of this essay, via the question of what sort of mistake regarding consent should exculpate. What *mens rea* should be required for rape will be affected by whether a force requirement is retained and how nonconsent is understood.

B. Consent

What should constitute consent for purposes of rape law? And what should constitute nonconsent?[155] Here is a first go at it: saying "yes" constitutes consent; saying "no" constitutes nonconsent or a withholding of consent. Actively participating in the intimacy, though not essential to consent, also constitutes consent; and physically or verbally resisting in a way other than saying "no" also constitutes nonconsent (though again is not essential to it). Would this do?

No. Importantly, *A* saying "yes" to *B* (or actively participating in the intimacy) does not constitute consent if on the occasion in question *B* had said (and in a way that did not appear to *A* to be joking), "I'll kill you if you don't agree to have sex with me."[156] "No" is rather less complicated; if *A* says "no" to X, *A* has not consented to it, period. However, my position on "no" turns on a view that not everyone shares, viz., that sexual consent—indeed, all consent—needs to be understood *not* as a mental state, but (to use J. L. Austin's term) as a "performative."[157] Consent is something one does. It is not something one feels. To consent to something is to agree to something, not to want something. (There is, as indicated above, the further detail that it is to agree reasonably freely to something, not to "agree" when a knife has been flashed at one; but my focus now is on the contrast between agreeing to something and wanting or desiring something.) A can desire something without agreeing to it—as, indeed, with sex, where A feels a strong desire for sex with B but for various reasons, such as A being married to C, chooses not to have sex with B and so declines B's invitation. One can also agree to something without desiring it (as when one agrees to give a housemate a ride to the metro station, realizing that the other's need for the ride is greater than one's own need to continue, without interruption, the proof one is working on).

If sexual consent is understood as sexual desire, saying "no" might well *not* constitute nonconsent. A could say "no" to B's overtures despite feeling sexual desire toward B (though the frequency with which this actually happens tends to be exaggerated, due no doubt to wishful thinking). Perhaps one reason why many people think that "no" does not constitute nonconsent is that they conflate sexual consent with sexual desire.[158]

Anyone who holds that A's "no" to B does not constitute nonconsent as long as A actually feels sexual desire toward B has reason to question the moral significance of consent thus understood as well as to wonder whether rape should even be understood as nonconsensual sex. It would be hard to regard rape as a serious crime if the essence of rape were having sex without desiring it. This is very likely one reason why force seems to many to be a crucial component of rape: they think of nonconsensual sex as simply sex that is not desired, and *that* does not sound like a serious crime. Surely if B (unequivocally) conveyed to A, in conditions that did not involve undue pressure, a willingness to have sex with A, the fact that A had sex with B when B did not desire sex should not be the basis for charging A with *any* crime, let alone a serious crime.

Clearly, it matters a good deal which way consent is understood: as basically akin to desire or as agreeing to something.

For purposes of holding people responsible for knowing whether another consented, it only makes sense to understand consent as something that, like promising, is "done"—something conveyed to another—rather than as desire (or any other mental state).[159] Why expect mind reading? And indeed in other areas of the law where consent converts something that would otherwise be a crime to something either innocuous or positively good, we understand consent as something conveyed, not as something felt. Whether you borrowed my car or are guilty of joyriding is (as far as the *actus reus* goes) a matter of whether I consented, and my consent is not a matter of how I feel or felt. If I told you that you were welcome to use my car on such-and-such a day, I consented to your doing so,[160] even if your request occasioned in me resentment and annoyance. How I felt is not the issue; it is a matter of whether

I told you that you could use it. If I wanted to let you borrow it but told you you could not (perhaps because I knew another party would be upset if I lent it to you), I did not consent, despite my warm feelings at the prospect of lending it to you.

Understanding sexual consent on the performative model (as something one does) rather than on the mental state model (as something one feels) is helpful in a number of ways. First, notice that one fear of false accusation of rape can be laid to rest if we are clear that consent is something done, not something felt: one fear is that someone might not want to have sex but only make that clear afterward and might then have grounds for saying she was raped. But on the performative model, if she gave every indication of wanting to have sex, in particular, if she said "yes" when asked, she has (unless the conditions were such as to vitiate consent) consented, whatever she in fact felt at the time. Likewise, as noted above, if one says "no," one has not consented, and what one feels is immaterial. Any claims on the part of an initiator to have seen that the other party—male or female—was sexually aroused are simply irrelevant; sexual arousal does not constitute consent and is perfectly compatible with nonconsent.[161]

C. Nonconsent, Force, and Resistance

As noted above, acceptance of the mental state conception of consent would motivate endorsement of the force requirement. But even some who accept the performative conception might endorse a requirement of force in addition to nonconsent.

The force requirement is best understood against the backdrop of the resistance requirement. The traditional requirement was "resistance to the utmost"; even when there was a threat of great and immediate bodily harm, resistance was required. Just how seriously judges took "to the utmost" is illustrated by the nineteenth-century Wisconsin case *Whittaker v. State*, summarized as follows by Stephen Schulhofer:

> The victim testified, "He had my hands tight and my feet tight, and I couldn't move from my place even." When she screamed for help, he threatened to use his revolver. Still, she tried once again to cry out. She testified, "I couldn't do any more, I got so tired out. I tried to save me so much as I could, but I couldn't save myself....I worked so much as I could, and I gave up."[162]

The jury convicted the man of rape, but the Wisconsin Supreme Court reversed the conviction, explaining that the "testimony does not show that the threat of personal violence overpowered her will" or that she was for any other reason "incapable of voluntary action."[163] The court elaborated: "submission..., no matter how reluctantly yielded, removes from the act an essential element of the crime of rape."[164] Thus even if she submitted because she believed that if she did not she would be killed, the *actus reus* requirement for rape was not met. It would be nice to be able to say that this position was soon abandoned, but as Schulhofer chronicles, the story was "endlessly repeated," and indeed in the early twentieth century, courts "intensified their insistence" that women resist to the utmost, invoking "modern science" to show that (unless she was unconscious at the time of the rape) her failure to prevent penetration generally means that she in fact was willing. In 1906, endorsing the rule[165] that a rape conviction requires proof that the alleged victim made "'the most vehement exercise of every physical means or faculty within [her] power,'"[166] the Wisconsin Supreme Court claimed that a woman "is equipped to interpose most effective obstacles by means of hands and limbs and pelvic muscles. Indeed, medical writers insist that these obstacles are practically insuperable in the absence of more than the usual relative disproportion of age and strength between man and woman."[167] A 1947 Nebraska Supreme Court case endorsed the position that submission counts as consent "no matter how reluctantly yielded" and, moreover, that "carnal knowledge, with the voluntary consent of the woman, no matter how tardily given *or how much force had hitherto been imposed*, is not rape" (my italics). In case this was not clear enough, they specified that "she must persist in such resistance as long as she has the power to do so until the offense is consummated."[168] Even in 1973 a New York appellate court decision set aside a rape conviction on similar grounds: rape "is not committed unless the woman opposes the man to the utmost limit of her power."[169]

What is behind the resistance requirement? After all, there is no such requirement for theft, robbery, or nonsexual assault.[170] The resistance requirement reflects the view that (a) a woman of honor will fight to the death to preserve it (or—once the requirement was toned down to require only "earnest" resistance rather than resistance to the utmost—maybe not to the death, but she will at least put up quite a fight, subjecting herself to considerable risk), and (b) it is not seriously wrong,[171] if wrong at all, for a man to force himself on a woman *unless* she makes her refusal unmistakably clear by screaming or fighting him and not "merely" by telling him clearly and firmly that she does **not** want this. Moreover, the screaming and fighting have to persist; otherwise he might think—and, the suggestion is, might reasonably think—that she is putting up "token resistance." Or, perhaps he would think he has won her over.

More needs to be said about honor. The notion seems to be that only a woman of honor is wronged, or harmed, by a rape (unless the rapist harms her by further violence or through damage inflicted by the rape). A promiscuous woman was not regarded as harmed or wronged by a rape since her honor was already lost. But honor is significant in another way, as well, dovetailing with (b): if she isn't a woman of honor, then, the thought was, probably she did consent or at least it is understandable if he thought she did. After all, if she has illicit sex with others, why not with me (reasons the defendant)? And if (he further reasons) she says "no," well, that's just token resistance, part of her attempt to look at least somewhat respectable. Thus, real resistance was the way to distinguish the virtuous woman—who should not be raped—from the slut, who was, in effect, fair game and, indeed, probably really wanted it or at least did not mind.

But all this is in the past, right? Not entirely. We see remnants of (a) and (b) in the ongoing interest in what the woman was wearing—as if wearing "provocative" clothes showed one to be a slut (the concomitant assumption being that sluts get what they deserve if they are raped, or that such women are always game to have sex, with anyone, at any time, in all circumstances), or "provoked" an attack,[172] or some-how amounted to consenting to sex.[173]

How much has the law changed with respect to the resistance requirement? The notion that the woman must fight to the death to preserve her honor has completely disappeared (from U.S. courts and statutes, anyway), but that either nonconsent is not enough or that "no" does not constitute nonconsent remains the norm. As Schulhofer writes, "Most courts still insist on some evidence of physical resistance. Verbal protests alone are not enough, unless there are threats and fear sufficient to make resistance seem futile."[174]

D. Should the Force Requirement Be Abolished?

Two possibilities should be distinguished: one is to abolish the force requirement altogether; another is to retain the force requirement for rape but have a lesser offense of nonconsensual sex for which force would not be required. I shall not be concerned to address considerations in favor of one of these changes over the other. As things stand, in the majority of U.S. jurisdictions, nonconsensual sex is not pun-ishable at all unless force is proven (or unless the person who does not consent is unconscious or for other reasons incapacitated, or underage).[175] Why might one think this a good arrangement?

To those who think it is hard to tell whether or not a woman is consenting and are concerned not to miss an opportunity for sex by taking "no" seriously if there is a chance that she doesn't really mean it, the resistance requirement made some sense; the same consideration would lead them to favor requiring force. Obviously, if one is unsure whether the "no" is intended to be taken seriously, one can ask; to some, though, this has its own considerable cost. They hold that it is much more romantic, or much more erotically charged, to leave things unstated and read off from the other's behavior whether or not she (or, for that matter, he) is consenting. I suspect that in many cases this attitude draws upon the notion that one may know better than the other person what she (or he) really wants, or will enjoy; if so, it reflects a picture of consent as a mental state. But it need not. One who views con-sent not as a mental state but, rather, as a relaying to the other of a wish to have sex might point out that such conveying is often done very subtly and argue that as the other person might be too shy or inhibited to say "yes" if asked, she needs to be helped to do what she possibly not only wants but knows she wants.

One underlying disagreement between those who think it best if nonconsensual sex is not punishable unless force is proven, and those who think that it should be punishable, concerns the comparative harms or losses in the following scenarios. In (a), when one party says "no" or "not now," the other stops and says something along the lines of "No to what I was just doing? Would oral sex be okay?"; some awkward-ness ensues, and the result is less sexual intimacy[176] than the two would otherwise have had and (let us imagine) have both enjoyed, as well as some significant disap-pointment on the part of at least one of the two. In (b), the person saying "no" expe-riences the horror of finding that the other is determined to have sex no matter what she or he says. Some authors write as if (b) is really not too bad as long as the man who is forcing himself on her is someone she knows; they even suggest that she knows he will not hurt her and that all she is suffering is "unwanted" sex. But typically the person on whom sex is being forced by a (supposed) friend does not know that, nor does she have reason to think that because he used to seem to be a perfectly decent person, surely he will not hurt her—beyond, of course, raping her.[177]

Both (a) and (b) are undesirable. But the loss in (b) is so much greater that it hardly makes sense to risk (b) in order to reduce the risk of (a). Likewise, the concern of the law should be to safeguard those who wish to refuse an invitation without having to resort to physical resistance to do so rather than to take care lest (god forbid!) the law create a strong incentive for talking to one's (presumed) partner to make sure that he or she is comfortable with what they are (or the initiator is) doing. We can acknowledge that while there is no particular reason to think that such a conversation would generally undermine the quality of the erotic experience (and there are reasons to think that it might improve it),[178] it is possible that sometimes it will;[179] but the loss of having sex forced on one despite one's verbal objections is far more serious.

The same point can be made about the alleged loss to any woman who would like to be able to say "no" without meaning it and then have her "no" ignored. Remarkably often a 1988 survey of female undergraduates at Texas A & M University is cited to show that women sometimes say "no" to sex without meaning it.[180] Those who rely on that study should bear in mind that it reports that two-thirds of those surveyed said they had *never* said "no" to sex without meaning it and that most of those in the one-third minority had done so only rarely. The study, if taken seriously, thus shows that far more often than not, the woman saying "no" to sex means it. But even if many more women said "no" to sex without meaning it, and even if (something not clear from the study, though a reasonable guess) those who did would lament a state of affairs in which their "no" was regularly taken seriously, it is clear which group—those who like to have their "no" taken seriously or those who prefer that it not be taken seriously—should be burdened. The burden of having to learn to say or show that one wants to have sex is far lighter than that of having to scream ("Help! I'm about to be raped!") or physically fight the seducer/rapist before one's refusal is taken seriously.[181]

Another argument in support of the status quo, according to which nonconsensual sex without force is not punishable,[182] is that it is unfair to punish initiators for not taking "no" seriously. How so? Let's assume the worry isn't about fair warning; those in favor of retaining the force requirement understand that the proposal is to change the law and then punish those who (after the law has been duly promulgated) violate it, not to punish without fair warning. Supposing the law is changed and duly promulgated (and aided by posters and brochures advising that "no" constitutes nonconsent and that mixed signals call for a conversation, not forging ahead), what is the objection? Some might claim that it involves an objectionable attempt to legislate behavior. Now, that it does can hardly itself be a problem; what law doesn't try to legislate behavior? The complaint must instead be that it is treating as a crime something that was not hitherto viewed as a crime and moreover is still not so viewed by many people. But doing so is objectionable only if we suppose that the criminal law should merely put a rubber stamp on—and add teeth to—widespread societal disapprobation of certain actions. This is implausible. Widespread societal disapprobation of x is neither necessary nor sufficient for criminalizing x. It may be, for example, that certain forms of harassment of atheists, or gays and lesbians, are viewed by a significant minority or even a majority in the United States as not wrong; yet this would not suffice to render unjust a law that made such harassment a crime. While there is, to be sure, some "legislation of behavior" when nonconsensual sex is treated as a crime (as there is when drunk driving is a crime), another way to describe what is going on is this: a serious harm is now recognized that hitherto was not. The harm of having sex inflicted on one despite one's refusal is a genuine harm. Those who ignore a refusal, even if they do not beat the person or threaten violence, are committing a serious wrong. That wrong, we now declare, is punishable. Where is the wrong in that (and in punishing those guilty of the crime accordingly)?[183]

A different argument is that there is more scope for error—for convicting the innocent—if we do not require force. This worry needs to be further specified. If it is not just the view that those who fail to take "no" for an answer in fact are guilty of no crime, what is the worry? Presumably it could be this: some who do take "no" seriously may still end up being convicted of rape if (say) after she says "no" they try unsuccessfully to persuade her, and then (looking annoyed), ask if a different sexual activity is okay, and when she says nothing, figure it is okay, when in fact she perceived the question as insistent and, out of fear, said nothing. Now, the first reply is that there is no reason to think that we need a force requirement to address that worry; instead, we need to address what, for the purposes of the law, should count as consent. *Should* saying nothing count as consent? I address this in the next section. But in addition, the worry that the defendant may have done his or her best to ascertain that the other person was consenting yet might have gotten it wrong can, and should, be addressed via the *mens rea* component. Honest mistakes may be possible; and in section F, I discuss what sorts of mistakes (if any) should exculpate.[184]

It bears mention that if we opt to retain a force requirement, a further matter would require discussion, namely, whether anything other than physical force, or a threat thereof, should satisfy the force requirement. What about the threats of a teacher to fail a student unless he has sex with him? A landlady's threats to evict a tenant (living in an area where affordable housing is very hard to come by) unless he has sex with her? A foster parent's threat to send his teenage foster child back to the orphanage unless she has sex with him? U.S. courts have traditionally been very reluctant to allow threats other than threats of physical force to count as force, partly for very bad reasons and partly because of the difficulty of differentiating threats from announcements, sometimes unobjectionable, that one is only willing to continue to do X for S (where X is something one is not obliged, by law or by one's role responsibilities or basic decency, to provide) if S agrees to sex.[185] Some object on these grounds to a statute adopted by the Pennsylvania legislature in 1995 that defines the "forcible compulsion" required for a rape conviction as compulsion "by use of physical, intellectual, moral, emotional or psychological force, either express or implied."[186] One solution, if the force requirement is retained and it is thought problematic to broaden the conception of force that is required for rape, would be to have a separate statute (or two) with a lesser penalty than rape and to limit liability to those whose threat involves a misuse of authority they have over the other person. In New Zealand, for instance, a crime carrying up to fourteen years of prison is that of "inducing sexual connection by coercion," where that includes "sexual connection with another person knowing that the other person has been induced to consent ... by ... [a]n express or implied threat ... to make improper use, to the detriment of the other person, of any power or authority arising out of any occupational or vocational position held by the person having sexual connection."[187] The same approach provides a way to criminalize, without treating as sexual assault, sexual blackmail.[188]

E. What Should Count as Nonconsent?

Supposing we agree that nonconsensual sex should be punishable even if force is not proven (and even if the victim is not a minor and not incapacitated), how should we understand nonconsent? To avoid undue complexity, I have spoken thus far as if nonconsent is simply saying "no" or something functionally equivalent (or pushing the initiator away). But we need now to consider whether nonconsent should instead be understood as the absence of affirmative consent.[189]

Two broad approaches can thus be distinguished. (1) The activity is nonconsensual if and only if one party[190] says or otherwise communicates "no"; or (2) it is nonconsensual in the absence of affirmative consent. Whether affirmative consent requires a verbal component is a further question.[191] There are variants to the first approach as well. One possibility is that strict liability be imposed once she has said "no" (and he has heard her); another is a rebuttable presumption of nonconsent once she has said "no." For our purposes, the exact details of what should be required, and the difficulties with each requirement, are of less interest than the underlying disagreements over what should count as nonconsent.

The fundamental disagreement is this: Is it the responsibility of the initiator to make sure that the other party indeed is agreeing to it? Or is it the responsibility of the person who does not want to have sex to convey that to the initiator (more precisely, to make it clear that she (or he) is not just ambivalent, or willing though not in the mood, but is declining)? Some may wonder why it would ever happen that the person who does not want to have sex would not say so. The answer is that he or she might be afraid of antagonizing the initiator, particularly if the initiator seems so determined to have sex that refusing looks futile and dangerous.

A plausible answer to the question about responsibility is that this depends on what, if any, relationship already exists between the two people. If there is an ongoing sexual relationship, then unless there is also a history of violence in the relationship, it seems fine for consent to be presumed unless otherwise indicated—as long as the presumption of consent is very easily overridden. If there is no prior sexual rela-tionship, or if it ended (or if there is any unclarity as to whether it ended), the pre-sumption should be nonconsent. It should be the responsibility of the initiator to make sure that the other party is agreeing to the activity. The reasons mirror those against requiring force: the worst-case scenario where the initiator checks with the other person is far less bad than the worst-case scenario where the initiator just assumes the other is consenting.

At this point I anticipate an admonition. "Let's not forget what we are doing. We are talking about what the elements of a crime are and what they should be. We are not devising rules of etiquette for sexual intimacy (or attempts at sexual intimacy). On the assumption that nonconsent remains a crucial component, and with the idea of eliminating the requirement of force, we are working out what should count as nonconsent. Let's continue to set the bar fairly low rather than hope to use the law as a vehicle for educating everyone on how to treat their (prospective) sex partners with greater respect and sensitivity. Dropping the force requirement is one thing, but let's not put the burden on the initiator to confirm before proceeding that a shy date really is happy to have sex with him (or her). We should rely on current social conventions and regard sex as consensual unless one party clearly indicates otherwise."

Now, were we to take that route, we would at least have to modify the position to say that sex is consensual unless (a) one party clearly indicates otherwise **or** (b) the circumstances or the demeanor of the noninitiator provide reason to suspect that he or she may be too shocked, confused, or afraid to express refusal.[192] We would also need to bear in mind the role played by wishful thinking in assessing whether the other person in fact is indicating that she does not want to proceed. But the route sketched proposes that we rely on social conventions. That calls for further comment.

Social conventions regarding sex are notoriously unsettled; moreover, much of what passes as "conventional" in this context wears on its face norms of male aggres-sion and female passivity. If the "convention" reflects a history of male entitlement, appeals to "convention"—even if not so intended—may be a sanitized way of ensur-ing that men's sexual access to women will not become restricted by inconvenient expectations that consent be obtained rather than presumed. Rather than rely on (alleged) conventions, we will need to steer people in the right direction by stipulat-ing that given x, y, or z, nonconsent is to be presumed. (I word this as I do to avoid saying that x, y, and z each constitutes nonconsent; it is more accurate to say that that there is a rebuttable presumption that they do.)[193] The power of wishful think-ing, abetted by norms of femininity and masculinity, can thus be undercut by explicitly saying that nonconsent is presumed if either party says "no." The legal upshot would be, as I see it, a requirement of due diligence that would be imposed if a "no" has been uttered. (Did he then say something along the lines of, "We won't do anything you don't want to do; just tell me if you want to stop; do you want to stop altogether, or just not do X?" Or did he say, "Oh come on, we're just getting started; you'll love this" or "What the hell do you think we came here for?!")

At this point an argument for requiring affirmative consent looms into view. If we are willing to impose a requirement of due diligence if either party says "no" (or otherwise expresses a wish to stop), why not impose it more generally so as to cover cases where she is so startled that she freezes and says nothing, as in the 1994 California case of *People v. Iniguez* (or in the rather similar case described to me by one of my students, whose roommate was raped at age sixteen by the drunken father of the children she had just babysat; she was, at the parents' suggestion, spending the night on the sofa so that they would not have to drive her home at so late an hour).[194] Imposing a requirement of due diligence would send a clear message that the initiator is not just to hope that sex can happen without resistance but, rather, to make sure, if there is any room for doubt, that the other person is consenting. It also would make it far more difficult for perpetrators to take advantage of the other person's fear, unease, and confusion and to deceive themselves into thinking that when they do so they are only seducing—only overcoming sexual inhibitions that she really wants to overcome—not raping.

The worry may persist that this is unfair and, more precisely, that it is imposing on everyone, with the force of the criminal law, a certain way of approaching sexual intimacy. As noted above, the worry would make sense if the idea were to prosecute without fair warning, but that of course is not the idea. The worry would also make *some* sense if rape (a) were not such a common crime, causing such serious damage to so many people, and (b) did not have a very low conviction rate compared to the number of offenses.[195] Were rape not nearly as frequent as it is, or were the conviction rate (or rate of conviction minus the overturning of convictions) not so low compared to the number of rapes, the proposed legal reform might more plausibly be seen as a way of using the law to educate everyone in greater sensitivity. And the criticism would then have some force (though it is by no means obvious that the law should never be used to educate, especially if doing so does not increase the risk of unjust convictions or excessively harsh sentences). But given the current situation, there is a real need to figure out ways we can—without running a significant risk thereby of convicting the innocent or of imposing unduly severe sentences—modify the law. Clarifying that without affirmative consent there is a presumption of nonconsent (except in ongoing relationships, free of violence) and indicating that we are in particular going to be looking for due diligence regarding consent seem to me to constitute the most promising approach. At the same time, in order to reduce the risk of unduly harsh penalties for nonconsensual sex where *A* took advantage of *B*'s unease and passivity and evinced a lack of concern for whether *B* was consenting, we might want a gradation of rape according to which merely nonconsensual sex (without physical force or even pressure on her) would incur no more than (say) a one-year prison sentence.

F. Mistakes and Culpability: The *Mens Rea* Question

Suppose *D* mistakenly believed *V* was consenting. Can he still be guilty of rape? In other words, should the laws be designed to preclude a conviction in such circumstances?

One position is that a mistaken belief that the victim was in fact consenting should preclude conviction; the defendant lacks the necessary *mens rea* if he thought she was consenting. Another is that only a reasonable belief that she was consenting precludes conviction. The third option is to say that even a reasonable belief that she was consenting should not preclude conviction.

The third option—a strict liability approach—makes some sense in jurisdictions where the force requirement is robust. But if the force requirement is dropped (as I think it should be), or so weakened as to be merely nominal, there is good reason to recognize the possibility of reasonable mistakes about consent. To be sure, mistakes about consent are generally avoidable with due diligence; all one has to do is ask. But even with due diligence, reasonable mistakes are, albeit extremely unlikely, possible, largely because of the possibility that *V* may misread the situation and, judging it to be dangerous, may act as if she is consenting. If we can imagine that (a) *V* thinks it pointless to refuse and dangerous even to appear reluctant and therefore feigns not only willingness but also enthusiasm; (b) *V* has excellent acting skills; and (c) *V*'s misreading of the situation is not due to anything in the circumstances (including *D*'s words, actions, and demeanor) that would have led a reasonable person to realize that *V* might be feeling threatened, a reasonable mistake on *D*'s part as to whether she is consenting is possible.[196] If *V* is a survivor of chronic sexual abuse, accustomed to refusal being pointless, and if *D* does not know this, the scenario is, sadly, all the more imaginable. (A very perceptive, sensitive man would hopefully pick up on subtle signs that she is only acquiescing out of fear, but it should not be a necessary condition for a mistake to be counted as reasonable that a very perceptive, sensitive man might well have made such a mistake. More generally, a lack of perceptiveness does not, and should not, suffice for criminal liability.)

The best approach thus seems to be to allow mistakes but to insist that a mistake must be reasonable to exculpate. That said, there is also reason for unease, since a jury instruction on mistakes, even with the restriction that they have to be reasonable mistakes, increases the risk of acquittals on such grounds as that he thought that because she chose to be in his company, went to his home alone with him, and accepted a drink that she was indeed consenting to sex with him—despite her firm, repeated "no." But this problem is better remedied by adding to the jury instructions that *a*, *b*, and *c* do not constitute consent (either severally or jointly) and that a belief based on *a*, *b*, and *c* that *V* was consenting does not count as reasonable.[197] Just as the law can specify that *x*, *y*, and *z* do not constitute adequate provocation, it can also stipulate that *a*, *b*, and *c* do not constitute consent. Moreover, it can also specify that if *d* (e.g., the complainant said "no"), there is a rebuttable presumption both that she did not consent and that he did not reasonably believe that she did.[198]

In discussing the standard of the reasonable person in criminal law, I emphasized the importance of distinguishing "reasonable" from "typical" or "ordinary" and not conflating "reasonable person" with "the sort of person we see all the time and certainly don't think of as a criminal." Mistakes based on a notion that a woman who dresses a certain way and chooses to go home with S is surely consenting to sex with S, whatever she may say, are not rendered reasonable just because they are familiar and reflect common views about women and "women's place." Moreover, such mistakes are mistakes of law, not mistakes of fact, and it is generally only the latter that provide a defense. A proper instruction on mistakes should point out that it is mistakes about what the complainant said, not generally about whether what the person said counts as consent, that may be grounds for acquittal. As the Supreme Court of Canada explained in *The Queen v. Ewanchuk*: "a belief that silence, passivity or ambiguous conduct constitutes consent is a mistake of law, and provides no defence. Similarly, an accused cannot rely upon his purported belief that the complainant's expressed lack of agreement to sexual touching in fact constituted an invitation to more persistent or aggressive contact. An accused cannot say that he thought 'no meant yes.'"[199]

I have been suggesting that a reasonable but mistaken belief that the complainant was in fact consenting should secure an acquittal. The problem that "reasonable" is often understood too broadly, with the result that such beliefs as that V consented because (though admittedly she did say "no") she was dressed provocatively (etc.) are treated as reasonable, is best addressed by providing guidance as to what does, and what does not, constitute either consent or reasonable grounds for a belief that V did consent and a reminder that only mistakes of fact, not mistakes of law, provide a defense.[200]

But should the belief have to be reasonable at all? It might be claimed that if D sincerely believed that V was consenting, despite her repeated, firm "no," he cannot be blamed for acting on his belief. The claim presumably would apply to beliefs in general, not only to beliefs about consent; I'll evaluate it accordingly.

The position that one cannot be blamed for acting on one's belief is highly implausible and certainly not a position generally reflected in the law; we would have no problem blaming, and punishing, someone who killed a U.S. president because she or he believed the leader ought to be killed.

A somewhat more plausible position is that S should not be held criminally liable for X unless S could have acted otherwise, and because S believed that p, S could not, at that time, have done otherwise than act on that belief (whether or not it was reasonable).[201] The idea here seems to be that, if at the moment when S did X S could not have acted otherwise (given the anger, the hatred, etc., that he brought to the situation or his confident belief that p), then S should not be criminally liable. That this too is not plausible—or at least, is not compatible with our practices of blaming and punishing—is evident from the fact that it would entail not holding someone responsible for causing a fatal car accident if, because of her intoxication, she could not have avoided hitting the pedestrian. We hold people responsible for avoiding putting themselves into such situations, for example, for not getting behind the wheel of a car while intoxicated, or when they know they have a medical condition that calls for not driving until tests indicate that their medication is effective. If S could not have done otherwise at that moment but only because S culpably placed herself in a situation where it was quite predictable that she would not be able to act responsibly, that she could not at that moment have done otherwise does not exculpate. Although my example concerns driving while impaired, the point holds more generally.

The position can be strengthened by inserting "nonculpably"; then the point can be put quite simply: that S was nonculpably unable to do otherwise should be a reason for not holding S criminally liable. Of course any position relying on the notion of inability to do otherwise requires fleshing out just what that inability amounts to. But we can ignore that, for the position does not provide substantial support for the view that negligence does not suffice for criminal liability. That S was nonculpably unable to do otherwise is a reason for not holding S criminally liable, but is not a reason for denying that negligence suffices for criminal liability. That there are some whose conduct, through no fault of their own, is sometimes going to deviate from the standard of care of a reasonable person in that situation is not a good reason to hold that negligence should never suffice for criminal liability. As noted above (drawing from H. L. A Hart),[202] we can hold that negligence suffices for criminal liability while at the same time allowing room for excuses so that those who nonculpably are unable to meet the reasonable person standard are not treated as culpable for that failure.

A much more plausible argument against the position that negligence (as defined in the MPC) suffices for criminal liability is that one should be criminally liable for negligence only if one's negligence reflects culpable indifference. This position certainly merits consideration, and has a bearing on negligent homicide, but it does not have any bearing on the question of whether negligence should be a sufficient *mens rea* for a rape conviction (or, framed in terms of mistakes, whether the *mens rea* requirement is met if the defendant believed, but unreasonably, that the complainant consented). Unreasonable mistakes about whether the complainant was consenting reflect culpable indifference (barring exceptional problems, which constitute excusing conditions). This is what demarcates unreasonable mistakes from reasonable ones. We call a mistake reasonable, in this context, when D is not at fault for failing to realize that V might not be consenting and for that reason failing to check to make sure he or she was. Otherwise, we think that D should have seen that it was at the very least unclear whether V was consenting. That D didn't take note of the signs that V was not consenting reflects—barring a special excusing condition—culpable indifference. One could hardly just be absentminded or lacking in foresight or insufficiently attuned to risks; failing to take note of obvious signs that V was not consenting is thus quite different from failing to notice a traffic light or failing to check before opening one's car door to make sure no bicyclists are zipping by. V is not a jogger or bicyclist who suddenly appears as one opens the car door; as Jennifer Temkin writes, "Unlike the cyclist whose presence is unknown, she is there right next to him."[203]

The correct position to take on the *mens rea* of rape is that reasonable beliefs that V was consenting negate the *mens rea*, but unreasonable beliefs do not. But this position is correct only if "reasonable" is not allowed too much elasticity. Instructions are in order to explain that "reasonable" does not simply mean "ordinary," and signposts are needed in the form of some indication of mistakes that do not count as reasonable for the purposes of the law.

G. Concluding Remarks on Rape

I have been suggesting that the law of rape (and sexual assault more generally) would do well to eliminate the force requirement altogether and to take non-consent, rather than consent, to be the presumption (except in ongoing relationships involving sex and not marred by the use of force to secure sexual compliance). Worries that the absence of a force requirement will render it too difficult for initiators to know whether the other person is consenting are addressed by (a) recognizing the possibility of mistakes and allowing that reasonable mistakes negate the *mens rea* but, at the same time, (b) clarifying what consent is—and what it is not—and (c) clarifying that because the "default" is nonconsent,[204] the initiator needs to seek affirmative consent of some sort and, if it is unclear, to seek clarification. I also argued that consent is best understood on the performative model, as something one does rather than something one feels, and that attention to this could go a long way toward both addressing worries that one could be charged with rape by someone who agreed to sex but later said she had not wanted to, and conveying that a "no" is to be taken as decisive, not as one among various signs to "read" in order to figure out "what she really wants."

V. Conclusion

I have sought in this essay to bring out some of the gender issues in the criminal law that are, or engage, issues of deep philosophical interest. I have taken care to avoid simply providing a report on "the feminist critique" or a sampling of feminist attacks on the law of self-defense, the provocation defense, and sexual assault laws. Too often, feminist scholarship or discussions of feminist objections read as if they are reporting the positions of a political party or a coalition of political parties. Instead, I sought to pinpoint what I take to be the serious problems, to trace those problems to their sources in the law, with attention both to the distinction between problems of application and problems rooted in the law, and to the interplay between problems of application and problems in the law itself. Problems of application are due in no small part to recalcitrant attitudes, but the attitudes may be recalcitrant in part because they are reinforced by what the laws express.

Long though this essay is, there are many topics I could not discuss, among them, statutory rape. Also of interest—and much further from what I did cover—is the general question of how much weight the fact that x is demeaning to women or has the effect of perpetuating women's subordination to men or of deepening gender polarization should have in determinations of whether x should be (or remain) illegal, or whether laws concerning x should otherwise be modified. This set of issues would need to be examined in the context of a broader discussion of the purposes of the criminal law, the expressive function (or lack thereof) of the law, and would best be carried out through both a general discussion and an examination of some specific areas where considerations that x is demeaning to women, and so on, are raised: for example, pornography and prostitution and perhaps also (considering the new cultural laws being debated in Europe) legislation restricting women from wearing a burqa in public.[205, 206]

NOTES

1. I have in mind so-called first world countries. Of course in many parts of the world things are far more dire; consider, for example, tolerance of forced marriages, even of little girls; tolerance of honor killings and dowry killings; and responding to reports of rape by prosecuting the rape victim for illicit sex. See, e.g., Nujood Ali and Delphine Minoui, *I Am Nujood: Age 10 and Divorced* (Random House, 2010); Rana Husseini, *Murder in the Name of Honor* (Oneworld Publications, 2009); and Seth Mydans, "In Pakistan, Rape Victims Are the 'Criminals'," *New York Times* (May 7, 2002), reporting a sentence of death by stoning for a woman who, in reporting that she was raped, had confessed to the crime of illicit sex (in her case adultery, proven by her having borne a child, conceived when her husband was in prison). The victim, Zafran Bibi, was freed in response to public outrage, though only after her husband claimed that the baby was his (conceived in a conjugal visit), and she recanted the claim to have been raped. As Mydans reports, although a death sentence was unusual, it is not at all unusual for a woman who reports a rape to be convicted of breaking the laws of zina. Prosecution of the rapist, by contrast, is rare. See Mydans, "Sentenced to Death, Rape Victim Is Freed by Pakistani Court," *New York Times* (June 8, 2002).

2. Osland v. The Queen, [1998] HCA 75, 159 ALR 170 (AHC, Dec. 10, 1998)). I take this to be significant for both its clear message that women are not full citizens and its practical implications. Women's attempts at independence are sabotaged, and a man who wishes to control (and perhaps batter and otherwise abuse) his wife is aided by the presence of such barriers to independence.

3. A related problem that deserves mention is that antigay violence finds some cover under this defense. See Robert B. Mison, Comment, "Homophobia in Manslaughter: The Homosexual Advance as Insufficient Provocation," *California Law Review* 80 (Jan. 1992): 133, and a reply by Joshua Dressler, "When 'Heterosexual' Men Kill 'Homosexual' Men: Reflections on Provocation Law, Sexual Advances, and the 'Reasonable Man' Standard," *Journal of Criminal Law & Criminology* 85, no. 3 (1995): 726–763. See also Dan M. Kahan and Martha C. Nussbaum, "Two Conceptions of Emotion in Criminal Law," *Columbia Law Review* 96, no. 2 (1996): 269–374.

4. Donna K. Coker, "Heat of Passion and Wife Killing: Men Who Batter/Men Who Kill," *Review of Law and Women's Studies* 2 (1992): 71–130, 72.

5. Caroline A. Forell and Donna M. Matthews suggest that in fact the defense is less readily available to women in the same situation. See *A Law of Her Own: The Reasonable Woman as a Measure of Man* (New York University Press, 2000), 171–172.

6. See Katherine K. Baker, "Gender and Emotion in Criminal Law," *Harvard Journal of Law & Gender* 28, no. 2 (2005): 447–466, esp. 461; Elizabeth Rapaport, "Capital Murder and the Domestic Discount: A Study of Capital Domestic Murder in the Post-Furman Era," *SMU Law Review* 49 (1996): 1508–1548, esp. 1517–1519; and Forell and Matthews, *A Law of Her Own*, 171.

7. This saying reportedly dates to 1697, when William Congreve wrote in *The Mourning Bride* (1697), "Heaven has no rage, like love to hatred turned, Nor hell a fury, like a woman scorned." *The Oxford Essential Quotations Dictionary* (American edition) (New York: Oxford University Press, 1998).

8. Coker emphasizes that many murder cases for which the jury is read an instruction on provocation are cases where the man killed because he was "scorned"—that is, she had left him or had announced an intention to leave him or in some other way rejected him. See also Martha Mahoney, "Legal Images of Battered Women: Redefining the Issue of Separation," *Michigan Law Review* 90 (Oct. 1991): 1–94. Homicides by women of their male partners are rarely responses to adultery or to the man leaving or threatening to leave, and far more often are responses to long-term physical and emotional abuse. See also Law Commission (U.K.), *Murder, Manslaughter, and Infanticide*, Law Com No. 304 (Nov. 28, 2006), pt. 5.6; and Susan S. M. Edwards, *Sex and Gender in the Legal Process* (London: Blackstone, 1996), 394–395. Also relevant are chapter 9 of Jeremy Horder, *Provocation and Responsibility* (New York: Oxford University Press, 1992); Victoria Nourse, "Passion's Progress: Modern Law Reform and the Provocation Defense," *Yale Law Journal* 106 (March 1997): 1331–1448; and Margo Wilson and Martin Daly, "Spousal Homicide Risk and Estrangement," *Violence and Victims* 8, no. 1 (1993): 3–16.

9. Indeed, in some jurisdictions—for example, Scotland—it cannot cover such cases. See Law Commission, *Murder, Manslaughter, and Infanticide*.

10. I offer reasons for thinking that we should not abandon it altogether in "Killing in the Heat of Passion," in *Setting the Moral Compass: Essays by Women Philosophers*, ed. Cheshire Calhoun (New York: Oxford University Press, 2004), 353–378. See also Joshua Dressler, "Why Keep the Provocation Defense? Some Reflections on a Difficult Subject," *Minnesota Law Review* 86, no. 5 (2002): 959–1002. For arguments favoring abolition, see Celia Wells, "The Case for Abolition," in *Rethinking English Homicide Law*, ed. Andrew Ashworth and Barry Mitchell (New York: Oxford University Press, 2000), 85–106; Matthew Goode, "The Abolition of Provocation," in *Partial Excuses to Murder*, ed. Stanley M. H. Yeo (Sydney: Federation Press, 1990), 37–60; and Horder, *Provocation and Responsibility*.

11. Maher v. People, 10 Mich. 212, 219 (1862).

12. Some would question my framing it in terms of culpability, but it is difficult to find a way to explain why one homicide seems worse than another (other than how much pain it inflicted or perhaps how exceptionally wonderful a person the victim was) unless we take into account what the action reflects about the character of the perpetrator and what it suggests concerning culpability. The quotation below from *Maher* brings this out.

13. *Maher*, 10 Mich. at 219.

14. *Id.* Blackstone's *Commentaries* draw a similar contrast: "manslaughter, when voluntary, arises from the sudden heat of the passions, murder from the wickedness of the heart" (cited in *Mullaney v. Wilbur*, 421 U.S. 684, 693 (1975)).

15. *Maher*, 10 Mich. at 219.

16. Horder, *Provocation and Responsibility*, 24; see also 28–30. Many law review articles on provocation begin with a history that speaks of five categories rather than four (and I followed suit in "Killing in the Heat of Passion"). This is because they are counting "chance medley" as one of the categories. Chance medley was actually a distinct species of voluntary manslaughter until the mid-nineteenth century; it was a separate defense, not a species of provocation.

17. Wells, "The Case for Abolition," 87.

18. The adultery was supposed to have been witnessed by *D* (or at least "reasonably inferable" from what *D* witnessed) to be adequate provocation, but that requirement was later relaxed. Laurie J. Taylor writes that "from 1871 to 1946, a line of English cases held that words alone could sufficiently provoke if those words confessed adultery" and that "American courts have held that discovery of a letter revealing completed adultery could sufficiently provoke a defendant, and that learning in other ways of a wife's infidelity sufficed as well." Comment, "Provoked Reason in Men and Women: Heat-of-Passion Manslaughter and Imperfect Self-Defense," *UCLA Law Review* 33 (1986): 1679–1735; quote at 1695–1696.

19. I am indebted in the next two paragraphs to Horder's discussion in chapter 5 of *Provocation and Responsibility*. See also Stephen Gough, "Taking the Heat out of Provocation," *Oxford Journal of Legal Studies* 19 (1999): 481–493.

20. If wrong at all! Consider the following ruling in a 1707 case: "when a man is taken in adultery with another man's wife, if the husband shall stab the adulterer, or knock out his brains, this is bare manslaughter: for jealousy is the rage of the man, and adultery is the highest invasion of property [citing a 1617 case] ... If a thief comes to rob another, it is lawful to kill him. And if a man comes to rob a man's posterity and his family, yet to kill him is manslaughter. So is the law though it may seem hard, that the killing in the one case should not be as justifiable as another." R. v. Mawgridge (1707) Kel. 119, 337; cited in Horder, *Provocation and Responsibility*, 39. That it is *as* justifiable seems to have been the view in some U.S. states. Georgia, New Mexico, Texas, and Utah treated the killing of a wife's lover as justifiable homicide, particularly if done to prevent consummation of an extramarital relationship. See Taylor, Comment, 1694. Texas did not repeal its "paramour statute" until 1973. See Kahan and Nussbaum, "Two Conceptions of Emotion in Criminal Law," 349.

21. *Mawgridge*, (1707) Kel. at 119.

22. R. v. Fisher, 8 C. & P. 183 (1837); cited in Horder, *Provocation and Responsibility*, 88.

23. The statement of Fisher's counsel contrasts interestingly to what Fisher himself said when taken into custody: Fisher defended his actions by saying that in killing a man whom he suspected of having abused his son, he had done only "what a father and an Englishman would have done under similar circumstances" (*Fisher*, 8 C. & P. 183). Fisher's counsel, by contrast, seeks not to defend, but to excuse it by reference to "desperation and madness."

24. See also Baron, "Killing in the Heat of Passion," and Nourse, "Passion's Progress." For discussion of whether the provocation defense should be understood as an excuse, or as a justification, see (among others) Baron, "Killing in the Heat of Passion"; Joshua Dressler, "Rethinking Heat of Passion: A Defense in Search of a Rationale," *Journal of Criminal Law & Criminology* 73 (1982): 421–470; and Vera Bergelson, "Justification or Excuse? Exploring the Meaning of Provocation," *Texas Tech Law Review* 42 (2009): 307–319.

25. Dressler, "Why Keep the Provocation Defense?", 975, quoting Adrian Howe, "More Folk Provoke Their Own Demise (Homophobic Violence and Sexed Excuses—Rejoining the Provocation Law Debate, Courtesy of the Homosexual Advance Defense)," *Sydney Law Review* 19 (1997): 359.

26. Dressler, "Why Keep the Provocation Defense?" 975, quoting Horder, *Provocation and Responsibility*, 192.

27. Dressler, "Why Keep the Provocation Defense?" at 977. His claim is reproduced more recently in "Objective versus Subjective Justification: A Case Study in Function and Form in Constructing a System of Criminal Law Theory," *in Criminal Law Conversations*, ed. Paul Robinson, Stephen Garvey, and Kimberly Ferzan (New York: Oxford University Press, 2009), 319–327 (combining the paper just quoted with his earlier "Rethinking Heat of Passion"). My discussion here overlaps my discussion in "Reframing the Issues: Differing Views of Justification and the Feminist Critique of Provocation," in Robinson et al., *Criminal Law Conversations*, 329–331.

28. The extent to which it trivializes the objections becomes more evident on closer inspection of his rejoinder (in the last quotation above). It could be understood in either of two ways. Is he saying that (a) the fact that men more often invoke the defense than women do is an insufficient reason to repeal it, or that (b) the fact that men more often invoke the defense than do women charged with murder is an insufficient reason to repeal it? In other words, whom is he comparing? Men who invoke the defense to all women, or men who invoke the defense to only those women who, having been charged with murder, might wish to avail themselves of the defense? Both (a) and (b) are true; neither fact is a sufficient reason to repeal the defense. It would be somewhat bizarre to think that feminists opposed to the provocation defense hold that either fact is a sufficient reason, but it would be particularly uncharitable to suppose that they generally take the fact in (a) to be a sufficient reason for repealing the provocation defense. The fact in (b), though hardly a reason for repealing a defense, would at least provide a reason to examine the defense to see if it is stacked against female defendants and, if so, how. When Dressler goes on to say "it is true that the provocation defense benefits men, but so do all other excuse and justification defenses, most of which are not considered controversial, because men, far more often than women, kill people for *all* reasons," it becomes clear that he was asserting (a). In fairness to Dressler, however, I want to acknowledge that there is a lot of bad scholarship, feminist and otherwise, so what he takes to be the abolitionist argument might well have been asserted as such somewhere in the legal literature; but in any event there are, and indeed he initially summarizes, far better feminist arguments for abolishing the defense.

29. See Horder, *Provocation and Responsibility*, chap. 9, and Law Commission, *Murder, Manslaughter, and Infanticide*.

30. For a discussion of the difficulties of prosecuting it and suggestions for how best to address them, see Michelle Madden Dempsey, *Prosecuting Domestic Violence* (New York: Oxford University Press, 2009).

31. To avoid unnecessary controversy, I'll ignore those involving political assassinations, even though I see no particular reason to assume that one cannot be roused to heat of passion by egregious misconduct, such as that noted above.

32. State v. Thornton, 730 S.W.2d 309 (Tenn. 1987).

33. State v. Furlough, 1993 Tenn. Crim. App. Lexis 769, 7.

34. The 1993 ruling indicates it was the same day; the indication in the 1990 ruling, overturning and remanding her murder conviction because, despite the defense's request, the jurors were not sequestered, is that it was the next day. State v. Furlough, 1990 Tenn. Crim. App. Lexis 293, 6.

35. State v. Furlough, 1993 Tenn. Crim. App. Lexis 769, 7.

36. One might think that Furlough should have been able to argue that she killed in defense of the child and, therefore, that the killing was justified. This will be addressed in sections II.E and III.

37. Note that in both these cases—though more so in *Thornton*—it is a stretch to say that there is a "sudden heat." Thornton's wife had conveyed not only that she was unhappy with the marriage but also that she wanted to end it and wanted to date other men. Moreover, he did not suddenly come upon them having sex; he watched through her window as they ate dinner, sat and read, and did laundry. His was a heat that intensified over time and, indeed, that intensified thanks to his putting himself in exactly the situation that would be most likely to intensify it: watching them for hours through her window. In *Furlough*, it seems likely that there was a sudden heat when she found him apparently on the verge of raping their young child, and then the heat—if indeed it had cooled down in those hours—was later reignited when he said he would "do it" to their child when they got home. That the timing requirements are not applied strictly in *Thornton* is evidence of something noted by Horder in *Provocation and Responsibility*: "Considerable latitude is given to male defendants who have killed on discovering their wives in an adulterous liaison, over such issues as pre-planning and the 'suddenness' requirement" (193).

Admittedly there are differences that explain greater sympathy with Thornton than with Furlough. She concealed the body, and when it was discovered, she lied to the police. In addition, she clearly shot to kill, whereas Thornton shot his victim in the hip (and indeed the victim died only several days later). On the other hand, shooting only to wound was less of an option for her; her history with *V* was one of ongoing violence against her (including, according to her testimony, ramming a hammer into her vagina in punishment for trying to flee from him), as well as violence against their daughter. And perhaps she would have gone to the police to report what she had done if women who kill their abusive husbands were more often shown the sympathy shown to men who kill their unfaithful wives (or their wives' lovers).

38. For a parallel comparison involving Canadian cases, see Dennis Klimchuk, "Outrage, Self-Control, and Culpability," *University of Toronto Law Journal* 44 (1994): 441–468, esp. 460.

39. Or what *D* reasonably believes to be such.

40. See note 39.

41. This is loosely suggested by Nourse, "Passion's Progress," though she says in a footnote that lawfulness is only a "guide to those kinds of outrage the law must protect" and "not a doctrinal standard" (n381). That the wrong must be serious (or justifiably believed to be such) is specified in Law Commission, *Murder, Manslaughter, and Infanticide*, and is part of the new "loss of control" defense replacing the provocation defense in England. See the Coroners and Justice Act 2009 (c.25), pt. 2, ch. 1, sects. 54–56 (text available at www.statutelaw.gov.uk/content.aspx?activeTextDocId=3637639). The Act also specifies that adultery does not count as sufficiently serious and indeed that in "determining whether the loss of control had a qualifying trigger," "the fact that a thing done or said constituted sexual infidelity is to be disregarded."

42. A curious remark of Camille Paglia's comes to mind here: "As a fan of football and rock music, I see in the simple, swaggering masculinity of the jock and in the noisy posturing of the heavy-metal guitarist certain fundamental, unchanging truths about sex. Masculinity is aggressive, unstable, combustible. It is also the most creative cultural force in history. Women must reorient themselves toward the elemental powers of sex, which can strengthen or destroy" (quoted in *Newsday*, January 27, 1991, 32).

43. It bears emphasis that it matters not only that the defendant receive the degree of mitigation due to him or her but also that the mitigation be the type of mitigation due, or, put differently, that the conviction—mitigation included—fit the crime. On this see John

Gardner, "The Mark of Responsibility," *Oxford Journal of Legal Studies* 23, no. 2 (2003): 157–171, esp. 159–161.

44. The argument might be that she is inured to it—an argument that would then be aided by the common assumption that the provocation defense has to require loss of self-control. After all, it might be said, if she has tolerated the violence before, why think that this time, but only now, she lost self-control? But it takes no more than ordinary familiarity with human emotions to realize that one may refrain multiple times from reacting with violence (or for that matter, with angry words) and yet another instance of the same sort of provocation may be the proverbial straw that breaks the camel's back.

45. I am speaking here of the provocation defense; the Coroners and Justice Act 2009, replacing the provocation defense with a loss of control defense, changes this. See note 49, below.

46. See State v. Perdue, 153 Ohio App.3d 213, 2003 Ohio 3481 (2003); and People v. DiMaggio, Cal. App. Unpub. Lexis 3873 (Cal. Ct.App., April 21, 2004), both discussed in Steven J. Sherman and Joseph L. Hoffman, "The Psychology and Law of Voluntary Manslaughter," *Journal of Behavioral Decision Making* 20 (2007): 499–519.

47. In England, loss of self-control was specifically required by Section 3 of the 1957 Homicide Act (in force until 2009), and in a 1949 case it was held that the loss of self-control had to be "sudden." Celia Wells asks, "Is it a coincidence that *Duffy*, the case which introduced [as A. Ashworth wrote] 'without the support of precedent' the word 'sudden', concerned a woman who killed her violent husband?" Thanks to *Duffy*, the provocation defense was not available to battered women who killed their batterers in a heat that was not so much sudden as a "slow boil." The situation changed only in 1996, when the court of appeal held in *R v Thornton* [1996] 2 Cr App R 108, that "sudden and temporary loss of self-control did not necessarily mean that there could be no time lag between the provocative event and the lost control." Quoted in Wells, "The Case for Abolition," 89. See also Law Commission, *Murder, Manslaughter, and Infanticide*, and the Ministry of Justice's response, *Murder, Manslaughter, and Infanticide: Proposals for Reform of the Law*, CP 19/08 (28 July 2008).

48. This differs considerably from one court to another and from one jurisdiction to another; many U.S. courts have recognized that the cumulative effect of ongoing abuse may produce, or constitute, a passion that generates the "heat" of passion.

49. In England, the Coroners and Justice Act 2009, replacing the provocation defense with a loss of control defense, has brought about major change concerning (a)–(e). It decidedly does not require anger, nor does it require that the "heat" (more precisely, loss of control) be sudden, nor that the loss of control be due to a single provoking incident. It does not indicate whether loss of self-control requires absence of premeditation and says nothing to suggest a no-cooling-off requirement.

50. State v. Furlough, 1993 Tenn. Crim. App. Lexis 769 at 11.

51. *Id*. at 7.

52. The reasoning put forward to support the claim of premeditation and deliberation is, however, bizarre. See text below corresponding to notes 56–58.

53. How much time elapsed before she killed him is not apparent, but it seems to have been no more than about ten minutes.

54. Horder, "Reshaping the Subjective Element in the Provocation Defence," *Oxford Journal of Legal Studies* (Spring 2005): 123–140; quotation at 124.

55. Horder, "Reshaping the Subjective Element in the Provocation Defence," 125.

56. A curious choice of words. Would not "rape" be more apt than "have sexual relations with"?

57. State v. Furlough, 1993 Tenn. Crim. App. Lexis 769, 12.

58. There was evidence—not, however, admitted at trial—of his expression of intent to have sex with other children, a reported assault on another young girl, and guilty pleas in 1980, 1982, and 1986 to, respectively, assault (reduced from a charge of sexual battery), sexual battery, and a harassing and obscene phone call. State v. Furlough, 1990 Tenn. Crim. App. Lexis 293.

59. State v. Furlough, 1993 Tenn. Crim. App., Lexis 769 at 12 (quoting an earlier case). This is implied but not stated; the court mentions that first-degree murder requires premeditation and deliberation, that deliberation (citing another case) "requires a period of reflection during which the mind is 'free from the influence of excitement, or passion,'" and that in "this case there was ample evidence of premeditation and deliberation." *Id.*

60. The requirement is, to be sure, ignored in cases that arouse sufficient sympathy, but it poses an obstacle that then helps to perpetuate the problems with the defense noted above.

61. State v. Hoyt, 21 Wis.2d 284 (1964). See also Devlin J's direction to the jury on the meaning of the subjective condition in provocation cases, approved by the court of appeal in *R v Duffy*: "Provocation is some act, or series of acts...which...actually causes in the accused, a sudden and temporary loss of self-control, rendering the accused so subject to passion as to make him or her for the moment not the master of his mind" (quoted by Horder in "Reshaping the Subjective Element in the Provocation Defense," 127). See also Horder's discussion of *R v Duffy* in *Provocation and Responsibility*, chap. 4.

62. A good place to start, if one wants to make sense of the notion, is Jeremy Horder, *Excusing Crime* (New York: Oxford University Press, 2004), chap. 2.

63. See Law Commission, *Murder, Manslaughter, and Infanticide*, pt. 5.19. The 2009 Coroners and Justice Act does not reflect this view, however; as noted above, it replaces the provocation defense with a loss of control defense.

64. Law Commission, *Murder, Manslaughter, and Infanticide*, pt. 5.18.

65. See, e.g., Stephen P. Garvey, "Passion's Puzzle," *Iowa Law Review* 90, no. 5 (2005): sect. I.

66. That there is no requirement in (a)(ii) that the fear be reasonable is, as I see it, unfortunate, but it is in keeping with English self-defense law, which, while requiring proportionality, does not require that the fear or the belief on which it is based be reasonable. Thanks to Jeremy Horder for explaining to me the reasons for the omission.

67. Presumably matters whose only relevance to the defendant's conduct is that they bear simply on his or her tolerance also are ruled out; that isn't specified, but I take it that is the intent, and probably it is thought to be encompassed by the restriction ("...bear simply on his or her general capacity for self-control").

68. Law Commission, *Murder, Manslaughter, and Infanticide*, pt. 5.11.

69. It is robust, that is, with respect to provocation. It is not robust with respect to fear (or more precisely, it is not robust insofar as it does not require that the fear, or the belief on which it is based, be reasonable, though it does require that the fear be fear of *serious* violence).

70. Section 210.3(1)(b) of the MPC replaces the heat of passion defense with an "extreme mental or emotional disturbance" defense. A "homicide which would otherwise be murder" is manslaughter if "committed under the influence of extreme mental or emotional disturbance for which there is reasonable explanation or excuse. The reasonableness of such explanation or excuse shall be determined from the viewpoint of a person in the actor's situation under the circumstances as he believes them to be." The comments explain that

one aim was to "abandon preconceived notions of what constitutes adequate provocation and to submit that question to the jury's deliberation" (sec. 210.3 Comment at 61).

71. The 2009 Coroners and Justice Act, however, allows the standard to vary according to sex as well as age. The relevant requirement for the "loss of control" defense is that "a person of D's sex and age, with a normal degree of tolerance and self-restraint and in the circumstances of D, might have reacted in the same or in a similar way to D" (sect. 54(1c)).

72. A note of clarification: since there is, on the Law Commission proposal, no requirement that her fear was reasonable, it would not be necessary to explain why she was fearful except insofar as such an explanation helps to overcome doubts that she really was fearful.

73. Law Commission (U.K.), *Partial Defenses to Murder*, final report, August 6, 2004, sect. 3.28.

74. On this see G. R. Sullivan, "Anger and Excuse: Reassessing Provocation," *Oxford Journal of Legal Studies* 13, no. 3 (1993): 421–429, esp. 426–428. See also Coker, "Heat of Passion and Wife Killing."

75. Exactly what we should regard as incompatible with having lost self-control is not altogether clear. Too often discussions of loss of self-control proceed as if it were obvious. Coker thinks it noteworthy that the abusive husbands and boyfriends she quotes spoke of being "out of control" at the time they subjected their respective female partners to violent beatings yet also reported thoughts reflecting "risk weighing behavior" (e.g., "but then I thought that if I went that far, she might leave me'"). These thoughts, Coker claims, "contradicts the loss of control excuse" (95). Coker also notes that "while describing their violence as 'out of control,' many men admit to intending to harm or frighten their partner" (96). Unlike Coker, I do not believe that either the intentions just mentioned or intending in general is incompatible with being out of control. But I am less concerned to figure out exactly what is and what is not compatible with losing self-control than to draw attention to such suppositions and especially to the fact that the notion of being "out of control" is dangerously malleable. Because it is such a slippery notion, and because when used in the strict sense that Coker has in mind it is exculpatory, we may be beguiled into thinking that "I lost control" is far more exculpatory than it actually is when the phrase is used (as it often is!) rather loosely.

76. Dressler, "Why Keep the Provocation Defense?" 974.

77. As in Spike Lee's *Jungle Fever* (Universal Pictures, 1991).

78. It is clearly a bad idea in the *criminal* law. The suggestion that sexual harassment needs to be keyed to a reasonable woman test, when the plaintiff is female, is more plausible, but since my focus is on the criminal law, I will not pursue that here.

79. In her *Rethinking the Reasonable Person* (New York: Oxford University Press, 2003), Mayo Moran provides evidence that gendered expectations play a large role already (in tort law as well as in the criminal law and with respect to children as well as adults), and also observes that specifying gender in formulating the standard would only make things worse.

80. On gender polarization, see Sandra Lipsitz Bem, *The Lenses of Gender* (New Haven, Conn.: Yale University Press, 1993).

81. The English Parliament decided otherwise, however; see note 71, above.

82. My own view is that this is very helpful indeed. So I do not mean to disparage the inclusion of specific constraints, indicating that *x* and *y* do not count as adequate provocation, as long as this is intended as a guide to understanding a general principle rather than as a substitution for it.

83. For an attempt to provide a guiding principle that does not involve the reasonable person, see B. Sharon Byrd, "On Getting the Reasonable Person out of the Courtroom," *Ohio State Journal of Criminal Law* 2, no. 2 (2005): 571–577.

84. See Moran, *Rethinking the Reasonable Person*, for extended discussion of these problems.

85. My use of "might well" instead of "would" might raise eyebrows. Often the standard is framed in terms of what a reasonable person would have done, but this seems to me generally to be a mistake and, in particular, clearly a mistake in the provocation defense. The reason it is generally a mistake is that the use of "would" suggests a definiteness about what a reasonable person would do, a definiteness that misleads, suggesting that the reasonable person represents exactly one person type. "The reasonable person" can be many different people. This is easier to recognize if "would" is used rather than "might." I discuss this at greater length in "The Standard of the Reasonable Person in the Criminal Law," in *Structures of Criminal Law*, ed. R. A. Duff, Lindsay Farmer, S. E. Marshall, M. Renzo, and Victor Tadros (forthcoming, Oxford University Press).

86. This is not intended as a complete list of the ways in which "reasonable" needs to be understood for the purposes of criminal law. Whether we work with this list or a longer one, one might claim that there is nothing that all the items on the list have in common, at least nothing having to do with reasonableness or with being a reasonable person. I disagree; they are all aspects of, and centrally require, self-governance.

87. See, for example, Dolores A. Donovan and Stephanie M. Wildman, "Is the Reasonable Man Obsolete? A Critical Perspective on Self-Defense and Provocation," *Loyola of Los Angeles Law Review* 14 (1981): 435–468.

88. A different and more meritorious objection to the reasonable person standard—but of relevance mainly to crimes for which negligence is a sufficient *mens rea* and for self-defense—is that one might run afoul of it despite one's best efforts. It is argued by some that unless one's action exhibits (at the very least) culpable indifference, one should not be criminally liable. See Victor Tadros, *Criminal Responsibility* (New York: Oxford University Press, 2005), and Moran, *Rethinking the Reasonable Person*.

89. Tadros, *Criminal Responsibility*, chap. 13.

90. See Masciantonio v. R [1995] A.J.L.R. 598, and Jonathan Herring's discussion in his "Provocation and Ethnicity," *Criminal Law Review*, July 1996, 490–493.

91. H. L. A. Hart, "Negligence, Mens Rea, and Criminal Responsibility," in *Punishment and Responsibility: Essays in the Philosophy of Law* (Oxford: Oxford University Press, 1968), 154.

92. But see Moran, *Rethinking the Reasonable Person*, chap. 7, and Tadros, *Criminal Responsibility*, chap. 13.

93. As Dressler writes, "In general, the defence contemplates the situation of two men of roughly equal strength in a one-time conflict, perhaps in a bar or on a street. Self-defence rules do not recognize the experiences of women and, in particular they do not contemplate the problems inherent in domestic violence circumstances, namely the dissimilar strength of the parties and the fact that the victim and her aggressor may be in nearly unceasing contact with each other." "Battered Women Who Kill Their Sleeping Tormenters," in *Criminal Law Theory: Doctrines of the General Part*, ed. Stephen Shute and A. P. Simester (New York: Oxford University Press, 2002), 259–283; quote at 273. Other relevant "domestic violence circumstances" that deserve mention include the dissimilar combat experience (one of the parties generally having far more practice attacking people than the other); societal pressures on women to "make the marriage work" or, at the very least, not to abandon it; and the tendency of many an abusive man to stalk, and sometimes kill, his female partner if she does leave. (See Coker, "Heat of Passion and Wife Killing.")

94. For details, see Joshua Dressler, *Understanding Criminal Law*, 4th ed. (Newark, N.J.: LexisNexis Matthew Bender, 2006), chap. 19.02.

95. The issues that arise in connection with battered women's self-defense claims may be slightly different when it is a third party who uses force to protect *V* against further attacks. The timing problem will not be as serious since a third party (e.g., *V*'s mother) together with *V* would have a better chance of thwarting an imminent attack than would *V* operating alone, though it may well enter in, particularly if the attacks on *V* occur only when her mother is not present. Note too that if battered woman syndrome is made pivotal to the self-defense claim of a woman who kills her batterer, this has implications for third parties who seek to aid her, since the third party is less likely to suffer from battered woman syndrome.

96. Dressler suggests that rather than revise self-defense laws, we should broaden the duress defense so that imminence would not be required, and duress could be a defense to homicide. Battered women who kill their batterers but cannot meet the requirements for self-defense might then be able to plead duress. Dressler, "Battered Women Who Kill," 278–280.

97. See Claire Finkelstein, "Self-Defense as a Rational Excuse," *University of Pittsburgh Law Review* 57 (1996): 621–649; and Reid Griffith Fontaine, "An Attack on Self-Defense," *American Criminal Law Review* 47 (2010): 57.

98. See Kimberly Kessler Ferzan, "Defending Imminence: From Battered Women to Iraq," *Arizona Law Review* 46 (2004): 213–262; and Jane Maslow Cohen, "Regimes of Private Tyranny: What Do They Mean to Morality and for the Criminal Law?" *University of Pittsburgh Law Review* 57 (1996): 757–808.

99. For discussion of justification, see my "Justification and Excuses," *Ohio State Journal of Criminal Law* 2 (Spring 2005): 387–413, and "(Putative) Justification," *Jahrbuch für Recht und Ethik* 13 (2005): 377–394.

100. 236 Kan. 461 (1985).

101. 324 N.C. 253 (1989).

102. The law on this is quite clear in the United States, but there are, among U.S. legal scholars, dissenters; see, e.g., Stephen P. Garvey, "Self-Defense and the Mistaken Racist," *New Criminal Law Review* 11 (2008): 119–171. It is also worth bearing in mind that, as noted above, English law does not have the same requirement. The force has to be reasonable in the circumstances as the accused believed them to be, but the belief need not be reasonable. See David Ormerod, *Smith and Hogan: Criminal Law*, 11th ed. (Oxford: Oxford University Press, 2005), 329.

103. I add this because, though not explicitly recognized in the law, there is still a step from holding a belief to taking action accordingly; and depending on the action taken, the bar for reasonableness in simply holding a belief should be lower than for reasonableness in taking action. Consider, for example, the difference between deciding to flee someone because one believes him to be dangerous and senses imminent danger from him, and deciding (in a situation where one doubts it is safe to flee) to shoot him for the same reason. One's reasons do not need to be as good for the former as for the latter (though of course we have to be careful not to burden the fearful person with careful weighing of evidence, much less of seeking confirmation before taking self-defensive action, given the imminence of the alleged danger).

104. The MPC approach is somewhat different, however. Rather than require that the belief be reasonable, it in effect holds that an unreasonable belief does not preclude self-defense as a defense to a murder charge but does preclude it as a defense to a charge of negligent homicide (and if the unreasonable belief is understood to involve recklessness, it also precludes a defense of self-defense to a charge of reckless homicide). The MPC requires only a belief—not a reasonable belief—on *D*'s part that the

force *D* is using is immediately necessary (see details at MPC secs. 3.04–3.08) but stipulates that if *D* is "reckless or negligent in having such a belief or in acquiring or failing to acquire any knowledge or belief which is material to the justifiability of his use of force," the justification is unavailable "in a prosecution for an offense for which recklessness or negligence, as the case may be, suffices to establish culpability" (sec. 3.09(2)). The MPC approach has apparently not been influential in state statutory reform. See Sanford H. Kadish, Stephen J. Schulhofer, and Carol S. Steiker, *Criminal Law and Its Processes: Cases and Materials*, 8th ed. (New York: Wolters Kluwer Law & Business, 2007), 749.

105. But see Garvey, "Self-Defense and the Mistaken Racist."

106. Dressler, *Understanding Criminal Law*, 237, drawing from *United States v. Peterson*, 483 F.2d 1222, 1230–31 (D.C. Cir. 1973), and *People v. Riddle*, 649 N.W.2d 30, 34 (Mich. 2002).

107. Dressler, *Understanding Criminal Law*, 239.

108. People v. Goetz , 497 N.E.2d 41, 48 (N.Y. 1986).

109. Doing so also facilitated helpful rulings on the admissibility of expert testimony on battered women syndrome.

110. I say "seems" because exactly how the standard was understood was not generally explained very precisely.

111. Or more plausibly, "a." After all, who belongs to only one group? See section III.E, below.

112. State v. Norman, 324 N.C. 253, 270–271 (1989) (dissent, quoting Eber, "The Battered Wife's Dilemma: To Kill or to Be Killed," *Hastings Law Journal* 32 (1981): 928–929).

113. As noted above, some do not think it is important to retain the classification of self-defense as a justification. See Finkelstein, "Self-Defense as a Rational Excuse"; but see also Hibi Pendleton, "A Critique of the Rational Excuse Defense: A Reply to Finkelstein," *University of Pittsburgh Law Review* 57 (1996): 651–676.

114. See, in particular, Martha Mahoney, "Legal Images of Battered Women: Redefining the Issue of Separation," *Michigan Law Review* 90 (1991): 1–94.

115. People will of course differ on which cases merit acquittal on self-defense grounds, and those who think that some cases where the woman believed, but not on reasonable grounds, that she needed to use lethal self-defensive force merit acquittal on self-defense grounds will have a different take from mine. I am in favor of retaining the status of self-defense as a justification and so oppose classifying as self-defense (imperfect self-defense excepted) instances in which one did not have the necessary reasonable belief.

116. See, e.g., State v. Hundley, 236 Kan. 461, 467 (1985): "Battered women are terror-stricken people whose mental state is distorted and bears a marked resemblance to that of a hostage or a prisoner of war. The horrible beatings they are subjected to brainwash them into believing there is nothing they can do. They live in constant fear of another eruption of violence. They become disturbed persons from the torture." For a discussion of *Hundley*, see my "Self-Defense: The Imminence Requirement," forthcoming in *Oxford Studies in Philosophy of Law*, ed. Leslie Green and Brian Leiter.

117. Sometimes the term "battered woman syndrome" is used differently, to refer to the abuser's "controlling mechanisms" and "the effect that those control mechanisms have" (quoting from the expert testimony of Dr. Lee Bowker, in *People v. Humphrey*, 13 Cal.4th 1073, 1078 (Cal. 1996). Thus understood, the term does not signify a pathology. The effects spoken of are (among others) heightened vigilance, necessary so that one can try to predict when the violence will occur, how severe it will be, and whether it will be directed at the children as well; skills one develops, out of necessity, at predicting the next outburst; and

barriers to fleeing (in particular, his threats of violence, and the increased danger to her if she does flee). I have no objections to reliance on "battered woman syndrome" thus understood (though the term itself is misleading); it does not, unlike the "pathologizing" version, conflate excuse and justification, and it is compatible with an objective reading of "reasonable" in the reasonable belief requirement.

118. See Stephen A. Saltzburg et al., *Criminal Law: Cases and Materials*, 3d ed. (Newark, N.J.: Matthew Bender, 2009), 799.

119. The preceding facts are taken from *State v. Norman*, 324 N.C. 253, 256 (1989). In his dissent, Justice Martin mentions that "the officer testified that the defendant's husband was interfering with ambulance attendants, saying 'Let the bitch die.' When he refused to respond to the officer's warning that if he continued to hinder the attendants he would be arrested, the officer was compelled to chase him into the house." *Norman*, 324 N.C. at 272). It is noteworthy that he was not arrested.

120. *Norman*, 324 N.C. at 272 (dissent).

121. *Id.* at 257. Phyllis, one of her daughters, testified that it was the third day in a row that he had ordered Judy not to eat anything.

122. *Id.* at 273 (dissent).

123. To be sure, the dissent mentions not only her conviction: she was incarcerated "by abuse, by fear, and by her conviction that her husband was invincible and inescapable." The mix is confusing, and very typical of discussions of battered women, leaving it unclear whether the problem is mainly the abuse itself, or the syndrome that developed as a result of it (and, relatedly, whether the claim is that the killing was justified, or that it should be excused).

124. People v. Goetz, 497 N.E.2d 41, 47 (N.Y. 1986).

125. This is not an unusual claim. See, for example, Donovan and Wildman, "Is the Reasonable Man Obsolete?"

126. *Goetz*, 497 N.E.2d at 52. Although the court used "or" after "rob him," I assume they intended "and"; presumably the defendant would have to believe not only that the other intended to injure or rob him but also that deadly force was necessary.

127. See Finkelstein, "Self-Defense as a Rational Excuse," 629.

128. State v. Leidholm, 334 N.W.2d 811, 817 (N.D. 1983).

129. And if someone fits into each category, would a self-defense instruction be given that asked whether a reasonable person who was bigoted, poorly educated, and narrow-minded and who believed in demonic possession might have believed it was necessary to use self-defense in the situation? (Or, to frame it differently, whether a belief that *p* would be a reasonable belief for someone who was bigoted, poorly educated, and narrow-minded and who believed in demonic possession?) Alternatively, would the defendant's counsel be asked to choose which attribute to highlight?

130. In jurisdictions that (generally with the addition of "reasonably" before "believed") have adopted the MPC version of the imminence requirement, according to which the defendant must have believed that the use of (lethal) force was "immediately necessary…on the present occasion" ($3.04(1)), the problem may be surmountable, at least in cases where the victim issued a clear and convincing threat before going to bed, explicitly indicating he would kill the defendant upon waking (and perhaps also—just to strengthen the case—that he would kill her relatives or friends if she tried to leave him during the night). In addition, a few courts in jurisdictions with the usual strict imminence requirement have removed a good portion of its bite, as, for example, in the following interpretation of the statutory imminence requirement: "A threat, or its equivalent, can support self-defense when there is a reasonable belief that the threat will be carried out.

Especially in abusive relationships, patterns of behavior become apparent which can signal the next abusive episode....Even an otherwise innocuous comment which occurred days before the homicide could be highly relevant when the evidence shows that such a comment inevitably signaled the beginning of an abusive episode." State v. Janes, 121 Wn.2d 220 (1993), cited in Kadish et al., *Criminal Law and Its Processes*, 772. (*State v. Janes* concerns a seventeen-year-old young man who killed the man who had subjected him, his brother, and their mother to emotional and physical abuse over several years.) The problem is also slightly ameliorated by the distinction, drawn by some courts, between "immediate" and "imminent" to allow that a danger may be imminent without being immediate. See State v. Hundley, 236 Kan. 461, 467 (1985).

131. Paul H. Robinson, *Criminal Law Defenses* (St. Paul, Minn.: West Publishing, 1984), sect. 131(c)(1) at 78.

132. I mention this to forestall an objection based on the following scenario, drawn up by Ferzan in her "Defending Imminence," 250. A, who is having an affair with C, is sure that B, C's husband, will kill him if he learns of the affair. He is also sure that B will at some point find out about it and that when he goes to kill A, A will be unable to defend himself. Assuming his beliefs are reasonable, Ferzan says, those who reject the imminence requirement have to allow that A may kill B when the danger is not imminent, since waiting until it is imminent is too dangerous. I address this objection in my "Self Defense: The Imminence Requirement."

133. See Ferzan, "Defending Imminence," 252–253, and my "Self-Defense: The Imminence Requirement."

134. It is evident also from the fact that imminence does not entail that retreat is impossible. The imminence requirement and the retreat requirement are separate requirements, yet the latter would be otiose if the imminence requirement entailed that retreat is impossible. At present the majority of U.S. states do not have a retreat requirement, but the reason given for not having one is never that the imminence requirement entails that one must retreat! On the contrary, removing or weakening the retreat requirement is assumed to be logically compatible with the imminence requirement—as indeed it is.

135. Further evidence that they are conflated is apparent in Victoria Nourse's finding that "imminence often operates as a proxy for any number of other self-defense factors—for example, strength of threat, retreat, proportionality, and aggression." Imminence has a spurious air of objectivity—after all, it is about whether the danger is a danger right away or only off in the distance—yet in fact the term is used in a variety of ways, and a denial that danger was imminent is often a catchall for saying it wasn't necessary to use lethal force. Nourse, "Self-Defense and Subjectivity," *The University of Chicago Law Review* 68 (2001): 1235–1301.

136. State v. Norman, 324 N.C. 253, 261 (1989).

137. See also Ferzan, "Defending Imminence," 253: "When a threat is imminent, the actor is in a 'do or die' situation. Conversely, if the aggressor's threat is not yet imminent, the need to act may not be apparent. The aggressor may change her mind. The defender may have time to seek out other alternatives to the use of force. A variety of other factors could foil the aggressor's plans." While it is true that the defender is more likely to have alternatives to the use of force when the threat is not imminent, the contrast is not as great as Ferzan's remarks suggest. When a threat is imminent (in the strictly temporal sense), it may still be the case that one can flee.

138. Nor, for that matter, can we always be sure afterward, though at least we know more then than I knew at the time I shot him; we know such things as that his gun was loaded, or that it was not.

139. The previous five paragraphs overlap with section 5 of my "Self-Defense: The Imminence Requirement."

140. See R. v. Pétel, [1994] 1 S.C.R. 3 (1994).

141. Thus Dressler writes, "Lethal self-defense is probably the weakest justification defence the law recognizes, and is very narrowly defined in order to maintain the principle that all human life, even that of an aggressor, should be preserved if at all possible." "Battered Women Who Kill," 272–273. See also his "Battered Women and Sleeping Abusers" and *Norman*, 253 at 260–261.

142. Dressler, *Understanding Criminal Law*, 243.

143. Dressler makes this point in *Understanding Criminal Law* (245), noting that this is especially likely to be the case when the assailant is armed with a gun.

144. The imminence requirement, if retained, could be revised in a way that would then parallel the retreat requirement: it could allow a self-defense claim to be available to one who reasonably believed that it would be dangerous to hold off on using force until such time as an attack was imminent.

145. Erwin v. State, 29 Ohio St. 186, 199 (1876). For discussion of the movement in the United States toward rejecting the (then) longstanding retreat requirement, see Richard Maxwell Brown, *No Duty to Retreat* (New York: Oxford University Press, 1991).

146. Due to space limitations, my discussion is limited to forcible rape and other sexual assault and will not include statutory rape.

147. This list of changes is not exhaustive. For a fuller discussion, see Stephen J. Schulhofer, *Unwanted Sex: The Culture of Intimidation and the Failure of Law* (Cambridge, Mass.: Harvard University Press, 1998). There is considerable debate about how effective the changes have been. See in addition to Schulhofer, Michelle J. Anderson, "All-American Rape," *St. John's Law Review* 79 (2005): 625–644; and Ilene Seidman and Susan Vickers, "The Second Wave: An Agenda for the Next Thirty Years of Rape Law Reform," *Suffolk University Law Review* 38 (2005): 467.

148. Lynne Henderson, "Rape and Responsibility," *Law and Philosophy* 11 (1992): 127–178, esp. pt. 1. The statistics that seemed to show that false claims of rape are more common than false claims of some other crimes turn out, on examination, to reflect the fact that many rape claims are "unfounded" for such reasons as that the complaint was not prompt or because the victim was not sufficiently distressed or "disheveled." See Emily Bazelon and Rachael Larimore, "How Often Do Women Falsely Cry Rape?" *Slate*, Oct. 1, 2009; available at www.slate.com/id/2231012 (accessed Dec. 3, 2010). For a vivid example of the readiness to think women claiming to be raped are lying, see Tom Gardner, "Woman Sues Police Who Didn't Believe Her Rape Report," *Las Vegas Sun*, March 23, 1999; available at www.lasvegassun.com/news/1999/mar/23/woman-sues-police-who-didnt-believe-her-rape-repor/ (accessed Dec. 3, 2010). When Jennifer W. reported the rape, the police scoffed at her, calling her a liar; apparently the reason they didn't believe her was that they found it incredible that the rapists drove her home. (When she called the next day to report the e-mail she had received from one of the rapists saying "I got away with rape," the response from the police sergeant was "You're a god-damned liar. Nobody in town believes you.") Only after the rapists raped a seventeen-year-old girl several weeks later did the police come to consider that she might not have been lying.

149. Sometimes the signs are subtle, not necessarily exhibiting a sense that date rape is not worth prosecuting, but reflecting a view that, without any (further) violence, it is not really all that bad. An in-depth, careful article on rape in a very good law review, for example, takes it for granted that a rape by someone one knows—for example, someone one had always regarded as a friend—would be unlikely (without an explicit threat or use

of force beyond that necessary to penetrate against the woman's will) to elicit any fear. See David Bryden, "Redefining Rape," *Buffalo Criminal Law Review* 3 (2000): 317–512, esp. 371. A sharp contrast is drawn between the rapist she knows she can trust not to inflict harm on her if she resists beyond saying "no" and the rapist she knows she can trust. But what trust would (or should) one have, no matter what her history with the man, if he makes it clear that despite her clear, emphatic "no!" he is going to have sex with her? As survivors of date rape report, one's thought (or feeling) is nothing along the lines of, "Well, with him I'm sure that if I scream and try to fight him off physically he will not do anything to hurt me; either he'll prevail and force himself on me, or he'll quit, so there is no danger in my resisting him"; rather, it is more along the lines of, "Oh my god, this isn't the same person. What has come over him? Is it drugs or what?" As for the aftermath, the following is a fairly representative report: "Ms. Serena, who had been going out with the man for several months before the attack, was so traumatized afterward that she moved to another town, changed jobs five times in six years and gained 50 pounds. Now, after counseling…she has regained her equilibrium. But she still refuses to date. 'I do not feel safe anywhere,' Ms. Serena said." Jane Gross, "Even the Victim Can Be Slow to Recognize Rape," *New York Times*, May 28, 1991, 8.

150. The National Institute of Justice report found that in 18 percent of open, unsolved rape cases, the forensic evidence had not been submitted to a crime lab; Human Rights Watch found more than 12,500 untested rape kits in the Los Angeles area alone. *New York Times* (editorial), "Respect for Rape Victims," Nov. 14, 2009, A22. It is hard to know what the apparent lethargy in submitting kits to the crime lab reflects. Another curiosity is the state's handling of the very serious problem of intentional drugging with a "date rape" drug to induce compliance and amnesia. In my community—and apparently this is not at all unusual—those who believe they have been so drugged and report that to the police may, with some luck, be able to obtain the necessary tests to confirm (or disconfirm) their suspicions but only if they are willing to foot the bill. Why wouldn't the state be interested enough in obtaining such evidence to pay for the medical tests? See Kelly Cochran, "A Story That's Far Too Common," *Indiana Daily Student*, May 16, 2010.

151. That the use of force is required for rape is the law in most of the United States. As Bryden, "Redefining Rape," explains, "In the great majority of states, unless the victim was underage or incapacitated, the prosecution must prove both that the intercourse was nonconsensual and that it was obtained by force (or a threat of force)" (355). For a comparison to other crimes, see note 170, below.

152. The relationship between the law and societal attitudes is sometimes darker than that: for many decades judges imposed a very strict requirement of "utmost resistance," overturning convictions because the woman did not resist enough. As one reads such cases as *Whittaker v. State*, 50 Wis. 519 (1880), it is noteworthy that general attitudes may have been more enlightened than the positions insisted on by judges, especially concerning how much resistance was necessary for a "sexual encounter" to constitute a rape.

153. Some scholars question treating nonconsent as essential to rape, though their objections are generally pragmatic rather than conceptual. One reform advocated in the 1970s, and proposed earlier in the MPC, was to drop the requirement of nonconsent in favor of a requirement that the defendant forced her to have sex. This reform was adopted to varying degrees in several states, most fully in Michigan. (See Schulhofer, *Unwanted Sex*, 31–32.) Conceptually, however, nonconsent was still part of the story: force mattered because it showed she did not consent. The intended shift was away from what she did or did not do to what he did; it was not, however, a conceptual shift. A more recent, and more radical, challenge to seeing nonconsent as the core of rape is Michelle Anderson's proposal

to require that sex be negotiated. "Negotiating Sex," *Southern California Law Review* 78 (2005): 1401. A short version of her article is published as "Rape Law Reform Based on Negotiation: Beyond the No and Yes Models," in Robinson et al., *Criminal Law Conversations*, 295–305.

154. Some jurisdictions require only force (the idea being that if the sex is forced, it is nonconsensual).

155. "Nonconsent" is admittedly a clumsy term to use here, and the question of what constitutes nonconsent might seem a little odd. The oddity reflects an underlying issue: should we understand nonconsent as anything that is not consent and, therefore, also understand anything that does not constitute consent to constitute nonconsent? Or is nonconsent something more particular, and does it require some action? My initial discussion of what nonconsent is takes as a starting point the traditional idea in law that nonconsent involves some action; later I will question that.

156. What if *B* said, "If you don't agree to have sex with me, you're not going to graduate from high school," where *B* is the high school principal and *A* is a student with borderline grades? Determining which threats vitiate consent is not a simple matter (and the same is true of fraud, which also can vitiate consent but presumably would not if it consisted of the initiator enhancing his or her appeal by, say, claiming to be a personal friend of a popular singer). Clearly, not all threats do; "If you refuse me again tonight, I'm not going with you to your cousin's wedding" would not; any threat of (nonnegligible) physical harm would; threats to fire, evict, expel from school, or prevent from graduating arguably do. For discussion of both current U.S. law on this and what it should be, see Schulhofer, *Unwanted Sex*, and Joan McGregor, *Is It Rape? On Acquaintance Rape and Taking Women's Consent Seriously* (Hampshire, U.K.: Ashgate, 2005). I touch on this topic briefly below in connection with the question of what sorts of threats should meet the force requirement, if a force requirement is retained. Other issues concerning consent include conditions—other than that of being threatened or deceived as to the identity of the initiator or the nature of the activity—that arguably vitiate or preclude consent, among them, (serious) intoxication, mental handicap of a sort that renders one incapable of sexual consent, and being below the age of consent. See Schulhofer, *Unwanted Sex*, and Alan Wertheimer, *Consent to Sexual Relations* (Cambridge: Cambridge University Press, 2003).

157. See J. L. Austin, *How to Do Things with Words*, 2nd ed., ed. J. O. Urmson and Marina Sbisà (Cambridge, Mass.: Harvard University Press, 1962), and his "Performative Utterances," in *Philosophical Papers*, 3rd ed., ed. J. O. Urmson and G. J. Warnock (New York: Oxford University Press, 1979), 233–252. See Brenda M. Baker, "Consent, Assault, and Sexual Assault," and Nathan Brett, "Commentary," in *Legal Theory Meets Legal Practice*, ed. Anne Bayefsky (Edmonton, AB: Academic, 1988), 223–238 and 253-257; Nathan Brett, "Sexual Offenses and Consent," *Canadian Journal of Law and Jurisprudence* 11 (Jan. 1998): 69–99; and Wertheimer, *Consent to Sexual Relations*. For alternative approaches to consent, see Heidi M. Hurd, "The Moral Magic of Consent," and Larry Alexander, "The Moral Magic of Consent (II)," both in *Legal Theory* 2, no. 2 (1996): 121–146 and 165–174.

158. Only one reason, though. There is also the following reason: some think that "no" may mean not "no" but something like: "I do want sex but don't want to say so, so please force yourself on me so that I can enjoy sex without taking responsibility for what I am doing"; they think this because they are aware that traditional female socialization discourages girls and women from openly expressing interest in having sex. Some, however, may have an inaccurate grasp of traditional socialization. The usual message is not that one should clearly say "no" when meaning "yes" and then (while repeating "no") wait for the

man or boy to push one down and rip one's bodice; the message, rather, was that nice girls showed some initial hesitation and had to be talked into it. I recall this most clearly from a picture book about Mr. and Mrs. Mushroom; when he proposed marriage, she first said "no" but then said "maybe" and, finally, "yes." But there was no suggestion that Mr. Mushroom should ignore her "no" and forcibly take her to the altar (or bedroom). Instead, he was to be patient and not give up hope that she would eventually consent to marry him. (I have been unable to locate this book, which I recall reading around 1959, and therefore need to acknowledge that my scholarship on this point is incomplete.)

For discussions of a 1988 study of women college students in Texas that provides evidence that some women indeed do occasionally say "no" when they do not mean it, see David Archard, *Sexual Consent* (Boulder, Colo.: Westview, 1998), esp. 31–37; Douglas N. Husak and George C. Thomas III, "Date Rape, Social Convention, and Reasonable Mistakes," *Law and Philosophy* 11, nos. 1–2 (1992): 95–126; Joan McGregor, "Why When She Says No She Doesn't Mean Maybe and Doesn't Mean Yes: A Critical Reconstruction of Consent, Sex, and the Law," *Legal Theory* 2 (1996): 175–208, and her *Is It Rape?*, esp. 207–216. The study is reported in Charlene L. Muehlenhard, "Misinterpreted Dating Behaviors and the Risk of Date Rape," *Journal of Social and Clinical Psychology* 6 (1988): 20–37. See also text below corresponding to notes 180–181.

159. For discussion of some complexities not addressed here, see Peter Westen, *The Logic of Consent: The Diversity and Deceptiveness of Consent as a Defense to Criminal Conduct* (Hampshire, U.K.: Ashgate, 2004).

160. Provided that you did not threaten me (though, as noted above, not all threats vitiate consent).

161. The view that sexual arousal constitutes consent no doubt is one reason for rape victims' hesitation to report the crime, and it would not be surprising if this were an even more serious obstacle to male victims reporting the assault to the police, particularly if the victim believes, or knows, that he was visibly aroused. It is instructive, in this context, to see how *People v. Liberta*, 64 NY2d 152 (1984), which widened the scope of New York's rape statutes by striking the exemption for women (as well as the marital exemption), addressed the claim that it is "physiologically impossible" for a man to be raped by a woman. The argument, the court of appeals wrote, "accepted by several courts (see People v Reilly, 85 Misc 2d 702, 706–707; Brooks v State, 24 Md App 334; Finley v State, 527 SW2d 553 [Tex Crim App])," was "premised on the notion that a man cannot engage in sexual intercourse unless he is sexually aroused, and if he is aroused then he is consenting to intercourse." What I wish to highlight is that in its reply, the *Liberta* court does not challenge the assumption that if a man is aroused he is consenting and, indeed, seems to endorse it: "'Sexual intercourse' however, 'occurs upon any penetration, however slight' (Penal Law, §130.00); this degree of contact can be achieved without a male being aroused and thus without his consent."

162. Schulhofer, *Unwanted Sex*, 19 (citing Whittaker v. State, 50 Wis. 519, 520 (1880)).

163. *Whittaker*, 50 Wis. at 520.

164. *Id.* at 522.

165. I do not mean to suggest, however, that the rule was always followed; we know that one tool European Americans used to terrorize African Americans and keep them from attaining anything close to full citizenship was to charge African American men with the rape of white women. The rules that generally protected white men who raped from prosecution and conviction were ignored when it was convenient; they were almost always ignored when an African American man was accused of raping a European American. See Angela Y. Davis, *Women, Race, and Class* (New York: Random House, 1981).

166. Brown v. State, 127 Wis. 193, 199 (1906) (cited by Schulhofer, *Unwanted Sex*, 19).

167. *Id.* at 200 (cited by Schulhofer, *Unwanted Sex*, 19–20).

168. State v. Cascio, 147 Neb. 1075, 1079 (1947) (cited by Schulhofer, *Unwanted Sex*, 20).

169. People v. Hughes, 343 N.Y.S.2d 240 (App. Div. 1973) (cited by Schulhofer, *Unwanted Sex*, 24). In this case a weaker principle could have been invoked to support their decision, but apparently they were happy to reaffirm not only that resistance was crucial but also that unless the woman resisted to "the utmost limit of her power," it was not rape.

170. There is a force requirement for robbery, but it does not require resistance. The Massachusetts Supreme Court (quoting an earlier ruling) explains the force requirement in robbery as follows in *Commonwealth v. Caracciola*, 569 N.E.2d 774, 777 (Mass. 1991): "the degree of force is immaterial so long as it is sufficient to obtain the victim's property 'against his will'." The court elaborates: "Thus, a purse snatching that is accomplished with force 'sufficient to produce awareness, although the action may be so swift as to leave the victim momentarily in a dazed condition,' is considered a robbery rather than a larceny which is theft without force." This explanation of the force requirement for robbery occurs in a ruling which, atypically for U.S. courts, rejects the position that physical force is a required element in rape cases. The court explains that the defendant's argument "asks us to assume that the Legislature intended to give greater protection to property than to bodily integrity. We decline to make such an unwarranted assumption." For more comparison of the force requirement for robbery and the force requirement for rape, see Susan Estrich, *Real Rape* (Cambridge, Mass.: Harvard University Press, 1988) or her "Rape," *Yale Law Journal* 95 (1986): 1087.

171. It might of course be wrong on "morals" grounds, such as adultery or fornication, if they are not married to each other. One does indeed find rape cases discussed as if the wrong, unless the victim is physically harmed (beyond the rape), is basically the same as that of consensual sex between two persons not married to each other.

172. See Henderson, "Rape and Responsibility," for discussion of the view that the victim bears some responsibility for his having raped her.

173. This view is singularly odd, and yet one does hear of consent being read off from the woman's clothing. This is all the more odd when, as is usually the case, the woman selected what clothing to wear knowing she would be seen by many people that day. (May all those people, at least all who have reached the age of consent, read off from her clothing, consent to sex with him or her?)

174. Schulhofer, *Unwanted Sex*, 31. Massachusetts and Pennsylvania courts are notable exceptions.

175. As of 2005, only fourteen states punish nonconsensual intercourse as a felony if force is not proven; an additional eight states treat such conduct as a misdemeanor, and in all other states such conduct is not punishable at all. See Anderson, "All-American Rape," 625.

176. Perhaps no less intimacy, but less sexual intimacy—if it makes sense to think of sexual intimacy as admitting of degrees in this way.

177. See note 149, above.

178. The thought here is that *eros* might be helped by a sense of safety and security, of being with someone one can trust, someone who shows that he or she views one as a person rather than merely as warm flesh (or, worse, as prey).

179. For a sympathetic presentation of the view that leaving things ambiguous is more exciting, see Jeffrie G. Murphy, "Some Reflections on Women, Violence, and the Criminal Law," in *In Harm's Way: Essays in Honor of Joel Feinberg*, ed. Jules L. Coleman and Allen Buchanan (Cambridge: Cambridge University Press, 1994), 209–230.

180. See note 158, above.

181. The arguments given for retention of the force requirement often appeal to the allegedly chilling effect on passion of "changing the rules" so that verbal refusal constitutes nonconsent and nonconsensual sex constitutes rape. It should be borne in mind that the current "rules" have a "chilling" effect on those who have to worry that saying "no" may well not be taken seriously (and, according to the law in the majority of jurisdictions, need not be). See McGregor's response to Husak and Thomas, who observe that a "proposal designed to make it more difficult for men to get away with rape might have the unanticipated effect of making it harder for some women to get what they want" (Husak and Thomas, "Date Rape, Social Convention, and Reasonable Mistakes," 114), in McGregor, *Is It Rape?* chap. 7.

182. Unless, as noted above, the nonconsenting person is underage or incapacitated.

183. To be sure, we need to be cautious lest we "overcriminalize." But here we have a serious, well-documented harm. For a discussion of overcriminalization, see Douglas Husak, *Overcriminalization* (New York: Oxford University Press, 2008).

184. Historically the force requirement has been allowed to do much of the work of a *mens rea* requirement since, obviously, if *A* forced *B* to have sex (where this means not just that force was used—as it might be in consensual "bondage" games—but that it was used to secure compliance), *A* cannot very well argue that he (or she) thought that *B* consented. This is especially clear when resistance to the utmost was required. Removal of the strict resistance requirement has already given the *mens rea* component a larger role. It is only in a very few instances that not even reasonable mistakes have been deemed exculpatory (though these few instances receive so much attention in casebooks in criminal law that one might get the impression that they are the rule rather than the exception). The only *mens rea* change that would be needed if the force requirement were removed altogether, I believe, is that in the few courts where reasonable mistakes are not now recognized as exculpatory, they would need to be so recognized.

185. See Sarah Conly, "Seduction, Rape, and Coercion," *Ethics* 115 (Oct. 2004): 96–121. Yet another issue is how to differentiate a threat from an offer. An offer to raise a grade in exchange for sex, though clearly very inappropriate, and grounds for serious disciplinary action, would hardly constitute force. A charge of sexual assault—unlike a charge of sexual harassment—would hardly be warranted. On threats and offers, see Wertheimer, *Consent to Sexual Relations*.

186. See discussion in Kadish et al., *Criminal Law and Its Processes*, 315–318.

187. S 129A(c) of *Crimes Act 1961*, 4th ed. (Wellington, New Zealand: Butterworths, 1997.

188. S 129A(b) addresses sexual blackmail.

189. It is worth noting that the answer given to the question of how nonconsent should be understood might be different if we supposed that the force requirement would remain in place. Likewise, whether or not we opt for a gradation, so that force is required for a rape conviction but not for conviction for a lesser crime, might also affect how we think nonconsent should be understood.

190. Or conceivably both parties, in a situation where a third party is forcing two people to have sex with each other.

191. See Archard, *Sexual Consent*; Heidi Malm, "The Ontology of Consent and Some Implications for the Law of Rape," 147 *Legal Theory* 2 (1996): 153; McGregor, "Why When She Says No She Doesn't Mean Maybe and Doesn't Mean Yes"; and Schulhofer, *Unwanted Sex*.

192. See People v. Iniguez, 872 P.2d 1183 (Cal. 1994).

193. Some may need to be told even that physical resistance generally constitutes nonconsent. Schulhofer reports the following description of an acquaintance rape: "'The

penetration was very violent. [He pushed me onto the floor, slammed me headfirst into a corner; and we struggled until he raped me.] When it was all over, he asked me if I usually fight so much during sex. I don't think it ever occurred to him that he had raped me.'" Schulhofer, *Unwanted Sex*, 48; quoting from Robin Warshaw, *I Never Called It Rape* (New York: Harper & Row, 1988). Brackets are Schulhofer's.

194. Here, as in *Iniguez* (see note 192), the victim was asleep until the man got on top of her and raped her. Here too she did not fight or scream, and here too she reported it promptly to the police. The police showed disbelief, kept trying to find inconsistencies in her story, and when they could not, nonetheless encouraged her to retract her complaint because going forward would "ruin a family." She did not withdraw her complaint, but the case never went forward.

195. The problem lies at every stage of the criminal process: the reporting of the crime; the "unfounding" by police who sometimes find a story fishy just because the rapist gave the victim a ride home or in some other way showed considerateness; prosecutorial decisions not to go forward; failing to send the rape kits to a lab; failing to convict; overturning convictions. See Henderson, "Rape and Responsibility," and Schulhofer, *Unwanted Sex*.

196. One might question whether this is a mistake at all: maybe on the performative model she is consenting. As I see it, however, the felicity conditions for consent are not met if she acquiesces out of fear. But this is a matter that calls for further work; it is not altogether clear just what the felicity conditions for consent are.

197. I probably would not have thought to add the second conjunct had I not read *R v Tawera* (14 CRNZ 290, 1996), which overturned a sexual assault conviction on the grounds that the evidence did not establish beyond a reasonable doubt "absence of belief in consent on reasonable grounds." The court did not question that lack of consent had been established but noted that the jury may have been "unduly concerned about the direction (correctly given) on s128A and the fact that a failure to protest or offer physical resistance does not by itself constitute consent. That kind of consideration may of course be highly relevant to whether there was consent, but it does not really bear on the critical issue of belief in consent." True, not specifically on the issue of whether he believed she was consenting, but how about the issue of whether he held that belief on reasonable grounds? (The governing statute allows only reasonable beliefs to defeat the *mens rea*, and S128A specifies that the "fact that a person does not protest or offer physical resistance to sexual connection does not by itself constitute consent to sexual connection.") In this instance, the forty-eight-year-old appellant apparently did indeed believe that his sixteen-year-old cousin was consenting, though there was nothing to point to in support of that belief except passivity and a lack of protest. Wise jurors!

198. In addition, jury instructions on mistakes can be restricted so that they are not provided unless certain conditions obtain. Breaking with its decision in *People v. Mayberry*, 542 P.2d 1337 (Cal. 1975), the California Supreme Court ruled in *People v. Williams*, 841 P.2d 961, 966 (Cal. 1992) that defendants are entitled to a jury instruction on the mistake defense only if the defendant produced "substantial evidence of equivocal conduct" on the victim's part "that would have led a defendant to reasonably and in good faith believe consent existed where it did not." See discussion in Saltzburg et al., *Criminal Law: Cases and Materials*, 405–406. (Franklin Mayberry had assaulted the victim, struck her when she refused to accompany him, and threatened to knock her teeth out; yet the court overturned his rape and kidnapping convictions, ruling that a failure to instruct the jury to acquit if he reasonably believed she was consenting was prejudicial.)

199. The Queen v. Ewanchuk, [1999] 1 S.C.R. 330, 356–357 (Can.). See also Moran, *Rethinking the Reasonable Person*, 295–300.

200. More accurately, only mistakes of fact negate the *mens rea*. (Mistakes of fact are only failure of proof defenses, not affirmative defenses, so it is somewhat inaccurate to speak of them as defenses. See Dressler, *Understanding Criminal Law*, 16.02.)

201. This position is suggested by Stephen P. Garvey, "Self-Defense and the Mistaken Racist."

202. Hart, "Negligence, Mens Rea, and Criminal Responsibility."

203. Temkin, "The Limits of Reckless Rape," *Criminal Law Review* (1983): 5–16; quote at 14.

204. Except, as noted above, in ongoing relationships involving sex and not involving any violence (or history thereof).

205. See Martha C. Nussbaum, "Veiled Threats?" *New York Times* (op-ed), July 11, 2010.

206. I am very grateful to John Deigh and David Dolinko for their comments on previous drafts, to Megan Mullett for research assistance, to R. A. Duff and Jeremy Horder for answering my questions about English law, and Joseph Hoffmann for answering my questions about U.S. law. Earlier drafts of this chapter were presented at the Chicago Roundtable (September 2008) and at the University of Texas Law School (November 2008). I would like to thank the discussants and especially my commentators, Kimberly Ferzan and Jane Maslow Cohen, for their stimulating discussion.

CHAPTER 14

....

PUNISHMENT

....

DAVID DOLINKO

I THE PROBLEM OF PUNISHMENT

....

When the state punishes a person convicted of crime, it imposes one or another form of deprivation, suffering, or "hard treatment" on that person: fines, imprisonment, perhaps even death. Treating a person in such a manner would ordinarily be considered an egregious violation of that person's rights. What—if anything—makes it morally legitimate (permissible, and possibly obligatory) for the state to inflict such hard treatment on those convicted of crime? This question of the *justification of punishment* has attracted the attention of philosophers since at least the time of Plato, whose Protagoras, in the dialog of that name, asserts:

> [N]o one punishes a wrongdoer in consideration of the simple fact that he has done wrong, unless one is exercising the mindless vindictiveness of a beast. Reasonable punishment is not vengeance for a past wrong—for one cannot undo what has been done—but is undertaken with a view to the future, to deter both the wrongdoer and whoever sees him being punished from repeating the crime.[1]

Over the centuries, theorists have made a host of attempts to defend the moral legitimacy of criminal punishment. A survey article—even one as lengthy as this one—cannot possibly do justice to the ever-increasing complexity and sophistication of the resulting debate. All that will be attempted here is an overview of two broad and competing categories of proposed justifications, the problems each encounters, and a sample of recent efforts to deal with those problems by combining features of the rival accounts or by developing a new justification.

The persistent and pervasive lack of consensus in the literature on punishment is evident as soon as one asks what punishment *is*. Some authors believe that *legal punishment*—the state's punishment of criminals—is only one of a variety of instantiations of the concept of punishment. A proper definition of this concept should apply across the board—to the punishment of children by parents, to the punishment of students by school authorities, and generally to "such informal punishments as kicking and punching, treating with coldness, coolness, aloofness, cutting dead, not speaking to, showing up, sending to bed without supper, for such varying 'offenses' as rudeness, jumping the queue, presumptuousness, conceit, cowardice, bad manners, bed-wetting, being a nuisance, etc."[2] Other writers confine their attention to legal punishment, which they regard as the "central" or "primary" case of punishment.[3]

Even partisans of the more expansive concept of punishment, however, recognize that legal or state punishment is a distinctive practice that calls for a justification of its own, rather than merely one instance of a broader practice that can be given an across-the-board justification.[4] Indeed, a strong emphasis on the unique nature of *state* punishment leads several writers to insist that this practice cannot be justified without addressing philosophical questions about the moral basis of and limits on state authority in general.[5] This claim is rejected explicitly by Michael Davis[6] and implicitly by the substantial number of theorists who simply discuss the justification of punishment without explicit attention to larger questions of political philosophy.

To keep this chapter within manageable bounds, I will focus exclusively on legal punishment, which I will discuss, to the extent possible, without tackling broader issues of political philosophy. Even so, there is no universally accepted account of what punishment is. One frequently used definition was put forward, with only minor differences, by Antony Flew,[7] Stanley Benn,[8] and H. L. A. Hart.[9] In Hart's version, "the standard or central case of 'punishment'" is defined "in terms of five elements":

(i) It must involve pain or other consequences normally considered unpleasant.
(ii) It must be for an offense against legal rules.
(iii) It must be of an actual or supposed offender for his offense.
(iv) It must be intentionally administered by human beings other than the offender.
(v) It must be imposed and administered by an authority constituted by a legal system against which the offense is committed.

Though widely accepted, this definition includes too much. It would classify as punishment such practices as deportation and tort liability for negligence per se (i.e., negligence based on the violation of a statute),[10] neither of which is normally considered *punishment*. (This is why, for example, a noncitizen unlawfully present in the United States can be punished by imprisonment and *then* deported without violating the constitutional prohibition of double jeopardy.)

In a very influential essay, Joel Feinberg contended that the Hart-Benn-Flew definition omits "an essential ingredient in legal punishment"—namely, "a certain expressive function: punishment is a conventional device for the expression of attitudes of resentment and indignation, and of judgments of disapproval and reprobation, on the part either of the punishing authority [it]self or of those 'in whose name' the punishment is inflicted."[11] Many philosophers and legal scholars agree that this symbolic significance of punishment is one of its central features.[12] We could incorporate Feinberg's expressive characteristic by adding to Hart's five conditions a sixth:

> (vi) It must express society's disapproval, resentment, condemnation, or reprobation of the offender's offense.

Yet even as supplemented, Hart's account is vulnerable to counterexamples. Deportation and damages for negligence per se can plausibly be said to lack the stigmatizing message of true punishment. But what of the *impeachment and removal of an American president*? This procedure not only satisfies Hart's criteria, but carries with it a strongly condemnatory message. Yet "it seems doubtful that we should consider impeachment a case of punishment" because "removal of the president is constitutionally authorized to protect the public, not to inflict 'unpleasant consequences' on the offending president."[13] Moreover, the Constitution explicitly authorizes the "punishment, according to law," of officials *after* they have been removed from office through impeachment.[14] The *disbarment* of an attorney is another example of a practice that satisfies all of Hart's criteria and clearly carries a condemnatory message, but whose status as "punishment" is debatable.[15]

For present purposes, however, there is no need to arrive at a precise set of necessary and sufficient conditions for punishment. We can understand punishment as an institution satisfying Hart's five principles plus the additional condition (vi). The core of the practice is the imposition of consequences generally believed to be painful or burdensome on someone found to have violated the law, as a condemnatory response to that violation, by persons vested with legal authority to impose these consequences.[16] This understanding is a sufficient basis for considering what, if anything, justifies punishment.[17]

Efforts to answer this question—so-called theories of punishment[18]—are usually divided into two categories: *consequentialist* and *retributive*.[19] Consequentialist theories are "forward-looking": they claim that the practice of punishment is morally legitimate because it brings about better consequences than would any alternative.[20] Consequentialists differ among themselves as to how the "goodness" of a state of affairs should be measured. Classical utilitarians like Bentham and Mill looked to *happiness* as the appropriate measure—either the *total* or the *average* happiness of persons in that state of affairs. Contemporary theorists are more likely to take the *satisfaction of the preferences* of these individuals as the relevant measure.[21] However they assess "goodness," consequentialists single out one or more of a number of consequences of punishment to explain why this practice maximizes "goodness." Punishment, it is said, can deter others from behaving as the criminal did ("general deterrence"), deter those punished from reoffending ("special deterrence"), alter the criminal's character or values so that he or she no longer wishes to commit crimes ("rehabilitation" or "reform"), disable unreformed offenders from committing new crimes ("incapacitation"), and reinforce the societal norms the criminal has violated ("normative validation"). Whatever mechanism consequentialists endorse, they agree that the deliberate infliction of suffering involved in punishment is in itself an evil, justified only instrumentally by its good consequences.

By contrast, retributive theorists regard punishment as an intrinsically good response to criminal behavior. It is intrinsically good because it "annuls" the crime, restores a proper balance of benefits and burdens in society, expresses an appropriate judgment of the criminal's act, or gives the criminal what he or she deserves. Retributive theories are thus "backward-looking." What justifies punishment, they claim, is not its consequences but its bearing the proper relationship to the criminal's prior offense.

Unfortunately, each kind of theory is open to serious objections. Let's consider first the difficulties of consequentialist theories, then those besetting retributivism, and finally efforts either to combine features of both or to develop some entirely different approach.

II Consequentialism and Its Discontents

Consequentialist theories of punishment, according to critics, suffer from a number of fatal defects. For one thing, a consequentialist theory must, in certain circumstances, endorse both punishing the innocent and not punishing the guilty. (We could call this the "maldistributed punishment" argument.) More fundamentally, such a theory cannot make sense of a notion allegedly central to the justification of punishment—the notion of *desert*. Finally, consequentialist theories call for "using" people without regard to their status as autonomous, rational creatures.

Maldistributed Punishment

Suppose, for example, that there is some method of deceiving both offenders and the general public into believing that offenders are punished, even though in fact they receive *no* punishment at all. We must imagine some more or less fanciful technique—systematic deception by officials sworn to secrecy, electronic stimulation of everyone's brain to implant false beliefs, futuristic methods of mass hypnosis or of subliminal suggestion, and the like. Though far-fetched, it is nevertheless *conceivable* that such a technique could be developed. If so, consequentialists ought to embrace a system of sham punishments.[22] Such a system would bring about the same good consequences as genuine punishment,[23] while inflicting far less actual suffering.[24]

More realistically, suppose that some nonpunitive technique is developed that costs much less than traditional punishment (both in money and in suffering) yet is more effective in reducing crime levels. (Such a technique might rely on psychotherapy, drugs, brain surgery, or similar methods.) A consequentialist would have to favor replacing punishment by this new system, provided its advantages are great enough. But such a shift would do violence to the sentiments of the vast majority of people, who believe that justice demands that the perpetrators of brutal, heinous crimes be made to suffer for what they have done.[25]

An even more disturbing implication of consequentialist theories, their critics say, is that there are unlikely but possible situations in which it would be proper to deliberately punish innocent persons. Such critics frequently employ variants of an example of H. J. McCloskey: A black man has raped a white woman in a virulently racist community, and white bigots are on the verge of mass lynchings of blacks. Suppose I have the ability to frame a particular black man, whom I—and I alone—know to be innocent. If I know that my doing so would save many lives while sacrificing only one individual, consequentialism would dictate that I am duty-bound to get the innocent man convicted.[26] Moreover, in certain circumstances a consequentialist theory would call for extremely brutal punishments, punishment out of all proportion to the gravity of the offense, and punishment of the offender's relatives.[27]

A short way of dealing with such examples is to concede that in such highly unusual, unlikely cases it *would* be proper to deliberately punish an innocent person or fake the punishment of the guilty, but to insist that these cases are simply too far-fetched and improbable for their conceivability to matter.[28] The anticonsequentialist will insist, however, that treating such injustices as "open moral possibilities" whose moral status is *contingent* on their likely effects betrays a failure to grasp their *intrinsic* wrongness[29]—a wrongness to which our deep-rooted moral intuitions alert us. Consequentialists have reacted in one (or both) of two ways: (1) by challenging reliance on intuitions about wildly unrealistic situations, and (2) by stipulating that the consequentialist calculus should be applied to *rules* or *institutions* rather than to individual acts.

(1) Our ordinary intuitions, it is said, have been shaped by, and are adapted to, the sorts of cases that we frequently encounter in the real world. Therefore, these intuitions cannot be trusted to yield correct results if applied to fanciful situations wholly different from any that actually arise.[30] If we accept this view, we can dismiss such hypotheticals as McCloskey's (let alone the science fiction scenarios!) as blatantly far removed from the ordinary run of cases in which alone our intuitive reactions are reliable. McCloskey's hypothetical itself, for example, has been attacked as resting on assumptions almost certainly false in the actual world—for example, that the real rapist will not strike again and that the deception will never come to light.[31]

(2) The second consequentialist response—*rule-consequentialism*—is the position that the criterion of maximizing utility applies only to the choice of *rules* (including institutions and practices), with the rightness or wrongness of particular acts assessed in accordance with the applicable rule. As applied to the institution of criminal punishment, rule-utilitarianism was given its classic formulation by John Rawls:

That a man is to be punished, and what his punishment is to be, is settled by its being shown that he broke the law and that the law assigns that penalty for the violation of it.

On the other hand we have the institution of punishment itself, and recommend and accept various changes in it, because it is thought by the (ideal) legislator and by those to whom the law applies that, as a part of a system of law impartially applied from case to case arising under it, it will have the consequence, in the long run, of furthering the interests of society.[32]

A rule-consequentialist can grant that it is perhaps possible to imagine a (wildly unrealistic) situation in which, say, framing an innocent person would have the best consequences. But to adopt a *rule* or *practice* of framing innocents whenever it is believed necessary would so corrode public confidence in the justice system, and so terrify everyone who realizes that he or she might one day be framed in this manner, that such a rule will surely have *worse* consequences than a system without deliberate scapegoating.[33]

Foes of consequentialism are unlikely to be swayed by this focus on rules, however. Who is to say that there *cannot* be a case in which framing an innocent person would yield the best consequences overall? To insist that the rule against scapegoating be followed in such cases "seems to introduce a kind of moral schizophrenia"— one knows that the best consequences would be produced by punishing the innocent individual, but knows, too, that the rules require releasing him.[34]

Indeed, a generalized version of this dilemma has greatly tarnished the once glittering appeal of rule-consequentialism. Consider a case in which compliance with a rule will have suboptimal consequences. The rule-consequentialist must choose between two equally unappealing alternatives. One is to insist that the rule be followed despite awareness that breaking it would produce the best consequences—a course of action that J. J. C. Smart famously derided as "rule-worship."[35] The other is to amend the rule by adding an exception clause that will yield the best results in this exceptional case. But adding exception clauses to cover *all* the exceptional cases will result in a system of rules extensionally equivalent to *act*-consequentialism, thus eliminating any supposed advantages of the retreat to rules.

In any event, anticonsequentialists will almost certainly dismiss rule-consequentialism on the ground that it suffers from the same fundamental defect as act-consequentialism. Under either approach, "considerations of guilt and innocence are at most contingently relevant to whether punishment is justified."[36]

Neglecting Desert

Retributivists often claim that the root of the problems just discussed—for example, scapegoating the innocent—lies in consequentialism's indifference to the concept of *desert*. "Utilitarians have never had much use for the notion of desert."[37] By contrast, as we shall see, retributivists frequently make desert the central notion in their justification of punishment.[38] A consequentialist evaluates actions or practices by looking exclusively to their consequences—what they will or are likely to bring about in the future. But a person's desert is determined by his *past* conduct, regardless of any effects his receiving what he deserves might have in the future. In particular, whether someone deserves punishment depends on what she has already done rather than on the actual or probable effects of her being punished. "To justify punishment merely by reference to its future consequences seems, *prima facie* at any rate, to take from the word 'desert' all its meaning."[39]

It has been objected that "desert" in fact *lacks* (much of a) meaning, because any theory whatsoever that distributes benefits and burdens can be described as giving people what they deserve. "[W]hatever is said to be properly allocated to (or withheld from) a person under the theory can be said to be therewith deserved (or not deserved) by that person."[40] This contention seems mistaken, however. As Joel Feinberg has emphasized, attributions of desert require a ground—a *desert basis*—and not everything can qualify as such a basis. For example, I might decide to distribute grades on the basis of how much I like each student, or on the basis of how much his or her family was willing to pay me, yet in neither case would my students properly be described as receiving the grade they *deserved*. In particular, "utility is not a desert basis for any deserved mode of treatment."[41]

Even so, desert is a vague, highly contested concept,[42] and retributivists have been faulted as unable to explain precisely *why* offenders deserve to suffer punishment.[43] Let us therefore put aside consideration of the consequentialist's antipathy to desert, and look at the often voiced yet elusive assertion that consequentialism involves improperly "using" persons and denies wrongdoers the "respect" they are due as autonomous, rational persons.

"Respect for Persons"

Consequentialist theories of punishment are often attacked for violating what is said to be the basic moral requirement of *respect for persons*. Unfortunately, there is little consensus on the precise meaning of what has been called "the elusive, near-empty notion of 'respect for persons.'"[44]

Kant, who brought this notion to prominence, is commonly interpreted as employing it to attack the consequentialist approach to punishment.[45] In a frequently cited passage, he asserted that legal punishment

> can never be inflicted merely as a means to promote some other good for the
> criminal himself or for civil society. It must always be inflicted upon him only
> *because he has committed a crime*. For a human being can never be treated merely
> as a means to the purposes of another or be put among the objects of rights to
> things: his innate personality protects him from this, even though he can be
> condemned to lose his civil personality.[46]

Consequentialists justify punishment by pointing to its alleged good results—deterring potential lawbreakers, incapacitating the offender, reforming her character, and so forth. But punishment, so conceived, involves "using" the offender. She is subjected to treatment she does not want in order to achieve the goals of the punishing authority or of the society in whose name it acts—goals she does not share. Thus the criminal is "treated merely as a means to the purposes of another," in disregard of his *dignity* as a rational, self-determining being[47] and of the *respect* owed to all persons.[48]

Hegel gave this objection to consequentialism a concise and uncharacteristically intelligible formulation when he likened punishment imposed as a deterrent to "the act of a man who lifts a stick to a dog": "It is to treat a man like a dog instead of with the freedom and respect due to him as a man."[49]

Contemporary opponents of consequentialism echo these themes. The consequentialist, they assert, sees the convicted criminal "as a being who may legitimately be used for attaining the objectives of others"[50] and is "punished because of the instrumental value the action of punishment will have in the future."[51] Antony Duff provides an exceptionally cogent formulation of this challenge to consequentialism:

> [I]f what justifies me in trying to persuade someone to modify her conduct is (my belief) that she *ought* to do so, the relevant reasons I should offer her are precisely and only those moral reasons that justify my belief that she ought to do so and my attempt to persuade her to do so. If instead I offer her prudential reasons for behaving differently, and particularly if I *create* those prudential reasons by threatening to inflict harm on her if she remains unpersuaded, I cease to treat or respect her as a rational moral agent; I am instead trying to manipulate or coerce her into obedience.[52]

Despite the persisting appeal of the "respect for persons" argument,[53] it is open to a variety of assaults. Consider, for example, Duff's contention that to threaten harm to someone whose behavior one seeks to change is to "cease to treat or respect her as a rational moral agent." Suppose that my neighbor plans to undertake construction on his house that will interfere with my ability to work at home. I ask him to compensate me for the inconvenience, but he refuses. I explain just why his conduct is morally wrong, but he shrugs it off. So I threaten to sue him. Am I now exhibiting disrespect for him as a rational moral agent? Or failing to treat him as such?

Indeed, I might argue that when I threaten to bring a lawsuit I am actually acknowledging—even appealing to—my neighbor's capacity for rational agency. I assume the neighbor will use his rationality to weigh the potential cost of litigation, and his likelihood of prevailing, against the cost of compensating me for the inconvenience, and will conclude that compensation is the more sensible alternative. The anticonsequentialist, however, could reply that on this analysis a robber who compels his victims to submit at gunpoint is "respecting their rational agency" by inviting them to balance the costs and benefits of handing over their valuables against those of suffering immediate death. Does the death threat, however, really leave its victims the opportunity to make a rational choice? And does my threat of litigation foreclose choice *in the same way* the robber's threat does?

Another course open to the consequentialist rests on observing that Kant forbids only treating people *solely* as means. There is nothing wrong with treating another person as a means *in some respects* (or to some extent) provided she is *also* treated as an end in herself. Although punishing a wrongdoer in order to deter other people from offending may seem to constitute "using" the person punished, a consequentialist could argue that other goals of punishment, such as reforming the offender's character, constitute benefits to the offender herself and thus do *not* treat her merely as a means.[54] Even so, consequentialism depicts punishment as aiming at all of these goals whether or not the person being punished wants them to be brought about. The criminal's character is to be reformed, for instance, regardless of the criminal's own wishes. Thus even goals other than the deterrence of other people are the purposes of the punisher or of "society," not of the offender. And the existence of these other goals therefore does not refute the contention that the consequentialist seeks to make use of the criminal as a means to achieve the objectives of others, not of the criminal himself.[55]

A consequentialist might insist that *any* practice of punishment, even if justified on retributive grounds, will inevitably involve "using" at least some persons—those wrongly found guilty of crimes. Any punishment system operated by humans will necessarily be fallible, and must therefore inflict punishment on some people who do not deserve it.[56] A retributivist who accepts any system of legal punishment must therefore be endorsing a system that she knows will punish some innocent people. She must accept this inevitable injustice to avoid the much greater injustice of failing to give any guilty persons their "just deserts." Thus the interests of the innocent persons who end up mistakenly convicted are sacrificed so that *others* may receive the punishment they deserve. The retributivist is thus "willing to trade the welfare of the innocents who are punished by mistake for the greater good of the punishment of the guilty."[57] But this is to *use* those erroneously punished for the overall benefit of society.

To be sure, the retributivist does not know who, exactly, ends up treated unjustly. Although she subjects everyone to a risk of unjust punishment, there is no one whom she knowingly and deliberately sacrifices for the greater good. Yet the terrorists who destroyed the World Trade Center were "using" their hapless victims to score a political point even if (as is quite certain) they were unaware of the identities of those in the towers.[58]

The belief that "using" criminal offenders is impermissible and that criminal punishment must "respect" offenders has been defended by the claim that the law "must justify its demands to [them] and offer [them] relevant moral reasons for obedience,"[59] and that "the policies relevant to the manner of treatment of criminals must ultimately be justifiable to everyone, including the criminals themselves, if they were to take up the moral deliberative perspective."[60] More generally, it is said that "[u]nderlying the various ideas of moral justification is a prohibition against treating people in such a way that they cannot share the purposes of those who are so treating them,"[61] and that the "requirement to respect other rational agents (as such) would have us confine our deliberations to what we could in principle justify to others who were willing to accept similar constraints."[62] Although many contemporary thinkers, like John Rawls and Thomas Scanlon, find such a principle congenial, it appears problematic.

What does it mean, exactly, to say that we could "in principle" justify our actions to others? Consider some wrongdoer—call her Sally. We are not saying that Sally will actually accept our proposed justification. And to say that she would *in principle* accept it seems surprisingly weak. "In principle" we could always justify to Sally our treatment of her—our only obstacle is the body of beliefs and desires Sally happens to possess. Were those suitably different, she would see things as we do. To be sure, we need to consider not just any arbitrary alteration in Sally's mind, but the desires and beliefs she would hold if she were a "rational moral agent."[63] But do we really show *respect* for Sally by offering her a justification that an *entirely different person*—a rational, other-regarding Sally—would accept? We appear to be relying on that appeal to one's "true self" that Isaiah Berlin condemned in his critique of "positive freedom"—the "monstrous impersonation" that equates "what X would want if he were something he is not" with "what X actually seeks and chooses."[64]

In short, both consequentialism and the criticisms leveled at it are beset by serious difficulties.

III THE MISFORTUNES OF RETRIBUTIVISM

The label "retributivism" has been applied to a variety of different accounts of the justification of punishment.[65] They share a belief that punishment is not, as consequentialists suppose, a necessary evil, but rather is an intrinsic good. And retributive theories characteristically base this belief on the claim that, regardless of its consequences, punishment is what wrongdoers *deserve*.

To say, however, that offenders deserve punishment is not yet to show that it is morally legitimate actually to inflict such punishment on them. A person may deserve treatment that, nevertheless, it would be wrongful to inflict on her. For persons have *rights*, and to give someone what she deserves may violate her rights. And "when the demands of desert conflict with those of rights . . . the latter usually appear to take precedence."[66]

As an example, imagine a rich man (Lear) with two sons. One (Jeremy) has always treated Lear with affection and respect, even caring for him (at great personal sacrifice) during his final illness. The other (Howard) is a lowlife who feels little regard for Lear and has neglected him almost completely. Yet Lear has always secretly admired Howard, wishing he himself had boldly defied the constraints of propriety, as Howard has. And Lear thinks Jeremy a priggish, overly repressed bore. Lear bequeaths a comparative pittance to Jeremy, leaving the bulk of his estate to Howard. Given their behavior, Jeremy deserved to inherit the estate, while Howard deserved to be cut out of the will. Yet the state will not set aside Lear's will and hand over to Jeremy what he, rather than Howard, deserves. To do so would violate Howard's *right* to the estate, a right he possesses despite deserving to inherit nothing.[67]

One defender of retributivism has objected that retributivists do not rely on the broad claim that it is always permissible to give an individual the treatment he deserves. Rather, they invoke the narrower claim that "when someone violates another's rights of a certain sort, then in virtue of this he deserves to be treated in ways which would otherwise violate his rights."[68] And the "Lear example is quite irrelevant to this view," because Howard has not violated any *rights* of Lear of the relevant sort.

Suppose, however, that Howard has tortured a number of victims. What he has done surely violates a very important right of his victims. It is a right of the relevant sort because it is a right whose violation the state "may legitimately make...illegal."[69] Yet one might believe both that Howard deserves to experience torture himself, and that it would be wrong to torture him, because that would violate Howard's *own* right not to be tortured.[70]

One possible response to this last example emerges from reflection on the incongruity of Howard's relying on the very right of which he has deprived others. Perhaps Howard has *forfeited* at least some of his rights? It may be morally impermissible to torture him even though he has tortured others, but perhaps it is morally permissible to deprive him of liberty for some period of time, because by grossly violating other people's rights he has forfeited some equivalent set of his own rights.[71]

This notion of forfeiture, however, faces objections well summarized by Warren Quinn, who imagines that Jones, "a generally decent young man," has foolishly stolen a neighbor's car:

> [S]uppose that the community in which Jones lives has the unjust practice of seizing and confining political dissenters. And suppose that shortly after his crime Jones, who also happens to be a dissenter, is officially seized and, for a time, quarantined to prevent the spread of his political views (views having nothing to do with his theft)....[W]e would naturally suppose that Jones's right to liberty had been violated by his community, even if he were confined only for a period that would constitute an acceptable punishment for his theft and were never punished thereafter.[72]

Quinn infers that "Jones has not forfeited his right without qualification" but forfeits it only "in that he may be subjected to a certain penalty (presumably the proper penalty for the crime) by certain people (presumably those with the right to punish him)"—so that the idea of forfeiture simply *means* that "the criminal's rights do not in fact stand in the way of his being punished" but provides no explanation of why this is so.[73]

Leaving forfeiture aside, retributivists may argue that what makes it morally permissible to give offenders the treatment they deserve is the particular kind of desert ascribed to offenders. They can argue that the *basis* for the wrongdoer's desert makes punishing him permissible, thus distinguishing examples where it would be wrong to treat someone as she deserves.

One group of retributivist theorists who have taken just this kind of approach have portrayed punishment as a matter of *reciprocity* or *fair play*. This approach enjoyed considerable popularity in the wake of Herbert Morris's influential essay "Persons and Punishment."[74] Morris depicted criminal punishment as an effort to restore an "equilibrium of benefits and burdens" in society that the commission of a crime upsets. Criminal laws, in this view, are constraints on behavior whose observance benefits everyone by ensuring that each individual will enjoy a sphere of autonomous action that is beyond interference by others. By violating these constraints, the criminal "has something others have—the benefits of the system—but by renouncing what others have assumed, the burden of self-restraint, he has acquired an unfair advantage."[75] He "achieves an excess of freedom over the law-abiding members of society."[76] Punishing such a criminal deprives her of this "unfair advantage," thereby restoring the proper balance of benefits and burdens.

Morris did not present this model of punishment as an argument in favor of retributivism, but rather as part of an effort to show that lawbreakers have a right to be punished rather than subjected to "therapeutic treatment." The model was subsequently adopted, however, by a number of retributivists, who put it forward as a moral justification for the practice of punishment.[77] Over time, however, this "fairness" picture was faced with so many objections that to one proponent it "seems no longer to play a significant role" in the ongoing debate about punishment.[78]

For one thing, the "benefit" of freedom from the burden of self-restraint ought to increase in step with the "burden" of obeying the law. If so, then "very serious crimes which most people feel little inclination to commit (e.g., murder) yield a lesser [benefit]—and hence deserve a lesser punishment—than those (like speeding or tax evasion) that test most people's self-restraint more severely."[79]

Richard Dagger has suggested that this objection evaporates once we "distinguish between the burden of obeying a particular law and the burden of obeying the law in general," and realize that it is freedom from the latter that constitutes the benefit derived from lawbreaking.[80] This move, however, implies that all crimes, from tax evasion to murder, yield the *same* "benefit" to the perpetrator. Dagger acknowledges this, saying that "the murderer and [the] tax cheater should be punished to the same extent for their crimes of unfairness." He immediately adds, however, that "This is not to say that the murderer and the tax cheater should receive the same punishment *tout court.*" The murderer, unlike the tax cheat, has in effect committed *two* crimes—a crime of unfairness *and* a crime against her particular victim. Punishment for the first will restore the balance of benefits and burdens, but the proper punishment for the second "must be justified and established on other grounds."[81]

Most retributivists, however, would reject Dagger's conclusion that retributive theory tells us only *that* punishing criminals is morally permissible, but not *how much* punishment is proper—for which we must appeal to "deterrence, reform, moral education, restitution"[82] and other consequentialist considerations.[83] Moreover, it is very implausible to assert that punishing a criminal eliminates her "unfair advantage" without leaving her unfairly *dis*advantaged, unless we have at least *some* idea of how much punishment we are talking about.

Michael Davis has championed a market-based method for assessing the "unfair advantage" different crimes yield, and argues that this method ensures that the more serious the crime, the greater the "unfair advantage."[84] Davis asks us to "imagine a society in which anyone subject to the law may bid on a small number of licenses to do what the law forbids."[85] The number of licenses for each crime would be "the maximum (taking into account unavoidable poaching) consistent with maintaining the desired level of social order."[86] A license could be used only once, but "could be bought and sold until 'cashed in' by being used."[87] Davis asserts that "the price of licenses should be a good *index* of the advantage criminals in our society unfairly take by doing the forbidden act."[88] And, crucially, the price of licenses would increase with the seriousness of the crime licensed. Partly, this is because fewer licenses will be issued for more serious crimes. More important, "the demand for licenses is likely to increase with the seriousness of the crime."[89]

This second claim, however, is unconvincing:

> What would you prefer, a license to steal or a license to torture? Although the latter is the more serious crime, surely vastly fewer people would find it an offense they might relish committing. Which would you prefer: a license to park overtime or a license to commit incest? Which would you prefer, a license to cheat on your taxes or a license to commit treason?[90]

Moreover, it is not clear that Davis's model is even coherent. The demand for a license will depend on the benefit prospective buyers believe it will give them. This, in turn, will depend in part on the penalty for what Davis calls "poaching"—committing a crime without the appropriate license. But, as R. A. Duff asks:

> [H]ow is that punishment to be fixed? If it is fixed by a meta-auction, selling meta-licenses for this meta-crime, an infinite regress beckons.... But if the sentence for poaching is not set by a meta-auction, then the model which was supposed to help us understand how to determine the appropriate levels of punishment turns out to depend on a system of punishments whose determinations it cannot itself explain.[91]

Davis concedes that there *would*, in fact, be poaching.[92] He suggests that "the society hosting the market punishes all *unlicensed* crime the same,"[93] and "so severely that buying a license seems a bargain in comparison"[94]—perhaps by "life imprisonment, death, or some inhumane penalty."[95] But imposing such draconian penalties on *all* poachers—even those whose unlicensed crime is, say, driving over the speed limit or painting graffiti on a school bus—is flatly inconsistent with Davis's assumption of "a relatively just society"[96] that is "much like ours."[97] In the end, then, Davis seems not to have demonstrated that more serious crimes yield a greater "unfair advantage."[98]

Another problem for the fairness theory arises from taking its central metaphor seriously. Suppose the lawbreaker really does obtain an unfair advantage: he enjoys the benefit conferred by the self-restraint of others (freedom from aggression and interference) without paying the price the law-abiding pay (restraining his own aggressive impulses). This "advantage" can be removed not only by exacting the unpaid "price" but by depriving him of the "benefit." This is easier to do than calculating just what penalties would be the equivalent of the "price" the criminal evaded—we simply need to stop restraining ourselves from aggression against the criminal. But this suggests that it would be morally proper to *outlaw* the criminal— that is, to permit the other members of society to subject him to their own aggressive conduct. Yet this is (one hopes!) an unacceptable course of action.

Ultimately, the strongest criticism of the fairness theory is that it relies on an incorrect view of what makes criminal actions wrong—that we punish wrongdoers because they are free riders. Some criminals can plausibly be thought of in this way—the tax evader, for instance, profits by casting off a burden that the rest of us bear. But it is "less plausible to argue that we all suffer a burden in abstaining from the core crimes of murder, rape, arson, robbbery, and burglary."[99] What makes rape, robbery, and murder so wrong is not that their perpetrator has benefited at *our* expense, but that he has inflicted terrible harm *on his victim*.[100] Retributivism must be supported in some other manner.

One idea quite unlike the fairness view was put forward by Hegel early in the nineteenth century. This idea is that punishment serves to cancel, negate, or *annul* the offender's crime.[101] Hegel expresses this idea in characteristically opaque language:

> The initial act of coercion as an exercise of force by the free agent, an exercise of force which infringes the existence of freedom in its concrete sense, infringes the right as right, is crime—a negatively infinite judgment in its full sense, whereby not only the particular . . . is negated, but also the universality and infinity in the predicate "mine" (i.e. my capacity for rights).[102]
>
> The sole positive existence which the injury possesses is that it is the particular will of the criminal. Hence to injure [or penalize] this particular will as a will determinately existent is to annul the crime, which otherwise would have been held valid, and to restore the right.[103]

Commentators have explicated these gnomic formulations. The criminal rejects his victim's capacity for rights—her personhood—as well as the entire regime of rights.[104] To leave the crime unpunished is to regard it as an innocent deed.[105] But "if the criminal is punished, the *status quo ante* crime is publicly restored; both the victim's moral status and her specific rights are vindicated."[106] In this way punishment—as "the negation of the negation"—reveals the *nullity* of crime[107]—its inherently contradictory nature.[108]

Hegel's position is anything but clear. Indeed, while most commentators agree that "Hegel is a true retributivist,"[109] a prominent Hegelian of the early twentieth century insisted that Hegel was not a retributivist at all.[110] His notion that crime must be "annulled," however, inspired a contemporary version of retributivism propounded by the late Jean Hampton. Punishment, Hampton conceded, cannot literally annul the criminal act itself—"but it can annul the false evidence seemingly provided by the wrongdoing of the relative worth of the victim and the wrongdoer."[111]

The criminal, says Hampton, treats her victim in a manner that fails to respect the victim's value as a human being,[112] "and by doing so, represents herself as elevated with respect to [him], thereby according herself a value that she does not have."[113] Retributive punishment, then, "is designed to vindicate the value of the victim denied by the wrongdoer's action through the construction of an event that not only repudiates the action's message of superiority over the victim but does so in a way that confirms them as equal."[114] It does this because it "is the defeat of the wrongdoer at the hands of the victim ... that symbolizes the correct relative value of wrongdoer and victim."[115] In this way punishment "can annul the message, sent by the crime, that they are not equal in value."[116]

This is an ingenious version of retributivism, but it is open to a number of objections. For example, if punishment aims at countering the false moral claims expressed by criminal acts, we need to know what makes it so important to nullify precisely *this species* of false moral claim. After all, the institution of punishment is hardly costless—it is "tremendously expensive, subject to grave error, and susceptible to enormous abuse."[117] And we "do not believe that it is somehow imperative to set up a social or governmental mechanism to seek out and correct false moral claims in general, nor even all false claims by one person to possess greater worth or value than another."[118] Many Americans seem to regard convicted felons as of lesser moral worth than themselves, yet the state takes no measures to combat this perception. Hampton's reply is that false moral claims justify governmental countermeasures only if they threaten or inflict serious harm.[119] But this amounts to conceding that punishment is justified by its harm-reducing consequences, rather than as the inherently appropriate response to criminal wrongdoing.[120]

Moreover, even if we believe that state punishment annuls false claims of superiority, this would *not* establish that punishment is morally permissible. Hampton herself acknowledges this point by asserting that torturing a torturer is wrong even though it would affirm the equal value of torturer and victim.[121] If torture would impermissibly violate the torturer's right not to be tortured, why would incarceration not violate her right to personal liberty?

As it happens, before Hampton developed her value-vindicating retributive theory, she had championed a quite different theory—punishment as *moral education*. That theory is one species of the currently prominent conception of punishment as a communicative enterprise, to which we now turn.

IV Punishment as Communication

Thinking of punishment as a form of moral education did not originate with Hampton.[122] Herbert Morris, a few years earlier, had expounded this idea, which he called a "paternalistic theory," as "one principal justification" for the institution of punishment.[123] Hampton, by contrast, initially championed moral education as "a full and complete justification" for punishment, a view she later renounced.[124] Morris and Hampton agreed, however, in depicting punishment as a form of communication.[125]

For Hampton, punishment is "a way of teaching the wrongdoer that the action she did (or wants to do) is forbidden because it is morally wrong and should not be done for that reason."[126] Its goal is not mere deterrence, but providing actual and potential offenders with moral reasons for freely choosing not to offend. Punishment, so conceived, "does not sanction the use of a criminal for social purposes,"[127] and does not "damage the autonomy of the criminal."[128] Rather, Hampton says, her moral education theory "attempts to justify punishment as a way to benefit the person who will experience it, a way of helping him to gain moral knowledge if he chooses to listen."[129]

Morris, too, depicts punishment as aimed at conferring a benefit. Its goal, he says, is "to promote a particular kind of good for potential and actual wrongdoers"—the good in question being "one's identity as a morally autonomous person attached to the good."[130] This involves appreciating the evil caused by one's wrongdoing, feeling guilt at one's deed, resolving to behave differently in the future, and conceiving of oneself as a responsible person worthy of respect.[131] Punishment, Morris believes, "permits purgation of guilt and ideally restoration of damaged relationships": it "communicates what is wrong" and "both rights the wrong and serves…as a reminder of the evil done to others and to oneself" in doing wrong.[132]

Now, it is certainly possible to use a form of punishment such as incarceration as an opportunity to subject the person being punished to measures designed to promote moral growth. But is there any reason to suppose, with Hampton and Morris, that the punishment *itself* can morally educate anyone?

Morris contends that through the punishment of wrongdoers "each citizen learns what is regarded as impermissible by society, the degree of seriousness [of] wrongdoing of different kinds, and the particular significance…of the evil underlying offenses."[133] In addition, punishment "permits purgation of guilt and ideally restoration of damaged relationships" as it "rights the wrong."[134] The first of these ideas can be applied to the particular individual punished as well as to the citizenry in general. Taken in the former manner, it seems unpersuasive—does the robber, rapist, or murderer not *know* his deeds are "impermissible" and "evil" until he is punished for them? It is more credible to suppose that the existence of the institution of punishment affects the citizenry at large—that leaving "serious wrongdoing" unpunished would "baffle our moral understanding" and erode the belief that what has gone unpunished really *was* serious wrongdoing. This, however, suggests that the particular offender being punished is being used to send a message to society at large—making Morris's theory as open as consequentialism to the charge of "not respecting" and "using" persons.

As for the "restoration of damaged relationships," note first that how punishment "rights the wrong" is a mystery.[135] Moreover, forgiveness and restored relationship are likely only if the punishment actually causes "a manifest change of heart on the criminal's part"—that is, only if he has been morally improved. But Morris treats this forgiveness *itself* as (a component of) "moral education." This creates a circular argument—"moral education will occur as a result of forgiveness, but forgiveness will occur only after the moral education has taken place."[136]

Hampton provides little explanation of how inflicting punishment would morally educate anyone. She does, however, say that punishment is "designed, in some sense, to 'represent' the pain suffered" by the victim of crime: "By giving a wrongdoer something like what she gave to others, you are trying to drive home to her just how painful and damaging her action was for her victims, and this experience will, one hopes, help the wrongdoer to understand the immorality of her action."[137] But, first of all, the most commonly used punishment—imprisonment—bears very little resemblance to the suffering of crime victims. Think, for example, of a store owner robbed at gunpoint: in what "sense" is the pain the robber inflicts "represented" by being locked in a cell for several years? The victim's was a relatively brief but terrifying, life-threatening experience; imprisonment is prolonged and not designed to create the fear of impending death. Moreover, it is unlikely that the criminal was not aware that what he was doing was painful to his victim.[138] Perhaps his awareness was not vivid, not emotionally charged and empathetic. But will punishment lead to deeper awareness of the harm he has caused? "Being subject to hard treatment is likely to shift the agent's attention from the nature of her previous wrongdoing to the nature of her current hardships," and is thus "as likely to deflect the agent's attention from her wrongdoing as to focus her attention on it."[139]

Even assuming that punishment can morally educate offenders, neither Hampton nor Morris explains why it is morally acceptable for the state to *compel* them to undergo this potentially beneficial experience. Morris points to our legitimate concern with the evil the criminal does to herself by her wrongdoing,[140] but this simply reiterates that punishment can benefit her. It does nothing to justify our compelling her to submit to punishment: we are not entitled to force a benefit—actual or potential—on an unwilling recipient.

R. A. Duff has developed a subtle and imaginative theory of punishment that is broadly similar to the "moral education" view. Like Hampton and Morris, Duff believes that punishment "aims to communicate something to the criminal"[141]—"a proper condemnation of his crime"[142]—and to bring about a form of moral growth. The hard treatment inflicted on the offender, Duff claims, is properly understood "as a species of secular penance"—"a burden imposed on an offender for his crime, through which, it is hoped, he will come to repent his crime, to begin to reform himself, and thus to reconcile himself with those he has wronged."[143] If successful, it will function "as a penance which the criminal comes to will for himself: the pain or suffering which began as a coercive attempt to attract and direct the unrepentant criminal's attention should become the penitential pain which the repentant criminal accepts for himself."[144] So viewed, Duff believes, punishment "respects and addresses the criminal as a rational moral agent"[145] and treats him not as an object to be manipulated but "as a moral agent *with* whom we are engaged in a communicative process," seeking "his participation, not merely his submission."[146] Like Morris, Duff maintains that one who commits a criminal act thereby harms not only others, but herself—"she separates herself from the values on which the community and her own well-being depend" and "damages or destroys her relationships with other members of the community."[147] In seeking to induce repentance and reconciliation, therefore, punishment "expresses a continuing concern for the criminal as a member of the community"[148] and "as a rational moral agent."[149]

Without pretending to do justice to Duff's rich and complex argument, we may take note of a number of objections. For example, Duff says that inflicting punishment on the offender is "a way of trying to focus his attention on his crime."[150] But, as noted earlier, subjection to hard treatment may be just as likely to focus the criminal's attention on her own suffering as on the harm she has caused.[151] Duff takes note of this objection without appearing to answer it.[152] Moreover, he describes punishment as "*forcing* the criminal's attention onto the implications of his crime."[153] Yet forcing people to attend to what they prefer to ignore seems a curious way of respecting their autonomy and rational moral agency.[154]

Even more strikingly, Duff depicts punishment as a form of public apology that we *require* from the wrongdoer.[155] Isn't this clearly a violation of her autonomy? Duff responds, in part, by noting that the criminal is not forced to *mean* what she says: "What matters is that the wrongdoer apologizes. We do not inquire into her sincerity."[156] Yet it is hard to see how a *compelled* and *insincere* "apology" is anything more than a meaningless ritual, or how such a sham apology could "reconcile the wrongdoer with those she has wronged."[157]

What punishment communicates to the criminal, Duff tells us, is "censure" or "condemnation of the crime."[158] At times, however, he seems to envisage a more ambitious communicative content, such as "communicating to [the criminal] the reasons which justify our condemnation of his conduct."[159] It is very hard to see how hard treatment could possibly communicate our *reasons* for censuring the criminal. Is it that "by forcibly reminding him how he dislikes having his own interests injured, we ... try to get him to see more clearly the wrongness of injuring the interests of others"? Duff rejects this suggestion,[160] but offers no alternative explanation of how punishment can communicate to the criminal "a better understanding of the nature and implications of his crime."[161]

Duff is as unenlightening as the "moral education" theorists about what *legitimates* or *justifies* our forcible, coercive interference with what would in a noncriminal be a person's rights. Like Hampton and Morris he relies on the claim that punishment actually benefits the criminal, without explaining why we are permitted to *impose* this benefit on someone who does not wish to receive it.

Finally, it is unclear why Duff believes that punishment, on his view, treats the offender with the respect due her as a rational and autonomous moral agent. Curiously, Duff himself, in criticizing a rival theory, tells us that in responding to a criminal:

> We may try to persuade him to obey the law, by appealing to the relevant reasons which justify its requirements; if he still breaks the law we may condemn and criticize him; we may even try to persuade him that he ought to seek or accept punishment; ... but we cannot impose that punishment on him, against his present and avowed will, and claim that in doing so we are treating or respecting him as an autonomous agent.[162]

V THE SEARCH FOR A MIXED THEORY

The "moral education" and "penitential" theories of punishment combine retributive and consequentialist features. Duff's theory, for example, "is retributive in that it is a response to [a] past crime whose meaning lies in the judgment on, and the condemnation of, that crime"[163] and that is intended to "bring offenders to suffer what they deserve to suffer."[164] Yet it is consequentialist in aiming to *reform* the criminal—to bring him "to repent his crime; to accept his punishment as an appropriate vehicle for his repentance; and thus to reform himself."[165] Similarly, Morris characterizes his moral education theory as both "comply[ing] with the demands of retributivism" and "supplementing" these by serving "deterrent values."[166]

There have been many other efforts to find some way of combining the best features of retributivism and consequentialism. Indeed, Douglas Husak claims "that almost all philosophers appreciate the need to construct hybrid syntheses of retributive and consequentialist elements."[167] One writer traces the quest for such a "mixed" or "hybrid" theory as far back as the eighteenth-century penal reformer Cesare Beccaria,[168] while others have argued that even Kant—commonly described as the most hard-core of retributivists—actually espoused a "mixed" theory.[169] A. C. Ewing claimed eight decades ago to have "found the basis of a possible treaty of reconciliation between the different views."[170] A more recent wave of hybrid theorizing was heralded by Anthony Quinton's assertion that "the two theories answer different questions: retributivism the question 'when (logically) *can* we punish?,' utilitarianism the question 'when (morally) *may* we or *ought* we to punish?'"[171] For Quinton, "retributivism is the view that only the guilty are to be punished"—that guilt is a *necessary* condition for punishment—which, he believed, was true by definition: "The infliction of suffering on a person is only properly described as punishment if that person is guilty."[172] And this in no way conflicts with the consequentialist insistence that "punishment must always be justified by the value of its consequences."[173] To be sure, hard treatment can be imposed on innocent people, "but this is not punishment, it is judicial error or terrorism."[174]

Many retributivists, however, would reject Quinton's description of their thesis:

> Retributivists assert that punishment is justified only if those who receive it deserve it, but that is not the connection between desert and punishment distinctive of retributivism. Rather, the more distinctive assertion of the retributivist is that punishment is justified if it is given to those who deserve it. Desert, in other words, is a sufficient condition of a just punishment, not only a necessary condition.[175]

Moreover, Quinton's "definitional stop" begs the crucial question: *why* limit hard treatment to guilty offenders, rather than adopting "other forms of social hygiene which we might employ to prevent anti-social behavior,"[176] such as detention of those judged *likely* to offend?

H. L. A. Hart, while rejecting Quinton's approach, proposed his own influential "two-question strategy"[177] for reconciling retributivism and consequentialism, based on a sharp distinction between questions about the *general justifying aim* of punishment and its *distribution*. To seek punishment's "general justifying aim" is to ask "why and in what circumstances it is a *good* institution to maintain"[178] or what "general aim or value its maintenance fosters"[179] or simply what is "the justification of punishment."[180] The question of "distribution" asks "Who may be punished?" (as well as how much).[181] Once we draw this distinction, says Hart, it is perfectly possible to believe *both* that the institution of punishment is justified by its consequences *and* that it is to be distributed according to desert. The consequentialist and retributive theories simply answer different questions.

Hart's distinction strongly resembles the one Rawls draws, discussed earlier, between justifying punishment as an institution and justifying particular instances of punishment. They differ, however, as to the status of the (retributive) principles governing the distribution of punishment. Rawls believes that punishment governed by these principles is a rule with better consequences overall than an institution that violates them, so that "ultimately punishment is justified in terms of a single value, utilitarianism."[182] Hart, by contrast, believes that the retributive principles of distribution "are to be understood as *different* from, *independent* of, and partly *conflicting* with" punishment's consequentialist justifying aim.[183] He believes punishment, like other social institutions, "can only be understood as a compromise between partly discrepant principles" that include "principles limiting the unqualified pursuit of [the] aim or value" it promotes."[184] Punishment as an institution is legitimated, for Hart, by the consequentialist principle—it produces the best results. But the retributive principles of desert "are meant to limit the pursuit of the utilitarian aim, to make sure that it is not sought in unjust ways, that the individual is not denied his rights and unjustly used by society, or even sacrificed to it, in ways which the unqualified pursuit of deterrence would call for."[185]

Although widely influential, Hart's theory is bedeviled by a number of problems. Observe, for one thing, that the theory assigns desert a purely negative role: the guilty are not to be punished more than they deserve, and the innocent not at all. But someone's deserving punishment "by no means entails the *duty* of the state to punish, which is based [solely] on the deterrent effects of punishment."[186] The punishment of Nazi war criminals, for example, was justified *only* if it deterred potential war criminals from committing new mass murders. But

> [t]his does not seem to be a very satisfactory answer.... [A]ssume, for the sake of argument, that...those remaining and those still to come are beyond deterrence.... The death sentences meted out at Nuremberg or the one given to Eichmann did not deter mass murderers who came later, such as Amin, [Pol] Pot, or Macias, and their henchmen.... [A]re we to conclude that the defendants at Nuremberg or Adolf Eichmann ought not to have been punished?[187]

This example is disturbing, but many retributivists would agree with Hart that desert by itself need *not* create a duty to punish.[188] John Finnis, for example, would take consequences into account:

[I]f it is unfair to law-abiding citizens not to punish criminals, it is more unfair to them to punish criminals when it is clear that the punishment will lead to more crime, more unfairness by criminals and more danger and disadvantage to law-abiding citizens.[189]

Even Michael Moore, who asserts that "officials have a duty to punish deserving offenders"[190] because desert is "a sufficient condition of a just punishment,"[191] acknowledges that the duty to punish can be overridden by other considerations.[192]

Richard Wasserstrom points to a more serious problem for Hart:

Hart's position is less a justification of punishment than a justification of the threat of punishment. It is clear that if we could convince the rest of society that we were in fact punishing offenders we would accomplish all that Hart sees us as achieving through punishment.... [I]t is the *belief* that punishment will follow the commission of an offense that deters potential offenders.[193]

If so, Hart's theory is open to the "sham punishment" objection discussed earlier.[194] Perhaps, however, we can disarm this objection by recalling that it relies on some implausible, science-fiction-type assumptions.

A third objection is that Hart's sharp distinction among the definition of punishment, its "general justifying aim," and its "distribution"

suggests that we can decide what punishment is and why we engage in it without knowing who is supposed to receive punishment—which seems preposterous.... Indeed, Hart himself inconsistently builds an answer to the "distribution" question into his supposedly separate "definition" of punishment, by specifying that punishment, in its "standard" or "central" case, "must be of an actual or supposed offender for his offense."[195]

Ironically, by building this "distribution" condition into his definition of punishment, Hart engages in the very maneuver for which he faults Quinton—accommodating retributivism by assuming that "punishment which is not deserved is not punishment."[196]

A final, more general objection to Hart's combination of retributive and consequentialist principles is that Hart does not explain how these two different principles relate to one another. As one critic complained, "we cannot escape the problems of one theory by simple addition of a separate, unconnected qualification."[197] Hart asserts, for example, that in sufficiently extreme cases the retributive ban on punishing the innocent may be overridden by the catastrophic consequences of not doing so,[198] but offers no guidance as to how to decide what situations are sufficiently "extreme."

Perhaps this is simply one of the line-drawing conundrums that are inescapable in a world of competing values. Michael Moore likens it to "the medieval worry of how many stones make a heap." Observing that "uncertainty whether it takes three, or four, or five, etc., does not justify us in thinking that there are no such things as heaps," he adds: "Similarly, preventing the torture of two innocents does not justify my torturing one, but destruction of an entire city does."[199]

Andrew von Hirsch and Uma Narayan have presented a different "mixed" theory that does try to explain the interrrelation of consequentialism and retributivism.[200]

Their point of departure is the existence of two aspects of punishment—it inflicts *hard treatment* on the offender, and in doing so it conveys society's *censure* or *reprobation* for his deed. Each of these features serves a distinct purpose. By threatening potential offenders with hard treatment, the criminal law "seeks to discourage criminal behavior." By conveying censure, "the law registers disapprobation of the behavior," giving citizens "moral and not just prudential reasons for desistence."[201] Von Hirsch cautions that the censuring function of punishment "has primacy"—the deterrent feature of punishment "operates only *within* a censuring framework."[202] The threat of hard treatment *supplements* "the normative reason conveyed by penal censure," helping fallible humans resist the temptation to do what they know is wrong.[203] In particular, the severity of the punishment for a given crime should be determined by the degree of censure that crime merits, *not* by the desired strength of the deterrent incentive the punishment will create.[204]

Narayan agrees. The censure component of punishment is justified because it "is a morally appropriate response to responsible wrongdoers,"[205] while hard treatment is the best "vehicle for the expression of censure" because of its "role in crime prevention."[206] And, like von Hirsch, Narayan regards the censuring function as primary.[207]

Both Narayan and von Hirsch acknowledge the possibility that censure could be conveyed without hard treatment.[208] They argue, however, that hard treatment is a superior method of censure because of its beneficial, crime-reducing consequences. Recall, however, that hard treatment is treatment that would ordinarily violate important rights of the person so treated, and that justifying punishment means explaining why no rights of an offender are violated by such treatment. The ability of hard treatment to convey censure does not explain this, given the possibility of nonpunitive censure. And even if hard treatment offers better consequences than such alternatives, our examination of consequentialist theories reveals how difficult it is to suppose that these consequences legitimate what would otherwise be rights-violations. The von Hirsch–Narayan theory, then, seems inadequate.

Some proponents of a "mixed" theory seek to justify punishment as a form of collective or societal *self-defense*. Ordinary, individual self-defense permits the use of force to ward off harm—a consequentialist justification—yet legitimates such force only if directed against an aggressor—a restriction paralleling the retributivist insistence on "desert." Self-defense thus offers a promising model of a "mixed" theory. The big problem, however, is that self-defense is a method of *preventing* wrongful harm, whereas punishment occurs *after* such harm has already taken place. This seems to make punishment a kind of retaliation, rather than defense. Several theorists have argued, nonetheless, that punishment and self-defense share a common justificatory structure.

Phillip Montague, for example, traces the permissibility of self-defensive force to a broader principle of distributive justice, which he contends also yields a justification of punishment.[209] Montague's principle applies to "forced-choice situations"—situations in which harm to *someone* is unavoidable, and one is able only to determine *who* will be harmed. In such situations, Montague contends, a principle he calls J applies:

> When members of a group of individuals are in danger of being harmed through the fault of some, but not all, members of that group; and when some person…is in a position to determine how the harm is distributed, even though the harm is unavoidable from that person's standpoint; then the person has a right (if a member of the threatened group) and is required (if not a member of the group) to distribute the harm among those who are at fault.[210]

Principle J will not directly justify individual instances of punishment, which are "not generally forced-choice situations."[211] Montague argues, however, that J does justify a society in creating a *system* or *institution* of legal punishment, because a society whose members include potential criminals does confront a forced-choice situation.

Let S be such a society. The potential criminals form a subclass S' of individuals who are willing and able to inflict harm on innocent members of S, and who will do so unless somehow deterred or prevented. Assume that "credible threats to their own well-being can deter them" and "that S can pose such threats by establishing and effectively implementing a system of legal punishment…that…places would-be offenders at significant conditional risk of being punished."[212] In this situation, harm is "unavoidable from the standpoint of S as a whole, though S does have some control over how this harm is distributed."[213] The existence of this unavoidable risk of harm is the fault of those in S', and thus principle J "presumptively requires S to establish a system of legal punishment."[214]

Punishment of individual wrongdoers is now *indirectly* justified:

> [I]f establishing a system of punishment is justified, then creating certain positions that system requires, with their attendant responsibilities, is justified, and the people who occupy those positions are certainly justified in fulfilling their responsibilities—that is, presumptively justified in participating in the punishment of individuals.[215]

Montague's argument has been criticized for treating all wrongdoers as an undifferentiated mass, all of whom are collectively responsible for all the crimes committed.[216] The reality, however, is that the threat of punishment will deter some of the individuals in S' but not others. Thus "S' can be subdivided into 'deterrables' and 'undeterrables.' A decision to establish a system of punishment is a decision to punish the undeterrables (or at least the undeterred) in order to deter the deterrables."[217] Thus Montague's strategy is open to one of the standard objections to consequentialist justifications of punishment—it "uses" the undeterrables as a tool by which we shape the behavior of the deterrables.

Another theorist, Warren Quinn, devised a very different argument for punishment as a variant of self-defense. Quinn's strategy involves likening punishment to an imagined science-fiction-type system of "mechanical-punishments" or "m-punishments." This imagined system employs "fantastically complex devices that can (at least as well as we can) detect wrongdoing…identify and apprehend those who are responsible, establish their guilt, and subject them to incarcerations (and perhaps other evils)."[218] A crucial feature of these devices is that once activated, they cannot be altered or turned off. Therefore, if the decision to activate the devices is morally permissible, no further human choice, in need of its own moral justification, is required to bring about each instance of actual punishment. Quinn argues, first, that activating these devices would indeed be permissible, simply as an exercise of our right of self-protection—we are defending ourselves from wrongful aggression by deterring would-be aggressors with the *threat* of punishment. Each actual instance of punishment is simply "an unavoidable empirical consequence"[219] of the decision to create that threat by deploying the m-punishment devices—a decision whose own justification rests on the deterrent value of the threat itself rather than on any property of the actual act of punishing.

Real-world punishment, of course, requires not merely an initial decision to *threaten* that offenders will be punished, but, in each particular instance, further decisions by human agents actually to *inflict* such punishment. Quinn argues, however, that real-world punishment is morally equivalent to "m-punishment." The crux of his argument is what could be called the *moral stability claim*: that the moral status of the offender's being punished does not change over time, because "a given state of affairs will be morally acceptable to x at all times if it is acceptable to him at any."[220] An offender who has a valid claim, after committing a crime, that punishment would violate his rights must have had the same grounds for this claim before the crime, when the threat of punishment was created.[221] But creating that threat was not morally objectionable, grounded as it was in our unproblematic right of self-protection.

Quinn's elegant reasoning rests, however, on contestable premises. The moral stability claim seems vulnerable to counterexamples. Suppose, for example, that on Monday John promises his neighbor Jane that he will drive her to the airport on Tuesday. On Sunday—before John's promise—Jane could not claim that the state of affairs *John's refusing to drive Jane to the airport on Tuesday* would violate any of her moral rights. On Tuesday, however, Jane can validly assert that this state of affairs would indeed violate her rights. In Quinn's terminology, *John's refusing to drive Jane to the airport on Tuesday* is a state of affairs morally acceptable to Jane on Sunday, but not acceptable on Tuesday.

Presumably, Quinn would respond by explaining "state of affairs" in a manner sufficiently fine-grained so that the state of affairs acceptable to Jane on Sunday was not the same as the one unacceptable to her on Tuesday. (E.g., Tuesday's state of affairs, unlike Sunday's, is the breach of a promise.) But the more fine-grained the concept of "state of affairs," the harder it becomes to understand how the state of affairs in which a potential offender is threatened, precrime, with punishment can be identical to that in which the offender actually is punished, postcrime, as Quinn's argument requires.

Even if we accept the moral stability claim, Quinn faces a different objection. He uses that claim to argue that Clem's being punished for theft is just as acceptable as Clem's being threatened, pretheft, with punishment. A critic can turn Quinn's argument around. If Clem does in fact steal, despite the threat of punishment, then we have learned that this threat is ineffective against him. Punishing Clem for theft cannot be justified as necessary to protect us against theft: indeed, had we known in advance that the threat of punishment would not deter Clem, we would have had no justification for threatening punishment in the first place. By virtue of the moral stability claim, then, since punishing Clem after the fact is morally objectionable, so was threatening to punish him before the crime![222]

The moral stability claim is not the only problematic move Quinn makes. Consider his first premise—that our right of self-protection justifies us in creating a real risk that an offender will be punished. Quinn employs analogies to defend this premise. In a state of nature, he says, one is entitled to protect oneself from assault by surrounding one's home with a very high fence. And if even the tallest fence "cannot stop some vigorous and agile enemies," one may "place dangerous spikes at the top of the fence in order to discourage those who would otherwise scale it." Now suppose that "our defender cannot arrange the spikes so that they offer a threat of injury to someone entering his territory but can arrange them so that they clearly offer a threat of injury to an enemy leaving his territory after an attack." Quinn argues that this, too, would be morally legitimate—it could make no morally relevant difference to a would-be attacker that the injury whose prospect is designed to discourage him will come later rather than sooner. "But building the second kind of fence is nothing more than creating an automatic cost to *follow* an offense."[223]

The reasoning is plausible. But push it further. Instead of spikes on the fence, our defender could equally justifiably "coat the fence with a visible, moderately toxic substance" that a would-be intruder could see would inflict the same degree of harm as would a spiked fence. But "now suppose that the prospect of becoming sick is not enough to deter most intruders" from scaling the fence, but that they would be deterred were the fence coated with "a second toxic substance" that would both sicken an intruder and "stick to the intruder's body for a long time and eventually infect all of his children." If Quinn's analogical argument justifies threatening to punish offenders for breaking the law, this extension of it should justify threatening to harm their innocent children as well. The repugnance of this conclusion indicates that something is wrong with Quinn's original argument.[224] Note that we cannot distinguish threats of harm to aggressors from threats of harm to their children by insisting that harming the children is something intrinsically, independently wrongful. For we would then be justifying threats to punish aggressors by a tacit appeal to the rightness of actually inflicting such punishment, when the whole point of Quinn's argument is to derive the rightness of inflicting punishment from the rightness of threatening it.

VI An Inconclusive Conclusion

The search for an acceptable justification of punishment continues.[225] As is characteristic of philosophical debates, it is unlikely that any proposal will ever win universal acceptance. But as is also characteristic of such debates, there has been a growing appreciation of the complexity of the questions involved, and a growing sophistication in the answers that have been propounded. An excellent illustration of this progress is an ingenious contribution recently offered by Mitchell Berman.[226]

Berman separates what he calls "core" cases of punishment from those "peripheral" cases that "involve imposition of punishment on persons who are not wrongdoers, either because no offence occurred or because, although it did, the individual was not responsible for it."[227] Put very roughly, he argues that "core" cases are justified on retributive grounds—an offender's suffering on account of her offenses "simply is not a bad," and the state "does not infringe the offender's rights" in inflicting such suffering.[228] "Peripheral" cases, on the other hand, are justified in consequentialist fashion, by looking to the multiple benefits produced by the practice of punishment as a whole. En route to these conclusions, Berman discusses the concept of "justification" and distinguishes two strategies for achieving it. And he presents a revisionist account of the rights that a person possesses. The supposed right against the purposeful infliction of suffering, he argues, is merely "a useful rule of thumb," commonly but not invariably implied by the truly basic right—the right to be treated with respect as a person.[229]

The arguments presented in this one article could easily keep theorists busy for a very long time. The quest for the justification of punishment may never come to an end, but there is every reason to anticipate a steady flow of novel and helpful insights along the way.

NOTES

1. *Protagoras* 324b–c, in Cooper 1997: 759.
2. Samek 1966: 220. See also Flew 1954: 294–295; McCloskey 1962: 316.
3. Benn 1958: 325–326; Hart 1968: 4–6; Philips 1986: 393–394; Scheid 1980: 453–454.
4. Zaibert 2006, however, strongly disagrees, insisting that state punishment cannot be understood unless it is viewed precisely as one species of a more general practice.
5. Lacey 1988: 13–15; Matravers 2000; Philips 1986.
6. Davis 1992: 18–41.
7. Flew 1954: 293–294.
8. Benn 1958: 325–326.
9. Hart 1968: 5.
10. Fletcher 1978: 410–412.
11. Feinberg 1970: 98.
12. E.g., Duff 1986: 235–262; Hampton, in Murphy & Hampton 1988: 123–143; Primoratz 1989: 149–154. An early version of this idea appears in chapter 4 of Ewing 1970, where "the essential part of punishment" is said to be the expression of society's disapproval. For a dissenting view, see Bedau 2001: 117.
13. Fletcher 1978: 410.
14. U.S. Constitution, article 1, section 3, clause 7.

15. For example, an attorney cannot invoke her privilege against self-incrimination simply because a truthful answer could lead to disbarment. Black v. State Bar, 7 Cal. 3d 676, 684 (1972); Zuckerman v. Greason, 20 N.Y.2d 430, 438–39 (1967), *cert. denied*, 390 U.S. 925 (1968).

16. Lacey 1988: 11–12. Richard Wasserstrom has objected to Hart's account of punishment as circular: it employs the notion of an "offense," yet the primary criterion for whether something *is* an offense is "to determine whether persons were liable to punishment were they to behave in this way" (Wasserstrom 1982: 475). The rough definition of punishment just presented in the text, however, does not use the concept of an offense, and seems essentially equivalent to Wasserstrom's own formulation. Punishment, he says, consists of deprivations that "are imposed because they are deprivations upon persons who are believed to have acted wrongly and in a way that is blameworthy by persons authorized to impose such deprivations in such circumstances." *Id.* at 477.

17. To ask for a "justification" of punishment may be to ask either of two quite different questions. "One concerns what could be called the 'rational justification' of the practice of punishment: *why*—for what reason or reasons—do we punish wrongdoers?" The other "asks, rather, for the 'moral justification' of punishment: why is it morally permissible to engage in this particular practice?" Dolinko 1991: 539. Moral justification is the sense in which "justification" is being used in this chapter.

18. Though standard, this use of "theories" has been criticized. "[T]heories of punishment are not theories in any normal sense. They are not, as scientific theories are, assertions or contentions as to what is or what is not the case.... [but rather] moral *claims* as to what justifies the practice of punishment—claims as to why, morally, it *should* or *may* be used." Hart 1968: 72.

19. This classification has been challenged, however: "The labels 'consequentialist' and 'retributive' are of increasingly little use as the theories that they are meant to group together have become so diverse." Matravers 2000: 4 n. 4.

20. "Consequentialism" is the general term for the view that the goodness of outcomes is the *only* relevant factor in determining the rightness or wrongness of actions, practices, or institutions. The term was introduced in 1958 by G. E. M. Anscombe, who contrasted it with "old-fashioned Utilitarianism" (Anscombe 1958: 12). Very often, however, the term "utilitarianism" is used in a broad sense to denote what I call "consequentialism." This broad usage appears in a number of the passages quoted in this chapter. In a narrower sense, "utilitarianism" refers to one particular (and historically prominent) variety of consequentialism.

Consequentialists disagree among themselves about what determines the "goodness" of states of affairs. *Welfarists* believe that it is determined by the amount of individual well-being in that state, with everyone's well-being counted equally. (Some welfarists look to the *total* amount of well-being, others to the average amount. Some look only to the well-being of persons, while others take into account the well-being of all sentient creatures.) "Utilitarianism" in its narrower sense refers to the combination of consequentialism and welfarism. See Kagan 1998: 60–61.

21. The term "utility" is commonly used to designate whatever it is that a particular brand of consequentialism regards as the determinant of "goodness" (hence calls for maximizing).

22. See, e.g., Primoratz 1989: 42–43.

23. As the arch-consequentialist Jeremy Bentham observed (while discussing the acquittal of an innocent man mistakenly believed guilty by the public at large):

In point of utility, apparent justice is everything; real justice, abstractedly from apparent justice, is a useless abstraction, not worth pursuing, and supposing it contrary to apparent justice, such as ought not to be pursued.

From apparent justice flow all the good effects of justice—from real justice, if different from apparent, none.

Bentham, *Principles of Judicial Procedure*, in 1 Bentham 1843: 21.

24. Actually, although this argument goes through with regard to deterrence, reform, and normative validation, it is difficult to see how sham punishments could actually *incapacitate* criminals. Perhaps they could be deceived into believing, for some period of time, that they are incarcerated and hence unable to victimize members of the public, even though they are in fact living quietly at home. Or perhaps we can simply imagine that the reduction in suffering and other costs of genuine punishment outweighs the loss in incapacitation.

25. Moore 1987: 183–185. A consequentialist might argue that the cost of a nonpunitive system would actually exceed that of punishment once we factor in this great increase in public dissatisfaction. The critic can assume, however, that the new system is so much less costly and more effective than punishment that its new benefits outweigh the added costs. The critic seeks only to show that there are *conceivable* circumstances in which consequentialists must favor abandoning punishment of the guilty.

26. McCloskey 1957: 468–469 and McCloskey 1965: 256. Some variant of this scenario turns up in Bagaric & Amaraseka 2000: 140–141, Matravers 2000: 17, Smart 1991: 364, Smilansky 1990: 257, Foot 1978: 23, and Nielson 1972: 223, to pick just a few examples.

27. Of course, such policies would not only inflict enormous suffering on those unjustly punished but would generate widespread fear and revulsion in the populace at large. "Yet if these iniquitous practices yielded sufficiently great pay-offs, consequentialists would take them to be morally justified. Perhaps torturing murderers would make murder so rare that the gain in deterrence would dwarf the anguish of the tiny group of murderers and their loved ones." Dolinko 2003: 76. Circumstances leading to such high payoffs for unjust punishments are surely unlikely—but "these things *could* happen—and, if they did, consequentialist reasoning would endorse torture and false convictions. Thus, consequentialism potentially justifies far too much." *Id.* at 77.

28. "[H]owever unhappy about it he may be, the utilitarian must admit that he draws the consequence that he might find himself in circumstances where he ought to be unjust. Let us hope that this is a logical possibility and not a factual one." Smart 1973: 71.

29. Duff 1986: 160; McCloskey 1965: 254–255. As G. E. M. Anscombe notoriously remarked: "[I]f someone really thinks, *in advance*, that it is open to question whether such an act as procuring the judicial execution of the innocent should be quite excluded from consideration—I do not want to argue with him; he shows a corrupt mind." Anscombe 1958: 17.

30. "[I]n order to use an appeal to our ordinary intuitions as an argument, the opponents of utilitarianism have to produce cases which are not too far removed from the sort of cases with which our intuitions are designed to deal, namely the ordinary run of cases. If the cases they use fall outside this class, then the fact that our common intuitions give a different verdict from utilitarianism has no bearing on the argument; our intuitions could well be wrong about such cases, and be none the worse for that, because they will never have to deal with them in practice." Hare 1979: 111. The argument is developed in detail in Hare 1981. For a counterargument, see Ten 1987: 18–32.

31. See Sprigge 1965: 276–77.

32. Rawls 1955: 6.

33. The two consequentialist moves just discussed are closely related. Thus Hare's objection to far-fetched, fanciful scenarios rests on his belief that "the principles which it is best for [people] to have are those which will lead them to make the highest proportion of right decisions in actual cases" (Hare 1979: 115). And this is tantamount to the rule-consequentialist position that the optimum set of *rules* or *practices* is the one that will lead to better consequences overall than any alternative set of rules.

34. Matravers 2000: 21.

35. Smart 1973: 10.

36. Montague 1995: 11.

37. Primoratz 1991: 388.

38. "Probably the most widely held assumption about retribution in punishment is the idea that it makes desert the central feature of just punishment." Bedau 1977: 52. Consider also James Griffin's remark that "Desert is necessary, in general, for the institution to be punishment and to be regarded as such." Griffin 1986: 277.

39. Ewing 1970: 15.

40. Bedau 1977: 52.

41. Feinberg 1970: 81.

42. Kelly 2002: 182.

43. Berman 2008: 258.

44. Griffin 1986: 269.

45. Kant has generally been treated as the retributivist par excellence. See, e.g., Murphy 1970: 140–144; Honderich 2006: 17–22; Ewing 1970: 13–21; Hodges 1957–58; Goldman 1965: 462–464. Several contemporary authors, however, have challenged this orthodox view of Kant as a thoroughgoing retributivist. In its place they have interpreted Kant as offering a *consequentialist* justification for having the institution of punishment at all, with retributive principles operating *within* this institution to determine how punishment should be distributed—that is, which individuals to punish and how much to punish them. See Scheid 1983, Byrd 1989, and Hill 1999. A different but related view is that Kant *did* espouse retributivism, but that a quite different view is much more compatible with his broader theory of right. Wood 2008, chap. 12.

46. Kant 1996: 105 (AKS 6:331).

47. "The capacity to set oneself an end—any end whatsoever—is what characterizes humanity (as distinguished from animality)." *Id.* at 154 (AKS 6:392). "Rational nature is distinguished from the rest of nature by this, that it sets itself an end." Kant 1997: 44 (AKS 4:437).

48. "Every human being has a legitimate claim to respect from his fellow human beings... [H]e is under obligation to acknowledge, in a practical way, the dignity of humanity in every other human being. Hence there rests on him a duty regarding the respect that must be shown to every other human being." Kant 1996: 209 (AKS 6:462).

49. Hegel 1952: 246 (addition to ¶ 99).

50. Primoratz 1989: 35.

51. Murphy 1973: 219.

52. Duff 1996: 14.

53. For some other examples, see Lewis 1972: 194–198; Morris 1976: 46–49; Sadurski 1985: 241.

54. Ewing 1970: 50–51; Gross 1979: 382–383.

55. The consequentialist might insist that an offender who does not want to be reformed is nevertheless benefitted by reformation and is therefore treated as an end, not merely as a means. But is subjection to such paternalism—"we know what's best for you

and will give it to you whether or not you want it"—genuinely compatible with being treated as an end in oneself?

56. Although I will speak of the "innocent," this category includes not only people who should have been found "not guilty" but also people erroneously found guilty of crimes more serious than what they actually committed—e.g., someone convicted of murder rather than manslaughter because the jury mistakenly disbelieved her story of provocation.

57. Schedler 1980: 189.

58. One might think of using the doctrine of double effect to rebut the claim that the retributivist necessarily "uses" the wrongly convicted. But see Dolinko 1992: 1633–1634.

59. Duff 1986: 184.

60. Hill 2003: 27.

61. Dworkin 1988: 31.

62. Hill 1992: 91.

63. "A system of law must seek the consent and the allegiance of the citizen as a rational moral agent." Duff 1986: 184.

64. Berlin 1969: 133. As Berlin explains: "It is one thing to say that I know what is good for X, while he himself does not . . . and a very different one to say that he has *eo ipso* chosen it, not indeed consciously, nor as he seems in everyday life, but in his role as a rational self which his empirical self may not know—the 'real' self which discerns the good." *Id.*

65. One writer has distinguished nine different "retributive" theories. Cottingham 1979. A subsequent author adds several more. Walker 1999.

66. Sher 1987: 194.

67. Dolinko 1991: 544.

68. Fischer 2006: 113.

69. *Id.* at 110.

70. Moreover, Fischer has no answer to the crucial question he himself raises: If "it is not always permissible for the state to give an individual what he deserves," then "why suppose that it is morally permissible for the state to give someone what he deserves in virtue of his violating the specified rights?" *Id.* at 117.

71. The notion of forfeiture plays this role in Goldman 1979 and McDermott 2001.

72. Quinn 1985: 332.

73. *Id.* at 333. An effort to rebut such criticism of the forfeiture idea appears in Morris 1991.

74. Morris 1976: 31–58 (originally published in *Monist* 52 [1968]: 475–501).

75. *Id.* at 34.

76. Dagger 1993: 481.

77. See, e.g., Murphy 1971; Finnis 1972; Sher 1987; Sadurski 1989, and Dagger 1993.

78. Dagger 1993: 474.

79. Dolinko 1991: 545–546.

80. Dagger 1993: 483.

81. *Id.* at 484.

82. *Id.*

83. See, e.g., Moore 1987: 100 (retributivists "are committed to the principle that punishment should be graded in proportion to desert"); Sadurski 1985: 237 ("The principle that punishments should be proportionate to crimes is one of the essential postulates of the retributivist theory"); Falls 1987; Sher 1987: 80 ("the benefits-and-burdens account equates amounts of punishment deserved with amounts of excess benefit received"); Davis

1992: 69 (defining retributivism as including the claim "that the only acceptable reason for punishing [a person] with such-and-such severity is that the punishment fits the crime").

84. Davis did not himself advocate fairness-based *retributivism*. He was concerned with "*how much to punish criminals* under the laws of a relatively just society" and "*not* the definition (or meaning) of punishment, its purpose (or function) as an institution, or its justification" (Davis 1992: 235).

But he has claimed that his method provides "an attractive analysis of unfair advantage" that can rebut criticisms of "that theory of criminal desert proportioning the (maximum) legal punishment for a crime to the unfair advantage the criminal takes by the crime" (Davis 1993: 133).

85. Davis 1992: 165.

86. *Id.* at 239.

87. Davis 1993: 140.

88. Davis 1992: 241.

89. *Id.* at 84.

90. Dolinko 1994: 511.

91. Duff 1990: 12–13.

92. Davis 1992: 244. He later equivocated, however, calling the assumption that no one will poach implausible "but still workable." Davis 1993: 151 n.24.

93. Davis 1993: 150.

94. Davis 1992: 244.

95. *Id.* at 111. In a subsequent paper, Davis contends that the penalty for poaching "should not produce *enough* injustice to undermine our assumption that the society in question is relatively just" (Davis 1996: 318; emphasis added). He also retracts his suggestion of an "inhumane" penalty for poaching. (*Id.* at 318 n.22). Oddly, however, he appears to regard life imprisonment for all poachers—even unlicensed speed-limit violators—as "humane." *Id.*

96. *Id.* at 246.

97. *Id.* at 239.

98. Other objections to Davis's market approach appear in Scheid 1995. Davis responds vigorously to the various objections in Davis 1996.

99. Fletcher 1978: 417–418.

100. See Wasserstrom 1977: 192–193, Duff 1986: 211–214, Hampton 1992: 1660–1661.

101. Hegel's account presents both an objective and a subjective justification of punishment. The subjective justification depicts punishment as the *right* of the criminal, because "his action is the action of a rational being and this implies that it is something universal and that by doing it the criminal has laid down a law which he has explicitly recognized in his action and under which in consequence he should be brought as under his right." Hegel 1952: ¶ 100. Only the objective justification is discussed in the text *infra*.

102. Hegel 1952: ¶ 95.

103. *Id.*, ¶ 99.

104. Knowles 2002: 144.

105. "[I]t would be impossible for society to leave a crime unpunished, since that would be to posit it as right." Hegel 1952, addition to ¶ 218.

106. Knowles 2002: 145.

107. "The nullity is that the crime has set aside right as such. That is to say, right as something absolute cannot be set aside, and so committing a crime is in principle a nullity: and this nullity is the essence of what a crime effects. A nullity, however, must reveal itself to be such.…A crime, as an act, is not something positive, not a first thing, on which

punishment would supervene as a negation. It is something negative, so that its punishment is only the negation of a negation." Hegel 1952: addition to ¶ 97.

108. "Being a negation of a right and a law, [crime] is only possible in the context of rights and the law. By negating its own presuppositions, an offense is immanently contradictory." Primoratz 1989: 72.

109. Primoratz 1989: 74.

110. McTaggart 1896.

111. Murphy & Hampton 1988: 131 (emphasis deleted).

112. *Id.* at 124.

113. Hampton 1992: 1677.

114. *Id.* at 1686.

115. Murphy & Hampton 1988: 125. To be sure, it is the *state* that inflicts this "defeat," not the actual victim. But the state does so as "an impartial agent of morality, with greater capacity to recognize the moral facts than any involved individual citizen" and "the institutional voice of the community's shared moral values." Hampton 1992: 1693, 1694.

116. Murphy & Hampton 1988: 131. Hampton asserts that because "to inflict on a wrongdoer something comparable to what he inflicted on the victim is to master him in the way that he mastered the victim," the wrongdoer's defeat means that "[t]he score is even." *Id.* at 128. But if the wrongdoer's initial "mastery" of the victim sends the "message" that the wrongdoer's value is superior, why doesn't the victim's defeat of the wrongdoer signify that the victim is of *superior* value?

117. Husak 1992: 450.

118. Dolinko 1991: 551.

119. Hampton 1992: 1679.

120. Also, given the abysmal prison conditions Americans tolerate, it could be argued that the belief in convicts' inferiority *does* inflict considerable harm. See, e.g., Dolovich 2004: 437–440.

121. Murphy & Hampton 1988: 135–137.

122. See, e.g., McTaggart 1896: 483; Ewing 1970: 80–125. Suggestions of a "moral education" view can be found in Plato. See *Gorgias* 476a–479e and *Laws* 860a–864b in Cooper 1997: 820–825, 1512–1522.

123. Morris 1981: 265.

124. Hampton 1992: 1659 n. 2.

125. Morris 1981: 264 (a "complex communicative act"); Hampton 1984: 215 (the state "punishes [a criminal] as a way of communicating a moral message to him").

126. Hampton 1984: 212.

127. *Id.* at 214.

128. *Id.* at 222.

129. *Id.* at 214.

130. Morris 1981: 265.

131. *Id.*

132. *Id.* at 268.

133. *Id.*

134. *Id.*

135. Possibly Morris is thinking of the "benefits and burdens" theory examined earlier. But he could mean "righting the wrong" to refer to the restoration of relationships itself. See *id.* at 267.

136. Shafer-Landau 1991: 203.

137. Hampton 1984: 227.

138. Indeed, for some sadistic criminals the very *reason* they commit crime is to inflict, and relish, their victim's suffering.

139. Narayan 1993: 177.

140. Morris 1981: 268.

141. Duff 1986: 234.

142. *Id.* at 236.

143. Duff 2001: 106.

144. Duff 1986: 261.

145. *Id.* at 238.

146. *Id.* at 263.

147. *Id.* at 256.

148. *Id.* at 256.

149. *Id.* at 234.

150. Duff 2001: 108.

151. See text at note 139.

152. Duff 1986: 242.

153. *Id.* at 261 (emphasis added).

154. One could respect the offender's rational agency without respecting her autonomy. But Duff explicitly values both. He says that his "main aim" is "to explore the implications of the Kantian demand that we should respect other people as rational and autonomous moral agents" (*Id.* at 6), and in a subsequent book he continues "[t]o address the offender as an autonomous moral agent, as a member of a normative community with autonomy as one of its central values" (Duff 2001: 118).

155. Duff 2001: 109–110.

156. *Id.* at 110.

157. *Id.* at 109. The other part of Duff's response is to suggest that the offender, when sentenced, should be given the chance to explain that she will not undergo her punishment as any form of apology. Punishment would still be justified, he thinks, as "an attempt to persuade her to repentance and self-reform." *Id.* at 111.

158. Duff 2001:107, Duff 1986: 236.

159. Duff 1986: 238.

160. *Id.* at 245.

161. *Id.* at 245.

162. *Id.* at 223.

163. *Id.* at 260.

164. Duff 2001: 107.

165. Duff 1986: 260.

166. Morris 1981: 271.

167. Husak 1992: 452.

168. Christopher 2002: 866–867 n. 128.

169. Hill 1999: 429. See Byrd 1989.

170. Ewing 1970: 95.

171. Quinton 1954: 134.

172. *Id.* at 137.

173. *Id.* at 139.

174. *Id.* at 137.

175. Moore 1997: 153–154.

176. Hart 1968: 6.

177. Zaibert 2006: 11.

178. Hart 1968: 4.

179. *Id.* at 10.

180. *Id.* at 7.

181. *Id.* at 11.

182. Ten 1987: 82.

183. Primoratz 1989: 137–138.

184. Hart 1968: 10.

185. Primoratz 1989: 138.

186. Primoratz 1989: 142.

187. *Id.* Macias, the dictator of Equitorial Guinea from 1968 to 1979, killed about a fifth of that West African country's population.

188. See, e.g., McCloskey 1968: 255–257; Ten 1987: 76.

189. Finnis 1972: 135.

190. Moore 1997: 154.

191. See text at note 175.

192. "*Within the set of conditions constituting intelligible reasons to punish*, the retributivist asserts, desert is sufficient, that is no other *of these* conditions is necessary. Of course, other conditions outside the set of conditions constituting intelligible reasons to punish may also be necessary to a just punishment." Consequently the retributivist "can happily agree" that desert, though always a reason to punish, is *not* always a conclusive reason. Moore 1997: 174. (Note, however, that the only outside conditions Moore mentions are nonforfeited rights of the offender—not the consequences of punishing him.)

193. Wasserstrom 1967: 111.

194. See text accompanying notes 22–24.

195. Dolinko 1991: 541.

196. Zaibert 2006: 143.

197. Lacey 1988: 49.

198. Hart 1968: 12.

199. Moore 1997: 724.

200. Von Hirsch 1993; Narayan 1993.

201. Von Hirsch 1993: 12.

202. *Id.* at 14.

203. *Id.* at 13.

204. *Id.* at 15–17.

205. Narayan 1993: 166.

206. *Id.* at 180.

207. "Only hard treatment that comports with a censuring function, and one that expresses an appropriate degree of censure[,] is permissible." *Id.*

208. "A condemnatory response to injurious conduct...can be expressed...in a purely (or primarily) symbolic mode." Von Hirsch 1993: 14. "[I]t might be argued that we should use our ingenuity to...create symbolic means of expressing degrees of censure in ways that do not involve the liberty-deprivations of hard treatment." Narayan 1993: 179.

209. A similar argument is presented in Farrell 1985.

210. Montague 1995: 42.

211. *Id.* at 59. Because punishment occurs after harm has already been done, someone deciding whether to punish a criminal would typically not be attempting to distribute *impending,* unavoidable harm.

212. *Id.* at 62–63.

213. *Id.* at 63.

214. *Id.* at 63.

215. *Id.* at 72.

216. Golash 2005: 110.

217. *Id.* at 112.

218. Quinn 1985: 337.

219. *Id.* at 340.

220. *Id.* at 366. By saying that a state of affairs is "acceptable" to x, Quinn means that x lacks the kind of objection "whose force would show the presence of some moral right and could, therefore, obligate us to see to it that the objectionable state of affairs did not obtain." *Id.* at 365.

221. "If…x can rightly object at t1 that trying to punish him harms his interests without furthering ours, he could have rightly objected at t1 that the punishment we then threatened might turn out to be like this. But both we and x then knew that although this unhappy result was a real possibility, it did not provide x with a legitimate objection." *Id.* at 366.

222. Golash 2005: 107–108.

223. Quinn 1985: 342–343.

224. Boonin 2008: 198–199.

225. Note that some authors believe that this search is futile, and that punishment simply *is not* justified. This thesis is defended, for example, in the recent books by Golash and Boonin.

226. Berman 2008.

227. *Id.* at 261.

228. *Id.* at 284.

229. *Id.* at 277.

BIBLIOGRAPHY

Anscombe, G. E. M. (1958), "Modern Moral Philosophy," *Philosophy* 33: 1–19.

Armstrong, K. G. (1961), "The Retributivist Hits Back," *Mind* 70: 471–490.

Bagaric, M., and K. Amarasekera (2000), "The Errors of Retributivism," *Melbourne University L. Rev.* 24: 124–189.

Bedau, H. A. (1977), "Concessions to Retribution in Punishment," in J. B. Cederblom and William L. Blizek, eds., *Justice and Punishment* (Cambridge, Mass.: Ballinger).

——— (2001), "Feinberg's Liberal Theory of Punishment," *Buff. Crim. L. Rev.* 5: 103–144.

Benn, S. I. (1958), "An Approach to the Problems of Punishment," *Philosophy* 33: 325–341.

Bentham, Jeremy (1843), *The Works of Jeremy Bentham*, ed. John Bowring.

Berlin, Isaiah (1969), *Four Essays on Liberty* (Oxford: Oxford University Press).

Berman, Mitchell (2008), "Punishment and Justification," *Ethics* 118: 258–290.

Boonin, David (2008), *The Problem of Punishment* (Cambridge: Cambridge University Press).

Byrd, B. Sharon (1989), "Kant's Theory of Punishment: Deterrence in Its Threat, Retribution in Its Execution," *Law & Philosophy* 8: 151–200.

Christopher, Russell (2002), "Deterring Retributivism: The Injustice of 'Just' Punishment," 96 *Nw. U. L. Rev.* 843–976.

Cooper, John M. (1997)(ed.), *Complete Works of Plato* (Indianapolis: Hackett).

Cottingham, John (1979), "Varieties of Retribution," *Philosophical Quarterly* 29: 238–246.

Dagger, Richard (1993), "Playing Fair with Punishment," *Ethics* 103: 473–488.

Davis, Michael (1992), *To Make the Punishment Fit the Crime* (Boulder, Colo.: Westview).

———— (1993), "Criminal Desert and Unfair Advantage: What's the Connection?," *Law and Philosophy* 12: 133–156.

———— (1996), "Method in Punishment Theory," *Law and Philosophy* 15: 309–338.

Dolinko, David (1991), "Some Thoughts about Retributivism," *Ethics* 101: 537–559.

———— (1992), "Three Mistakes of Retributivism," *UCLA Law Review* 39: 1623–1657.

———— (1994), "Mismeasuring 'Unfair Advantage': A Response to Michael Davis," *Law and Philosophy* 13: 493–524.

———— (2003), "State Punishment and the Death Penalty," in R. G. Frey and C. H. Wellman, eds., *A Companion to Applied Ethics* (Oxford: Blackwell) 75–88.

Dolovich, Sharon (2004), "Legitimate Punishment in Liberal Democracy," *Buffalo Crim. L. Rev.* 7: 307–442.

Duff, R. A. (1986), *Trials and Punishments* (Cambridge: Cambridge University Press).

———— (1990), "Auctions, Lotteries, and the Punishment of Attempts," *Law and Philosophy* 8: 1–37.

———— (1996), "Penal Communications: Recent Work in the Philosophy of Punishment," *Crime and Justice: A Review of Research* 20: 1–95.

———— (2001) *Punishment, Communication, and Community* (Oxford: Oxford University Press).

Dworkin, Gerald (1988), *The Theory and Practice of Autonomy* (Cambridge: Cambridge University Press).

Ewing, A. C. (1970), *The Morality of Punishment* (Montclair, N.J.: Patterson Smith) (originally published 1929).

Falls, Margaret (1987), "Retribution, Reciprocity, and Respect for Persons," *Law & Philosophy* 6: 25–51.

Farrell, Daniel M. (1985), "The Justification of General Deterrence," *Phil. Rev.* 94: 367–394.

Feinberg, Joel (1970), *Doing and Deserving: Essays in the Theory of Responsibility* (Princeton: Princeton University Press).

Finnis, John (1972), "The Restoration of Retribution," *Analysis* 37: 131–135.

Fischer, John Martin (2006), "Punishment and Desert: A Reply to Dolinko," *Ethics* 117: 109–118.

Fletcher, George (1978), *Rethinking Criminal Law* (Boston: Little, Brown).

———— (2007), *The Grammar of Criminal Law,* vol. 1, *Foundations* (Oxford: Oxford University Press).

Flew, Antony (1954), "The Justification of Punishment," *Philosophy* 29: 291–307.

Foot, Philippa (1978), *Virtues and Vices* (Oxford: Oxford University Press).

George, Robert P. (1993), *Making Men Moral* (Oxford: Oxford University Press).

Golash, Deirdre (2005), *The Case against Punishment* (New York: New York University Press).

Goldinger, Milton (1965), "Punishment, Justice and the Separation of Issues," *Monist* 49: 458–474.

Goldman, Alan H. (1979), "The Paradox of Punishment," *Phil. & Pub. Affairs* 9: 42–58.

Griffin, James (1986), *Well-Being* (Oxford: Oxford University Press).

Gross, Hyman (1979), *A Theory of Criminal Justice* (New York: Oxford University Press).

Hampton, Jean (1984), "The Moral Education Theory of Punishment," *Phil. & Pub. Affairs* 13: 208–238.

———— (1992), "Correcting Harm versus Righting Wrongs: The Goal of Retribution," *UCLA L. Rev.* 39: 1659–1702.

Hare, R. M. (1979), "What Is Wrong with Slavery," *Phil. & Pub. Affairs* 8: 103–121.

———— (1981), *Moral Thinking* (Oxford: Oxford University Press).

Hart, H. L. A. *(1968), Punishment and Responsibility* (Oxford: Oxford University Press).

Hegel, G. F. W. *(1952), Philosophy of Right*, trans. T. M. Knox (Oxford: Oxford University Press).

Hill, Thomas (1992), *Dignity and Practical Reason in Kant's Moral Theory* (Ithaca: Cornell University Press).

———— (1999), "Kant on Wrongdoing, Desert, and Punishment," *Law & Philosophy* 18: 407–441.

———— (2003), "Treating Criminals as Ends in Themselves," *Annual Review of Law and Ethics* 11: 17–36.

Hodges, D. C. (1957–58), "Punishment," *Philosophy and Phenomenological Research* 18: 209–218.

Honderich, Ted (2006), *Punishment: The Supposed Justifications Revisited* (London: Pluto Press).

Husak, Douglas (1992), "Why Punish the Deserving?," *Nous* 26: 447–464.

Kagan, Shelly (1998), *Normative Ethics* (Boulder, Colo.: Westview Press).

Kant, Immanuel (1996), *The Metaphysics of Morals*, trans. Mary Gregor (Cambridge, Cambridge University Press).

———— (1997), *Groundwork of the Metaphysics of Morals*, trans. Mary Gregor (Cambridge: Cambridge University Press).

Kelly, Erin (2002), "Doing without Desert," *Pacific Philosophical Quarterly* 83: 180–205.

Knowles, Dudley (2002), *Hegel and the Philosophy of Right* (London: Routledge).

Lacey, Nicola (1988), *State Punishment* (London: Routledge).

Lewis, C. S. (1972), "The Humanitarian Theory of Punishment," in R. Gerber & P. McAnany, eds., *Contemporary Punishment: Views, Explanations, and Justifications* (South Bend: University of Notre Dame Press) (originally published 1954).

Mackenzie, M. M. (1981), *Plato on Punishment* (Berkeley: University of California Press).

Markel, Dan (2001), "Are Shaming Punishments Beautifully Retributive?," *Vanderbilt Law Review* 54: 2157–2242.

Matravers, Matt (2000), *Justice and Punishment* (Oxford: Oxford University Press).

McCloskey, H. J. (1957), "An Examination of Restricted Utilitarianism," *Philosophical Review* 66: 466–485.

———— (1962), "The Complexity of the Concepts of Punishment," *Philosophy* 37: 307–325.

———— (1965), "A Non-utilitarian Approach to Punishment," *Inquiry* 8: 249–263.

McDermott, Daniel (2001), "The Permissibility of Punishment," *Law & Philosophy* 20: 403–432.

McTaggart, J. M. E. (1896), "Hegel's Theory of Punishment," *International J. Ethics* 6: 479–502.

Montague, Phillip (1995), *Punishment and Societal-Defense* (Lanham, Md.: Rowman and Littlefield).

Moore, Michael (1987), "The Moral Worth of Retribution," in F. Schoeman, ed., *Responsibility, Character, and the Emotions* 179–219.

———— (1997), *Placing Blame* (Oxford: Oxford University Press).

Morris, Christopher (1991): "Punishment and Loss of Moral Standing," *Canadian J. Phil.* 21: 53–79.

Morris, Herbert (1976), *On Guilt and Innocence* (Berkeley: University of California Press).

———— (1981), "A Paternalistic Theory of Punishment," *American Philosophical Quarterly* 18: 263–271.

Murphy, Jeffrie (1970), *Kant: The Philosophy of Right* (New York: St. Martin's Press).

—— (1971), "Three Mistakes About Retributivism," *Analysis* 31: 166–169.

—— (1972), "Moral Death: A Kantian Essay on Psychopathy," *Ethics* 82: 284–298.

—— (1973), "Marxism and Retribution," *Philosophy & Public Affairs* 2: 217–243.

Murphy, Jeffrie, and Hampton, Jean (1988), *Forgiveness and Mercy* (Cambridge: Cambridge University Press).

Narayan, Uma (1993), "Appropriate Responses and Preventive Benefits: Justifying Censure and Hard Treatment in Legal Punishment," *Oxford J. Leg. Stud.* 13: 166.

Nielsen, Kai (1972), "Against Moral Conservatism," *Ethics* 82: 219–231.

Philips, Michael (1986), "The Justification of Punishment and the Justification of Political Authority," *Law and Philosophy* 5: 393–416.

Primoratz, Igor (1989), *Justifying Legal Punishment* (Atlantic Highlands, N. J.: Humanities Press International).

—— (1991), "Utilitarianism, Justice, and Punishment: Comments on Smart and Flew," *Israel Law Review* 25: 388–397.

Quinn, Warren (1985), "The Right to Threaten and the Right to Punish," *Phil. & Pub. Affairs* 14: 327–373.

Quinton, Anthony (1954), "On Punishment," *Analysis* 14: 133–143.

Rawls, John (1955), "Two Concepts of Rules," *Phil. Review* 64: 3–32.

Sadurski, Wojciech (1985), *Giving Desert Its Due* (Dordrecht: Reidel).

—— (1989), "Punishment, Social Justice, and Liberal Neutrality," *Law & Philosophy* 7: 351–373.

Samek, Robert (1966), "Punishment: A Postscript to Two Prologomena," *Philosophy* 41: 216–232.

Schedler, George (1980), "Can Retributivists Support Legal Punishment?," *Monist* 63: 51–64.

Scheid, Don (1980), "Note on Defining 'Punishment,'" *Canadian Journal of Philosophy* 10: 453–462.

—— (1983), "Kant's Retributivism," *Ethics* 93: 262–282.

—— (1995), "Davis, Unfair Advantage Theory, and Criminal Desert," *Law & Philosophy* 14: 395–409.

Shafer-Landau, Russ (1991), "Can Punishment Morally Educate?," *Law & Philosophy* 10: 189.

Sher, George (1987), *Desert* (Princeton: Princeton University Press).

Smart, J. J. C. and Williams, Bernard (1973), *Utilitarianism: For and Against* (Cambridge: Cambridge University Press).

—— (1991), "Utilitarianism and Punishment," *Israel Law Review* 25: 360–375.

Smilansky, Saul (1990), "Utilitarianism and the 'Punishment' of the Innocent: The General Problem," *Analysis* 50: 256–261.

Sprigge, T. L. S. (1965), "A Utilitarian Reply to Dr. McCloskey," *Inquiry* 8: 264–291.

Ten, C. L. (1987) *Crime, Guilt and Punishment* (Oxford: Oxford University Press).

Walker, Nigel (1999), "Even More Varieties of Retribution," *Philosophy* 74: 595–605.

Wasserstrom, Richard (1967), "H. L. A. Hart and the Doctrines of *Mens Rea* and Criminal Responsibility," *Univ. of Chicago Law Review* 35: 92–126.

—— (1977), "Some Problems with Theories of Punishment," in J. B. Cederblom and William L. Blizek, eds., *Justice and Punishment* (Cambridge, Mass.: Ballinger).

—— (1982), "Capital Punishment as Punishment," *Midwest Studies in Philosophy* 7: 473–502.

Von Hirsch, Andrew (1993), *Censure and Sanctions* (Oxford: Oxford University Press).

Wood, Allen W. (2008), *Kantian Ethics* (Cambridge: Cambridge University Press).

Zaibert, Leo (2006), *Punishment and Retribution* (Aldershot, England: Ashgate).

....

CHAPTER 15

THE DEATH PENALTY
AND DEONTOLOGY

....

CAROL STEIKER

AT first glance, moral disagreement about the permissibility of capital punishment appears to have the same general contours as many other debates about the permissibility of killing or severely harming human beings, such as those regarding war, state-sanctioned torture, or euthanasia. In each of these debates, there are inevitably some absolutists who believe that the practice in question is always wrong, arrayed against those who believe that the practice is sometimes justified or even required. Moreover, the absolutists in these debates tend to support their categorical stances on deontological grounds—that is, on grounds that the practice in question is wrong as a matter of principle regardless of its potentially good consequences—while their opponents tend to argue for the conditional permissibility of the practice in question on consequentialist grounds. This rough sketch (deontological, categorical ban v. consequentialist, conditional permissibility) does not capture all the nuances of any particular debate, but the general shape of the central dispute is surely recognizable. At a very general level, this description captures the death penalty debate as well: a core of absolutists relies on the inherent wrongness of state killing, in contrast to proponents who urge that the beneficial social functions of capital punishment (usually deterrence of murder, but also incapacitation of the perpetrator and "closure" for the families of murder victims) justify its imposition, at least in some circumstances.

But the death penalty debate is unusual, perhaps even unique, by virtue of the fact that the only fully developed deontological account of the general practice of state punishment—retributivism—appears to require (or at least permit) the practice of capital punishment. Immanuel Kant, the progenitor of modern retributivism, certainly thought so. In Kant's view, a wrongdoer's voluntary choice to commit a crime justifies the infliction of a parallel evil in return; respect for the autonomy of the wrongdoer requires that "the undeserved evil which any one commits on another is to be regarded as perpetrated on himself."[1] Moreover, under Kant's strong view of the demands of retributivism, a society is not merely authorized to execute murderers, it is duty-bound to do so: "[W]hoever has committed Murder must *die*."[2] Kant used a vivid metaphor to illustrate how this duty exists independent of any benefit that a society might expect to reap from executing murderers: he argued that even a society on an island that was about to disband and scatter throughout the world (i.e., a society on the brink of extinction) would have a duty to execute "the last Murderer lying in the prison."[3]

There are many variations on Kant's strict version of the demands of retributivism, but most of these also appear to require or at least permit capital punishment. Some retributivists argue that it is not respect for the wrongdoer's autonomy, but rather respect for the equality of the victim that gives rise to the duty to punish. In this view, punishment is required to "annul" the wrong done to the victim[4] or to "restore[] the equilibrium of benefits and burdens" that the wrongdoer has upset by renouncing the burden of self-restraint that others have voluntarily assumed, thus gaining an unfair advantage.[5] Sometimes this equality-based version of retributivism takes on an expressive cast: punishment is required to undo the "demeaning message" of the low status of the victim promulgated by the crime.[6] All of these variations on Kantian retributivism, however, simply develop additional or alternative grounds for asserting a deontological duty to punish crime commensurate with wrongdoing. In light of such a duty, capital punishment appears to be a moral imperative of the penal law, absent some sufficient countervailing moral prohibition against the practice.

Some proponents of retributivism back away from its mandatory aspect and argue that wrongdoing provides merely "a license to punish the offender" rather than a duty to do so.[7] Under this view, sometimes called a "mixed" theory of punishment, a criminal sanction is justified not by virtue of its being deserved by a wrongdoer, but rather "by reference to the effects [it] is likely to have on the offender or on the fabric of law and morality in general."[8] This view rejects the Kantian notion of a duty to punish and the general retributive account of criminal punishment as an affirmative moral good in its own right. But it accepts that society is authorized to punish an offender up to the ceiling of retributive desert, should utilitarian benefits warrant such punishment. Thus, this softer version of retributivism permits, though it does not require, the infliction of capital punishment when it is deserved.

Consequently, those whose wish to assert the categorical, deontological wrongness of capital punishment have their work cut out for them, given that the leading deontological account of punishment appears to permit or require the practice. Some opponents of the death penalty ground their categorical opposition to the death penalty in their religious faith. While this approach is indeed a deontological, as opposed to consequentialist, rejection of capital punishment, religious abolitionists resort to a source of moral imperative that overcomes the retributive case for capital punishment solely by reference to a moral trump that is convincing only to other believers. Other (secular) death penalty opponents assert the categorical wrongness of executions regardless of their social consequences, but they need to offer a convincing account of the source of that wrongness. Rare indeed is the abolitionist who also opposes all possible uses of lethal force by state actors, whether in law enforcement or in war. If *some* state killing is justified, how to counter the claim that state killing is justified as proportionate, deserved punishment? Categorical opponents of capital punishment need to offer a moral grounding for their abolitionism that can overcome or refute the existing justification for the practice offered by the well-developed discourse of retributivism.

The deontological case against capital punishment is underdeveloped,[9] most likely because public debate about capital punishment tends to be dominated by consequentialist arguments. Many abolitionists, at least of the secular variety, tend to cede the issue of absolute morality and to argue instead that capital punishment is wrong *in practice* on the grounds of its cost, its disputed deterrent effect as well as its inverse potential for "brutalization," the inadequacy of legal procedures (especially the lack of adequate defense counsel), the proven likelihood of error, the persistent evidence of arbitrariness and discrimination in its application, or some combination of the above. This move to consequentialist terrain can leave the impression that the retributive case for capital punishment is unassailable and that there is little to be said regarding nonconsequentialist, categorical opposition to the death penalty. This essay will attempt to correct that misimpression by surveying, developing, and critically examining the leading deontological arguments *against* capital punishment.

Deontological arguments against capital punishment tend to fall roughly into two categories: (1) those that argue entirely within retributivism, asserting only that the requirements of retributivism are not met in the context of capital punishment, and (2) those that argue that some other moral value trumps the retributive case for capital punishment. The line between these categories can sometimes blur because, as we shall see, the moral values that are generally asserted as trumps—such as equality and dignity—are often essential to (or at the very least compatible with) retributivism itself. But the distinction between the two kinds of arguments is useful in that the second kind of argument, unlike the first, requires the development of a moral account of punishment beyond the well-trod terrain of retributivism.

Despite these differences, most deontological arguments of either sort against capital punishment begin in the same place, at the most obviously vulnerable point of the Kantian argument in favor of the death penalty for murderers—the lex talionis. Despite its appealing symmetry, simplicity, and biblical resonance, the lex talionis runs into some immediate and obvious difficulties. First of all, it is simply impossible, as Kant himself recognized, to punish some offenses by their exact likenesses (Kant gave the examples of pederasty and bestiality). Moreover, even when it might be technically possible to mirror an offense in its punishment, it is clearly morally repugnant to do so in the case of some offenses (Kant gave the example of rape, but one could surely add torture and mutilation). Thus, many have argued within the Kantian tradition that punishment must be proportional to the offense, but not necessarily an exact likeness of the offense.[10] This move opens up the dual questions of (1) whether execution is always or ever proportional punishment for murder, and (2) if so, whether death falls in the rape, torture, and mutilation camp of "morally repugnant" punishments, even if proportional. These two questions invite the two main types of anti–death penalty arguments described above, which will be addressed in turn.

I The Requirements of Retributivism

The central requirements of retributivism are that punishment be deserved and proportional to an offender's wrongdoing. Kant assumed that death is always a deserved and proportional punishment for the crime of murder. However, this assumption is vulnerable to attack both at the level of individual culpability and at the level of systemic distribution of death sentences.

A Social Conditions and Individual Desert

A quick tour of any modern death row or a casual perusal of the social histories of any group of death-sentenced inmates will immediately confirm the common-sense view that capital murderers are generally an extremely disadvantaged and damaged lot. They often have experienced multiple forms of societal deprivation (poverty, racism, poor education, inadequate nutrition, inadequate housing, inadequate health care, police violence, inadequate police protection from private violence, etc.), and they often suffer from unameliorated internal conditions that are thought to reduce their culpability for their criminal offenses (brain damage or other cognitive impairments, mental illness, drug or alcohol addiction, ongoing trauma from childhood abuse, etc.). While not every single capital murderer fits this description, surely the "typical" capital murderer does. What relevance does this portrait of the modal capital murderer have for the retributive case for the death penalty? There are at least three possible arguments that the endemic social and personal disadvantage of capital murderers undermines the retributive justice of executing them.

1. Reduced Culpability.

First, the deprivation and dysfunction suffered by most capital murderers undermine the claim that they fully "deserve" society's most serious punishment. If the wrongdoing for which an offender has been convicted is the predictable result of conditions unchosen by the offender, then the voluntariness on which desert is premised is called into question.[11] At its most extreme, the recognition that social deprivation and internal dysfunction are "criminogenic" in the sense that they "cause" crime can amount to a deterministic view of human action that requires a complete rejection of the retributive case for the practice of punishment at all. Clarence Darrow's plea for the lives of the infamous thrill killers Leopold and Loeb urged the sentencing judge to accept that "intelligent people now know that every human being is the product of the endless heredity back of him and the infinite environment around him."[12] But one needn't go so far as to reject the possibility of free will in order to recognize that circumstances can impinge on freedom in a way that diminishes, even though it does not eradicate, responsibility for wrongdoing. While death as punishment for murder might be proportionate in the abstract, if the punishment of death is routinely imposed on murderers whose circumstances have greatly impinged on their freedom of action, then perhaps the Kantian assumption of equivalence breaks down: "[T]he strongest argument for such disproportionality lies in the reduced culpability of most convicted capital offenders."[13]

A retributive supporter of capital punishment has recourse to a number of possible responses to this blanket argument of reduced culpability. First, whereas many or even most capital murderers may have suffered from societal or individual circumstances that suggest reduced culpability for their offenses, surely not every capital murderer has a similarly strong claim to limited voluntariness (unless one accepts some version of Darrow's determinism). Think of Adolf Hitler, Timothy McVeigh, or Osama bin Laden—it is implausible to suggest that the death penalty would be a disproportionate punishment for their crimes on the grounds of their reduced culpability. For an argument to count as a categorical or deontological objection to capital punishment, it must explain why the practice is always wrong as a matter of principle, not merely in some (or even many) applications. It is clear that retributivism requires that all circumstances that might reduce an offender's culpability be fully and fairly considered in mitigation of his offense, as the U.S. Supreme Court currently requires in capital cases.[14] Moreover, it surely follows from this requirement that individual death sentences produced by such a process may be criticized on retributive grounds for failing to give adequate weight to the offender's reduced culpability. But it is not immediately apparent how the accumulation of such criticisms offers grounds for a categorical (as opposed to a merely prudential) repudiation of capital punishment.[15]

A second and quite different sort of response to the abolitionist argument from reduced culpability might suggest that for many capital offenders, the death penalty as it is currently imposed should already be viewed as a kind of "discount" off of proportional punishment. After all, mass murderers, or murderers who rape or torture their victims, or murderers whose victims linger in pain before dying receive the punishment of only a single and relatively quick and painless death. Today we generally do not, for reasons that will be explored below,[16] try to modulate the sentence of death by adding gruesome tortures in cases of more grievous murders, as some earlier societies did.[17] Consequently, one might rebut the reduced culpability argument by suggesting that most murderers are already receiving a reduced penalty from what either the lex talionis would impose or what might seem "proportional" in some more abstract way to the heinousness of their offenses. One possible response to this rebuttal is an argument that death sentences have their own distinctive cruelty, especially in the United States, where inmates often spend years or even decades living under the threat of execution without any certainty about when or whether it will be carried out.[18] On the other hand, however, much of the delay between death sentence and execution is welcomed or even affirmatively sought by death row inmates and their lawyers as a means to gain strategic legal advantage or simply to prolong life. Hence, it becomes difficult to know whether to consider lengthy delay as a harm or a benefit to any particular death row inmate. But even if lengthy delay of execution is counted as a serious harm to death row inmates, the recognition that death (even delayed death) is not, in fact, the worst punishment that can be (or has ever been) imposed complicates any claim that murderers' reduced culpability automatically renders death a "disproportionate" punishment for their murders, no matter how numerous or heinous.

2. *Shared Societal Responsibility.*

The prevalence of extreme societal deprivation among capital murderers might be thought to reduce their culpability in a different way—comparatively, rather than absolutely. A society that generates deprived capital murderers both tolerates and benefits from the profound social inequality that drives the deprivation. Jeffrey Reiman develops this argument as follows: "[W]hen crimes are predictable responses to unjust circumstances, then those who benefit from and do not remedy those conditions bear some responsibility for the crimes and thus the criminals cannot be held *wholly* responsible for them in the sense of being legitimately required to pay their full cost."[19] He explains, "In arguing that social injustice disqualifies us from applying the death penalty, I am arguing that unjust discrimination in the *recruitment* of murderers undermines the justice of applying the penalty under foreseeable conditions in the United States."[20] The moral conflict created by the disjuncture between collective responsibility for criminogenic conditions and the imposition of individual criminal responsibility is perfectly captured by a *New Yorker* cartoon that depicts a jury foreperson delivering the verdict "We find that all of us, as a society, are to blame, but only the defendant is guilty."[21]

Reiman's argument resonates with some familiar moral and legal principles of compensatory justice. When more than one agent is causally responsible for a single cognizable harm to a victim, all of the responsible agents may share in the obligation to compensate the victim—but generally *in proportion* to their roles in bringing about the harm.[22] The law of comparative negligence recognizes that joint tortfeasors, though they may bear responsibility individually to fully compensate the victim, nonetheless have a right of contribution from each other for the others' fair share of liability.[23] Similarly, when victims are found to have negligently contributed to the harms inflicted by a tortfeasor, the tortfeasor's liability is reduced by the amount of the victim's contributory negligence.[24] Reiman's argument appears to appeal, at least implicitly, to these principles in questioning the justice of holding murderers fully responsible for their offenses. Under Reiman's view, either society is jointly liable with the murderer for the murder victim's harm or society *is* the victim of the crime but is contributorily negligent in bringing about the harm it suffers through murder. Either way, society should bear its fair share of responsibility for the crime, which would necessarily diminish the murderer's share.

Reiman's implicit appeal to these principles of compensatory justice, however, can be countered both with other, competing aspects of compensatory justice and with conflicting moral and legal principles of retributive justice. Within compensatory justice, the foundational doctrines of duty and proximate cause often work to completely absolve "remote" wrongdoers who set the stage for subsequent intentional wrongdoing.[25] Thus, Reiman's reliance on the intuition from general principles of compensatory justice that liability for harm should be shared among all responsible actors is undercut by the fact that more specific doctrines of compensatory justice often limit or cut off entirely the liability of remote and less culpable actors in favor of full responsibility for immediate and more culpable actors. Moreover and even more powerfully, retributive justice rejects the basic intuition that the multiplicity of agents responsible for a harm affects the degree of their responsibility. A criminal wrongdoer is generally not absolved, even partially, of wrongdoing simply by dint of the involvement of others in the same crime.[26] Rather, well-established principles of accomplice liability hold that each accomplice should receive the full penalty for the harm caused, even if the actions of others were necessary for the harm to occur. The degree of each wrongdoer's criminal liability in the context of joint wrongdoing tends to track the wrongdoer's culpability (mens rea) rather than the wrongdoer's "share" of causation. Criminal law, in contrast to tort law, recognizes that multiple actors can each be 100 percent responsible for wrongful harms, and that full punishment of one does not in any way reduce the justification for punishing the others.

In partial exception to this principle, older Anglo-American common law and some of current European civil law allows the liability of accomplices to be modulated according to the particular role each played in the offense. But this modulation is premised on the idea that the lesser role played by some participants suggests their lesser culpability for the crime, not on the notion that the greater liability of the principal actor somehow diminishes an accomplice's "share" of liability. Moreover, the most common way of apportioning joint criminal liability gives full responsibility to the "principal"—"the actor or absolute perpetrator of the crime."[27] Thus, even the minor extent to which the criminal law might be seen as modulating responsibility in a joint context would not undermine the full responsibility of a murderer for a murder he directly committed, whatever social forces might be in play in the background. Even accepting Reiman's judgment that unjust societies are to some extent responsible (morally, if not legally) for the crimes of their disadvantaged members, Reiman does not explain why it inevitably follows that disadvantaged murderers are less than fully responsible themselves for their murders.

One might think that the best account of why society's responsibility for social injustice undermines the full responsibility of murderers for their crimes lies in the causal connection between social injustice and crime. The criminal law *does* accept this kind of reason for modulating the extent of criminal liability. Perhaps the most analogous context is the partial defense of provocation: the Anglo-American common law modulates responsibility for murder when the murder victim is responsible for "provoking" the perpetrator and causing the perpetrator to act with less than full voluntariness.[28] Reiman's claim that social inequality leads to "unjust discrimination in the *recruitment* of murderers" seems to invoke some similar causal claim that the social deprivation of most murderers undermines the voluntariness of their criminal acts. But Reiman seems to want to distance himself from such an idea ("My argument does not claim that criminals, murderers in particular, cannot control their actions.").[29] Moreover and more to the point, the claim that societal deprivation causes murderers to kill is a claim about their absolute, rather than comparative, responsibility for their crimes and thus dissolves into the first argument about the "reduced culpability" of capital murderers discussed and challenged above in the preceding subsection.[30]

3. *Failure of Reciprocity.*

A final way the existence of societal deprivation might be thought to undermine the retributive justice of executing deprived murderers is an argument that society has failed to carry out its end of the "social contract" that creates obligations for citizens and thus lacks the moral right to punish citizens for violating the law. Jeffrie Murphy has developed this argument as follows:

> The retributive theory really presupposes what might be called a "gentlemen's club picture" of the relation between man and society—i.e., men are viewed as being part of a community of shared values and rules. The rules benefit all concerned and, as a kind of debt for the benefits derived, each man owes obedience to the rules. In the absence of such obedience, he deserves punishment in the sense that he owes payment for the benefits.... But to think that [this] applies to the typical criminal, from the poorer classes, is to live in a world of social and political fantasy.... If justice, as both Kant and Rawls suggest, is based on reciprocity, it is hard to see what these people are supposed to reciprocate for.[31]

Murphy's argument could be contested directly on his proposed terrain of reciprocity. While it is uncontestable that many societies (and the United States in particular) tolerate a high level of social and economic inequality, it is surely debatable whether these inequalities amount to such a complete breakdown of the social contract that the most deprived members of society have no obligation to obey the law. After all, even the most disadvantaged do receive *some* benefits from society in terms of roads and public utilities, regulation of air and water quality and the food supply, welfare and disability entitlements, housing, schooling, medical care, policing, and military defense, among other things, even if the relatively more advantaged receive disproportionate benefits. Egalitarians may agree with John Rawls that societies have an obligation to pursue and achieve distributive justice,[32] but it does not necessarily follow that a failure to do so automatically renders illegitimate criminal punishment of the disadvantaged. Indeed, one scholar has argued that application of Rawlsian principles would demonstrate that criminal punishment is indeed legitimate, even in an only "partially compliant" society in which "background con-ditions" are unjust.[33] Moreover, one might that think that capital murder would be the very *last* criminal prohibition whose enforcement would be rendered illegiti-mate by inequality, given that (1) socially disadvantaged murderers disproportion-ately murder socially disadvantaged victims, and (2) such murders, unlike, say, drug dealing, are rarely committed in direct pursuit of improving the perpetrator's dis-advantaged status.

However, even accepting Murphy's account of the way inequality undermines retributive justice, for our purposes the account crucially fails to distinguish the special wrongness of capital punishment. Murphy was not addressing the justice of any particular form of punishment; he was addressing the legitimacy of criminal punishment altogether. Hence, the sweep of his conclusion:

> [W]e may really be forced seriously to consider a radical proposal. If we think that institutions of punishment are necessary and desirable, and if we are morally sensitive enough to want to be sure that we have the moral right to punish before we inflict it, then we had better first make sure that we have restructured society in such a way that criminals genuinely do correspond to the only model that will render punishment permissible—i.e., make sure that they are autonomous and that they do benefit in the requisite sense.[34]

This argument explains why social inequality might render *all* criminal punishment illegitimate but does not offer any grounds for distinguishing the punishment of death from any other sort of punishment.

B Procedural Failings and Systemic Desert

Any argument premised on social deprivation as grounds for challenging the retrib-utive justice of capital punishment—including all three versions examined above—runs into the very first objection noted with respect to the "reduced culpability" claim: not *every* capital murderer is the victim of social deprivation, and thus argu-ments from deprivation do not appear to be categorical or deontological arguments for the *intrinsic* wrongness of capital punishment. Rather, they appear to be contin-gent claims that our processes for imposing the death penalty fail to eliminate a class (perhaps a very large one) of murderers who do not deserve the ultimate pen-alty. Arguments that capital punishment is applied in an arbitrary or even racially discriminatory manner, as well as arguments about the unacceptable likelihood of executing innocent people, are of the same general cast: they appear to be objec-tions to capital punishment *in practice* rather than as a matter of absolute morality. This characterization of such arguments is reinforced by the fact that claims about arbitrariness, discrimination, and error are often elaborated in public discourse from an identifiably consequentialist perspective. For example, one frequently hears arguments that arbitrariness in the application of the death penalty undermines its deterrent effect, that racial discrimination contributes to the further marginaliza-tion of already disadvantaged groups and undermines the perceived legitimacy of the criminal law, and that errors allow the real murderers to go free while imposing huge costs on entirely innocent people and their families.

Can arguments from such systemic failures fairly be viewed as categorical objections to capital punishment? The U.S. Supreme Court apparently thought so, in ruling that the arbitrary and capricious application of the penalty prior to 1972 rendered the punishment "cruel and unusual" under the Eighth Amendment and abolishing the practice in its ruling in the landmark case *Furman v. Georgia*.[35] Although the claim that arbitrary application of the death penalty renders it unconstitutional sounds like a claim about inadequate *procedures*, the Court had rejected that claim when it was brought under the seemingly more appropriate due process clause.[36] By accepting the claim under the *substantive* prohibition of the cruel and unusual punishments clause, the Court appeared to equate the claim of systemic breakdown with a claim about the *nature* of the punishment of death. It is hard to say exactly what the Court meant by its holding in *Furman*, given that the five justices in the majority all authored separate opinions and that the Court soon constitutionally reinstated capital punishment by upholding several new state statutory schemes for imposing the death penalty.[37] But Murphy has offered a defense of the *Furman* Court's recourse to the substantive language of the Eighth Amendment by developing a deontological argument against a *system* of imposing capital punishment that is arbitrary and capricious—that is, that runs an unacceptable risk of executing both those who are "totally innocent of any wrongdoing and those whose conduct, though meriting conviction of something (e.g. manslaughter), does not merit conviction of an offense of supreme gravity (e.g. murder in the first degree)."[38] Murphy recognizes that *all* criminal punishment is imposed through processes that are arbitrary and capricious to a similar extent and that it would be absurd to reject entirely any possibility of criminal punishment. Thus, he takes as his task the development of an argument that the death penalty is qualitatively different from all other punishments and that arbitrariness in the system of imposing such a penalty amounts to a categorical wrong to all capital defendants.

In Murphy's view, the distinctiveness of capital punishment arises from two features: "Death is a greater harm than loss of liberty because it is (a) totally *incompensable* and (b) represents *lost opportunity* of a morally crucial kind."[39] As for incompensability, Murphy notes that it is "both logically and empirically impossible"[40] to compensate someone who has been executed in error. Moreover, Murphy argues, the fact that contract law forbids people to bargain away their lives, while it allows them to bargain away a large part of their personal liberty (for example, by joining a volunteer army), demonstrates society's recognition of the special incompensability of death. As for lost opportunity, Murphy proposes that "the most important thing within a human life…is the *development of one's own moral character*."[41] To cut off any possibility of this development is to impose a penalty of "exceptional moral gravity."[42] In light of the substantive gravity of the death penalty, concludes Murphy, the government acts with insufficient respect for citizens as people with rights if it maintains a legal system that threatens such a serious interference with basic interests "in a casual and irresponsible way."[43] Of course, this objection could be met by repairing the irresponsible system, but if this is not done or is not possible to do, the rejection of capital punishment should count as a deontological one, in Murphy's view—that is, one derived from rights that individuals bear as a matter of principle, prior to and regardless of the social utility of such rights.[44]

Murphy's argument from the risks of arbitrariness, bias, and error faces challenges from his fellow retributivists. According to them, and to Kant himself, the "respect for persons" on which Murphy seeks to ground his argument requires death as a punishment for murderers as a consequence of respect for their rational autonomy, and the retributive justice of such executions is not erased or overshadowed by the unavoidable costs imposed by the inevitability of mistakes. On the question of arbitrariness and bias, many have argued that the overinclusion of poor and minority defendants in capital cases should be remedied by the greater inclusion of rich and powerful defendants, rather than by invalidating the sentences of the unlucky but deserving denizens of death row. For example, Louis Pojman proposed "broadening, not narrowing, the scope of capital punishment" to include businessmen the likes of Kenneth Lay and Bernard Madoff, who caused such serious harm to so many people, as a way of promoting equality in the application of the death penalty.[45] Randall Kennedy has argued that those who call for abolition of capital punishment on the basis of its racially discriminatory application do so only because they reject the justice of capital punishment to begin with; if they accepted that capital punishment was a public good (as retributivists do), then they would call (as Pojman does) for its broader application, not its abolition: "From the perspective of a proponent of capital punishment, abolition as a remedy for race-of-the-victim disparities is equivalent to reducing to darkness a town in which street lights have been provided on a racially unequal basis; the norm of equality is enforced but at the cost of a reduction in services to all."[46] The most pithy expression of the retributivist position in favor of the death penalty despite its unequal application is Ernest van den Haag's: "[U] nequal justice is the only justice we have, and certainly better than equal injustice—giving no murderer the punishment his crime deserves."[47]

These rebuttals all assume that the death sentences produced by an arbitrary and discriminatory legal process are, for the most part (the question of innocence will be addressed below) retributively sound—that is, deserved and proportional to the wrongdoing of those who received them. But as Stephen Nathanson has noted, van den Haag's appeal to the "justice" of death sentences despite their arbitrary distribution "fail[s] to distinguish (a) the claim that judgments concerning *who deserves to die* are arbitrarily made, from (b) the claim that judgments concerning *who among the deserving shall be executed* are arbitrarily made."[48] Nathanson cites the seminal book of Charles Black, who was the first to elaborate in detail the insuperable obstacles to developing a capital justice process free from the risks of arbitrariness, discrimination, and error from which Murphy's deontological argument proceeds.[49] If, as Black claims, it is impossible for a legislature to give adequately constraining guidance in advance on the question of who deserves to live and die, then local prosecutors and sentencing judges and juries will inevitably be guided by their diverse values and sympathies, and the reliability of capital verdicts ensured only by the variable safeguards afforded by local law enforcement techniques. Under such circumstances, permitting capital punishment to continue is choosing a system that regularly and unavoidably will impose death on those who do not "deserve" it—not merely on the occasional wholly innocent defendant, but routinely in selecting the defendant, who though guilty of some form of homicide, is not properly eligible, in retributive terms, for the penalty of death.[50]

The problem of the risk of executing the "wholly" innocent is often treated as a problem separate from and more serious than the general arbitrariness of the capital justice process. As a matter of classification, it appears that Black got it right in describing "caprice" and "mistake" as a unitary problem: "capriciousness" in designating who deserves death represents a moral error of exactly the same kind (though not the same degree) as complete "mistake" about who committed the underlying crime. In each case, retributive justice is not done, because the defendant is punished in excess of what he or she deserves. But accepting that "mistakes" involving the execution of wholly innocent people are more extreme and provoke a special kind of horror, opponents of capital punishment like Murphy, Nathanson, and Black must determine how high a risk of such mistakes a system can justly tolerate. Or, lumping in the problem of "capriciousness" as I want to do, they must explain how high a risk of "capriciousness" a system can justly tolerate. For we can all surely identify *some* death sentences—those imposed on Timothy McVeigh, John Wayne Gacy, and Ted Bundy, to name a few—that don't seem to pose any problem at all of capriciousness or mistake. It seems extreme to insist that the possibility of *any* caprice or mistake at all automatically dooms the death penalty. After all, the legal process is a human process and is thus necessarily subject to error. And we risk the loss of innocent human life to error all the time—in medicine, air travel, bridge building, and war, to name just a few disparate social endeavors. Even if the horror of wrongful execution should set a higher standard of reliability for the death penalty than for ordinary criminal punishments, as Murphy maintains, it still remains to be specified just how high that standard is and whether our current system meets it or could be adjusted to meet it.

In short, both Murphy's deontological account of how arbitrariness fails to "respect" citizens and Nathanson's explanation of how arbitrariness creates a system that routinely fails to produce retributive justice need to address the question of the permissible quantum of capriciousness and mistake that their accounts elide (essentially by assuming that our current system fails any permissible quantum).

II OTHER MORAL VALUES AS TRUMPS

Murphy and Nathanson's abolitionist arguments from arbitrariness could be seen as entirely retributivist in nature (hence their placement in section I of this essay): Murphy's "respect for persons" is an injunction he derives from retributivism (and indeed, sees as a virtue of retributivism), and Nathanson's reliance on the concept of "desert" appears to be obviously retributive. Yet both arguments could also be viewed as appealing to some moral value outside of retributivism: Murphy's claim that citizens have a right to procedural due process (and to a kind of "super due process" for capital punishment)[51] might be seen to invoke a broader moral or political account of the relationship of citizen to state, and Nathanson's argument could be portrayed as grounded in a right to equal treatment rather than a right not to be punished more than one deserves. A retributivist could try to claim that procedural implications flow from retributivism (as Murphy does), or that equality of persons is a central commitment of retributivism (as Hegel did),[52] but there is clearly room for competing characterizations here.

This section will take up deontological challenges to capital punishment that seem a bit further from retributivism's core commitments to desert and proportionality (which dominated the arguments addressed in the preceding section). It is possible that one could cast these further arguments, too, in retributivist terms and argue that they demonstrate that capital punishment is wrong simply because it fails to meet the demands of retributive justice. But it is also possible and sometimes more plausible to see these arguments as asserting some good that competes with the moral good of retributivism rather than derives from it. That is, while it makes sense to say "It is unjust as a matter of retributive justice to impose capital punishment," it also makes sense to say "Even if the imposition of capital punishment satisfies retributive justice, there are other intrinsic moral goods that outweigh, or 'trump,' the good of pursuing retributive justice." It may seem odd to use the word "trump" here, as it often is used to indicate how matters of moral principle or right supersede consequentialist concerns. But moral principles can supersede or pose side constraints on one another. It is this kind of "trumping" that is at issue in the arguments that follow.

A Dignity

This essay started with the widely shared moral intuition that some punishments are "clearly morally repugnant" even when they do *not* exceed what offenders might be said to deserve as proportional to their wrongdoing.[53] We do not, after all, rape rapists or torture torturers. Why might this be so? Kant himself suggested a rationale for this forbearance in his rejection of rape as a punishment for rapists and his further insistence that the imposition of the death penalty on an offender "must be kept free from all maltreatment that would make the humanity suffering in his Person loathsome or abominable."[54] This injunction seems premised on a respect for what Kant calls "the humanity" of people or what many current moral theorists call human "dignity." Kant treats this principle as part and parcel of retributivism, derived from the same wellspring of respect for the distinctive capacities of human beings that requires their punishment for wrongdoing. But there is some obvious tension between requiring punishment commensurate with desert while at the same time forbidding "maltreatment" that degrades human dignity. Kant did not appear troubled by this potentially far-reaching contradiction, and he clearly found nothing wrong with the punishment of death for murder (or for that matter, of castration for rape!). However, other moral and legal theorists have attempted to elaborate Kant's defense of dignity so as to move the death penalty to the rape and torture side of the prohibitory line.

Murphy develops a very tentative and ambivalent case for opposing capital punishment on dignitary grounds. He acknowledges that some images of the imposition of the death penalty seem dehumanizing, but suggests that perhaps death is not inevitably or *intrinsically* brutal and dehumanizing, contrasting the harrowing description of the imposition of the death penalty in Truman Capote's *In Cold Blood* with the dignified, self-administered execution of Socrates depicted in Plato's *Phaedo*.[55] Thus, in Murphy's view, death is different from (not as degrading as) torture, because torture "is a process whose very point is to reduce [a person] to a terrified, defecating, urinating, screaming animal."[56] Nonetheless, Murphy's recognition that the punishment of death eradicates the executed offender's opportunity for any further moral development leads him to reconsider whether capital punishment can truly be squared with human dignity: "[I]t is by no mean's clear that one can show respect for the dignity of a person as a person if one is willing to interrupt and end his most uniquely human capacities and projects."[57] But Murphy's embrace of his own reasoning is only tentative ("there is perhaps a case to be made that the punishment of death is degrading after all");[58] he places primary emphasis on his argument from arbitrariness.[59]

Reiman takes up the human dignity banner in developing an account of why capital punishment is a "horrible thing," like torture, that civilized societies should forswear. He argues that executions share two features that render torture "especially awful"—"intense pain and the spectacle of one human being completely subject to the power of another."[60] Moreover, Reiman submits that knowledge of an impending execution provokes a particularly intense kind of psychological pain; he explains that a "humanly caused" and "foreseen" death lacks "the consolation of unavoidability" that accompanies death from natural causes and adds the "terrible consciousness of...impending loss."[61] Reiman thus concludes that forgoing the death penalty "is an advance in civilization" at least "as long as our lives are not thereby made more dangerous."[62] (That is, so long as there is no clear proof that the death penalty is "a better deterrent to the murder of innocent people than life in prison.")[63] Reiman's argument from dignity, while less ambivalent about the special awfulness of the death penalty than Murphy's, is more contingent in that it recognizes a consequentialist override of the dignitary case against capital punishment.

Justice William Brennan, alone among the justices who struck down capital punishment under the Eighth Amendment in *Furman*, developed an account of the constitutional prohibition on "cruel and unusual punishments" based on the concept of human dignity. He adduced four principles that would allow courts to determine whether a particular punishment violated the admittedly amorphous concept of dignity: (1) the degree to which a punishment is severe and degrading; (2) the probability that a punishment is inflicted arbitrarily; (3) the rejection of a punishment by contemporary society; and (4) the extent to which a punishment fails to serve penal purposes more effectively than a less severe punishment. Justice Brennan's approach is something of an amalgam of arguments that this essay is attempting to untangle, but his first principle addressing the extent to which a penalty is "severe or degrading" is the closest to what Murphy and Reiman seem to mean by affronts to "dignity." Justice Brennan argued that physical and mental pain was part of what rendered penalties "severe or degrading," but that it was not the only thing; rather, punishments such as the rack and the wheel were affronts to dignity because "they treat members of the human race as nonhumans, as objects to be toyed with and discarded. They are thus inconsistent with the fundamental premise of the [cruel and unusual punishments] Clause that even the vilest criminal remains a human being possessed of common human dignity."[64] Justice Brennan concluded that the death penalty was an affront to dignity because of the physical pain associated with execution,[65] the mental anguish experienced by those awaiting execution (often for prolonged periods),[66] and the complete and irrevocable foreclosing of any possibility of a future.[67] Thus, Brennan's position melds features of both Murphy's and Reiman's accounts. The irrevocable foreclosing of the future echoes Murphy's central concern, while the emphasis on psychological pain and the treatment of murderers as "nonhumans" echoes Reiman's concerns with the special anguish of the condemned and the complete subjugation enacted by execution.

Arguments about whether death (or any punishment) is unacceptably degrading to human dignity have an elusive quality. Violations of human dignity appear to be a matter of degree on a subtly shaded and multidimensional spectrum. Thus, the charge of "degradation" or "dehumanization" could be leveled, with some plausibility, at most punishments: incarceration is being caged like an animal; compelled community service is like slavery; registration and community notification of sex offenders is like ostracism and banishment, and so on. Whether one agrees with any particular claim seems to be as much a function of gut level response as of rational discernment. For example, one of the most chilling examples of "dehumanization" in punishment that I have witnessed was as a young public defender on a tour of the local jail. A deputy warden conducting the tour was explaining to us how the inmates wore indestructible identification bracelets to permit quick and accurate counts of the jail population. As he spoke, our group passed an inmate mopping the floor, and the warden casually and without prelude lifted the man's wrist for our inspection. The inmate stood stock still, eyes averted, until the warden finished his demonstration. The warden then, still without a word to the inmate, dropped the inmate's arm and motioned us on our way. The warden was not *trying* to humiliate the inmate, but the warden's assumption of unchallenged access to and control over the inmate's body was viscerally disturbing, in much the same way that Reiman found the complete subjugation involved in execution horrifying. Similarly, Murphy cites studies suggesting that long-term incarceration is "a kind of slow torture and psychic mutilation" that amounts to "a kind of death (of personhood)," concluding that if such studies are correct, then such punishments "*should* no doubt be banned on Eighth Amendment grounds."[68]

But therein lies the rub: if incarceration (or at least long-term incarceration) is *also* degrading (along with the death penalty), then we may find ourselves without sufficiently serious punishments to impose in response to the most serious offenses. Imagine a court sentencing Adolph Hitler to eight to twelve years in prison, with time off for good behavior—surely, one would have to take seriously objections that such a punishment was simply an inadequate response to Hitler's crimes. Kantian retributivism would hold that such a disproportionately lenient sentence fails to respect the rational autonomy (and thus the humanity) of Hitler himself, while more equality-based versions of retributivism would hold that such a sentence fails to respect the equality (and thus the humanity) of Hitler's millions of victims.

In short, reliance on dignity as a moral principle that constrains the duty to punish according to retributive desert runs into difficult line-drawing problems, at least in the context of capital punishment. Proponents of such arguments need to show *both* how the death penalty is sufficiently like rape and torture *and* how it is sufficiently unlike long-term incarceration (or some other punishment sufficiently severe to constitute an adequate response to the most heinous murders). Failure to do the former fails to make out a dignity claim at all, and failure to do the latter runs into competing dignity claims from within retributivism.

B Civilization

Reiman's depiction of the death penalty as a "horrible thing" to inflict on offenders fits well within the category of dignitary arguments against capital punishment. But Reiman also invokes a different sort of argument: "Torture is to be avoided not only because of what it says about *what* we are willing to do to our fellows, but also because of what it says about *us*."[69] In Reiman's view, torture "demonstrates a kind of hard-heartedness that a society ought not parade."[70] Rejection of such official demonstrations of hard-heartedness "continues the taming of the human species that we call civilization" and thus rejection of torture (and by analogy rejection of the death penalty) "is part of the civilizing mission of modern states."[71] Reiman invokes Emile Durkheim to make the link between penal policy and social progress, citing Durkheim's "first law of penal evolution," which takes the amount of penal force a society uses against its own people as "an inverse measure of its justness."[72]

Reiman's appeal to the "civilizing mission of modern states" owes a debt to sociologist Norbert Elias's influential two-volume work "The Civilizing Process."[73] In the first volume, Elias traces the development of Western sensibilities from the Middle Ages to the modern period, describing the slow transformation of attitudes regarding a wide range of social behaviors, such as interpersonal violence, sexual behavior, bodily functions, table manners, and social etiquette. Elias identifies a commonality in these diverse changes that he deems "the civilizing process"—"a tightening and a differentiation of the controls imposed by society upon individuals, a refinement of conduct, and an increased level of psychological inhibition as the standards of proper conduct became ever more demanding."[74] In the second volume, Elias shows how these changes were engendered by (and in turn enabled) the expansion of social interdependence, first in court society and then in bourgeois market society.

Although Elias (in contrast to Durkheim) pays scant attention to penal practices, sociologist David Garland has built on Elias's work to explore changes in punishment practices and understandings, arguing that the history of punishment conforms closely "to the general developmental pattern which Elias identifies."[75] Garland describes the decline in public displays of the suffering of convicts and of the condemned: "the sight of this spectacle becomes redefined as distasteful, particularly among the social elite, and executions are gradually removed 'behind the scenes'—usually behind the walls of prisons."[76] Moreover, "the idea of doing violence to offenders becomes repugnant in itself, and corporal and capital punishments are largely abolished, to be replaced by other sanctions such as imprisonment."[77] Garland cites the work of Pieter Spierenburg, who offered an essentially Eliasian account of the change in corporal and capital punishment practices in the Netherlands from the early seventeenth century onward: "as the sense of repugnance or embarrassment at the sight of violence developed among the ruling groups, they gradually brought about the privatization of punishment and a reduction in the display of suffering."[78] Carolyn Strange offers an important nuance to this account in her study of the debates in Canada in the mid-twentieth century about the permissibility of corporal and especially capital punishment.[79] Strange notes that the changes in sensibility that Elias identified do not easily or inevitably lead to changes in penal policy such as the abolition of capital punishment; rather, "refined sensibilities about pain and suffering could coexist, albeit uneasily, with rationales for the retention of state punishment"[80] because both opponents and supporters of bodily punishment could frame their arguments with claims of "civilizing objectives: to instill respect for law; to instruct others on costs of violating law; to hurt as little as possible; to ensure fair and equal justice."[81]

One obvious problem with relying on Elias's account of the civilizing process for developing a moral argument against the death penalty is the fact that Elias's work is fundamentally sociological rather than normative. Elias's careful description of centuries of changing social sensibilities and their likely causes and effects cannot be rendered normative without the imposition of some external normative framework. David Garland offers the beginning of such a framework by observing that Elias's description of the effect of changing sensibilities or "culture" on social practices has an important corollary: social practices—in particular, *punishment practices*—undoubtedly affect sensibilities or culture as well. "It is a two-way process.... Penal institutions are thus 'cause' as well as 'effect' with regard to culture."[82] While Garland's project, like that of Elias, remains essentially sociological rather than normative, his recognition that penal institutions are not mere cultural artifacts, but rather dynamic forces in the creation of culture, offers a perspective from which one can critically assess them.

This kind of critical assessment of the meaning and influence of penal institutions is evident within the historical accounts that Garland, Spierenburg, and Strange offer. For example, Strange describes at length the concerns voiced by

Canadian reformers about the brutalizing effect of corporal and capital punishment "on those who administered and observed the infliction of pain and death,"[83] the unsavory responses of "[u]nruly crowds—uncivilized witnesses who scandalously derived pleasure from death,"[84] and the "decivilizing effects" of executions on other prisoners.[85] As legal scholar Scott Altman explains in an analogous context, social practices may alter the sensibilities not only of people whom they directly affect but also of people who observe them practiced as part of their society.[86] These altered sensibilities may be salutary or they may be lamentable; Altman labels arguments about the desirability or undesirability of altering social practices that are based on projected changes in participants' and observers' changed sensibilities "modified-experience" arguments.[87] Thus, a normative argument emerges from Eliasian observations about the civilizing process: the practice of the death penalty will have the effect of brutalizing not only the people most directly involved in it (the prison guards and executioners, the prisoners, and the immediate observers) but also all the rest of the members of a society that engages in the practice.

Indeed, there is perhaps special reason to worry about the "modified experience" effects of punishment practices (as compared to other kinds of social practices, such as the medical technologies Altman addresses). Most obviously, criminal punishment is officially performed in the name of the public and thus directly calls on "the people" to feel implicated in its imposition. Moreover, the formal procedures surrounding charging, conviction, and imposition of sentence constitute a self-consciously solemn morality play that enacts with high drama rituals of blame and shame. Think of the common practice of holding "perp walks" whereby charged defendants are paraded before the press, the formal rituals of the trial process, and the demand that a convicted defendant stand up and face the court for the imposition of sentence. These rituals engender—and indeed are meant to engender—a sense of public satisfaction in the punishment of convicted criminals, a mood of congratulation and even celebration as "justice is done." These emotions are so common and so emotionally resonant that crime and courtroom dramas continue to proliferate in films and on television. When these emotions are tied to extremely brutal forms of punishment—such as the torturous punishments of old or, as Reiman would argue, today's death penalty—they require the public to suppress their "civilized" responses of unease and revulsion in the face of overt brutality and pain and replace them with the feelings of satisfaction and celebration that the rituals of criminal justice are designed to elicit. This is the "modified experience" that concerns critics who oppose the death penalty on grounds of "civilization" or "brutalization."

This argument against the death penalty runs into two quite different types of objections. First, the argument from civilization has an essential empirical component—a claim about the nature of the effects of executions on the sensibilities of people who live in a society that carries them out. But, as Strange noted in the Canadian experience, the meaning and effects of executions are highly contested. Instead of seeing a "brutalizing" or "decivilizing" ritual, supporters of capital punishment see in the execution of heinous murderers the public expression of the terrible wrongness of murder, of deep compassion for innocent murder victims and their families, and ultimately of the great sanctity of human life. Thus, the abolitionist claim that capital punishment brutalizes the society that practices it needs something more than mere assertion.

Empirical studies, however, have not yet offered and are unlikely to be able to offer a resolution of this dispute about the effects of a regime of capital punishment. One empirical researcher who studied the deterrent effects of the death penalty in the United States in recent decades found that when the data from different jurisdictions were aggregated, a strong deterrent effect was found.[88] But when the same data were disaggregated by state, only six of the twenty-seven states exhibited a deterrent effect, while thirteen states exhibited a "brutalization" effect (that is, a rise in the execution rate correlated with an *increase* in the homicide rate).[89] Joanna Shepherd, the researcher on both studies, sought to explain the disparate results by hypothesizing that capital punishment deters only when executions rise above a substantial numerical threshold; below such a threshold, it may have the "brutalization" effect its detractors fear.[90] However, so few states in the United States execute large numbers of inmates that the data for a robust comparison between vigorously executing states and others simply do not exist. More fundamentally, even if the data did exist and it became absolutely clear that large numbers of executions could substantially reduce the murder rate, there would still be debate about which was more "brutalizing" to society: the large number of executions or the increased homicidal violence society would endure without them.

The second objection to arguments from "civilization" or "brutalization" is more fundamental, as it rejects such claims as claims of principle. Arguments about whether capital punishment brutalizes or deters are simply arguments about whether, all things considered, the benefits the practice offers outweigh the costs it entails. This is not a deontological argument at all; it is an argument within consequentialism about what, precisely, the consequences of capital punishment are for a society that adopts it. Even if the argument takes the form that "at any time, in any circumstance, for any crime, the bad consequences of the practice will always outweigh the good," the argument still remains one about consequences and not about moral principle. Indeed, Reiman seems to concede as much about his own argument from civilization, through his concession that his argument is contingent on the lack of a proven marginal deterrent effect of capital punishment.[91]

C Brutalization and Moral Agency

I want to explore a way to cast the argument from civilization as an argument from moral principle rather than as an argument about the desirable (or pernicious) consequences that might flow from abolishing the death penalty. Accepting the argument from civilization's descriptive premise that the maintenance of a highly visible and salient practice like capital punishment will affect people's sensibilities over time, one must ask whether the sensibilities that are affected and the way they are affected have any special moral salience. If they do, then there is an argument that certain moral sensibilities must be protected and fostered as a matter of protecting human moral agency. This may sound like an appeal to virtue ethics rather than a deontological argument (that is, a concern with character rather a concern with moral rules or principles), but it is not. The argument I seek to develop is not concerned with certain sensibilities as goods in themselves, but rather as preconditions for the moral agency that deontological accounts of human nature presume.

As explored above, proponents of the argument from civilization worry that the ability to inure ourselves to the suffering inflicted by execution and, indeed, to celebrate such suffering as just, will over time erode human capacities such as empathy and compassion. Theorists of human nature from Aristotle to Rousseau have recognized that human capacities are not constants, unaffected by the nature of social organization and communal practices. The modern sociologists whose work was sketched above take their task to be the exploration and unraveling of the complex interaction among society, culture, sensibility, and capacity. These works recognize that claims about human nature, or "what people are like," or "what is fair to expect from people" vary widely over time and place. These claims vary not just because people think about themselves differently in different times and places, but because they actually *are* different in different times and places. This is the essential descriptive premise of the sociology from which the claim from civilization derives.

Deontological theories of right cannot distance themselves as completely as they might like from the shifting sands of sociology. While deontological theories of justice generate rules that exist prior to and independent of their consequences in the world, such theories depend (either explicitly or implicitly) on some conception of human nature. Kant's categorical imperative depends on the human attribute of rational autonomy: people must have the capacities both to *reason* about the consequences of universalizing their actions and to *choose* to act, thus willing their voluntary actions as universal law. But the exercise of rationality embodied in the Golden Rule–like categorical imperative requires not merely a Mr. Spock–like logic chopping but also an ability to imagine the effects of one's actions on people entirely different from oneself.[92] For example, to recognize the degree of moral wrongness of racial discrimination requires the ability of a member of the majority race to imaginatively enter into the experience of a member of an oppressed minority group. The "universalizing" thought experiment required by the categorical imperative (or the imagining of different possible positions in society from behind the Rawlsian "veil of ignorance") becomes impossible in a diverse society without assuming some capacity for empathy as well as a capacity for reason. If the capacity to imaginatively enter into the consciousness of others is truly blunted or diminished, then the preconditions for moral choice are eradicated. Thus, deontologists as well as consequentialists should heed the argument from civilization.

But, as discussed above, we cannot be certain that the argument from civilization is in fact empirically correct. We might worry that we will damage crucial moral sensibilities through the maintenance of practices like capital punishment, but it is very hard to prove that such damage is actually occurring or will ever occur. Why then should we ban a practice that we might believe reduces the murder rate, or makes victims' families feel better, or simply is the clear preference of political majorities? There are two related answers to this question. The first is to analogize the moral case for the protection of qualities essential to moral agency to the democratic case for the protection of rights essential for democratic self-governance. We give specially protected status to rights such as free speech and political equality, for example, in order to ensure that the preconditions for democratic self-governance continue to exist. If moral self-governance is analogized to political self-governance, then human capacities that are essential preconditions for moral agency need the same strong protection accorded to bedrock political rights. That is, even a possible threat to their continued existence needs to be taken very seriously. Another way to think about the need for this special protection and what it might entail is through the concept of the "precautionary principle," which holds in its strongest version that if an action or policy might cause severe or irreversible harm to the public or to the environment, in the absence of a scientific consensus that harm would not ensue, the burden of proof falls on those who would advocate taking the action.[93] This principle need not be embraced in its strongest form for its thrust to be helpful here: the greater and more irreversible the potential harm from an action or policy, the higher the burden on the proponents of such an action, in the face of substantial uncertainty about its effects.

This argument from moral agency offers a way to view the argument from civilization as an argument grounded in moral principle, rather than as one defined solely in consequentialist terms. However, the power of the argument from moral agency is directly linked to the power of the case for believing that the empirical foundation of the argument from civilization in fact exists. Moreover, the argument from moral agency depends on a further claim, partly moral and partly political, that more than a rudimentary capacity for empathy is necessary for moral agency— that is, that the damage done by the "decivilizing" or "brutalizing" effects of capital punishment is substantial enough to erode true moral agency. Such a conclusion may need to be based on a kind of "faith" about the nature of human moral agency not entirely different from the religious "faith" that animates much opposition to the death penalty.

CONCLUSION

The foregoing is meant to be a survey of the landscape of deontological or categorical objections to the practice of capital punishment. Though not by any means exhaustive, this sketch of the various possible approaches fills the vacuum left by the frequent ceding of the moral field by nonreligious opponents of capital punishment. I have sought to complicate and question rather than to champion any particular approach. The foregoing analysis both highlights the complicated relationship between arguments that might at first blush appear to be consequentialist and arguments from moral principle and suggests avenues for further research, discussion, and debate.

I thank Glenn Cohen, David Dolinko, John Goldberg, and Jeffrie Murphy for very helpful comments on an earlier draft.

NOTES

1. Immanuel Kant, *The Philosophy of Law* (W. Hastie tr., 1887, Edinburgh: T & T Clark), at p. 196 (comma omitted).

2. *Id.* at p. 198 (comma omitted).

3. *Id.*

4. G. W. F. Hegel, *The Philosophy of Right* (S. W. Dyde tr., 1996, Amherst, N.Y.: Prometheus Books), at p. 91.

5. Herbert Morris, *On Guilt and Innocence* (1976, Berkeley: University of California Press), at p. 34.

6. Jean Hampton, *An Expressive Theory of Retribution, in Retributivism and Its Critics* (W. Cragg ed., 1992, Stuttgart: Franz Steiner Verlag), at p. 13. *See also* R. A. Duff, *Trials and Punishments* (1986, Cambridge: Cambridge University Press), and R. A. Duff, *Punishment, Communication, and Community* (2000, Oxford: Oxford University Press) (developing an account of punishment as a mode of communication between a political community and its citizens). It is fair to ask whether such "expressive" or "communicative" accounts of punishment are truly retributive or even deontological, as they are often claimed to be, in that these accounts seem to be premised at least in part on the good consequences that flow from the expressive or communicative aspects of criminal punishment. *See* Michael Moore, "The Moral Worth of Retribution," in *Responsibility, Character, and the Emotions* (F. Schoeman ed., 1987, Cambridge: Cambridge University Press), at p. 181 (distinguishing retributivism from "denunciatory" theories of punishment); Joel Feinberg, *The Expressive Function of Punishment, in Doing and Deserving: Essays in the Theory of Responsibility* (1970, Princeton: Princeton University Press), at pp. 95–118 (arguing that the social effects of denunciation are the primary goal of expressive theories of punishment).

7. H. L. A. Hart, *Punishment and Responsibility: Essays in the Philosophy of Law* (2nd ed. 2008, Oxford: Oxford University Press) at p. 236.

8. *Id.* at pp. 236–237.

9. Underdeveloped does not mean completely *un*-developed. In recent decades, a handful of scholars have directly addressed the deontological case against capital punishment. This essay's catalog cannot reproduce all of their diverse accounts in their entirety, but it tries to give a sense of the nature and scope, as well as the strengths and weaknesses, of deontological argument on the topic. *See* Robert S. Gerstein, "Capital Punishment— 'Cruel and Unusual'?: A Retributivist Response," 85 *Ethics* 75 (1974); Dan Markel, "State, Be Not Proud: A Retributivist Defense of the Commutation of Death Row and the Abolition of the Death Penalty," 40 *Harv. C.R.-C.L. L. Rev.* 407 (2005); David McCord, "Imagining a Retributivist Alternative to Capital Punishment," 50 *Fla. L. Rev.* 1 (1998); Jeffrie G. Murphy, "Cruel and Unusual Punishments," in *Retribution, Justice, and Therapy: Essays in the*

Philosophy of Law (1979, Dordrecht: Reidel); Robert A. Pugsley, "A Retributivist Argument against Capital Punishment," 9 *Hofstra L. Rev.* 1501 (1981); Jeffrey H. Reiman, "Justice, Civilization, and the Death Penalty: Answering van den Haag," 14 *Phil. & Pub. Aff.* 115 (1985).

10. *See, e.g.,* Andrew von Hirsch, *Doing Justice: The Choice of Punishments* (1976, New York: Hill and Wang); Jeremy Waldron, "Lex Talionis," 34 *Ariz. L. Rev.* 25 (1992).

11. Thomas Nagel describes the ascription of responsibility in such cases as a species of problematic "moral luck": "Where a significant aspect of what someone does depends on factors beyond his control, yet we continue to treat him in that respect as an object of moral judgment, it can be called moral luck." Thomas Nagel, "Moral Luck," in *Mortal Questions* (1979, Cambridge: Cambridge University Press), at 26.

12. Maureen McKernan, *The Amazing Crime and Trial of Leopold and Loeb* (1989: Notable Trials Library), at p. 254.

13. Carol S. Steiker, "No, Capital Punishment Is Not Morally Required: Deterrence, Deontology, and the Death Penalty," 58 *Stan. L. Rev.* 751, 766 (2005).

14. *See* Woodson v. North Carolina, 428 U.S. 280, 304 (1976) (holding that the capital sentencing process "requires consideration of the character and record of the individual offender and the circumstances of the particular offense as a constitutionally indispensable part of the process of inflicting the [death] penalty").

15. For consideration of arguments that a *system* of capital punishment may be categorically objectionable if it produces a predictable pattern of unjust applications, see the discussion below in section 1.B.

16. For consideration of arguments against, for example, raping rapists or torturing torturers, see the discussion below in section 2.

17. *See* Michel Foucault, *Discipline and Punish: The Birth of the Prison* (A. Sheridan tr., 1975, New York: Vintage Books), at pp. 3–6 (describing in detail the horrifically torturous execution of Damiens the regicide in Paris in 1757).

18. *See, e.g.,* Knight v. Florida, 528 U.S. 990 (1999) (Breyer, J., dissenting from denial of certiorari) ("It is difficult to deny the suffering inherent in a prolonged wait for execution.").

19. Reiman, *supra* note 9, at p. 132, n. 20.

20. *Id.* at p. 133, n. 22.

21. Michael Maslin, Cartoon, *New Yorker,* Feb. 24, 1997, www.cartoonbank.com (cartoon no. 29638).

22. *See generally* Richard A. Epstein, *Cases and Materials on Torts* (9th ed. 2008, New York: Aspen), at pp. 403–404.

23. *See id.* (contrasting the right of contribution that joint tortfeasors can pursue after having fully compensated the victim with the even more limited liability of joint-and-several tortfeasors, who are liable from the start only for their share of the victim's harm rather than for the full amount of damages).

24. *See id.* at pp. 327–360 (tracking the movement, both by legislation and at common law, away from the even stricter traditional rule which foreclosed any tort recovery at all for negligent plaintiffs toward the principle of comparative negligence).

25. For example, in many contexts, courts hold that the actions of a present, intentional tortfeasor constitute a superseding cause that negates the liability of a more remote, merely negligent actor. *See* Restatement (Second) of Torts, § 442 (1965).

26. *See generally* Sanford H. Kadish, Stephen J. Schulhofer, & Carol S. Steiker, *Criminal Law and Its Processes: Cases and Materials* (8th ed. 2007, New York: Aspen), at pp. 589–632.

27. *Id.* at p. 590 (quoting 4 Blackstone, *Commentaries,* ch. 3).

28. This is the classic liberal account of the common law partial defense of provocation, which reduces murder to voluntary manslaughter. *See id.* at pp. 390–410.

29. Reiman, *supra* note 9, at p. 132 n.20.

30. *See supra* subsection I.A.1.

31. Jeffrie Murphy, "Marxism and Retribution," 2 *Phil. & Pub. Aff.* 217, 240 (1973).

32. John Rawls, *A Theory of Justice* (1971, Cambridge, Mass.: Harvard University Press).

33. Sharon Dolovich, "Legitimate Punishment in Liberal Democracy," 7 *Buff. Crim. L. Rev.* 307, 351 (2004).

34. Murphy, *supra* note 31, at p. 240.

35. 408 U.S. 238 (1972).

36. McGautha v. California, 402 U.S. 183 (1971).

37. Gregg v. Georgia, 428 U.S. 153 (1976); Proffitt v. Florida, 428 U.S. 242 (1976); Jurek v. Texas, 428 U.S. 262 (1976).

38. Murphy, *supra* note 9, at p. 239.

39. *Id.* at p. 241.

40. *Id.* at p. 241.

41. *Id.* at p. 242.

42. *Id.* at p. 243.

43. *Id.* at p. 238.

44. As Murphy explains his project: "What I wish to explore in this essay…is how far one can go with a purely deontological conception of constitutional restrictions and a purely retributive conception of punishment. It turns out, I think, that one can go pretty far." *Id.* at p. 244, n. 5.

45. Louis P. Pojman, "Why the Death Penalty Is Morally Permissible," in *Debating the Death Penalty: Should America Have Capital Punishment?* (H. A. Bedau & P. G. Cassell eds., 2004, Oxford: Oxford University Press), at p. 73.

46. Randall L. Kennedy, "McCleskey v. Kemp: Race, Capital Punishment, and the Supreme Court," 101 *Harv. L. Rev.* 1388, 1440 (1988).

47. Ernest van den Haag, "Refuting Reiman and Nathanson", 14 *Phil. & Pub. Aff.* 165, 174 (1985).

48. Stephen Nathanson, "Does It Matter If the Death Penalty Is Arbitrarily Administered?," 14 *Phil. &. Pub. Aff.* 149, 154 (1985).

49. Charles Black, Jr., *Capital Punishment: The Inevitability of Caprice and Mistake* (2nd ed. 1982, New York: Norton).

50. Reiman appears to agree that Nathanson's account of the relevance of arbitrariness is a moral, as opposed to a prudential, reason to oppose the death penalty: "Moral assessment of the way in which a penalty will be carried out may be distinct from moral assessment of the penalty itself, but, since the way in which the penalty will be carried out is part of what we will be bringing about if we institute the penalty, it is a necessary consideration in any assessment of the morality of instituting the penalty." Reiman, *supra* note 9, at p. 132, n. 22.

51. *See* Margaret J. Radin, "Cruel Punishment and Respect for Persons: Super Due Process for Death," 53 *S. Cal. L. Rev.* 1143 (1980).

52. *See* Hegel, *Philosophy of Right, supra* note 4.

53. *See supra* p. 443.

54. Kant, *The Philosophy of Law, supra* note 1, at p. 198.

55. Murphy, *supra* note 9, at p. 237.

56. *Id.* at p. 233.

57. *Id.* at p. 243.

58. *Id.* at p. 243.

59. *See supra* section I.B.

60. Reiman, *supra* note 9, at pp. 139–40.

61. *Id.* at p. 140.

62. *Id.* at p. 138.

63. *Id.* at p. 142.

64. Furman v. Georgia, 408 U.S. 238, 272–273 (1972) (Brennan, J., concurring).

65. "[I]t appears that there is no method available that guarantees an immediate and painless death." *Id.* at p. 287.

66. "[T]he process of carrying out a verdict of death is often so degrading and brutalizing to the human spirit as to constitute psychological torture." *Id.* at p. 288 (quotation marks omitted).

67. "The unusual severity of death is manifested most clearly in its finality and enormity. Death, in these respects, is in a class by itself." *Id.* at p. 289.

68. Murphy, *supra* note 9, at p. 240.

69. Reiman, *supra* note 9, at p. 141.

70. *Id.* at p. 141.

71. *Id.* at p. 142.

72. "The intensity of punishment is the greater the more closely societies approximate to a less developed type—and the more the central power assumes an absolute character." Emile Durkheim, *Two Laws of Penal Evolution, Economy and Society* 2 (1973), at p. 285, quoted in *id.*, at pp. 136 & 148.

73. Norbert Elias, *The Civilizing Process*, vol. 1, *The History of Manners* (E. Jephcott tr., 1978, Oxford: Blackwell), and vol. 2, *State Formation and Civilization* (E. Jephcott tr., 1982, Oxford: Blackwell).

74. David Garland, *Punishment and Modern Society: A Study in Social Theory* (1990, Chicago: University of Chicago Press), at pp. 217–218.

75. *Id.* at p. 224.

76. *Id.* at p. 224.

77. *Id.* at p. 224.

78. *Id.* at p. 228 (citing Pieter Spierenburg, *The Spectacle of Suffering: Executions and the Evolution of Repression* (1984, Cambridge: Cambridge University Press).

79. Carolyn Strange, "The Undercurrents of Penal Culture: Punishment of the Body in Mid-Twentieth-Century Canada," *Law & History Review* 19.2 (2001), www.historycooperative.org/journals/lhr/19.2/strange.html.

80. *Id.* at para. 60.

81. *Id.* at para. 64.

82. Garland, *supra* note 74, at p. 249.

83. Strange, *supra* note 79, at para. 11.

84. *Id.* at para. 54.

85. *Id.* at para. 55.

86. Scott Altman, "(Com)modifying Experience," 65 S. *Cal. L. Rev.* 293 (1991) (addressing the effects on public sensibilities of new medical technologies such as fetal genetic engineering, in vitro fertilization, and surrogacy).

87. *Id.* at p. 294.

88. Hashem Dezhbakhsh, Paul Rubin & Joanna M. Shepherd, "Does Capital Punishment Have a Deterrent Effect? New Evidence from Postmoratorium Panel Data," 5 *Am. L. & Econ. Rev.* 344 (2003).

89. Joanna M. Shepherd, "Deterrence versus Brutalization: Capital Punishment's Differing Impacts among States," 104 *Mich. L. Rev.* 203 (2005).

90. *Id.*

91. *See* Reiman, *supra* note 9, at p. 142.

92. In light of the release of the eleventh *Star Trek* feature film, it may be unnecessary to explain that Mr. Spock is a fictional character from an alien race of Vulcans who do not feel human emotions.

93. *See* Cass R. Sunstein, *Laws of Fear: Beyond the Precautionary Principle* (2005, New York: Cambridge University Press) (explaining various versions of and critiquing the precautionary principle).

CHAPTER 16

....

MERCY

....

R. A. DUFF

1 THE PROBLEM OF MERCY

....

Without trying to offer a definition of mercy, we can say, roughly and with some artificiality, that

A shows B mercy when, although it would be Φ for A to impose a certain burden on B, A imposes no such burden, or imposes a lighter burden, out of compassion for B.

Three examples will illustrate the three main types of case that fit this specification: only the third will directly concern us here.

(a) It would be within A's power, and in accordance with A's usual practice as a mugger, to rob B of all B's money and valuables; but, moved by B's plea that he needs the money to buy food for his family, A takes nothing (or, moved by B's pleading, A leaves B with the valuable memento of his dead wife).

(b) It would be permissible for A, in terms of A's moral and legal rights, to demand that B pay A the money he owes, and to take B to court if he refuses to pay; but, moved by B's plight (the fact that paying the money would leave B very badly off), A remits the debt.

(c) It would be consistent with the demands of retributive justice for A, as the sentencing judge, to impose a moderately heavy custodial sentence on B for the crime for which B has been convicted; but, moved by B's plight (the fact that B is suffering from a serious and painful illness), A suspends the custodial sentence, or imposes a much lighter, noncustodial sentence.

It is cases like (c) that will concern us in what follows,[1] both because our interest is in mercy within the criminal law, and because it is only in cases like (c) that mercy seems to raise any serious problems; but it is worth spelling out the crucial differences between (c) and the other kinds of case.

In case (a), it would of course be wrong for A to impose such a burden on B; A can hardly claim moral credit for curtailing a mugging on which he should never have embarked. But, so long as he was motivated by genuine compassion for B (and not, for instance, by mere whim or by some prudential calculation), we can count his action as merciful, and see it as at least mitigating the seriousness of his crime: it showed that he was not *totally* deaf or blind to his victims as fellow human beings; his crime would have been even worse, and he would have shown himself in an even worse light, had he not shown such (admittedly minimal) mercy. It might be argued that mercy ("strictly speaking") must involve the remission of a burden that the agent has at least the right to impose: but while that is certainly where mercy is displayed as a virtue, we should not deny that it can also be discerned, in at least a tenuous or etiolated form, in cases like (a). However, our main concern is with mercy of a kind that conflicts or is at odds with other moral considerations—which is clearly not true in case (a); A's merciful impulse in that case simply moves him to do something that he anyway ought to do, or to commit a less serious wrong than he would otherwise have committed.

In cases like (b), we can normally offer a more unqualified moral approval of A's action, and of A as its agent.[2] Sometimes, if the debt is small relative to A's resources and the burden on B of paying it would be very serious, we might think that A ought to remit it, as a matter of minimal decency or humanity;[3] in other cases, while we might not say categorically that A ought to remit the debt, we will see it as the decent thing to do; and in yet other cases we will admire A for treating B mercifully even at some cost to herself. Sometimes, of course, we will instead see A's mercy as misguided: if, for instance, B's plight is not serious (and largely B's own fault), and remitting the debt would be burdensome for A, we might either talk of mercy that is misguided, or deny that A showed mercy—for if mercy is a virtue, its exercise must be guided by practical wisdom, which in this case A has not shown. The key point, however, is that when what is remitted is a debt that B owes to A, so that it would be permissible rather than obligatory or required for A to demand full payment, A's mercy does not conflict with other moral demands, and thus does not raise the kinds of problem that concern us here.

In cases like (c), by contrast, we might suppose that justice requires, rather than merely permitting, the imposition of the custodial sentence: if the judge is to do punitive justice, she must—not merely may—impose that sentence. It is therefore here rather than in cases like (a) or (b) that we find the supposed paradox of mercy. On the one hand, mercy is supposed to be a virtue: merciful action might not be a matter of duty or right, but is nonetheless admirable in its place—and it seems natural to think that it sometimes has a place in the criminal court. On the other hand, if punitive mercy involves imposing a sentence lighter than that which is required by justice, punitive mercy seems to involve injustice: how then can it be virtuous, or admirable?

This question can usefully be analyzed into two slightly more precise questions. First, is mercy relevant to criminal law, in particular to criminal sentencing, at all: is it ever proper for a sentencer to act mercifully, or for others to appraise a sentencer's decisions as merciful or as unmerciful? Or should we rather say that, while mercy is a virtue that we should exercise in many contexts, it has no place in our courts of

criminal justice? Second, if mercy can play a role in the criminal courts, if it is something to which sentencers should sometimes attend in deciding what punishment
to impose, and in terms of which we should sometimes judge their actions, is its
relevance internal or external to the criminal law? Does its relevance flow from the
very aims of the criminal law, from the very values and principles by which the
criminal law is, or should be, structured; is it in virtue of their role as officers of
the criminal law that sentencers should sometimes be merciful? Or do the demands
of mercy come from outside the criminal law: do they constitute an intrusion into,
rather than an aspect of, the criminal law's normative structure?[4]

Before tackling these questions, four preliminary points are worth making.
First, I have talked so far of mercy as a virtue, as it often seems natural to talk: we
commend the merciful person, and admire her merciful actions. Now we could use
"mercy" and its cognates in a way that implies that a merciful disposition is always
virtuous, and merciful action always right. We could say, in an Aristotelian spirit,
that mercy is the mean, of character and of action, in relation to leniency: the mean
between the vices of hard-heartedness and soft-heartedness. On this understanding, we never have to ask whether it is appropriate to be merciful, since to describe
a response or action as merciful is to describe it as appropriate. We must ask instead
whether and when, to whom and in what ways, it is appropriate to be lenient—
questions that must be answered by the exercise of practical wisdom and the moral
perception that it includes; to be merciful is to be lenient "at the right time, about
the right things, toward the right people, for the right end and in the right way."[5]
Or we could use "mercy" and its cognates in a way that leaves such normative issues
more open: we could understand mercy as leniency motivated by concern or compassion for the well-being of the person to whom it is shown, leaving it to be determined when, to whom, and how it might be appropriate to be merciful. On the
former understanding, the question is whether mercy can ever be shown in the
sphere of criminal justice: those who argue that it cannot must of course recognize
that sentencers can be motivated to leniency by compassion for the convicted
offender, but would deny that this constitutes mercy. On the latter understanding,
the question is not whether mercy can be shown by sentencers and by other officials
of a criminal justice system, since it clearly can be; the question is whether it can
ever be appropriate to be merciful or to show mercy in that context. I doubt that
ordinary usage is determinate enough to decide between these two understandings,
but for the sake of simplicity I will follow the latter: judges and other officials in the
criminal justice system can indeed show mercy, by remitting penal burdens out of
concern for the offender's good; the question is whether, when, and why they can be
justified in doing so.

Second, I have assumed that mercy is a matter of motive as well as of conduct
(this is one difference between mercy and leniency). A mugger leaves his victim
unrobbed only because he sees richer pickings elsewhere; a creditor remits a debt
only because he thinks it will make him look good; a judge mitigates an offender's
sentence only because she was bribed to do so: such actions are not merciful, or acts
of mercy—any more than is a gift motivated purely by the expectation of later profit

an act of generosity.[6] We might urge the creditor to remit the debt, because it would be merciful to do so: but doing so is merciful only if it is done for the very reason that makes it merciful. Those reasons, furthermore, have to do with the interests or plight of the person to whom mercy is shown. A creditor might remit a debt out of concern not for the debtor, but for another needier creditor whom the debtor will now be able to pay: her action might be admirable and virtuous, but is not on this interpretation an act of mercy. A judge might remit an offender's sentence not out of concern for the offender, but in return for his assistance to the police (and as an incentive to other offenders to do likewise): whether or not we think this appropriate, it is not an act of mercy. Leniency counts as mercy only when it is motivated by concern for the good of the person to whom it is shown.[7]

Third, if mercy is not a matter of justice, it discriminates between offenders whose penal desert is relevantly similar: in the example given above, B's punishment is reduced because of his illness, while C, who committed a similar offence in similar circumstances but is not ill, receives no such reduction. This is not to say, however, that mercy is a matter of caprice.[8] The sentencer has reason to show mercy to B—it is not a mere whim; and if the same or a relevantly similar reason applied in C's case, she should see reason to reduce his punishment, too. We have not yet discussed whether C or anyone else has cause for complaint about the leniency shown to B: if mercy in such contexts is unjustified, because it is at odds with the requirements of penal justice, C might have reason to complain that he is treated unjustly in comparison to B—that although they were similarly guilty of similarly serious crimes, he is punished more severely than B. His complaint would then be that the sentencer's decision to reduce B's punishment was arbitrary, because based on inappropriate or irrelevant reasons; but he cannot deny that it was based on reasons.

Fourth, mercy in sentencing seems most obviously problematic on a positive retributivist view of punishment: if we take it to be a requirement of justice that offenders be punished in proportion to their penal deserts (to the seriousness of their crimes), we must wonder how it could ever be appropriate to show mercy to an offender. It is also, however, problematic in a similar way if we view it from the perspective of negative retributivism, according to which it is permissible—as far as justice is concerned—rather than required to punish offenders to the extent that they deserve.[9] It is true that if we attend only to B and his penal deserts, justice is not now flouted if he is punished less than he deserves. But the principle of proportionality in punishment is also a principle of relative or ordinal proportionality, concerning the ways in which offenders are punished relative to each other: offenses of similar seriousness should receive punishments of similar severity.[10] As we have just seen, mercy discriminates between offenders whose penal desert, as determined by the seriousness of their offenses, is relevantly similar. When B's sentence is mitigated, as an act of mercy, C surely has grounds to complain that penal justice has not been done as between him and B: for he did not deserve a harsher sentence than B—but that is just what he has received. Even from the perspective of negative retributivism, mercy is therefore still problematic, just because it treats differently offenders between whom there is no difference in penal desert.

Since most contemporary theories of punishment incorporate at least a negative version of retributivism, this means that mercy is problematic for most contemporary penal theories. It is also problematic for purely consequentialist theories, according to which punishment is to be justified solely by reference to its beneficial effects. More precisely, a practice or act of punishment is justified, for a consequentialist, insofar as it is an efficient, that is, cost-effective, way of achieving certain goods that it is appropriate for the state to pursue. Now, either the offender's interests and well-being are to be included in the calculus of costs and benefits, or they are not. If they are not to be included,[11] then there is no room for mercy within that penal perspective, since mercy precisely involves a concern for the offender's good. If they are to be included, then the determination that it would be appropriate or legitimate to impose this punishment on B must be based on the calculation that this would efficiently serve the ends of the penal system, *despite the harm or suffering that it inflicts on B*. But this leaves no room for a merciful remission of the punishment out of concern for B's good: for that would be to give B's interests a quite unjustified double-weighting—to count them both within the penal calculus, and then again in deciding to show mercy.

In the remainder of this essay I will discuss three examples of what might count as mercy in criminal sentencing, in order to see whether mercy can plausibly play a role in punishment; and, if it can, how it is related to penal justice and to the aims and logic of the criminal law.

2 THREE EXAMPLES

The first example is designed to bring out most starkly the (apparent) paradox of mercy. Alan has been convicted of a nontrivial but not dramatically serious crime: perhaps theft or fraud of a kind that could be punished by a fairly short prison sentence. At the sentencing stage it is revealed that his wife has just died, or that he has been diagnosed with a terminal illness; the judge, moved by compassion for his suffering, discharges him without formal punishment, or replaces the prison term that she would otherwise have imposed with a lighter, noncustodial sentence.[12] His bereavement or diagnosis postdated his commission of the offense: so there is no suggestion that it mitigates the offense or reduces his culpability for its commission; he still deserves whatever punishment he deserved before he suffered this tragedy. Nor could we plausibly say that his formal, legal punishment should be remitted or reduced because he has "already suffered enough"—because his bereavement or illness should be seen as a "natural" punishment for his crime that reduces or removes the need for formal punishment: that would be a morally crass response both to his crime and to what he has now suffered.[13] The mercy that Alan is shown involves relieving him of the punitive burden that he deserves to suffer—and that is suffered by his codefendant, Bill, who committed the same offense, with the same kind of culpability, but has suffered no such tragedy.

The second example involves leniency that is grounded in factors more closely connected to the offender's commission of the crime for which he has been convicted. Chuck has also been convicted of a nontrivial but not dramatically serious crime: he assaulted someone with whom he got into an argument over a parking space; or he stole from a neighbor. He has a record of similar offenses, and a background that was in various serious ways deprived and disadvantaged: he grew up in an unstable, violent home, received little education, or training in skills that might help him find employment, and has been unemployed for most of his (so far quite short) adult life. He is certainly not eligible for any recognized legal defense: he was not acting under exculpatory provocation, or duress (either by threats or of circumstances); he is not mentally disordered; he knew what he was doing, and had the capacity to refrain from doing it. But yet, the judge thinks, given his background and upbringing; given the harsh and brutal environment in which he grew up; given the hand fate has dealt him: he merits our compassion. Rather than imposing the custodial sentence that would usually be imposed, she therefore imposes only a suspended sentence, and tries to make sure that he is offered some suitable support and training;[14] she and he see this as an act of mercy.

The third example is of repentance. David has committed a serious crime, and he initially denied it and did his best to evade detection and prosecution. After his arrest, however, he has a change of heart, earnestly repents his crime, pleads guilty, and expresses his determination to do anything he can to make reparation for his crime. His repentance can make no difference to the seriousness of his offense or to his guilt as its perpetrator—it cannot alter the past; he surely therefore still deserves whatever punishment he deserved before he repented (a punishment that he might now accept more willingly). But, moved by his repentance, the judge imposes a much lighter sentence than she would otherwise have imposed: as she and he might see it, she shows him mercy.

Three kinds of response are in principle available to each of these examples. First, we could argue that mercy is unjustified: the sentencer has no adequate reason for leniency; mercy, whatever its moral merits in other contexts, has no place in a criminal court. Second, we could argue that mercy is justified, as a matter of penal justice: leniency is warranted by the principles and goals that structure the criminal justice system itself. Or we could argue, third, that mercy is justified, but not as a matter of criminal justice: mercy conflicts with the demands of penal justice, but should sometimes defeat them. I will argue that each example merits a different response, and that in some cases (those to which the third response is appropriate) we should therefore give mercy an essentially disruptive role in the criminal law: mercy is sometimes justified as an intrusion into the criminal law of values that lie outside its normative structure. The main point of the discussion of these examples, however, will not be to persuade readers of any particular response to them; it will be to clarify the different ways in which mercy can be viewed and assessed in the criminal law.

3 MERCY, NOT JUSTICE

In the first example, of Alan and his tragedy, it seems obvious that mercy is at odds with the demands of penal justice, since what he has now suffered can make no difference either to his guilt or to the punishment he deserves.

We might be tempted to avoid this conclusion by portraying the punishment he deserves as something permissible rather than mandatory: just as a creditor may demand payment from his debtor, but may also permissibly remit the debt out of compassion for the debtor, so, too, a society may, through its criminal courts, impose deserved punishments on those who violate its laws, but also has the right to remit such punishments out of compassion. The metaphor of punishment as a debt the criminal owes is a prevalent one; if we take it that that debt is owed to his fellow citizens collectively (since it is their shared norms that he has violated), why should we not say that they may then mercifully remit the debt—that is, that the sentencer could be authorized to show mercy on their behalf and in their name?[15] This would reconcile mercy with penal justice: showing mercy does not violate any demand of justice.

One problem with this suggestion is that the metaphor of punishment as a debt stands in serious need of explanation before we can determine either whether it is useful or whether the debt is one that could be remitted (quite apart from the question of who would have the right to remit it). Such an explanation would require the articulation of a complete penal theory—a task we cannot embark on here. That theory would need to hold that the justifying aim of punishment is neither to assist the pursuit of some consequential good (for we have seen that there is no room for mercy within a consequentialist perspective) nor to satisfy requirements of justice, which demand that the guilty suffer their just deserts (for such demands cannot be so easily waived), but perhaps to satisfy the reasonable desires or wishes of those in whose name and on whose behalf it is imposed: desires or wishes that they could reasonably demand be satisfied, but could also reasonably decide not to press, out of compassion for the person whom their satisfaction would burden. This line of thought might lead us back to the kind of retributivism espoused by Stephen, according to whom punishment should satisfy "the feeling of hatred and the desire of vengeance" that crime "excites in healthily constituted minds";[16] or to the "fair play" model, according to which punishment restores that fair balance of benefits and burdens that crime disturbs, by imposing on the offender a burden to wipe out the unfair advantage he took over the law-abiding in committing his crime.[17] This is not the place to discuss the serious objections that both these kinds of account face.[18] All we need note here is that if they are to make room for mercy in this way, they must portray punishment as optional—as something we collectively have the right to demand, but are also entitled to remit. Surely, however, if we are to provide an adequate justification of a practice as onerous and oppressive as criminal punishment, we must do more than this: we must be able to show that we have not merely the right to punish offenders (a right we need not exercise) but also a duty to do so—a duty grounded either in the harms that, for a consequentialist, punishment will avert, or in the demands of retributive justice. But a duty to punish cannot be waived in the way that the right to exact a debt can be waived.[19]

Alan deserves the punishment the merciful judge remits, and we must assume that its imposition would serve the proper aims of the penal system: that is why the remission counts as an act of mercy rather than as a sentencing decision mandated by the system's principles of sentencing (retributivist, consequentialist, or both). But, it might now be argued, does this not show that mercy is unjustified in this or any other criminal case?[20] Mercy is indeed a virtue, and merciful actions are properly admired, in their proper place; but that proper place is never the criminal court. Someone who is a judge might have the virtue of mercy, and might exhibit it in various contexts: but it is not a virtue that bears on her exercise of her judicial duties in sentencing. She might be tempted to reduce an offender's sentence out of compassion for his plight, but that would be a temptation to vice: to the vice of excess in relation to leniency. As a virtue, mercy involves showing leniency "at the right time, about the right things, toward the right people, for the right end and in the right way."[21] But the sentencing stage of a trial is never "the right time," offenders being sentenced are never "the right people," their sentences are never "the right things" for the exercise of compassionate leniency: just as there is no such thing as virtuous, legitimate murder,[22] so there can be no such thing as virtuous or legitimate judicial mercy in sentencing.

The argument for this rejection of mercy in the context of criminal punishment is simple. In a justified system of criminal law and punishment, the punishment to which an offender is liable serves some important systemic goal—whether that goal is understood in retributivist or in instrumental terms. Since punishment is of its nature painful or burdensome, the goal(s) it serves must be such as not merely to permit it but to require it: how else could a state justify imposing such burdens on a citizen than by showing that this is necessary to achieve some important end? It follows, therefore, that mercy involves hindering the achievement of the goals that punishment serves—that is, that the sentencer who shows mercy puts the interests of the offender whose merited punishment she remits ahead of those interests (of the victim, or of the polity as a whole, or of justice) that punishment serves. Now in cases of individual or private action, when the only interests significantly at stake are my own, mercy might be permissible—even admirable. I have the right to impose a burden on another person (to exact payment of a debt, for instance), but it is a right I am not required to exercise: I also have the right to prefer my debtor's interests to my own interests, to sacrifice an interest of mine for his sake, and to waive the debt; doing so might indeed be admirable. But matters are different for the state and its officials. Their proper function is to serve the interests of the polity and its citizens—however those interests are to be defined; the more particular function of officials is to play their part in maintaining the institutions that are created to serve the state's overall goals. The criminal law is one such institution, and the job of its officials is to serve its proper goals, whether those be understood in retributivist or in consequentialist terms: since, as we have seen, the mercy that the sentencer shows Alan cannot be justified in terms of those goals, it cannot be justified; as an official, a servant of the polity, she does not have the right to put the offender's interests above those of the polity.

An analogy will help to clarify this point. A teacher grading students' work is playing a formal role in a particular institution, within which grading has (we suppose) a point. While the institution of education serves a range of goals, to which grading contributes, one central purpose of grading has to be to give the work the grade it deserves (though there is plenty of room for controversy about just what determines desert); we might use grades to encourage students to work more assiduously, but it is important to their role in the system that they be justified by the quality of the work for which they are to be given. Now a teacher might know that a student whose exam he is grading has suffered some serious tragedy since producing the work—she has just been bereaved, or diagnosed with a serious illness. Might it then be legitimate for the teacher to show "mercy": to give the work a pass although it clearly does not meet the standard for such a grade, or to give it a higher grade than it merits? The answer is surely "No": to do so would be inconsistent with the proper aims of the practice of grading (it would make nonsense of the practice), and with the teacher's responsibilities as an examiner. The teacher should of course be moved by the student's plight, as anyone should be, and should perhaps try to find a way of helping the student, not just as a fellow human being but as her teacher;[23] but his activity as a grader should not be affected.

One could no doubt imagine extreme cases in which an insistence on giving the work the grade it deserves would cause disaster—the student's death, for instance; perhaps in such a case the examiner should not give the deserved grade but should refuse to grade the work at all, or even (if that would not avert disaster) give an undeserved grade. But that would be true only in the most extreme cases, and would involve abandoning or suspending the practice of grading; it does not show that mercy has a role *within* that practice. Similarly, those who argue that mercy has no place in sentencing might agree that there could be emergencies in which justice must give way to disaster-averting necessity, when the judge should not impose a deserved sentence; but that would be to suspend the normal practice of punishment, rather than to give mercy a place within that practice.[24]

The core of this argument against mercy is, I think, right. Mercy is at odds with justice, understood here as a matter of inflicting deserved punishments; it is at odds with the aims of criminal punishment as a distinctive institution, whether we understand those aims in roughly retributivist or in consequentialist terms; it cannot be integrated into a criminal justice system, since it is precisely *not* motivated either by an understanding of the offender's penal desert, or by a judgment about what disposal would most efficiently serve the penal system's further goals. But, I will argue, that does not show that mercy should not play a role in sentencing; it shows, instead, that mercy constitutes an intrusion of other values into the criminal justice system—an intrusion that can sometimes be justified.

This argument can usefully begin with an example from outside the context of criminal law and punishment—an example of moral rather than legal mercy.

A friend has done me some moderately serious wrong: perhaps he has betrayed my trust in quite a serious way, or used something that I told him in confidence to his own advantage, in a way that causes me serious embarrassment or loss. I go to his home to confront him—to "have it out with him." I might not know whether our friendship can survive—much depends on how he responds to me; but my immediate aim is to confront him forcefully with what he has done, to make clear how wrong it was, to communicate my hurt and my anger. I intend, that is, to criticize and censure him: my aim is to get him to understand, and ideally to accept, the moral condemnation that is appropriate to the wrong he has done. But when I reach his house, he greets me with the news that his wife has just died. At once (or so we might hope) my anger is replaced by sympathy: even if I did not know his wife myself, I share in his grief, and feel for him in his loss. As for my complaint against him, my determination to call him to account for the wrong he did me, of course I do not pursue it; indeed, one might hope that a true friend would simply forget about it—it would be pushed from her mind by the friend's plight. I do not mention it myself as the reason for my visit, or as something that we need to talk about; if he raises it (perhaps because he feels guilty), I will brush it aside—"We needn't [we shouldn't] think about that now."[25]

This seems a wholly natural and proper response; indeed, we would think it grotesque if I insisted on discussing the wrong he had done me. It is not strictly a matter of mercy, since "mercy" suggests a relationship of effective authority that gives me the right, perhaps even a duty, to impose something on him, which is not true of my relationship to my friend. But it is a moral analogue of one kind of legal mercy: by understanding what it means, and why it is so obviously appropriate, in the moral case we can come to understand the role of one kind of mercy in the context of criminal punishment.

Why does his wife's death make it so obviously inappropriate for me to insist on talking about the wrong he did me, and castigating him for it? Since his bereavement postdated the wrongdoing, it does not constitute any kind of excuse for or mitigation of that wrongdoing: it was and remains true that he deserves severe moral criticism for what he did. Nor should we say that I withhold criticism because he has already suffered (or been punished) enough by his wife's death: it would be—at best—morally crass thus to connect his wife's death to the wrong he did to me, as if it could be seen as a kind of "natural punishment" for it. The point is rather that my criticism would be an attempt to get him to focus on, to attend carefully to, the wrong that he did me: but given what he has now suffered, it would be callously inhuman to expect him to do so. Indeed, the point is stronger than that. As his friend, my attention should now be focused on his bereavement, not on the wrong that he did, and it is not merely natural or understandable but wholly proper that that is where his attention is focused: there would be something not just strange or unusual, but morally disturbing, about a man whose beloved wife had just died, and whose attention was focused on the wrong he had done to a friend. In other cases, however, the focus of his attention on something other than the wrong that he did might be understandable rather than morally appropriate. Suppose that he had just been told by his doctor that he was suffering a terminal illness: we might think it heroic if he managed none-theless to think repentantly about the wrong that he had done me (whereas we would not be inclined to talk of heroism in the case of bereavement), but it would still be inappropriate for me to try to make him think about it, or to claim that he ought to do so; it is reasonable that he should focus on his illness.

I have chosen an extreme example, in which it seems obvious that, even when the wrong committed was moderately serious, the wrongdoer's present suffering should drive it from the wronged person's mind, and would understandably (even properly) also drive it from the wrongdoer's mind. If we think about possible varia-tions on the example, we will see that an idea of proportionality has some role to play: the less serious the wrong, the less terrible the wrongdoer's current suffering needs to be to make it proper to turn our attention away from the wrong to the suf-fering (my friend failed to turn up to meet me for dinner, but when I visit him to castigate him I find that he has just been burgled); some wrongs might, however, be so serious that they cannot be thus put aside. A further point to note about such examples is that the most natural response to the wrongdoer's present suffering is not to mitigate my criticism of him, but to put it aside altogether. Perhaps—at least or especially if he raises the matter—I would dwell on it briefly, and in tones or terms more moderate than I might otherwise have used; but more probably I would simply refrain altogether from even a moderated form of the criticism that I would otherwise have offered—and that he certainly deserves.

Turning now to mercy in the criminal court, and to the example of Alan, we can see why the judge might properly show mercy by remitting his sentence—and why this involves the intrusion into the criminal court of values external to the criminal law's logic.

One essential purpose of criminal punishment is the communication of an appropriate message to the offender—a message of censure or condemnation: whatever else punishment is meant to achieve, by way either of retribution or of consequential benefit, this expressive or communicative purpose is integral to its character as punishment.[26] Now communication is something on which the com-municator focuses (her aim is to get the message across) and on which she thus implies that the person with whom she is trying to communicate should focus: when I talk to you, I expect you to listen. Given the message of censure that punish-ment aims to convey, and the very forceful means (imprisonment, fines, compul-sory community service) through which the message is to be conveyed, that focus is quite insistent: the court, acting on behalf of the polity as a whole, insists on focus-ing on the crime, and insists that the offender should focus on it, too—that he should hear, and attend to, the message that his punishment conveys. But this is surely not what we demand that Alan focus on; nor indeed should it be our focus as his fellow citizens (and thus the court's focus, as acting on our behalf). Just as it was entirely appropriate for my friend's attention to be focused on his bereavement or illness, and would have been inappropriate for me to insist on discussing his wrong-doing, so it is here entirely appropriate for Alan's attention to be focused on his own tragedy—and for the court to recognize that by remitting his punishment.[27]

Is this to say that it should be part of a sentencer's role to temper justice with mercy: that an adequate account of the judge's judicial responsibilities in a criminal trial must include, if not a duty to be merciful, at least room for the discretionary exercise of mercy—a discretion that, we might think, a judge should sometimes exercise? This is how Tasioulas portrays the matter.[28] Mercy, he insists, does conflict with penal justice: for justice demands that Alan be punished, while mercy remits his punishment. But that conflict arises, and must be resolved, within the practice of punishment, understood in appropriately pluralist terms. The "formal overarching justification" of punishment is indeed "the communication of justified censure"; and we have seen that such a justification makes no room for mercy. But that purely formal justification does not constitute a "substantial justification in its own right": a penal practice that has that formal aim can and should serve a variety of substantive values—retributive justice, but also such values as mercy and crime prevention.[29] Some grounds for leniency are admittedly "extraneous" to a theory of punishment, or to "the logic" of punishment, and can therefore conflict with the proper aims and principles of a penal system; but mercy involves grounds for leniency, including those that obtain in cases like Alan's, that are "integral to" the logic of punishment, understood in pluralist terms.[30] Although Tasioulas thus rightly insists that mercy and justice cannot be reconciled, I think that he understates the depth of conflict between them: the conflict between mercy and justice is a conflict not within the normative structure or logic of criminal law, but between that normative structure and another that, in these cases, intrudes into the criminal law; it might be right for the judge to show mercy, but in doing so she is no longer acting simply as a judge.

The criminal law, and thus the criminal court as part of the criminal law, is focused on wrongdoing: it defines certain kinds of conduct as wrong and provides, through its courts and penal institutions, for those who commit such wrongs to be called to account, condemned, and punished for them. This must also be the focus of the judge, as an officer of the law: it is her responsibility to administer the law, and to attend only to what is legally relevant. Within that focus, from that distinctive perspective, Alan's present tragedy has no relevance, since it does not bear on the nature or seriousness of his wrongdoing or on the censure he deserves for it: the eyes of the criminal law must be blind to that tragedy.

This is an important feature of the criminal law as a distinctive, and limited, institution. In my dealings with my friend, I am properly concerned with all aspects of his life—with the tragedy he has suffered and with the wrong he has done me; it is as his friend that I should be moved from castigating him for his wrongdoing to sympathizing with his plight. But the law should not take such an all-embracing interest in its citizens. This is a crucial aspect of liberal criminal law—that it concerns itself with only a limited area of our lives.[31] It defines criminal offenses, as wrongs that are its business; it requires courts to determine whether defendants committed such wrongs, to appraise their culpability (as defined by the law) in doing so, and to determine what sentence will be appropriate, given the aims of punishment, for those who are convicted; it demands of its citizens not only that

they refrain from committing wrongs that it defines as criminal, but that they
answer for such wrongs, through the criminal process, if they do commit them. But
it does not and should not take an interest in further aspects of their lives or characters: that would be to intrude into what is not its business.

Given the character of the criminal law as a limited institution, the criminal
court is also a distinctively limited, formal arena in which the various participants
have particular, limited, roles to play. The defendant, jurors (if there is a jury), judge
or magistrate, and counsel are there not as citizens who have come together for an
unconstrained moral discussion about the defendant and his past deeds but as play-
ers in this particular game—a game that defines their roles for them.[32] The defendant is on trial for his alleged commission of a criminal offense, and only those
aspects of his life and character that bear directly on that charge are relevant in the
court. His belief or disbelief in God; his sexual orientation; his fidelity or infidelity
to his spouse or partner; his tastes in food, music, literature, or sport; his good or
bad table manners: all these are irrelevant to his trial on a charge of dangerous driving. Similarly, the judge who determines his punishment must act as a sentencer:
her attitudes toward and beliefs about religion, sexuality, marriage, aesthetics, etiquette, and so on are irrelevant to her task; her treatment of the defendant should
not be affected by the extent to which she would approve or disapprove of such
aspects of his life.[33] In determining both guilt (if that is part of her role) and sentence, she should, as a judge, attend only to those aspects of his life and conduct that
bear directly on whether he committed the offense, on his culpability in doing so,
and on the suitability to his offense of such punishments as the law makes available;
the tragedy that he has suffered has no bearing on these issues, and is therefore
irrelevant to her strictly judicial role.

But offenders are not just offenders, and sentencers are not just sentencers.
The criminal law constitutes one perspective on the defendant, and the sentencer,
qua sentencer, must see him through that perspective—a perspective from which
his present tragedy is invisible. Now in maintaining a system of criminal law, in
authorizing its officials to take this perspective, we must believe that it is one that
it is often, perhaps even normally, appropriate to take; we should, normally, take
crime seriously, which is to say that we should, normally, seek to call to account
through a criminal trial those who commit such wrongs. If Alan is indeed guilty of
theft or fraud, it is (normally) appropriate that the criminal law should focus its
attention, and try to focus his attention, on that wrong by the process of trial, conviction, and punishment: there might be many other matters in his life that concern him, and to which he would rather attend; but as a citizen he should attend,
as should the judge who sentences him, to this wrongdoing. But sometimes things
are not normal. Sometimes other aspects of the offender, as a human being, demand
our attention, and reasonably occupy his attention. Sometimes the sentencer, not
as a judge but as a fellow human being, should not close her eyes to those other
aspects: which is to say that she should not continue to see and to respond to the
offender simply as a sentencer dealing with an offender. Alan's present suffering
might be such that it is quite reasonably salient both for him and for the sentencer:

it is that, rather than his crime, that demands his and her attention. That suffering cannot figure *within* the judge's deliberations, qua sentencer, about what punishment is appropriate, qua punishment, to his crime: rather, it undermines the propriety of taking (only) that perspective on this offender. Qua sentencer, she should impose the punitively appropriate sentence; but sometimes a sentencer should not act simply or only as a sentencer. That is why Card rightly separates justice "as a virtue of persons" from justice as a "virtue of social institutions" and argues that "mercy is an expression of justice as a virtue of persons who have the right to punish, but not an aspect of the social or legal justice of the institution by which they get that right."[34]

(Here, too, considerations of proportionality play a role: the less serious the crime, the less dramatic or terrible the offender's current suffering needs to be to make it proper to turn our attention away from the crime to the suffering; and some crimes are no doubt so serious that they cannot be thus put aside. There is also the question of whether this account can explain mitigations as well as complete remissions of sentence. At first glance it might seem that it cannot do so. To refrain from any punishment, beyond that integral to the conviction that the defendant has suffered,[35] is to recognize that his and our attention should be on his suffering, rather than on his crime; but to impose even a reduced sentence is to try to get him to attend to his crime. This might be true if mitigation was just a matter of imposing a lighter sentence of the same kind—fewer years in prison, a smaller fine, fewer hours of community service—than the offender would otherwise have had to undergo; but there might be room for merciful mitigation as a matter of changing the mode of punishment to one that makes less total, all-embracing demands on the offender. Imprisonment could be replaced by some noncustodial sentence on these grounds. Prison is a total institution that gives the offender no respite from his crime; he is imprisoned, living within a penal structure, twenty-four hours a day and seven days a week. By contrast, a community service order leaves more of the offender's time and life intact, and thus leaves him more space to attend to other matters: it does not demand his total attention.)

Mercy, as thus understood in this kind of example, is therefore not a consideration that can operate *within* the perspective of criminal punishment: it is not a virtue of sentencers, qua sentencers; it is not a virtue internal to the role of sentencer within a system of criminal law. It is, rather, a virtue of the human beings who fill that role. A sentencer should recognize the importance of her role and its duties, of the criminal justice system of which that role is part, and of the perspective that structures that system: but as a human being (and citizen) she should also be able to put the criminal law in its place, and to recognize that in some cases (cases that must be unusual, if the criminal law is to be possible) that fall within the reach of the criminal law and its focus on public wrongdoing, it is not appropriate for her to think and act purely from within the perspective of the criminal law—purely within the confines of her role.

We can read the English Court of Appeal's judgment in *R v. Bernard* in the light of this interpretation of mercy:

> an offender's serious medical condition may enable a court, as an act of mercy in the exceptional circumstances of a particular case, rather than by virtue of any

general principle, to impose a lesser sentence than would otherwise be appropriate.[36]

The "general principle[s]" of sentencing have no room for such factors, which do not bear on the penal appropriateness of a sentence; but sometimes, exceptionally, a judge may or should look beyond that perspective, and allow other values—a concern for the defendant simply as a suffering fellow—to intrude.

I have argued so far that in the kind of case exemplified by Alan, the criminal law should make room for mercy; but that in doing so it allows the intrusion of values and concerns that are extrinsic rather than internal to its own normative structure as a distinctive institution. The same is not, however, true of the other two examples given in section 2.

4 MERCY AND EQUITY

Chuck's case is very different from Alan's. Alan's suffering, I have suggested, moves us to turn our attention away from his offense; by contrast, what we learn of Chuck's early life and background moves us to view his offense, and him as the offender, in a different light. He is not eligible for a recognized legal defense; we do not suppose that he is not now a responsible agent, or that he is simply the helpless victim of his heredity, environment, and upbringing—if we supposed that, we would think that he should not have been convicted at all, which is not the case we are imagining. But we recognize, and the sentencer recognizes, that he faced far greater obstacles than most of us face in growing up—that it would have been far harder for him than it has been for most of us to become the kind of person who would not commit that kind of crime; and for that reason we think it appropriate that he receive a lighter sentence, as well as the offer of help.[37] Perhaps somewhat analogously, someone who is convicted of murder might receive a much lighter sentence (if this is legally possible) when it turns out that what he committed was voluntary euthanasia: even if we agree that euthanasia should be criminal, this defendant's motives, the context of the killing, should lead us to see his action, and him as its perpetrator, in a different and much less harsh light; the law might not formally count "mercy-killing" as a distinct and lesser offense, but the judge should surely adjust the sentence in the light of these morally mitigating factors.[38]

It might seem, and has seemed to a number of theorists,[39] that any mitigation of sentence based on considerations such as these is not properly a matter of mercy: "relaxing the penalty of a general law in a 'deserving case' is not mercy at all but mere justice."[40] The sentencer is not remitting what justice demands or allows (which is what mercy involves); she is, rather, doing penal justice. For justice includes equity, which involves an attention to particularities of individual cases that are not captured by the system's rules. The criminal law's rules for offenses and defenses might be generally just: it defines as crimes what are indeed usually wrongs that merit public condemnation; it generally distinguishes wrongs that differ from each other significantly as to character or seriousness; it generally recognizes as defenses, whether partial or complete, the kinds of factor that negate responsibility or culpability. But rules are inevitably imperfect: they cannot do justice to the subtly variegated particularities of individual cases, which means that their rigid and exceptionless application will sometimes do injustice in particular cases. If the rules are well formulated, their application will usually do justice: but those who are to apply the rules (in this context, sentencers) must be left with a zone of discretion within which they can make the kinds of variation or exception that justice itself requires. Such discretion is especially appropriate, we might also think, at the stage of sentencing. Perhaps it is important that at the stage of verdict, when the defendant is either convicted or acquitted, the law sends out a clear message, and draws as bright a line as can be drawn between conduct that is legally permissible and conduct that is not; but sentencing can be a more nuanced, individualized affair, in which justice can be done to the particularities of the individual case.[41] If this is what "mercy" involves, there is no conflict between mercy and justice: rather, the "moral ideal" of mercy is a "norm [that] fulfills and completes a conception of justice that lies itself at the basis of the rule of law."[42]

This is not to say that mercy, conceived as a matter of justice-completing equity, is quite unproblematic. There are difficult questions about the discretion sentencers should have: how far should it extend; how should it be checked or controlled? There are equally difficult questions about the grounds on which sentencers should show leniency: is it appropriate to show Chuck this kind of mercy, or should we insist that, as a matter of penal justice, no such disadvantages in a person's background should be taken to mitigate his guilt?[43] But these questions are not our concern here: I want instead to suggest that even here there is conflict of a kind between "mercy" and "justice"—that here, too, mercy can constitute an intrusion into the criminal law of values that are in some ways external to it.

Our criminal law formally recognizes only a limited range of exemptions and excuses.[44] It counts defendants as criminally responsible agents, who can be held to account for what they have done, unless they meet the strict criteria of nonresponsibility—infancy or serious mental disorder that radically impairs their capacities for rational thought and action; it thus sets the bar of responsibility very low. It also holds responsible defendants fully culpable for their criminal actions unless they can point to some immediate and drastic kind of pressure that very seriously undermined their capacity or opportunity to avoid committing the offense. A defendant can plead self-defense (he used possibly fatal force in response to an immediate attack on his physical safety); or duress by threats (he committed the crime only because he was threatened with otherwise unavoidable serious harm); or necessity (he committed the crime to avoid imminent and otherwise unavoidable serious harm); or perhaps provocation as at least a partial defense (his victim provoked the attack by seriously wronging him):[45] but if none of these kinds of dramatic and exceptional factors obtain, he has no defense. Now this is not just a matter of practical convenience—a matter of having relatively clear rules that cover the majority of cases, and that can leave unusual cases to the discretion of officials. There are two good reasons of principle why a liberal criminal law should recognize such a limited and tightly constrained set of exemptions and excuses.

First, it matters (or should matter) greatly to citizens that they be recognized and treated as responsible agents, who can take control of their own lives and answer for their actions; the state should, therefore, be very slow to deny this status to a citizen, and should do so only for those who are manifestly lacking in those modest rational capacities that are required for adult social life.[46] Nor should the state inquire into the extent to which or the sense in which citizens who are now minimally rationally competent can legitimately be held responsible for having become the kinds of people they are: what matters is to engage with them as they now are, as citizens who can be held responsible for what they now do;[47] the question of what (if anything) it means to be responsible for becoming the kinds of people we are, and of whether we are thus responsible, is not one that should concern legislators.

Second, we have noted that the criminal law "abstracts" defendants from their contexts:[48] it does not aim to judge the whole person; its interest is only in the defendant's relationship to the particular offense for which he is being tried. Its perspective is in this way a very shallow one: it does not seek, and its courts must not seek, to delve into the depths of the defendant's character or soul, into the various conditions that made him the person he is, or into all the circumstances that lay behind his crime. It asks whether (assuming that he satisfies the fairly modest conditions of responsible agency) he committed the offense charged; and it exempts him from conviction and punishment, if he did commit the offense, only if he can point to some quite starkly abnormal feature of the context in which it was committed that renders it clearly justifiable or its agent clearly excusable. The criminal law does not seek to judge us as our friends or family will (we must hope) judge us. We expect from them a sympathetic and intimate understanding that, while by no means blind to our faults and wrongdoings, sees them in the broader, deeper context of our lives and characters—and thus, we might hope, can often see them in a less unqualifiedly condemnatory light.[49] But we should not expect the criminal law to take this perspective on us: its perspective is simpler, shallower, more limited. That is why the example with which Nussbaum begins her discussion of the implications of classical Graeco-Roman ideas of equity "for contemporary political and legal issues" is apt as illuminating an important aspect of our private, personal lives, but unhelpful as a guide to the way in which the criminal law should judge us.[50] David Copperfield's understanding of and attitudes toward Steerforth are quite properly conditioned by their shared history and by his knowledge of Steerforth's background, upbringing, and whole life; but we should not expect a criminal court to take that kind of view of him.

Why not? Because a liberal state should not take that kind of intrusive (and so potentially oppressive) interest in its citizens' lives and souls. It should regulate our overt dealings with each other, and identify and condemn wrongs that we commit in the course of such dealings; but while its offense definitions and its judgments should be grounded in moral standards of wrongdoing and culpability, it should not try to reproduce the depth and nuances of our moral thought. We may expect our friends and families to deal with us as intimates, but we should expect the law, and especially the criminal law, to take a more detached stance, which tries to deal only with the more superficial aspects of our lives. That is why various factors that will properly make a difference to our moral understanding of and responses to our friends (such as Chuck's unfortunate background) will not figure in the criminal law's perspective.

We could of course accept such a conception of the criminal law, but argue that its limits should be modestly weakened: that we should, perhaps, recognize "seriously disadvantaged background" formally as at least a mitigating factor, if not as a formal defense.[51] Similarly, we might argue that even if euthanasia properly remains criminal, it should (at least when it is at the request of person killed) be formally distinguished from murder as a separate and lesser offense.[52] Sometimes, no doubt, this will be the right view to take—I think that it is right in the case of euthanasia, for instance. But sometimes we will recognize that the criminal law cannot make room within its perspective for factors that would affect our moral responses— I think that this is probably true of a case like Chuck's, even if we have some moral sympathy for him. We might then say that in that case the law and the court must remain blind to such factors: if the law does not formally recognize them as mitigating, the judge must ignore them in passing sentence.

Now it is true that if the criminal law, understood as the kind of limited practice I have sketched here, is to be possible, it must normally be possible and legitimate to exclude consideration of such factors; it must normally be possible for courts to pass judgments on defendants that, although they exclude from consideration a range of factors that would bear on a more intimately personal moral understanding of their actions, can nonetheless be accepted as just by those defendants and by others. But the qualifying "normally" is crucial: for surely there can be cases— perhaps Chuck's is one—in which what is normally possible and legitimate is no longer possible. Just as in a case like Alan's the judge might find that she cannot stick unwaveringly to the criminal law's perspective, so (though for different reasons) she might find in a case like Chuck's that she cannot maintain the law's rigid exclusion from consideration of the factors that make his life and actions (to sympathetic moral eyes) more of a tragedy than a crime; she might therefore be tempted, and might decide, to show mercy in sentencing him.

I do not claim to have shown that this kind of mercy is ever really permissible; indeed, I am not sure whether it is, although I have argued that there is at least a case to be made for it. My primary aim has rather been to show that there is logical space for it—that it is an instance of mercy, whose merits or demerits we can discuss; but also that, as in Alan's case, mercy constitutes an intrusion into the perspective of the criminal law of concerns and values that are not part of it. It is true that in this case, unlike Alan's, the concerns to which a merciful judge appeals are closely connected to those of the criminal law, since they have to do with the justice of condemning the defendant as a wrongdoer: but they are still extrinsic to the law, since they have to do with dimensions of justice that the criminal law properly excludes from its normal purview. Some will argue that this is one of the ways in which liberal criminal law is riven by contradictions or "antinomies" that undermine any claim that it is a rational, principled human practice. It tries to abstract defendants from their social contexts and backgrounds, but cannot consistently do so, since contextual and background factors constantly irrupt in the courts; it is committed to maintaining a limited, abstracting perspective that it also proves impossible to maintain.[53] It is true that to give mercy such a role in the criminal law is to introduce a kind of conflict that cannot be neatly resolved; it is, as I have argued, to allow values and concerns that belong to perspectives distinct from that of the criminal law to intrude into the law, and thus to disrupt the legal process. But it is by now a familiar claim that, while life would be much easier if values never conflicted, the world—the normative world of values—is not like that; we face a world of diverse and irreconcilable values, which make ineluctably conflicting demands on us.[54] Rationality must then embrace conflict, rather than shun it as contradiction: rational moral thinkers will face, rather than deny or try to eliminate, the conflicts with which the normative world presents them. Sometimes those conflicts flow from different roles that we fill, from different normative perspectives to which those roles belong: this is true, I have been arguing, in the case of mercy in the criminal law.

5 MERCY AND REPENTANCE

We must turn, finally, to the case of David, the now repentant offender who pleads guilty and seeks to make amends for his crime. This example raises two questions. First, does such repentance warrant some mitigation of punishment: should a repentant offender be punished less severely than he would have been punished had he shown no such repentance?[55] Second, if such mitigation is warranted, is this a matter of mercy—or simply of penal justice?

From the perspective of penal justice, understood as a matter of penal desert, it is hard to see how repentance, however heartfelt and genuine, could be relevant. It could be argued to be relevant if we took a wholly character-based view of the grounds for punishment, which holds punishment to be ultimately justified not by the particular crime for which the offender has been convicted, but by the reprehensible character trait revealed by that crime;[56] for we could then say that the offender's later repentance casts a new and more favorable light on his character. But such a radically character-based view of criminal liability is not plausible, at least for a liberal system of criminal law: the criminal law is concerned with, and punishes us for, what we do, not what we are; its focus is on our actions, not on our deeper character.[57] Now it is true that if repentance follows *immediately* on the crime, if the offender is struck by remorseful horror at what he has done as soon as he does it, this might affect our judgment of the criminal action, and thus of the wrongdoer's penal desert: an action that is so immediately repented and disowned is perhaps not as culpable as one that is not thus repented.[58] But when the repentance comes later, it cannot affect the seriousness of the offense, or the offender's culpability in committing it; it therefore cannot affect the severity of the punishment he deserves for committing the offence.[59]

Some would therefore give a firmly negative answer to the first question: the repentant offender deserves, and should therefore receive, a punishment as onerous as would have been imposed had he not repented; his repentance is commendable (it is, indeed, one of the aims of punishment) but should not mitigate his punishment.[60] However, others argue that repentance can still make some mitigation of sentence appropriate, but as a matter of mercy rather than of penal justice.[61]

Tasioulas argues, on the basis of his pluralist account of punishment,[62] that the sentencer can legitimately "widen [her] field of vision beyond the wrongful act—to take account of the nature of the agent and his broader circumstances," so long as this works to the benefit of the offender, and the further factors that she considers are so connected to the wrongful act as to "make them bear on justified censure for wrong-doing." Repentance satisfies both conditions (the second, because repentance is "the hoped-for consequence of punishment"); so although it cannot affect the offender's penal desert or rights, "there is an unavoidable sense of excess in insisting on the full infliction of deserved hard treatment [when] the offender has already repented"—which is to say that his repentance is a reason to show mercy.[63] That "excess" is not, on this view, a matter of penal injustice—of a disproportionality between the offense and the punishment: for Tasioulas insists that retributive desert is independent of that "hoped-for consequence" of repentance. Nor does the "sense of excess" express the idea that repentance, which is indeed a painful and burdensome process closely connected to the offense, is itself a kind of punishment, so that the formal punishment imposed on the offender by the criminal law can be reduced in the light of this informal punishment that he has already and informally imposed on himself by repenting: that would again be to make repentance-based leniency a matter of penal justice—of ensuring that the total punishment, informal and formal, does not become disproportionate to the offense. We are to accept that the full punishment is fully deserved, but also feel that it would be excessively harsh given the offender's repentance—although the repentant offender himself will presumably not regard the punishment as unduly harsh, but will be ready to undergo it as what he deserves.

I cannot do justice here to the depth and subtlety of the account of mercy that Tasioulas offers,[64] or to the broader question of whether repentance should make any difference at all to an offender's sentence. My own view is that it should not. Repentance is indeed a proper aim of punishment: the punishment that the offender is required to undertake or to undergo should both provide a structure within which he can be brought to confront and (or so we must hope) repent his crime, and provide the formal means by which he can, by accepting punishment, express his repentance to his victims and to the wider community; punishment should thus be a two-way communicative process through which the polity communicates to the offender the censure that his crime deserves, and the offender can communicate back to the polity his own recognition of the wrong he has done. But both dimensions of this two-way communication are important, and even if we might think that the offender's own repentance makes the first less vital, it does not make the second any less necessary: for the prescribed punishment is the way in which a repentant offender can formally express his repentance.[65] This view depends, however, on a particular and contentious account of punishment as communication, and will not persuade those who find such an account implausible.

One final point is worth noting here. Tasioulas talks of "an unavoidable sense of excess in insisting on the full infliction of deserved hard treatment" on an already repentant offender. We should indeed have such a sense when we contemplate the harsh punishments imposed in our existing systems of criminal justice: when we think, for instance, of a repentant offender sentenced to a long term in the brutal environment of one of our prisons. But we should also have that sense when we contemplate the punishments that we so often inflict on unrepentant offenders, and the oppressive harshness that characterizes so many of our penal institutions and practices. If we then try to imagine a penal system that is less oppressive and inhumane, which imposes punishment that are less destructive, and more respectful of the moral status of those on whom they are imposed, we might be less likely to feel such a "sense of excess" in contemplating the full punishment of repentant offenders.[66] If the punishment that is deserved in such a radically reformed system is, for instance, a relatively (to contemporary eyes) short term in a civilized prison, or a noncustodial sentence of constructive community service and probation, should we feel so reluctant to impose it on a repentant offender?

6 A VERY BRIEF CONCLUSION

I have discussed three kinds of case in which it might be argued that a sentencer could—or even should—show mercy to an offender. My aim has not been to argue that mercy is indeed justified in such cases; I have real doubts about the propriety of mercy in at least the second and third kinds of case. But the point of discussing these three kinds of case has rather been to explicate the logic of mercy, as something distinct from (indeed, opposed to) retributive justice, and to show how it *could* nonetheless play a role in a system of criminal justice. Its role is different in each kind of case. In the first kind of case (discussed in section 3) mercy cannot be grounded in the aims or values of the criminal law itself; it is, rather, an intrusion into the criminal law, a voice that speaks from outside the criminal law in tones that belong to a quite distinct normative perspective. Here there is a clear conflict between justice and mercy, and the question is when, if ever, mercy can properly defeat justice. In the second kind of case (discussed in section 4), mercy is also an intrusion into the logical structure of the criminal law, but is grounded in values from which that structure itself ultimately derives; the conflict here is not between mercy and justice as such, but between mercy and justice as it is artificially (and justifiably) defined within the system of criminal law. In the third kind of case (discussed in section 5), mercy still conflicts with retributive justice; but if Tasioulas is right, it can be, and is, justified in terms of the aims and values of the criminal justice system itself.

There is therefore no neat conclusion to be reached either about the relationship between mercy and criminal justice (for there is no single such relationship) or about the legitimacy of mercy in sentencing (or in other parts of the criminal justice system); the most I can hope to have achieved here is to clarify the various ways mercy might figure in the context of criminal law, and the different questions it raises.

NOTES

1. Although I will focus, as theorists generally focus, on judicial sentencing as the context in which mercy is at stake in criminal law, it can be an issue in any context in which some burden of penality (see D. Garland, *Punishment and Welfare* (Oxford: Oxford University Press, 1985), x) may be compassionately lightened—by police officers deciding whether to pursue an investigation into a suspect, by prosecutors deciding whether to charge a suspect or what charge to pursue, by those who administer punishment. I assume that the issues in these other contexts will be relevantly similar to those that arise in the context of sentencing.

2. Only "normally," because there could be cases in which remitting B's debt makes A unable to satisfy other, more stringent, moral demands.

3. We need not discuss here the question of whether, in extreme cases, it might be denied that A has the moral right to demand payment.

4. Compare the distinction that Tasioulas draws between grounds for leniency that are "integral to" and those that are "extraneous to" a theory of punishment, or to "the logic" of punishment (J. Tasioulas, "Punishment and Repentance" (2006) 81 *Philosophy* 279, 318–9); and Card's distinction between justice "as a virtue of persons" and justice "as a virtue of social institutions" (C. Card, "On Mercy" [1976] 81 *Philosophical Review* 182, 188–93).

5. Aristotle, *Nicomachean Ethics*, II.6.1106b; see books II–IV generally.

6. See, e.g., Card, n. 4 above, 186–7; J. Tasioulas, "Mercy" (2003) 103 *Proceedings of the Aristotelian Society* 101, 102–3. Contrast D. Markel, "Against Mercy" (2004) 88 *Minnesota Law Review* 1421, 1436–8, defining mercy to encompass leniency "motivated by bias, corruption or caprice."

7. This is true at least of noninstitutional actions. If an institution's rules provide for the exercise of mercy by its officials, an official can exercise (what the institution counts as) mercy from corrupt motives. The use of the "executive grant of clemency" in the United States provides an interesting case study in this context: see K. Moore, *Pardons: Justice, Mercy, and the Public Interest* (Oxford: Oxford University Press, 1989).

8. For a contrary view, see R. Harrison, "The Equality of Mercy," H. Gross & R. Harrison (eds.), *Jurisprudence: Cambridge Essays* (Oxford: Oxford University Press, 1992), 107, 107–8; see also G. Rainbolt, "Mercy: In Defense of Caprice" (1997) 31 *Nous* 226. For critique, see Tasioulas, n. 6 above, 104–7; also Card, n. 4 above, 186–7.

9. On "negative" as against "positive" retributivism, see D. Dolinko, "Some Thoughts about Retributivism" (1991) 101 *Ethics* 537, 539–43.

10. On relative or ordinal proportionality, as against absolute or cardinal proportionality, see A. von Hirsch, *Censure and Sanctions* (Oxford: Oxford University Press, 1993), 18–19.

11. Consequentialists will of course typically, and rightly, insist that the effects of punishment on the offender must figure in the calculus of costs and benefits; I mention the possibility of excluding them only because that is what is sometimes suggested by the rhetoric of the "war on crime," and by theorists who argue that offenders forfeit their moral standing (see, e.g., C. Morris, "Punishment and Loss of Moral Standing" (1991) 21 *Canadian Journal of Philosophy* 53.

12. Compare *Bernard* [1997] 1 Cr. App. R.(S.) 135. Alan has still, of course, suffered the pain of being brought to court and convicted, which counts as a kind of punishment. In such a case, however, one could also imagine the prosecutor deciding not to prosecute him, as an act of mercy; see n. 1 above.

13. See D. Husak, "Already Punished Enough" (1990) 18 *Philosophical Topics* 79. Matters are more complex if the offender's loss resulted from his crime (a reckless driver causes a crash that kills his wife, for instance). We cannot pursue here the question of whether it can make sense to see such loss as a "natural punishment": see P. Winch, "Ethical Reward and Punishment," in his *Ethics and Action* (London: Routledge, 2002), 210.

14. Compare the examples discussed, in more nuanced detail, in M. Nussbaum, "Equity and Mercy" (1993) 22 *Philosophy & Public Affairs* 83; C. Bennett, "The Limits of Mercy" (2004) 17 *Ratio* 1, 5–9; Tasioulas, n. 6 above, 116–7.

15. See J. G. Murphy, "Mercy and Legal Justice," in J. G. Murphy and J. Hampton, *Forgiveness and Mercy* (Cambridge: Cambridge University Press, 1988), 162, 177–80.

16. J. F. Stephen, *Liberty, Equality, Fraternity* [1873] (ed. J. White; Cambridge: Cambridge University Press, 1967), 152. See also T. Honderich, *Punishment: The Supposed Justifications Revisited* (London; Pluto Press, 2005), 28–9, 231–3.

17. See classically J. G. Murphy, "Marxism and Retribution" (1973) 2 *Philosophy & Public Affairs* 217. For what is perhaps the most plausible version, see R. Dagger, "Playing Fair with Punishment" (1993) 103 *Ethics* 473, and "Punishment as Fair Play" (2008) 14 *Res Publica* 259.

18. See Honderich, n. 16 above, ch. 2, Postscript .; R. A. Duff, *Punishment, Communication and Community* (New York: Oxford University Press, 2001), 21–5, and further references there.

19. There is also the problem, noted above (at nn. 9–10), that remitting Alan's punishment seems unjust to Bill, whose offense was the same as Alan's but who now receives a harsher punishment.

20. See Markel, n. 6 above, for a developed and detailed argument to this conclusion.

21. See n. 5 above.

22. Aristotle, *Nicomachean Ethics*, III.1, 1110a .

23. This is one respect in which the analogy does not hold: whilst a judge should feel for the defendant as a fellow human being, it is not clearly part of a judge's responsibilities to offer or seek such help.

24. See, e.g., Markel, n. 6 above, 42–3. Given Markel's broad definition of "mercy," this would count as an exercise of mercy; but if we so define mercy that acts of mercy must be motivated by compassion for the offender's plight, it is unlikely that such emergencies would justify mercy, as distinct from leniency.

25. The "now" is best read as "given what has now happened," but could of course be taken to leave open the possibility that I will return to the matter at some later date: that

I am postponing rather than abandoning my intended criticism of him. Whether it will be proper to return to the matter later will depend on a range of factors: on the seriousness of the wrong, on the seriousness of what has befallen him and the length of time for which it (quite properly) occupies his and our attention; on the ways in which it changes him and us.

26. Some version of this (as presented here, vague and general) claim is common to many penal theories. See, classically, J. Feinberg, "The Expressive Function of Punishment," in his *Doing and Deserving* (Princeton, N.J.: Princeton University Press, 1970), 95; for different retributivist versions of the claim, see von Hirsch, n. 10 above; Duff, n. 18 above; Tasioulas, n. 4 above. For a consequentialist account that posits an expressive function for punishment, see J. Braithwaite and P. Pettit, *Not Just Deserts* (Oxford: Oxford University Press, 1990).

27. Why should this lead us to a remission, rather than just a deferral, of punishment? See n. 25 above. Perhaps deferral would be appropriate for a serious crime; but for lesser crimes remission might be grounded on an informal analogue of a statute of limitations, together with the thought that deferring punishment would unreasonably extend the whole penal process.

28. See Tasioulas, n. 6 above, n. 4 above; also "Repentance and the Liberal State" (2007) 4 *Ohio State Journal of Criminal Law* 487.

29. Tasioulas, n. 4 above, 285.

30. See Tasioulas, n. 4 above, 318–9; and n. 4 above and accompanying text.

31. See further Duff, n. 18 above, 56–72, and *Answering for Crime* (Oxford: Hart, 2007) chs. 4, 6.

32. To call it a game is not to imply that it is either unimportant or detached from reality; the term "game" here carries the kind of meaning it has in Wittgensteinian talk of "language games."

33. This is one of the ways in which the criminal law involves "abstraction": it abstracts the defendant from the rich particularities of his or her life and its context. See, e.g., A. W. Norrie, *Crime, Reason and History: A Critical Introduction to Criminal Law* (2nd ed.; London: Butterworths, 2001), 21–23; and at n. 53 below.

34. Card, n. 4 above, 189.

35. Although in some cases that would merit mercy if they were carried through to conviction, the prosecutor might properly decide not to bring the case to trial at all; see n. 1 above.

36. [1997] 1 Cr. App. R.(S.) 135, 138: the case is cited by N. Walker, *Aggravation, Mitigation and Mercy in English Criminal Justice* (London: Blackstone Press, 1999), 2134, and by Tasioulas, n. 6 above, 117–8.

37. If we also think that the disadvantages he has suffered were at least in part the result of serious injustices in our political, social, and economic arrangements, and of our collective failure as a society to attend to the well-being of the vulnerable, we might also question our right to call him to account now for his crime (see Duff, n. 18 above, 179–201): but that would be a different kind of doubt about the legitimacy of his punishment. To show mercy, in the context of the criminal law, presupposes the right to punish; it is that very right that this kind of question puts in doubt.

38. Given the significance of the label "murder," and the mandatory life sentence for murder in English law, it is quite likely that the mercy-killer would be charged with or convicted of manslaughter rather than murder, even though his action fitted the legal definition of murder; but we can focus here on a case in which he is convicted of murder. See further at n. 52 below.

39. See, e.g., Murphy, n. 15 above, 169–72; Tasioulas, n. 6 above, 110–4; Markel, n. 6 above, 1435–6, 1473–5; S. P. Garvey, "Is It Wrong to Commute Death Row? Retribution, Atonement and Mercy" (2004) 82 *North Carolina Law Review* 1319, 1325–30.

40. P. Geach, *Truth and Hope* (Notre Dame: University of Notre Dame Press, 2001), 96, quoted by Tasioulas, n. 6 above, 114.

41. Compare the notorious case of *Dudley and Stephens* [1884] QBD 273, in which the court declared firmly that the defendants, who had killed and eaten a fellow-sailor in order to avoid dying from starvation after being shipwrecked, must be convicted of murder, but the death sentence was then commuted to six months' imprisonment.

42. Nussbaum, n. 14 above, 109.

43. See Bennett, n. 14 above. On the general issue about the bearing of social deprivation on criminal liability, see R. Delgado, "'Rotten Social Background': Should the Criminal Law Recognize a Defense of Severe Environmental Deprivation?" (1985) 3 *Law and Inequality* 9; B. Hudson, "Beyond Proportionate Punishment: Difficult Cases and the 1991 Criminal Justice Act" (1995) 22 *Crime, Law and Social Change* 59; W. Heffernan & J. Kleinig (eds.), *From Social Justice to Criminal Justice* (New York: Oxford University Press, 2000); A. von Hirsch & A. J. Ashworth, *Proportionate Sentencing* (Oxford: Oxford University Press, 2005), ch. 5.

44. On the distinction between exemptions (which negate responsibility) and excuses (which negate culpability but not responsibility) see J. Gardner, "The Gist of Excuses" (1998) 1 *Buffalo Criminal Law Review* 575; V. Tadros, *Criminal Responsibility* (Oxford: Oxford University Press, 2005), 124–29.

45. On the range of defenses recognized by English and American criminal law, see A. P. Simester & G. R. Sullivan, *Criminal Law: Theory and Doctrine* (4th ed; Oxford: Hart, 2010), chs. 17–22; M. D. Dubber & M. G. Kelman, *American Criminal Law: Cases, Statutes, and Comments* (New York: Foundation Press, 2005), ch. 7.

46. Compare J. Gardner, "The Mark of Responsibility" (2003) 23 *Oxford Journal of Legal Studies* 157; see also Bennett, n. 14 above.

47. See, e.g., N. Lacey, *State Punishment: Political Principles and Community Values* (London: Routledge, 1988), 65–68.

48. See at n. 33 above.

49. Compare Iris Murdoch's discussion of the "just and loving gaze" that we should turn on other people: *The Sovereignty of Good* (London: Routledge, 1970).

50. Nussbaum, n. 14 above, 105–8.

51. See n. 43 above.

52. See at n. 38 above; and see Law Commission, *Murder, Manslaughter and Infanticide* (No. 304; London: Stationery Office, 2006), Part 7, recommending that "mercy killing" should be a partial defense on a charge of murder.

53. See, e.g., Norrie, n. 33 above; also "'Simulacra of Morality': Beyond the Ideal/Actual Antinomies of Criminal Justice," in R. A. Duff (ed.), *Philosophy and the Criminal Law* (Cambridge: Cambridge University Press, 1998), 101; in response, see R. A. Duff, "Principle and Contradiction in Criminal Law: Motives and Criminal Liability," in the same volume, 156.

54. See, e.g., I. Berlin, "The Pursuit of the Ideal," in his *The Crooked Timber of Humanity* (London: Murray, 1991) 1, 12; S. Hampshire, *Morality and Conflict* (Oxford: Blackwell, 1983); Tasioulas, n. 6 above.

55. As seems in fact to happen, if we interpret the mitigation of sentence standardly received by offenders who plead guilty as grounded in the repentance that such pleas might be taken to express: but see A. J. Ashworth, *Sentencing and Criminal Justice* (4th ed.;

Cambridge: Cambridge University Press, 2005), 163–71. I leave aside here the difficult questions that arise about the sincerity of offenders' expressions of repentance: for a very useful discussion, see J. G. Murphy, "Remorse, Apology and Mercy" (2007) 4 *Ohio State Journal of Criminal Law* 423, 436–46, arguing that repentance should figure as grounds for executive clemency rather than at the sentencing stage, because there is then available "a more reliable evidential foundation upon which to base judgments of sincerity" (444).

56. See, e.g., M. D. Bayles, "Character, Purpose and Criminal Responsibility" (1982) 1 *Law and Philosophy* 5; Lacey, n. 47 above, ch. 3.

57. For the justification of this dogmatic claim, and some of the qualifications that it requires, see M. S. Moore, *Placing Blame: A General Theory of the Criminal Law* (Oxford: Oxford University Press, 1997), ch. 13; Duff, n. 31 above, ch. 5.

58. See Tasioulas, n. 4 above, 308.

59. See Tasioulas, n. 4 above, 306–10.

60. See Duff, n. 18 above, 118–21.

61. See especially Tasioulas, n. 4 above; n. 28 above; see also von Hirsch and Ashworth, n. 43 above, 172–8.

62. See at nn. 28–30 above.

63. Tasioulas, n. 4 above, 317–8.

64. But see R. A. Duff, "The Intrusion of Mercy" (2007) 4 *Ohio State Journal of Criminal Law* 361, 383–7.

65. See further Duff, n. 18 above; C. Bennett, "Taking the Sincerity out of Saying Sorry: Restorative Justice as Ritual" (2006) 23 *Journal of Applied Philosophy* 127.

66. This point is especially relevant to debates in the United States about mercy in relation to the death penalty. It is hard not to feel a sense of gross excess when we contemplate the execution of a manifestly repentant murderer (see, e.g., the cases discussed in Murphy, n. 55 above; Garvey, n. 39 above, and "'As the Gentle Rain from Heaven': Mercy in Capital Sentencing" (1996) 81 *Cornell Law Review* 989; M. Sigler, "Mercy, Clemency, and the Case of Karla Faye Tucker" (2007) 4 *Ohio State Journal of Criminal Law* 455.

CHAPTER 17

ALTERNATIVES TO PUNISHMENT

STEPHEN P. GARVEY

WE should begin with some distinctions. If someone says that we should try to find an alternative to punishment, they might mean that we should try to find alternative forms of punishment: something other than the traditional or dominant forms in use today, especially imprisonment. Indeed, a number of authors have made the case for greater use of "intermediate sanctions," such as intensive probation supervision, so-called day fines, or home confinement.[1] Another, and more controversial, alternative involves so-called shaming penalties.[2] A person convicted of driving while intoxicated affixes a bumper sticker to his car: "Convicted: DWI." A shoplifter stands in front of Wal-Mart bearing a sign: "I am a thief; I stole from Wal-Mart." The wisdom of these alternative punishments continues to be the subject of debate, as sometimes does their legality.

Someone who says we should try to find an alternative to punishment might also mean that we should try to find an alternative *theory* of punishment. A theory of punishment purports to tell us when and why it is at least permissible to treat a person in a way that would ordinarily be impermissible. For example, when, if ever, is it permissible to confine a person against her will? Traditional theories look to the future or to the past for an answer. *Consequentialist* theories focus on the future: punishment is permissible if and when punishing an offender maximizes good consequences.[3] Punishment works for the common good. *Rehabilitative* (or reform) theories likewise focus on the future: punishment is permissible if and when punishing an offender makes her a better person, even at the cost of otherwise diminished social good.[4] Punishment works for the offender's good. *Retributive* theories focus on the past: punishment is permissible if and when the offender deserves to be punished for a past transgression.[5] Punishment is an end in itself, since doing punishment means doing justice.

An alternative theory of punishment presents itself as an alternative not reducible to one of these traditional theories or justifications. For example, Antony Duff has offered one such alternative, according to which "[c]riminal punishment...should communicate to offenders the censure they deserve for their crimes and should aim through that communicative process to persuade them to repent those crimes, to try to reform themselves, and thus reconcile themselves with those whom they wronged."[6] For Duff, punishment should ideally be a form of "secular penance."[7] Such an account is neither utilitarian nor rehabilitative, since the relationship between punishment and the goods it achieves is said to be necessary, not contingent. Nor it is retributive, since deserved punishment is not an end in itself, but a (necessary) means to other ends.

The task at hand is to examine alternatives to punishment in neither of these senses, as alternative forms of punishment or alternative theories of punishment. Instead, the task is to examine *alternatives to punishment* itself. Those who say that we should end state punishment and replace it with something else are *penal abolitionists*.[8] They conclude for one reason or another that punishment is not justified, and perhaps cannot be, no matter what form it takes and no matter what the offense for which it is imposed. All efforts to come up with a justification have so far failed, and perhaps are bound to fail. This conviction, then, motivates the search for some alternative. If we cannot justifiably punish, then what, if anything, should we be doing instead?

Penal abolitionists must therefore answer at least two questions: First, why is punishment never justified? Second, what, if anything, should replace it?[9]

1 PUNISHMENT AND ABOLITION

1.1 Defining Punishment

In order intelligibly to explain why punishment should be abolished, and why that which replaces it is not punishment, we need some account of that which is to be abolished and replaced: punishment. Settling on an account of what punishment is turns out to be more difficult than one might initially suspect. How best to define punishment was a matter of considerable debate in philosophical circles in the 1950s, and from that debate emerged what can fairly be described as a consensus view, which has since come to be known as the Flew-Benn-Hart definition of punishment (after Antony Flew, Stanley Benn, and H. L. A. Hart). Flew originally proposed the definition,[10] which Benn and Hart later embraced.[11] I will refer to it as the *standard definition*. According to Hart's influential formulation, the "standard or central case of [state] 'punishment'" involves five elements:

1. It must involve pain or other consequences normally considered unpleasant.
2. It must be for an offense against legal rules.

3. It must be of an actual or supposed offender for his offense.
4. It must be intentionally administered by human beings other than the offender.
5. It must be imposed and administered by an authority constituted by a legal system against which the offense is committed.[12]

Three features of this definition warrant additional comment. First, it portrays punishment as necessarily "retributive" in the *limited sense* that punishment is imposed *for an offense* already done. Punishment necessarily looks back to some offense the actor committed.[13] A retributive theory of punishment would then go on to say that the actor's culpable commission of the offense permits the state to punish him for it, whereas a consequentialist theory would go on to say that his punishment for the offense is permissible if and only if it serves the common good, and a rehabilitative theory would then go on to say that his punishment for the offense is permissible if and only if it serves his good.

Second, one might object that this definition forecloses at least one question any definition should leave open: Is it possible for the state to punish someone it believes to be innocent of any offense? According to the standard definition, the state cannot punish someone it believes to be innocent: punishment must be of an actual or supposed offender. The state can on the standard account *victimize* someone it believes is innocent, but it cannot *punish* her. Consequently, it makes no sense to ask whether the state is ever permitted to punish an actor it believes to be innocent. But insofar as we should be able to ask that question, the standard definition can easily be amended such that punishment must be of an actual or supposed offender for her offense, *or* of a person the state *represents* as having committed an offense, even though it believes she has in fact committed no offense.[14] With the definition so modified, the state can punish an actor who it believes to be innocent, though it cannot punish an actor whose innocence it openly acknowledges.

Third, one might object that the standard definition is incomplete. Imagine that you decide, as you often do, to park in the spot reserved for handicapped drivers. Your usual luck runs out this time, and you return to find a ticket under your windshield wiper. When all is said and done, you end up having to pay a fine—or is it a user fee? You surely have no choice but to hand money over to some state functionary, but in being so compelled are you being punished, or are you really just paying the fee you are required to pay (albeit after the fact) for the privilege of parking where you are permitted to park if and only if you pay the required fee?

According to the standard definition, one *could* say that you *are* being punished. Go through the criteria: Handing over money is unpleasant. You are required to hand it over because you committed an offense: you parked where you were not supposed to have parked. The folks taking your money are human beings; they take your money intentionally; and they take your money in the name of the law, which is the authority against which you have committed the offense. There you have it: The payment you make is a punishment.

But *is* it? One could admit that all of the conditions laid out in the standard definition are met but nonetheless intelligibly insist that you are not being punished. One could insist that your payment should instead be characterized as a mere *penalty*. If so, then the standard definition is incomplete. It leaves out whatever it is that distinguishes punishments from penalties, and thus leaves us unable to tell whether you are being punished or (merely) penalized.

This line of thought is famously associated with Joel Feinberg, who argued that the standard definition ignored the *expressive dimension* of punishment. According to Feinberg, "punishment is a conventional device for the expression of attitudes of resentment and indignation, and of judgments of disapproval and reprobation, on the part either of the punishing authority himself or of those 'in whose name' the punishment is inflicted."[15] The hardship of punishment is therefore like a language. It constitutes a medium or vehicle by and through which the state expresses its indignation toward, and thus condemns or censures, the offender for his offense. Punishments have meaning. They express condemnation or censure. Penalties don't.

This insight brings two more in tow. First, according to one model of communication, the state expresses indignation only if indignation is what it intends to express. What the state expresses depends on what it intends. Consequently, a state-imposed hardship is not a punishment unless the state intends its imposition to express indignation at what the offender has done and thus to condemn or censure her for doing it. (Notice here that state punishment presupposes that it makes sense to ascribe mental states like intentions to corporate entities like the state.)

Inasmuch as punishment's existence depends on the state's intent, problems will naturally arise when the state's intent and the conventions it uses to express that intent diverge, assuming that the state's intentions have an existence independent of the conventions it uses to express them. For example, sometimes the state may *say* that its intent is not to condemn, but what it *does* may suggest otherwise. Imagine that John Doe is convicted of child molestation. He is sentenced to imprisonment, and he begins to serve his time. Meanwhile, the state enacts a sexual predator law pursuant to which John and others like him can be detained in what the state calls a "treatment facility" after their time is up, provided the state determines that they are dangerous and that they suffer from a mental abnormality.

When John has finished his sentence, the state duly diagnoses him as abnormal and solemnly concludes that he is dangerous. He therefore finds himself confined to a treatment facility. The state might say that it does not intend the additional time in the treatment facility to express condemnation, but the more the treatment facility looks and runs like a prison, the more inclined one will be to take what the state does, and not what it says, as the true expression of its intentions. Actions sometimes speak louder than words.

Or consider the opposite problem. Sometimes the state may *say* that its intent is to condemn, but what it *does* might again suggest otherwise. Imagine Jane Doe is convicted of vandalism. When the time comes to impose a sentence, the judge decides to compel Jane to perform community service, thereby intending to express

the law's intent to condemn Jane for her offense. According to the standard definition, when Jane starts to remove spray paint from the sides of subway cars, she is
being punished. But onlookers might think otherwise. When they see members of
the local neighborhood beautification society cleaning the adjacent car, they might
doubt that the state really intended to condemn Jane's conduct. Cleaning subway
cars is a good way for those performing it to express their civic pride, but a poor way
for the state to express its condemnation.[16] If someone says "hot" when he means
"cold," one might fairly question his competence as a user of the English language.
Similarly, one might sometimes question the competence of a judge (and thus the
state in whose name he speaks) as a user of the language of punishment.

Second, inasmuch as it makes no sense to condemn those who are not responsible for what they have done, neither does it make any sense to punish them.[17] Nor
a fortiori does it make sense to punish creatures who are *incapable* of bearing such
responsibility. For example, although one might speak of "punishing" one's dog for
not doing as ordered, it makes better sense to say that the dog is being disciplined.[18]
Assuming that a dog cannot be a bearer of responsibility, punishing her is not in the
conceptual cards, even though one might believe otherwise because one erroneously believes that dogs are capable of bearing responsibility.

Punishment is often said to be a sign of respect. We can now see why. Responsible
agents who do wrong are punished; nonagents (like dogs) who fail to do as instructed
are disciplined. Punishment is therefore a sign of respect to this extent: it tells us
that the authority imposing the punishment believes that the subject bearing the
punishment is a responsible agent, and not a dog.[19]

In sum: for present purposes punishment is a hardship intentionally imposed
on one person in the name of another person or entity with the authority or standing to impose such a hardship (in our case that authority being the state), where
that hardship is imposed for a wrong with respect to which the person bearing the
hardship is (or is represented as being) responsible, and where that hardship is (or
is represented as being) imposed with the intent to condemn or censure the person
for the wrong he has (or is represented as having) done.

1.2 Two Forms of Abolitionism

Based on this account of what punishment is, we can distinguish two forms of abolition. A *positive abolitionist* says that the state should get out of the business of condemning and punishing altogether. As the positive abolitionist sees it, punishment
presupposes an actor who is responsible for whatever she did to warrant punishment, but in fact, no one is ever responsible for anything she does. *None* of us is an
agent capable of bearing the responsibility punishment presupposes. As such, none
of us possesses what would be needed to qualify as participants in the game of condemning and punishing.[20] Thus, no matter who or what the authority, whether it be
the state, a university, or a parent, it makes no sense to condemn and punish.[21]

A *negative abolitionist*, unlike a positive abolitionist, does not insist that the
state should get out of the condemning business, but he does, like the positive

abolitionist, insist that the state get out of the punishing business. The negative abolitionist believes, contrary to the positive abolitionist, that we are responsible agents and thus that we are fit targets for condemnation when we do wrong. The negative abolitionist is nonetheless an abolitionist because he insists that the state refrain from expressing its condemnation through the *hardship* inherent in punishment. The state must do away with punishment and express its condemnation in other ways.[22] Theories of punishment are efforts to justify the hardship inherent in punishment, but according to the negative abolitionist, none of those efforts has so far been successful, or at least none has succeeded in carrying its burden of proof. Consequently, punishment must end. So whereas the positive abolitionist says that punishment is incoherent, because punishment presupposes responsibility, and no one is responsible, the negative abolitionist says not that punishment is incoherent but that it needs to be justified and no such justification has so far persuasively been given. The jury remains out, and so long as the jury remains out, punishment must stop.

1.3 Alternatives to Punishment

The alternatives to punishment turn out to be rather limited. In fact, they boil down to two. First, an abolitionist might say that a system of *compensation or restitution* should replace punishment. If an actor has caused material harm to another, the state should require her to make the victim whole. She should be forced to pay compensation or make restitution in order to restore the status quo ante. Second, an abolitionist might say that a system of *preventive intervention* should replace punishment. Insofar as an actor is dangerous and likely to cause harm in the future, the state should take steps to prevent her from doing so. Alternatives to punishment therefore aim to remedy past harm caused and to prevent future harm.[23]

Of course, we already have a regime whose goal is make whole those who have suffered harm at the hands of another: the tort system. All abolitionists tend to agree that the existing tort system, or something like it, should be kept in place to remedy harm, and for some of these, nothing more is needed. No system of prevention need be installed. Let the existing civil-law tort system do all the work. As some put it, this approach would *civilize* the criminal law: civilization through punishment's elimination.[24] Punishment would cease to exist, as might the criminal law itself.

Other abolitionists are less parsimonious. They argue that a system of prevention is needed in addition to a system of compensation.[25] All such systems exercise control over a person so long as he is dangerous, but the two forms of abolitionism support different recommendations as to the structure this system might take.[26] For a negative abolitionist, the state can continue to convict responsible agents when they commit crimes, which conviction expresses condemnation, albeit only through words (i.e., speech acts). But it can go no further. It can impose no hardship intended to express condemnation beyond conviction. In other words, it can condemn, but it cannot punish. Instead, once the actor is convicted and formally censured, he would straightway enter the state's prevention system, and how he is treated once inside would depend primarily on how dangerous he is thought to be.

Unlike the negative abolitionist, the positive abolitionist must jettison the concept of crime altogether. The positive abolitionist believes that none of us is capable of bearing the responsibility that punishment presupposes. Without responsibility, condemnation makes no sense, and without condemnation, crime makes no sense. Some positive abolitionists might nonetheless say that the state should wait until we have done something before we can come within the jurisdiction of its preventive system. We at least have to act. But others might say that the state should be free to rope us into the system whenever it determines that we are dangerous. Why wait until someone has actually done something dangerous? That would be too late, or at least later than need be. In any event, whatever it takes to enter the state's preventive system, once one finds oneself there, how one is treated would again depend primarily on how dangerous one is thought to be.

The subsequent sections of this chapter explore these forms of abolitionism in more detail. For each one, beginning with negative abolitionism, we ask the two questions any abolitionist can fairly be expected to answer: Why abolish punishment? What is the alternative? The final section examines restorative justice, a recent and prominent school of thought, and in particular whether, as some have claimed, it represents an abolitionist challenge to punishment itself, and if so, what kind.

2 NEGATIVE ABOLITIONISM

2.1 Why Abolish Punishment?

The negative abolitionist begins from the premise that when a state causes a citizen to bear a burden, with the intent thereby to condemn the citizen for something she has done or failed to do, its action stands in need of justification. Indeed, without some such justification, punishment itself would be a crime. The fine collector would be guilty of theft; the jailer of kidnapping; the executioner of murder; and so on. The law provides these state functionaries with a legal justification, commonly known as a "public authority" defense.[27] But what the negative abolitionist wants to know is whether that legal justification has a moral justification to back it up. Can the hardship inherent in punishment be morally justified?

Providing such a justification is what a theory of punishment purports to do. Its limited purpose is to explain why the state is at least permitted to cause a responsible agent to bear a hardship for the wrong he has done, with the intent to cause him to bear such a hardship, in order to express its condemnation of his wrongdoing. The traditional theories, once again, are consequentialism (which purports to justify punishment's hardship based on its anticipated contribution to the common good), rehabilitation (which purports to justify punishment's hardship based on its anticipated contribution to the offender's good), and retribution (which purports to justify punishment's hardship because the offender deserves it, and perhaps only because he deserves it).

Now, you might find one or more of these theories persuasive. Or you might not. You might, for example, believe (as many do) that a thoroughgoing commitment to consequentialism would lead to a world in which no one should want to live, since a consequentialist state would under the right (if rare) circumstances be permitted, or perhaps even obligated, to punish a person it knows to be innocent, or not punish a person it knows to be guilty, provided that the anticipated good of punishing or not punishing outweighs the anticipated bad, as it sometimes will.[28] If these implications are too much to swallow, then you are not apt to find utilitarianism very attractive. Likewise, you might believe that rehabilitation leads to an unhappy world, since a state committed to rehabilitation is one that makes it its business to perfect its citizens, to get them to live the kind of life the state believes they should be living, even if perfection is not what they want. Consequently, if you are committed to the proposition that people should be free to choose for themselves how to live their lives, provided the choices they make do not harm or risk harming others, rehabilitation won't do.[29]

That leaves retribution. Some so-called negative retributivists maintain that a state is permitted to punish a person if the anticipated good of doing so outweighs the anticipated bad, but only if the state believes that the person punished is guilty of a crime, and only if the punishment imposed on the person does not exceed the punishment she deserves.[30] This account of retribution is really a form of consequentialism in which the state's pursuit of good consequences is subject to limitations. Such an account guarantees that only the guilty are punished, and that they are punished no more than they deserve. What it does not guarantee is that all the guilty are punished, or that they are punished as much as they deserve. Someone committed to this account of retribution must let the guilty go free, or punish them less than they deserve, if punishing them, or punishing them as much as they deserve, would yield no net good.[31] If these consequences tarnish the appeal of negative retribution, consider positive retribution.

Positive retributivists insist that the state is not only permitted but also obligated to punish an offender as much as she deserves (but no more), just because she deserves it.[32] The punishment must fit the crime. Different theories of positive retribution are efforts to explain why one should believe, as all positive retributivists do, that the guilty ought to bear punishment's burden to the full extent that they so deserve. For example, is it because the guilty are free riders who flout the law while the rest of us bear the burden of obedient restraint, such that punishment is warranted as an after-the-fact burden the guilty should have borne before-the-fact but did not?[33] Or is it just because the belief that the guilty deserve to suffer best explains other beliefs we would be loathe to abandon?[34] You might find one of these explanations persuasive, but even if you do, you might still wonder how we can really tell what punishment fits what crime. How can we tell what punishment a crime really deserves? The worry here is that we cannot tell, and that any claim that this punishment is the one that fits the crime is more-or-less arbitrary.[35]

If you end up with doubts about all of the prevailing theories of punishment, what do you do? The possibilities are two. You could resolve your doubts in favor of punishment. You could believe, perhaps on faith, that punishment cannot be unjustified, and that someday some such justification will appear on the horizon. It must be true, you hope, that the state is at least sometimes permitted to impose burdens on wrongdoers in order to condemn their wrongdoing. Or you could resolve your doubts against punishment, and if so, you would become a negative abolitionist. You would conclude that nothing warrants punishment's hardship, so that unless and until some persuasive justification for imposing such a hardship comes along, the state should not impose it. But if the hardship must stop, so, too, must punishment. The two go hand in hand.

2.2 What Is the Alternative?

What the negative abolitionist objects to is the hardship or burden intrinsic to punishment. Nothing more. His abolitionism commits him to the elimination of punishment only because he is committed to the elimination of punishment's hardship. Everything else can more or less remain the same. The civil justice system, or something serving its usual function, would remain in place to provide compensation to the victims of crime for any material harm they suffer. The criminal justice system would also remain in place, as would the concept of crime itself. The negative abolitionist is free to have a penal code and the apparatus needed to enforce it. He can have trials, and he can have convictions: formal condemnations. But there he will draw the line. The only action the state can take to express its condemnation is *speech*. It can *speak* to an offender, but it cannot *do* anything to him, nor can it force him to do anything on pain of its doing something worse to him if he refuses.

But what happens to an offender after he is convicted? One possibility would be nothing. He might be liable in tort to make amends for any harm he has caused, but other than that, he would free to go about his business. Another possibility would be that he enters a system of preventive intervention justified in the name of *self-defense*. An actor who commits a crime is not punished for his offense, but that offense nonetheless warrants a rebuttable presumption that he will in the future cause harm, just as he has caused or risked it on the present occasion. In order to forestall and defend against that anticipated (although not imminent) harm, he is brought within the state's preventive system. Keep in mind that the negative abolitionist's preventive system is one of limited jurisdiction. The negative abolitionist continues to believe that most people are capable of bearing responsibility for what they do. Consequently, in order to respect our status as responsible agents, the negative abolitionist imposes an important limit on the state's prevention system: no one can come within its jurisdiction unless and until he chooses to commit a crime, no matter how dangerous the state otherwise believes him to be. Sexual predator laws provide a glimpse of what such a system might look like.

Before sexual predator laws came onto the scene, a state could only exercise coercive control over someone in one of two circumstances. First, if the person committed a crime, and if he was responsible at the time he committed it, he could be convicted and punished.[36] Second, if the person was nonresponsible (due to mental illness) and presented a danger to himself or others, he could be civilly committed, even if he had committed no crime or otherwise caused harm to anyone. In other words, responsible actors were punished, provided they committed a crime; nonresponsible actors were civilly committed, provided they were dangerous. Punishment and prevention were kept separate: punishment was reserved for responsible actors who commited crimes, and prevention for nonresponsible ones who were dangerous.

Sexual predator laws combine punishment and prevention. Most criminals are released from state control once their time is up. Not sexual predators. Their time may be up, but they are not then automatically released from the state's grip. On the contrary, if they are dangerous, they remain in its control, and they remain in its control until the state says that they are no longer dangerous. The reasons the state gives to justify this continued control are superficially similar to the reasons it gives when it subjects someone to civil commitment: something is wrong with him mentally, and he is dangerous to himself or others. The difference is this: someone who is civilly committed is not only dangerous, he also suffers from a mental disease or defect sufficient to render him nonresponsible. In contrast, the sexual predator, though also considered dangerous, suffers from a "mental abnormality" or "personality disorder" *insufficient* to render him nonresponsible. The state continues to detain him based in the end on little more than its belief that he is dangerous.[37]

The preventive system associated with negative abolitionism would be similar to the one associated with sexual predator laws, with two differences. First, whereas sexual predator laws reach only actors who commit sexual offenses, the negative abolitionist's prevention system would cover anyone who commits a crime. Second, whereas sexual predator laws have three steps (conviction, punishment, prevention), the negative abolitionist's regime would have only two (conviction, prevention). The punishment step would be eliminated because the hardship associated with that step is precisely what the negative abolitionist wants to abolish.

Consequently, crimes would no longer mark the line over which an actor must choose to step before the state can punish him. They would instead mark what Joel Feinberg has called the "clutch line": the line over which an actor must choose to step before he can come into the state's clutches, where he will stay as long as the state believes that he remains dangerous, but only so long as the state so believes.[38] Indeed, in a negative abolitionist's world, an offender guilty of a serious crime who presented no risk of future wrongdoing would be released immediately, whereas one guilty of a minor crime who presented a substantial risk of future wrongdoing would be held until he no longer presented such a risk, perhaps into old age.

One final point. A negative abolitionist who adopted a preventive system would permit the state to interfere with the liberty of its citizens (provided they committed a crime and provided they were dangerous), but any such system must nonetheless respect their status as responsible agents. Consequently, the means used to restrict an actor's liberty would be the least restrictive necessary to secure the community's safety. If house arrest and a leg monitor would suffice without any additional risk to the community, then placing someone in a secured facility away from home would be unjustified. Likewise, an actor subject to the system would be entitled, if she so chose, to participate in treatment or educational programs whose goal would be to enable her to join sooner rather than later the ranks of the nondangerous, and the state would be obligated to provide such opportunities.

3 POSITIVE ABOLITIONISM

3.1 Why Abolish Punishment?

The negative abolitionist rejects the hardship intrinsic to punishment because none of the prevailing theories of punishment persuades her that the state is permitted to impose such hardship. Nonetheless, the negative abolitionist doubts not that people can bear responsibility for their actions, nor does she question the state's authority to condemn wrongdoers, so long as that condemnation is limited in form to a criminal conviction. A negative abolitionist state would continue to convict its citizens for the crimes they commit, but it would not punish them. A positive abolitionist state would go further. It would abolish not only punishment's hardship. It would abolish punishment itself. Indeed, it would abolish the entire category of crime. Why?

The short answer is that crime only makes sense with punishment, and punishment only makes sense with responsibility. But according to the positive abolitionist, no one is ever responsible for what he does or chooses to do. Thus, if responsibility goes, so, too, does punishment; and if punishment goes, so, too, does crime. A positive abolitionist can reach the conclusion that no one is ever responsible for what he does or chooses to do in two different ways. One is to embrace what is generally known as *alternative-possibilities incompatibilism*; the other is to embrace what is generally known as *source incompatibilism*.

3.1.1 *Alternative-Possibilities Incompatibilism*

A positive abolitionist might believe that no one is responsible for what he does or chooses to do unless he could have done or chosen to do otherwise: unless he has free will. We are not responsible for what we do or choose to do unless what we do or choose to do is *up to us*. Now, if it turns out that the state of the world at any moment in time could not (in light of the laws of nature) have been any different from what it actually was, then determinism is true. Every event (including human choices and actions) has a cause, and whatever happens in the world was destined to happen. Consequently, no one has the capacity to do or choose to do otherwise than she actually did or chose to do: no one has free will, and no one is responsible for what she does or for the choices she makes.

This position is commonly known as *alternative-possibilities incompatibilism*.[39] Free will requires alternative possibilities: some alternative to the way the world actually turned out must have been possible. The future must be a garden of forking paths. Determinism is incompatible with the existence of such possibilities. Moreover, according to alternative-possibilities incompatibilism, determinism is true, and as such, free will does not exist. Inasmuch as responsibility depends on free will, no one is responsible for what he does or chooses to do, and if no one is responsible for what he does or chooses to do, then punishment must go, root and branch.

Standing in direct opposition to alternative-possibilities incompatibilism is *libertarianism* (no relation to political libertarianism).[40] According to one prominent form of libertarianism, we *do* have the capacity to do or choose to do otherwise than we actually do or choose to do.[41] The laws of nature bind the physical world, but we are exempt from those laws. On the contrary, we have the capacity to do or choose to do otherwise precisely because we have the power to act contrary to those laws. Determinism governs the rest of the world, but not us. Whatever happens in the world is not destined to happen because we have the power to act outside the causal laws of nature. We have contracausal freedom: a spark of the divine. Consequently, we *are* capable of bearing responsibility for what we do or choose to do.

Alternative-possibilities incompatibilists and libertarians are on opposite sides of the fence, but they nonetheless agree that the freedom that consists in the capacity to do or choose to do otherwise (and with it the capacity to bear responsibility) is incompatible with determinism and the laws of nature. Both are therefore committed to incompatibilism. They disagree on which—freedom and responsibility or determinism and the laws of nature—must go in order to resolve the incompatibility. Alternative-possibilities incompatibilists side with determinism and the laws of nature, rejecting freedom and responsibility. Libertarians side with freedom and responsibility, rejecting determinism and the laws of nature (as least so far as human choice and action is concerned).

Others begin from a different premise altogether, and so sidestep the debate between alternative-possibilities incompatibilists and libertarians. That debate begins from the common premise that freedom and the possibility of responsibility that goes along with it depend on the capacity or power to do or choose to do otherwise. *Compatibilists* reject this premise. They say that responsibility does not require the capacity or power to do or choose to do otherwise.[42] Some other, less divine capacity will suffice. According to what is probably today's most prominent form of compatibilism, the capacity that responsibility requires is the capacity to respond to moral reasons, not the capacity to do or choose to do otherwise, and this capacity, unlike the capacity to do or choose to do otherwise, is perfectly compatible with determinism and the laws of nature.[43] Consequently, even if we are all destined to do as we do, we are still responsible for what we do, provided that what we do results from the exercise of our capacity to respond to reasons, and when such a reasons-responsive action constitutes a crime, the state is free to punish us for it.

With these distinctions in mind, here is another way of looking at positive abolitionism *qua* alternative-possibilities incompatibilism. Under existing law, an actor who commits what would otherwise be a crime will be neither convicted nor punished if he was insane at the time. Most jurisdictions speak of insanity in cognitive terms: a person is insane if he lacked the capacity to realize that what he was doing was a crime. A few also speak of insanity in volitional terms: a person is insane if he lacked the capacity to conform his conduct to the law's demands. Yet despite what the law says, some scholars fairly argue that insofar as the criminal law rests on compatibilism, what it really means (or should mean) when it says that an actor is insane is that he lacked the capacity to respond to reasons.[44]

Now imagine what would happen if the criminal law abandoned compatibilism and joined ranks with the alternative-possibilities incompatibilist. In that case, the law would presuppose that the capacity needed to underwrite responsibility was the capacity to do or choose to do otherwise, not just the capacity to respond to reasons. It would also presuppose that this capacity cannot coexist with the truth of determinism and that determinism is indeed true. The upshot would be that none of us possesses the capacity needed to underwrite responsibility, and so none of us is responsible. In other words, the criminal law would come to regard us all as "insane," all of the time, in which case the criminal law may as well close up shop: precisely the conclusion to which the positive abolitionist is led.

Inasmuch as it presupposes compatibilism, the criminal law has no need to fear the determinism that leads the positive abolitionist to regard us all as insane, and as such, it can proceed with business as usual.[45] But what if we, those subject to the criminal law, are not compatibilists? What if we are instead libertarians, at least pretheoretically (i.e., before we think hard about the question)? In other words, what if we, like the positive abolitionist, believe that responsibility requires the capacity to do or choose to do otherwise, but unlike the positive abolitionist, we believe that determinism is false because we possess this contracausal capacity?[46] We would in that case be on the side of the criminal law, believing that people by and large are responsible for the choices they make and the actions they perform.

But now imagine that the progress of modern neuroscience persuades us that we cannot do or choose otherwise.[47] We do not, it turns out, have any spark of the divine. Any belief to the contrary is really nothing more than an article of faith. What then?

If we continued to believe that responsibility required the contracausal capacity to do otherwise, we would rationally be forced to abandon our libertarianism. Yet we could take no refuge in compatibilism, at least not if we continued to affirm what compatibilism denies: that responsibility requires the capacity to do or choose to do otherwise. Alternative-possibilities incompatibilism would be the only option left, and our newfound belief in determinism would lead us to abandon the criminal law and join ranks with the positive abolitionist. Such a world would be one in which the criminal law, true to its belief in compatibilism, could in good faith continue to convict and punish, but it would do so without legitimacy in the eyes of those it condemned, since those it condemned would not see themselves as responsible for what they had done. Thus, though modern neuroscience may be no direct threat to the criminal law, it poses an indirect threat inasmuch as it threatens to undermine the criminal law's legitimacy among those subject to it.[48]

We have so far have been assuming that alternative-possibilities incompatibilism leads naturally to penal abolition and the end of punishment. However, an alternative-possibilities incompatibilist might insist that her incompatibilism does not commit her to penal abolition. On the contrary, she might insist that determinism is incompatible not with punishment but with the retributive *theory* of punishment. Punishment can continue to exist if determinism is true, and its continued existence is justified if and because the good consequences it produces outweigh the bad, even if no one is responsible for the choice or action for which he is punished. Alternative-possibilities incompatibilism in the metaphysics of free will, so the argument goes, leads to utilitarianism in the theory of punishment, not to abolition.[49]

This line of thought is surely mistaken. Inasmuch as punishment presupposes responsibility, and insofar as determinism is incompatible with responsibility (as the alternative-possibilities incompatibilist maintains), determinism is incompatible with punishment and does indeed lead to abolitionism. The only way an alternative-possibilities incompatibilist could rescue punishment from oblivion would be to say that an actor is responsible for an action whenever "punishing" him brings about more good than bad.[50] But that gets it backward. It makes sense to say that a person can only be punished for what he has done if and because he is responsible for it. It makes no sense to say that he is only responsible for what he has done if and because he is "punished" for it. Punishment presupposes responsibility, not the other way around

Other alternative-possibilities incompatibilists might recognize that incompatibilism commits them to abolition, but nonetheless insist that a world without punishment is not, as some have claimed,[51] a world in which no one is treated with the respect that punishment is said to signify. Although punishment in today's world marks the distinction between agents worthy of respect (who are punished), and nonagents unworthy of it (who are dealt with in some way other than with punishment), a world without punishment would be a world in which, so the argument goes, agents and nonagents would be treated alike—and with respect. Agents who caused harm would not be punished in such a world. They would instead be subject to the same regime as would nonagents who caused harm. Consequently, no basis would exist for claiming that agents got respect, while nonagents got none. Both would be treated in the same way, ostensibly with respect.

This line of thought is surely mistaken, too. It presupposes that the way we respond to a person is what makes her worthy or unworthy of respect. But that gets it backward, too. The way we respond to a person is not what makes her worthy of respect. On the contrary, the fact that a person is worthy of respect is what makes us respond to her in this way or that. We respond to her in one way rather than another because she is worthy of respect. We do not make her worthy of respect because we respond to her in this way rather than that. Thus, the positive-abolitionist world may be a world in which everyone is treated alike, but it is a world in which *no one* is treated with respect, because no one is believed to be an agent worthy of such respect.

3.1.2 *Source Incompatibilism*

Alternative-possibilities incompatibilism is probably the most common route to positive abolitionism. But we can imagine another. Alternative-possibilities incompatibilism embraces the claim that free will and responsibility require the capacity to do or choose to do otherwise, together with the further claim that no one possesses this capacity in light of the truth of determinism. But one might well think that our responsibility for what we do or choose to do does not depend on our possession of any capacity to do or choose to do otherwise at the moment of action or choice. It might well be true that we could not have done otherwise at that moment, but so what? We might still be responsible for what we do, *provided* that whatever determines the way we act or choose to act at the moment we so act or choose can be said to have its sources or origins *in us*. Insofar as we are the ultimate source of what determines what we do or choose to do, we remain responsible for what we do or choose to do. But, unfortunately, if determinism is true, we are never in fact the source or origin of what we do or choose to do. Nature is. We are back to incompatibilism, usually known as *source incompatibilism*, and from there to abolition.

Imagine that John Doe robs a bank. Why did he rob the bank? He wanted to get the money in the bank's vault, he believed that robbing the bank was the best way to get the money, and these reasons caused him to act as he did. If the story stopped there, we would be at a loss to understand why the source incompatibilist would refuse to permit the state to punish John. But of course the story does not end there. It turns out that John had been brainwashed or otherwise coercively manipulated. His desire to get the bank's money and his belief that robbing the bank was the best way to get it were implanted in him. Consequently, the reasons causing him to act were not *his* reasons. They were the brainwasher's reasons. One might therefore be inclined under these circumstances to say that John is not responsible for the robbery. It was not really John who robbed the bank, because the reasons causing John to act were not really John's.

The source incompatibilist takes this idea to its extreme. The reasons causing John to act are not his reasons because the brainwasher implanted him with those reasons. The source incompatibilist believes that no meaningful difference exists between John when he robs the bank and the rest of us whenever we do anything, since the reasons causing all of us to act have likewise been implanted in us. The culprit is not another person, but the laws of nature. Nature has "brainwashed" us, such that the reasons causing any of us to act are reasons for which none of us is ultimately responsible.

Here is another way to look at it. An actor who commits what would otherwise be a crime will be excused if she acted under duress. In many jurisdictions, an actor who commits a crime because she was brainwashed into doing so would not be able to claim duress as a defense. Duress is commonly available only if a third party threatens the actor with death or serious bodily injury unless she does as the third party tells her to do. In contrast, the Model Penal Code expands the traditional duress defense, such that an actor will be excused on grounds of duress if he "engaged in the conduct charged to constitute an offense because he was coerced to do so by the use of or a threat to use...unlawful force against his person...that a person of reasonable firmness in his situation would have been unable to resist."[52] Moreover, according to the Code's drafters, this language was meant to allow a brainwashed actor to argue that she acted under duress.[53] The source incompatibilist can be understood to take this logic one step further (or perhaps many steps further), portraying us all as if we had been brainwashed, not at the hands of another, but at the hands of nature. For the source incompatibilist, we always act under duress.

In sum: positive abolitionism rests on the claim that no one is responsible for anything he does or chooses to do, and one can get to this global denial of responsibility either through alternative-possibilities incompatibilism or source incompatibilism. Both roads lead to Rome.

3.2 What Is the Alternative?

Like the negative abolitionist, the positive abolitionist would preserve some system designed to compensate those who suffer harm at another's hands. The positive abolitionist would also establish a preventive system, which might take one of two different forms.

The first form mirrors in structure and rationale the preventive system associated with negative abolitionism. True, the positive abolitionist, unlike the negative abolitionist, regards none of us as capable of bearing the responsibility needed to underwrite condemnation and punishment. Nonetheless, he might still regard us as being capable to responding to reasons. Moreover, although the positive abolitionist regards this capacity as insufficient to underwrite censure and punishment, he might nonetheless regard our possession of it as sufficient to inform the rationale on which his preventive system is based, as well as to impose constraints on its operation. As such, the system would be based on some appeal to self-defense; it would require the actor to do something before coming within the system's jurisdiction; it would restrict an actor's liberty only so far as necessary; and it would offer opportunities for treatment, education, and the like. Indeed, the only real difference between the positive abolitionist's preventive system and that of the negative abolitionist would be the name attached to whatever the actor must do to enter the system. The negative abolitionist would call it a crime. In contrast, inasmuch as the positive abolitionist would eliminate the category of crime altogether, he must come up with another name: perhaps "quasi crime."

The positive abolitionist's preventive system might also assume a more ominous shape. Begin with the rationale of such a system, and imagine now that the positive abolitionist regards us as not only incapable of bearing responsibility for what we do, but also incapable of responding to reasons. She sees us instead as capable only of responding to incentives that make no appeal to reason: to pleasure and pain, much as one imagines is true of animals. Moreover, once we are so regarded, the positive abolitionist's preventive regime becomes a system based not so much on self-defense as on *quarantine*. A person infected with a contagious disease is quarantined to safeguard the public health if and when he is identified as a carrier of the contagious bug, whether or not he has in fact infected anyone else with the disease he carries. The bug his body carries makes him dangerous. In a brave new world of pure preventive detention, the actor *becomes* the bug. The person his body carries makes him dangerous.[54] Consequently, an actor would come within the jurisdiction of the preventive system once he is identified as *being* dangerous, whether or not he has *done* anything to cause or risk harm to anyone else.

The internal structure of this preventive regime might also look very different. For insofar as its inhabitants are regarded as little more than dangerous animals lacking any hint of agency, the state is presumably free to treat them as it might any dangerous animal. The only constraints on how the administrators of such a system treat its inhabitants would be those constraints that they elect to respect out of some sense of compassion. If the administrators are without compassion, or if their sense of what compassion requires is distorted or perverse, then nothing stands in the way of such "rehabilitative" techniques as aversive conditioning, lobotomies, and the like. Think *Clockwork Orange*. Indeed, such a regime of prevention is really a zoo full of more or less dangerous animals: human animals, but animals all the same. Remember the humans in *Planet of the Apes*? Of course, animals should be treated humanely, not because they are human but just because they are sentient creatures. In fact, those who can be adequately disciplined and trained not to bite should be released if the cost of keeping them confined is more than the probable harm they might cause if released. Those that cannot be trained must be detained indefinitely—or else put down.[55]

4 RESTORATIVE JUSTICE

Sometimes the rhetoric of restorative justice, with its emphasis on restitution and community service and opposition to imprisonment, implies that restorative justice is an alternative *form* of punishment. At other times the rhetoric of restorative justice, with its hostility toward retribution, implies that restorative justice is an alternative *theory* of punishment.[56] At still other times the rhetoric of restorative justice, with its talk of ending punishment, implies that restorative justice is an *alternative* to punishment itself. For present purposes, this last and most ambitious claim is the most important: Is restorative justice a form of abolitionism?

Answering this question is not easy. Restorative-justice practitioners and proponents tend to agree more or less on the practices that *constitute* restorative justice, but they tend to disagree about how to *characterize* those practices.[57] Those who participate in the practices of restorative justice, as well are those who observe those who participate in those practices, do or observe more or less the same thing, but they offer different accounts of what they are doing or observing. Agreement on practice has not translated into agreement on theory.

Let me begin with a hopefully uncontroversial description of the practice of restorative justice. A person commits a crime. He pleads guilty to the offense charged. The judge enters a judgment of conviction, but does not enter a sentence imposing punishment. Instead, the now-convicted offender agrees to participate in a restorative-justice conference.[58] Present at this conference are a facilitator, the victim and his supporters, and the offender and his supporters (and maybe a representative of the "community" as well). Each party tells his story. If all goes well, the conference culminates in an agreement setting forth sundry obligations that the offender must discharge, usually requiring the offender to make restitution or perform community service. The terms of the agreement are subject to judicial review in order to ensure that they are not too harsh, and perhaps to ensure that they are not too lenient. If the parties fail to reach an agreement, the offender is treated as he would have been had he never joined the conference to begin with.

If this account of the practice of restorative justice is accurate, what does it tell us about the theory or philosophy of restorative justice? Is it an abolitionist theory, or something else? For starters, nothing in this account suggests that restorative justice is allied with positive abolitionism. Restorative justice practitioners and theorists are rightly concerned about ameliorating the causes of crime, but they break ranks with those, like some cognitive neuroscientists, who move from the premise that crimes, like everything else, have causes to the conclusion that no one is responsible for committing them. Restorative justice does not seem to presuppose that none of us is capable of bearing responsibility for what we do. On the contrary, getting offenders to accept responsibility is a prominent restorativist theme. Nor are restorativists keen to purge the concept of crime itself from our vocabulary. If so, then restorative justice should not be understood as an example of positive abolitionism.

Existing practices associated with restorative justice nonetheless suggest that restorative justice is most plausibly portrayed as a form of negative abolitionism. Existing restorative-justice practice seems to presuppose that offenders are responsible agents who are neither exempt nor excused for what they do, and that what they do is properly characterized as a crime that is fairly subject to the formal censure of the state in the form of a criminal conviction. What would make restorative justice an example of negative abolition would be its rejection of the hardship associated with punishment. The state is free to condemn an offender through what it says to him, but it cannot go further and condemn him through imposed hardship.

The state's role is carefully circumscribed. It enters the picture only at the beginning and at the end of the restorative process: it convicts the offender at the beginning, and it reviews the burden he has agreed to bear at the end. Nowhere does the state impose any burden or hardship on the offender in order to condemn him for his crime, and as such, at no point does the state punish him.

But whether restorative-justice practices can really be understood as an example of weak abolitionism depends on how one understands what does or should go on during the most salient part of the restorative process: the conference. Everyone acknowledges that a successful conference results in an agreement, and that as part of this agreement the offender must *do* something. Moreover, that something is presumably a hardship or a burden for him, albeit one he agrees in some sense to shoulder. If so, then whether or not restorative justice can fairly claim to be an example of negative abolitionism depends on two questions.

First, are the victim and his supporters state actors when they assume the role of conference participants? If not, then the hardship the offender agrees to bear cannot constitute *state* punishment, though it might constitute punishment imposed in the name of some other authority. Now, the conduct of the victim and his supporters, as well as the conduct of other conference participants, is subject to little legal regulation. The process is meant to be informal. Nonetheless, the victim's job description requires him, together with his supporters, to determine, albeit through a negotiated process, the burden the offender will be obligated to bear. It would therefore seem fair to say that the victim has temporarily assumed a role something like that of a judge, and as such he becomes a state actor *pro tem*. The victim may speak for himself, but in so doing, he also speaks for the state. Indeed, he can speak for himself only because the state permits him to speak. If the conference did not thus proceed under the auspices of the state, restorative justice would end up being a form of state-sponsored and -regulated vigilantism.

Second, what is the intent of the victim and his supporters when they sign off on the burden or hardship memorialized in the agreement? If their intent is to condemn, then the burden the offender must bear is the burden of a punishment, however else it might differ from the burden he would have been forced to bear had a judge sentenced him. Moreover, whatever a victim might *say* is his intent, one cannot help but suspect that in most cases the victim will in fact intend the offender's burden to be, at least in part, an expression of condemnation. The victim presumably resents the wrong the offender has done to him, and if so, then the hardship the offender bears is easily seen as a way for the victim to express that resentment, and expressing resentment is condemning. If so, then restorative-justice advocates are mistaken if and when they describe the burden the offender bears as restitution or community service or whatnot, and *not* as punishment. Instead, the burden the offender bears *is* punishment *in the form of* restitution or community service or whatnot.

But what if the restitution or community service does *not* come with any intent to condemn the offender for what he has done? Moreover, a restorativist might claim that the burden the offender bears *should not* come with any such intent.

What then? In that case, restorative justice would indeed be an example of negative abolitionism. The state formally condemns the offender for his crime in the form of a criminal conviction. The victim, too, may condemn him through the words he speaks at the conference. But the burden associated with the restorative acts the offender must undertake would be nothing more than that: a burden, indistinguishable from the burden associated with any effort to repair a material harm. As long as the burden an actor bears is imposed without any expression of condemnation, then whatever else is being done to him, he is not being punished. Thus, whether restorative justice is in fact an example of weak abolition depends on the mind of the victim: Does the victim intend the burden the offender bears to express condemnation?

Why might a restorativist believe that victims should not regard the offender's burden with condemnation in their heart? John Braithwaite has gestured toward one answer. The "restorativist," he writes, "has [a] more segmented view of human actors [including offenders] as *multiple selves*."[59] If that claim is taken at face value, then perhaps some restorativists believe that all wrongdoers suffer from a form of split personality: one self commits the wrong, and the other is an innocent bystander. Assuming that both personalities are responsible actors, and therefore fair subjects of condemnation, one might nonetheless refrain from punishing the guilty personality inasmuch as punishing him entails knowingly imposing hardship on the innocent personality. Thus, whereas the negative abolitionist rejects the hardship associated with punishment because none of the prevailing theories of punishment has persuaded her otherwise, the restorativist might reject the hardship of punishment because its imposition can never fail to be unfair: punishing the guilty invariably means imposing hardship on an innocent. Better that the guilty go free than an innocent suffer.[60]

A more plausible answer begins with the hope that the conference itself will conform to a special script, unfolding as follows. The victim and offender are present, together with their supporters. The victim begins. He tells of his anger at, and resentment toward, the offender for what he has done, and he expresses those sentiments in no uncertain terms. Then something nearly miraculous happens. Far from turning a deaf ear to the victim's outpouring, the offender is overcome with remorse. He offers his heartfelt apology and genuinely repents his wrongdoing. In response, the victim finds that he can no longer hold onto his resentment, and when resentment departs, forgiveness arrives. He no longer has any desire to express his resentment, either in words or deeds. Indeed, he no longer has any resentment to express. Consequently, any burden to which the victim and offender thereafter agree cannot constitute a punishment, because the victim does not (cannot) intend it to be an expression of resentment. The victim and offender might see the burden the offender agrees to bear as nothing more than a way through which offender compensates the victim for any material harm he has suffered.

Yet they might see it as something else entirely. They might see it as a way for the offender to expiate his guilt (which persists despite the victim's forgiveness) or as a way to for him to express how deeply and sincerely sorry he is. The offender would freely accept and undertake the burden, not just as an incident to making material amends, but as the hardship he must bear in order to rid himself of guilt or express his remorse. In other words, what would otherwise be a punishment becomes instead a penance, and inasmuch as a penance is not a punishment, the hardship associated with the practice of restorative justice would be an alternative to punishment. The offender is treated as a responsible agent. He is condemned, albeit only in words, for what he has done: the state goes first when it convicts him; the victim goes next, with his own expressions at the conference. But the burden the offender willingly bears when he leaves the conference is not a punishment because the victim does not intend it to express condemnation. Insofar as the offender's burden constitutes something more than just the cost associated with making material amends, seeing it as a secular penance is probably the best way to see it.

We can now make better sense of the controversy surrounding the theoretical status of restorative justice. Is it or is it not an example of abolitionism? Controversy exists because the answer is that it depends, and it depends in particular on how the conference unfolds and on the purpose the victim and offender ascribe to the burden the offender agrees to bear. If that burden's purpose is to express the victim's resentment, then restorative justice is not an alternative to punishment: it is at best an alternative theory of punishment. On the other hand, if it is meant to express nothing (i.e., if it is merely an incident of making material amends) or if it is meant to expiate the offender's guilty or to express his repentance, then restorative justice is indeed an alternative to punishment itself, and not merely an alternative theory of it.

NOTES

I'm grateful to Mitch Berman, David Dolinko, and Doug Husak for written comments on an earlier version of this chapter. I'm also grateful to John Deigh and David Dolinko for inviting me to contribute to this volume, and to participants at the roundtable discussion sponsored by the University of Illinois College of Law Program in Law and Philosophy and graciously hosted by Heidi Hurd and Michael Moore for their comments. Larry Alexander provided especially helpful remarks on that occasion.

1. See, e.g., Michael Tonry & Mary Lynch, "Intermediate Sanctions," in Michael Tonry (ed.), *Crime and Justice: A Review of Research*, vol. 20 (Chicago: University of Chicago Press, 1996), 99.

2. See, e.g., Dan Kahan, "What Do Alternative Sanctions Mean?," *University of Chicago Law Review* 63 (1996), 591. Forced labor could be another alternative form of punishment. One author has proposed such an alternative, but he characterizes it as an alternative to punishment, not as an alternative form of punishment, inasmuch as the state's purpose in forcing an offender to work is something other than to condemn him for the crime he has committed. See Goeffrey Sayre-McCord, "Criminal Justice and Legal Reparations as an Alternative to Punishment," *Philosophical Issues* 11 (2001), 502, 506–07.

3. See, e.g., Jeremy Bentham, *An Introduction of the Principles of Morals and Legislation* (London: T. Payne & Son, 1789), ii.

4. See, e.g., Jean Hampton, "The Moral Education Theory of Punishment," *Philosophy and Public Affairs* 13 (1984), 208; Herbert Morris, "A Paternalistic Theory of Punishment," *American Philosophical Quarterly* 18 (1981), 263. It is of course possible, and indeed common, to understand rehabilitation as simply one way among others of maximizing good consequences.

5. See, e.g., Michael Moore, "The Moral Worth of Retribution," in Ferdinand Schoeman (ed.), *Responsibility, Character, and the Emotions: New Essays in Moral Psychology* (Oxford: Oxford University Press, 1987), 179; Herbert Morris, "Persons and Punishment," *Monist* 52 (1968), 475.

6. R. A. Duff, *Punishment, Communication, and Community* (Oxford: Oxford University Press, 2001), xvii.

7. *Id.* at xix.

8. Penal abolitionists are not necessarily anarchists, although anarchists are necessarily penal abolitionists inasmuch as they advocate abolition of the state itself. Some writers describe themselves as abolitionists because they believe that "[p]unishment...means the same thing as retribution," and they reject retribution. See Michael L. Corrado, "The Abolition of Punishment," *Suffolk University Law Review* 35 (2001), 257, 260. I adopt here what I take is the more conventional view according to which retribution is one thing and punishment another: retribution is a theory purporting to explain when and why an authority is permitted to impose something called punishment.

9. Another alternative to *state* punishment would of course be punishment imposed in the name of some authority other than the state, in which case one might say, not that punishment has been *abolished*, but that it has been *relocated* to another authority, or at least that punishment is *retained* in the hands of that authority.

10. Antony Flew, "The Justification of Punishment," *Philosophy* 29 (1954), 291, 293–95.

11. Stanley I. Benn, "An Approach to the Problems of Punishment," *Philosophy* 33 (1958), 325, 325–26; H. L. A. Hart, "Prolegomenon to the Principles of Punishment," *Proceedings of the Aristotelian Society* 60 (1959–60), 1, 4–5. For a thoroughgoing critique of the standard definition, together with a proposed alternative, see Leo Zaibert, *Punishment and Retribution* (Aldershot, England: Ashgate, 2006).

12. Hart, above n. 11, at 4–5. Some have argued that for one reason or another some or all existing states lack the standing or authority to impose punishment. The usual thought here is that the state has somehow treated unfairly those over whom it claims the authority to punish, such that its authority to punish those whom it has treated unfairly is undermined. See, e.g., Jeffrie G. Murphy, "Marxism and Retribution," *Philosophy & Public Affairs* 2 (1973), 217.

13. See, e.g., Richard A. Wasserstrom, "Punishment," in *Philosophy and Social Issues* (Notre Dame: University of Notre Dame Press, 1980), 112, 121.

14. See, e.g., Steven Sverdlik, "Punishment," *Law and Philosophy* 7 (1988), 179, 181.

15. Joel Feinberg, "The Expressive Function of Punishment," *Monist* 49 (1965), 397, 400. See also Henry M. Hart, Jr., "The Aims of the Criminal Law," *Law and Contemporary Problems* 23 (1958), 401, 404 ("What distinguishes a criminal from a civil sanction and all that distinguishes it, it is ventured, is the judgment of community condemnation which accompanies and justifies its imposition.").

16. See Kahan, above n. 2, at 625–30.

17. Ascriptions of responsibility usually presuppose that the person to whom responsibility is ascribed satisfies two general conditions, one of which relates to the actor's

knowledge, and the other to his freedom. Where an actor's responsibility for acting contrary to the law is at issue, the knowledge (or epistemic) condition provides an answer to this question: Under what circumstances does an actor lack the knowledge necessary to hold him responsible for acting contrary to its demands? The freedom condition provides an answer to this question: Under what circumstances does an actor lack the freedom necessary to hold him responsible for acting contrary to its demands? So-called strict liability crimes represent a potential violation of the epistemic condition for ascribing responsibility, not the freedom condition.

18. See Zaibert, above n. 11, at 33.

19. Cf. Kent Greenawalt, "Punishment," in Joshua Dressler (ed.), *Crime and Justice* (New York: Macmillan, 2d ed., 2002), 1282. ("In typical cases of punishment, persons who possess authority impose designedly unpleasant consequences upon, and express their condemnation of, other persons who are *capable of choice* and who have breached established standards of behavior.") (emphasis added).

20. One might also be led to positive abolition, not because one believes that no one is ever responsible for what they do or choose to do (and thus that punishment is incoherent), but rather because one believes that a world with some alternative to punishment would all things considered be a better place than a world with punishment.

21. Indeed, one might go on to say, not only that punishment makes no sense, but that normativity itself makes no sense. We should not only give up the practice of punishment, we should give up any practice associated with ascribing responsibility, with blaming—or praising.

22. One could loosely say that a criminal conviction itself is "punishment." Moreover, although it has been said that the criminal process is a punishment, see Malcom M. Feeley, *The Process Is the Punishment: Handling Cases in a Lower Criminal Court* (New York: Russell Sage Foundation, reprint ed., 1992), 199, that cannot be correct. Prior to conviction, the actor has not authoritatively been found to have committed any offense for which he can be punished. The burden an actor bears in being forced to endure a trial must therefore be justified, if at all, on the same basis as any other burden a citizen is required to bear.

23. Someone whose commitment to the abolition of punishment followed from his commitment to the abolition of the state (i.e., an anarchist) would endorse neither a system of compensation nor a system of preventive intervention inasmuch as each requires the continued existence of something called the state.

24. See, e.g., David Boonin, *The Problem of Punishment* (Cambridge: Cambridge University Press, 2008), 216; Deirdre Golash, *The Case against Punishment* (New York: New York University Press, 2005); Randy E. Barnett, "Restitution: A New Paradigm of Criminal Justice," *Ethics* 87 (1977), 279, 289; Jan Narveson, "Moving from Punishment to Compensation," *Canadian Journal of Law & Jurisprudence* 5 (1992), 57. Golash does contemplate the "detention of an individual until opportunity or motive for commission of a specific crime that he clearly intends has passed," Golash, *id.* at 160, and in a later article Barnett contemplates the preventive detention of responsible agents who clearly communicate an intention to violate another's rights. See Randy E. Barnett, "Getting Even: Restitution, Preventive Detention, and the Tort/Crime Distinction," *Boston University Law Review* 76 (1996), 157, 165.

25. Small-scale preventive regimes, although seldom much noticed as such, are already at work alongside the existing system of punishment. For example, sexual predator laws constitute a preventive regime inasmuch as they permit the detention of responsible agents who are believed to be dangerous, provided they have been convicted of a crime (and have

already discharged the punishment assigned to that crime). The detention ends when the actor is no longer dangerous. Likewise, pretrial detention constitutes a preventive regime inasmuch as it permits the detention of responsible agents who are believed to be dangerous, provided that the state has "probable cause" to believe the actor has committed a crime. The detention ends when the actor is either acquitted or convicted. Finally, so-called *Terry* stops constitute a preventive regime inasmuch as they permit the police to detain ("stop") responsible agents, provided the police suspect that a crime is "afoot," even if they have no reason to believe that the person has committed a crime (not even an inchoate crime). If the police further believe the detained person is dangerous, they can "frisk" him. The detention ends when the suspicions of the police are either confirmed or disconfirmed. If confirmed, such that the suspicion that a crime is "afoot" ripens into probable cause to believe that the actor has in fact committed a crime, the actor may then enter the pretrial detention system.

26. Nonabolitionists have advanced different ways of dealing with responsible agents who are dangerous. See, e.g., Stephen J. Morse, "Blame and Danger: An Essay on Preventative Detention," *Boston University Law Review* 76 (1996), 113, 152 (punishment of dangerous actors for failing to take steps to render themselves nondangerous); Paul Robinson, "Punishing Dangerousness: Cloaking Preventive Detention as Criminal Justice," *Harvard Law Review* 114 (2001), 1429, 1454 (postpunishment preventive detention). For criticisms of Morse's proposal, see Michael Louis Corrado, "Punishment and the Wild Beast of Prey: The Problem of Preventative Detention," *Journal of Criminal Law and Criminology* 86 (1996), 778; Richard L. Lippke, "No Easy Way Out: Dangerous Offenders and Preventive Detention," *Law and Philosophy* 27 (2008), 383, 399–406; Philip Montague, "Justifying Preventative Detention," *Law and Philosophy* 18 (1999), 173.

27. See, e.g., Paul H. Robinson, *Criminal Law Defenses*, vol. 2 (St. Paul: West, 1984), § 141(a), at 113–15.

28. See, e.g., Heidi M. Hurd, "Expressing Doubts about Expressivism," *University of Chicago Legal Forum*, 2005 (2005), 405, 412–13.

29. Idem. at 409.

30. See, e.g., Hart, above n. 15, at 9.

31. See, e.g., Hurd, above n. 28, at 414.

32. See Moore, above n. 5, at 182 ("For a retibutivist, the moral responsibility of an offender...gives society the *duty* to punish.").

33. See Morris, above n. 5, at 483–84.

34. See Moore, above n. 5, at 183.

35. See, e.g., Hurd, above n. 28, at 415–16. For one prominent attempt to describe an approach by which at least to assess the seriousness of one crime compared to another, see Andrew von Hirsch et al., "Gauging Crime Seriousness: A 'Living Standard' Conception of Criminal Harm," in Andrew von Hirsch & Andrew Ashworth, *Proportionate Sentencing: Exploring the Principles* (Oxford: Oxford University Press, 2005), 186.

36. If an actor was not responsible (due to mental illness) at the time he committed the offense, he would be acquitted on grounds of insanity. If he remained nonresponsible (due to mental illness) at the time of his acquittal, and if he was also found to be dangerous to himself or others, he could be civilly committed. In contrast, if he was either no longer nonresponsible (due to mental illness), or if he was but presented no danger to himself or others, he would be released.

37. See Stephen J. Morse, "Uncontrollable Urges and Irrational People," *Virginia Law Review* 88 (2002), 1025, 1069–70.

38. Joel Feinberg, "Crime, Clutchability, and Individuated Treatment," in Joel Feinberg, *Doing and Deserving* (Princeton: Princeton University Press, 1970), 252, 265.

39. See Derk Pereboom, "Source Incompatibilism and Alternative Possibilities," in David Widerker & Michael McKenna (eds.), *Moral Responsibility and Alternative Possibilities* (Aldershot, England: Ashgate, 2003), 185, 186.

40. For an overview, see Randolph Clarke, *Libertarian Accounts of Free Will* (Oxford: Oxford University Press, 2003). See also R. Jay Wallace, "Moral Responsibility and the Practical Point of View," in R. Jay Wallace, *Normativity and the Will: Selected Essays on Moral Psychology and Practical Reason* (Oxford: Clarendon Press, 2006), 144, 154 (defending libertarianism from within the "normative framework of practical reason").

41. See, e.g., Timothy O'Connor, *Persons and Causes: The Metaphysics of Free Will* (Oxford: Oxford University Press, 2000); Thomas Pink, *Free Will: A Very Short Introduction* (Oxford: Oxford University Press, 2004).

42. Some compatibilists argue that responsibility does require the capacity to do or choose to do otherwise, but insist that determinism is compatible with this capacity. Thus, while most modern compatibilists reject the claim that the capacity to do or choose to do otherwise is necessary for responsibility, some latter-day classical compatibilists accept that claim but reject the further claim that determinism is incompatible with such a capacity, and they reject that further claim because they endorse a conditional analysis of the what it means to say that an actor "could have done or chosen to do otherwise." See, e.g., Michael Smith, "Rational Capacities," in Sarah Stroud & Christin Tappolet (eds.), *Weakness of Will and Practical Irrationality* (Oxford: Clarendon Press, 2003), 17; Kadri Vihvelin, "Freedom, Foreknowledge, and the Principle of Alternative Possibilities," *Canadian Journal of Philosophy* 30 (2000), 1. For a critical appraisal of this effort to revive classical compatibalism, see Randolph Clarke, "Dispositions, Abilities to Act, and Free Will: The New Dispositionalism, 118 *Mind* (2009), 323.

43. See, e.g., Nomy Araply, *Merit, Meaning, and Human Bondage: An Essay on Free Will* (Princeton: Princeton University Press, 2006); John Martin Fischer & Mark Ravizza, *Responsibility and Control: A Theory of Moral Responsibility* (Cambridge: Cambridge University Press, 1998); R. Jay Wallace, *Responsibility and the Moral Sentiments* (Cambridge, Mass.: Harvard University Press, 1996). Another prominent form of compatibilism says that an actor is responsible for an act if he endorses or otherwise identifies with the reasons causing his actions. See, e.g., Harry G. Frankfurt, "Freedom of the Will and the Concept of a Person," *Journal of Philosophy* 68 (1971), 5; Gary Watson, "Free Agency," *Journal of Philosophy* 72 (1975), 205; Susan Wolf, "Sanity and the Metaphysics of Responsibility," in Schoeman, above n. 5, at 45.

44. See, e.g., Michael S. Moore, "Mental Illness and Responsibility," *Bulletin of the Menninger Foundation* 39 (1975), 308, 318; Stephen J. Morse, "Excusing and the New Excuse Defenses: A Legal and Conceptual Review," in Michael Tonry (ed.), *Crime and Justice: A Review of Research*, vol. 23 (Chicago: University of Chicago Press, 1998), 329, 341.

45. See, e.g., Stephen J. Morse, "The NonProblem of Free Will in Forensic Psychiatry and Psychology," *Behavioral Sciences & the Law* 25 (2007), 203.

46. According to one relatively recent analysis of the relevant experimental literature, the "folk" in fact have "have incompatibilist intuitions under some conditions and…compatibilist intuitions under others." Manual Vargas, "Philosophy and the Folk: On Some Implications of Experimental Work for Philosophical Debates on Free Will," *Journal of Cognition & Culture* 6 (2006), 239, 240. More specifically, "incompatibilist intuitions are elicited in abstract, low-affect contexts, and compatibilist intuitions are elicited in concrete, high-affect contexts." Idem. at 247.

47. See, e.g., Joshua Greene & Jonathan Cohen, "For the Law, Neuroscience Changes Nothing and Everything," *Philosophical Transactions of the Royal Society* 359 (2004), 1775, 1778 ("In modern criminal law, there has been a long tense marriage of convenience between compatibilist legal principles and libertarian moral intuitions. New neuroscience…will probably render this marriage unworkable."). But see Shaun Nichols, "After Incompatibilism: A Naturalistic Defense of the Reactive Attitudes," *Philosophical Perspectives* 21 (2007), 405, 406 (predicting that "if people come to accept determinism, things will remain pretty much the same").

48. According to some observers of recent debates, we can live with the thought that mental causes determine our choices and actions. We would therefore be prepared to abandon our libertarianism in favor of compatibilism. What we cannot live with is the thought that our mental states are reducible to physical ones. If so, then modern science is no threat to the criminal law if all it does is cause us to believe that determinism is true. It is a threat if it causes us to believe that reductionism is true. See, e.g., Adina Roskies, "Neuroscientific Challenges to Free Will and Responsibility," *Trends in Cognitive Sciences* 10 (2006), 419, 422–23. See also John Monterosso, Edward B. Royzman, & Barry Schwartz, "Explaining Away Responsibility: Effects of Scientific Explanation on Perceived Culpability," *Ethics & Behavior* 15 (2005), 139, 155 ("[I]n viewing mind and body as two mutually exclusive attributional suspects (as opposed to alternative levels of analysis), the stage is set so that advances in the physiological behavioral sciences progressively shrink what is left to attribute to the intentional agent.").

49. See, e.g., Greene & Cohen, above n. 47, at 1783.

50. See, e.g., J. J. C. Smart, "Free-Will, Praise and Blame," 70 *Mind* (1961), 291, 302 ("The ascription of responsibility…[has] a clear pragmatic justification which is quite consistent with a wholehearted belief in metaphysical determinism."). See also Richard J. Arneson, "The Smart Theory of Moral Responsibility and Desert," in Serena Olsaretti (ed.), *Desert and Justice* (Oxford: Clarendon Press, 2003), 233; Manual Vargas, "Moral Influence, Moral Responsibility," in Nick Trakakis & Daniel Cohen (eds.), *Essays on Free Will and Moral Responsibility* (Newcastle on Tyne: Cambridge Scholars Press, 2008), 90.

51. See, e.g., Christopher Slobogin, "A Jurisprudence of Dangerousness," *Northwestern University Law Review* 98 (2003), 1, 31.

52. American Law Institute, *Model Penal Code* (Philadelphia: American Law Institute, 1985), § 2.09, at 37.

53. Idem. § 2.09, at 376.

54. Discussions about the design of preventive systems usually and properly assume that the system will make mistakes: some dangerous actors will be brought into the system when they are not in fact dangerous, or will be kept there longer than they need to be. (The converse error will also happen: some dangerous actors will slip through the system.) It is hard to imagine what it would be like to live in a world in which some people would be able perfectly to predict what someone else will do. Science fiction gives a glimpse. The agents at Pre-Crime in the film *Minority Report* can with the help of the three so-called pre-cogs see perfectly into the future. (Of course, that is not quite right: sometimes the pre-cogs disagree among themselves, which is why minority reports exist in the first place.) A crime can be seen before it happens. But why can't the Pre-Crime agents see themselves stopping the crime, such that the crime they see happening in the future in fact never happens? Perhaps the pre-cogs can't see that far. But what if they could? See generally Roy Sorensen, "Future Law: Prepunishment and the Causal Theory of Verdicts," *Noûs* 40 (2006), 166.

55. For an engaging defense of this so-called objective attitude against the criticisms usually laid at its doorstep, see Tamler Sommers, "The Objective Attitude," *Philosophical Quarterly* 57 (2007), 321.

56. John Braithwaite and Philip Pettit claim that the good of "nondomination," which is the touchstone of their "republican" political theory, "commends restorative justice as an attractive way of dealing with known criminal offenders and victims." John Braithwaite & Philip Pettit, "Republicanism and Restorative Justice: An Explanatory and Normative Connection," in Heather Strang & John Braithwaite (eds.), *Restorative Justice: Philosophy to Practice* (Aldershot, England: Ashgate, 2000). If the claim here is that the punishment, if any, associated with restorative-justice practices are justified if and because it maximizes nondomination, then restorative justice as a theory of punishment is a consequentialist theory, and as such, it must grapple with the problems that traditionally beset any such theory. See David Dolinko, "Restorative Justice and the Justification of Punishment," *Utah Law Review*, 2003 (2003), 319.

57. See, e.g., Gerry Johnstone & Daniel W. Van Ness, "The Meaning of Restorative Justice," in Johnstone & Van Ness (eds.), *Handbook of Restorative Justice* (Cullompton, England: Willan, 2007), 5, 6 ("[R]estorative justice...is a deeply *contested* concept.").

58. Of course, if he does not agree, the court will sentence him as it would any other offender. If the default sentence is in the offender's eyes worse than anything he can imagine would emerge from his participation in a conference, then it might be more accurate to say that his participation is actually coerced. For an interesting account that treats an offender's nonnegotiable participation in a restorative-justice conference itself as a punishment, see Christopher Bennett, "Taking the Sincerity out of Saying Sorry: Restorative Justice as Ritual," *Journal of Applied Philosophy*, 23 (2006), 127, 128.

59. John Braithwaite, "Narrative and 'Compulsory Compassion,'" *Law & Social Inquiry* 31 (2006), 425, 443 (emphasis added). See also Jean Hampton, "The Nature of Immorality," *Social Philosophy & Policy* 7 (1989), 22, 32 (arguing that immorality, according to the "Manichean explanation," is "presented as the result of a force within each of human being which struggles with and overpowers that person's 'true self,' while good is the result of that 'true self' prevailing over the 'evil force.'").

60. But see Walter Sinnott-Armstrong & Stephen Behnke, "Responsibility in Cases of Multiple Personality Disorder," *Philosophical Perspectives* 14 (2000), 301, 320–21 (arguing that a person with multiple personality disorder can fairly be punished provided that the "alter in charge at the time of the crime" was sane).

Name Index

....

Subject Index

CPSIA information can be obtained
at www.ICGtesting.com
Printed in the USA
BVHW060901130619
550776BV00001B/1